Great British Drawings

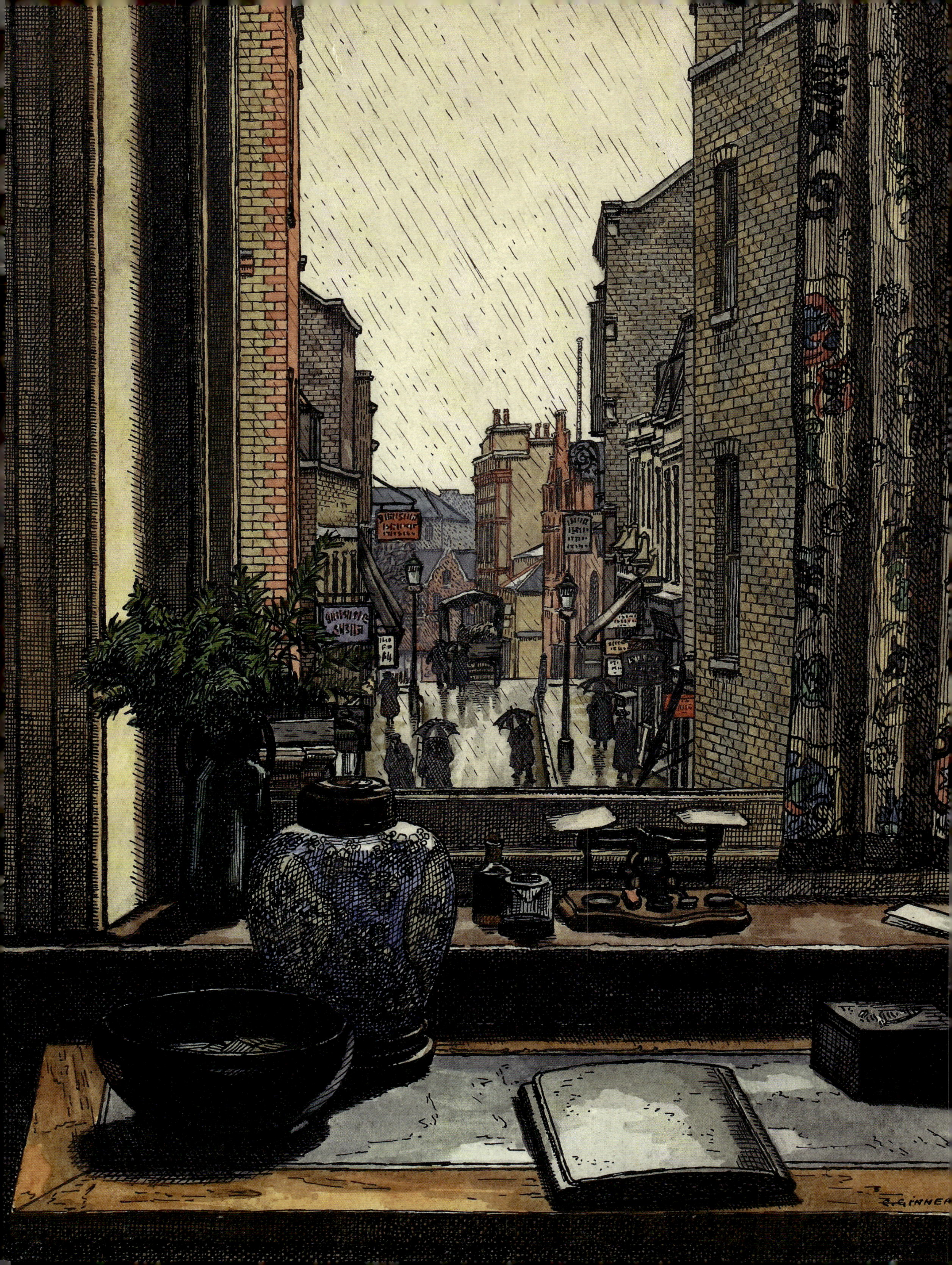

COLIN HARRISON
with Caroline Palmer, Katherine Wodehouse
& Harry Dickinson
Essays by Susan Owens & Timothy Wilcox

GREAT BRITISH DRAWINGS

Ashmolean Museum
Oxford 2015

ASHMOLEAN

GREAT BRITISH DRAWINGS
Ashmolean Museum, Oxford
26 March – 31 August 2015

Exhibition supported by Lowell Libson Ltd
and The Friends of the Ashmolean

British Library Cataloguing-in-Publication Data
A catalogue record for this book is available from the British Library

ISBN 978 1 85444 296 3

Published by the Ashmolean Museum, University of Oxford
General Editor: Katherine Wodehouse
Designed and typeset in Verdigris by Dalrymple
Printed and bound in Belgium by Albe de Coker

Front cover: John Sell Cotman, *A Ruined House*, *c.* 1807–10 (cat. 33)
Back cover: Dante Gabriel Rossetti, *Proserpine*, 1871 (cat. 68)
Frontispiece: detail from Charles Ginner, *Flask Walk: Rain*, *c.* 1924 (cat. 90)

For further details of Ashmolean titles please visit:
www.ashmolean.org/shop

LOWELL
LIBSON LTD
BRITISH ART

UNIVERSITY OF
OXFORD

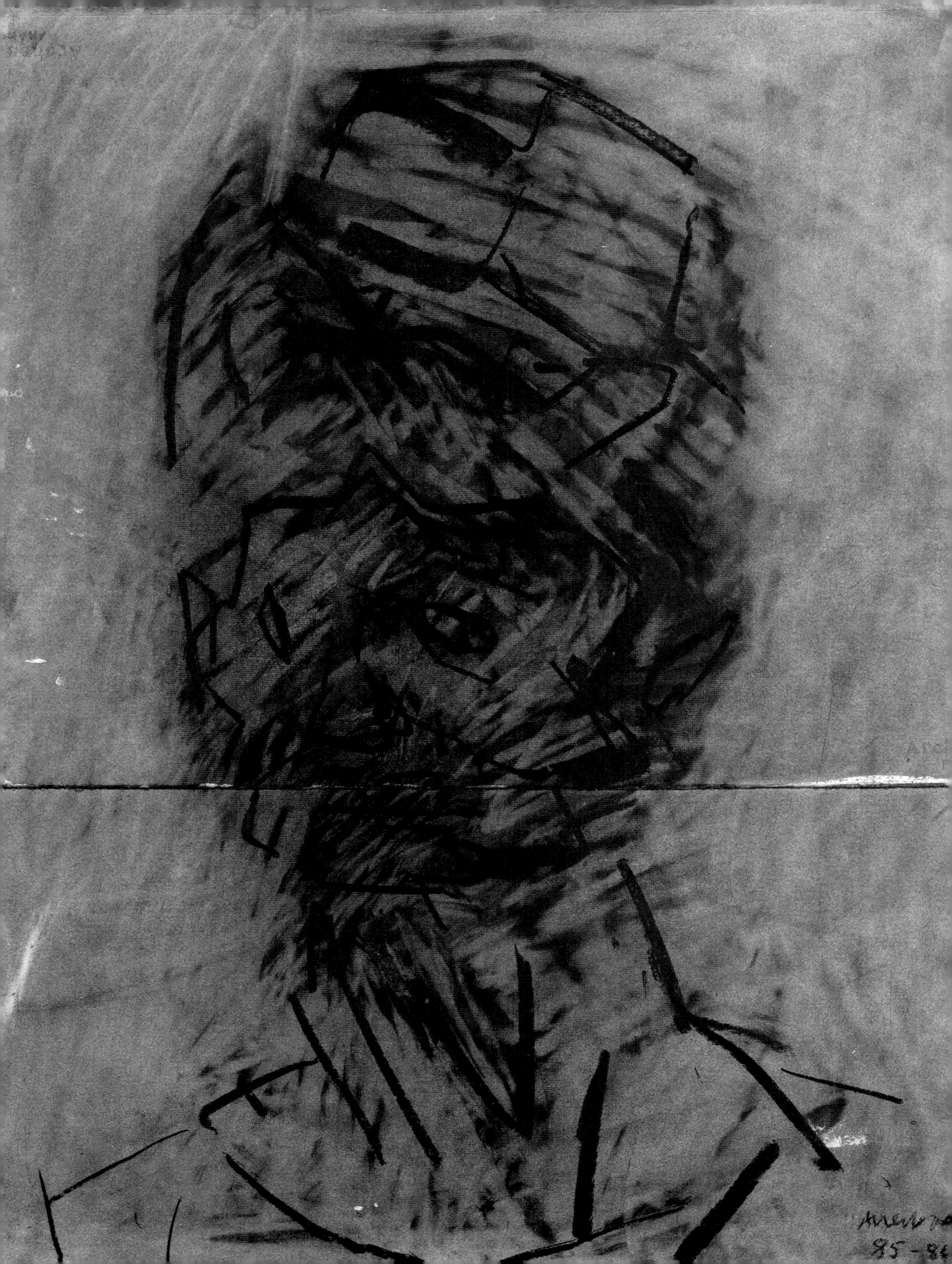

Foreword

The Ashmolean's exceptional collections of drawings, watercolours, and prints are among its greatest treasures and no school is better represented than the British. This catalogue and the exhibition it accompanies celebrate this extraordinary richness with drawings ranging from Flemish artists working in England in the seventeenth century, to those created by contemporary British artists. One of the great pleasures of looking at drawings is their immediacy, the way in which they can reveal the artist's working and thinking processes. It is not therefore surprising to find that artists themselves have often collected and treasured the drawings of their predecessors and peers.

The Ashmolean's collection has at its heart the great collection of Raphael and Michelangelo drawings collected by Sir Thomas Lawrence. Among the British drawings is the notable donation by John Ruskin of his beloved Turner watercolours in 1861, as well as his extensive gifts to the Drawing School he established in 1871, which were formally transferred to the Ashmolean after the Second World War. This year we are also thrilled to have received, through the Government's Acceptance in Lieu scheme, the great portrait by Frank Auerbach of his wife, Julia, which was among the many drawings by the artist in the collection of Lucian Freud (cat.113).

Ruskin believed that art could change lives, encouraging the viewer to see his or her natural and man-made surroundings in a more constructive and sympathetic way, and that every member of the public deserved to enjoy great works of art; beliefs that continue to be upheld by the provision of the Museum's Western Art Print Room. The exhibition of *Great British Drawings* has been selected by Colin Harrison, Senior Curator of European Art. Although drawn almost exclusively from the Ashmolean's own collection we are delighted that two private collectors have lent works which perfectly complement our own holdings. Finally, it is a great privilege to be able to display three drawings from the collection of caricatures formed by Jeffrey Archer.

The exhibition would not have been possible without the substantial support of Lowell Libson Ltd and the Friends of the Ashmolean, to whom we extend much thanks. It forms the centrepiece of a British season over the coming summer, with associated exhibitions of *Love Bites: Caricatures by James Gillray*, and *An Elegant Society: Adam Buck, Artist in the Age of Jane Austen*.

XA STURGIS *Director, Ashmolean Museum*

Detail from Frank Auerbach, *Head of Julia* (cat. 113)

Acknowledgements

This exhibition has been selected from the collection of some 10,000 British drawings and watercolours in the Ashmolean Museum. It opens with one of the most sensitive of all seventeenth century portraits, by the first great native-born English artist, Samuel Cooper, and closes with portraits by three of Britain's most celebrated living artists, Frank Auerbach, David Hockney, and Tom Phillips. Between come a wide variety of landscapes and figure studies, portraits and still lifes, including drawings and watercolours, chosen on the grounds of quality and condition rather than solely for their historical importance. There are a number of prominent absentees: there is no Sandby or Varley, Lawrence or Constable, and a host of names working after the First World War. It is a particular cause of satisfaction that three private collectors have agreed to lend important works from their collections. The watercolours by John Robert Cozens and David Cox far eclipse any by these artists in the Ashmolean; and the works by Keith Vaughan, William Gear, Bryan Winter, Colin Self, and Cecil Collins enable us to show some of the many aspects of British art in the twentieth century. The loans of caricatures from Jeffrey Archer have been arranged through his personal assistant, Alison Prince, and through Chris Beetles. Finally, several items on long-term loan to the Ashmolean, from the Christopher Sands Trust and two anonymous collections, are included. We are greatly indebted to all these lenders.

I am grateful to my three collaborators on the catalogue entries, Caroline Palmer, Katherine Wodehouse, and Harry Dickinson, and to the authors of the essays, Timothy Wilcox and Susan Owens. In addition to writing entries, Katherine Wodehouse has masterminded the production of the catalogue from beginning to end. We are indebted to David Gowers and Anne Holly for their expert photography, as well as to the work of Amy Taylor in our Picture Library. Eunice Lee assisted with third party image and rights acquisition. Thanks are likewise due to Robert Dalrymple, our catalogue designer. We also recognise the vital contribution of our Exhibitions and Design teams as well as our Registrars and Paper Conservators.

For help with particular artists, we are grateful to Alessia de Quincey, Tom Cain, Patrick Conner, Briony Llewellyn, Martyn Gregory, Susan Sloman, Sophie Bowness, and Timothy Wilcox. The whole exhibition has benefited immeasurably from the wise counsel of Lowell Libson.

COLIN HARRISON *Senior Curator of European Art*

Detail from Edward Lear,
Constantinople from Ayoub (cat. 42)

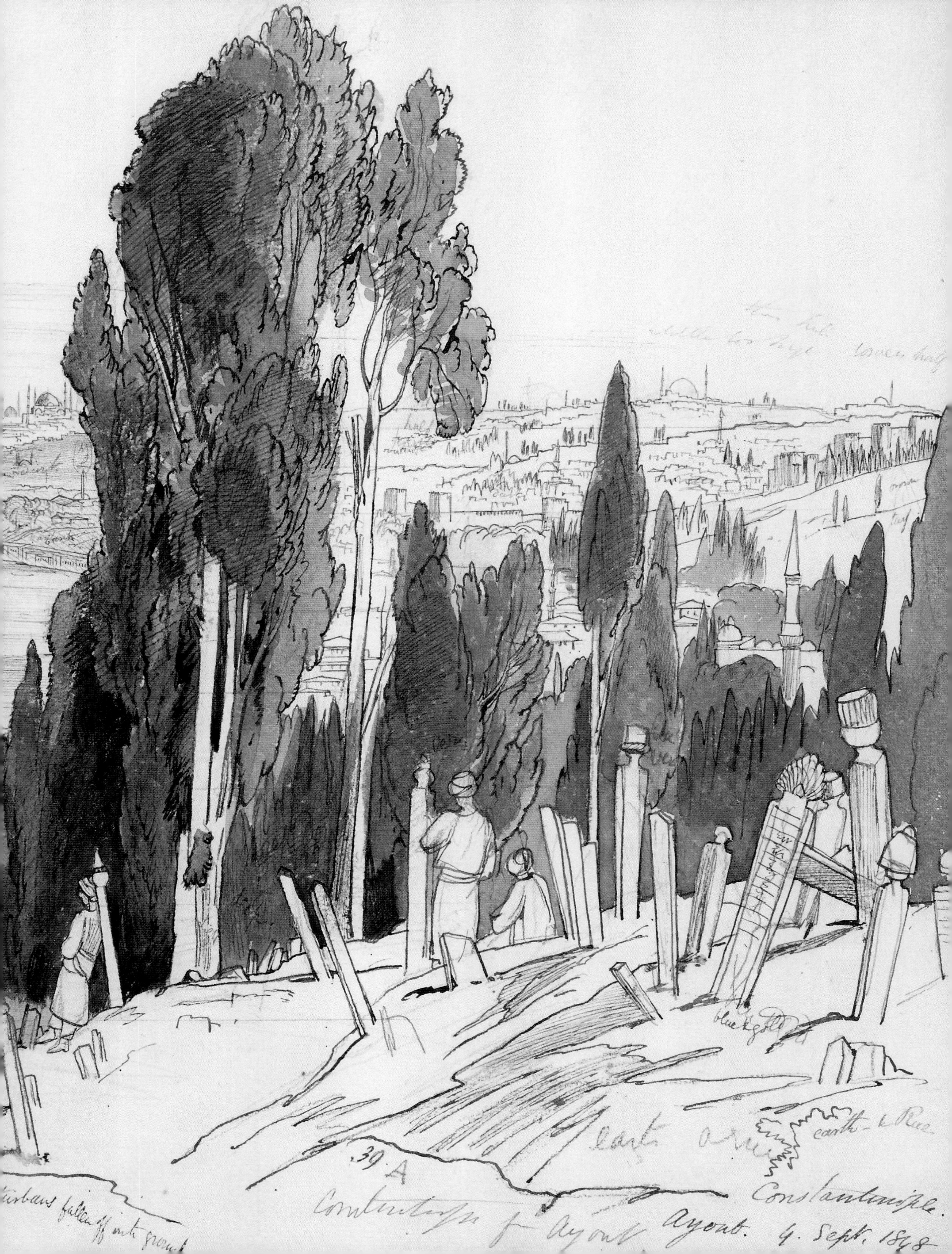

blue & gold
earth – & Rue
39 A
Constantinople.
Ayoub. 4. Sept. 1848

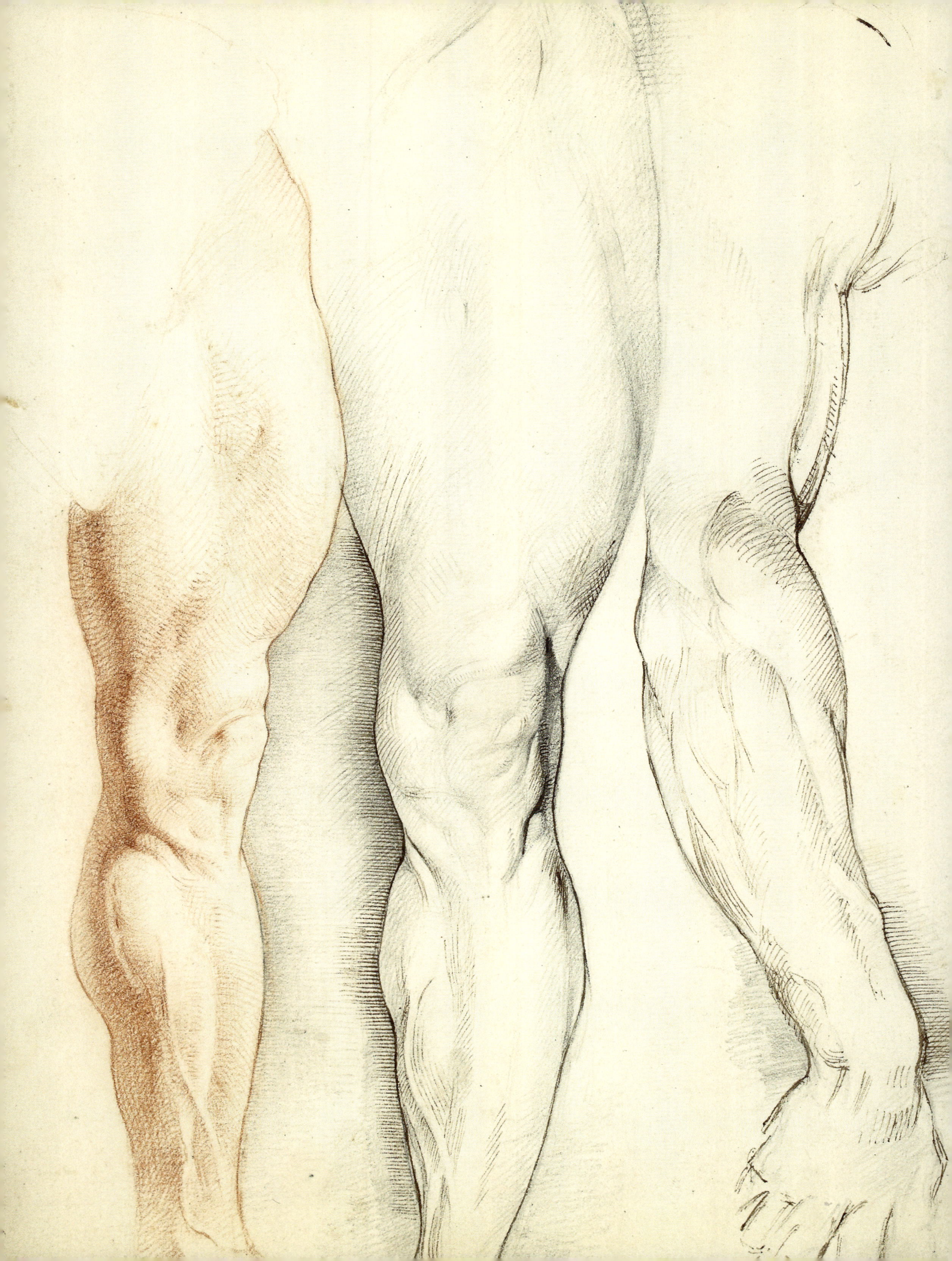

Learning to Draw

Susan Owens

Detail from George Richmond, *'Boswood's Thigh' and the right arm of Michelangelo's 'David'* (cat. 21)

For centuries, drawing and learning have been closely connected. As a means of co-ordinating the mind and hand, and inculcating habits of observation, the practice of drawing was considered essential in preparing an artist for a career as a painter or sculptor. Consequently, the process of learning to draw remained at the heart of art academies from the sixteenth century until the third quarter of the twentieth. The most effective way of teaching artists to draw has not, however, been the subject of such universal accord. Each institution brought with it particular values and principles, dictating what students studied, how (and indeed if) they were taught, and the kinds of drawings they were expected to produce. Just as important as what went on inside these academies were the rebellions against them, when artists rejected institutional values and sought alternatives. The history of learning to draw is a vital thread in the narrative of British art, marked by a succession of conflicting theories and practices, power struggles and revolts.

England approached the concept of the art academy with caution. In Italy, by contrast, there had been an unbroken tradition of official institutions since the sixteenth century, with the foundation of the *Accademia del Disegno* in Florence in 1563 and the *Accademia di S. Luca* in Rome in 1593. In France, the *Académie royale de peinture et de sculpture* was established in 1648, a full 120 years before its English equivalent, the Royal Academy. The English attitude can be seen in a treatise on miniature painting written by the courtier Edward Norgate in the second quarter of the seventeenth century. He noted that on the Continent, there was 'another way of Designing, that is by frequenting the Academy' and, with the air of somebody explaining the faintly amusing activities of foreigners, described this academy as:

> *a Roome where in the middle, a hired Long sided Porter or such like is to be set, stand or hang naked sometimes in a posture for two or three howres. This fellow is surrounded by a number of Painters, who make him their Model, and drawe him as he appeares to every one. By this practice they pretend to greate skill in the naked Anatomy, and Muscles of the Body …*[1]

Norgate was sceptical about the point of this practice, and related that no less an authority than Rubens had told him that artists had been known to attend the Academy 'for twenty Yeares together to little or noe purpose'.[2]

Rubens's reservations presumably arose from his doubts about the usefulness of studying life-drawing in an academic vacuum, rather than as part of a process that would lead to a finished work.[3] In contrast, Norgate's were caused by his lack of familiarity. In England, from the Middle Ages until the eighteenth century, an artist would typically enter the studio of an established master as an apprentice, to be introduced to the range of tasks involved in that particular practice. Within this studio context, drawing would normally have been taught as a key skill in the planning of a painting or sculpture – but not privileged as an activity to be pursued separately. Signs of change came in the 1670s, when the highly successful portrait painter Peter Lely responded to an increasing number of requests from young artists to be taken on as apprentices by setting up an informal academy next door to his studio in Covent Garden.Here he supervised drawing from the life model.[4] That established artists should take on students and teaching life drawing was the norm in Lely's native Netherlands, and could be regarded as the expansion of an existing system rather than a departure from it.

At the same time, however, there was a growing awareness of the advantages of the situation on the Continent. As a consequence, a desire for a comparable system of art training in England began to be voiced. A drawing manual published in 1674 considers the widespread practice of drawing in foreign art schools, particularly in Rome, and advocates 'a diligent and serious imitation, that the Art of Drawing and Painting here in *England* might flourish, as much as in any part beyond the Seas, not have any occasion to give precedency or pre-eminence to any foreign Artist whatsoever'.[5] Towards the end of the seventeenth century, small schools or drawing classes began to emerge. Clubs such as the Society of the Virtuosi of St Luke and the Rose and Crown Club offered a professional arena for discussions concerning the state of the arts in England.

When the first formal academy opened in England, it was not a state institution with a hierarchical structure, as in France, but an organisation set up by artists and for artists, open to anyone on payment of a guinea's subscription fee. The Great Queen Street Academy was established in 1711 in a house in the West End of London, with the illustrious portrait painter Sir Godfrey Kneller at its head. This new academy was designed to cater for a broad range of art professionals rather than one specific group; under Kneller, the twelve directors – elected by the members – included the portraitists Jonathan Richardson and Thomas Gibson, the pastellist Edward Luttrell, the history painters Louis Laguerre, Antonio Pellegrini and James Thornhill, the sculptor Francis Bird, and the engraver Nicholas Dorigny. The contemporary chronicler of the art world, George Vertue, remarked that many 'excellent painters and Artists joynd to study there to cultivate knowledge in a more extensive way than had ever been before in England'.[6] As well as the opportunity to draw from the life model, the Academy provided a professional and social forum for painters, sculptors and engravers, both established and aspiring, as well as visiting foreign artists. It reflected the increasing professionalization of the artist, and his growing status as a gentleman rather than a craftsman, and promised to be a cohesive and galvanising force for England's painters and sculptors.

Following Continental practice, the human figure was the principal object of study at Great Queen Street. This focus became a sort of ideological pivot: building on the native tradition of portraiture, it also fostered a knowledge of anatomy, and thus potentially raised standards by making figures as convincing as faces. Horace Walpole's complaint that Richardson, one of the most successful portraitists of the era, 'drew nothing well below the head ... His attitudes, draperies, and backgrounds are totally insipid and unmeaning' suggests that the lack of such training was indeed something of a disadvantage.[7] At the same time, the centrality of the life model at the Academy seemed to signal a national ambition to progress beyond the portrait to subject pictures, both secular and religious, for which competence in drawing the human figure in a range of expressive poses was the essential building block. The market for such pictures was now so strong that foreign paintings were being imported in large numbers to meet the demand. English artists needed to compete with these imports, and putting the human figure at the heart of the first native academy indicated an intention to do just that.

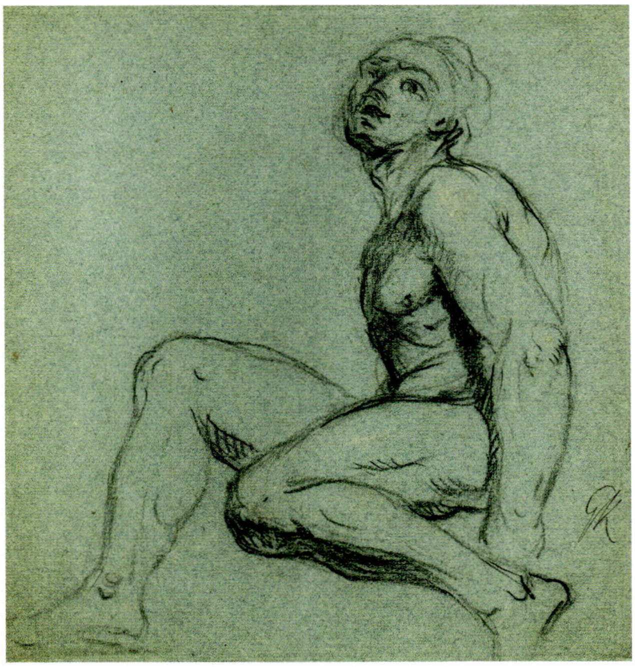

Fig. 1 | Godfrey Kneller (1646–1723), *Seated male nude*, *c.* 1711. Black chalk on blue paper. British Museum, London, 1888,0719.71 © Trustees of the British Museum

One of the roles of the Academy's directors was to establish the life model's pose. Vertue mentions how one of them, Pelligrini, who 'drew very often' at the Academy, 'had an extraordinary readynes in setting the moddel well'.[8] This role was more important than it might at first appear. Not only could a model be positioned in ways that were useful for an artist planning a subject picture, but his pose could also convey elevated cultural references. A life drawing by Kneller himself records a model whose pose emulates a figure painted by Annibale Carracci on a ceiling in the Palazzo Farnese in Rome – illustrating the ways in which Old Master compositions were brought to bear on academic training (fig. 1).[9]

The Academy in Great Queen Street does not seem to have offered formal instruction, although advice was freely given by its members. Vertue relates how the young Joseph Highmore, later to become a painter of portraits and conversation pieces, 'came into the accademy under Sr. G. Kneller about ye 3d or fourth Year after it was sett up'. He noted that Highmore's 'continual application improv'd him much in the fundamentals of that Science, his daily access to all the eminent Artists & their free communicateing to him their instructions … was of great advantage to his improvement without much cost or expence', giving a sense of the collaborative atmosphere that prevailed in the early academy.[10]

Theories of art training were much discussed at this time. In the early 1720s Vertue himself set out a scheme in his notebook for an academy and drawing school 'For the Improvement of the ART of Delineing in this NATION'.[11] Vertue's attendance at Kneller's Academy from its foundation in 1711 had shaped his experience of art training, although whether his ideas reflected aspects of the existing system or sought to complement what was possibly a rather *laissez-faire* one is debatable. In any case, his proposed course was certainly more rigorous than that offered at Great Queen Street. Vertue believed in a progressive system, derived from contemporary drawing manuals, in which students worked diligently through a number of stages. This began with copying, and Vertue recommended that the school should be equipped with exemplary drawings of the 'Rudiments' that every student should emulate: 'Eys nose mouth facces hands feet &c. Arms leggs bodies each being pasted on a Cartoon' (a large sheet of paper so that they could be propped up and to make them durable).[12] The next step was for the student to 'copy drawings that are done after statues, Busts or Casts, described on Grey paper or Blew hightned with black and white only'.[13] It was only after this stage – which 'may consist of 50 drawings all which must be copyd carefully' – that the student would be permitted to draw casts of Antique sculpture.[14] Vertue's proposed school is particularly interesting for its principle that the student should initially learn to draw by looking at other drawings, rather than working out his own way of representing objects on paper. Presumably the intention was to inculcate particular methods of outlining, hatching and shading.

Although they apparently managed to avoid so rigorous a curriculum, the Great Queen Street Academy and its successors created a climate in which artists were able to establish a common vocabulary for drawing. Whereas through the apprenticeship system an artist would learn the stylistic traits of his immediate master, an academy fostered the ideal conditions in which to share ideas about drawing methods and techniques more widely. This was partly achieved through the provision of exemplary drawings. When in 1720 another academy was in the process of being set up, Vertue proposed that each director should 'give or present to the Accademy, one Accademy figure of his own Drawing there in that Accademy done. to be kept or preserved by the Treasurer. in one large Cover folio & for that purpose provided only'.[15] A drawing by Jonathan Richardson of 'James Figg the Gladiator', who,

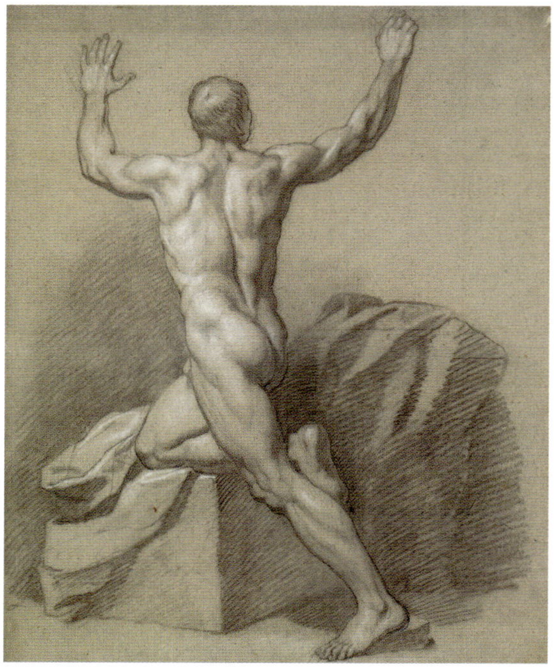

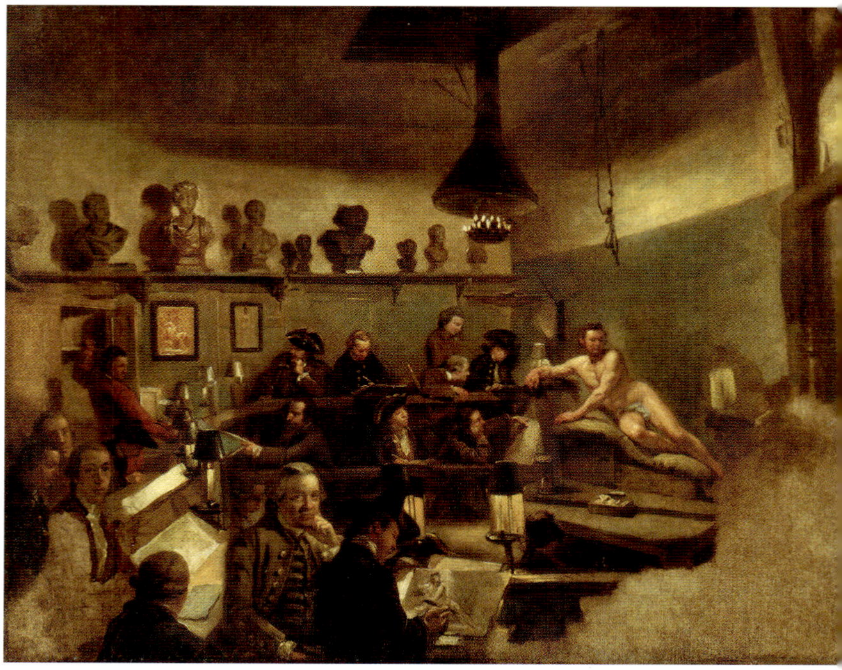

as well as posing for artists, ran an academy of arms, was probably a demonstration drawing of this kind, made in 1714 for the Great Queen Street Academy (cat. 6).[16] As might be expected of a drawing by a portraitist, this study represents a distinct individual, rather than a generic muscular body. It is likely that such exemplary drawings of nudes were supplemented by established artists' working drawings. There is evidence that Kneller took the head studies he made as preparation for his portraits into the Academy for students to study and copy.[17]

In 1720 the Great Queen Street Academy was superseded by a new institution just off St Martin's Lane, set up by Louis Chéron and John Vanderbank. Both artists had attended the Great Queen Street Academy from its inception, and Vertue records that Chéron's 'talent in delineing' was 'soon distinguishd' and that his drawings were 'much immitated by the Young people'.[18] Born in Paris, Chéron had been trained at the French *Académie*. Here his drawings had been so admired that he was twice awarded the *Prix de Rome*. Emphatically hatched to create the illusion of volumetric form, his powerful, heroic nudes introduced an unprecedented rigour to academic drawing in England (fig. 2). Although influential, Chéron's French drawing style was not, however, universally admired; Vertue, for instance, found his drawings 'generally heavy'.[19]

It appears that Chéron and Vanderbank introduced the practice of employing female as well as male models – to make the academy 'more inviting to subscribers', as Hogarth suggested, perhaps not entirely seriously.[20] This put the new academy in the vanguard, as those on the Continent did not employ female models until nearly 100 years later.[21] However, it closed after only four years, in 1724, when Vanderbank was obliged to leave the country in order to avoid imprisonment for debt.

In the same year Sir James Thornhill, who had previously taken over the governorship of the Great Queen Street Academy from Kneller, set up a free drawing academy in a room in his own home in Covent Garden.[22] This was eventually succeeded in 1735 by the 'second' St Martin's Lane Academy, founded by Thornhill's son-in-law William Hogarth and the portrait painter John Ellys, with the 'neglected apparatus' Hogarth had inherited from the older artist.[23] Vertue noted: 'this Winter 1735 an Accademy for Life sett up in St Martins lane where several Artists go to Draw from the life. Mr Hogarth principally promotes or undertakes it'.[24] Hogarth himself described how, in 'a room big enough for a naked figure to be drawn after by thirty or forty people', he provided 'a proper table for the figure to stand on a large lamp iron stove and benches in a circular form'.[25] A painting by Johann Zoffany representing the academy's room reveals the configuration of the space, how the nude figure was lit and, on an upper shelf, the plaster busts that could serve in the absence of a life model (fig. 3). It was, Hogarth later declared, 'as perfect an academy as any in Europe'.[26]

Hogarth was an unlikely founder of an art academy. In his treatise *The Analysis of Beauty*, published in 1753, he voiced his scepticism about the effectiveness of academic training, citing the example of 'those gentilmen who have

Fig. 2 | Louis Chéron (1660–1725), *Kneeling male nude seen from behind*, *c.* 1720–4. Black and white chalk on grey paper. British Museum, London, 1953,1021.11.83 © Trustees of the British Museum

Fig. 3 | Johann Zoffany (1733–1810), *A Life Class at St Martin's Lane Academy*, 1761–2. Oil on canvas, unfinished. Royal Academy of Arts, London, 03/621 © Royal Academy of Arts, London

Fig. 4 | William Hogarth (1697–1764), *Seated female nude*, *c.* 1720–4. Black and white chalk on grey paper. British Museum, London, 1960,0409.113 © Trustees of the British Museum

labour'd with the utmost assiduity abroad surrounded with the works of the great masters, and at home at academys for twenty years together without gaining the least ground'; indeed, he added ominously, 'nay, some have rather gon backwards'. Instead, he advocated the simple habit of being observant: 'if I have acquired anything in my way it has been wholly obtain'd by Observation by which method be where I would with my Eyes open I could have been at my studys'.[27]

Nothing if not patriotic, Hogarth was incensed at the thought of English artists travelling abroad to study when England could produce its own home-grown facilities:

Everything requisite to compleat the consummate painter or sculptor may be had with the utmost ease without going out of London at this time going to study abroad is an errant farce and more likely to confound a true genious than to improve him do skyes look more like skies trees more like tree[s] [28]

What distinguished his own academy from what he called the 'pompous parading one at paris' was its lack of hierarchy.[29] Indeed, Hogarth stated that he 'became an equal subscriber with the rest signifying at the same time that superior and inferior among artists should be avoided especially in this country'.[30]

In contrast to the French *Académie*, where a disciplinarian oligarchy dictated an approved manner of drawing, no particular drawing style was imposed at St Martin's Lane. In fact Hogarth even quoted with approval Voltaire's observation that 'after that establishment [the *Académie*] no work of genious appeard for says he they all became imitators and mannerists'.[31] The democratic ethos instilled by Hogarth in the St Martin's Lane Academy created the conditions for free-style drawing based on observation rather than on academic formulae. Hogarth's own life drawings are decidedly sensuous in comparison with Chéron's, representing the bodies and faces of individual models rather than stereotyped figures (fig. 4). When he voiced a preference for a 'blooming young girl of fifteen' to the 'stony features of a ... venus', Hogarth was pitting an English sensibility and toleration of individuality against the severe classical tradition promoted by Chéron.[32]

The portrait painter Allan Ramsay was also a member at St Martin's Lane. Like many artists of his generation, he had made an extended visit to Rome, and studied at the French Academy, which was open to visiting students for life-drawing classes. His drawing of a female nude (cat. 8), although probably made during a later trip to Italy in the 1750s, is a sensitive study, softly modelled in chalks. If Ramsay brought a French sensibility to his drawing, it was the lively sensuality of Boucher rather than the formal academicism of Chéron.

In the 1750s and early 1760s other arenas for drawing emerged in London.One of these was the Duke of Richmond's sculpture gallery in Whitehall, which opened in 1758. Here students had access to a treasure trove of casts of classical statuary and made drawings under the guidance of the sculptor Joseph Wilton and the Florentine decorative painter Giovanni Battista Cipriani.

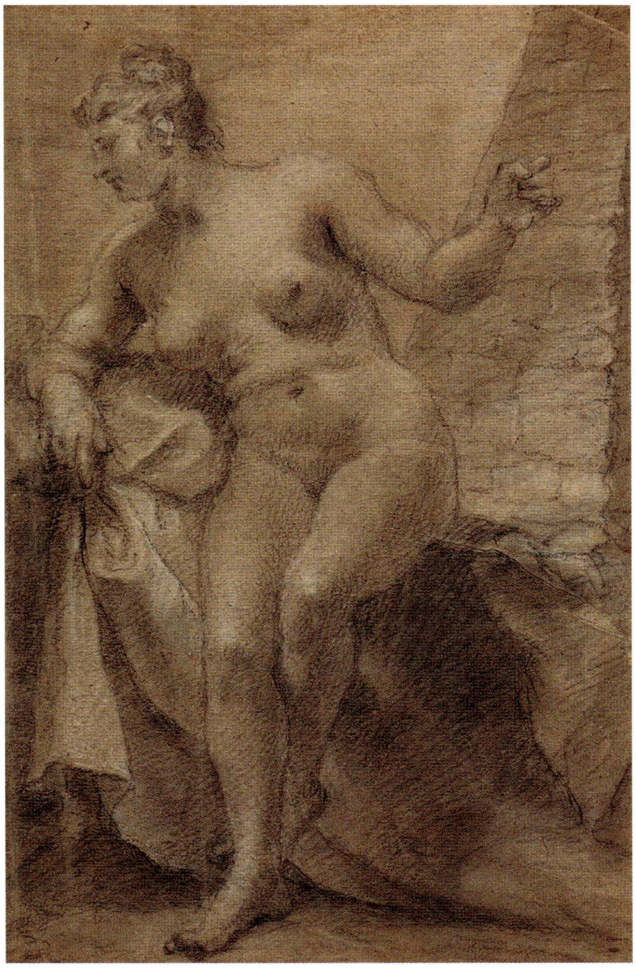

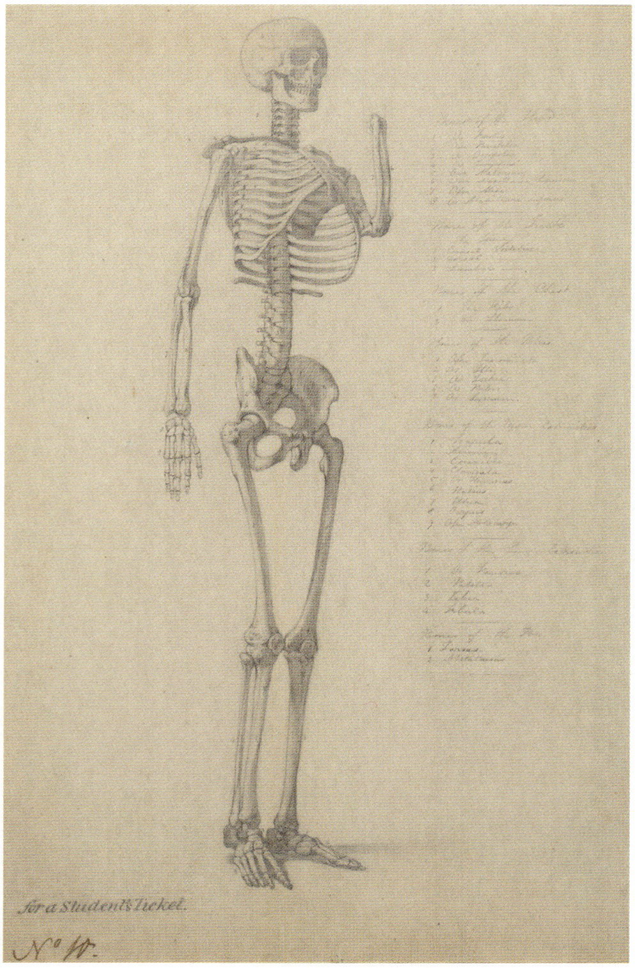

Fig. 5 | Edward William Frost (1810–1877), *Annotated study of a skeleton*, *c.* 1829. Graphite on paper. Victoria and Albert Museum, London, E.424–1948 © Victoria and Albert Museum, London

Another was a drawing school with large premises in Beaufort Buildings on the Strand, run between 1754 and 1761 by William Shipley, founder of the Society for the Encouragement of Arts, Manufactures and Commerce. He favoured a broad-based drawing course, which extended beyond the life class and was aimed at the education of future designers and craftsmen, with the intention of assisting 'such manufactures as require Fancy and Ornament, and for which the knowledge of Drawing is absolutely necessary'.[33] Shipley's pupils included John Hamilton Mortimer, Richard Cosway, Ozias Humphry, Joseph Nollekens, and William Pars.

It might have seemed that there had never been more varied opportunities for young artists to study. Yet the establishment of the Royal Academy in 1768 had the effect of channelling this momentum, expressive of the growth and confidence of a British school, into a narrower course. For the first time, the new institution offered the opportunity to study from the antique and from the life under the same roof. It also introduced a hierarchical system and a strict degree of control over admission and student practice that had not previously been seen in English art education.

In an address to mark the official opening of the Royal Academy of Arts in January 1769, its first President, Joshua Reynolds, was immensely unflattering about the state of art education in Britain. 'One advantage', he said, 'I will venture to affirm, we shall have in our Academy, which no other nation can boast. We shall have nothing to unlearn.'[34] Complaining about the standard of drawing at other schools of art, and no doubt thinking of the St Martin's Lane Academy, he said

> *… the Students never draw exactly from the living models which they have before them. It is not indeed their intention; nor are they directed to do it. Their drawings resemble the model only in the attitude. They change the form according to their vague and uncertain ideas of beauty, and make a drawing rather of what they think the figure ought to be, than of what it appears.*[35]

This was more or less the same point made by Hogarth in 1753, although Reynolds expressed it with more rhetorical panache. The practice of observation, it seems, was not straightforward.

Surprisingly little was put in writing at this stage about the aims of the Royal Academy, beyond the founder members' intention, expressed in a petition presented to George III in November 1768, to provide 'a well-regulated School or Academy of Design'.[36] But it was perhaps inevitable that an organisation on this scale would demand a more rigorous discipline than had been imposed at either Great Queen Street or St Martin's Lane. This discipline found its expression in the imposition of a two-tier system in the Academy. First, a student had to be accepted as a Probationer, after which he was required to submit a finished drawing from one of the casts, and annotated drawings of an écorché figure and a skeleton (fig. 5). If the Probationer's drawings were approved, he would then receive a student's ticket and be enrolled in the Antique Academy, where:

Fig. 6 | Edward Francis Burney (1760–1848), *The Antique School at New Somerset House*, c. 1780. Pen and ink with watercolour on paper. Royal Academy of Arts, London, 03/7484 © Royal Academy of Arts, London

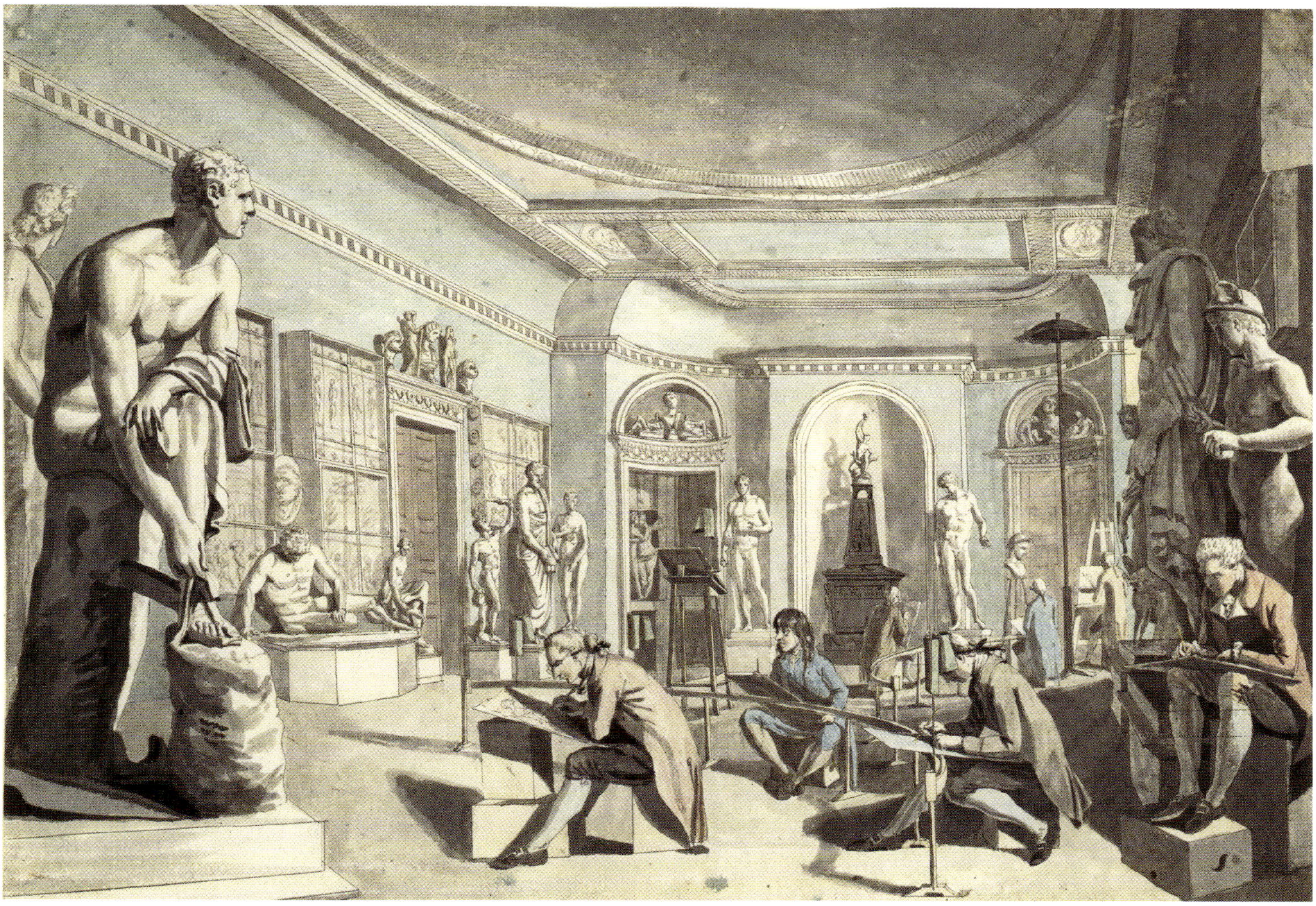

There shall be Weekly, set out in the Great Room, One or more Plaister Figures by the Keeper, for the Students to draw after, and no Student shall presume to move the said Figures out of the said Places where they have been set by the Keeper, without his leave first obtained for that Purpose.

When any student hath taken possession of a Place in the Plaister Academy, he shall not be removed out of it, till the Week in which he hath taken it is expired.[37]

The system posited the antique as the first stage of a progressive system. For the first time, the student was obliged to spend a considerable period drawing from casts of classical sculpture in the Antique Academy (fig. 6). Only when he had submitted satisfactory drawings was he admitted to the Life Room. As Benjamin West, Reynolds's successor as President, put it, proficiency was 'not to be gained by rushing impatiently to the school of the living model; correctness of form and taste was first to be sought by an attentive study of the Grecian figures'.[38]

For Reynolds, the antique was the lifeblood of artistic excellence:

The principal advantage of an Academy is, that ... it will be a repository for the great examples of the Art ... By studying these authentick models, that idea of excellence which is the result of the accumulated experience of past ages, may be at once acquired'.[39]

He invested these exemplary works with properties that were all but magical, believing that they enabled the student to receive 'at one glance, the principles which many Artists have spent their whole lives in ascertaining.[40]

The rigidly structured nature of the Royal Academy, in which students began their training in the Antique

Fig. 7 | William Mulready (1786–1863), *Study of a plaster cast of the Pancrastinae*, *c.* 1800. Black and white chalk on grey-green paper. Victoria and Albert Museum, London, 6000 © Victoria and Albert Museum, London

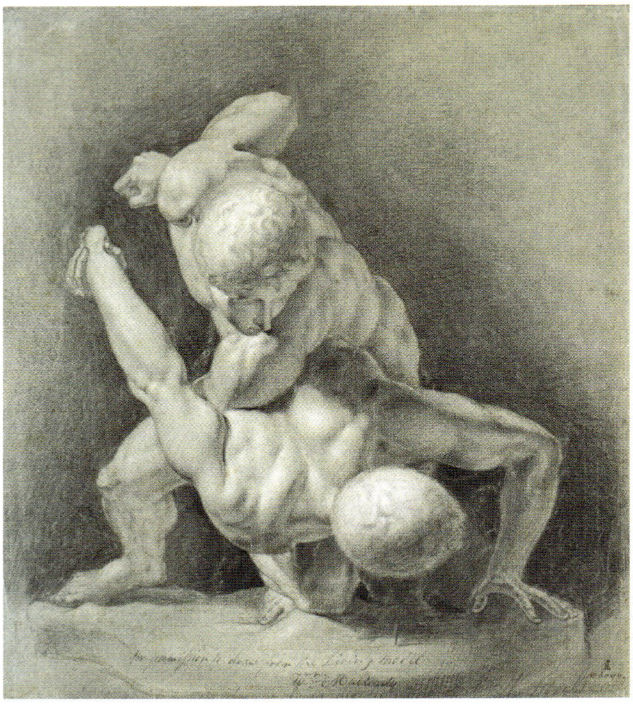

Academy and were eventually examined for their fitness to draw from the living model, was a force for conformity. Students were expected to produce drawings that demonstrated their ability to represent the subtle gradations of light and shadow on three-dimensional forms – and, because of the element of competition, they strove to make their works fit this requirement. An inscription on a work of about 1800 by William Mulready (fig. 7) records that the drawing was submitted 'For permission to draw from the living model', and it exemplifies the painstaking modelling that was most likely to earn the artist a passport to the Life Room. Strokes of the chalk have been smoothed out with a stump, a tool of rolled leather or paper, and gestural marks indicative of individual draughtsmanship suppressed. There was no room in the system for the rapid sketch or the exploratory study.

Nonetheless, while the rules engendered a climate of conformity, the teaching offered by the Royal Academy was not particularly rigorous. Indeed, in his inaugural address Reynolds had spoken favourably of what he called 'an atmosphere of floating knowledge', in which students learned principally from one another.[41] In terms of tuition, the Academy had a system of 'Visitors' who taught in rotation. Nine Royal Academicians were elected annually to fulfil this role, which demanded that for one month each year they would attend the Antique Academy or the Life Room to supervise the students' drawings and, in the latter case, to set the model's pose.

It was a system that militated against consistency. One Visitor discouraged strong outlines, and, according to an account of 1803, even erased them when he found them in a student's work:

... if by chance a student made an error in his drawing by too powerful an outline or too marked a development of muscular action, Mr Wilton would gently come up to the draughtsman's side, and collecting his delicately white ruffles between the tips of his fingers and the palm of his hand, begin to rub over the offending parts, smudging the white with the black chalk, saying, 'I do not see those lines in the figure before you'.[42]

The approach of the Swiss-born artist Henry Fuseli, appointed Keeper of the Royal Academy in 1804, presented a stark contrast. Fuseli was moved to intervene decisively when he detected a student too greatly absorbed in producing fine degrees of shading:

Woe to the poor student who depended on his elaborate finishing. After having been a week or ten days working up his drawing with the softest chalk, stumping, dotting, stippling, until he had nearly worn his eyes out, the Keeper would stealthily come behind him, and looking over his shoulder would grasp the porte-crayon, and, standing at arm's length from the drawing, would give so terrific a score as to cut through the paper and leave a distinct outline on the board beneath; and then would say, by way of encouragement to future exertion, 'There, Saar, there, you should have a boldness of handling and a greater fwreedom of tooch'.[43]

Nevertheless, in general, Royal Academy drawings were expected to be carefully shaded – a style that was compatible with the smooth surface quality of plaster casts, but that also conformed to an early nineteenth-century taste in oil paintings. Because of its versatility, the material most often used for students' drawings was black chalk. Dense enough to be sharpened to a point and used for linear work, it was also capable of broad, sculptural effects and could be rubbed with a stump to create subtle tonal gradations.

A student needed to have attained a high standard of proficiency in drawing before the Royal Academy would admit him, and as a result a number of private art schools were established which offered preparatory tuition.One of the best known was run by Henry Sass from premises in Charlotte Street, where William Powell Frith, William

Holman Hunt and Dante Gabriel Rossetti all studied. Sass had unshakable confidence in his abilities, once claiming: 'I met [David] Wilkie, and he said to me, "Sass, you could teach a stone to draw;" and SO IT IS'.[44] Sass offered a disciplined elementary course in which students began by drawing outlines and eventually progressed to drawing from the round. Even then, the first object to be drawn was a huge plaster ball, 'by the representation of which in Italian chalk and on white paper', wrote Frith, a student in the 1830s, 'the student was to be initiated into the first principles of light, shadow, and rotundity.'[45] Only when he had mastered the 'awful ball' was the student permitted to progress to 'a gigantic bunch of plaster grapes' and, eventually, to casts of classical sculpture.[46] It was a long and arduous process.

Hunt too recalled the intensely disciplined drawing technique that was taught at Sass's, which imitated the 'dot-and-lozenge' method found in eighteenth-century line engravings:

Many students who worked there shaded their drawings with the most regular cross hatching, putting a dot in every empty space; thus the figure was blocked out into flat angular surfaces, which, ultimately blended by half-tints, produced the required modelling[47]

Such discipline paid off when it came to applying to the Academy. As Hunt recalled, 'Sasse's [*sic*] school in particular was recommended by Academicians, and the drawings that issued from it, with their mechanical precision, were favoured by the examiners'.[48] Not only did Sass's insistence on rigorous cross-hatching and stippling drum the grammar of drawing into the student, but it was also intended to instil discipline – although on many talented but independently minded students, such as Rossetti, it must have had the opposite effect.

A comment later made by John Everett Millais suggests that at the Royal Academy, the style and 'finished' quality of a drawing eventually began to be valued at the expense of its accuracy – a weakness that was exposed when the student moved to the Life Room:

We find students straight from the Antique school, who have drawn the Gladiator and Apollo most correctly and admirably, quite incapable of drawing the living model, because they cannot draw well enough, yet it is only too common to find modest faithfulness to nature ignored for the work which seems to say – 'see how well I am drawn, and how much learning there is in me'.[49]

The apparently simple principle expressed by Reynolds at the outset, that students should draw, not 'what they think the figure ought to be', but what 'appears', seemed to remain tantalisingly out of reach.

From the early seventeenth century to the early twentieth, British artists avidly sought out Old Master prints and drawings, incorporating the subjects, styles and techniques they found in them into their own work. Lely, Richardson, Reynolds and Thomas Lawrence, each of whom played an important role in the development of a national school, all assembled great collections. As time went on and a powerful Establishment became more entrenched, artists began to look beyond the accepted canon, finding in certain Old Masters an authoritative alternative to the *status quo*. This is vividly illustrated by William Blake's famous annotations to Reynolds's *Works*, which begin on the title page with his furious accusation: 'This Man was Hired to Depress Art'. A few pages later Blake describes the following encounter with George Michael Moser, the first Keeper of the Royal Academy Schools:

I was once looking over the Prints from Rafael & Michael Angelo. in the Library of the Royal Academy Moser came to me & said You should not Study these old Hard Stiff & Dry Unfinished Works of Art, Stay a little & I will shew you what you should Study. He then went & took down Le Bruns & Rubens's Galleries. How I did secretly Rage. I also spoke my Mind … I said to Moser, These things that you call Finished are not Even Begun how can they then, be Finished? The Man who does not know The Beginning, never can know the End of Art.[50]

Blake himself had initially learned to draw not at the Royal Academy, but at Pars's drawing school and as an apprentice to the engraver James Basire, and his linear drawing style in part resulted from this training. Nonetheless, even as a youth he had acquired prints after Michelangelo and Raphael, who, as his altercation with Moser suggests, were, together with Albrecht Dürer, his great artistic

Fig. 8 | Samuel Palmer (1805–1881), *Studies of leaves from a sketch-book*, c. 1824. Pen and brown ink on paper. British Museum, London, 1964,1104.1.14
© Trustees of the British Museum

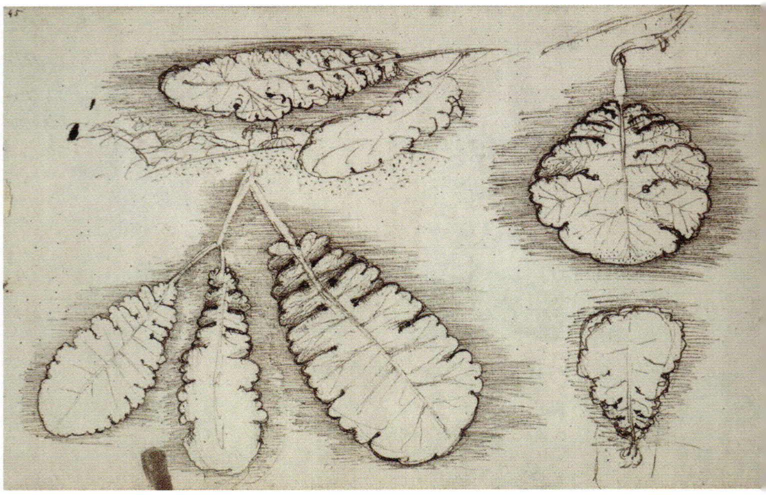

heroes. The powerful contours of Michelangelo's figures in particular were a vital source of inspiration for Blake in the development of his own intense vision. Blake knew the works of these masters largely through the medium of engravings; they fed back into his belief in the power of the crisp outline, by which he distinguished the good from the corrupt: 'the more distinct and sharp and wiry the bounding line, the more perfect the work of art; and the less keen and sharp this external line, the greater is the evidence of weak imitative plagiarism and bungling … Leave out this line and you leave out life itself.'[51]

In the last three years of his life, Blake transmitted his reverence for Michelangelo and Dürer to a group of idealistic young artists, including Samuel Palmer, Edward Calvert, and George Richmond. They called themselves 'the Ancients', despising what they regarded as the pomposity and conventionality of contemporary art, and seeking more authentic models to help them define their own artistic identity. Blake became an inspirational figure for the group, whose members sought to emulate his idiosyncratic vision as much as the Old Masters he discussed with them.

Palmer was one of the most inventive and least conventional draughtsmen of his generation. His most fertile period as an artist, from the mid-1820s to the mid-1830s, coincided with his residence in the secluded village of Shoreham in Kent. The hills and lanes of this place, his 'valley of vision', inspired him to create some of the most intense and numinous landscape drawings in the whole of English art (cat. 22). These works were deeply informed by his knowledge of masters, both old and new. Notes in a sketchbook of 1824 find Palmer mulling over the problems of representing natural forms: 'Though I hope we shall all be severe outlinists, I hope our styles of outline may all be different as the design of Michael Angelo from his equal, Blake, and the outline of Albert Dürer from that of Andrea Mantegna. There is no line in nature, though excessive sharpness.'[52] Another mentor, the artist John Linnell, encouraged him to look specifically at prints by Dürer and Lucas van Leyden, and in the same sketchbook Palmer made drawings of natural forms with the fine wiry lines and stippling strokes he had learned from engravings by these masters (fig. 8).

The impact of Michelangelo on British artists in this period can be seen in a drawing of 1828 by another 'Ancient', George Richmond, which juxtaposes studies of the muscular thigh of a male model with one of the right arm of Michelangelo's *David* (cat. 21). This is an unconventional drawing for the period, not shaded like the approved kind of academic study, but an incisive and detailed study of musculature. It emulates studies by Michelangelo himself, which Richmond must have seen in the collection of Sir Thomas Lawrence, President of the Royal Academy – not only in its fine hatching and attention to contour, but also in its partial use of red chalk, a material that was strongly associated with drawings by Italian Renaissance artists. With a different chemical make-up from black chalk, red was almost indelible, and so, although ideal for representing flesh tones, it was seldom used in nineteenth-century Britain for academic studies. With this accomplished drawing Richmond measured himself against the Renaissance figure who, for him and his fellow Ancients, was among the greatest masters of all.

If, for Blake, Reynolds was the man 'Hired to Depress Art', for Dante Gabriel Rossetti and his fellow members of the Pre-Raphaelite Brotherhood in the mid-nineteenth century he was simply 'Sir Sloshua'. They despised the tired academic conventions he represented. Rather than his lofty generalisations, they were interested in the specific, the detailed, the localised. As their name suggests, they found what they were looking for in non-canonical masters: artists of the early Renaissance, little regarded at the time and known as 'Primitives'. A key source of inspiration was a volume of engravings by Carlo Lasinio, *Pitture a fresco del Campo Santo di Pisa*, published in 1828, which reproduced frescoes by Benozzo Gozzoli and Giotto among others. William Holman Hunt later described

Fig. 9 | Sir John Everett Millais (1829–1896), *The Race Meeting, or The Gambler*, 1853. Pen and black ink on off-white paper. Ashmolean Museum, Oxford, WA1947.335

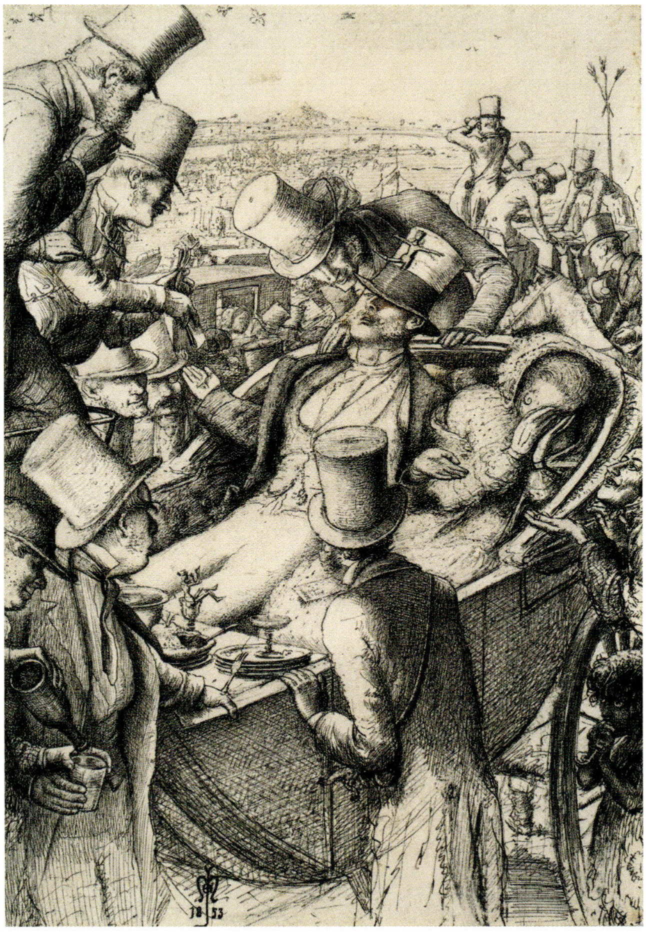

these images of fourteenth and fifteenth-century frescoes as being 'remarkable for incident derived from attentive observation of inexhaustible Nature'.[53] As well as mining these prints for figure types and compositional ideas, the Pre-Raphaelites were also struck by their linearity – although this was more characteristic of the engravings than of the original frescoes. Even so, the linear outlines that they associated with early Renaissance art touched a vital chord, offering the group an exciting alternative to the soft chiaroscuro which – after Raphael – still exerted a powerful force on British art, especially at the Royal Academy Schools. Millais and Rossetti in particular both exploited the capacity of pen and ink to create compelling and complex linear drawings, whether for portraits or book illustrations (fig. 9 and cats 64 and 66).

The other key influence for Rossetti, and for his follower Edward Burne-Jones, was Albrecht Dürer. When Rossetti first met Burne-Jones in 1856, he described the younger artist's drawings in a letter to William Bell Scott as 'marvels of finish & imaginative detail, unequalled by anything except perhaps Albert Dürer'.[54] In the late 1850s, and encouraged by Ruskin, both artists produced extraordinarily detailed drawings on medieval themes which closely emulated the elaborate detail of Dürer's line engravings (cat. 71). The materials that Burne-Jones used for these drawings combined the archaic with the modern. He drew *with* a fine steel nib of the kind that came into common use in the 1830s, and which alone could produce the needle-sharp lines he sought; but he drew *on* sheets of vellum, which has a smoother surface than paper and so is capable of receiving finer detail – and which brought with it connotations of medieval manuscripts.

Unlike the members of the Pre-Raphaelite Brotherhood, Burne-Jones had little formal training beyond attending evening classes at the Birmingham School of Design and, once in London, life classes at the private art school run by James Matthews Leigh. As an artist outside the 'system', he had less immediate need to rebel against it; and in the absence of any sustained academic training, he looked to Old Master drawings, studying them both at London exhibitions and during visits to Italy, and incorporated styles and techniques derived from them into his work. He was also an avid collector of photographs, to which he evidently referred in his studio practice. As he wrote to a friend who had offered to procure some for him: 'I want them all. Select some for me, will you … choose as you would for yourself. You know what I like – all helpful pieces of modeling and sweet head-drawing, and nakeds by Leonardo and M. Angelo and Raphael.'[55]

Burne-Jones's knowledge of Old Master drawings occasionally even prompted him to emulate them by experimenting with metalpoint, a medium commonly used by artists of the early Renaissance, but which had been more or less abandoned at the beginning of the sixteenth century. Metalpoint involves drawing with a stylus (usually an alloy of silver) on paper specially prepared with a slightly abrasive coating, often attractively coloured. Burne-Jones's life drawing of Antonia Caiva (cat. 76) has

Fig. 10 | John Ruskin (1819–1900), *Study of Gneiss Rock, Glenfinlas*, 1853–4. Lampblack, bodycolour and pen and ink over graphite on wove paper, with some scratching out. Ashmolean Museum, Oxford, WA.RS.REF.089

a metalpoint base, but he has subsequently gone over most of the contours with graphite, a material capable of a richer, more emphatic line. More often than working in the rather intractable medium of metalpoint itself, Burne-Jones resorted in the early 1870s to using a hard grade of graphite. Sharpened to a fine point, such graphite could imitate the crisp contours and pale silvery lines associated with Florentine drawings (cat. 75).

The man who helped to foster Burne-Jones's love of Italian art, taking him on his first visit to Italy in 1862, was John Ruskin, the most influential art critic of the nineteenth century. In contrast to Hogarth, Ruskin was a born pedagogue: his entire mission might be summed up as a determination to instil a knowledge and love of art in the British people. Yet, paradoxically, he had no desire to create artists. Although in the 1850s he taught drawing at the Working Men's College in London, and in 1871 founded his own Drawing School in Oxford, he wanted less to teach drawing than to train his students in the appreciation of works of art and habits of observation. In the preface to his manual *The Elements of Drawing* (1857), Ruskin claimed that he 'would rather teach drawing that my pupils may learn to love Nature, than teach the looking at Nature that they may learn to draw'.[56]

Ruskin's teaching methods were unconventional. When William Bell Scott visited the drawing class at the Working Men's College he was shocked by what he found: students bent over desks 'trying to put on small pieces of paper imitations by pen and ink of pieces of rough stick crusted with dry lichens!'.[57] He was baffled that they should waste their time labouring over such trifles when they could have been drawing conventional art school props such as 'beautiful ornamental objects' or the human figure.[58] Ruskin would have replied that Scott was missing the point. For him, nature in any form was worth studying, and drawing was the most certain route to understanding it.

A student's account of these classes gives a vivid impression of Ruskin's enthusiasm and lateral thinking, not to mention his generosity:

For one pupil he would put a cairngorm pebble or fluor-spar into a tumbler of water, and set him to trace their tangled veins of crimson and amethyst. For another he would bring lichen and fungi from Anerley Woods. Once, to fill us with despair of colour, he bought a case of West Indian birds unstuffed, as the collector had stored them, all rubies and emeralds. Sometimes it was a fifteenth-century Gothic missal, when he set us counting the order of the coloured leaves in each spray of the MS. At other times it was a splendid Albert Dürer woodcut ... One by one, he brought for us to examine his marvels of water-colour art from Denmark Hill[59]

For Ruskin, a student's drawing style was unimportant beside his close observation of these glorious examples of art and nature. When it came to gathering visual material for use at his Drawing School in Oxford, Ruskin assembled a characteristically eclectic group of prints, drawings, photographs and watercolours. He also added many of his own drawings; some had been made many years previously, others he made especially for the School. Such exemplars were in stark contrast to the classical sculptures at the Royal Academy, and to the casts of ornament and other didactic material to be found in the government schools of design.

Ruskin's passionate belief in the artist's obligation to record the actual detail of natural form, rather than to represent it in conventional terms, was born out of personal experience. He recorded an epiphany in his unconventional autobiography, *Præterita*:

... one day on the road to Norwood, I noticed a bit of ivy round a thorn stem, which seemed, even to my critical judgement, not ill 'composed'; and proceeded to make a light and shade pencil study of it in my grey paper pocket-book [...] When it was done, I saw that I had virtually lost all my time since I was twelve years old, because no one had ever told me to draw what was really there! All my time, I mean, given to drawing as an art; of course I had the records of places, but had never seen the beauty of anything, not even of a stone – how much less of a leaf![60]

For Ruskin, the focal point of art, from being distant and ideal, rushed to the foreground. In his landscapes, the particular takes precedence over the general to the extent that scale can be hard to establish: what at first appears to be a distant forest might turn out to be a wild strawberry plant. A drawing he made of gneiss rock (fig. 10) at Glenfinlas in 1853 took by his own account about two months to complete, reflecting his painstaking attention

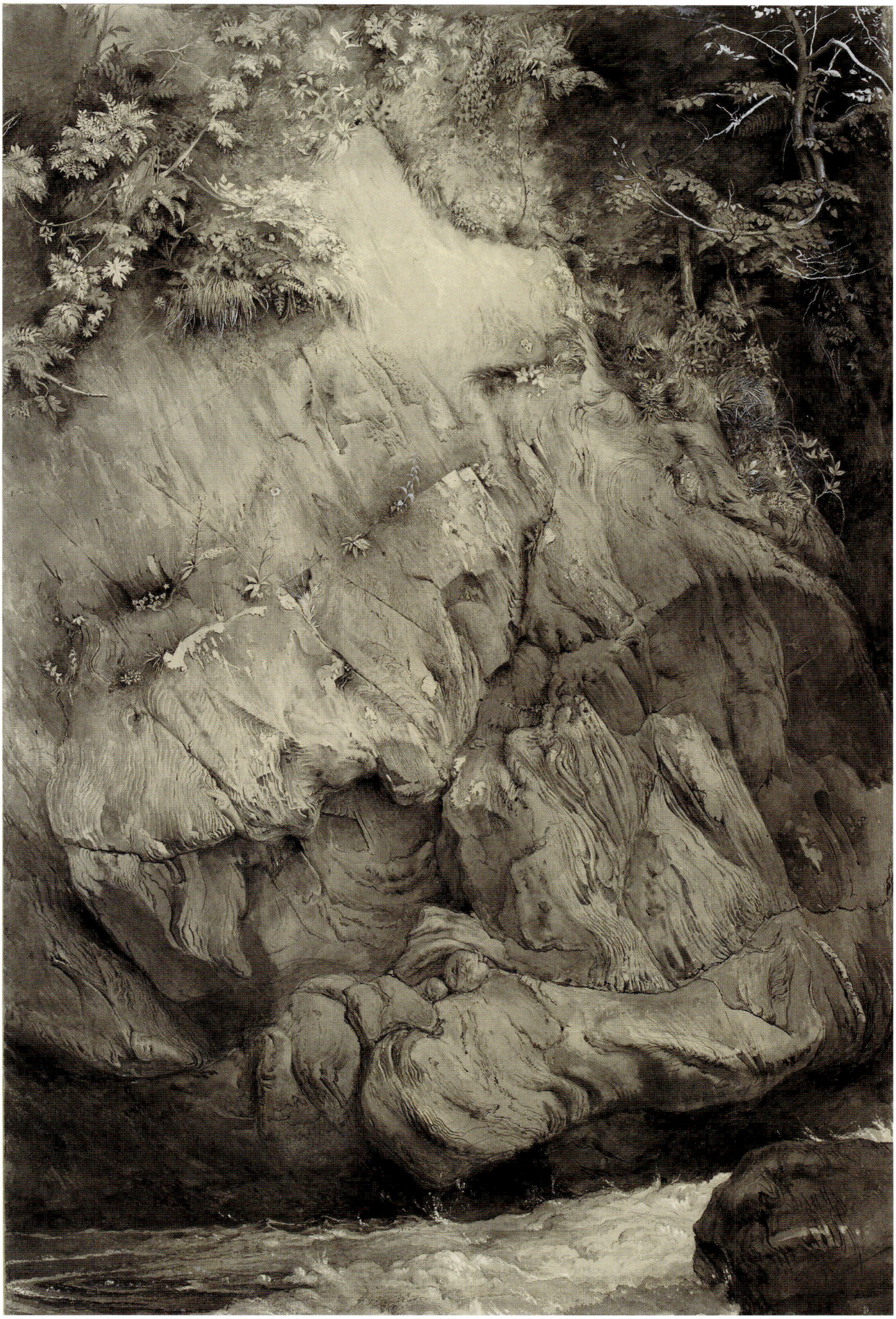

to the smallest detail of natural form – which was precisely the basis of his educational mission.

The Professorship of Fine Art at Oxford, which Ruskin took up in 1869, was funded by a generous bequest made by the wealthy art collector Felix Slade. At University College London, Slade not only founded another Professorship, but also an institution that would change the course of drawing in Britain: the Slade School of Fine Art. Although founded in the same year as Ruskin's Drawing School, the Slade was to take a very different direction. The first Professor, Edward Poynter, had trained in Paris at the *École des Beaux-Arts* and as a pupil of the Swiss painter Charles Gleyre. This experience convinced him of the superiority of the French system of art education, which privileged drawing from the life model. He thus ensured that French principles were at the heart of the new school's ethos.

In his inaugural lectures, Poynter voiced his opposition to the Royal Academy, where, he complained, 'every kind of difficulty would seem to be put in the way of study from the life'.[61] Poynter was fundamentally opposed to a system which 'reverses the natural order of things; for until the student knows something of the construction of the human body from the living model, it is impossible he can understand the generalised and idealised forms in Greek sculpture'.[62] He therefore recommended the practice that he had known in France, of 'constant study from the life-model', as the central tenet of the Slade.[63] Poynter's other target was the idea, enshrined within the Royal Academy's system, that a drawing was an end in itself, rather than a means 'to obtain a thorough knowledge of the human figure'.[64] For Poynter, as for Ruskin, drawing was a way of understanding the world, and he considered the kind of finely graded shading practiced by Royal Academy students to be a trivial waste of time.

Poynter's successor at the Slade was the Dijon-born artist Alphonse Legros, whose teaching method was described by Randolph Schwabe, a student and later Professor at the Slade as 'a return to the practice and tradition of draughtsmanship among the old masters'.[65] Legros's spoken English was poor, and his comments to individual students were, as one recalled, 'laconic and somewhat bleak'.[66] He therefore taught by demonstration, making drawings in front of a class. One former student remarked that 'the watchers probably learnt more in that silent lesson than during three times the amount of verbal instruction'.[67]

In the Life Room at the Slade, students were encouraged to make rapid, linear sketches from the model as well as more lengthy studies. Under the charismatic teacher and later Slade Professor, Henry Tonks – an ex-surgeon once credited as 'the great leader of that great revival of the art of drawing' – both long and short poses were held.[68] One pose was held for the morning and afternoon session. This was followed, towards the end of the afternoon, by a period devoted to short poses, held for only three or four minutes each, to allow the students to make a number of rapid studies. Tonks's method of teaching was also based on demonstration; he would often sit down next to the student and draw on the side of their sheet. William Coldstream, a student in the 1920s, recalled that students were 'encouraged to draw in pencil, sight size, making each pencil stroke clear and deliberate' and to 'start with a very faint line, and increase the strength of the mark as the drawing progressed'.[69]

In the late nineteenth and early twentieth centuries, the centre of British art education shifted decisively to the Slade. Most of those who went on to shape the art of the new century were Slade-trained, among them Augustus John, Gwen John, William Orpen, Stanley Spencer, Paul Nash, David Bomberg, Harold Gilman, and Ben Nicholson. Tonks described this period at the Slade as 'a crisis of brilliance'. Augustus John in particular was regarded as the most talented draughtsman of his generation, his skill prompting comparisons with the Old Masters. The fast-paced and fluent sketching – what he called 'intelligent drawing' – that he had learned at the Slade became the basis for his later figure studies.[70] One of his academic drawings of a male nude (fig. 11) remained in the Life Room long after his departure, pinned up on the wall by Tonks as an exemplary drawing. Wyndham Lewis, a student at the Slade between 1898 and 1901, remembered it as 'a large charcoal drawing in the centre of the wall of the life-class of a hairy male nude, arms defiantly folded and a bristling moustache, [which] commemorated [John's] powers with almost Gascon assertiveness'.[71]

Fig. 11 | Augustus John, (1878–1961), *Standing Male Nude*, 1897. Black chalk on paper. University College London Art Museum, SDC 6711 © UCL Art Museum, University College London, UK / Augustus John / Bridgeman Images

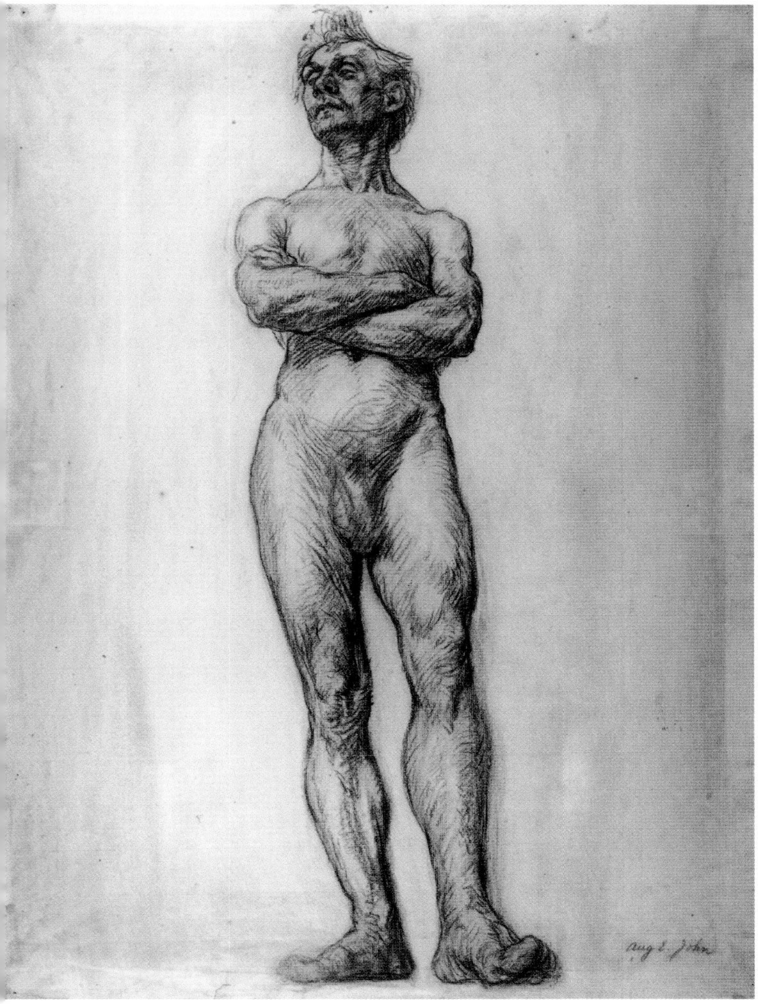

Visible corrections around the edges give the impression of vitality, of the planes and shadows of a real body, not conveyed by the idealised smooth transition from light to shade of traditional academic drawings. If drawing at the Royal Academy had become moribund and conventional, at the Slade it was the driving force.

Although French academic principles were embedded in the Slade's teaching, it was to contemporary French art that many of its students turned. A principal catalyst for this was the two exhibitions of Post-Impressionism organised by Roger Fry at the Grafton Gallery in London in 1910 and 1912. These introduced the work of artists including Cézanne, Gauguin, Van Gogh, and Picasso to a generation of Slade students – much to the chagrin of Tonks, who had enjoined them to stay away from such dangerous influences. In terms of drawing, the impact on British artists of this exposure to the Continental *avant-garde* is especially evident in the work of Harold Gilman. His engagement with Post-Impressionism, particularly the drawings of Van Gogh, is reflected in the expressive dots and thick-nibbed dashes of his drawing style (cat. 89).

The artist who exerted the most powerful influence on twentieth-century British art was, without doubt, Picasso. The influence of his sinuous, confident line stretched right across the century, as vividly present in Ben Nicholson's 1920s *View of the Harbour at St Ives* as in David Hockney's drawing of *Henry Writing, Lucca*, dated 1973 (cats 93 and 112). Artists instructed in draughtsmanship at art schools re-learned to draw by appropriating and adapting aspects of Picasso's protean work, excited by the new possibilities it revealed.

If the first schools of art to be established in England helped artists compete with foreign rivals by providing opportunities to draw from the life model, giving them the tools to aspire beyond portraiture to more diverse subjects, the Royal Academy and the Slade – although espousing different philosophies – were also essentially concerned to equip artists to depict the human figure. In the early twentieth century, however, the rise of non-figurative art began to destabilise the academic system. What the academy had to offer began, to some, to seem irrelevant and insular, its authority inevitably compromised as young artists engaged with progressive European art. In addition, a proliferation at this time of independent exhibiting societies offered alternative groups and new professional forums. Increasingly, artists with an eye on Continental developments began to organise things for themselves – which brings the story full circle.

Notes

1. Edward Norgate, *Miniatura or the Art of Limning*, ed., Jeffrey M. Muller and Jim Murrell (New Haven and London, 1997) p. 108.
2. *Ibid.*
3. Norgate (1997) pp. 209–10, n. 307.
4. See Ilaria Bignamini, 'George Vertue, Art Historian and Art Institutions in London, 1689–1768: a Study of Clubs and Academies', *Walpole Society*, 54 (1988) p. 61.
5. William Gore (Wilhelmus Goeree), *An Introduction to the General Art of Drawing*, trans. J. L. (London, 1674) p. 11.
6. 'Vertue's Note Book', *Walpole Society*, 18 (1929–30) Vertue I, p. 16.
7. Horace Walpole, *Anecdotes of Painting in England; with some account of the principal artists; and incidental notes on other arts; collected by the late Mr. George Vertue; and now digested and published from his original MSS*, 4 vols (Twickenham, 1771) IV, pp. 15–16.
8. 'Vertue's Note Book', *Walpole Society*, 18 (1929–30) Vertue I, p. 39.
9. See Bignamini (1988), p. 66.
10. 'Vertue's Note Book', *Walpole Society*, 22 (1933–4) Vertue III, p. 29.
11. 'Vertue's Note Book', *Walpole Society*, 20 (1931–2) Vertue II, pp. 150–5.
12. Vertue (1931–2), p. 150.
13. *Ibid.*
14. *Ibid.*
15. Vertue (1931–2) p. 128.
16. Carol Gibson-Wood does not accept the attribution of this drawing to Richardson.Carol Gibson-Wood, 'Jonathan Richardson as a Draftsman', *Master Drawings*, 32, no. 3 (1994) pp. 203–29 (pp. 227–8, n. 46), and Carol Gibson-Wood, *Jonathan Richardson: Art Theorist of the English Enlightenment* (New Haven and London, 2000) p. 237, n. 66. However, as the handling seems to me to be consistent with that of Richardson's other chalk drawings, I see no reason to doubt it.
17. The Courtauld has Kneller's preparatory study for a portrait of William Congreve (*c.* 1709; D.1952.RW.1399), alongside two drawings by lesser hands that are apparently copies of it (D. 1952.RW.2438 and D.1952.RW.3549). The last has a study of a male nude on the *verso*, suggesting an academic context.
18. 'Vertue's Note Book', *Walpole Society*, 22 (1933–4) Vertue III, p. 22.
19. *Ibid.*
20. Michael Kitson, 'Hogarth's "Apology for Painters"', *Walpole Society*, 41 (1966–8) p. 93, line 358.
21. See Bignamini (1988) p. 67.
22. The date at which Thornhill took over is uncertain, but it was in either 1715 or 1716. See Bignamini (1988) p. 71, n. 27.
23. Kitson (1966–8), p. 93, line 362.
24. 'Vertue's Note Book', *Walpole Society*, 22 (1933–4) Vertue III, p. 76.
25. Kitson (1966–8) p. 94, lines 378–9 and 383–5.
26. Kitson (1966–8) p. 93, lines 367–8.
27. William Hogarth, *The Analysis of Beauty*, ed., Ronald Paulson (New Haven and London, 1997) p. 122.
28. Kitson (1966–8) p. 85, lines 170–4.
29. Kitson (1966–8) p. 92, line 328.
30. Kitson (1966–8) p. 94, lines 385–7.
31. Kitson (1966–8) p. 92, lines 329–31.
32. Kitson (1966–8) p. 86, lines 202–3.
33. D. G. C. Allan, *William Shipley: Founder of the Royal Society of Arts: A Biography with Documents* (2nd ed., London, 1979) p. 80.
34. Joshua Reynolds, *Discourses on Art*, ed., Robert R. Wark (New Haven and London, 1997) p. 16.
35. Reynolds (1997) p. 19.
36. From the petition presented to George III on 28 November 1768, Royal Academy General Assembly Minutes, I, 1–4, here quoted from James Fenton, *School of Genius: A History of the Royal Academy of Arts* (London, 2006) p. 89.

37. Royal Academy, Council Minutes, 2 January 1769, I, pp. 4–6. Here quoted from Sidney C. Hutchison, *The History of the Royal Academy, 1768–1986* (2nd edn., London, 1986) p. 31.
38. Prince Hoare, *Academic Annals of Painting, Sculpture, & Architecture* (London, 1809) p. 182.
39. Prince Hoare (1809) p. 15.
40. *Ibid.*
41. Reynolds (1997) p. 16.
42. Quoted in William Whitley, *Art in England 1800–1820* (Cambridge, 1928) p. 82.
43. *Ibid.*
44. William Powell Frith, *My Autobiography and Reminiscences*, 3 vols (London, 1887–8) I, p. 40.
45. Frith (1887–8) I, pp. 25–6.
46. *Ibid.*, p. 26.
47. William Holman Hunt, *Pre-Raphaelitism and the Pre-Raphaelite Brotherhood*, 2 vols (London, 1905) I, p. 34.
48. *Ibid.*
49. Pierpont Morgan Library, New York, Millais Papers and correspondence, Bowerswell Papers, J55, 'To the art student', 29 May 1875.
50. http://www.blakearchive.org/exist/blake/archive/erdman.xq?id=b12.8, page xlvii, accessed 19 September 2014.
51. Allan Cunningham, *The Lives of the Most Eminent British Painters, Sculptors and Architects*, 6 vols (2nd ed., London, 1830–3) II, pp. 165–6.
52. Ed., A. H. Palmer, *The Life and Letters of Samuel Palmer, Painter and Etcher* (London, 1972) p. 16.
53. Hunt (1905) I, p. 133.
54. Letter to William Bell Scott, 7 February 1857, letter 57.12 in *The Correspondence of Dante Gabriel Rossetti: the Formative Years 1835–1862*, 2 vols, ed., William E. Fredeman (Cambridge, 2002) II, p. 171.
55. Georgiana Burne-Jones, *Memorials of Edward Burne-Jones*, 2 vols (London, 1904) II, pp. 20–1.
56. *The Complete Works of John Ruskin*, ed., E. T. Cook and Alexander Wedderburn, 39 vols (London, 1903–12) XV, p. 13.
57. William Bell Scott, *Autobiographical Notes*, 2 vols (London, 1892) II, p. 10.
58. *Ibid.*, pp. 9–10.
59. Ruskin (1903–12) V, p. xl.
60. Ruskin (1903–12) XXXV, p. 311.
61. Edward Poynter, *Ten Lectures on Art* (London, 1879) p. 100.
62. Poynter (1879) p. 101.
63. Poynter (1879) p. 107.
64. Poynter (1879) p. 103.
65. Randolph Schwabe, 'Three Teachers: Brown, Tonks and Steer', *Burlington Magazine*, 82 (1943) pp. 141–6 (p.142).
66. William Rothenstein, *Men and Memories: Recollections of William Rothenstein 1872–1900*, 2 vols (London, 1931) I, p. 24.
67. Quoted in Emma Chambers, 'The cultivation of mind and hand: teaching art at the Slade School of Fine Art 1868–92', in *Governing Cultures: Art Institutions in Victorian London*, ed., Paul Barlow and Colin Trodd (London, 2000) p. 109.
68. Sybil Vincent, 'In the Studio of Professor Henry Tonks', *Studio* (February 1937) p. 84.
69. William Coldstream, from an interview recorded in ed., Lynda Morris, *Henry Tonks and the 'Art of Pure Drawing'* (Norwich, 1985) p. 8.
70. Augustus John, *Chiaroscuro: Fragments of Autobiography: first series* (London, 1952) p. 41.
71. Percy Wyndham Lewis, *Rude Assignment: A narrative of my career up-to-date* (London, 1950) p. 119.

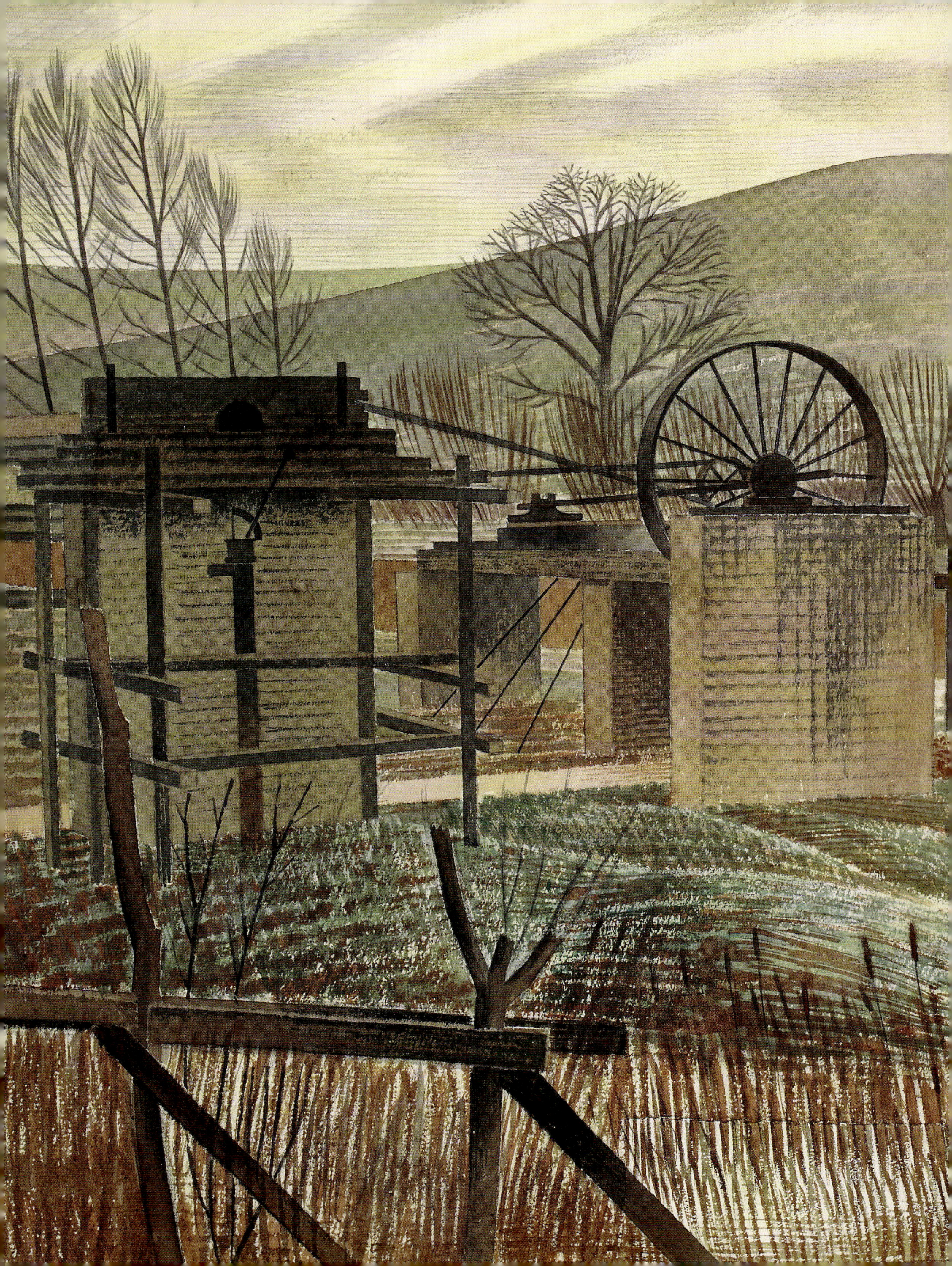

Questions of Identity: the Place of Watercolour in British Art

Timothy Wilcox

Detail from Eric Ravilious, *The Brickyard* (cat. 96)

The exhibition of British Art mounted by the Royal Academy in 1934, the largest survey of its kind before or since, included more than 200 watercolours, about one-eighth of the 1,632 items. Most were packed into the Large South Room, where they were seen by Nikolaus Pevsner, then a newly arrived German immigrant. Two decades later Pevsner delivered his now famous Reith Lectures on *The Englishness of English Art*, and recognised that the status accorded to watercolour painting in England was 'never equalled in any other country'.[1] Since it was part of his self-imposed brief to account for the ways in which the particular forms of English art reflected the English character, Pevsner needed to suggest some link, some unique reason why the medium flourished so conspicuously in these islands; as far as he could see, one of the more compelling answers was that watercolours are usually small. 'They gave an unquestionable tone of liberal-mindedness to a suburban villa, and were the cheerfullest possible decorations for a moderate-sized breakfast-parlour opening onto a nicely-mown lawn', wrote the critic John Ruskin in 1879, of William Henry Hunt and Samuel Prout, two watercolourists he admired but who, despite his own best efforts, came to encapsulate the limited horizons and lack of visual sensibility of the British middle classes.[2] Was Pevsner's 'small' a barely disguised metaphor for 'small-minded'?

These guarded assessments stand in stark contrast to the claims made for watercolour painting in the opening decades of the nineteenth century. The Society of Painters in Watercolours, relaunching itself in 1821, prefaced its catalogue with the statement that 'Painting in Water Colours may justly be regarded as a new art, and, in its present application, the invention of British Artists'.[3] The claims of modernity, paired with a patriotic rewriting of art history, proved highly congenial to the British public, who considered themselves the masters of post-Napoleonic Europe. The stylistic and technical eclecticism of the eighteenth century was consigned to history; watercolour painting was redefined to apply only to those practitioners who used transparent washes, without the aid of the opaque bodycolour (previously the norm among works designed for display). 'Hence, we

Fig. 12 | Joseph Stadler, after Augustus Charles Pugin (1769–1832) and Thomas Rowlandson (1756/7–1827), *Exhibition of watercolour drawings, Old Bond Street* from *The Microcosm of London*, 1808. Hand-coloured aquatint. Ashmolean Museum, Oxford, Hope Library, V.K.11

now behold in the paintings in water-colours, a boldness, richness, and daring splendour of effect, which in some degree emulate the power of paintings in oil; incorporating with these properties, those peculiar to water-colours, the British school has, at length, achieved the honour of having created a new, and most captivating style of art'.[4]

The writer of this self-congratulatory paragraph was William Henry Pyne, an artist who had been one of the sixteen founder members of the Society of Painters in Watercolours in 1804. Their first exhibition opened in the spring of 1805, coinciding with the exhibition at the Royal Academy, and they remained the only artist-led exhibiting body to rival the Academy. Even if the main pretext for the watercolourists' secession had been the poor treatment of drawings and watercolours in the Royal Academy exhibitions – where they were relegated to the lower floor, hung opposite windows and left to jostle with the marbles and casts of the Antique Room – there was a further, unspoken, cause of resentment: regulations forbade any artist who did not paint in oils from applying for membership of the Academy, even at the lower rank of Associate. The growing band of specialist watercolour painters, emboldened by the example of Thomas Girtin, whose grand landscapes of Wales had been hailed as the finest the Royal Academy exhibition had yet witnessed, was thus excluded from the professional status and social prestige, not to mention the business opportunities, monopolised by the established body.

The first exhibition of the new Society was a considerable commercial success: 160 of the 275 works were sold, and the artists paid themselves a dividend from the entrance receipts of more than 11,000 visitors.[5] Among the latter were several Royal Academicians, who admitted to being favourably impressed; Thomas Lawrence, already a noted collector of drawings, was one of the buyers. What began as perhaps no more than a curiosity (the first Watercolour Society exhibition was almost completely overlooked by the periodical press) quickly became a phenomenon.[6] By 1809 its attendance had doubled, and the Royal Academy could no longer simply ignore the upstart. Yet despite a reversal in its regulations in 1812, again admitting the creators of drawings or watercolours to the rank of Associate, very few applied and none was elected.

The rivalry between the two institutions was not relaxed until the 1870s, when Sir John Gilbert, President of the Watercolour Society, became the first artist elected concurrently to membership of the Royal Academy.[7] By then the damage had been done, however, and a strong sense of the exclusivity of watercolour as a completely independent practice had firmly taken root. In reality, leading watercolourists such as Peter De Wint, Copley Fielding and William Turner of Oxford also sent oils to the Royal Academy, and David Cox even came to prefer the medium at the end of his life. Only with the passing of this entire generation (Fielding died in 1855, Cox in 1859, Turner in 1862) did a new atmosphere emerge in which the institutions regarded each other with respect rather than antagonism.

The Society of Painters in Watercolours set the agenda for the future of the medium in numerous ways, which have subsequently become so entrenched that their initial novelty is hardly recognised. As the one early image of their exhibition gallery shows, most of the displayed works were landscapes (fig. 12); but this was not the case every year. Two of the original members, Samuel Shelley and Stephen Rigaud, were figure painters, while Joshua Cristall exhibited both figures and landscapes; Robert Hills was primarily an animal painter and Nicholas Pocock a marine artist. Just as watercolour was not entirely synonymous with landscape, so the careers of the men (the first woman, Anna Byrne, was elected when the membership expanded in 1806) were not completely given over to the creation of paintings for exhibition. Watercolour may have given them a crucial identity, individually and collectively, but the Society's members remained teachers, writers, printmakers, illustrators and, in the case of Cornelius Varley, scientist and inventor.

In 1805 Britain was at war against the Napoleonic armies, and the Continent was inaccessible to travellers. The vast majority of the landscapes hung in the exhibition were necessarily of British subjects, suggesting from the outset some patriotic intent, real or implied.[8] The bubble burst in 1812 when, in the face of falling receipts, the Society disbanded; they must have been grateful to have avoided the fate of a newer, rival group, the Associated Artists in Watercolours, some of whose exhibits were

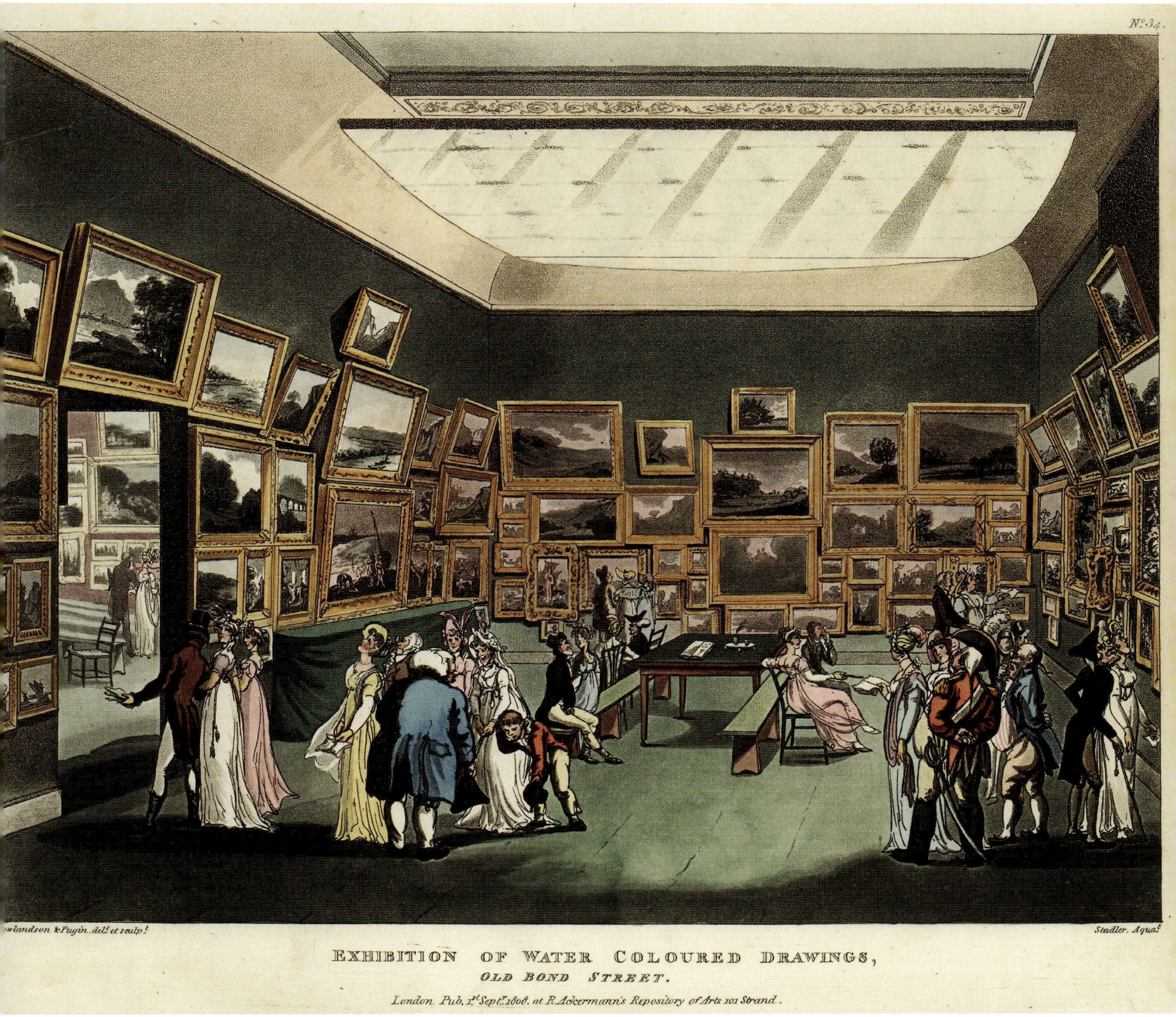

seized as surety for debt. It was at this moment – in the autumn of 1812, when the movement was at its lowest ebb – that the first historical account of British watercolour painting appeared. It was published in Ackermann's *Repository of Arts*, the monthly periodical issued by the picture dealer and artists' supplier who had profited by the recent enthusiasm for watercolour among professionals and amateurs alike, and who consequently had a great deal to lose. The series of articles, 'Observations on the rise and progress of painting in watercolours', cited Paul Sandby as the pre-eminent artist of the earlier generation whose work 'opened the way to every subsequent improvement'.[9] Having recently been dubbed 'the father of modern landscape painting in watercolours', Sandby enjoyed the unique status of an Academician who, over a 40-year period, had shown nothing but works on paper in the annual exhibition.[10] These ranged widely throughout the British Isles, with a predominance of views of Windsor Castle, itself a symbol of patriotism and monarchical authority.[11]

Fig. 13 | Louis Ducros (1748–1810), *Falls of Tivoli*, c. 1780.
Watercolour and bodycolour on paper. Stourhead, The Hoare Collection
© National Trust Images/John Hammond

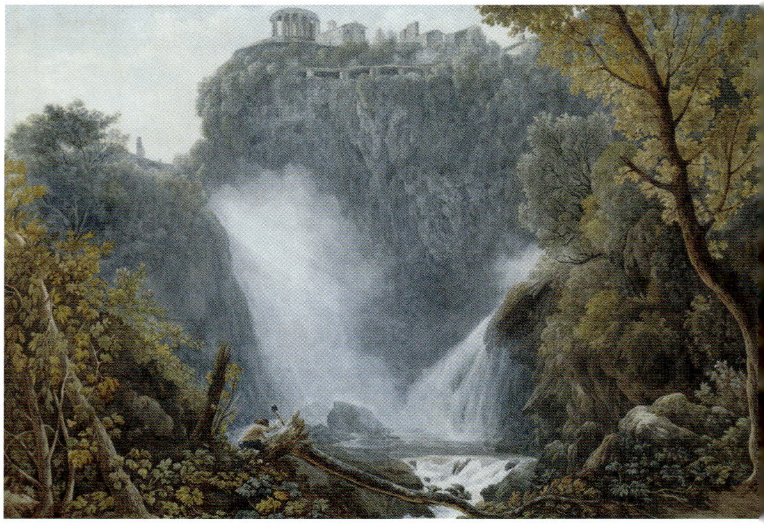

Following Sandby, the two artists judged to have made the greatest contribution to watercolour landscape were John Robert Cozens and John 'Warwick' Smith. Both had concentrated on views of Italy, but it was the landscape itself which was said to have inspired them; at no stage are any of the foreign artists whom they encountered in Rome referred to, let alone mentioned by name. So began the isolationist account of the development of British watercolour painting, in which the scenery alone – formerly Italian and now, by implication, the native landscape – took sole credit for the merits of the art. The 'Observations' conclude with an appeal for a new generation of patrons (unmasking the Society's thinly veiled ulterior motive as a marketing operation), without paying the least regard to the realities of international relations in the later eighteenth century. At that time, for every watercolour painted by Cozens or Smith, British Grand Tourists had offered commissions to an eclectic array of Continental artists, of whom the German Jakob Philipp Hackert, the Swiss Louis Ducros and the Italian Giovanni Battista Lusieri have only lately received due recognition.[12]

The foundation of the Society of Painters in Watercolours, and in 1807 the appearance among its ranks of 'Warwick' Smith, an artist who had previously survived entirely on private patronage and never exhibited in public, marks a watershed of a different sort. The eighteenth-century watercolour was generally classified as a somewhat luxurious illustration, collected as much for its documentary as for its artistic value, and as such was more at home in a gentleman's library, mounted into bound albums or kept loose in portfolios with maps and large engravings. A notable exception was made by Richard Colt Hoare at Stourhead in Wiltshire. As well as displaying framed Italian views by Cozens and Smith, he showed them in the company of highly elaborate watercolours by Ducros, acquired in Rome during two journeys in 1785–7 and 1788–91 (fig. 13). In his *History of Modern Wiltshire*, published in 1822, Hoare claimed, with exaggerated self-importance, that the advances in watercolour painting over the previous three decades owed much – indeed almost everything – to the example of Ducros. To the extent that his richly coloured depictions of Roman architecture may well have spurred the young Turner to a greater chromatic range in the watercolours of Salisbury he made for Hoare from 1798 to 1803, Ducros may indeed have made some contribution to recent developments in Britain. However, such a bold proposition, especially when made within the pages of a large antiquarian tome, could hardly be accommodated in the freshly minted master narrative of British supremacy, and Hoare's suggestion was promptly forgotten for more than a hundred years.[13]

In any case, the situation was considerably more complex. It was not Ducros's surface dazzle so much as the near-monochrome watercolours of Cozens which opened up unforeseen possibilities – not only to Turner, but to an entire generation of painters exposed to his work at the London house of Dr Thomas Monro. Monro employed Turner, Girtin and other young artists, including John Varley and John Sell Cotman, to make copies of compositions by Cozens. It was less the subjects themselves, scenes in the Roman Campagna or the Bay of Naples, than the subtlety of Cozens's wash technique which made the greatest impression; through the extreme refinement of his graduated colour, Cozens evoked the fabled clarity of the Italian atmosphere, and an almost infinite spatial recession. These were the very features recalled by John Henderson, Junior, whose father had been a regular visitor to Monro's house and must have seen the copies in progress: 'the graduations are beautifully and tenderly marked and are full of light possessing much of these qualities for which Turner afterwards became so renowned'.[14] The shift of emphasis from a linear to a tonal medium demonstrated that the watercolour landscape could make its own distinctive contribution to aesthetic debates centring on the value of outline – debates that more often raged around the figures of Michelangelo or Raphael.[15]

Fig. 14 | J. M. W. Turner (1775–1851), *The Junction of the Greta and the Tees at Rokeby*, 1816–8. Watercolour over graphite, with scratching out and use of the brush handle, on wove paper. Ashmolean Museum, Oxford, WA.RS.STD.002

At the sight of the art treasures assembled in the Louvre, the British artists who visited Paris in 1802 had cause to reflect on their own national art and whether, less than four decades after the foundation of their own Royal Academy, such a thing as a national style could yet be identified. The consensus recorded by the Academician Joseph Farington was that *drawing* was most highly valued in France (despite the cessation of military hostilities, still the culture Britain measured itself against), while in Britain, the style was more *painterly*.[16] The watercolours of Cozens and the brush drawings of Gainsborough thus acquired signs of Britishness, no less effective for being applied retrospectively. Francis Towne, who had once protested that he 'never exhibited a drawing', succumbed to the new trend early in 1805, and mounted a one-man-show of nearly 200 of his finished sketches.[17] In order to accommodate contemporary taste, he reworked many to increase their tonal range and to reduce the intrusive linear effect of his virtuoso penwork.

John Robert Cozens provided a model for the new, independent, painterly watercolour in one further respect: none of his watercolours was engraved. The sets of Welsh aquatints by Paul Sandby, and the Italian and Lake District views published by 'Warwick' Smith, played a key role in promoting the names and reputations of these artists, far beyond the value of the images themselves. The founder members of the Society of Painters in Watercolours may have wished to free themselves from watercolour's usual associations with the commerce of publishing and the artisanal craft of engraving; but, in doing so, they forfeited the wider dissemination of their work. Something of a rearguard action was launched in the 1820s, with Robert

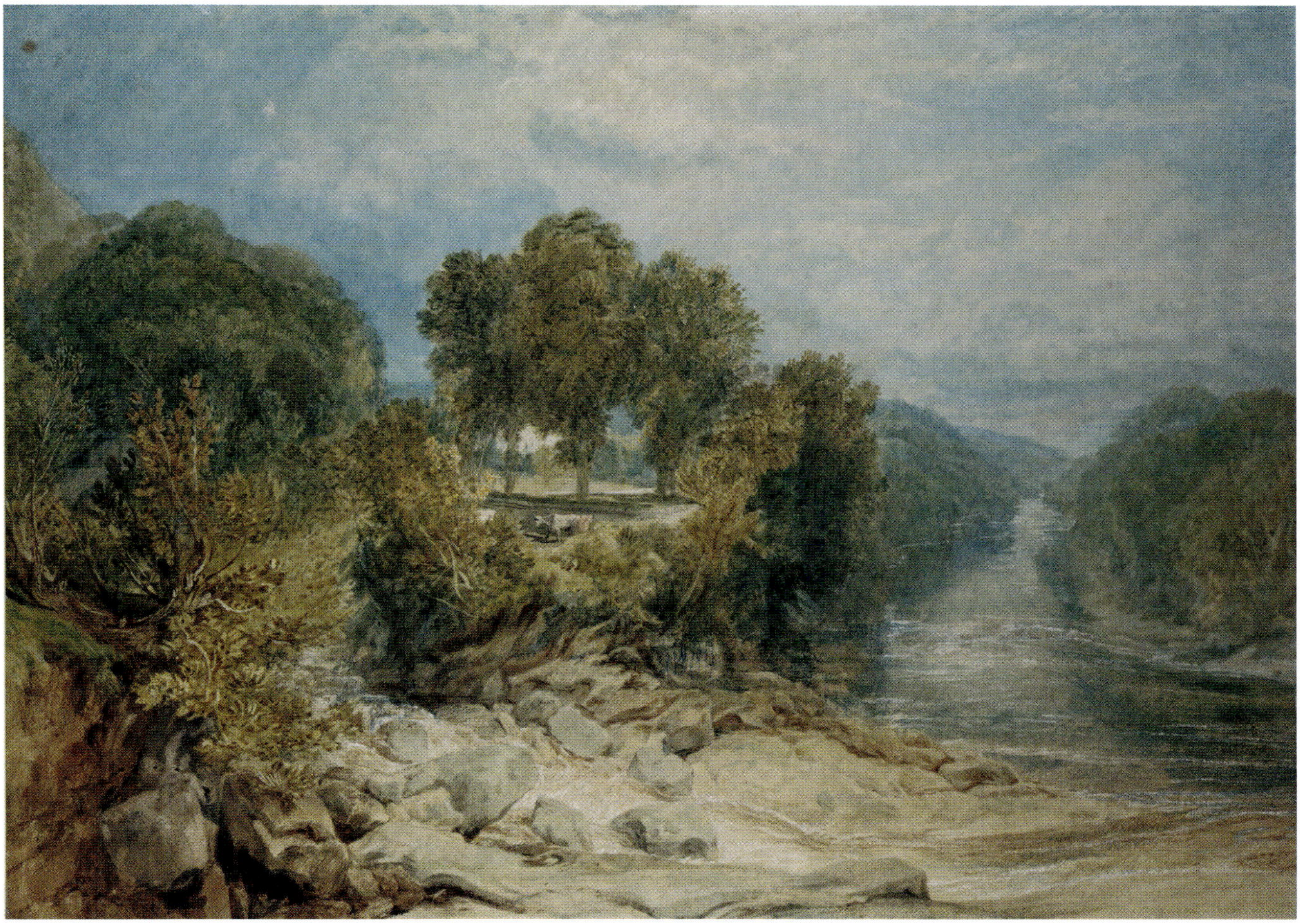

Fig. 15 | John Frederick Lewis (1804–76), *A Frank Encampment in the Desert of Mount Sinai, 1842*, 1856. Watercolour, bodycolour and graphite on slightly textured, beige wove paper mounted on board. Yale Center for British Art, Paul Mellon Collection, B1977.14.143

Fig. 16 | Alfred William Hunt (1830–96), *Durham from the Red Hills*, *c.* 1860–5. Pencil and watercolour on paper. Ashmolean Museum, Oxford, WA1918.7.63.18

Bowyer's *Facsimiles of Watercolour Drawings* (1825); and in 1831 the Society took matters into its own hands with the folio, *Gallery of the Society of Painters in Watercolours*.[18] This came in response on the one hand to the inception of a 'New Society of Painters in Watercolours', and on the other to the exhibitions of Turner's watercolours for the *Picturesque Views in England and Wales*, which demonstrated how those members of the public who could not afford such consummate pinnacles of watercolour art were happy to enjoy them by proxy through the medium of engraving (cats 44 and 45).[19]

When Ruskin began his defence of Turner in the first volume of *Modern Painters* (1843), it was the *Picturesque Views in England and Wales* that he most frequently discussed, along with the twenty subjects engraved for Dr Thomas Whitaker's *Richmondshire*, left incomplete at the author's death in 1821. Ruskin ultimately owned thirteen of the hundred or so *England and Wales* watercolours. He also managed to acquire four of the Yorkshire subjects, one of which, *The Junction of the Greta and Tees at Rokeby*, he gave to his Drawing School in Oxford in 1875 (fig. 14).[20] He considered these drawings to have 'the most heart in them, the most affectionate, simple, unwearied, serious finishing of truth'. Such comments follow directly on Ruskin's observation that 'whatever is to be truly great and affecting must have on it the strong stamp of the native land. Not a law this, but a necessity, from the intense hold on their country of the affections of all truly great men … if we are now to do anything great, good, awful, religious, it must be got out of our own little island, and out of these very times, railroads and all'. Thinking of Turner, Ruskin partially excused landscape from this directive, but only because the sentiments aroused by Turner's latest views of Switzerland must have been sparked initially in Britain: 'the law of nationality will hold with him only so far as a certain joyfulness and completion will be by preference found in those parts of his subject which remind him of his own land'.[21]

Ruskin's discussion of Turner implicitly affirmed the status of watercolour art by citing without discrimination oils, watercolours and even the prints of the *Liber Studiorum*, as long as they illustrated the principles he sought to expound. The contemporary landscape painters, whose flickering lights rendered Turner's only more incandescent by comparison, were also predominantly watercolour specialists: David Cox, Copley Fielding, Peter De Wint. Ruskin's father made his first purchases from the Society of Painters in Watercolours in the early 1830s. He was entirely typical of the middle-class, suburban collectors who for several decades in the

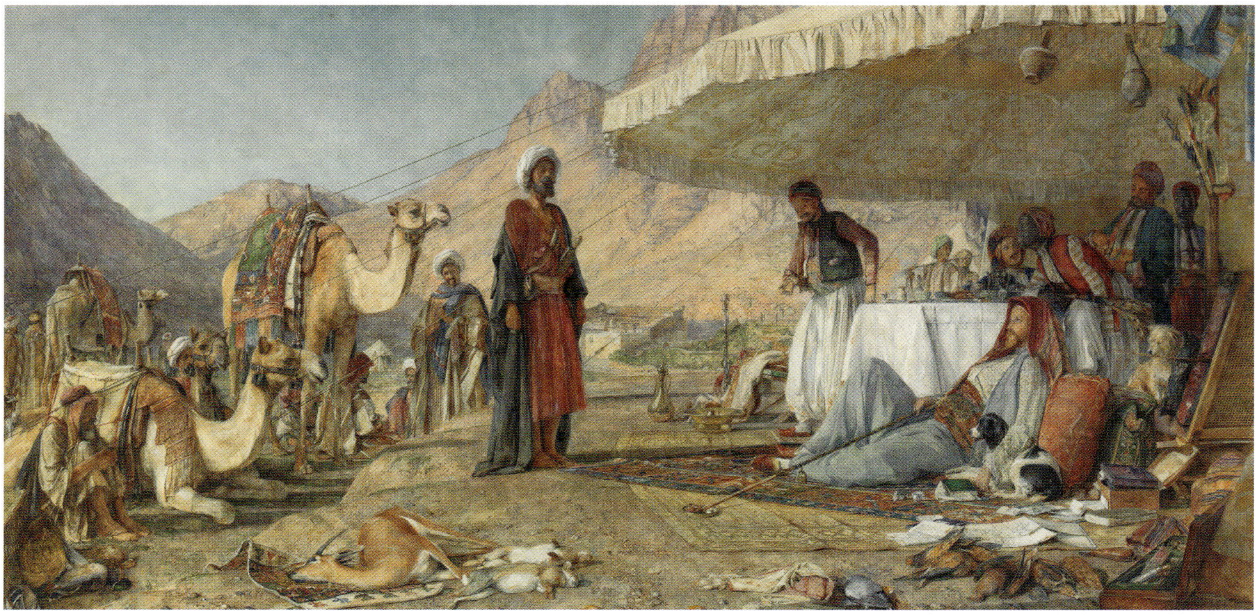

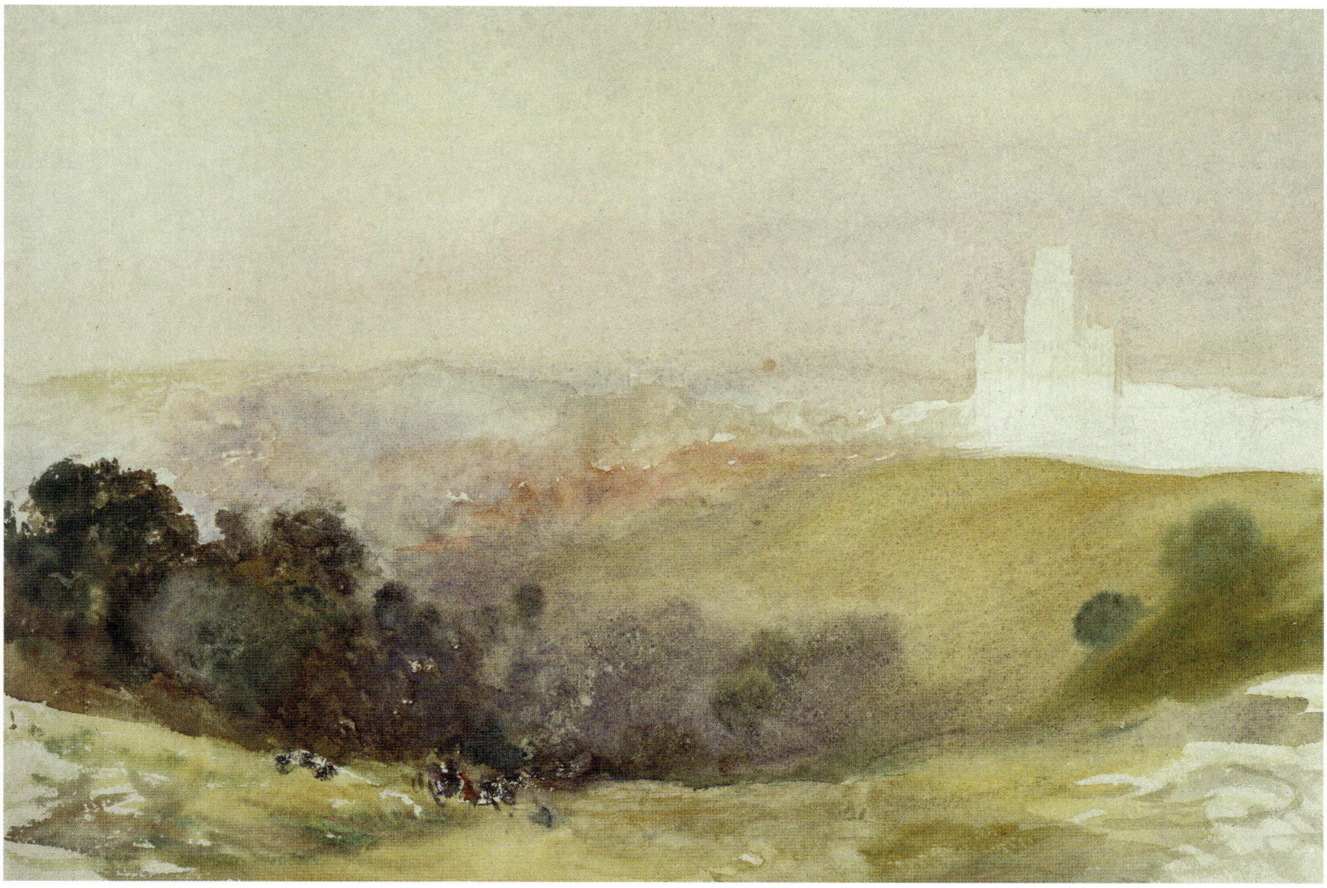

middle of the nineteenth century helped make this institution not only the rival to the Royal Academy, but arguably its superior, at least in popularity and volume of sales.[22] The fact that their client list was headed by Queen Victoria, far from upsetting this assertion, only redoubled its power, since the possession of watercolours by members of the two watercolour societies was itself a potent mark of the domesticity she wished the royal household to exemplify.[23] The parity of the Society of Painters in Watercolours and the Royal Academy and the media they represented (taking for granted that the Royal Academy could not compete as far as watercolour art was concerned) was further reinforced by the publication of Ruskin's *Academy Notes*, which in 1856 extended their coverage to include the Society of Painters in Watercolours.

His review opened with John Frederick Lewis's *A Frank Encampment in the Desert of Mount Sinai, 1842*. 'I have no hesitation in ranking it among the most wonderful pictures of the world,' Ruskin declared, 'nor do I believe that, since the death of Paul Veronese, anything has been painted comparable to it in its own way' (fig. 15).[24] Ruskin admired the colour, the quality of light and, above all, the miniaturist's handling of fine detail. Twenty years later he set it alongside a work by Turner from the Yorkshire series as representing 'unsurpassable standards' in the art of watercolour.[25] By then the tide had well and truly turned, however, leaving Lewis as a high-water mark of minute intricacy largely superseded by a different aesthetic entirely: the sketch.

Paradoxically, it was again Ruskin who set this process in motion. In his *Academy Notes* for 1859 he castigated virtually the entire membership of the watercolour societies for their want of true poetic sentiment, and their concentration on the particular to the detriment of any breadth or unity as a whole. Following Turner's death in 1851, Ruskin, as one of his executors, took on the task of organising his legacy to the nation, and it is hard not to see his change of position as the result of sifting and sorting through all the drawings and watercolour sketches in the Turner Bequest. He completed a preliminary selection in 1857 and later created a display of 338 sheets, exhibited at Marlborough House in the spring of 1858.[26] While the finished watercolours had become relatively familiar, the sketches were completely unknown: nothing like them had been seen in public before. They were studied with profit by watercolourists in Ruskin's orbit, such as Alfred William Hunt (fig. 16) and Albert Goodwin, as well as by existing admirers, including Samuel Palmer, and new converts, among them James McNeill Whistler and Hercules Brabazon Brabazon.[27]

Whistler, American by birth but resident in Paris and later London, acted as an intermediary between Britain and France. The scenes of the River Thames he titled *Harmony* or *Nocturne* were conceived entirely in terms of colour, like Turner's sketches, and executed in thin veils of translucent paint, handled more like watercolour than oil. For his part, Brabazon was an affluent amateur who for decades avoided exhibiting his work. When he eventually consented to a one-man show, at the Goupil Gallery, London in 1892, he was hailed as a bridge between the British tradition and the new art of the Impressionists, an artist who had 'gathered from Turner the hints that extraordinary genius flung out of a technique partly transparent, partly opaque, embracing the full range of resource in the medium, and adapted to express by its speed and suggestiveness the most fleeting actions and exquisite surprises of colour'.[28] The closing remarks were surely calculated to suggest a comparison with the most recent canvases of Monet, while the emphasis on Turner's varied use of the watercolour medium undermined the entrenched orthodoxy that still saw only the transparent technique as the true embodiment of tradition.

An earlier challenge, again Anglo-French in origin, had come in the mixed techniques employed by Richard Parkes Bonington in the 1820s. However, this had been effectively suppressed by the Society of Painters in Watercolours who roundly condemned any artist who had recourse to the pernicious, supposedly Continental, use of bodycolour. So the landscapes shown by William Havell in 1827 were euphemistically described as 'not popular with the members owing to the free use of body colour'; a stricture so severe that, in the following year, Havell resigned to concentrate on oil painting, though with little success.[29] In his review of the Society's exhibition of 1840, the novelist William Makepeace Thackeray singled out Frederick Tayler: 'we are led bitterly to deplore the use of that fatal white-lead pot, that is clogging and blackening the pictures of so many of the water-colour painters nowadays. His large picture contains a great deal of this white mud'.[30] Later artists sought to head off criticism by exploiting the layman's confusion over terminology, especially where artist's materials were concerned. Marcus Huish, sometime editor of *The Art Journal*, related how George Pinwell 'answered the query of one of his would-be purchasers whether he used Chinese white with the reply, "Chinese white! God forbid. I only use body colour"'.[31]

By the turn of the twentieth century the Royal Watercolour Society, as it had become in 1881, was firmly part of the establishment, and was again called upon by more conservative voices in the press to stand firm in its resistance to foreign innovation. Watercolour was by now held to be responsible for 'carrying on the continuity of one branch of our national culture' and for keeping 'at least one stream of English art pure and wholesome', in contrast to the painters in oils who 'have been blown about by every wind of doctrine'.[32]

That watercolour was a quintessentially English art could not be doubted; the difference now was that, instead of being considered innovative, it was valued, in some quarters at least, for being reactionary. As long as cosmopolitanism was understood to be one of the defining characteristics of modernism, which was transplanted, or, rather grafted, on to national schools across the world, watercolour remained a potent symbol of Englishness. In the hands of its most original exponents, the choice of material did not in itself imply a resistance to new ideas; on the contrary, it symbolised a duality, a state of flux in which tradition and modernity sought to co-exist. One work that came to embody this very condition was John Sell Cotman's *Greta Bridge*. This watercolour of 1805 was acquired by the British Museum in 1902 and first reproduced in colour in 1903.[33] It immediately gained talismanic status, and remained for half a century the touchstone to which the vast majority of British landscape painting deferred. Cotman was given an enormous retrospective at the Tate Gallery in 1922 (at that date an honour that had been accorded to neither Turner nor Constable), at which *The Times* pronounced, 'There is no English landscape painter – perhaps no English painter at all except Hogarth – so interesting to the modern artist'.[34]

Laurence Binyon, who had been largely responsible for the acquisition of the Cotman by the British Museum and had written the essay accompanying its reproduction in 1903, concluded his seminal volume on *English Water-colours* with a chapter entitled 'Revival'. In a bid to naturalise the supposedly foreign implant of Post-Impressionism, Binyon noted that, 'there was no need to invoke Cézanne, for Cotman was there to show the way by his mastery of structural design'.[35] Binyon recognised such qualities in the watercolours of Paul Nash and Eric Ravilious, but he would have discovered other, intriguingly hybrid, responses within the ranks of the Royal Watercolour Society. William Russell Flint, elected President in 1936, was avowedly un-English in adapting Cotman's broad flat washes to the depiction of clear Mediterranean skies; he gave the screw a further twist in populating his beach scenes with figures culled from Art Deco fashion illustration. Leonard Russell Squirrell was one among many commercial illustrators who found in Cotman an ideal model for railway posters celebrating British landscape with the attention-grabbing brevity of a headline in block capitals. The watercolour Squirrell donated to the Royal Watercolour Society on his election in 1941 was rather more subtle: a half-demolished building with unmistakeable echoes of Cotman's *Ruined House* (cat. 33), but executed in a range of pastel shades that are entirely contemporary (fig. 17).

By this date, thanks to the German Luftwaffe, such sights were becoming all too familiar. At the onset of war in 1939, the Pilgrim Trust had inaugurated an ambitious programme to commission artists to make watercolours of buildings throughout England and Wales that were perceived to be under threat. Rather than simply using photography, the *Recording Britain* scheme chose watercolour, partly to provide employment for trained artists who were suffering from the contraction of their market, and partly to reassert national pride in an art form held to be distinctively British. Even the leading modernist critic Herbert Read, reviewing the first exhibition of the resulting watercolours in 1941, recognised the apt choice of materials, since this 'modest craft' was one 'for which, among the nations of the world, [the British] have shown a supreme ability'.[36] John Piper was one of the few artists in the scheme who is widely known today. Whether working in oils, mixed media or print, all his architectural work owes a strong debt to Cotman, both for his stark depiction of ruins and his assertive geometry. In an article he wrote in 1942 to mark the centenary of Cotman's death, Piper described him (somewhat unfairly) as an artist 'obsessed by death and decay in old buildings', a reason for the 'present sympathy' with him, since 'the texture of walls in bombed cities is a prominent reality at the moment'.[37] Piper thus added Cotman to the cast of British eccentrics, which included William Blake and Samuel Palmer, whose dogged individualism was in itself a powerful expression of the British character.

Fig. 17 | Leonard Russell Squirrell (1893–1979), *The last phase: demolition at Stoke Street, Ipswich*, 1938. Watercolour and bodycolour on paper © Royal Watercolour Society, London

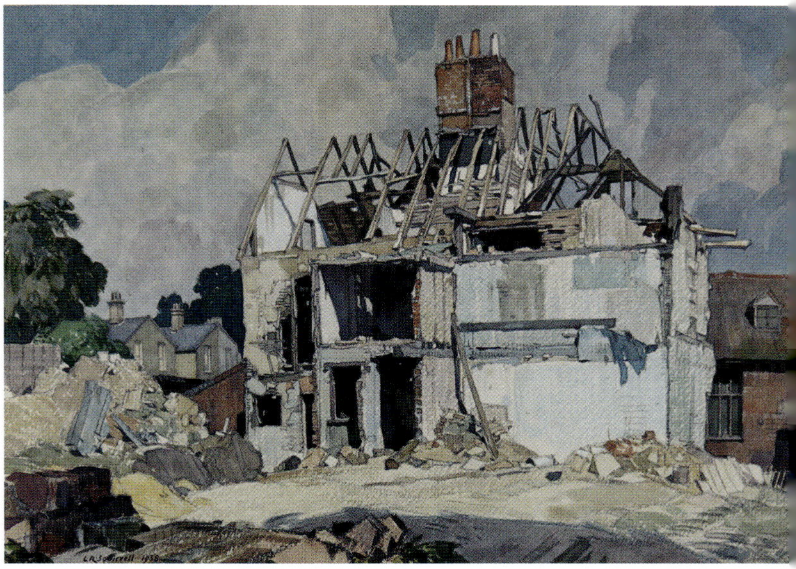

Recording Britain is now recognised as the final flowering of a 200-year-old tradition which, after the Second World War, all but vanished. The various pressures of international modernism, the increase in scale typical of the New York action painters, the possibilities offered by the new medium of acrylic – all seriously undermined the qualities of watercolour, which, apart from its combination with other drawing media in quick sketches, for decades became a virtual ghetto for the amateur. The art so strongly associated with Britishness appeared to have lost its credibility in an era which was epitomised by the disintegration of the British Empire.

It has taken a post-colonial consciousness to recognise that watercolour, in addition to its use as highly successful propaganda to boost national self-esteem at home, was also effective as a national representative overseas.

Fig. 18 | Anonymous Delhi artist, *Recruits to the regiment of Skinner's horse*, *c.* 1815–20. Opaque watercolour on paper © The British Library, Add. Or. 1261

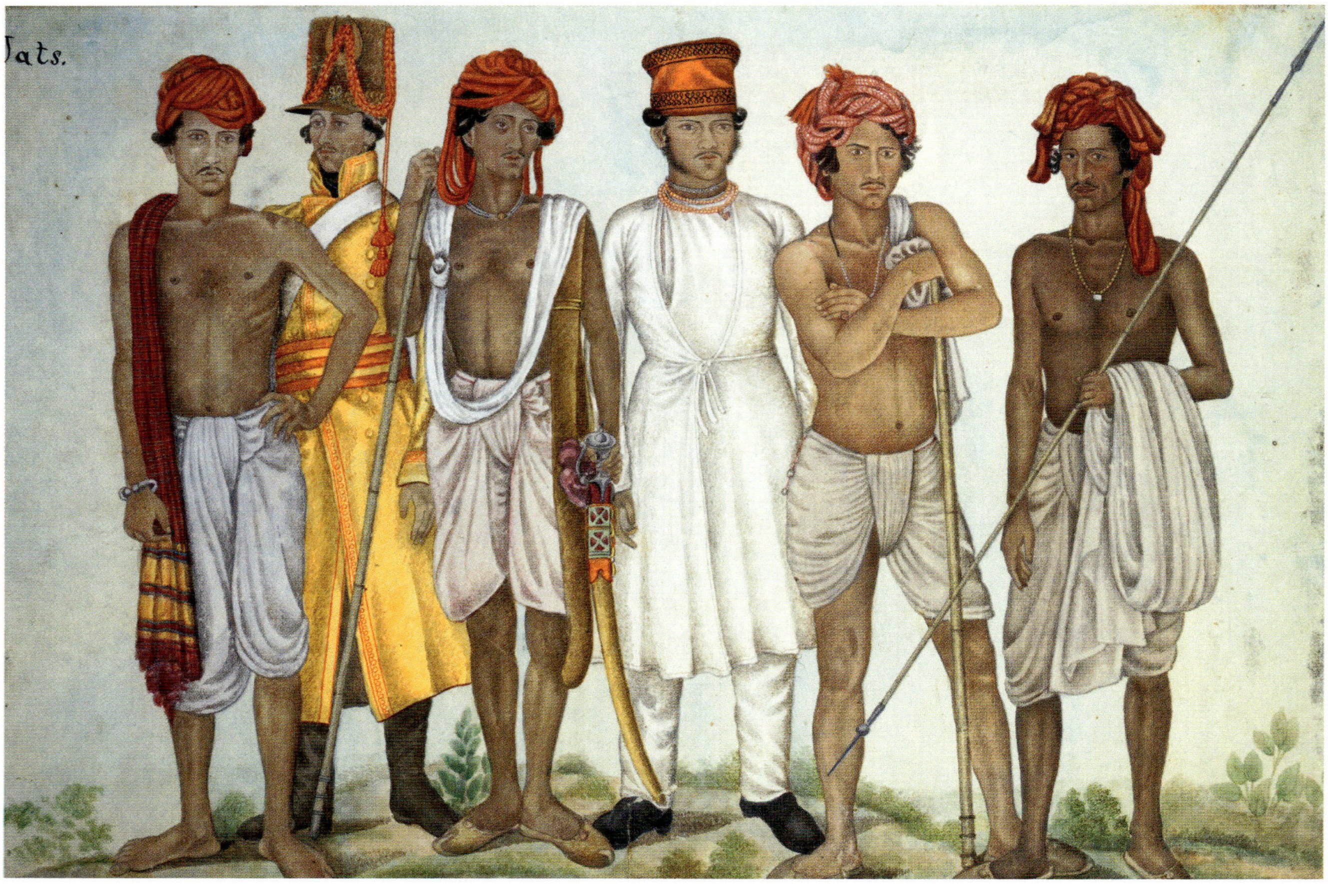

When a large group of watercolours was included in the British section of the first International Exhibition held in continental Europe, the *Exposition Universelle* of 1855, the impact was inescapable. J. F. Lewis, recently elected President, received an enquiry from the Comte de Persigny, French ambassador in London, asking about the constitution and rules of the Society of Painters in Watercolours, presumably with a view to founding a comparable organisation in France. In the event, the *Société des aquarellistes français* was not founded until 1885.[38] Lewis would have been unaware that nearly three decades earlier, none other than Eugène Delacroix had made a similar enquiry. The arch-romantic was a highly enthusiastic and committed watercolourist, using the medium as a gesture of independence from the Académie, and as an expression of the *anglomanie* which was a vital strain of French culture in the 1820s.[39]

In the late eighteenth century watercolour had been added to travel sketches to give a further layer of scientific veracity by official draughtsmen such as John Webber, in the Pacific with Captain Cooke, or William Alexander, who accompanied Lord Macartney's mission to China.[40] The retraining of the court artists of Delhi in English methods of observation and wash drawing marked an important step in the exportation of national cultural values by the colonising power. The portraits of young recruits drawn in the Himalayan foothills for William and James Fraser are a moving testimony from artists who have already accepted a process of westernisation, creating memorials of individuals about to undergo a similar fate (fig. 18).[41]

The prominence of watercolour painting throughout the English-speaking world is a direct consequence of its vogue in nineteenth-century Britain, and is arguably one of the more potent ways by which the medium perpetuates its connexion with these shores. This is also true of Canada and Australia, and even more so of the United States of America. The first watercolour society in Australia, the Australian Watercolour Institute, was not founded until 1923, but it was even then modelled on the now century-old Royal Watercolour Society.[42] Watercolour was already promoted as a significant art form in the Antipodes; among the first purchases for the National Gallery of Victoria in 1905 was *Okehampton*, one of Turner's prestigious *Picturesque Views in England and Wales*.[43]

Just as the Australian watercolourists were motivated by a combination of solidarity and the desire to maximise their market in the aftermath of the First World War, so the American Society of Painters in Watercolors (soon renamed the American Water Color Society), founded in 1867, was in part a fresh initiative following the conclusion of the American Civil War in 1865. The parallels with its British antecedent, itself a product of a long period of conflict, are not hard to perceive. Winslow Homer, perhaps America's greatest ever watercolourist, joined the Society in 1876. He spent eighteen months in Britain in 1881–2 and, although the expressive and technical brilliance of his later watercolours cannot be directly attributed to this trip, most of which was spent among the artists' colony in the tiny Northumberland fishing village of Cullercoats, the sight of his recent work holding its own in vast mixed exhibitions in Newcastle and London must at the very least have helped to build his confidence in the medium and his ability with it.[44]

It is surely from Homer that the vibrancy of the twentieth-century American watercolour springs. On his death in 1910 the great East Coast museums – Boston, Brooklyn, the Metropolitan – vied for the remains of his studio. By the 1920s critics were confidently reinterpreting watercolour as a quintessentially American phenomenon: 'Watercolor painting ... seems particularly suited to the American temperament. Its swiftness and spontaneity reflect our swift intensity of living', wrote one reviewer in 1926.[45] A mid-century survey in Minneapolis inspired an article entitled 'Watercolor, the American medium?'; it was echoed by another in 1962 which considered that the question mark was unnecessary.[46] For a more recent scholar, writing in the 1990s, the appeal of this view of early modern American painting was due in part to the perception that watercolour had not been 'recently identified with any particular country'.[47] Were the British, previously so proud of their watercolour heritage, now quietly disowning it?

Debates about national identity, its formation and cultural expression, rarely acknowledge the innovative role played by the founder members of the Society of Painters in Watercolours. These artists contrived a pact with the public which lasted the length of the nineteenth century – through which, for better or worse, the unique prominence of watercolour painting could be seen as an expression of the British character. Ruskin, delivering his first lectures as Slade Professor in Oxford in 1870, grandly dismissed the entire enterprise as tantamount to a lack of ambition in the present and a lack of concern for posterity: 'the extended practice of watercolour painting, as a separate skill, is in every way harmful to the arts; its pleasant slightness and plausible dexterity divert the genius of the painter from its proper aims and withdraw the attention of the public from excellence of higher claim'.[48] He sneered at the way in which the watercolour had become a commodity, when marketing and sales were arguably one of the greatest successes of the whole movement, one which America and Australia were happy to emulate. The preponderance of landscape painting appealed not only to the first-generation inhabitants of the suburbs of industrial towns; the innate conservatism of rural life supplied equally potent imagery for the economically depressed decade of the 1930s.

The present survey provides ample evidence that excellence in watercolour painting was never confined to one period, nor to one place. The rhetoric it inspired was effective, far beyond the aspirations of those who devised it. Watercolour has shown itself robust and resilient; whether these characteristics constitute further aspects of its supposed Britishness, it would be futile to judge. They do nevertheless suggest the art form, for all its colourful past, also has a rosy future.

Notes

1. Nikolaus Pevsner, *The Englishness of English Art* (London, 1956, rev. ed., Harmondsworth, 1964) p. 169. See also Andrew Causey, 'English Art and 'The National Character', 1933–34', in ed., David Peters Corbett, Ysanne Holt and Fiona Russell, *The Geographies of Englishness: Landscape and the National Past, 1880–1940* (New Haven and London, 2002) p. 295. For the purposes of this essay 'English' and 'British' are used interchangeably, as they have been in most discussions of national identity during the time period covered here.
2. John Ruskin, *Notes on Prout and Hunt*, 1879; *The Complete Works of John Ruskin*, ed., E. T. Cook and Alexander Wedderburn, 39 vols (London, 1903–12) XIV, p. 373.
3. John Gage, 'Turner: A Watershed in Watercolour', in ed., M. Lloyd, *Turner* (National Gallery of Australia, Canberra, 1996) p. 106.
4. 'On Painting in Water Colours', *Somerset House Gazette* (1823) p. 31.
5. Greg Smith, *The Emergence of the Professional Watercolourist: Contentions and Alliances in the Artistic Domain, 1760–1824* (Aldershot, 2002) p. 9.
6. The only periodical to notice the 1805 exhibition was the *Morning Post*. Greg Smith, personal communication.
7. Simon Fenwick, *The Enchanted River: Two hundred years of the Royal Watercolour Society* (Bristol, 2004) p. 79.
8. The only exceptions were the view of Paris, St Denis and Florence by John Claude Nattes. In 1807 views of Italy by John 'Warwick' Smith, an elder statesman of the medium who claimed some of the credit for introducing a more 'painterly' approach to landscape, made an appearance.
9. 'Observations on the rise and progress of painting in watercolours', *Ackerman's Repository*, vol. VIII (November 1812) p. 259.
10. 'Memoir of Paul Sandby', *Monthly Magazine* (1811) p. 440; see Timothy Wilcox, *The Triumph of Watercolour: The early years of the Royal Watercolour Society 1805–55* (London, 2005) p. 67. A founder member of the RA, and thus not subject to the later requirement to exhibit oils, Sandby had painted in this technique only at the outset of his career, before the foundation of the Academy.
11. Luke Herrmann, *Paul and Thomas Sandby* (London, 1986) pp. 69–72.
12. See Simon Reynolds, 'Jakob Philipp Hackert und die britischen Sammler' in Klassik Stiftung Weimar, *Jakob Philipp Hackert. Europas Landschaftsmaler der Goethezeit* (Hamburg, 2008) pp. 70–4; Lindsay Stainton, 'Ducros and the British' in Iveagh Bequest, Kenwood, *Images of the Grand Tour: Louis Ducros 1748–1810* (London, 1985) pp. 26–30; Aidan Weston-Lewis, *Expanding horizons: Giovanni Battista Lusieri and the Panoramic Landscape* (Edinburgh 2012) *passim*. Publications in English on the host of other eighteenth-century watercolourists who had no contact with the British are sparse indeed, and are indicative of an abiding insularity, despite the national affection for the medium. The British Museum's *French Landscape Drawings and Sketches of the Eighteenth Century*, from as long ago as 1977, remains a rare exception.
13. C. F. Bell, 'British water-colour painters: James Moore Collection', *The Walpole Society*, V (1915–17) pp. 56–7; the grounds for his support of the influence of Ducros are questioned by Lindsay Stainton, *loc.cit.*
14. 'Account of a visit by Joseph Jenkins to Mr Henderson, ... 15 January 1856', Simon Fenwick and Greg Smith, *The Business of Watercolour: A guide to the archives of the Royal Watercolour Society* (Aldershot, 1997) p. 279.
15. See, for example, George Cumberland, *Thoughts on Outline* (1796) as discussed in David Bindman, *Blake as an Artist* (Oxford, 1977) pp. 102–3.
16. Joseph Farington, *Diary*, 29 September and 3 October 1802, quoted in John Gage, '*The British School* and the British School', in ed., Brian Allen, *Towards*

a Modern Art World (New Haven and London, 1995) p. 117.
17. Timothy Wilcox, *Francis Towne* (London, 1997) p. 163.
18. J. L. Roget, *A History of the 'Old Water-colour' Society, now The Royal Society of Painters in Water-colours*, 2 vols (London, 1891) I, pp. 554–5.
19. Eric Shanes, *Turner's Picturesque Views in England and Wales 1825–1838* (London, 1979) pp. 10–15, details the tortuous history of the engravings, with the plates and the remaining stock bought up by Turner himself in 1840. Withholding the coppers and failing to sell the impressions privately, Turner effectively removed the series from circulation until after his death.
20. Eric Shanes (1979) p. 16, and L. Herrmann, *Ruskin and Turner* (London, 1968) pp. 96–7. See also Stephen Wildman, 'Aquarelles de J. M. W. Turner dans la collection de John Ruskin', in *Ruskin – Turner. Dessins et Voyages en Picardie Romantique* (Amiens, Musée de Picardie, 2003) pp. 135–48.
21. Ruskin (1903–12) III, p. 232.
22. Ann Sumner, *Ruskin and the English Watercolour: from Turner to the Pre-Raphaelites* (Whitworth Art Gallery, Manchester, 1989) p. 7.
23. See Delia Millar, *The Victorian Watercolours and Drawings in the Collection of Her Majesty the Queen*, 2 vols (London, 1995).
24. Ruskin (1903–12) XIV, p. 74.
25. *Ibid.*, p. 340.
26. Ian Warrell, 'Turner's legacy: the artist's bequest and its influence', in Katharine Lochnan *et al.*, *TurnerWhistlerMonet* (London, 2004) p. 69.
27. Andrew Wilton, 'The Legacy of Turner's watercolours', in Eric Shanes, *Turner: The Great Watercolours* (Royal Academy of Arts, London, 2000) pp. 46–55; Chrisotpher Newall, *The Poetry of Truth: Alfred William Hunt and the Art of Landscape* (Oxford, 2004) pp. 11–12.
28. D. S. McColl, in *The Spectator*, quoted in Wilton (2000) p. 55.
29. Felicity Owen, *William Havell, 1782–1857* (London, 1981) pp. 31–3.
30. William Makepeace Thackeray, 'A pictorial rhapsody', *Fraser's Magazine* (July 1840) in *Critical Papers in Art* (London, 1904) p. 137.
31. Marcus Bourne Huish, *British Water-colour Art* (London, 1904) p. 202.
32. *The Times*, 13 April 1881, quoted in Greg Smith, 'An art suited to the 'English Middle Classes'? The Watercolour Societies in the Victorian period', in ed., Paul Barlow and Colin Trodd, *Governing Cultures: Art Institutions in Victorian London* (Aldershot, 2000) p. 121.
33. Ed., Charles Holme, *Masters of English Landscape Painting* (London, 1903) Special plate, opp. p.JSC iv.
34. *The Times*, 8 April 1922.
35. Laurence Binyon, *English Water-Colours* (London, 1933, 2nd ed., 1944), pp. 167–8.
36. *The Listener*, 24 July 1941, quoted in David Mellor, Gill Saunders and Patrick Wright, *Recording Britain: A Pictorial Domesday of Pre-War Britain* (London, 1990) p. 12.
37. John Piper, 'John Sell Cotman', *Architectural Review* (July 1942) pp. 9–11.
38. J. L. Roget (1891) II, p. 91 ; Timothy Wilcox, 'Magnificence et crasse, le classique et le pittoresque, les aquarellistes anglais en France', 1880–1855, in *Napoléon III et la Reine Victoria: Une visite à l'Exposition Universelle de 1855* (Musée National du Château de Compiègne, 2009) p. 188.
39. Patrick Noon, 'Diamonds that flatter and ravish the eye: the ascendancy of watercolour', in Patrick Noon, *Constable to Delacroix: British Art and the French Romantics* (London, 2003) pp. 232–7.
40. William Hauptmann, *John Webber, 1751–1793: Pacific Voyager and Landscape Artist* (Manchester, 1996); Susan Sloman, *William Alexander: Image of China* (London, 1980).
41. Mildred Archer and Toby Falk, *India Revealed: The Art and Adventures of James and William Fraser 1801–35* (London, 1989); Joachim K. Bautze, *Interaction of Cultures: India and Western Painting, 1780–1910. The Ehrenfeld Collection* (Alexandria, Virginia, 1998).
42. Jean Campbell, *Australian Watercolour Institute 1923–1980*, www.awi.com.au/home/History.aspx, accessed 13 November 2014.
43. Basil Burdett, *The Felton Bequests: A Historical Record 1904–1933* (Melbourne, 1935).
44. William H. Gerdts, *Winslow Homer in Cullercoats*, Yale University Art Gallery Bulletin, 36, no. 2 (spring 1977), pp. 18–35.
45. M. Breuning, 'Contemporary Watercolor Painters', *International Studio* (January 1926) quoted in Barbara Dayer Gallati, 'Language, Watercolor and the American Way', Linda S. Ferber and Barbara Dayer Gallati, *Masters of Color and Light: Homer, Sargent and the American Watercolor Movement* (Washington, 1998) p. 167.
46. Edgar Preston Richardson, 'Watercolour, the American medium?', *Art News* (April 15–30, 1945) pp. 20–22, 29–30; Frederic Whitaker, 'Watercolor, the American medium', *American Artist* (June 1962) pp. 64–75. See Carol Troyen, 'A War Waged on Paper: Watercolor and Modern Art in America', in Sue Welsh Reed and Carol Troyen, *Awash in color: Homer, Sargent and the Great American Watercolour* (Museum of Fine Arts, Boston, 1993) pp. xxxv–lxxiv.
47. Marilyn S. Kushner, *The Modernist Tradition in American Watercolors 1911–1939* (Mary and Leigh Block Gallery, Northwestern University, Chicago, 1991) p. 2, in Ferber and Gallati (1998) p. 145.
48. Ruskin (1903–12) XX, p. 120.

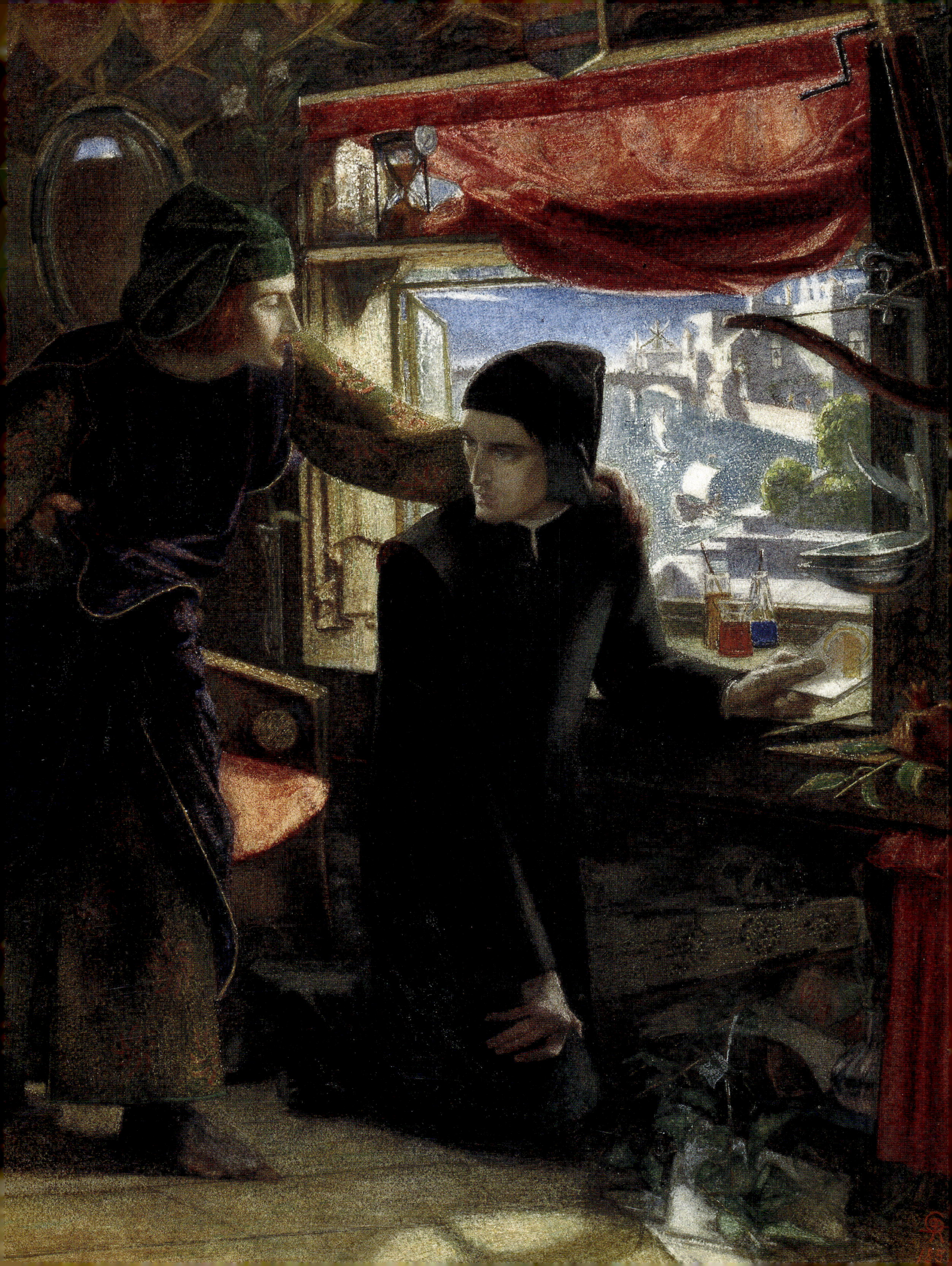

British Drawings in the Ashmolean Museum

Colin Harrison

Detail from Dante Gabriel Rossetti, *Dante drawing an Angel on the Anniversary of Beatrice's Death* (cat. 62)

The collection of British drawings in the Ashmolean Museum is one of the largest and most representative in the world.[1] As with other parts of the collections belonging to the University of Oxford, its formation has been long and complex, and created largely by gifts and bequests, often from old members of the University. When the Ashmolean Museum was opened in 1683, it housed not only the natural and man-made curiosities assembled by Elias Ashmole and the Tradescants, but also the library they had formed. Among the most celebrated volumes is a collection of drawings of fruits known as 'Tradescant's Orchard'. This and many other such volumes could be said to be the first British drawings to enter the collection. However, they were transferred at an early date to the Bodleian Library, which remains an important repository of British drawings, especially those relating to topography and natural history. The earliest acquisition now in the Ashmolean is William Faithorne's portrait of John Aubrey, which was presented to the Museum in 1689 (fig. 19).[2]

However, it was not until the inauguration of the University Galleries in 1845 that the University consciously began to collect fine art for display, rather than to decorate a library or to be consulted in the same way as books. The acquisition of the celebrated drawings by Michelangelo and Raphael from the collection of the portrait painter Sir Thomas Lawrence enabled the new institution to become almost the first after the British Museum to include permanent displays of drawings. Benefactors including the first Earl of Ellesmere (1851) and Chambers Hall (1855) no doubt saw their gifts as complementing the Lawrence drawings, and it is perhaps ironic that Hall gave his best English drawings, a splendid series of watercolours by Thomas Girtin, to the British Museum, reserving for the University Galleries his superlative groups of etchings by Rembrandt, Ostade, and Claude Lorrain; drawings by Rembrandt, Claude, and Leonardo da Vinci; and oil sketches by Rubens and Van Dyck. Among other British artists, he had a predilection for Richard Wilson, and included several oils and drawings in his gift. These joined the watercolours commissioned by the University Press to decorate the Oxford Almanack, which had been deposited in the Galleries in 1850; among the artists represented were Peter de Wint and J.M.W. Turner (cats 32 and 47).

Fig. 19 | William Faithorne (?1616–1691), *John Aubrey*, 1666.
Black lead and wash, with red chalk and graphite, on vellum.
Ashmolean Museum, Oxford, WA1904.3

Fig. 20 | Paul Sandby (1731–1809), *Leith*, 1747.
Watercolour and some coloured chalk over indications in graphite, on paper.
Ashmolean Museum, Oxford, WA.B.I.IV.240.131

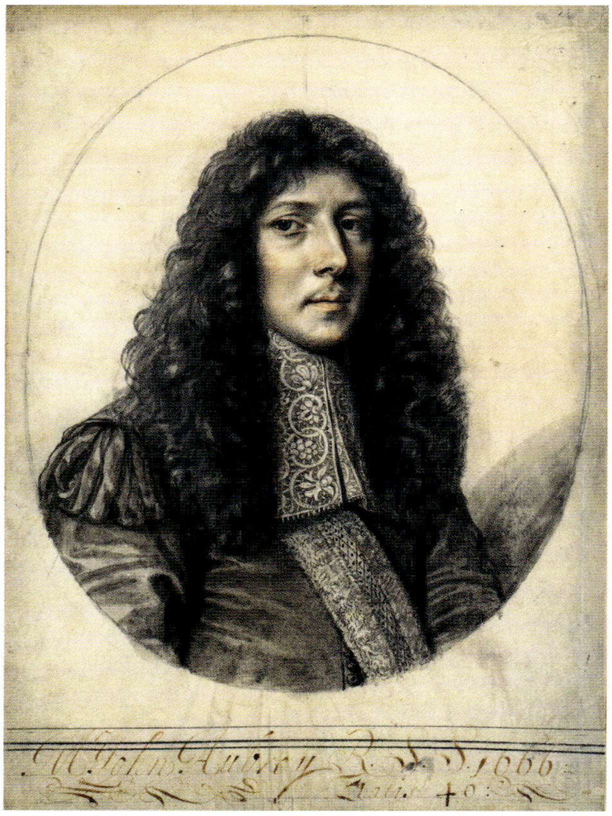

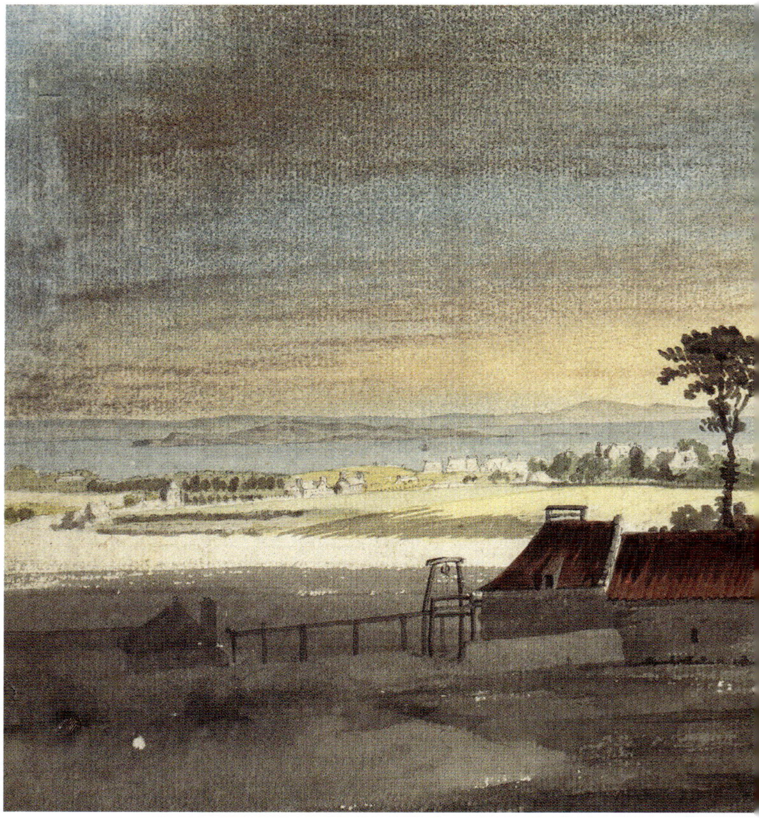

Whereas Hall had a distinctive taste for the sketchy and his motives in collecting were primarily aesthetic, the purpose of the next benefactor of British drawings was unashamedly didactic. As an undergraduate at Christ Church, John Ruskin would no doubt have examined attentively the early Italian paintings given in 1828 and 1834 by W. T. H. Fox-Strangways, later fifth Earl of Ilchester; but would certainly have been aware that there was nothing comparable in most other colleges. As a 'graduate of Oxford', he devoted his first major publication, *Modern Painters* (1843) to J. M. W. Turner, and it was on the completion of the final volume of this series in 1860 that he decided to give to his old University 38 watercolours by Turner, together with 12 leaves from a sketchbook that are now attributed to William Turner of Oxford (cats 46 and 54). As he wrote to his old friend, Henry Acland, 'I don't care to keep 1500 pounds worth of him in my table drawers, while I go abroad – or work at political matters'.[3] Ruskin's gift was housed in specially made cabinets in the Turner Room at the top of the stairs in the University Galleries, next door to the large Raphael Gallery where Lawrence's drawings were displayed. Some years later, in 1869, Ruskin was appointed the first Slade Professor of Fine Art at Oxford. He noted that

I conceive it to be the function of this Professorship … to establish both a practical and critical school of fine art for English gentlemen: practical, so that, if they draw at all, they may draw rightly; and critical, so that, being first directed to such works of existing art as will best reward their study, they may afterwards make their patronage of living artists delightful to themselves in their consciousness of its justice.[4]

In 1871 he established his own Drawing School in the University Galleries. His teaching consisted largely of providing examples of works of art to copy, which he arranged in several series with ostensibly different functions, Educational, Rudimentary, and Reference, which were stored in frames in specially constructed bookcases.

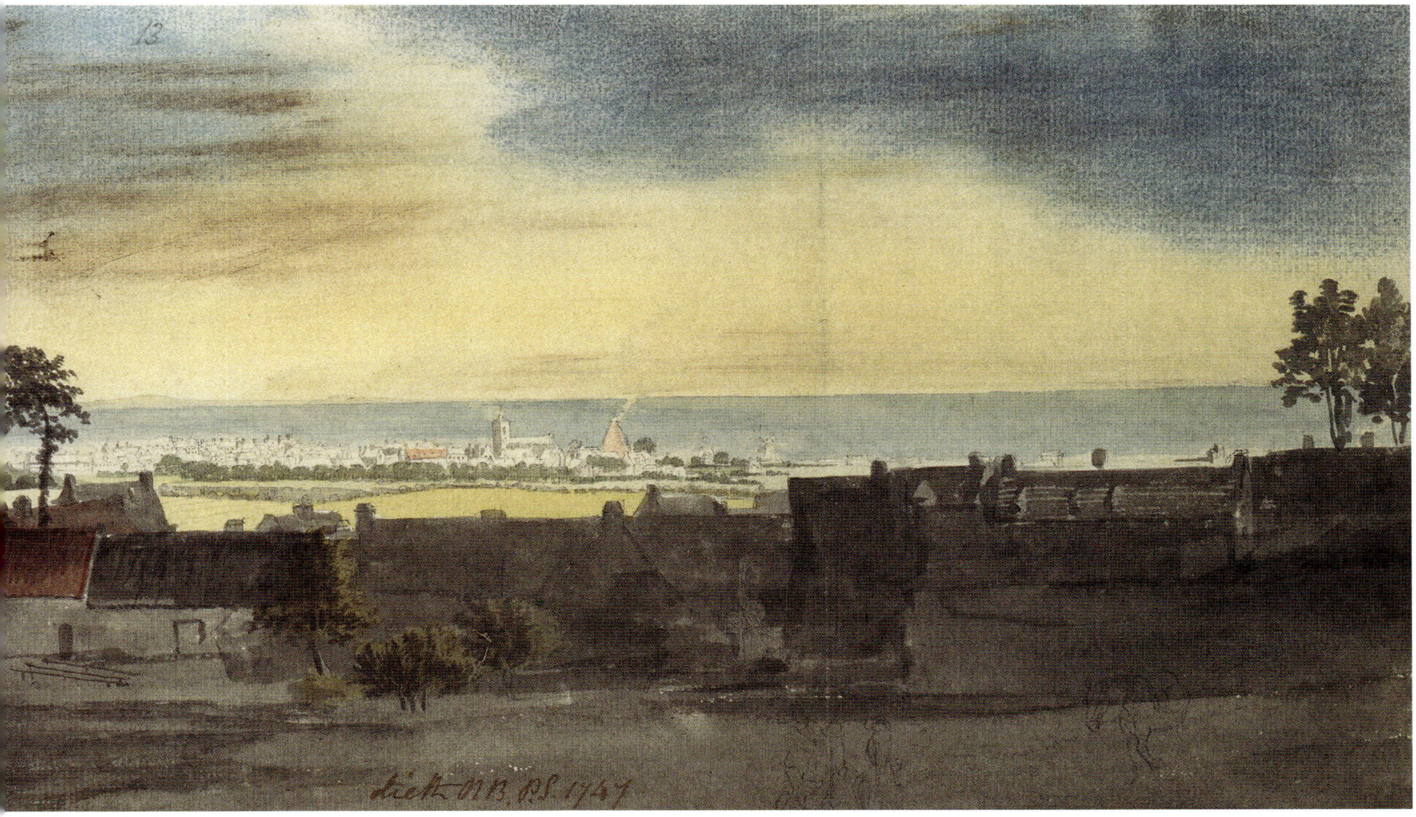

The contents of these series were fluid, as Ruskin added and subtracted items, but they included a large group of his own drawings, as well as further examples by Turner (cats 53, 55–6, 58). Unfortunately, his efforts were unsuccessful, and he admitted in 1884 that, 'As for the undergraduates, I never succeeded in getting more than two or three of them into my school, even in its palmiest days'.[5] Ruskin also ensured that a selection of Turner sketches and watercolours from the artist's bequest to the nation was exhibited in Oxford from 1879 to 1906.

Although Ruskin was an early supporter of the Pre-Raphaelite Brotherhood, he included no examples of their work in his teaching collection. Another of their early patrons, Thomas Combe (1796–1872), had collected their work from 1851 onwards, and the death of his widow in 1893 brought their fine collection to the University Galleries. It consisted primarily of oil paintings, but included several portrait drawings, and one of Rossetti's most intense watercolours (cat. 62).

Numerically, the three most extensive gifts in the nineteenth century came not from collectors of works of art, but from collectors of imagery, some of which happened to be works of art. The first was the eccentric antiquary, Francis Douce (1757–1834), who bought books, drawings, and prints illustrating the manners and customs of earlier times.[6] Among the incomparable riches in his bequest to the Bodleian Library was the largest surviving group of drawings by James Barry (cat. 18). Douce's drawings and fine prints were subsequently transferred to the University Galleries in 1863, while the Bodleian Library retained his collection of manuscripts.

The second great iconographical collection was formed by Alexander Hendras Sutherland (1753–1820) and his wife, Charlotte Hussey (1782–1852), who were able to take advantage of the huge quantities of prints and drawings on the market during the years of the wars with France, allowing them to amass their vast collections, specifically designed to augment Lord Clarendon's *History of the*

Fig. 22 | Hubert Andrew Freeth (1912–1986), *Sir Karl Theodore Parker*, 1952. Pen and red ink, with watercolour on paper. Ashmolean Museum, Oxford, WA1968.461 © Martin, Tony & Richard Freeth

Fig. 21 | William Strang (1859–1921), *Charles Francis Bell*, 1910. Three coloured crayons on a pale ochre preparation on paper. Ashmolean Museum, Oxford, WA1927.19

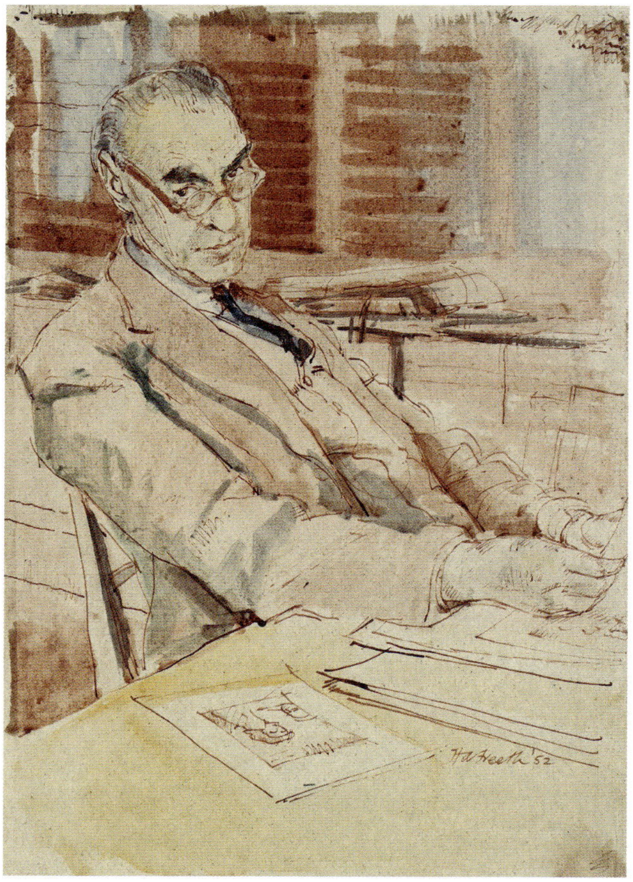

Rebellion (1702–3) and Bishop Burnet's *History of his own Time* (1724–34), as well as a few lesser titles. They eventually amassed nearly twenty thousand prints and almost 1,500 drawings, predominantly British, to illustrate the characters, events, and places mentioned in their chosen texts. Among the drawings was the famous series of representations of the royal palaces, the panorama of London, and other sites, made by Anthonis van der Wyngaerde (active *c.* 1544–1570) at the behest of Philip II of Spain, husband of Queen Mary of England. The collection also boasts several drawings for the first comprehensive topographical survey of Scotland by Jan Wyck (*c.* 1645–1700), and three of Paul Sandby's most beautiful early drawings, again views in Scotland (fig. 20).[7] Among the dozens of portrait drawings are notable groups by George Vertue, Hubert-François Gravelot, and George Perfect Harding. Mrs Sutherland left clear instructions that the grangerised volumes should not be dismembered, and the only item from her collection in the present exhibition is the splendid Lely drawing of Sir Henry de Vic (cat. 2).

The third of these great accumulations of prints and drawings was formed by the Revd Frederick William Hope (1797–1862), who acquired tens of thousands of prints and a few drawings, of portraits and topographical subjects, which he presented together with his entomological collection to the University in 1850. The fund given to expand the collection has since the 1930s been spent on portrait drawings (cats 5–7, 40).

The Keeper who was most single-minded in building up the collection of British drawings, though his range also extended to sculpture and Renaissance plaquettes was Charles Francis Bell (1871–1966, fig. 21).[8] As the nephew of Sir Edward Poynter through his mother, and the descendant of the great sculptor Thomas Banks, Bell might have been expected to enjoy Victorian art of all kinds, but his sympathies were less catholic. Apart from the punctilious cataloguing of the greater part of the collection he inherited when the Ashmolean Museum was united with the University Galleries in 1908, Bell laid a particular emphasis on the British watercolours. In 1912 he succeeded in securing for the University one of the most important and interesting collections formed by an amateur artist, James Moore, in relation to his own research into architectural antiquities. This included not only Moore's own sketches, but also watercolours by Dayes, Girtin, J. M. W. Turner, and others. Moore was not associated with Oxford, but his descendant Edward Mansel Miller (d. 1912) was a Fellow of Magdalen College. It was on the death of his sister, Miss H. L. Miller in 1915 that her portion of the collection became available, and her trustees ceded it to the University at a very advantageous rate, to which Magdalen College contributed generously. Among the highlights was the extraordinary little drawing by Dayes of Durham Cathedral (cat. 31).

On the same occasion, Francis Pierrepont Barnard and Thomas Girtin, great grandsons of the artist Thomas Girtin, presented a number of related works. Bell cultivated Barnard assiduously. He had inherited works by Girtin and had formed a representative collection of English watercolours. Having begun his career as a

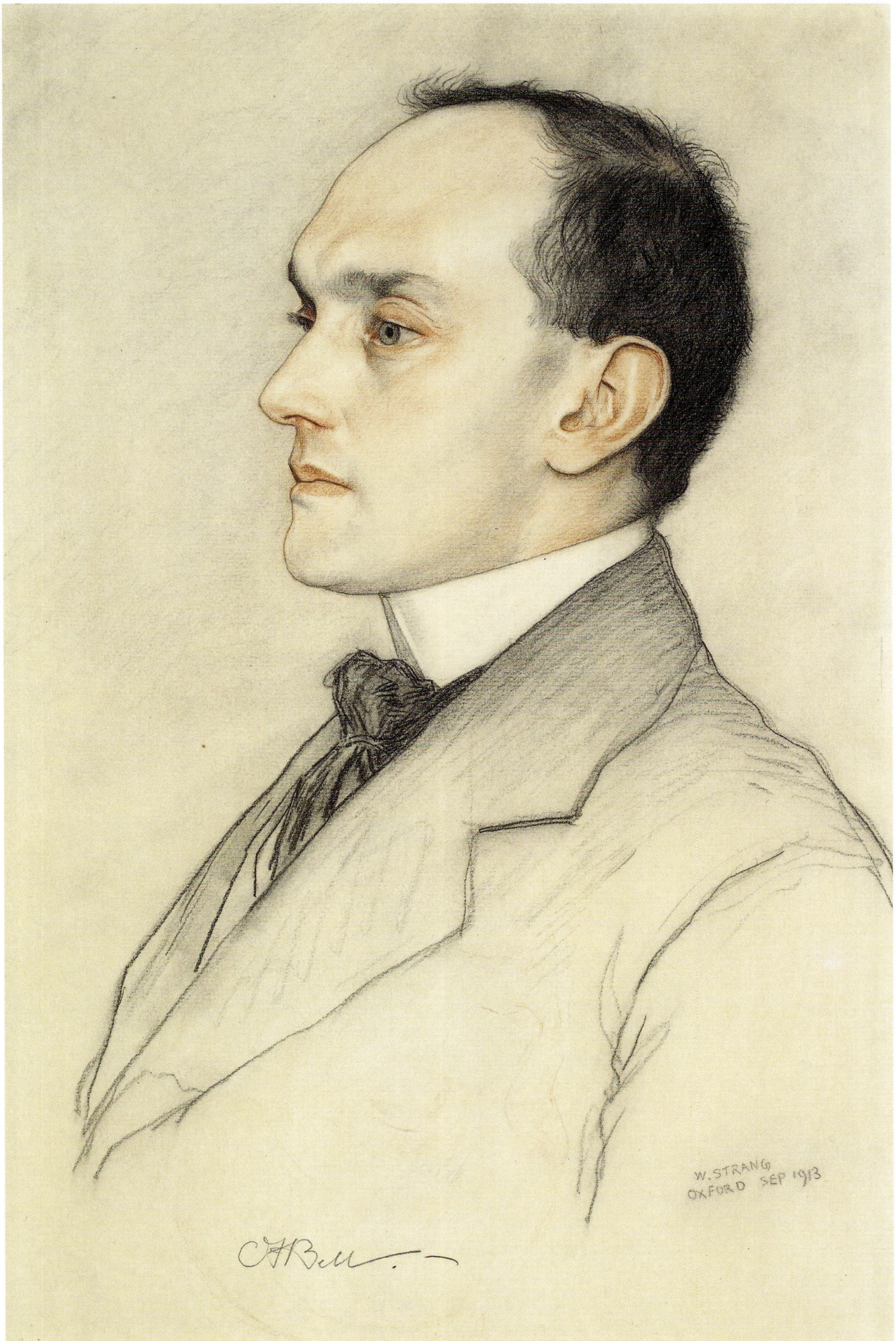
W. STRANG
OXFORD SEP 1913

headmaster, Barnard moved to Liverpool as Professor of Medieval Archaeology. On the transfer of the Oxford coin collections from the Bodleian to the Ashmolean, he was appointed curator of coins in 1921, having earlier been elected an Honorary Fellow of his old college, Pembroke. His collection of watercolours was displayed in a special gallery in his house at Bilsbury, Lincolnshire. Bell was understandably dismayed when Barnard wrote to say early in 1927 that his investments had collapsed and he felt obliged to sell the collection. Fortunately, this came to nothing, and the arrival of Barnard's bequest in 1934 transformed the holdings of English watercolours (cats 27–8).

Among the other benefactors during Bell's period of office, one of the most remarkable was A. E. Anderson (d. 1938), who told Sir Sydney Cockerell, Director of the Fitzwilliam Museum, that 'I simply cannot resist buying a beautiful work of art when I see it, and, as there is no room in my tiny cottage, there is nothing like presenting them to the great public museums, where they will have a safe refuge for many years to come. I should hate a sale for distribution far and wide after they have been collected together with such loving care'.[9] The Ashmolean was one of several beneficiaries, which also included the Whitworth Art Gallery, Manchester, the Fitzwilliam Museum, Cambridge, and the National Gallery, London (cats 23, 29, 34).

Bell's successor as Keeper was Kenneth Clark, who in turn was succeeded by Dr K. T. Parker (1895–1992, fig. 22). From a wholly different background, he had studied on the Continent, obtaining a doctorate in English literature at Zurich, and became one of the leading specialists in the world in Old Master drawings. He arrived in Oxford with a distinct prejudice against the polite English watercolours with which his predecessors had grown up, and coined the widely repeated epigram that 'the only thing worse than an English watercolour is a faded English watercolour'.[10] Nevertheless, although his attention was focused primarily on Old Master drawings, which he bought with almost unparalleled brilliance, he also acquired some of the most significant British drawings in the collection. For example, he bought the six sepia drawings by Samuel Palmer of 1825 in 1941, but only because their owner, J. G. Overbury, feared for their safety during the Blitz (cat. 22). It is largely thanks to Parker that the Ashmolean now has outstanding collections of drawings by Palmer, John Frederick Lewis, and Sir David Wilkie. He also bought Pre-Raphaelite works when they were available at very low prices, and made numerous gifts himself (cat. 79). His unerring sense of quality can also be seen in the selection of drawings he made from those distributed by the War Artists' Advisory Committee in 1947 (cats 98–101).

Since the 1930s, many collectors and dealers have made significant donations to the Ashmolean. On the whole, they have been wide-ranging collections in which works by British artists were outnumbered by those of other nationalities. Nonetheless, the bequests of Mrs W. F. R. Weldon (1937) and Francis Falconer Madan (1962) brought many important British drawings and watercolours (cats 13–4, 19, 66, 70). Another notable gift of carefully chosen works by British artists was that of Luke Herrmann, a former Assistant Keeper, who in 2002 distributed to several museums and galleries the drawings that he had inherited from Sir Bruce Ingram. Among those received by the Ashmolean were charming watercolours by George Chinnery and J. F. Lewis (cats 37, 39), which perfectly complement the drawings bought from Ingram's heirs in 1963 (cats 38, 119).

Parker had little interest in modernism, the abstract or the contemporary, and the same was largely true of benefactors to the Ashmolean in the twentieth century. It is only in recent years that an attempt has been made to acquire drawings by living artists. The portrait of Sir Salman Rushdie by Tom Phillips (cat. 114) is part of a representative selection of the artist's works on paper bought in 2009. Other modern drawings have been presented by or through the Contemporary Art Society (cat. 104). The Acceptance in Lieu scheme has also, in this as in other areas of the collection in the Ashmolean, been fundamental, and enabled the acquisition of major drawings by Ben Nicholson (cat. 93) and, most recently, Frank Auerbach (cat. 113). In spite of these acquisitions, there are still many gaps in the Museum's collection of British drawings. It must therefore be hoped that the enormous generosity of the Ashmolean's many past benefactors can be matched by those of the future.

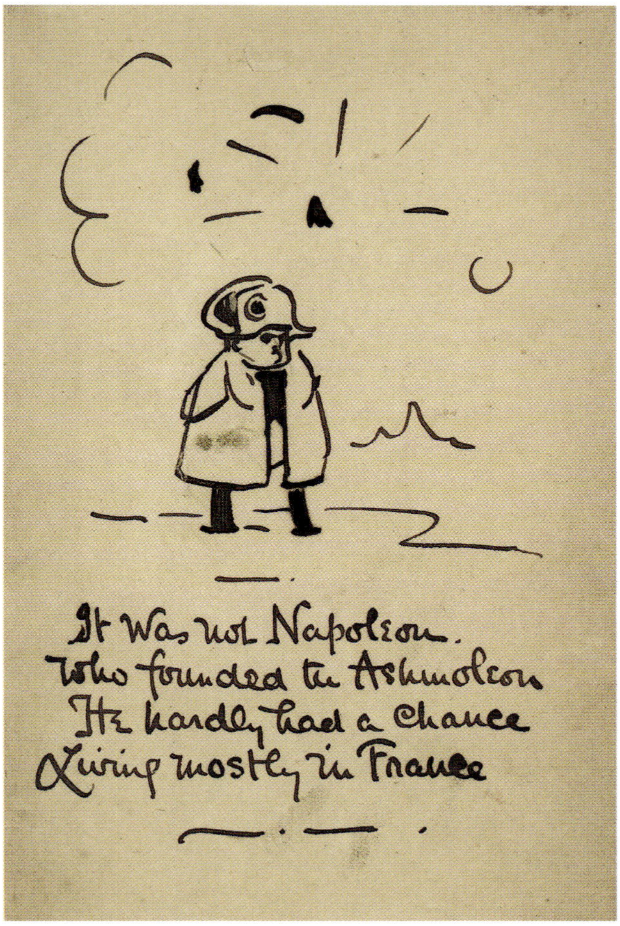

Fig. 23 | Gilbert Chesterton (1874–1936), *Napoleon: an illustrated clerihew*. Pen and black ink on pale brown paper. Ashmolean Museum, Oxford, WA1983.166

Notes

1. This essay is based on the introduction to David Blayney Brown, *Catalogue of the Collection of Drawings at the Ashmolean Museum, Oxford, IV: Early English Drawings* (Oxford, 1982), supplemented by Jon Whiteley, *Catalogue of the Collection of Drawings at the Ashmolean Museum, Oxford, VII: French School* (Oxford, 2000), and Christopher Brown, *Master Drawings* (Oxford, 2013).
2. Brown (1982) no. 123.
3. Luke Herrmann, *Ruskin and Turner: A Study of Ruskin as a Collector of Turner, based on his gifts to the University of Oxford, incorporating a Catalogue Raisonné of the Turner Drawings in the Ashmolean Museum* (London, 1968) p. 31.
4. Robert Hewison, *Ruskin and Oxford: The Art of Education* (Oxford, 1996) p. 17.
5. Hewison (1996) p. 24.
6. See *The Douce Legacy: An Exhibition to commemorate the 150th Anniversary of the Bequest of Francis Douce 1757–1834* (Oxford, 1984).
7. Brown (1982) nos. 234–6, 1650–2.
8. See the obituary by Sir Francis Watson in *The Walpole Society*, XLI (1968), pp. IX–X.
9. *The Times*, 26 November 1938.
10. Colin Harrison, 'Parker, Sir Karl Theodore (1895–1992)', *Oxford Dictionary of National Biography* online edn. (2007) http://www.oxforddnb.com/view/article/51272, accessed 5 February 2015.

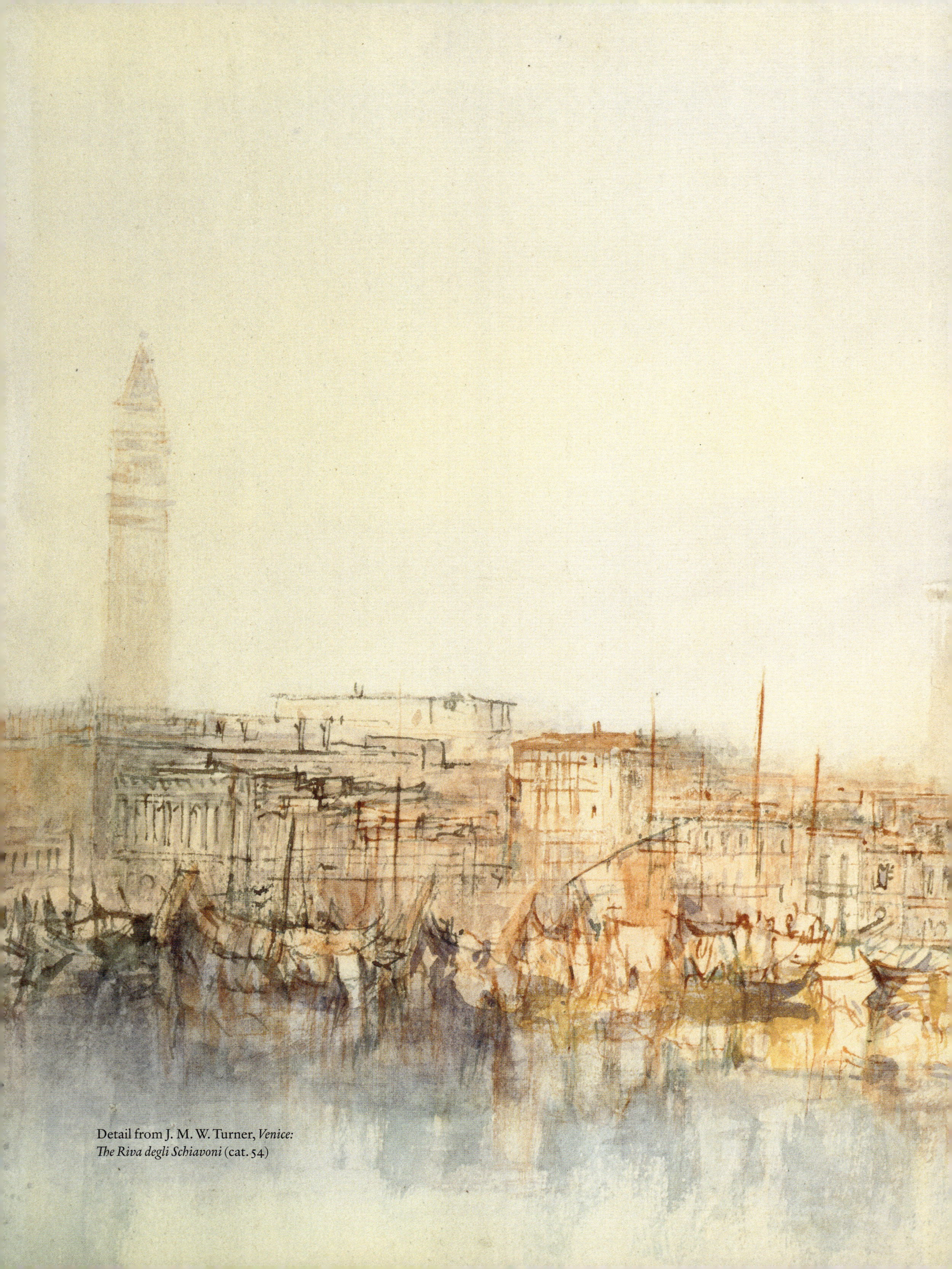

Detail from J. M. W. Turner, *Venice: The Riva degli Schiavoni* (cat. 54)

Great British Drawings

Catalogue

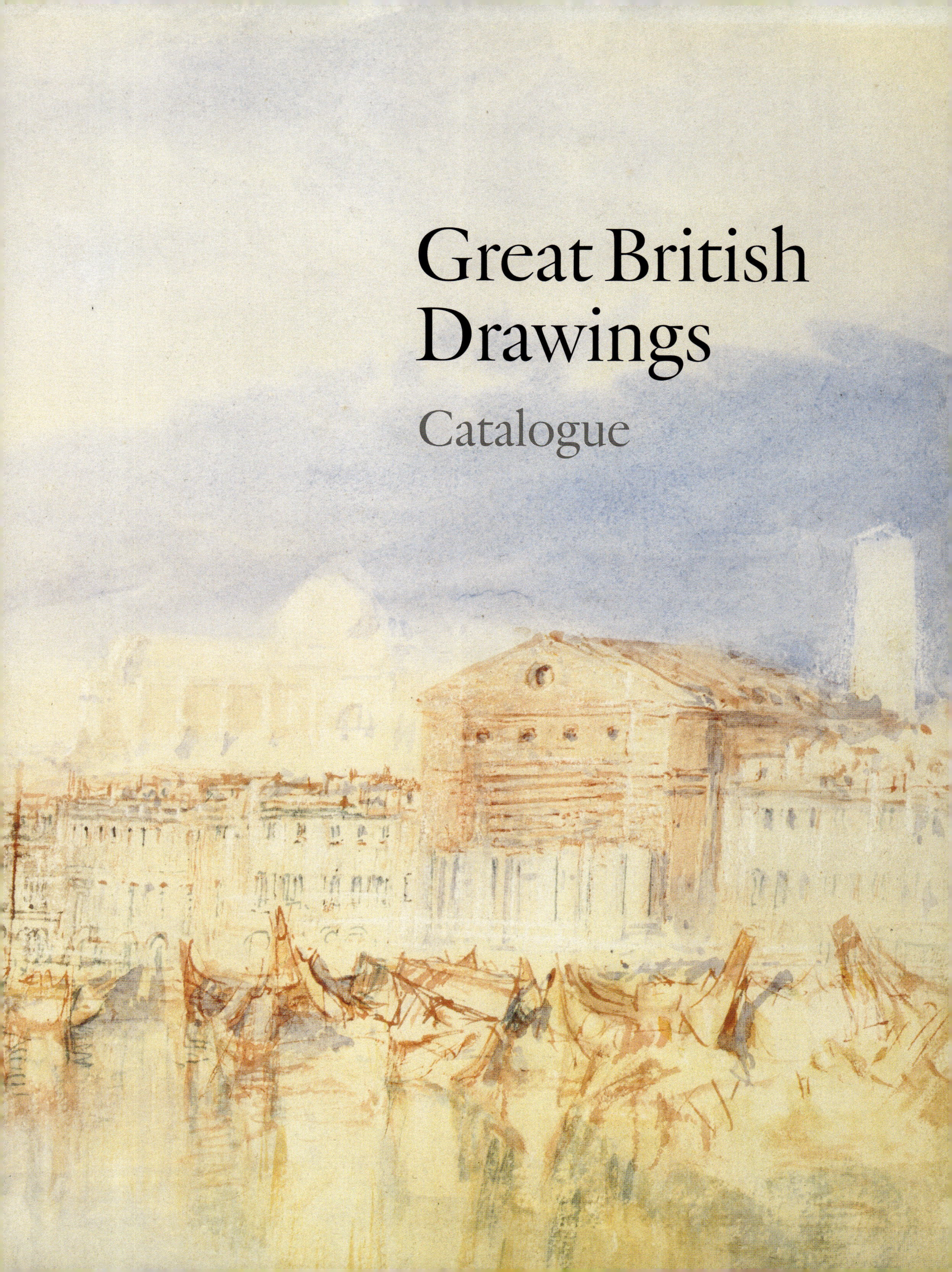

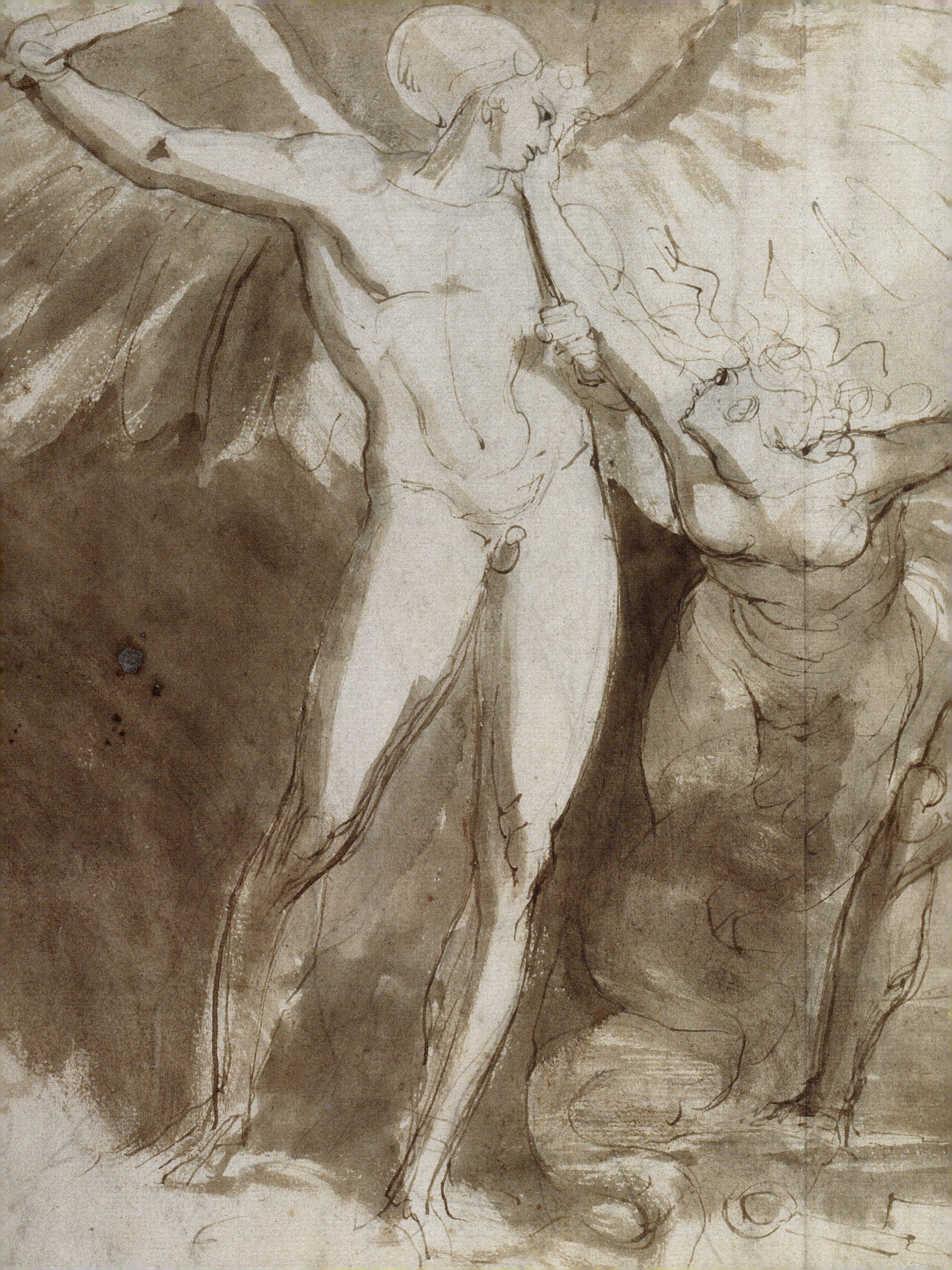

Likeness Sensibility & Vision

1650–1830

Detail from Henry Fuseli,
Satan, Sin, and Death (cat. 16)

1

SAMUEL COOPER 1609–1672
Thomas Alcock, c. 1650

Black chalk heightened with white on paper
17.7 × 11.3 cm
Inscribed on the backboard of the original frame: *This Picture / was drawne for mee / at the Earle of West- / -morelands house / at Apethorpe, in / Northamptonshire / by the Greate, tho' little, / Limner, the then famous / Mr. Cooper of Covent / Garden: when I was / eighteen years of / age / Thomas Alcock / preceptor.*
Bequeathed by Dr Richard Rawlinson, 1755
WA1897.33

LITERATURE: Foskett (1974) no. 141; Brown (1982) no. 115; Stainton and White (1987) no. 74; Rutherford (2013) no. 43

Described in 1669 by Cosimo III de' Medici as 'a tiny man [*piccinetto*], all wit and courtesy', Samuel Cooper is perhaps best known for his 'warts and all' portrait of Oliver Cromwell of the early 1650s, though in 1663 he was also appointed Court painter to Charles II following the Restoration.[1] Only a handful of drawings by Cooper survive, but the quality of this portrait reveals him to be a highly skilled draughtsman. The black chalk is applied with confident economy, creating the soft shading of the face and loose curls of the hair with a freedom unexpected in a miniature painter. Edward Norgate, in his *Miniatura, or the Art of Limning* (*c.* 1646), specifically praised Cooper's 'crayon drawings', or pastels, for their 'likeness, neatness and roundness'.[2]

The turn of the head, the relaxed mouth and steady gaze of the young man bear a strong resemblance to a drawing thought to show Cooper's uncle, John Hoskins, suggesting a similar date.[3] The inscription on the back of the original frame identifies the subject as one Thomas Alcock, though there has been some conjecture as to who this may have been. He has most recently been identified as the author of the dedicatory epistle to a manuscript of *The Famous Pathologist, or the Noble Mountebank*, presented in 1687 to Lady Anne Baynton, daughter of John Wilmot, Earl of Rochester (1647–1680). This describes how Rochester, aided and abetted by Alcock, disguised himself as an Italian quack doctor 'Alexander Bendo' and as a 'grave Matron' to gain access to ladies' bedchambers. These escapades were said to have taken place *c.* 1675–6, after Rochester had been expelled from Court for his lascivious behaviour. If this is indeed the case, then the wide-eyed innocence of Alcock's expression belies his somewhat dubious morality.

The title 'preceptor' indicates the role of tutor, and Alcock was employed by Mildmay Fane, 2nd Earl of Westmorland, to teach his numerous offspring, probably from about 1645. (Fane was imprisoned in the Tower of London in 1642–3.) A patron of the poet Robert Herrick, Fane wrote masques and poetry, and six of his 'politicized entertainments' were performed at his seat, Apethorpe, during the 1640s. His nephew, Francis Fane (d. 1691), was a friend of Rochester, so Alcock could have come to know the poet through his association with the Fanes.

This drawing once belonged to the antiquary Dr Richard Rawlinson (1690–1755) who bequeathed it to the Bodleian Library, together with a large collection of books and manuscripts. One wonders whether Rawlinson, as a clergyman, would altogether have approved of Alcock's antics. CP

1. Quoted in Rutherford (2013) p. 115.
2. *Ibid.*
3. Stainton and White (1987) no. 80.

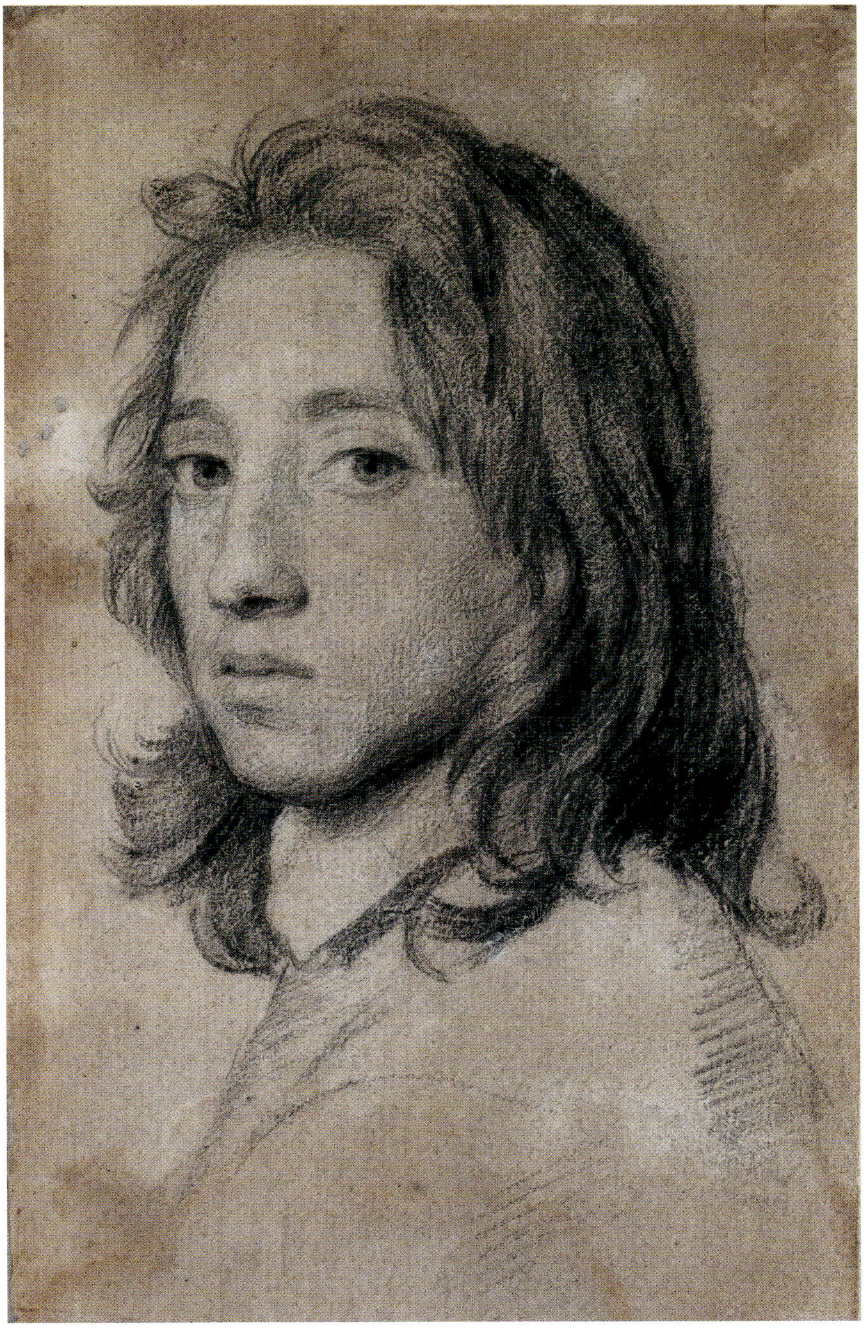

2

SIR PETER LELY 1618–1680

Sir Henry de Vic, Chancellor of the Order of the Garter, c. 1665–70

Black oiled chalk, heightened with white, on blue-grey laid paper
49 × 31.8 cm
Inscribed: *Chancellor of the Order*; the original inscription: *De Canclier ven d Ordre / de mantel violet fluweel* [purple velvet mantle], is now beneath an engraved portrait of the artist in Sutherland's Grangerised copy of Dibdin's *Bibliographical Decameron* (Bodleian Library)
Presented by Mrs A. H. Sutherland, 1837
WA.B.II.722

LITERATURE: Millar (1978) no. 114; Brown (1982) no. 154; White, Whistler, Harrison (1992) no. 89

Seen as the successor to Van Dyck as the most prominent portrait painter in England, Lely was appointed principal painter to Charles II in 1661. The 30 or so drawings he made of members of the Order of the Garter have been described as 'among the most powerfully baroque drawings ever produced in England'.[1] Now scattered among numerous collections, they illustrate the procession that took place annually on 23 April, the Feast of St George. The elaborate ceremonies of the Order were revived following the Restoration, with the formal robes being completely redesigned.

Lely may have been inspired by an oil sketch he owned by Van Dyck showing *Charles I and the Knights of the Garter in Procession* (1638).[2] This served as model for tapestries to decorate the Banqueting Hall in Whitehall. Lely's drawings are also related to prints designed by Wenceslaus Hollar (1607–1677) for Elias Ashmole's *Laws and Ceremonies of the Most Noble Order of the Garter* (1672). Here Sir Henry de Vic (*c.* 1599–1671), a Guernsey-born courtier appointed Chancellor in 1660, holds himself formally erect, as befits his position. Lely displays great skill in his representation of the fall of light over the heavy velvet mantle, in contrast to the mechanically repeated vertical pleats of Hollar's figures. The three-tasselled purse carried by de Vic is very similar to Hollar's print of the Bag of the Seal of the Garter, while the large tassel dragging on the floor also appears in Hollar's etching showing the Chancellor's mantle.[3] These accurate details suggest access to the ceremonial robes themselves.

There is no evidence of a specific commission for the procession drawings. However, as offsets exist for several of them, they were probably working drawings of some kind; a double offset of this drawing is in the British Museum.[4] The fact that the figures are sometimes shown in pairs implies that they formed part of a larger compositional whole, rather than being individual portraits; but the high degree of finish suggests that they were commissioned by an important client.[5] As Lely's friend, the architect Hugh May, carried out renovations for Charles II at Windsor in the 1670s, Lely may have designed a scheme for tapestries or mural decoration for the new state apartments there.

This fine drawing was originally bound into an extra-illustrated edition of Bishop Burnet's *History of his own Time* (1724–34), where it illustrated a reference to Burnet's tenure as Bishop of Salisbury from 1689. De Vic was the last lay Chancellor of the Order, and following his death the role was conferred on the Bishop of Salisbury. CP

1. Millar (1978) no. 114.
2. Ashmolean Museum, WA2002.55.
3. British Museum, 1855,0811.175 and 1871,1209.2274.
4. 1946,0713.1267.a.
5. Stainton and White (1987) pp. 129–37.

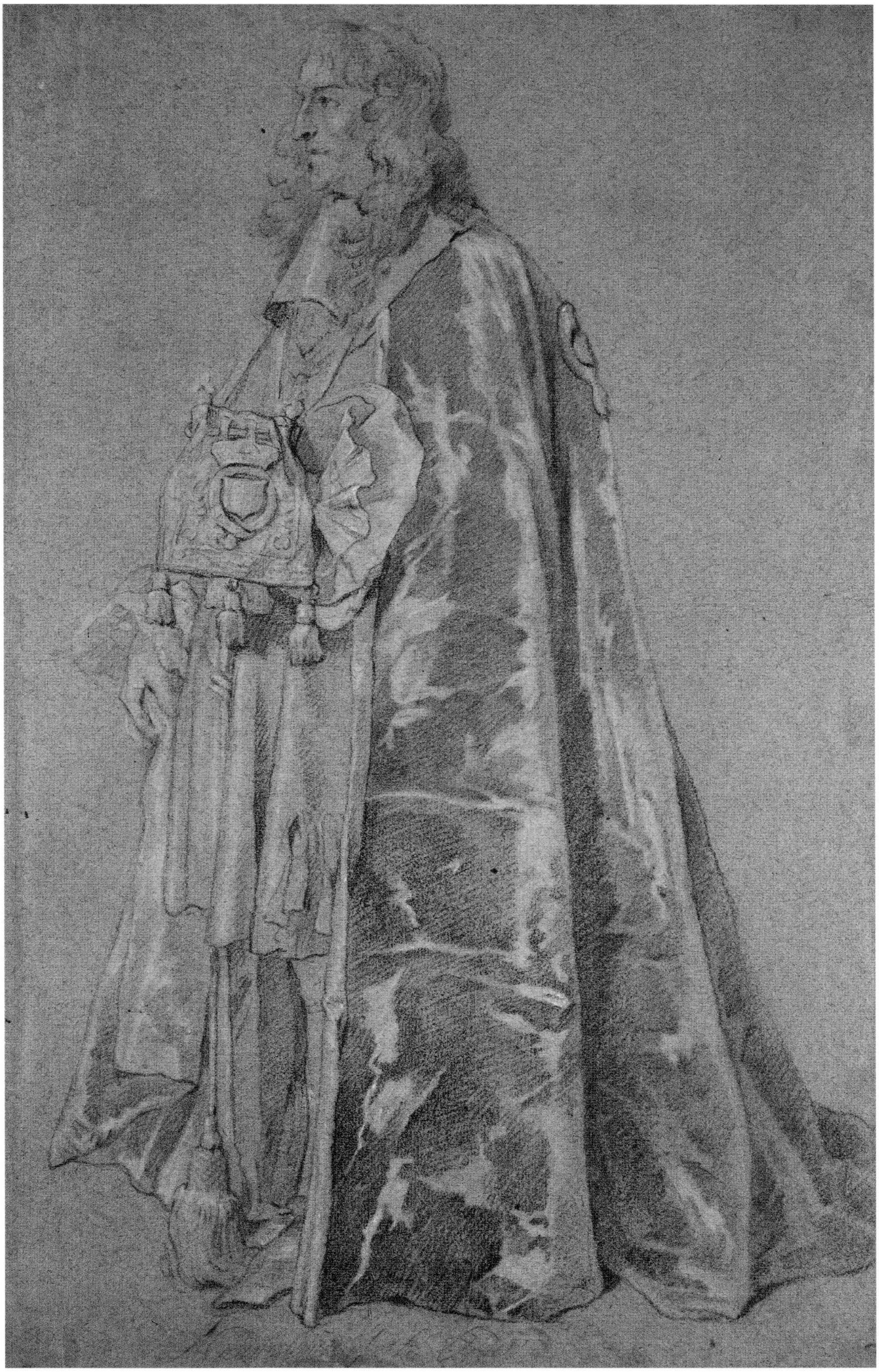

3

EDMUND ASHFIELD 1640–1679

Portrait of an Unknown Man, 1673

Coloured chalk with some bodycolour on buff laid paper
26.8 × 21.8 cm
Signed and dated: *EA F 1673*
Purchased, 1955
WA1955.34

LITERATURE: Brown (1982) no. 56; Jeffares (2006) p. 38

According to Neil Jeffares, the pastellist Edmund Ashfield was born in Little Missenden, Buckinghamshire, the son of Hampden Ashfield and the grandson of Sir Edmond Ashfield of Chesham, to whom Henry Peacham dedicated his treatise on drawing, *Graphice*, published in 1634. Bainbrigg Buckeridge described Ashfield as 'a gentleman well descended' in his 'Essay Towards an English School of Painters' of 1706.[1]

The antiquary Thomas Hearne (1678–1735) praised Ashfield in 1709 as having 'a Genius for painting, especially for Craons', while Buckeridge noted that he was the first to increase the number and variety of tints in pastel, using them to paint in imitation of oils 'with equal force and beauty'.[2] Most of his known works date from between 1673 and 1676, and according to Buckeridge he practised 'with deserved applause', charging as much as £10 a head for his portraits.[3] He seems to have moved from his London home in Holborn Row, Lincoln's Inn Fields, to Tickenham Court in Somerset following his marriage to the wealthy heiress, Eleanor Goodricke, in 1676.

In his *Epitome of Painting* (1683), the pastellist Edward Luttrell (*c.* 1650–1737), who appears to have been trained by Ashfield, explained how his master freed pastel from its role as a preparatory medium for the making of engraved portraits and 'brought itt to a perfection', so that it came to be valued in its own right. Ashfield's memory will never die, he declared, 'Butt ever flourish whiles tyme permitts those admirable pictures to endure … as Monuments of his Ingenuity'.[4] The extraordinary state of preservation of this drawing shows how brilliant pastels were in colour and indicates why such works came to be highly prized by contemporaries as finished portraits, increasingly valued on a par with oil paintings, though somewhat cheaper.

The tonal depth and high level of finish in this magnificent portrait – one of the earliest by Ashfield to survive – demonstrates the new, more painterly use of coloured chalks. However, the buff paper is still used as a middle tone in the white stock under the sitter's chin and in the sleeve, in the traditional manner. The richness of tone in the hair and eyes rivals the qualities of oil painting, while the glints of pure white picked out in the eyes, lip, and brooch are dazzling in their intensity. Such unabashedly eye-catching qualities were to lead later eighteenth-century commentators, including the satirist John Wolcot (alias 'Peter Pindar'), to criticise pastel as a 'meretricious' and showy medium, not worthy of the serious consideration of connoisseurs. CP

1. Buckeridge (1754) dedication.
2. Quoted in Neil Jeffares, http://www.pastellists.com/Articles/Ashfield.pdf, accessed 9 January 2015.
3. Buckeridge (1754) p. 355.
4. Quoted in Neil Jeffares, http://www.pastellists.com/Articles/Ashfield.pdf, accessed 9 January 2015.

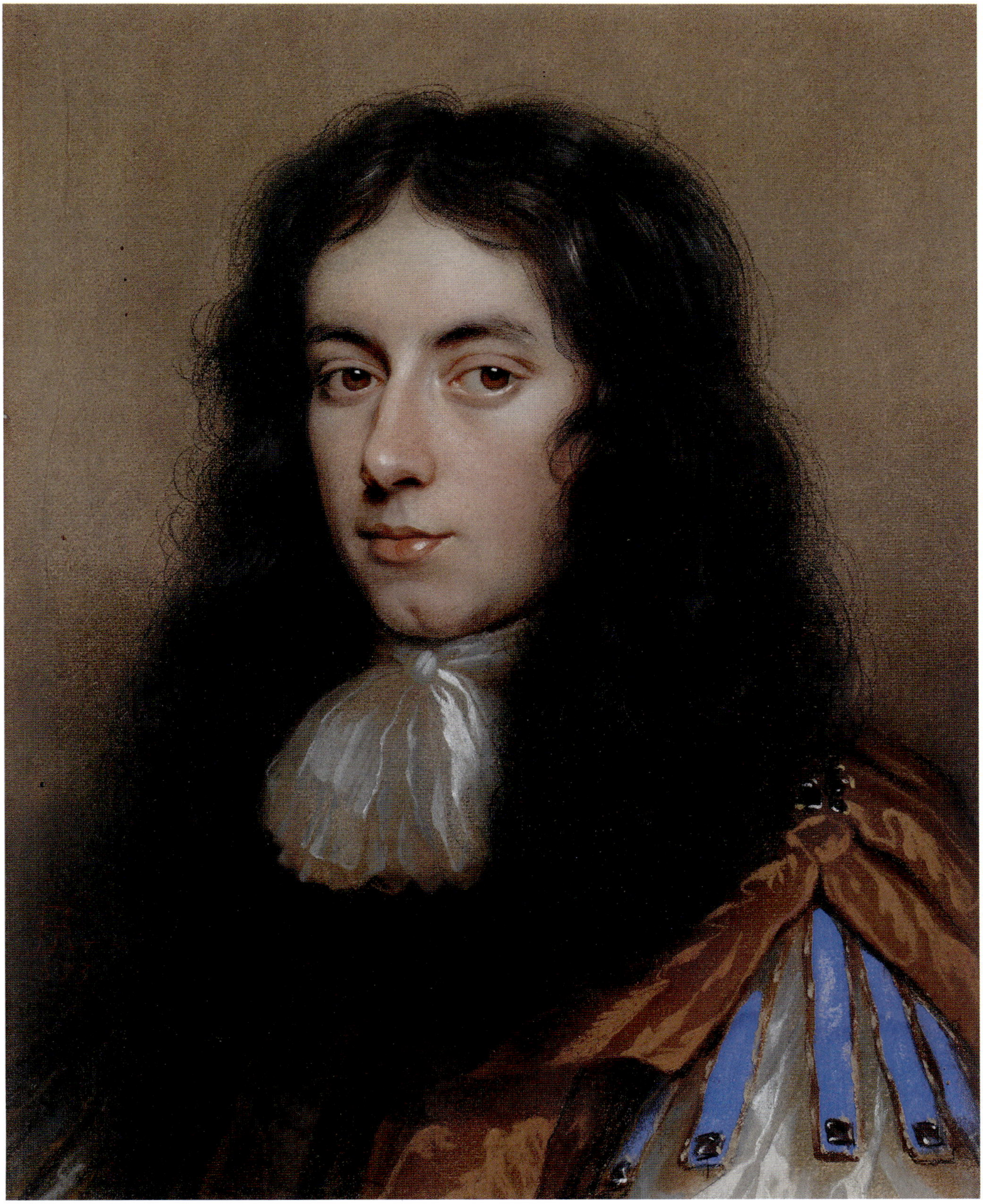

4

WILLIAM FAITHORNE ?1616–1691

Portrait of a Man, probably Thomas Dare, 1679

Pastel and black chalk on cream laid paper
26.7 × 21.6 cm
Inscribed and dated: *To the Kings most Excelent Maj:tie / January: 26. 1679. / W. Faithorne delt*
Purchased, 1940
WA1940.50

LITERATURE: Brown (1982) no. 125

Having trained initially as an engraver, William Faithorne fought for the Royalist cause beside his master, Robert Peake, in the early 1640s, and was imprisoned following the two-year siege of Basing House. The delicate details of this sensitive portrait in pastel and chalk suggest the influence on Faithorne's style of his extended period of banishment in Paris during the Civil War, between 1647/8 and 1651/2. There, he absorbed the French vogue for highly finished portrait drawings, notably those by the portrait engraver Robert Nanteuil (1623–1678).

On his return to London in 1651/2 Faithorne established a print shop at Temple Bar, dealing in foreign prints and artists' materials. He became highly regarded for his engraved frontispieces, book illustrations and, especially, his portrait prints, considered by Horace Walpole to represent the very best produced in seventeenth-century England. In 1660 he was appointed 'engraver in copper' to Charles II. The diarist Samuel Pepys records a visit to Faithorne's shop on 7 November 1666, when he especially admired a portrait in coloured chalks, a highly fashionable medium in this period: 'The picture in chalke is the finest thing I ever saw in my life, I think'.[1] A prolific yet subtle draughtsman, Faithorne here uses the buff colour of the paper to create a halo of light round the subject's head, lifting the effect of the formal wig with its tight curls.

Shortly after the date of this work, Faithorne retired from his shop to Blackfriars, where he concentrated on producing chalk portraits. This example is presumed to represent the wealthy Dissenter Thomas Dare II (1643–1685), who was an eminent silversmith and one of the burgesses of Taunton, Somerset. Examples of his work can be found in the Bishop's Palace in Wells and the Museum of Somerset. In January 1679, Dare presented a petition to Charles II, requesting that he take action against Popish Recusants; the scroll is depicted in his right hand. Having been jailed for sedition, he fled to Holland, where he became Paymaster General of the doomed Monmouth Rebellion of 1685. Shortly after landing on the Dorset coast, an unfortunate altercation took place over a horse between Dare and the Scottish cavalry commander of the rebellion, Andrew Fletcher of Saltoun. Infuriated at being whipped by Dare, Fletcher shot him dead, instantly depriving Monmouth of valuable financial backing and local West Country influence.

Bainbrigg Buckeridge quotes the following lines of verse: 'A Faithorn sculpsit is a charm can save / From dull oblivion, and a gaping grave.'[2] Dare's portrait does not appear to have been engraved, but his appearance is nonetheless preserved. CP

1. http://www.pepysdiary.com/diary/1666/11/07/, accessed 9 January 2015.
2. Buckeridge (1754) pp. 371–2.

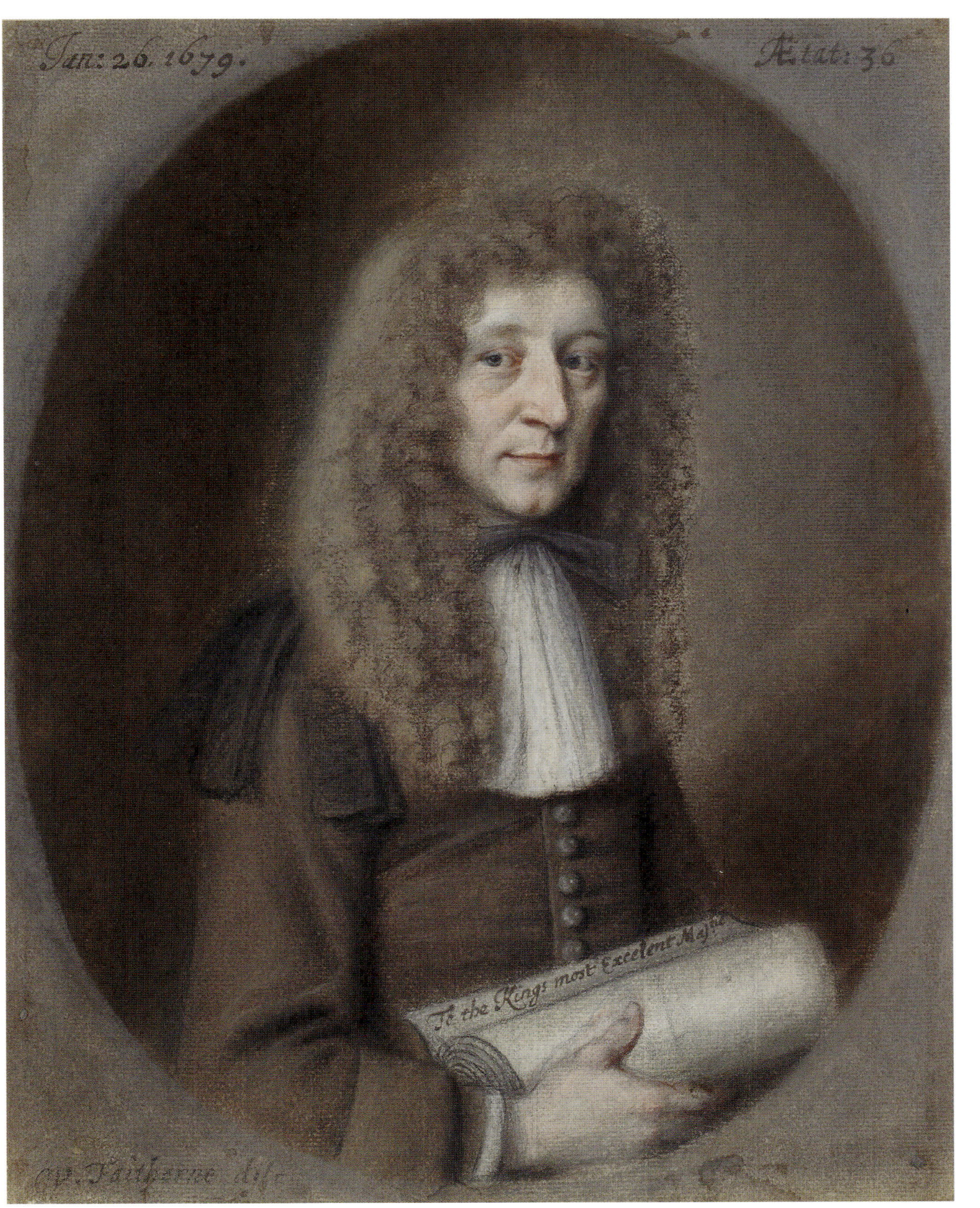
Jan: 26. 1679.
Ætat: 36
To the Kings most Excelent

5

SIR GODFREY KNELLER 1646–1723

Henry Aldrich, Dean of Christ Church, 1696

Black chalk heightened with white, on rough grey laid paper
29.2 × 23.3 cm
Purchased (Hope Fund), 1934
WA1934.412

LITERATURE: Brown (1982) no. 151; Stewart (1971) no. 44; Stewart (1983) III no. 34

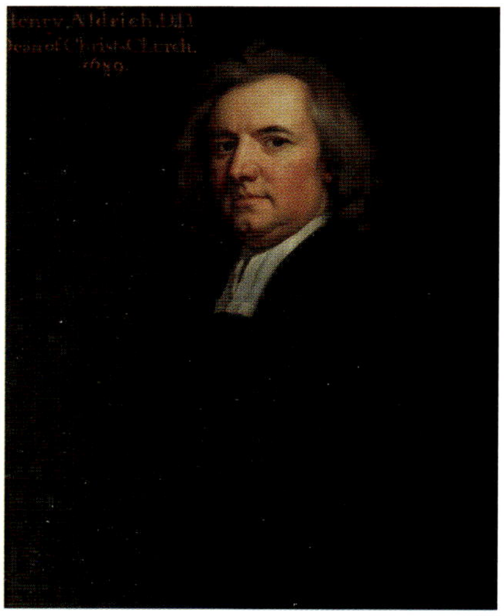

Fig. 24 | After Godfrey Kneller (1646–1723), *Henry Aldrich, Dean of Christ Church*, 1696. Oil on canvas. Christ Church, University of Oxford, LP 105 © By permission of the Governing Body of Christ Church, Oxford

James Northcote, assistant to Sir Joshua Reynolds, remarked in the 1810s that Kneller's works had fallen in esteem, for 'the great mass of his works are such hasty slobbers, that they are scarcely fit to be seen'.[1] This lively portrait with its vigorous handling demonstrates the unfairness of this judgment, underlining the genius of Kneller at his best: George Vertue described him as 'the Morning Star for all other Portrait Painters in his Time'.[2]

Vertue particularly praised Kneller's ability to capture a true likeness. This rapidly executed sketch has all the immediacy of a portrait taken from life, catching the essential qualities of Dean Aldrich (1648–1710). An erudite logician, collector, composer, and amateur architect, he must have been a highly sympathetic and stimulating sitter. Aldrich became Vice-Chancellor of the University of Oxford in 1692, and it was partly through his good offices that Kneller was awarded an honorary doctorate in 1695. This is undoubtedly a preparatory study for the portrait of Aldrich now at Christ Church, probably occasioned by this event; it is dated 1696 from a mezzotint by John Smith.[3]

Kneller introduced into England the practice of drawing heads full-size so that they could be transferred directly on to canvas, rather than being squared up; the fact that the painting is in reverse of the drawing suggests that he used an offset method for transfer. The study is similar in technique to Kneller's portrait of the engraver Peter Vanderbank, with its deft application of highlights and fluent curves of loosely falling hair.[4] The sharpest touch of white and the darkest touch of black appear below and above Aldrich's right eye respectively, drawing us into his gaze. Multi-directional hatching around the jowls and forehead describe the forms in the manner of an engraving, while Kneller's characteristic zigzag shading can be found beneath the right eye, around the chin and in the ear lobe. There is a Baroque verve in the drawing that reflects the lively intelligence of the sitter.

In the painting, the head is tilted back slightly, giving Aldrich a somewhat guarded expression. He appears more idealised than in the drawing, acquiring a magisterial air at the expense of humour. In reality Aldrich had a reputation as a *bon viveur* and 'punner of the first value', producing a translation from Latin of a popular poem on drinking:

If all be true that I do think,
There are five reasons we should drink,
Good wine, a friend, or being dry,
Or lest we should be by and by,
Or any other reason why.[5] CP

1. Quoted in Stewart (1971) p. 6.
2. Quoted in J. Douglas Stewart, 'Kneller, Sir Godfrey, baronet (1646–1723)', *Oxford Dictionary of National Biography*, online edn. (2010), www.oxforddnb.com/view/article/15710, accessed 6 January 2015.
3. National Portrait Gallery, D11585.
4. British Museum, P,7.214.
5. Quoted in Suttle (1940) p. 128.

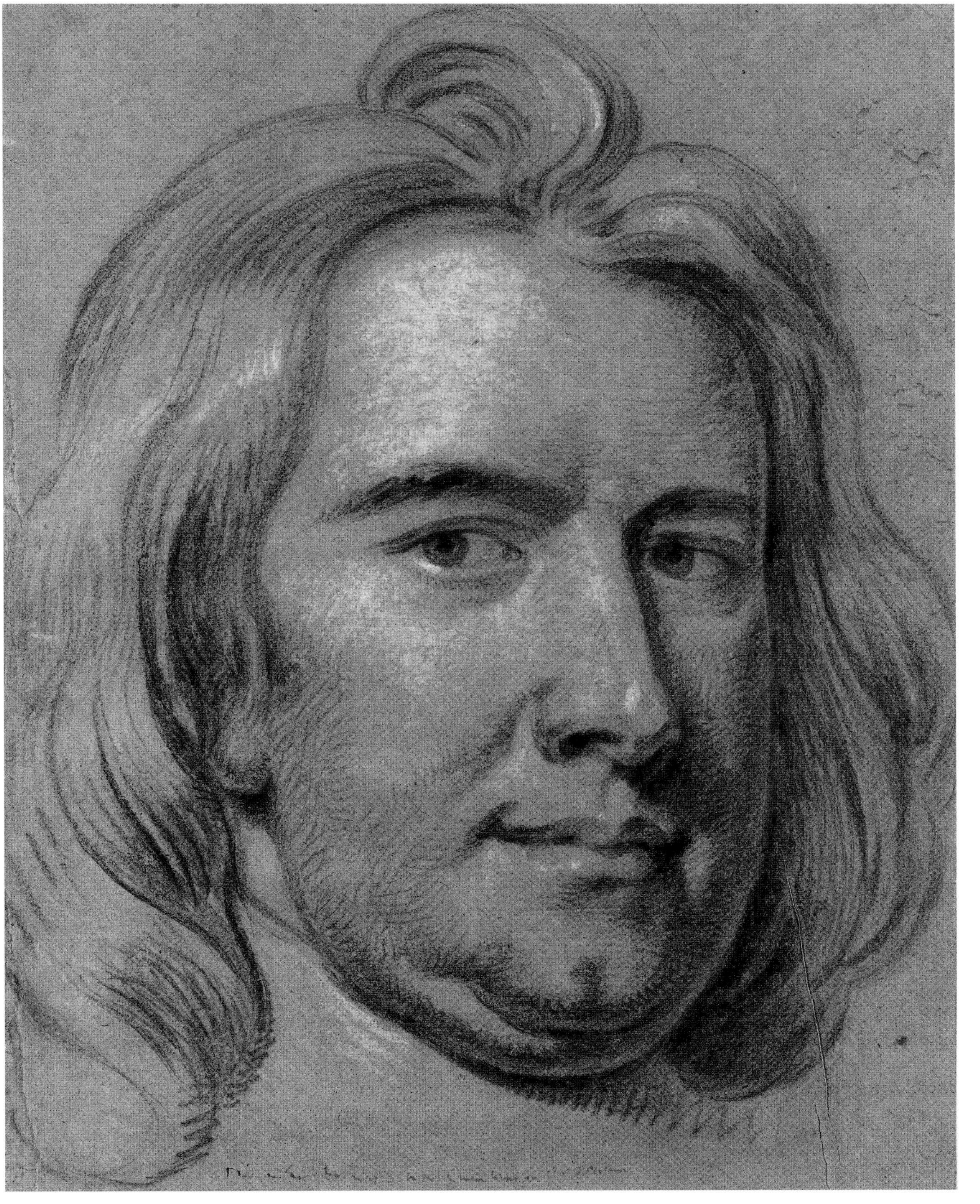

6

JONATHAN RICHARDSON 1665–1745

James Figg, 1714

Black, white and pink chalks on blue laid paper
29 × 22.5 cm
Inscribed by Richardson the Younger: *Figg Gladiator ad Vivum 14*. Inscribed: *1714*
Purchased (Hope Fund), 1945
WA1945.135

LITERATURE: Brown (1982) no. 1532; Stainton and White (1987) no. 182

James Figg (before 1700–1734) was a prize-fighter born at Thame in Oxfordshire, where the name of a public house still records his fame. The fact that this drawing describes Figg as a 'Gladiator' rather than a bare-knuckle boxer ties his use as a model to the academic tradition, conjuring up images of the classical statues later used as examples in the Royal Academy drawing schools, including the 'Borghese Gladiator'.[1] This Antique statue actually shows a swordsman, which is appropriate since Figg ran a school for arms in London from *c.* 1714, instructing his students in fencing and the use of the backsword and quarterstaff. He opened an amphitheatre in Oxford Road (now Oxford Street), where sporting competitions and exhibitions of swordsmanship were held, and also taught the arts of self-defence to wealthy pupils from the gentry and nobility. In 1729, as a result of these social contacts, he was appointed gatekeeper of Upper St James's Park.

Figg's fame led to his being portrayed in William Hogarth's engraving *Southwark Fair* (1734), where he regularly demonstrated his skill in different forms of combat. He sits astride a horse on the far right of the print, grim-faced, with sword raised.[2] A similarly focused, frowning expression appears in Richardson's study of Figg, inscribed in the handwriting of the artist's son as having been taken from the life. Soldiers and prize-fighters such as Figg were often selected by artists to act as life models because of their well-defined musculature. They may also have been seen to embody the spirit of Greek classical art through their physical prowess and bravery; the inscription under John Faber's mezzotint (1727–9) of Figg, after a painting by John Ellys, celebrates 'The Vigour of his Arme, the Quickness of his Eye'.[3]

The loose handling of this drawing is in strong contrast to the tight control of Richardson's portrait of Dr Mead (cat. 7), partly dictated by the medium of black chalk, which lends itself to sweeping strokes and soft modelling. Richardson has used more blending and smudging here than in some of his other chalk drawings, which are often sharply hatched in all directions. The modelling of the muscles in the arms and concern for an exact outline to the figure seem to be the artist's primary focus. The use of black chalk with white heightening, employing the blue of the paper as a middle tone, is typical of life-drawing techniques in this period, and the style of Kneller's Great Queen Street Academy in particular. CP

1. See, for example, Musée du Louvre, MR 224.
2. British Museum, 1868,0822.1515.
3. National Portrait Gallery, D1948.

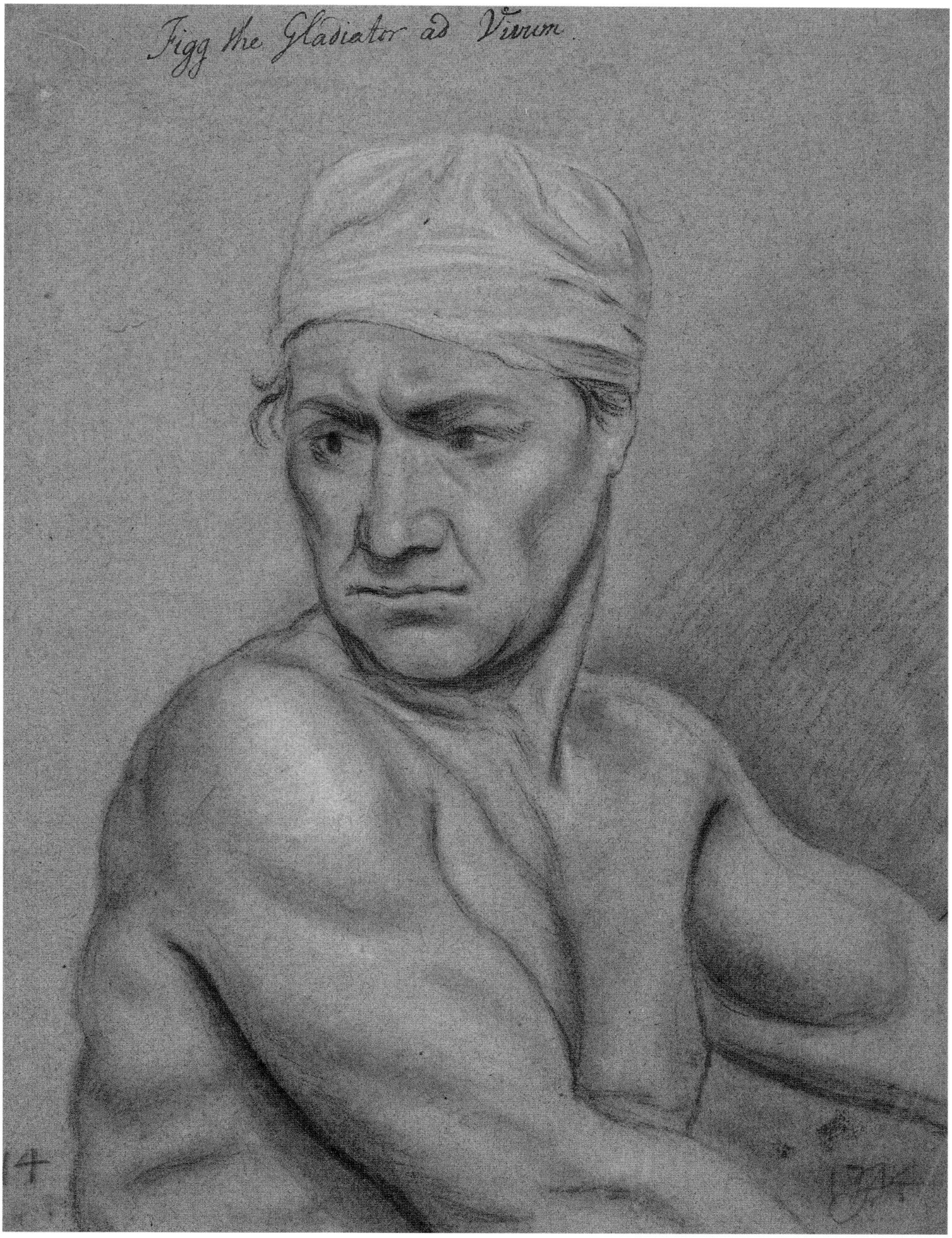
Figg the Gladiator ad Vivum
14

7

JONATHAN RICHARDSON 1665–1745

Dr Richard Mead, c. 1739

Graphite on vellum
17.8 × 13.8 cm
Inscribed on old mount: *Dr Mead*
Purchased (Hope Fund), 1938
WA1938.110

LITERATURE: Brown (1982) no. 1534

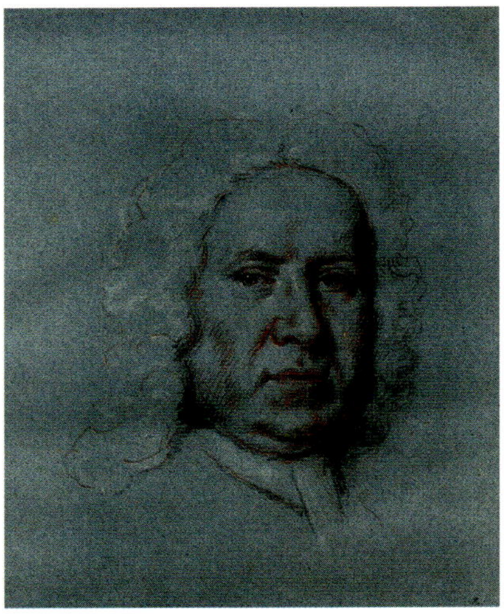

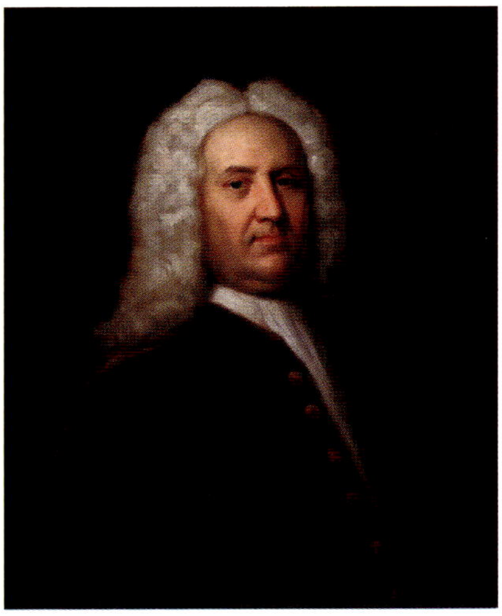

Fig. 25 | Jonathan Richardson the Elder (1665–1745), *Portrait of Dr Mead*, 1738. Red, black and white chalk on blue paper. British Museum, London, 1902,0822.37 © Trustees of the British Museum

Fig. 26 | Jonathan Richardson the Elder (1665–1745), *Portrait of Dr Mead*, *c.* 1738. Oil on canvas. National Portrait Gallery, London, 4157 © National Portrait Gallery, London

At his death in 1745, Jonathan Richardson left almost 550 of his own portrait drawings to his son. These can be broadly divided between carefully finished studies in plumbago, or graphite, on vellum, and looser sketches in black and/or red and white chalks on blue paper, such as that of James Figg (cat. 6). Carol Gibson-Wood has plausibly argued that the more finished portraits might have been designed for the purposes of private contemplation – part of a personal album depicting people of importance in Richardson's life. This would have acted as a form of *memento mori*, in line with his theory of portraiture as a genre that encouraged moral improvement through contemplation of the deeds of great men.[1]

Certainly, the life of Richard Mead (1673–1754) was an inspiring one. He rose to eminence in the field of medicine, as well as being a respected bibliophile and collector of antiquities, curiosities, and works of art. Best known, perhaps, for his support for the Foundling Hospital, one of the first venues for the public viewing of art in Britain, Mead also made his personal collection available to artists and to the public.

This portrait seems to have been based on a detailed drawing in coloured chalks on blue paper in the British Museum. Dated 5 October 1738, it was doubtless preparatory to Richardson's portrait of Mead, produced *c.* 1738 (fig. 26). There is no doubt that this was a working drawing from life – a second attempt at drawing Mead's lips has been made in the lower left part of the sheet. The portrait gives Mead a fuller, blander face, and lacks the sensitivity and psychological penetration of the drawing.

The Ashmolean portrait on vellum is most closely connected with a profile portrait of Mead.[2] The two works must have been made at the same time, as they use the same media and are of the same size; the heads both measure exactly 8 cm from hairline to chin. The profile was produced as an etching, though there does not appear to be an equivalent print for the full-face version.[3]

The quality of drawing in the Mead portrait is deft and precise, deliberately emulating the technique of Old Master drawings in silverpoint which Richardson admired and collected. Dense hatching in closely packed parallel strokes describes the surface of the face, while the hair is more economically drawn with repeated calligraphic curves, highly characteristic of this artist. The handling displays great delicacy without losing the spontaneity of the original sketch. CP

1. Gibson-Wood (1994) pp. 203–29, especially pp. 209–13.
2. Ashmolean Museum, WA1936.193.
3. British Museum, Q,1.107.

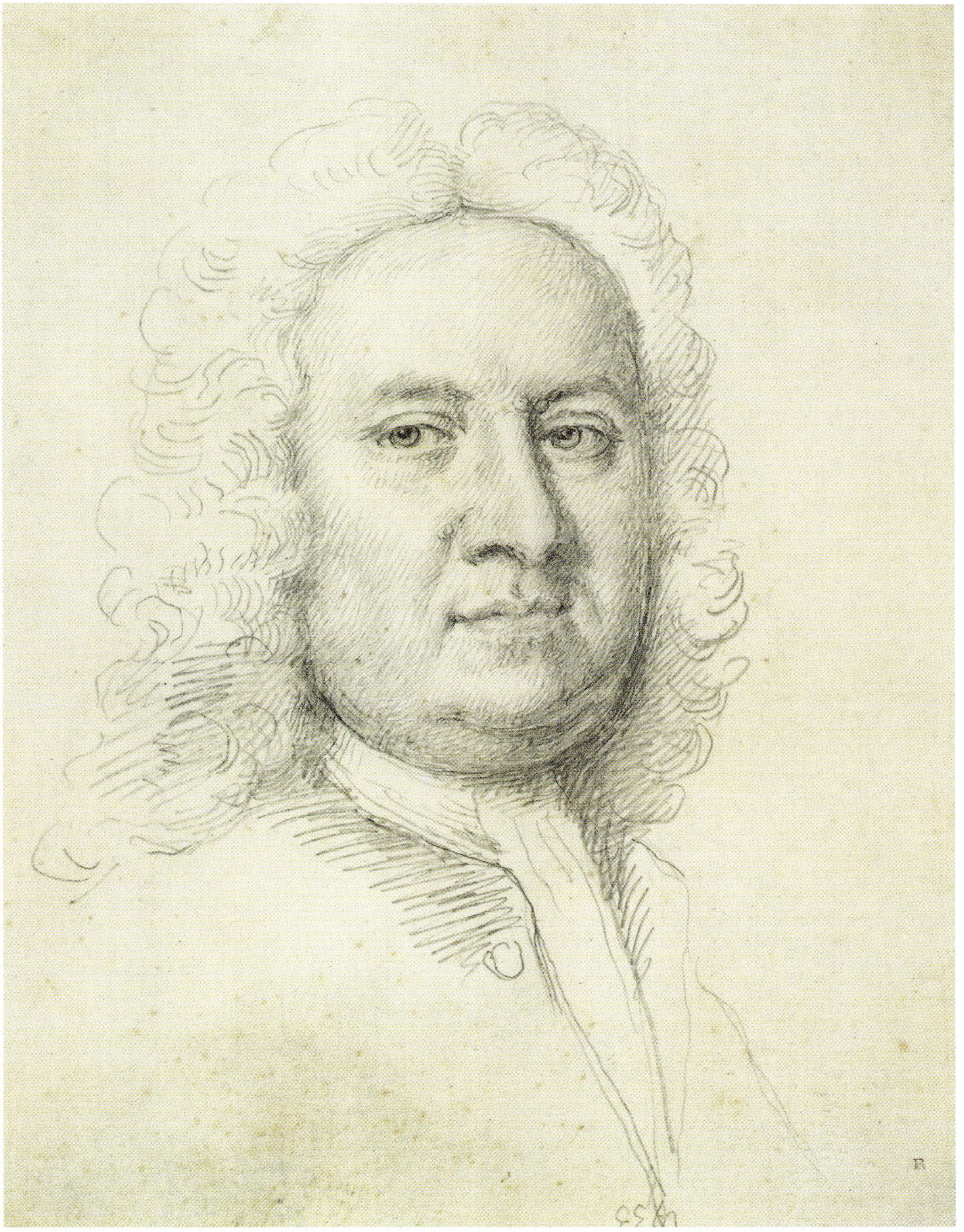

8

ALLAN RAMSAY 1713–1784

A Nude Woman seen from Behind, probably 1754–7

Black and white chalk touched with red on blue paper
41 × 27.5 cm
Presented by Percy Moore Turner, 1942
WA1942.24

LITERATURE: Brown (1982) no. 1508

Allan Ramsay's father, the distinguished poet and author Allan Ramsay (1684–1758), joined a group of friends in establishing the short-lived Academy of Saint Luke in Edinburgh in 1729, where the artist made his first copies after Old Master drawings and casts of Antique sculptures. He later studied with Hans Hysing (1678–1752) in London, and made the first of his four journeys to Italy in 1736–8. With strongly antiquarian interests, he made drawings of classical statues in the Uffizi in Florence, and in Rome. Although Ramsay was formally instructed by the portrait and history painter Francesco Imperiali (1679–1740), he also frequented the life class in the French Academy.

In spite of this assiduous study, on his return to England, George Vertue complained that 'I don't understand, when he draws in the Accademy [*sic*] from human nature he has any great skill or practice therein'.[1] Nevertheless, Ramsay quickly became the most prominent portrait painter in London, his sitters including leading Scottish and English aristocrats. In 1745 he was summoned to Holyroodhouse to paint the young Pretender, Prince Charles Edward Stuart, and his portrait of Flora MacDonald became one of the most popular of the century.[2] In his *Dialogue on Taste* (1755), Ramsay explained his conception of the 'natural portrait', which owed much to his French contemporaries.

It has been convincingly argued that Ramsay's second visit to Italy, from 1754 to 1757, marked a period of decisive change in his style, away from the slight hardness and glassy surface of the early portraits towards a softness and malleability characteristic of his last decade.[3] In Rome he took lodgings on the unfashionable Viminale, far from the high life of the Piazza di Spagna. The architect Robert Adam noted that he was thus able to 'preserve the greatest part of his time for painting, drawing and reading … and as Mrs Ramsay is of so good a family and Mumpy [as Ramsay was known] himself so rich they are no discredit'.[4] They did, nevertheless, hold a popular weekly salon. Apart from painting a few portraits, Ramsay's principal purpose was again to continue his studies. He went regularly to the French Academy, where, under its new Director, Charles-Joseph Natoire, life drawing had taken on greater importance, and where students were encouraged to make landscape drawings in the open air. Most surviving drawings from this period are of the male model, and it is possible that this female nude was made at the St Martin's Lane Academy in 1758, after Ramsay's return to London. Whatever the precise circumstances of its creation, its delicacy and refinement certainly owe much to the example of Natoire.[5] CH

1. Quoted in Brown (1982) p. 518.
2. Ashmolean Museum, WA1960.76.
3. Campbell (2013) p. 25.
4. Ingamells (1997) p. 797.
5. Smart (1992) p. 119.

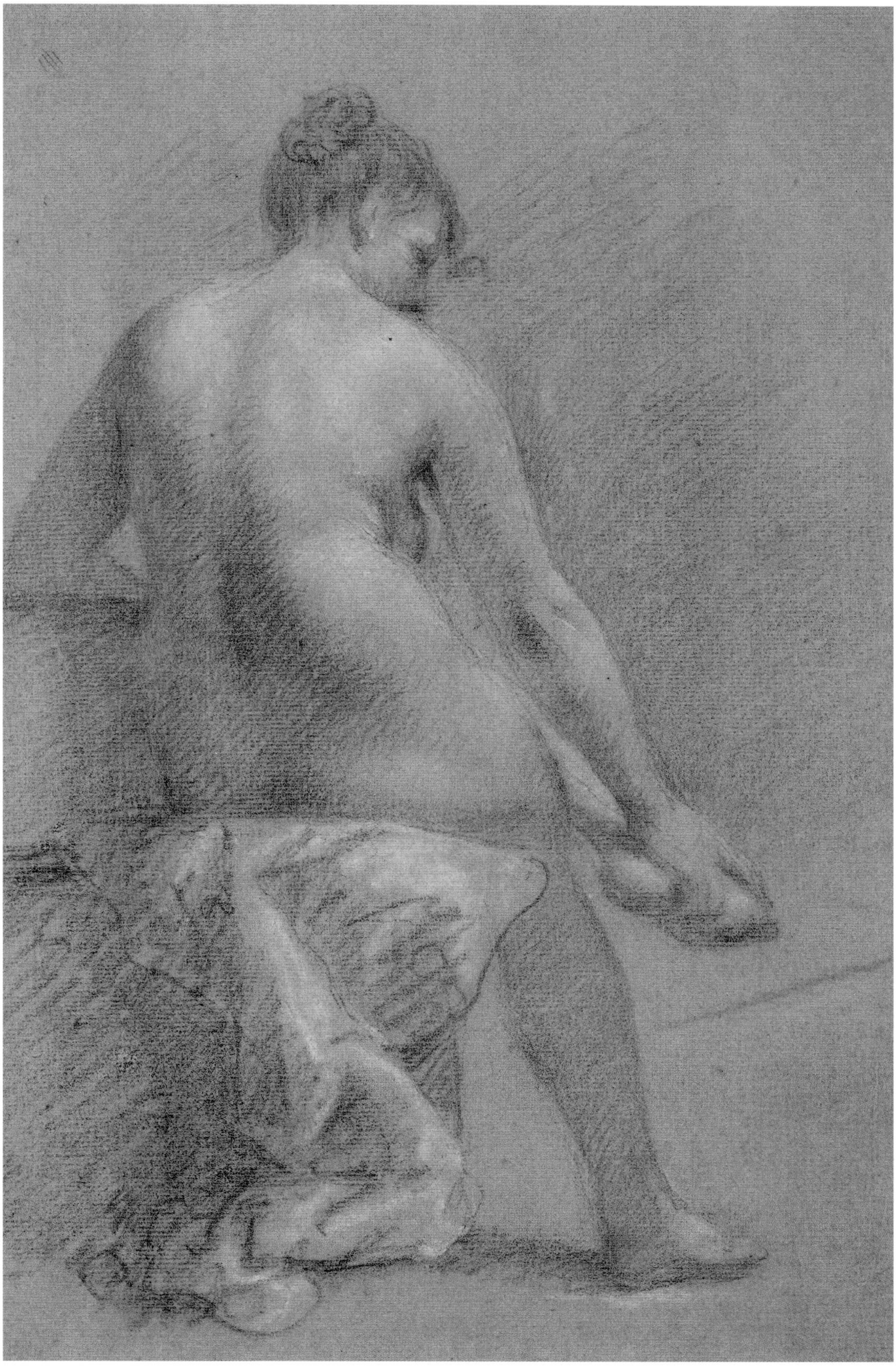

9

SIR JOSHUA REYNOLDS 1723–1792

Study of Charity, c. 1778

Pen and brown ink with wash over indications in graphite on paper
29 × 18 cm
Lent by the Warden and Fellows of New College, Oxford, 1997
LI838.1

LITERATURE: Postle (1995) pp. 168–85; Mannings (2000) no. 2116

In 1777 Thomas Jervais was appointed to complete the stained glass renovation begun at New College, Oxford, in the mid-1760s. He recommended that Benjamin West provide the designs, but in July the commission was awarded to Sir Joshua Reynolds, partly through the negotiations of Thomas Warton, an academic who was also a friend of the artist. Reynolds was best known as a portraitist, but once elected to the Presidency of the newly created Royal Academy of Arts in 1768, he campaigned vigorously to raise the status of British art. His *Discourses* promoted artistic practice based upon a close study of the Antique and drawing after the live model, while he increasingly produced 'fancy' pictures and in 1773 exhibited his first major history painting, *Count Ugolino and his Children*.[1]

Reynolds had ample opportunity to study Antique sculpture and paintings by the Old Masters during his time in Italy in 1750–2, and he probably drew from the life model at the St Martin's Lane Academy. Yet he later privately confessed that his draughtsmanship of the human figure was not as adept as it might be.[2] This is certainly borne out by this typically swift sketch of the figure of Charity, for the centre of the lower register in the New College west window, as the principal of the seven Virtues. Reynolds was originally requested to make 'drawings or cartoons', but recounted that 'he had been so long in the use of the pallet and brushes, that he found it easier to him to paint them to drawing'.[3] This had the additional benefit of providing a coloured exemplar for Jervais and enabling Reynolds to exhibit the preparatory paintings, judiciously advertising the commission to his London audience.

This early study follows Ripa's *Iconologia* (first published 1593), in which Charity suckles an infant held in her left arm with two children at her feet. The additional infant is a departure from Ripa's emblem, and the lively pen-work indicates the improvisatory nature of the drawing. Reynolds later simplified the group and, sensitive to the *mores* of eighteenth-century society, removed the element of nudity. Furthermore, he based the subsequent compositions upon an engraving of an Antique statue of Niobe, while using Mrs Sheridan (née Linley) as a model, astutely combining his theoretical promotion of the Antique with the depiction of a recognisable celebrity. *The Nativity* for the window's upper register, inspired by Correggio's *La Notte*, also featured Mrs Sheridan, developed from an earlier, abortive plan, led by Reynolds, to decorate St Paul's Cathedral. The New College commission received mixed reviews upon completion in 1785, but this initial study is an undeniably charming depiction of innocent merriment. KW

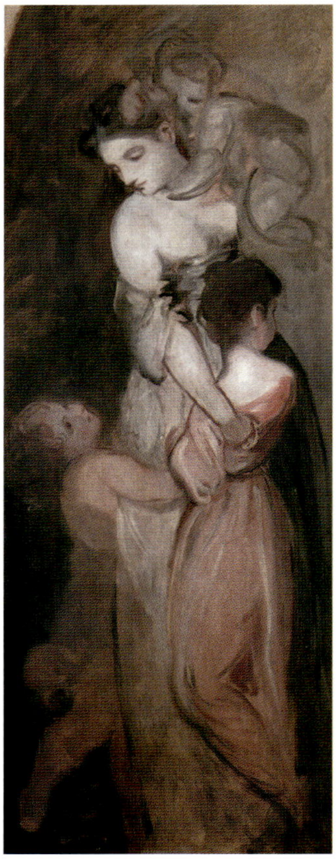

Fig. 27 | Sir Joshua Reynolds (1723–1792), *Charity*, *c.* 1778. Oil on canvas. Ashmolean Museum, Oxford, WA1855.158

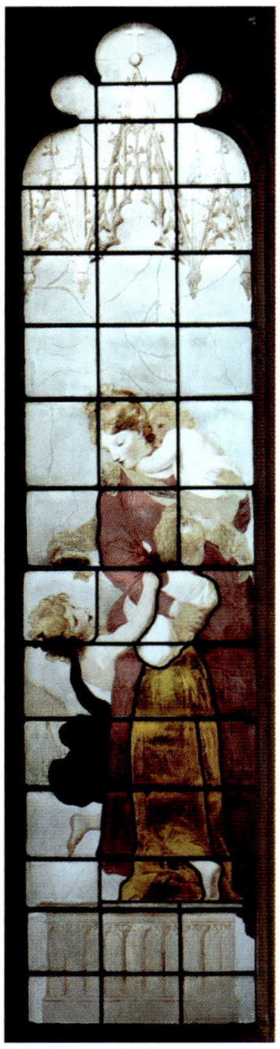

Fig. 28 | Thomas Jervais (d. 1799) after Sir Joshua Reynolds, *Charity*, *c.* 1778–9. Stained glass. New College, University of Oxford, © Courtesy of the Warden and Scholars of New College, Oxford / Bridgeman Images

1. Knole, National Trust, 12993; Mannings (2000) no. 2172.
2. Postle (2005) p. 271.
3. Mannings (2000) p. 545.

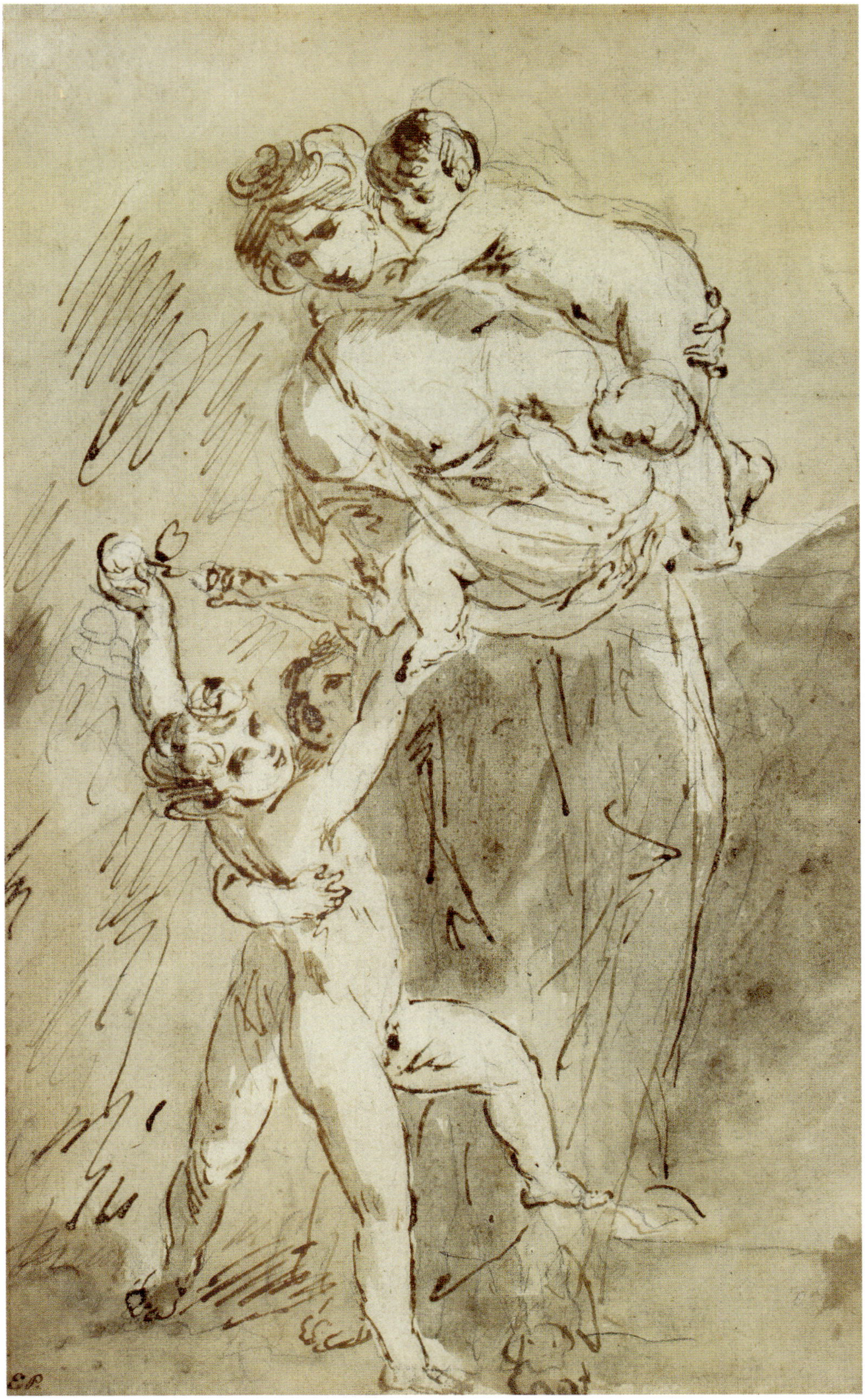

10

CHARLES GRIGNION II 1753–1804
Tan-Che-Qua, 'Chitqua' RA, 1771

Black and white chalk on buff paper
51.2 × 36.4 cm
Provenance unrecorded
WA.OA252

LITERATURE: Brown (1984–5) p. 10

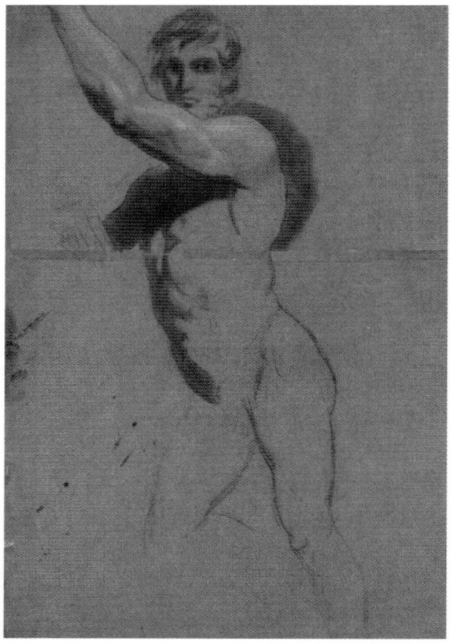

Fig. 29 | Charles Grignion II (1754–1804), *Study of a male nude*, *c.* 1771. Black and white chalk with stump on buff paper. Ashmolean Museum, Oxford, WA.OA252 (*verso*)

This large, impressive study shows 'Chitqua' (*c.* 1728–1796), a Chinese artist and modeller of portraits in clay, who travelled to England from Canton in 1769. Chitqua's arrival in London caused great interest: he had an audience with King George III and received commissions for his portraits from the tea merchant, Thomas Todd, and the porcelain manufacturer, Josiah Wedgwood. James Boswell described him as an 'ingenious artist' and Wedgwood's partner, Thomas Bentley, as 'a goodnatured, sensible man, very mild in his temper and gentle in his motions'.[1] His portrait was taken by John Hamilton Mortimer (1770–1), and in 1770 he exhibited one of his full-length clay figures, a 'model of a Gentleman', at the Royal Academy.[2] Chitqua visited the Academy Schools in the spring of 1771; he appears in the far left-hand corner of Johan Zoffany's famous painting of the Academicians (1771–2), engaged in conversation with the miniature painter Jeremiah Meyer.[3]

Charles Grignion the Younger, nephew of the Huguenot engraver Charles Grignion (1721–1810), was admitted to the Royal Academy in 1769, after winning prizes for drawing from the Society of Arts, and studied with Giovanni Battista Cipriani. There are 8 portrait drawings by Grignion II of Royal Academicians in all, probably produced when they were sitting to Zoffany for his painting *The Academicians of the Royal Academy* (1772). The drawing of the painter Charles Catton (1728–1798), also in the Ashmolean, is specifically inscribed 'Drawn at the Royal Academy / while standing to Zoffany'; it shows Catton together with the leg of the nude model.[4] Another of Grignion's drawings, portraying Dr William Hunter, the Academy's Professor of Anatomy, is similarly inscribed, and posed as in Zoffany's painting.[5] The muscular male nude study on the *verso* of the Ashmolean's Chitqua sheet also suggests the context of an Academy life-drawing class. Although the figure is not posed as in the Zoffany painting, his left arm is raised above his head, while in Zoffany's work the model is having his right arm placed in a rope sling, to support it while holding just such a pose.

A second drawing by Grignion of Chitqua in profile was one of the eight drawings described above, sold in the Fitzroy-Newdegate sale of 1952.[6] The technique of that drawing appears closer to those of Catton and Hunter, being more broadly hatched, and with Chitqua's chin is tilted upwards, as in the Zoffany painting. The Ashmolean's more finished study, idealising the sitter to a greater degree, could have been taken at a second sitting, perhaps with a painted portrait in mind. CP

1. Quoted in Brown (1984–5) p. 10.
2. Royal College of Surgeons, London, RCSSC/P 242.
3. Royal Collection, IN 400747.
4. WA1952.28
5. Hunterian Museum, Glasgow, GLAHA42340.
6. Piper (1952) pp. 198–9.

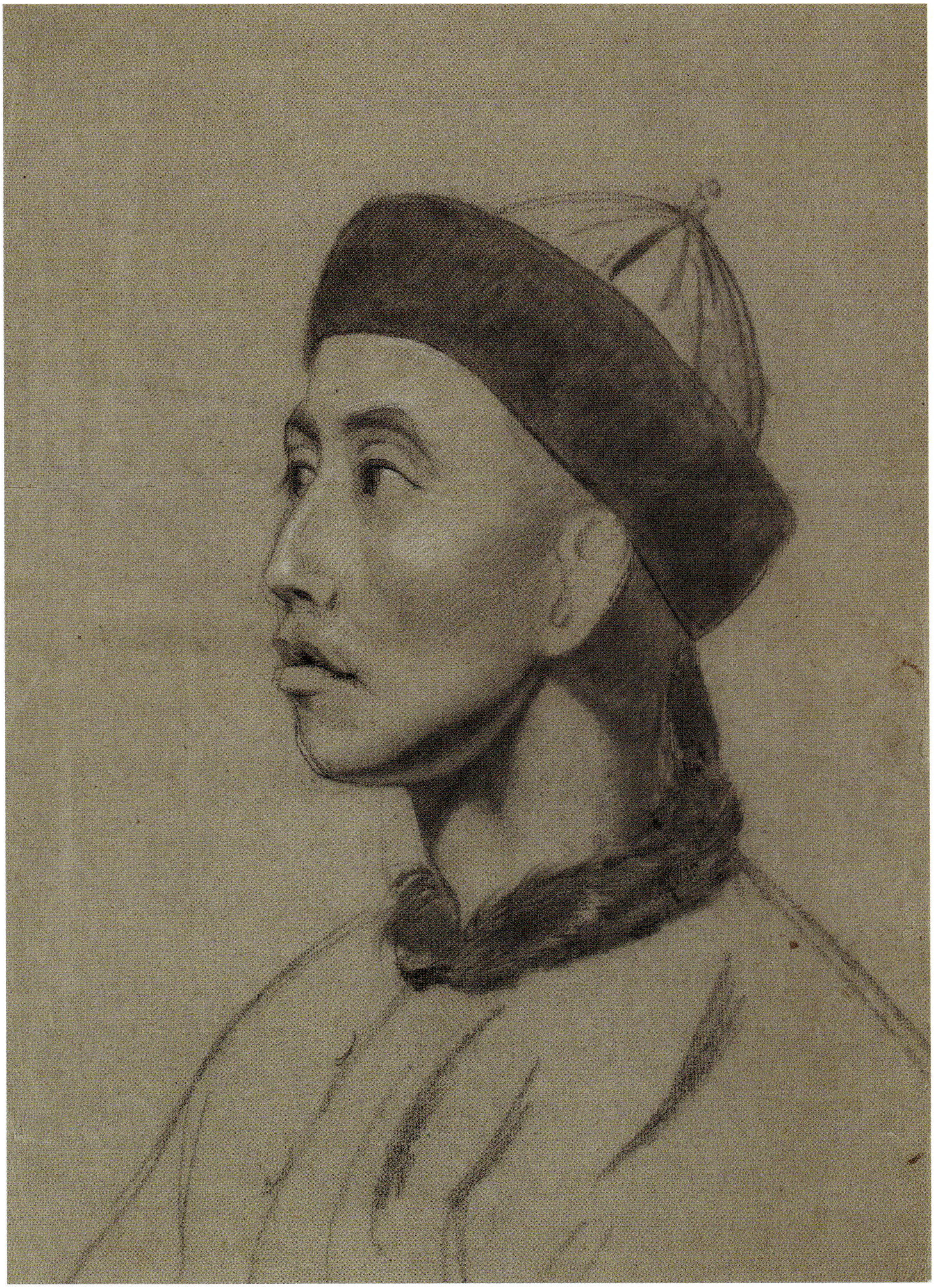

11

THOMAS GAINSBOROUGH 1727–1788

Study of a Woman, seen from the back, c. 1760–70

Black chalk and stump, heightened with white, on greyish-brown paper
49.4 × 30.8 cm
Bequeathed by Mrs Alice Jessie Mott, in memory of her husband Charles Egerton Mott, 1959
WA1959.9

LITERATURE: Hayes (1970) no. 30; Brown (1982) no. 673; Rosenthal and Myrone (2002) no. 68

Gainsborough moved from Ipswich to Bath in 1759 to exploit his talents among the city's wealthy seasonal residents. Second only to London as a centre for fashionable celebrity, Bath attracted visitors from the upper reaches of society as well as hosts of musicians, actors, and ambitious businessmen. Increasingly engaged on full-length portraits but rarely employing a drapery painter, Gainsborough made a series of costume studies, sometimes using articulated dolls, to examine the elaborate folds and textures of contemporary fashions. He simultaneously developed a fluid painting style, perfectly suited to capturing the sumptuous flamboyance of eighteenth-century dress and subtle nuances of movement.

Born in Sudbury, Suffolk, described by one contemporary source as 'Populous and Wealthy, being enrich'd by the Clothing-Trade', Gainsborough came from a family which was historically involved in the town's staple industry.[1] His sister was established as a milliner in Bath from 1762, so Gainsborough would have been well aware that his sitters' attire might cost more than the commissioned portraits in which it was commemorated. The extravagant sophistication of the fashionable world was not lost on the artist, who, taking Van Dyck as his model, sought to create portraits of equivalent opulence and grace. The pace at which fashions changed allows the drawing to be dated to the 1760s, owing to the popularity of the mushroom-shaped hat.

Drawn from life, the superbly varied handling of black and white chalks communicates a sense of the woman's movement as well as the luxurious layering of her costume, conveying the weight of her skirts, the diaphanous lightness of her apron and the frothy lace of her sleeves. The mid-tones of the paper are exploited to suggest a sense of volume with great economy, a technique developed from the example of Gainsborough's teacher, Hubert-François Gravelot (1699–1773). While the drawing remains primarily a study of drapery rather than of anatomy, as indicated by the clumsiness of the left foot, there is a refined eroticism in the dip between the shoulder blades uncovered by the slipping shawl and the revealing of the woman's right ankle.

This was one of a group of studies kept by Gainsborough that he bequeathed to his wife. They subsequently passed to his younger daughter, Margaret and then to his great-nephew Richard Lane, who published a lithograph of the work in January 1825. When it was offered for sale at Christie's in February 1831 it was among a lot described as 'drawings by Gainsborough ... received by the late Miss Gainsborough as favourite studies of her father'. KW

1. Quoted in Rosenthal and Myrone (2002) p. 17.

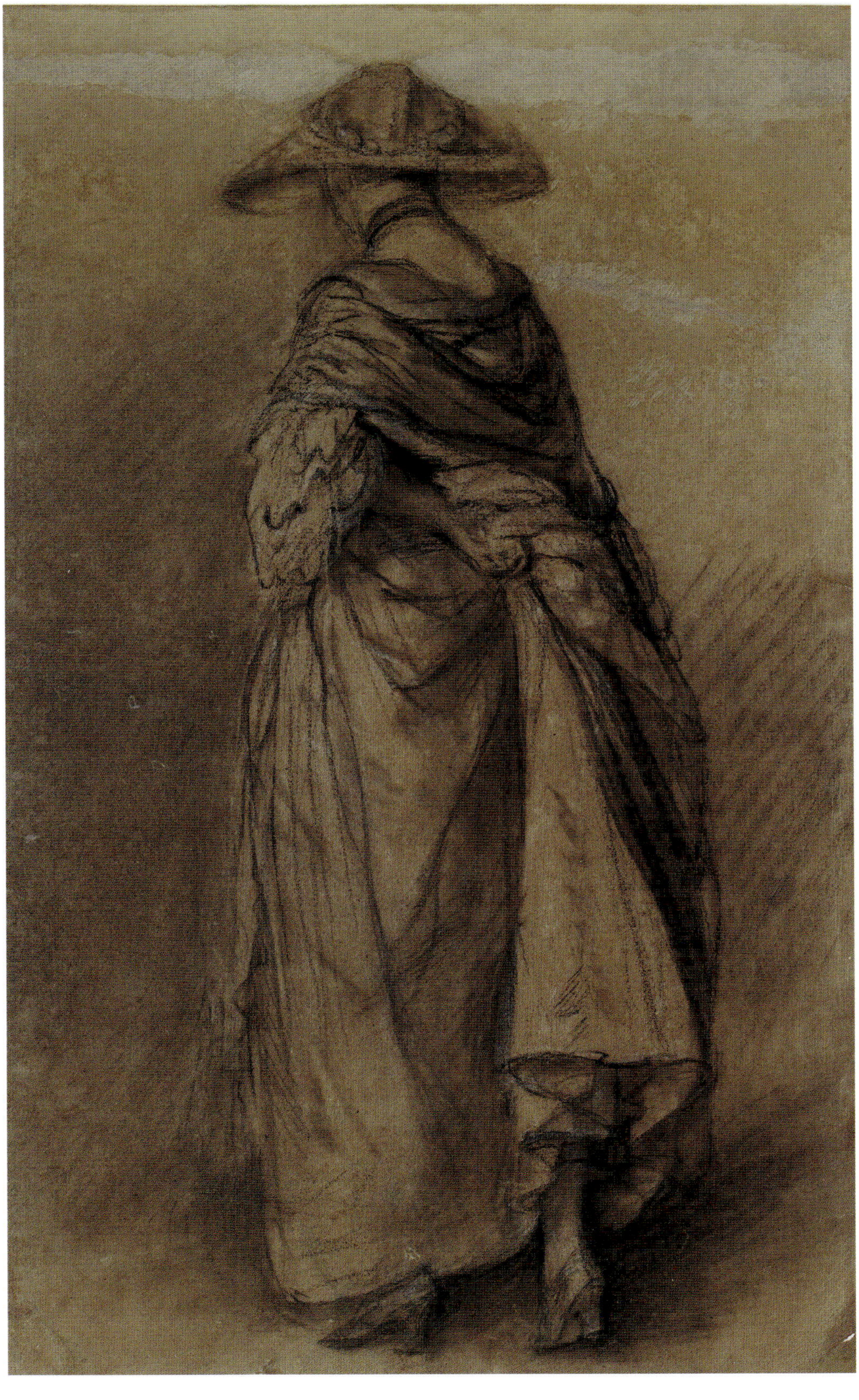

12

GEORGE ROMNEY 1734–1802

A Lady Leaning on a Pedestal, 1777–8

Pen and brown ink and dark bistre washes over graphite on paper
40.5 × 30.5 cm
Presented by John Ruskin to the Ruskin Drawing School, 1875
WA.RS.STD.029.b

LITERATURE: Brown (1982) no. 1559

This bold wash drawing was one of four by Romney in the Standard Series in Ruskin's Drawing School showing full-length female figures. They were 'among the most valuable examples of art in the rooms', according to Ruskin, who included them to demonstrate the ease of execution possible using a loosely applied flat wash.[1] Ruskin believed these drawings to be the work of Romney's great rival as the most fashionable portrait painter in London, Sir Joshua Reynolds, which is perhaps hardly surprising, given their resemblance to Reynolds's classicising portraits of women.[2]

This study most closely resembles Romney's portrait of Elizabeth Capel, daughter of the 4th Earl of Essex, who in 1777 married John, 3rd Lord Monson. Painted in 1778, the work was presumably commissioned to commemorate her marriage.[3] Though the pose is the same as in the final portrait, with upturned head, gracefully folded arms, and crossed ankles, the details of the background differ. The powerfully shadowed balustrade at the lower right of the drawing disappears in favour of a pillared one, while in the upper right of the painting there appears a domed classical building, perhaps suggesting the Temple of Vesta at Tivoli.

Romney has employed bistre ink to map out the broad contrasts of light and shade within his final composition, demonstrating 'the dominant power of *chiaroscuro*' in his approach, and exemplifying Ruskin's claim that 'A really great painter can leave every form as he would finally have it, with dark wet blots of water-colour thus thrown'.[4] After his return from Rome in 1775, Romney worked increasingly in this broad, spontaneous style. He often painted straight onto the canvas and made no preparatory drawings; according to John Wesley, he did 'more in an hour than Sir Joshua did in ten'.[5] Drawings such as this demonstrate the rapidity of Romney's working methods and his increasing confidence as a draughtsman.

On the *verso* of this work is an even more freely executed sketch in graphite. This imaginary composition features numerous figures in violent action, and children sheltering with their kneeling mothers. The sheet therefore unites the twin aspects of Romney's art: his productive public portrait business, carried on by day, and his private passion for literary and historical subjects, primarily indulged at night. CP

1. Ashmolean Museum, WA.RS.STD.030, WA.RS.STD.033, WA.RS.STD.034. Ruskin (1903–12) XXI, pp. 259–60.
2. See, for example, *Lady Elizabeth Compton* (1780–2; NGA, Washington DC).
3. Private collection. A mezzotint after this painting by Norman Hirst, *Lady Monson: The Setting Sun* was published in 1907. Ten years before sitting to Romney, Elizabeth had been painted by Reynolds with her younger brother, George, Viscount Malden; Mannings (2000) no. 308.
4. Ruskin's catalogue description to *Sepia sketch of Leafage*, WA.RS.RUD.290.
5. Wesley's Journal, 5 January 1789.

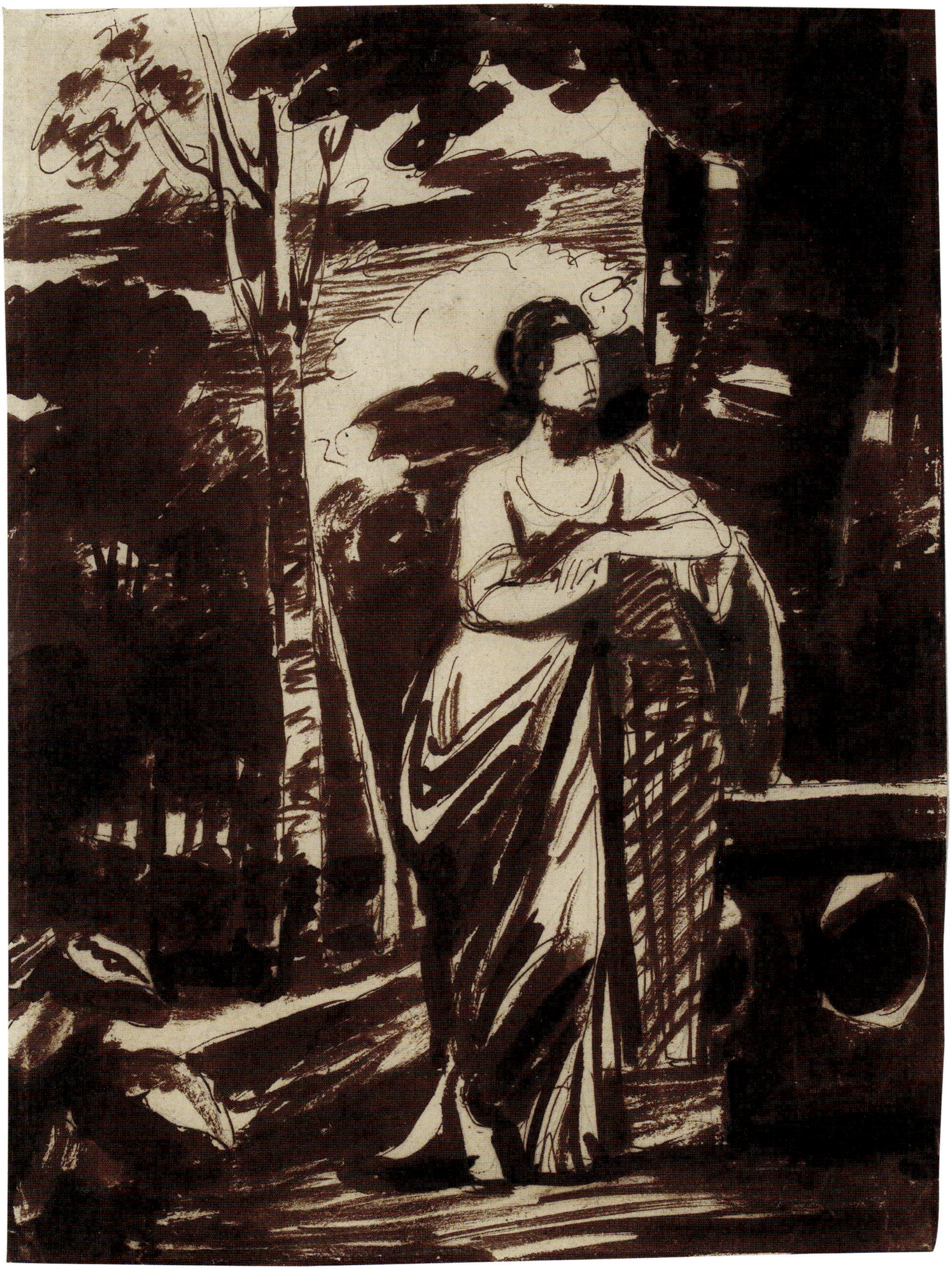

13

THOMAS GAINSBOROUGH 1727–1788
Milkmaid with two cows, 1770s

Black chalk and stump heightened with white, on coarse paper prepared with pink
24.1 × 32.3 cm
Bequeathed by Francis Falconer Madan, 1962
WA1962.17.67

LITERATURE: Hayes (1970) no. 404; Brown (1982) no. 681

During his early years in Suffolk, Gainsborough sketched assiduously from nature, in black chalk or pencil. However, as his fame grew and his portrait painting practice expanded, he left behind the meticulous naturalism of such early masterpieces as *Cornard Wood* (1748; National Gallery). After his move to Bath in 1759, he became resolutely opposed to painting actual views. As he told Lord Hardwicke, 'with regard to real Views from Nature in this Country, he has never seen any Place that affords a Subject equal to the poorest imitations of Gaspar or Claude ... if His Lordship wishes to have anything tolerable of the name of G. the Subject altogether, as well as figures etc must be of his own Brain'.[1]

During his mature years, Gainsborough drew compulsively, both as a form of instruction, and as a recreation in the evening after the day's work painting portraits. One of his acquaintances, William Henry Pyne, recorded that he had more than once 'seen him make models, or rather thoughts, for landscape scenery, on a little old-fashioned folding oak table', using cork or coal for foreground rocks, sand, and clay for the middle distance, lichens and mosses for bushes and broccoli for trees.[2] These three-dimensional 'thoughts' were not designed to be drawn, but were rather a symptom of Gainsborough's restless creativity. In fact, his landscape drawings were wholly imaginary, for, as he told his friend, William Jackson, 'a person able to collect in the Mind, will certainly groupe in the Mind also; and if he cannot master a number of Objects, so as to introduce them in friendship, let him do but a few'.[3] Almost invariably, Gainsborough's landscapes included figures: 'A regular Composition in the Landskip way should [incorporate] figures to fill a place (I won't say stop a Gap) or to create a little business for the Eye to be drawn from the Trees in order to return to them with more glee.'[4]

This drawing remains on its original mount signed by the artist, indicating that it was probably given away; Gainsborough made it a rule never to accept money for his drawings. It is unusual in concentrating on a close-up view of a milkmaid and two cows, one standing seen from the side, the other sitting and seen from the front, leaning against a tree. The composition is balanced on the right by another tree. The style is purposeful and deliberately inelegant: rough strokes in black and white chalks reflect the essential rusticity of the scene, and the pink-brown wash over the sheet gives it an appealing warmth. CH

1. Quoted in Sloman (2011) p. 5.
2. Quoted in Sloman (2011) p. 8.
3. Quoted in Sloman (2011) p. 8.
4. Quoted in Belsey (2002) p. 33.

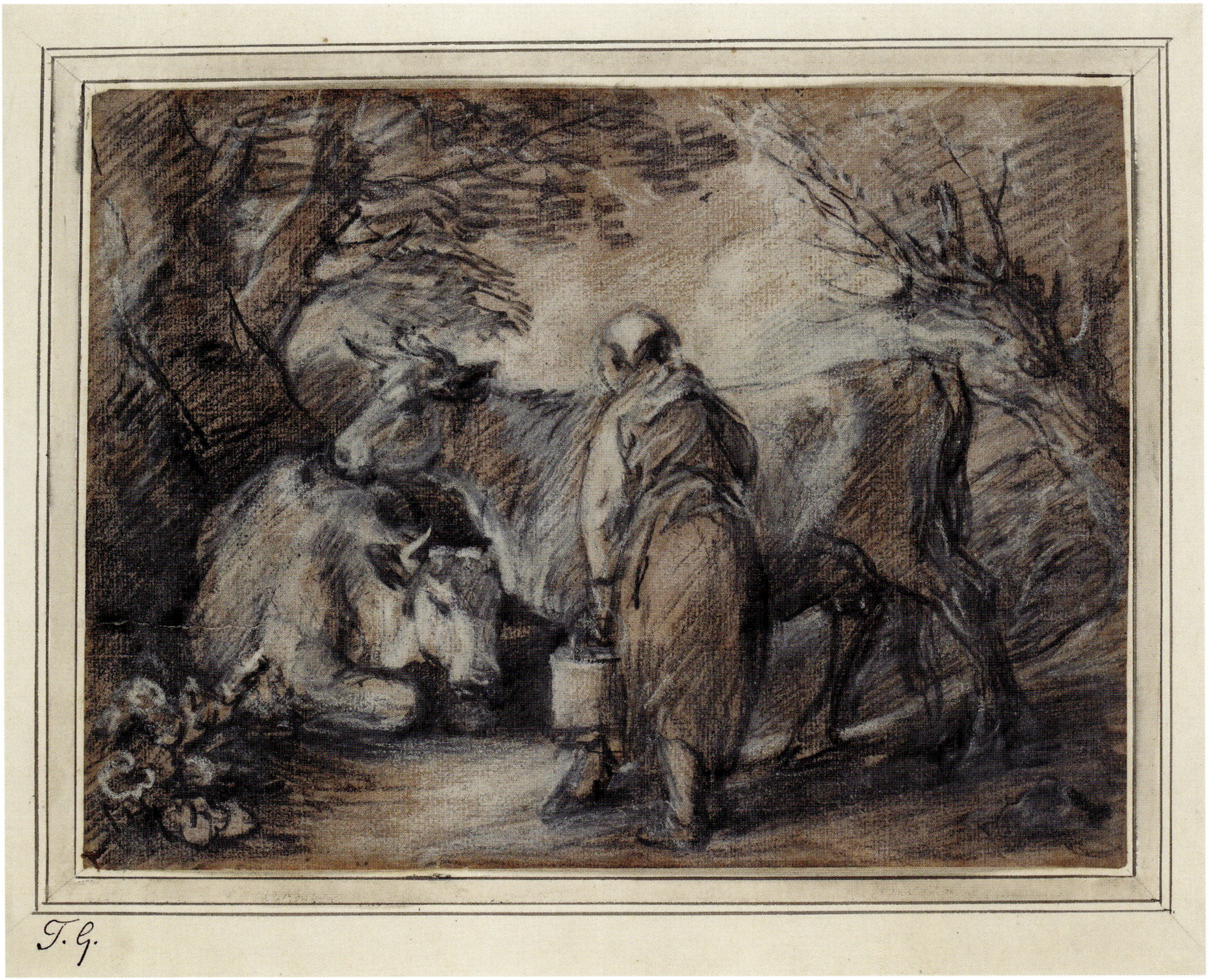
T. G.

14

THOMAS GAINSBOROUGH 1727–1788

Italianate Landscape with Travellers on a Winding Road, 1775–9

Black chalk with watercolour and bodycolour, on paper, varnished
22.5 × 30.9 cm
Bequeathed by Francis Falconer Madan, 1962
WA1962.17.66

LITERATURE: Hayes (1970) no. 370; Brown (1982) no. 680

As the supply of sitters for his practice as a portrait painter in Bath dried up, Gainsborough moved to London in 1774, settling at the grand address of Schomberg House in Pall Mall. He became increasingly experimental, both in subject matter and technique, which caused mounting strain in his relations with the Royal Academy, of which he had been a founder member in 1768. Yet after his death the President, Sir Joshua Reynolds, devoted his annual Discourse to the praise and analysis of Gainsborough's genius, as founded on a sincere love of art and a desire to excel. Although he did not recommend Gainsborough as a model for students, Reynolds acknowledged that 'all those odd scratches and marks, which, on close examination, are so observable ... this chaos, this uncouth and shapeless appearance, by a kind of magick, at a certain distance assumes form, and all the parts seem to drop into their proper places; so that we can hardly refuse acknowledging the full effect of diligence, under the appearance of chance and hasty negligence'.[1]

In his drawings, Gainsborough used an almost bewildering variety of techniques; as his friend William Jackson observed, 'No man ever possessed methods so various in producing effect, and all excellent – his washy, hatching style, was here in its proper element'.[2] His most elaborate drawings were begun in Indian ink with white chalk highlights. They were then dipped in skimmed milk to fix the chalk, and reworked with wash and watercolour, before being varnished three times with spirit varnish, on both sides so that the paper did not curl. Because Gainsborough's compositions were imaginary, and generally drawn in the evening, they are infinitely various. Here, he has adapted elements of the classical landscapes of Claude Lorrain and Gaspard Dughet – Italianate rustic buildings and an elegant bridge – and incorporated them in an airy composition, animated by a figure on horseback with an attendant in the foreground, a man resting by the side of the road, and other figures crossing the bridge.

An inscription on the *verso* notes that this drawing was given by the artist to the father of Miss L. Loscombe, 'an amateur and antiquarian'. This was possibly Benjamin Loscombe, who served as High Sheriff of Bristol in 1778 and was the son of a wealthy merchant, Joseph Loscombe (d. 1772). CH

1. Reynolds (1975) pp. 257–8.
2. Rosenthal (1999) p. 254.

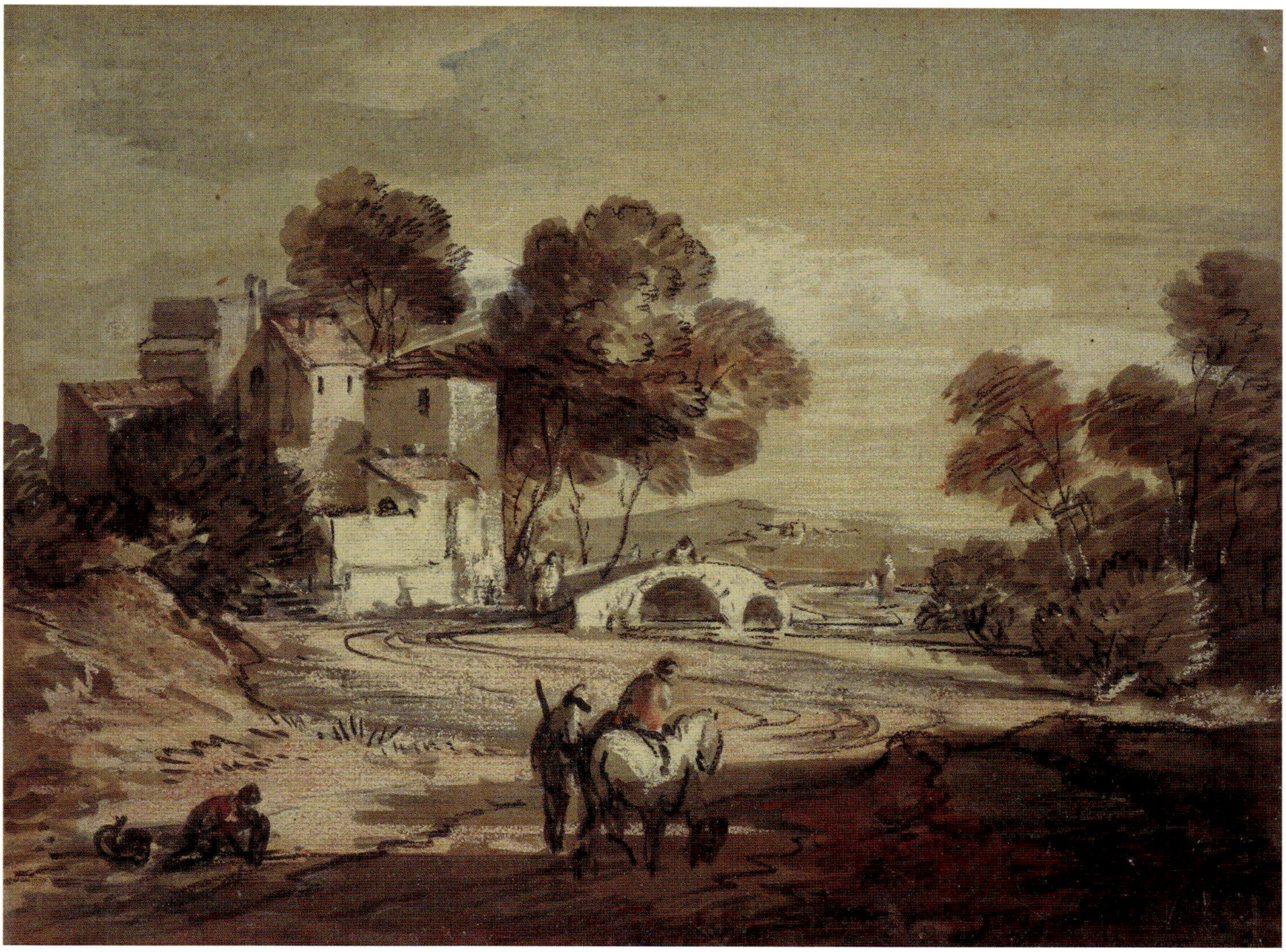

15

THOMAS ROWLANDSON 1756/7–1827

Landscape with Cattle Fording a Stream, c. 1795–1800

Pen and brown and black ink and watercolour over indications in graphite on paper
24.1 × 38.1 cm
Bequeathed by Miss Selina Adelaide Philippa Boyle, 1967
WA1967.52.38

LITERATURE: Brown (1982) no. 1591; Hayes (1990) no. 55

Rowlandson was admitted to the Royal Academy Schools in 1772 at the age of only 15. He became one of the most successful satirical printmakers of his age, producing social and political caricatures with a somewhat Hogarthian flavour. Being partly of French Huguenot extraction, he made frequent trips to France before the Revolution of 1789. From 1780, influenced by French artistic practise, he began to produce tinted watercolour drawings, moving away from the pure pen and grey wash that he had favoured previously.

The extensive collection of watercolours formed by the diplomat Sir John Crampton (1805–1886) included a large group by Rowlandson, purchased in 1855.[1] Although several of these works by Rowlandson were sold in 1923, possibly because they were thought morally dubious, many remained in the family by descent, and 16 were bequeathed to the Ashmolean in 1967. Two of the landscapes may be views of Cornwall. That shown here is very close to a version in a private collection inscribed 'The river Camel, Cornwall'; the undulating hills certainly resemble other views of Cornwall made by Rowlandson in the late 1790s.[2] Both works could have been drawn during one of many visits to Devon and Cornwall, to stay with his friend and patron, the banker and *bon viveur* Matthew Michell (1751–1817), on the Hengar estate near Bodmin.

The subject of horses and cattle fording a stream was often repeated by Rowlandson. It owes much to the work of Gainsborough, as well as to more distant models including Claude and Rubens. Rowlandson had studied Gainsborough's landscapes closely in the 1780s, producing aquatint and soft-ground etchings after his work for the series *Imitations of Modern Drawings* (*c.* 1784–8).[3] Rowlandson's fine penwork offers a picturesque variety of foliage, using marks very similar to those employed by Gainsborough in his drawings. The branches of the central and foreground trees have a rococo feel in their tightly twisted, snaking shapes, which contrast with the soft feathering of the shrubs on either side of the five-barred gate.

This wonderfully winding composition is beautifully lit, the dark foreground to the left balancing the fresh tints of the group in the bright stream and the sun-washed distant hills. The active movement of the animals towards the right contrasts with the stillness of the figures resting in the shade to the left, and the second dog sitting patiently in front of one of the tumble-down farm cottages. CP

1. McEvansoneya (2009) p. 104.
2. See Brown (1982) no. 1590. This was described as a view of 'Cornwall' on a former mount.
3. See also Ashmolean Museum, WA1974.238–41, for a set of Rowlandson's sepia landscapes after Gainsborough, 1789.

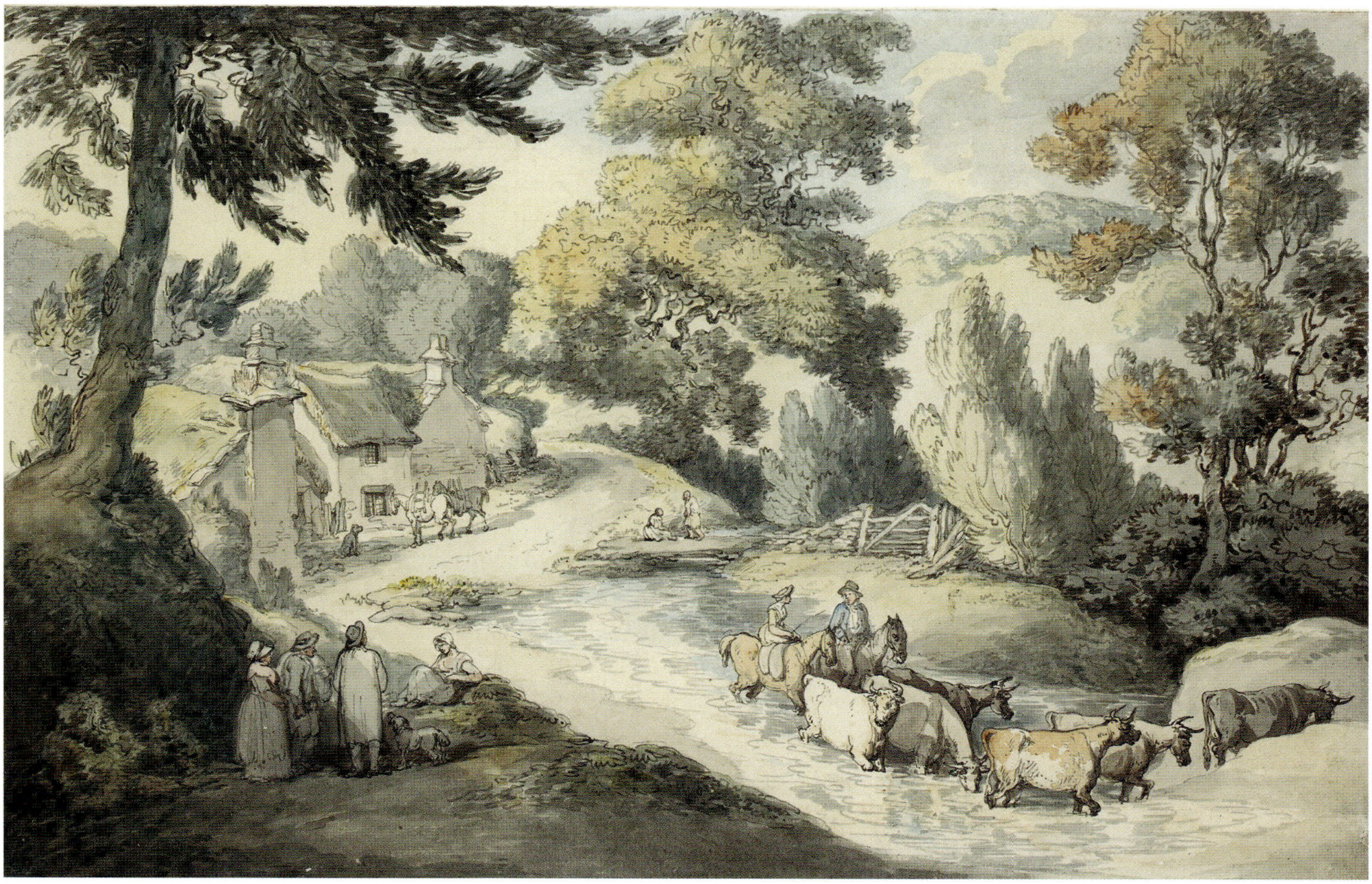

16

HENRY FUSELI 1741–1825
Satan, Sin, and Death, 1776

Pen and brown ink and wash over pencil on paper
27.1 × 38.4 cm
Dated: *Roma oct. 76*. Inscribed: *16*
Bequeathed by Dr Grete Ring, 1954
WA1954.70.198

LITERATURE: Schiff (1973) no. 480; Brown (1982) no. 658

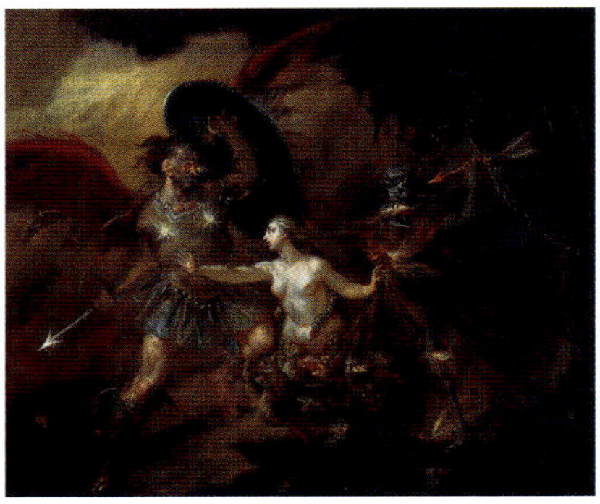

Fig. 30 | William Hogarth (1697–1764), *Satan, Sin, and Death (A Scene from Milton's 'Paradise Lost')*, *c.* 1735–40. Oil on canvas. Tate, London, T00790 © Tate, London 2014

William Hogarth's rare excursion into history painting, *Satan, Sin, and Death* (*c.* 1735–40; Tate), was one of the most influential of all his works, in spite of the low opinion of the artist's contemporaries, who generally found it absurd. When an engraving of the picture was published in 1767, the original belonged to the celebrated actor, David Garrick. The episode is one of the most dramatic in Milton's *Paradise Lost*, and was first selected for illustration by Sir John Medina in an edition of 1688. At the gates of Hell, Satan, who is on his way to tempt Adam and Eve, prepares to fight Death, but they are stopped by Sin, the 'snaky sorceress that sat Fast by hell gate, and kept the fatal key' (II.724–5), who explains that Death is the result of the incestuous union between herself and Satan, and that they must all three work together for the destruction of the human race. In Hogarth's painting, Satan on the left wears the costume of a Roman centurion, while Death is portrayed in the traditional form of a skeleton. Sin herself is 'fair above' with 'serpent coils and encircling dogs' below, as Milton described.

Fuseli left his native Switzerland in 1763 and, apart from a protracted period of study in Rome, 1770–8, remained in England for the rest of his life, becoming an influential figure in the Royal Academy. He was encouraged in his ambitions as a history painter by Sir Joshua Reynolds, whom he met in 1768. During his years in Rome, he studied the works of Michelangelo and his followers, and adopted their muscular, contorted forms. It was while he was in Rome that he made this drawing of *Satan, Sin, and Death*. He had been familiar with Milton's poem for many years, since one of his mentors in Zurich, Johann Jakob Bodmer had translated it into German. In adapting the composition of Hogarth's painting, which he must have seen in the original or known through a reproduction, Fuseli has overcome many of its weaknesses. All three figures are nude, and the muscular male figures have a great strength that Hogarth's lack. Sin is pale, with outspread wings, and contrasts dramatically with Death, no longer a skeleton but a true Michelangelesque nude. The penwork is characteristically rapid and nervous, with the wash very swiftly applied.

When in 1799–1800, Fuseli came to paint the same subject for his Milton Gallery, an attempt to emulate the success of Alderman Boydell's Shakespeare Gallery in providing a permanent display of history paintings in London, he used a similar composition to even greater dramatic effect.[1] CH

1. Los Angeles County Museum of Art, 59.56.

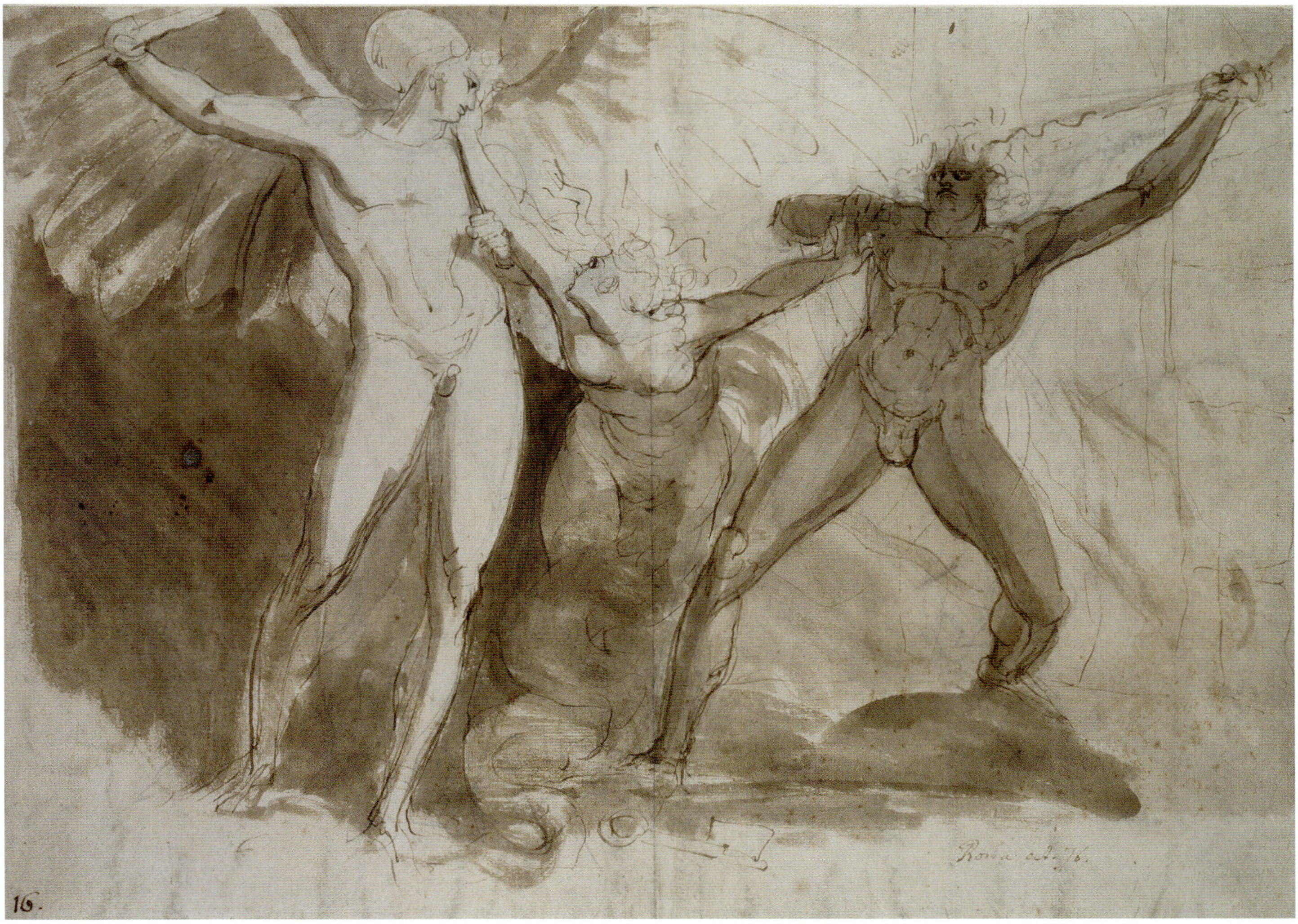
16.
Roma ad. 76.

17

JOHN HAMILTON MORTIMER 1740–1779

Monsters, ?1779

Pen and black ink with watercolour on paper
41.9 × 28.2 cm
Bequeathed by the Revd Robert Finch, 1830
WA1971.72

LITERATURE: Brown (1982) no. 1440; Sunderland (1986) no. 148

One of the most original and ambitious artists of the eighteenth century, Mortimer was also one of the most restless; he became notorious for his dissolute living and died at the early age of 38. Although he initially began studying as a portraitist, he always wanted to be a history painter, and found the studio of Robert Edge Pine (1730–1788) sympathetic to his ambition. He also made life drawings at the St Martin's Lane Academy. After winning prizes for history painting awarded by the Society of Arts in 1763 and 1764, Mortimer's career seemed assured. On the second occasion, the winning entry was a huge painting of *St Paul Preaching to the Antient Druids in Britain*, typically a subject from national history rather than the Bible or classical authors.[1]

In the early 1770s Mortimer became more extravagant in dress and behaviour. He modelled himself on a great proto-Romantic hero, the Neapolitan artist Salvator Rosa (1615–1673), a specialist in wild landscapes populated by *banditti*. In 1770 Mortimer exhibited a painting entitled *An Incantation*, showing a grotesque witch casting a spell in a cave, while a young woman cowers before her and a skeleton gestures towards a book of incantations behind her.[2] This composition was indebted to Rosa's *Saul and the Witch of Endor* (Louvre, Paris), which Mortimer would have known from engravings, and which also inspired imitations by Henry Fuseli, Benjamin West, and William Blake. Mortimer also made paintings, drawings, and etchings of *banditti* that earned him the nickname 'the English Salvator'.

The present drawing is one of the most extraordinary of what Mortimer's contemporary, Edward Edwards, called his 'horrible imaginings'. In the centre, an emaciated and almost naked man, with claws for feet, triumphs over a winged figure with a dragon's tail and snakes for hair. John Sunderland has suggested that this may be the 'washed drawing' shown as *Satan and Death* at the Royal Academy in 1779, shortly after Mortimer's own death. The freedom of the penwork owes much to his study of drawings by Guercino (1591–1666), which were extremely popular with English collectors. The use of watercolour, however, is unusual, and would seem to confirm the suggestion that this is an exhibition drawing.

Mortimer's influence on the younger generation of artists was considerable, especially among the caricaturists. Both Thomas Rowlandson and James Gillray adopted his exuberant line, and frequently, his emaciated types in some of their most powerful prints. CH

1. Now in the Guildhall, High Wycombe; Sunderland (1986) no. 13.
2. Sunderland (1986) no. 36.

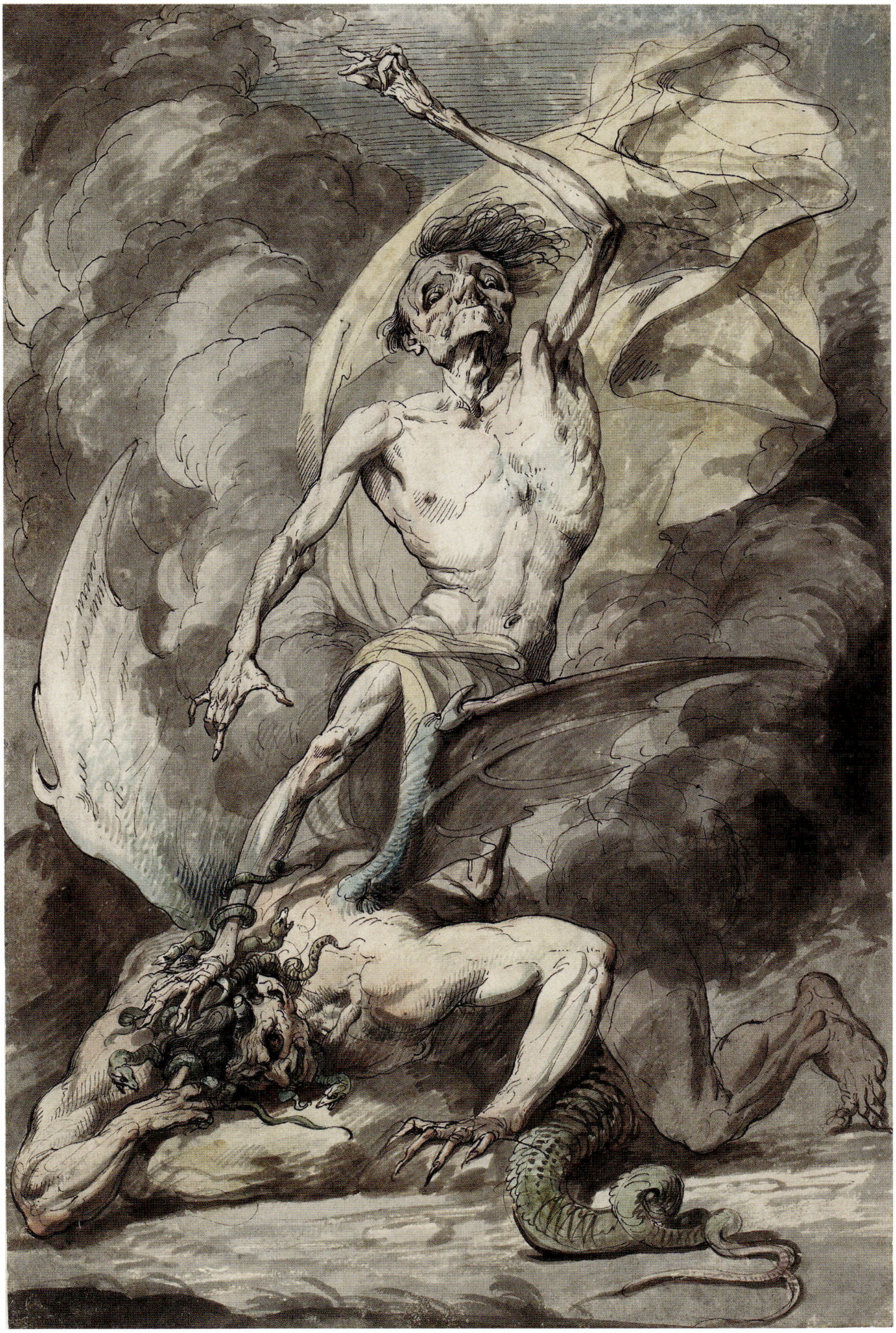

18

JAMES BARRY 1741–1806

Allegory of the Union of Britain and Ireland, 1800–1

Pen and black ink and grey washes over indications in graphite
70.5 × 52.9 cm
Signed: *Jas. Barry Invt.* Inscribed: *Holy Evangelists*
Bequeathed by Francis Douce, 1834
WA1863.1065

LITERATURE: Pressly (1981) no. D40; Brown (1982) no. 360; Pressly (1983) no. 88

Drawings by the Irish artist James Barry are comparatively rare. This is surprising given that he devoted his career to the genre of history painting, which necessarily required extensive and elaborate preparation. The group of Barry's drawings in the Ashmolean is the largest in existence, and comprises about a quarter of those surviving. They were nearly all bought by the antiquary Francis Douce, most at the studio sale in 1807.

This drawing was sent to William Pitt in 1800. Barry described it in a letter to Pitt as 'a design for a picture and an engraving on the subject of the happy union of Great Britain and Ireland', in the hope that the government would commission a painting of this subject.[1] The Act of Union between Great Britain and Ireland was passed on 1 January 1801, following the dissolution of the Irish parliament, and united the legislatures of the two countries. Barry was optimistic that Catholic emancipation and other reforms would follow, in spite of the resignation of Pitt as Prime Minister. When he received no reply from Pitt, he suggested to the Royal Society of Arts that this design and another should be used for paintings to replace the portraits of Gainsborough and Reynolds in the Great Room. Although the majority of members approved of this proposal, the President, the Duke of Norfolk, objected for political reasons.

In this composition, which combines allegorical with historical figures, Great Britain and Ireland are shown as equal; the scale held by the angel is perfectly balanced. The New Testament they hold refers to their shared Christian faith. In front of the altar is a group representing Aesop's fable of the father, his sons, and the bundle of sticks, which cannot be broken together but only singly. A medallion of George III and Queen Charlotte hangs beneath a ram's head. In the background on the right, personifications of envy, deceit, destruction, war, and folly are dispersed by divine thunderbolts held by an angel. In front of them a politician explains the benefits of the union.

This sheet was followed by two others in which the composition is considerably simplified, the historical figures removed, and some poses altered.[2] However, in a long inscription on the back of the second, Barry noted that, 'Perhaps my first thought was better'. CH

1. Quoted in Brown (1982) p. 188.
2. British Museum; Pressly (1981) nos. D42–3.

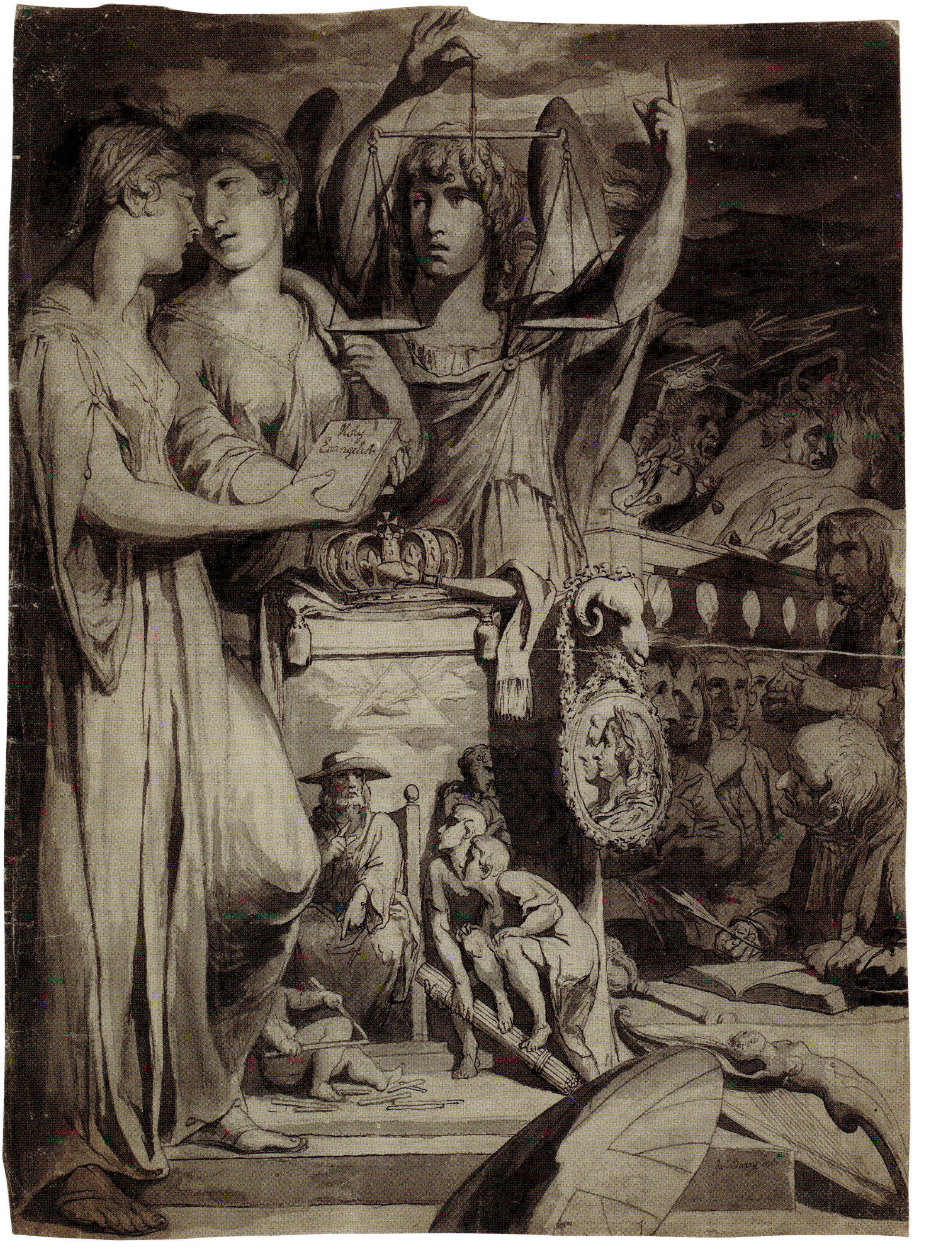
Holy Evangelists

19

WILLIAM BLAKE 1757–1827

The Baptism of Christ, c. 1803

Pen and black ink and watercolour over indications in graphite on paper
31.3 × 34.8 cm
Inscribed: *WB inv*. Inscribed on the mounting board: *This is my beloved Son, in whom I am well pleased / Mattw; ch: 3rd. v. 16th / And Jesus, when he was baptized, went up straightaway out of the water: and lo, the heavens were opened unto him, and he saw the Spirit of God descending like a dove and resting upon him.*
Bequeathed by Francis Falconer Madan, 1962
WA1962.17.57

LITERATURE: Butlin (1981) no. 475; Brown (1982) no. 386

In 1799 Blake received a commission for 50 small paintings at one guinea each from Thomas Butts, to whom he had probably been introduced by the artist John Flaxman. A clerk in the office of the Commissary General of Musters, Butts was to prove Blake's most loyal patron. Subsequently, he commissioned an extensive series of watercolours, on which Blake worked from 1800 to 1805 but with some produced as late as 1809, of which the *Baptism* is one of about 80 known. Like the earlier series of tempera paintings these were of biblical subjects, with the exact selection of scenes left to Blake.

From 1800 to 1803 Blake lived at Felpham, near Chichester, under the aegis of William Hayley. During this time he confessed to Butts that he had undergone a conversion related to his experience of walking on the seashore, and had emerged from unhappiness into the 'light of day', 'to Embrace Christianity and Adore him who is the Express image of God'.[1] The Baptism marks the first revelation of the divinity of the adult Christ, and while the later inscription identifies the source in Matthew chapter 3, by depicting the Baptist rather than Christ witnessing the descent of the Holy Spirit, Blake follows John 1.32–4.

Reworking the iconography of his tempera of the *Baptism*, Blake simplified and reduced the number of figures, moderated the rapturous mood and reversed the figure of Christ so that, most unusually, he faces away from the viewer.[2] All four gospels mention the opening of the heavens, but without any indication of the flaming glory of the ranked angels, singing accompanied by lyre, cymbals, and tambourines. It is possible that Blake's colour palette here also alludes to the promise that Christ will baptise with fire rather than water. While baptising with his right hand, John raises his left in a gesture of blessing. Christ's quiet modesty is in contrast to the Baptist's ecstatic expression and dynamic musculature, which make him as prominent as the Messiah. This is entirely consistent with Blake's characterisation of himself as a prophet. This image of compelling grace, exquisitely balancing serenity and revelation, demonstrates Blake's profound understanding of the Bible as a stimulus to the imagination rather than an authoritarian text. KW

1. 22 November 1802, quoted in Rowland (2010) p. 3.
2. *c.* 1799–1800; Rhode Island School of Design Museum of Art, 32.219; Butlin (1981) no. 415.

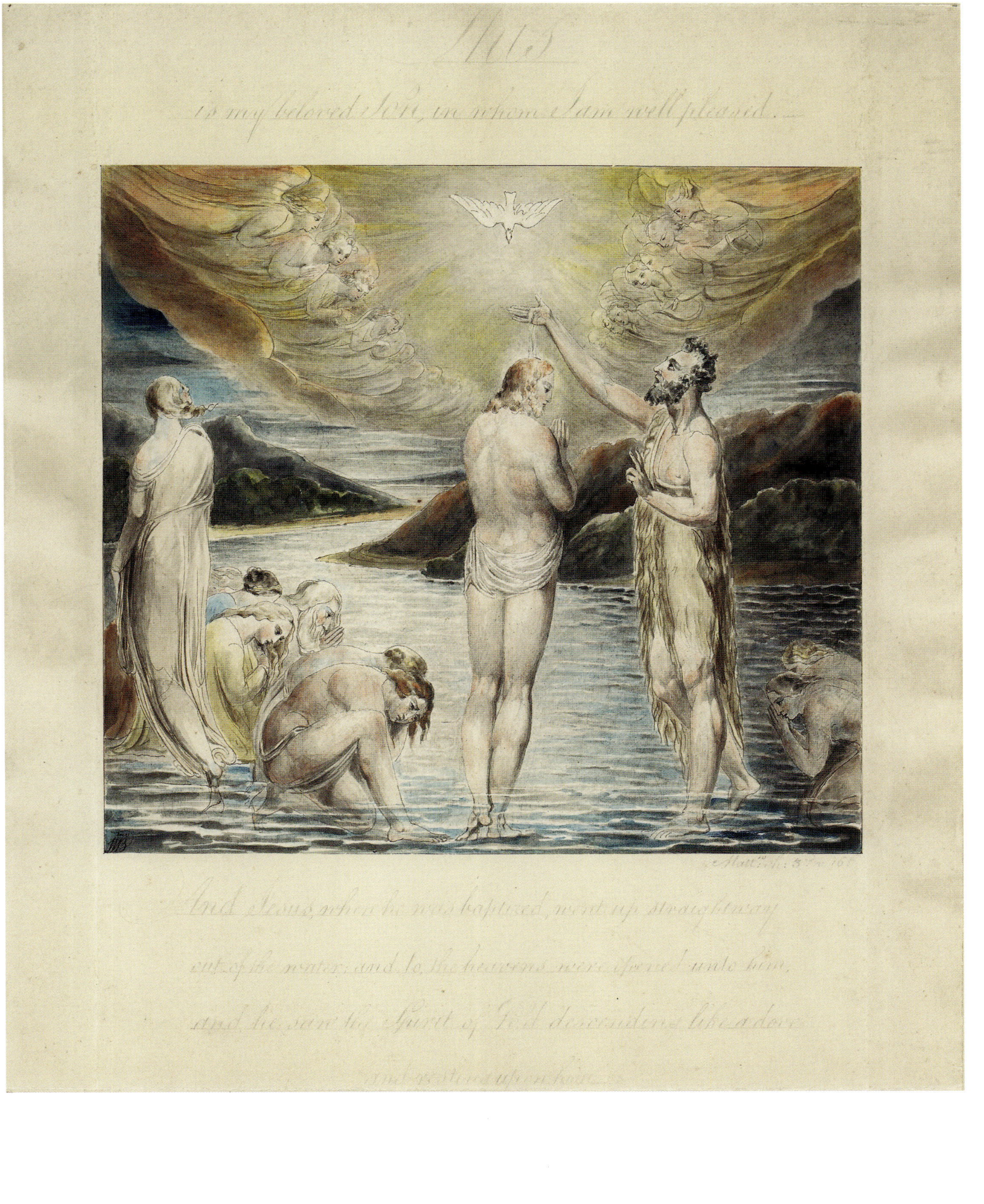
This
is my beloved Son, in whom I am well pleased.
And Jesus, when he was baptized, went up straightway
out of the water: and lo, the heavens were opened unto him,
and he saw the Spirit of God descending like a dove
and resting upon him

20

WILLIAM BLAKE 1757–1827

The Deity from whom proceed the Nine Spheres (illustration to Dante's Divine Comedy, Paradiso XXVIII*), 1825–7*

Watercolour and some pen and black ink over indications in graphite on paper
51.9 × 36.7 cm
Presented by The Art Fund, 1918
WA1918.4

LITERATURE: Butlin (1981) no. 812.97; Brown (1982) no. 389; Klonsky (1980) no. 100

Struggling with ill health and living in penury at 3 Fountain Court, off the Strand, Blake met his fellow artist, John Linnell in 1818. Their friendship resulted in some of Blake's most influential work, including in the summer of 1824 Linnell's commission of the illustrations for *The Divine Comedy*. Blake produced 102 water-colours; some completed, others barely begun, with Blake apparently preferring to move back and forth rather than work in a sequential manner.[1] He also created seven engravings, indicating that publication was eventually intended.

Blake had some knowledge of Italian from his years in Sussex, where he learned ancient and modern languages. He had annotated Boyd's edition of the *Inferno* (published 1785) in 1800, but now began to wrestle in earnest with Dante's monumental epic. He further instructed himself in Italian, reading Sessa's edition of 1564 as well as the 1819 edition of H. F. Cary's first complete English translation of the poem. Visiting Blake on 9 October 1824, Samuel Palmer found him nursing a leg injury but 'hard-working on a bed covered with books sat he up like one of the Antique patriarchs, or a dying Michael Angelo. Thus and there was he making in the leaves of a great book (folio) the sublimest designs from his (not superior) Dante'.[2] Blake created the watercolours on Kent paper from the 1790s, subsequently bound into a volume. His last act of interpretative illustration, they demonstrate the cherished centrality of the book in his artistic achievement.

While revering Dante as a poet, Blake undoubtedly took issue with his theology and politics. His annotation 'Every thing in Dante's Comedia shews that for Tyrannical Purposes he has made this World the Foundation of All' may account for the reconfiguration of Dante's Pseudo-Dionysian cosmology in this sheet.[3] Blake substituted the Earth for the Deity as the point around which the spheres revolve, giving this drawing a hierarchical rather than a concentric arrangement. Possibly owing to the constricted space, he also conflated the innermost (here uppermost) sphere of the Seraphim with that of the Deity, who should reside separately. The difficulty of interpreting this illustration signals the complex nature of the *Paradiso*, in which Dante repeatedly requires his heavenly guide Beatrice to explain sights that are otherwise beyond comprehension.

Nonetheless, this drawing intriguingly reveals Blake's artistic process. Beginning in graphite, he broadly sketched simplified forms, such as the oval bisected by two lines for the head of the Deity. Next he developed these outlines with diluted ink and brush, before meticulously resolving details using pen and ink. Watercolour washes applied at various stages evoke the limpid beauty of the divine light of Paradise. KW

1. 72 illustrations for *Inferno*, 20 for *Purgatorio* and 10 for *Paradiso*: Butlin (1981) nos. 812.1–102.
2. Quoted in Hamlyn and Phillips (2000) p. 74.
3. *Homer Bearing the Sword and his Companions*, Harvard Art Museums, Fogg Museum, 1943.442; Butlin (1981) no. 812.7.

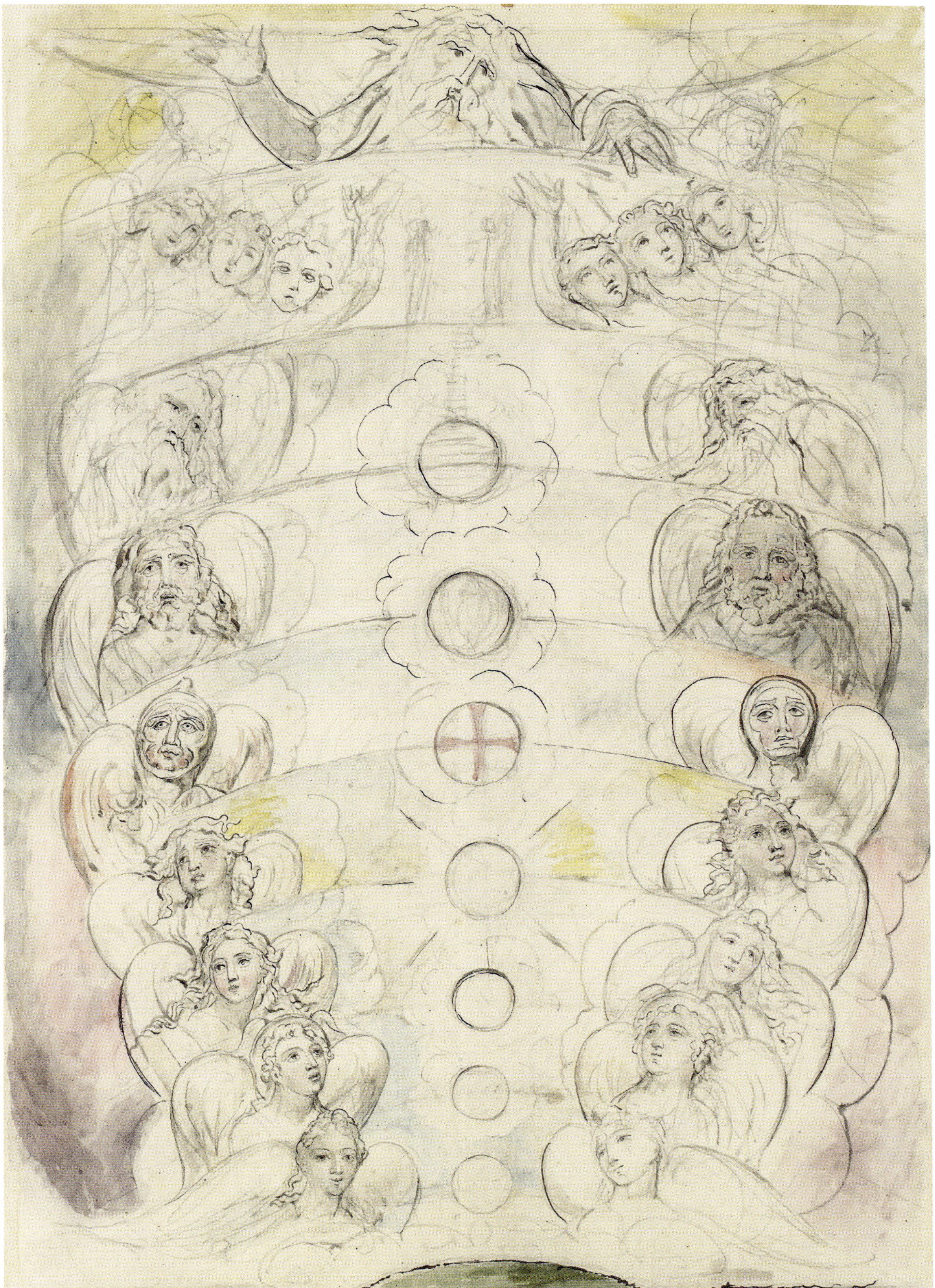

21

GEORGE RICHMOND 1809–1896
'Boswood's Thigh' and the right arm of Michelangelo's 'David', 1828

Red chalk, graphite and pen and brown ink on off-white wove paper
26.9 × 18.7 cm
Signed and dated: *GR 1828* and inscribed under the appropriate studies, *Boswood's Thigh* and *M Ange*
Purchased (Eldon Fund) with the assistance of The Art Fund and the Fenton Arts Trust, 2002
WA2002.27

LITERATURE: Sloman (2001) no. 6

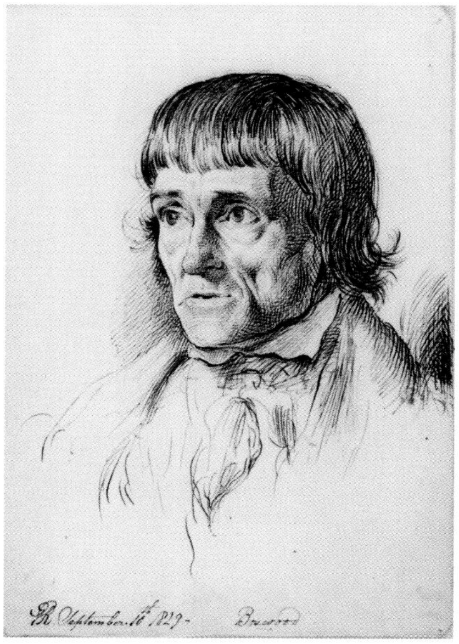

Fig. 31 | George Richmond (1809–1896), *Boswood*, 1829. Pen and ink. Formerly private collection, Prof. Philip Rieff, Pennsylvania

It might have seemed natural that Richmond, as the son of a miniature painter, would become an artist. He began drawing the Antique marbles in the Towneley and Elgin galleries of the British Museum when he was only 12 years old, and enrolled at the Royal Academy Schools in December 1824, when he was still 15. From the evidence of several early drawings, he clearly admired the idiosyncratic style of the Keeper, Henry Fuseli, but his greatest influence was the aged William Blake, whom he met early in 1825.

For a few years Richmond experimented with Blake's technique of 'fresco' (pigment mixed with glue rather than oil). Indeed, Blake instructed him in anatomy for his first exhibit at the Royal Academy, *Abel the Shepherd* (1825).[1] His second submission to the Royal Academy in 1826, *The Creation of Light*, was even further indebted to Blake and to the Old Masters the elder artist revered above all, Dürer and Michelangelo; and was rejected.[2] He continued to make drawings of historical subjects, a few of which he developed into paintings, until the early 1830s. However, following his marriage in 1831, he increasingly relied on portraiture for his income, becoming one of the most successful portrait painters of his day.

In spite of his precocious start, Richmond continued his education at the Royal Academy Schools until at least 1828. This remarkable sheet includes two studies from the life class, and one from a cast. The identity of 'Boswood' is unknown, but his features and anatomy were recorded in other drawings by Richmond.[3] A cast of the right arm of Michelangelo's *David* had hung in the Antique Room of the Royal Academy since the 1770s. In his diaries, Richmond noted in June 1827 that he had made 'A finished drawing of Michael Angelos Arm'; and a year later, he further 'made a model of MA Arm'.[4] Since Richmond went through his portfolios towards the end of his life identifying and dating them, it is possible that this sheet may have been drawn on the earlier occasion. It is unusual in consciously emulating the work of the Old Masters, in particular Michelangelo, in style and medium, especially in the use of red chalk. It is likely that Richmond had been able to examine some of the exceptional collection of Michelangelo's drawings belonging to the President of the Royal Academy, Sir Thomas Lawrence (1769–1830). CH

1. Tate; see most recently Phillips (2014) nos. 238–9.
2. Tate; Phillips (2014) no. 236.
3. See fig. 31 and Sloman (2001) no. 7.
4. Quoted in Sloman (2001) no. 6.

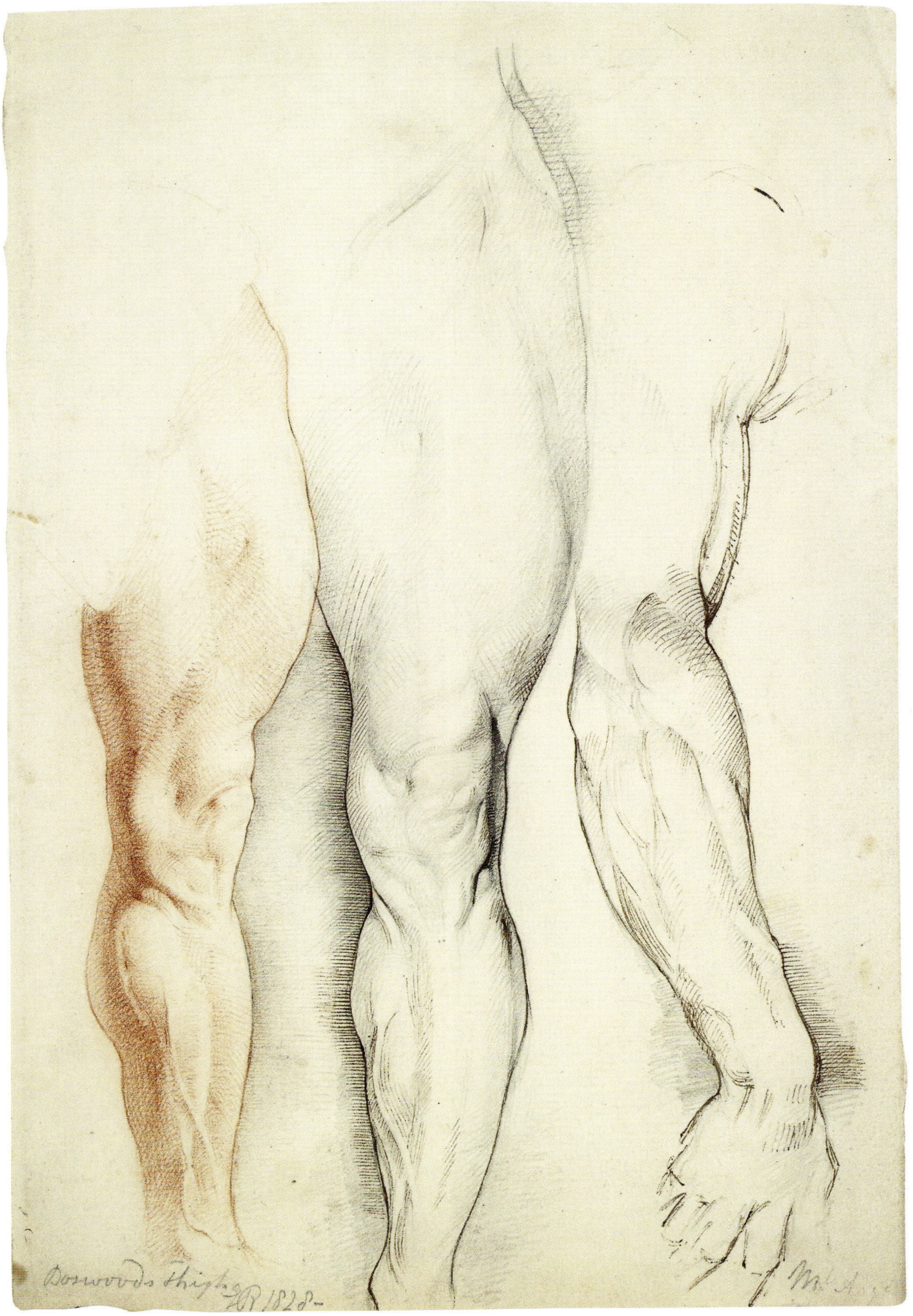
Boswoods thigh
1828-

22

SAMUEL PALMER 1805–1881
The Valley with a Bright Cloud, 1825

Pen and brush in sepia mixed with gum arabic, on paper, varnished
18.8 × 23.2 cm
Signed and dated: *SAMUEL PALMER / 1825*
Inscribed on the old mount: *This our life, exempt from public haunt, / Finds tongues in trees, books in ye running brooks, / Sermons in stones, and good in every thing / As you like it*
Purchased, 1941
WA1941.105

LITERATURE: Brown (1983) no. 8; Lister (1988) no. 54; Vaughan, Barker, Harrison (2005) no. 11

Palmer's meeting with the elderly William Blake in the early months of 1824 comprehensively changed his life. He had been a precocious but conventional landscape painter, having sold his first exhibited work at the age of 14. Blake gave him the confidence to pursue a wholly new genre of painting, the visionary landscape. Palmer and his young friends equated the aged artist with the Interpreter in Bunyan's *Pilgrim's Progress*, the man who showed Christian the way to what would be profitable for his soul's salvation.

Even before he met Blake, Palmer would have known his woodcut illustrations to Robert Thornton's *The Pastorals of Virgil* (1821). Ignoring the menacing tone of many of these images, Palmer described them as 'visions of little dells, and nooks, and corners of Paradise, models of the exquisitest pitch of intense poetry'.[1] The new direction in Palmer's art can be seen in the sketchbook begun on 15 July 1824, in *The Repose of the Holy Family* (1824–5) and the six sepia drawings of 1825.[2] The last best represent Palmer's Neo-Platonic vision of the English countryside, the reflection of divine munificence as praised in Psalm 104, 'The earth is full of thy riches'.

The Valley with a Bright Cloud is one of the six drawings which in later life Palmer had mounted in a single frame, with a quotation beneath each one. However, it is almost certain that this was a consequence of their fragility, and their failure to sell when several were exhibited individually at the Royal Academy in 1825 and 1826. They are the most original and most Romantic of all Palmer's works. The technique, thick lines drawn with the brush in ink mixed with gum arabic, and the finer detail in pen, is unique in the history of English art, though ultimately derived from Blake's 'fresco', pigment mixed with glue. Once completed, the composition was varnished with a layer of gum arabic, which would quickly have turned brown, as Palmer expected.

Here, in the only daylight scene (all the others take place at twilight), the rounded hills recall those surrounding Dulwich or, more probably, the village of Shoreham in the Darent valley, where one of Palmer's grandfathers lived. They are drawn in the strong outlines advocated by Blake, with the perspective abbreviated and distorted. The most prominent sign of man is the huge felled log in the foreground, another expression of God's bounty. The billowing clouds are a more conventional symbol of divine immanence. CH

1. Palmer (1892) pp. 15–6.
2. All in the Ashmolean; Lister (1988) nos. 46, 53–8; Vaughan, Barker, Harrison (2005) nos. 10–15, 28.

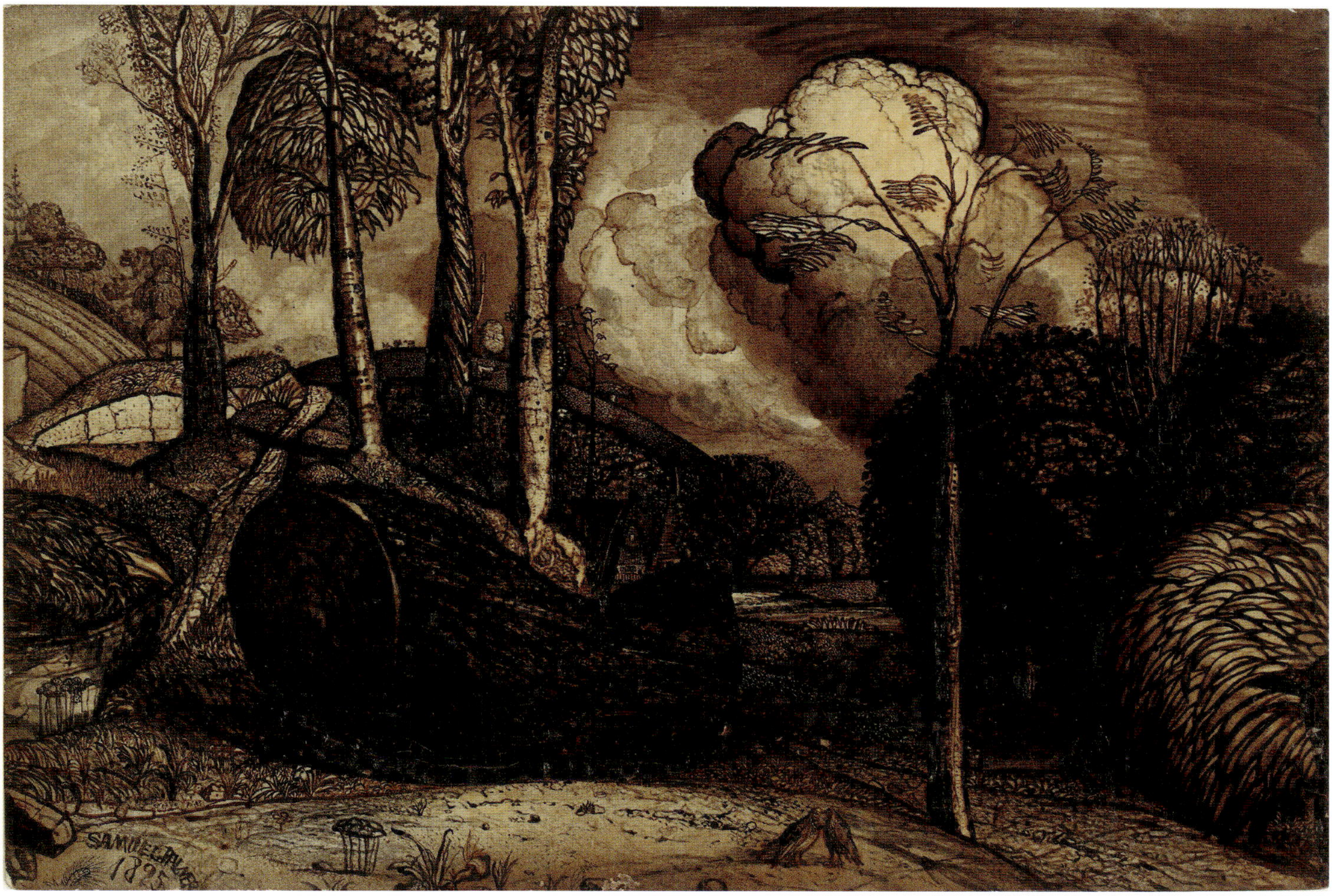

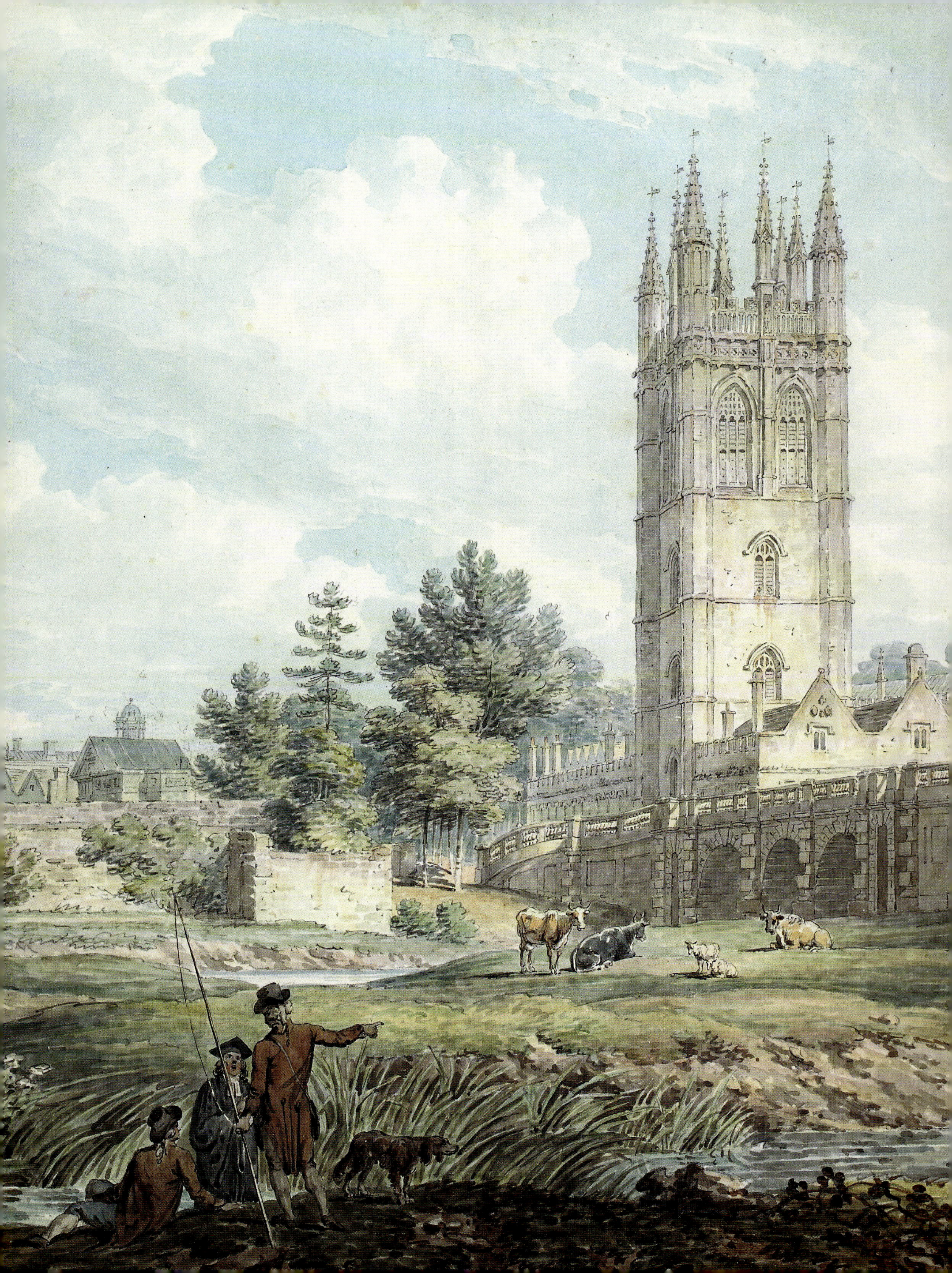

Travel & Topography

The Golden Age of Watercolour

Detail from Edward Dayes, *Magdalen College and Bridge, Oxford, from the river* (cat. 30)

23

JOHN ROBERT COZENS 1752–1797

Vesuvius and Somma from the Mola at Naples, 1782

Watercolour over indications in graphite on paper
30.5 × 45.5 cm
Presented by A. E. Anderson, through The Art Fund, 1924
WA1924.2

LITERATURE: Bell and Girtin (1934–5) no. 322; Brown (1982) no. 473; Hawcroft (1988) no. 112

Thirty years after his father, the drawing master Alexander Cozens (1717–1786), had visited Italy, John Robert Cozens set out on his first tour with the wealthy classical scholar, Richard Payne Knight (1751–1824). The men made a brief tour of the Alps, and arrived in Rome in November 1776. Cozens was to remain in Rome until 8 April 1779, exploring the city and the surrounding Campagna, working up his Swiss sketches for Payne Knight, and also making large watercolours of Sicily based on sketches by Charles Gore and Philipp Hackert. During this period Cozens gradually abandoned the tightly drawn style of his earliest work, with very limited monochrome washes, in favour of more brightly coloured and atmospheric views. Most remarkable are his darkly romantic watercolours of craggy Swiss mountains and waterfalls, and of caverns in the Campagna.

After three years living in Bath, where he worked for, among others, his father's pupil and friend William Beckford (1759–1844), Cozens set off on his second visit to Italy in May 1782. He travelled as one of Beckford's large retinue, journeying through the Tyrol to Padua, Venice, and Rome, before arriving at Sir William Hamilton's villa at Naples in early July. On the way he began the first of seven sketchbooks which eventually covered much of the Italian tour, with notable gaps.[1] Beckford left Naples in September, but Cozens stayed until December. He made sketches of subjects in the city and along the coast, though Hamilton told Beckford that he was 'indolent'.[2]

This watercolour represents one of the few scenes painted by Cozens in Naples for which there is no related drawing in his sketchbooks. The view was taken from the entrance to the Mola, close to the Castel Nuovo, with the smoking peak of Vesuvius visible on the left. The old harbour was a centre of great social activity, and a favourite place for a stroll after dinner. Cozens has used its angular shape, with the lighthouse in the corner, to provide a strong foreground, animated with groups of soldiers, nuns, and even a running dog. In the harbour itself are several ships, their masts and booms carefully delineated. Above all, however, this watercolour is remarkable for its brooding atmosphere: the south wind blows across the bay and a storm whips up the sea on the right, while clouds cast shadows over the whole panorama. CH

1. Now in the Whitworth Art Gallery, Manchester.
2. Quoted in Hawcroft (1988) p. 80.

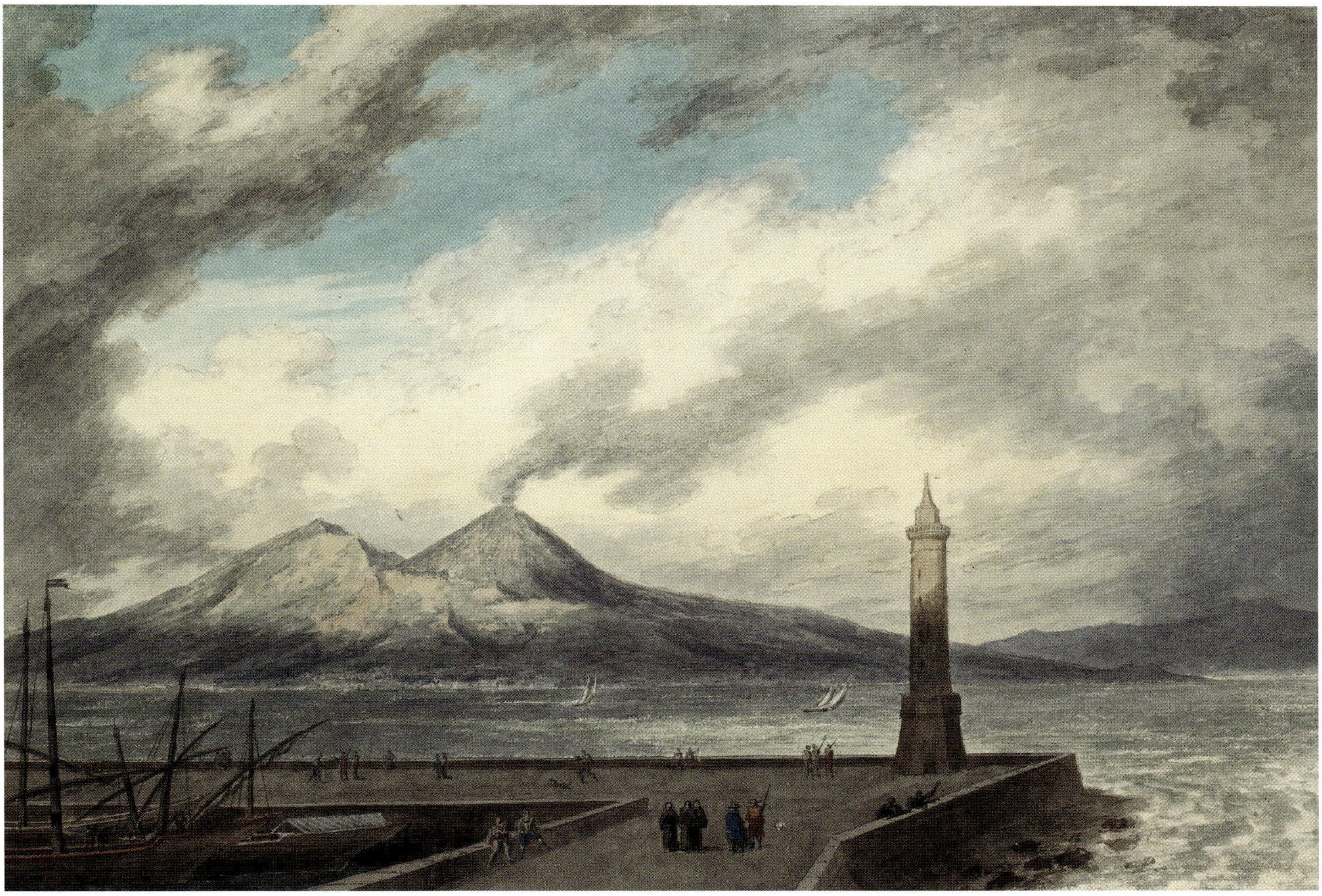

24

JOHN ROBERT COZENS 1752–1797

Villa Madama, near Rome, 1782–3

Watercolour and bodycolour on paper
26.7 × 36.8 cm
Lent from a private collection
L12224.1

LITERATURE: Bell and Girtin (1934–5) no. 362

After nearly five months in Naples and the surrounding area (see cat. 23), Cozens travelled back to Rome, alone, in December 1782. His movements are not documented until 15 September 1783, and it is generally assumed that he remained in Rome, working on a series of watercolours for his patron, William Beckford. On their outward journey, Beckford and Cozens had stopped at Venice so 'that Cozens may sketch some of my favourite isles with their morisco Towers and waving cypresses', and there is no doubt that, to some extent, Beckford dictated the subjects that Cozens should paint.[1] However, since no sketches for many of the Roman subjects survive, and Beckford had long since left Italy, it has been suggested that these watercolours were made direct from nature while Cozens was unaccompanied in 1783. He would no doubt have learnt this practice, which was unusual among English artists, from his German and French contemporaries, such as Jacob Phillip Hackert (1737–1807), who were in Rome at the same time. On the other hand, it is also possible that a batch of sketchbooks is missing. Moreover, whereas Beckford had a particular interest in architecture and antiquities, his protégé did not. The choice of subjects would therefore explain why so many of these watercolours show the gardens of famous monuments, rather than the monuments themselves. The villas of suburban Rome – Ludovisi, Mattei, Negroni, Lante, Barberini, Borghese – and those in the vicinity, such as the Villa Mondragone at Frascati, are all subordinate to the vegetation of the gardens, portrayed in dramatic effects of light and weather.

This majestic watercolour, which has not been exhibited since 1923, is one of the most romantic of all the series. The Villa Madama, on the Monte Mario to the north-west of Rome, was initially designed by Raphael, and became a favourite spot from which to enjoy panoramic views over the city. Cozens shows the Villa perched on the hillside, with dense woods behind it, and cypresses standing guard to the side. The landscape is dark and stormy, save for a dramatic patch of clear sky; a second, in the distance, is brilliantly reflected in the waters of the Tiber below. On the right, two women and a child hurry past to avoid the approaching storm. It is such emotionally charged works that caused Constable to describe Cozens as 'the greatest genius that ever touched landscape'.[2]

Cozens produced 94 finished watercolours for Beckford, who sold them in 1805, after which they became widely dispersed. The *Villa Madama, near Rome* was described in the sale catalogue as a 'capital drawing embellished with an elegant group of figures'.[3] It later belonged to the greatest of all English collectors of drawings, the portrait painter, Sir Thomas Lawrence. CH

1. Quoted in Bell and Girtin (1934–5) p. 17.
2. Hawcroft (1971) p. 10.
3. Christie's, 10 April 1805, lot 85.

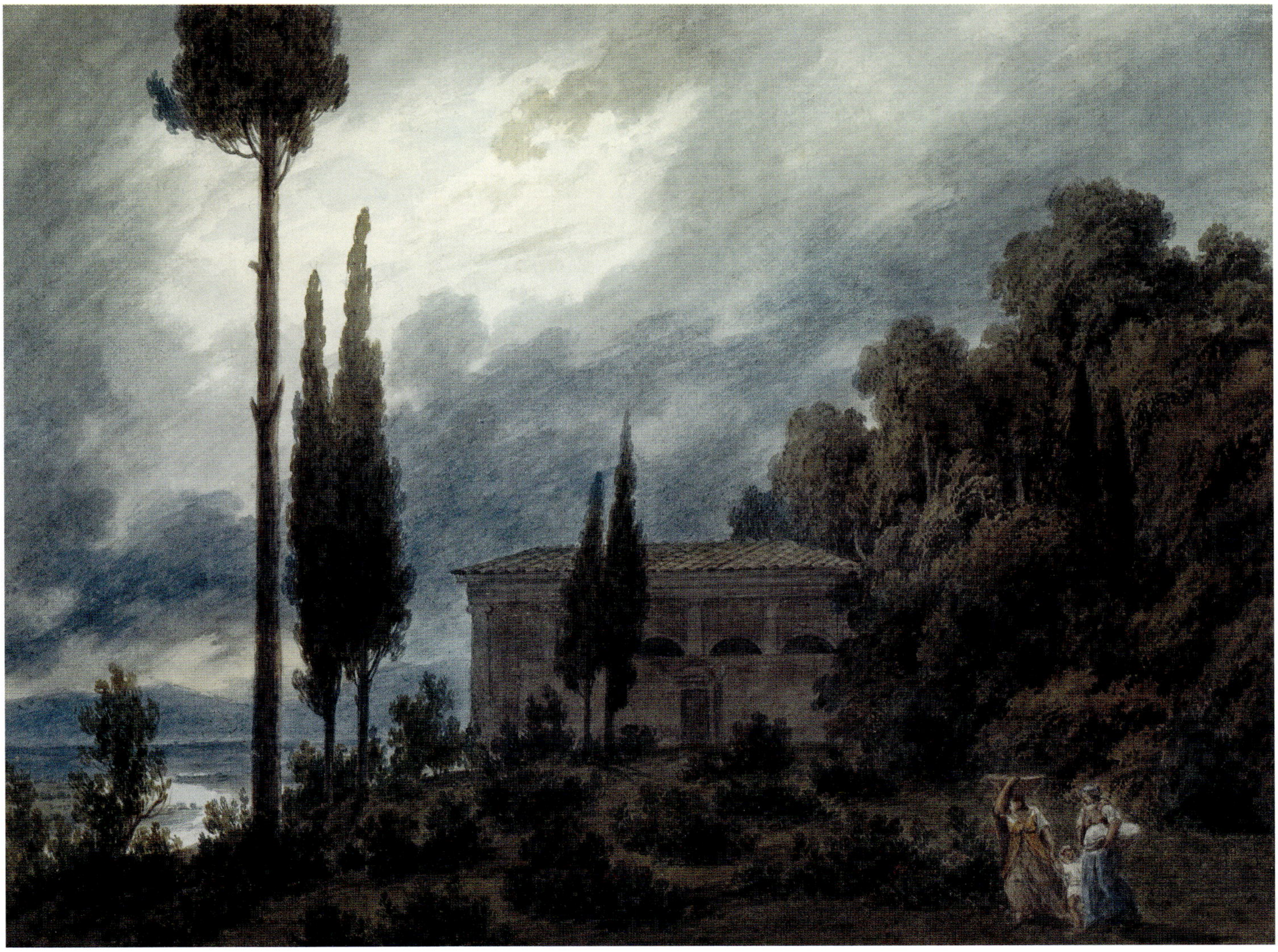

25

FRANCIS TOWNE 1739/40–1816

A View of the Cascade in the Groves at Ambleside, 10 August 1786

Pen and brown ink and watercolour on paper
37.7 × 26.5 cm
Signed and dated: *F. Towne / delt. 1786*
Inscribed on the back of the artist's mount: *A View from the Cascade in the Groves at Ambleside, the Head of the Lake of Windermere drawn on the spot by Francis Towne August 10th 1786 / NB The paper this is drawn on I brought myself from Rome*
Presented by the Misses Merivale, 1922
WA1922.8

LITERATURE: Brown (1982) no. 1823; Wilcox (1997) no. 57

Towne is the most eccentric and enigmatic figure in the so-called 'Golden Age' of the English watercolour. Trained in London as a coach painter, he settled in Exeter *c.* 1764, swiftly establishing himself as the leading drawing master in this prosperous provincial centre. He earned nearly £1000 a year and therefore had no need to sell his pictures, though he continued to exhibit in London. Towne is now remembered for his remarkable studies made on the spot, in which outlines are as important as subtlety of colouring. His practice was to begin a drawing in graphite or pen, then apply watercolour, finally reworking the drawing in pen and ink. The work would be signed on the front, and mounted. He generally made an inscription on the back of the drawing, which would be transferred to the back of the mount. These elaborate watercolours were not originally intended for exhibition, but as private studies for the development of oil paintings.

Known for his diffidence and modesty, Towne was not adventurous in his subject matter. He made a short tour of Wales in 1777, and an extended expedition to Rome and Naples, returning over the Alps, in 1780–1. At the suggestion of two of his Exeter friends, James White and John Merivale, he accompanied them to the Lake District in August 1786, spending just over a fortnight based at Ambleside, at the northern end of Lake Windermere. Towne explored the area thoroughly, armed with two sketchbooks and about 15 larger sheets of paper. He was especially fascinated by the secluded falls of Stock Gill, just above Ambleside, of which he made three elaborate drawings.[1] The present sheet is the most accomplished, indeed widely acknowledged as one of the artist's masterpieces. The first of the companion drawings is similar in composition, taken from a point slightly nearer the waterfall; the second is entirely different, featuring a distant view including blue sky and a variety of green foliage. In the Ashmolean drawing, the white of the water offers a brilliant contrast with the shaded rocky hillside, its almost geometric shape answered by the exuberant penwork in the foreground. Overhead, the sun shines brightly through the canopy of trees, creating subtle patterns in the leaves above. CH

1. Tate, and private collection; Wilcox (1997) nos. 58–9.

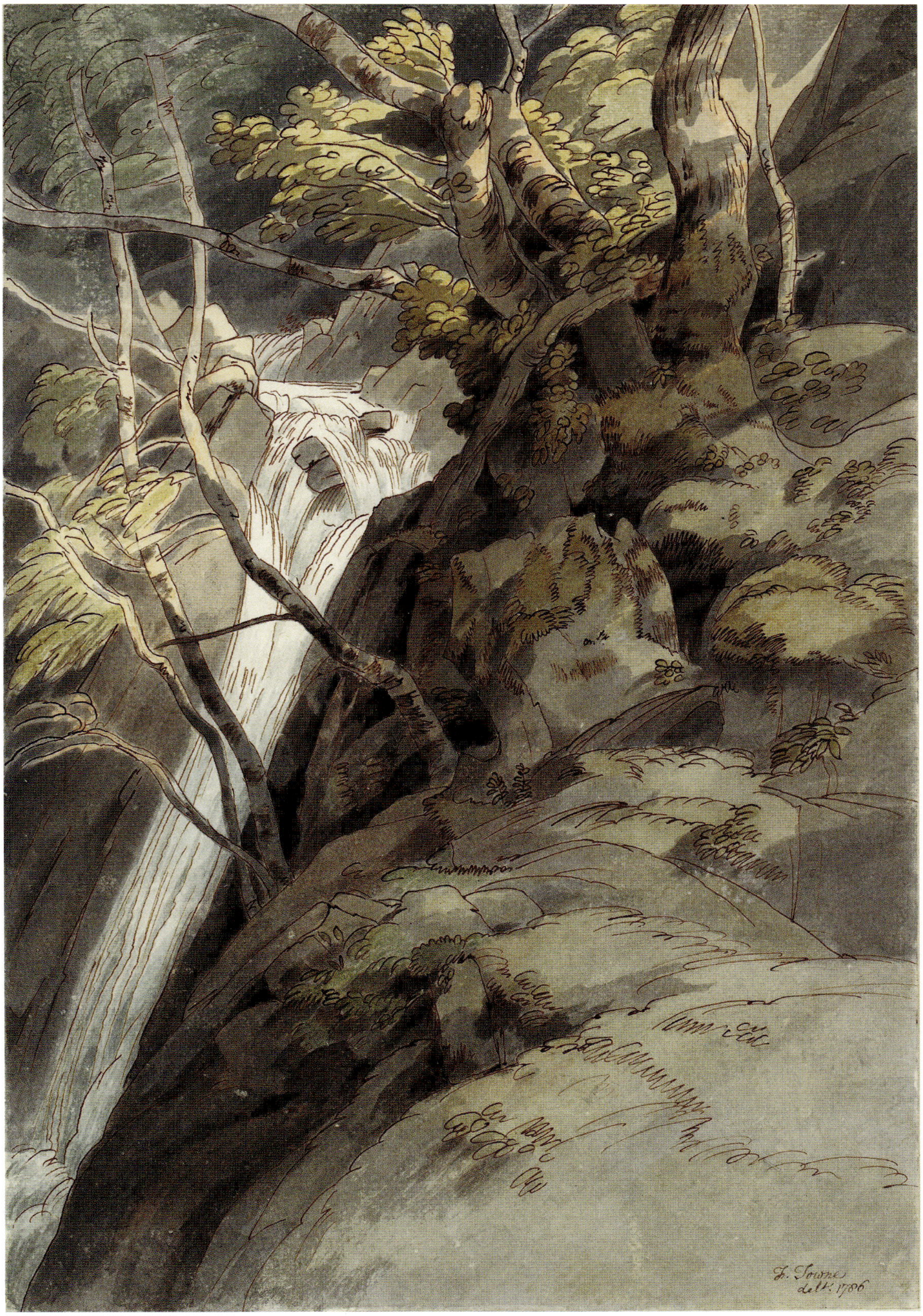

J. Towne
delt. 1786

26

GEORGE AUGUSTUS WALLIS 1761–1847

The Ruins of Selinunte, c. 1792

Watercolour and bodycolour with pen and brown ink over an etched outline on paper
53.8 × 75.5 cm
Presented by Revd S. H. Scott, 1937
WA1937.114

LITERATURE: Brown (1982) no. 1856; Bailey (1975–6) fig. 17

The Scottish painter George Wallis is barely known today, yet he once enjoyed a European-wide reputation. The collector William Young Ottley, who owned several of his paintings, made bold claims for his talents in landscape, which united 'the wildness of *Salvator Rosa* with the classic chastity of *Nicolo Poussin*'.[1] Shortly after travelling to Italy in 1788, funded by the Earl of Warwick, Wallis was taken to Sicily in 1792 as the protégé of Thomas Hope (1769–1831). Shortly afterwards, he returned to the island in the company of Lord Berwick. Settling in Rome in 1794, he acted primarily as a picture-dealer for British travellers. His landscapes were praised by Madame de Staël and Goethe, but he seems to have been a rather unreliable character according to Samuel Taylor Coleridge, who lodged with him in Rome. Whatever his personal failings, this watercolour certainly reflects Ottley's judgment regarding the 'grandeur of his conceptions'.[2]

Selinunte, on the south-west coast of Sicily, boasts some of the most impressive remains of the ancient Greek world. Selinus, the most westerly colony of Magna Graecia, was established in 628 BC, but what Hannibal did not destroy in 409 BC was further shaken by earthquakes, leaving a vast ruined temple complex. The confused heaps of fallen masonry lie on a site overlooking the Mediterranean, making this a scene ripe for Romantic musings. Here we see the colossal wreckage of shattered columns from the Temple of Apollo.

Wallis has added several visiting shepherds to give a sense of scale and to enliven the scene, lending it a timeless, Arcadian air. A blue cloak draws the viewer's attention to two men resting at the centre, while the diagonals of the fallen pillars and an animated figure to the left lead the eye towards a man in the middle distance, who seems to be carving his initials into a column. The work is dominated by muted blues, greens, and browns, with considerable penwork hatching and outlining in the vegetation and architecture. The watercolour is added over a faintly printed etching, which also appears in reverse on the back of the sheet. The Raphaelesque figure with his hand raised does not feature in this print, which may explain why he appears rather overworked.

Apart from a brief return to London *c.* 1806, Wallis spent most of his life abroad – in Rome, Spain (where he acquired Velázquez's *'Rokeby' Venus*, now in the National Gallery, London), Heidelberg, and finally Florence. His grandiose tomb in the Protestant cemetery there, erected by his appropriately named son Trajan, is adorned with a portrait medallion and an inscription recording his 'genius and science in the art of painting'.[3] CP

1. Ottley sale catalogue of 1814, quoted in Paley (2008) p. 46.
2. Paley (2008) p. 46; see also Bailey (1975–6) pp. 34–57.
3. http://www.florin.ms/sculptors.html, accessed 7 January 2015.

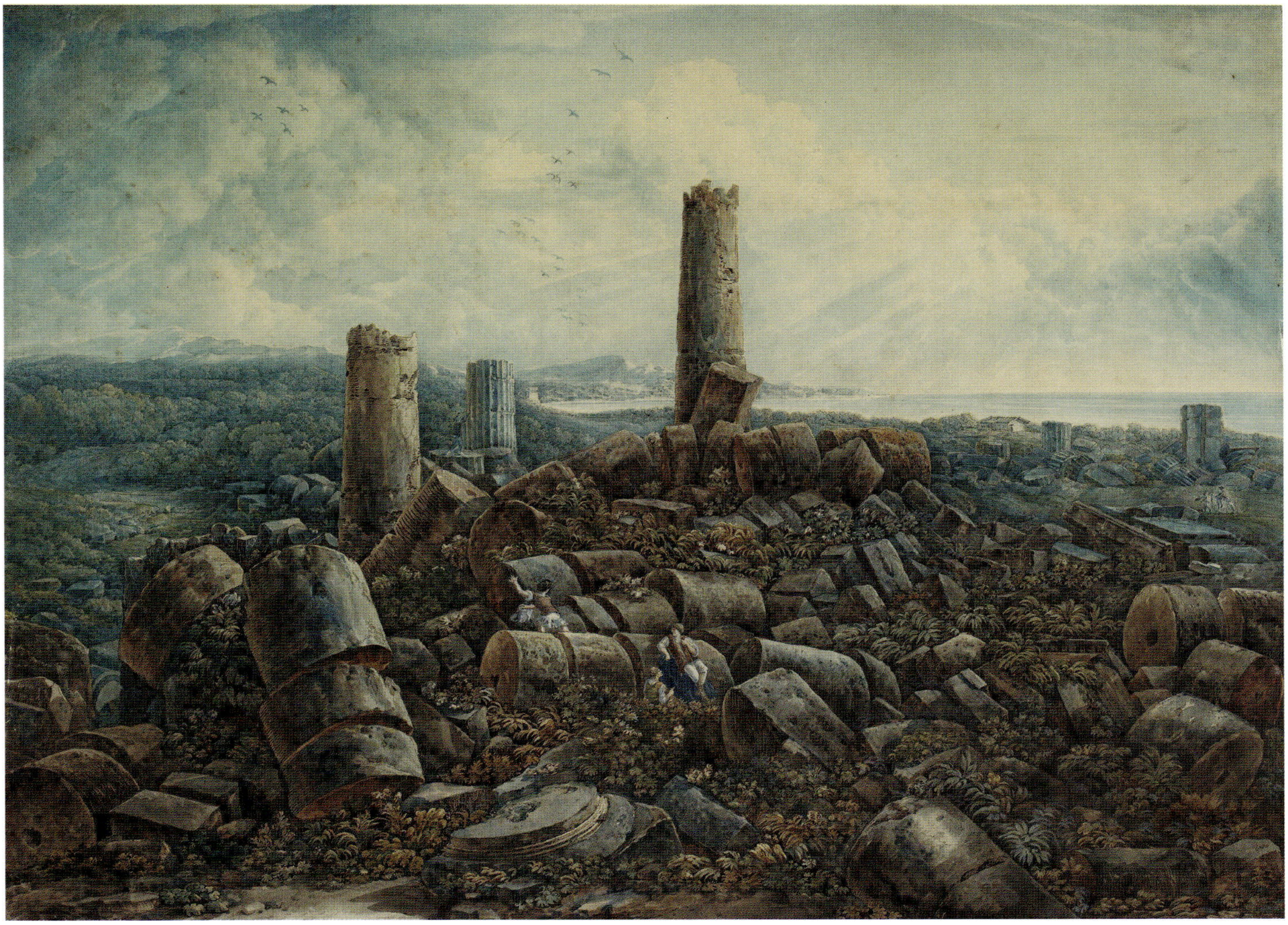

27

THOMAS GIRTIN 1775–1802

Crowland Abbey, Lincolnshire, c. 1793

Watercolour over indications in graphite on paper
33.2 × 30 cm
Signed: *Girtin*
Bequeathed by Professor and Mrs Francis Pierrepont Barnard, 1934
WA1934.126.1

LITERATURE: Girtin and Loshak (1954) no. 50; Brown (1982) no. 708

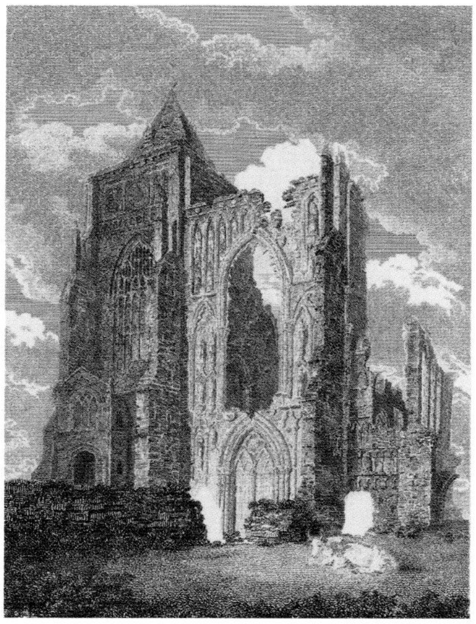

Fig. 32 | Bartholomew Howlett (1767–1827) after Thomas Girtin (1775–1802), *Croyland Abbey*, 1797. Engraving. Ashmolean Museum, Oxford, WA1934.126.2

Among the antiquaries surveying the historical remains of the British Isles in the late eighteenth century, none was more enthusiastic than James Moore (1762–1799). A wealthy linen draper from Southwark, he made a series of tours which resulted in such publications as the unillustrated *List of the Abbies, Priories and other Religious Houses, Castles etc in England and Wales* (1786) and *Monastic Remains and Ancient Castles in England and Wales, Drawn on the Spot by James Moore* (1791–3), with plates finished and engraved by Jacob Schnebbelie, official draughtsman to the Society of Antiquaries.

Following Schnebbelie's death in 1792, Moore turned to artists such as Edward Dayes to work up his sketches into watercolours suitable for engraving. Girtin had been apprenticed to Dayes in 1789, and was commissioned by Moore to make independent watercolours from his sketches. In 1792 or 1793, he began work on a series of about 60 watercolours based on sketches made throughout mainland Britain, for which he was apparently paid six shillings a day. Apart from providing a regular income, this work enabled Girtin to become familiar with Gothic architecture and introduced him to a wide circle of antiquaries. There is no suggestion that he regarded it as demeaning hack work. Indeed, his first exhibit at the Royal Academy, in 1794, was a large *View of Ely Minster* based on a sketch by Moore.[1]

Crowland Abbey was based on two of Moore's sketches, and probably made in 1793, although Girtin accompanied Moore on a tour of the Midlands in 1794 which took in Lincolnshire. The work was engraved in 1797 and published in Bartholomew Howlett's *Selection of Views in the County of Lincoln* in 1805. Until the Dissolution of the Monasteries, the abbey was one of the richest Benedictine foundations in England, largely rebuilt in the thirteenth century. Girtin's watercolour is not a mere dry record of this noble ruin, but a virtuoso evocation of its architecture, its stones painted in the most subtle gradations of grey, blue, and brown, against an atmospheric sky. CH

1. Ashmolean Museum, WA1916.1; Girtin and Loshak (1954) no. 65; Brown (1982) no. 714.

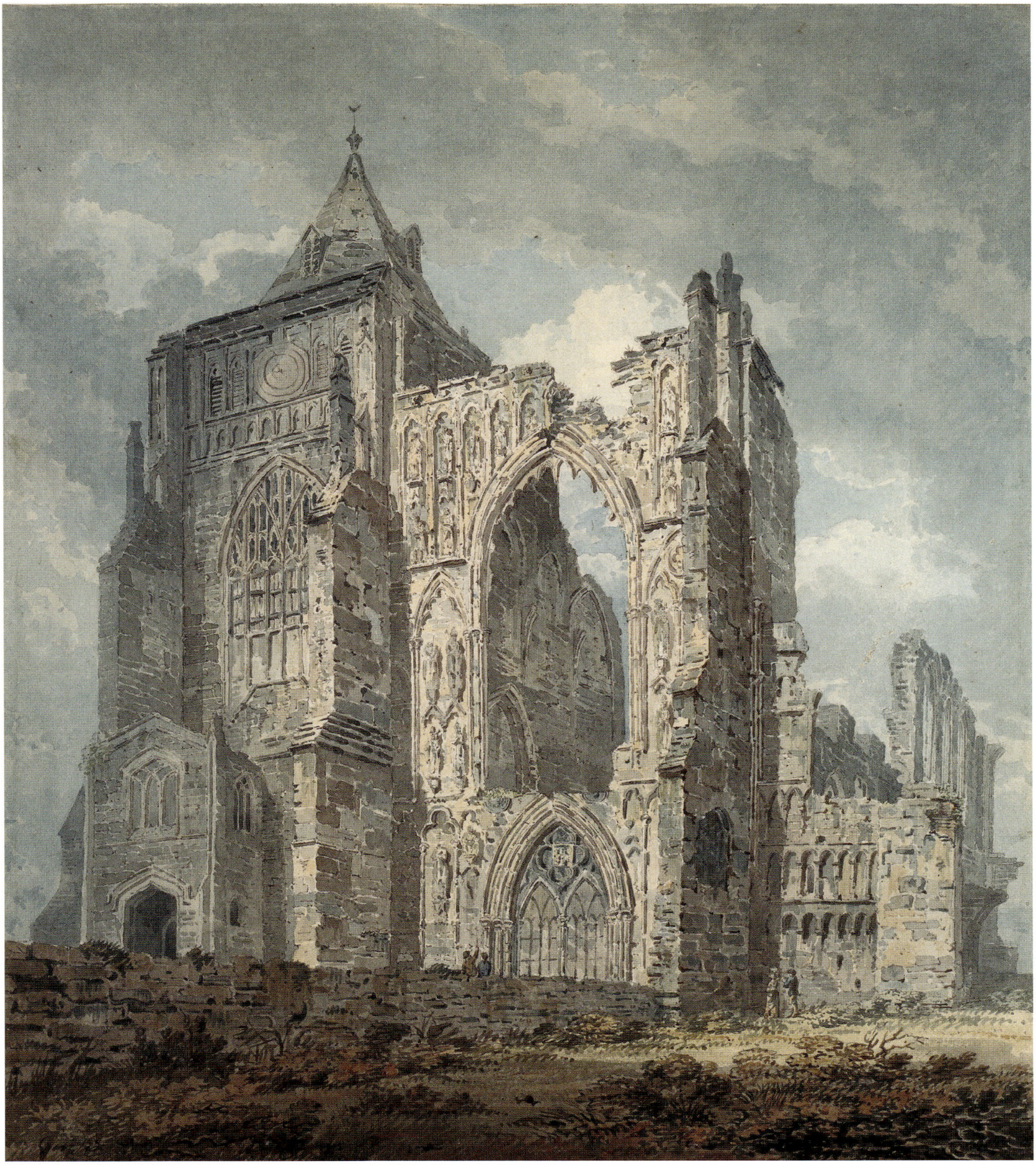

28

THOMAS GIRTIN 1775–1802
Dunottar Castle in a Thunderstorm, c. 1794

Watercolour over indications in graphite on paper
16.5 × 22.5 cm
Bequeathed by Mrs Francis Pierrepont Barnard, 1934
WA1934.118

LITERATURE: Brown (1982) no. 717; Girtin and Loshak (1954) no. 72; Smith (2002) no. 36

James Moore (see cat. 27) made an extensive tour of Scotland in 1792, with the intention of recording the country's most notable antiquities for future publication. He set out from York on 13 August, reached Kelso in the Borders on 20 August and spent some days in Edinburgh. From there he moved west, turned north towards Perth, and then travelled up the east coast to Aberdeen, where he arrived on 5 September. Moore's tour continued west to Inverness, then down the Great Glen to Dunstaffnage, before going across to Inveraray, and finally through Glasgow to Carlisle and the Lake District. The only published result of this tour was the *Twenty-Five Views in the Southern Part of Scotland*, which included monuments in the Lowlands and as far north as Dunkeld. The majority of views were engraved after watercolours by Edward Dayes. He also worked up a number of Moore's sketches, presumably intended to be engraved for a companion volume dealing with the northern part of Scotland.[1]

This small watercolour has until recently been called *Dunstanburgh Castle*, with the building on the clifftop identified as the Lilburn Tower. However, Greg Smith has conclusively shown that the subject is Dunottar Castle, near Stonehaven, based on James Moore's sketch in pencil and blue and grey wash dated 5 September 1792.[2] It was thus one of the series on which Girtin's master, Dayes, worked in 1792, though Girtin's own involvement with Moore dates from 1793–4. The site is one of particular importance in Scottish history: it was at Dunottar that William Keith, Earl Marischal, the hereditary keeper of the Honours of Scotland, the crown and other regalia, hid them from Cromwell's armies after the coronation of Charles II at Scone on 1 January 1651. During a siege of the castle later in the year, the Honours were smuggled out and hidden in a nearby church, before being returned to Edinburgh at the Restoration in 1660.

Girtin must have been aware of the historical significance of Dunottar, and has completely transformed Moore's sketch to create an elemental drama of thunder and lightning, wind and rain, with huge waves crashing against the coast. The castle itself is seen from the south, a diminutive tower house standing on top of the cliff. It is almost overwhelmed by nature – there is nothing antiquarian about this scene. The low viewpoint, in which the ostensible subject is framed by billowing rocks, and the restricted palette make this small watercolour one of the artist's most sublime. It was not engraved. CH

1. Brown (1982) nos. 491–507.
2. Yale Center for British Art; repr. Smith (2002) p. 58.

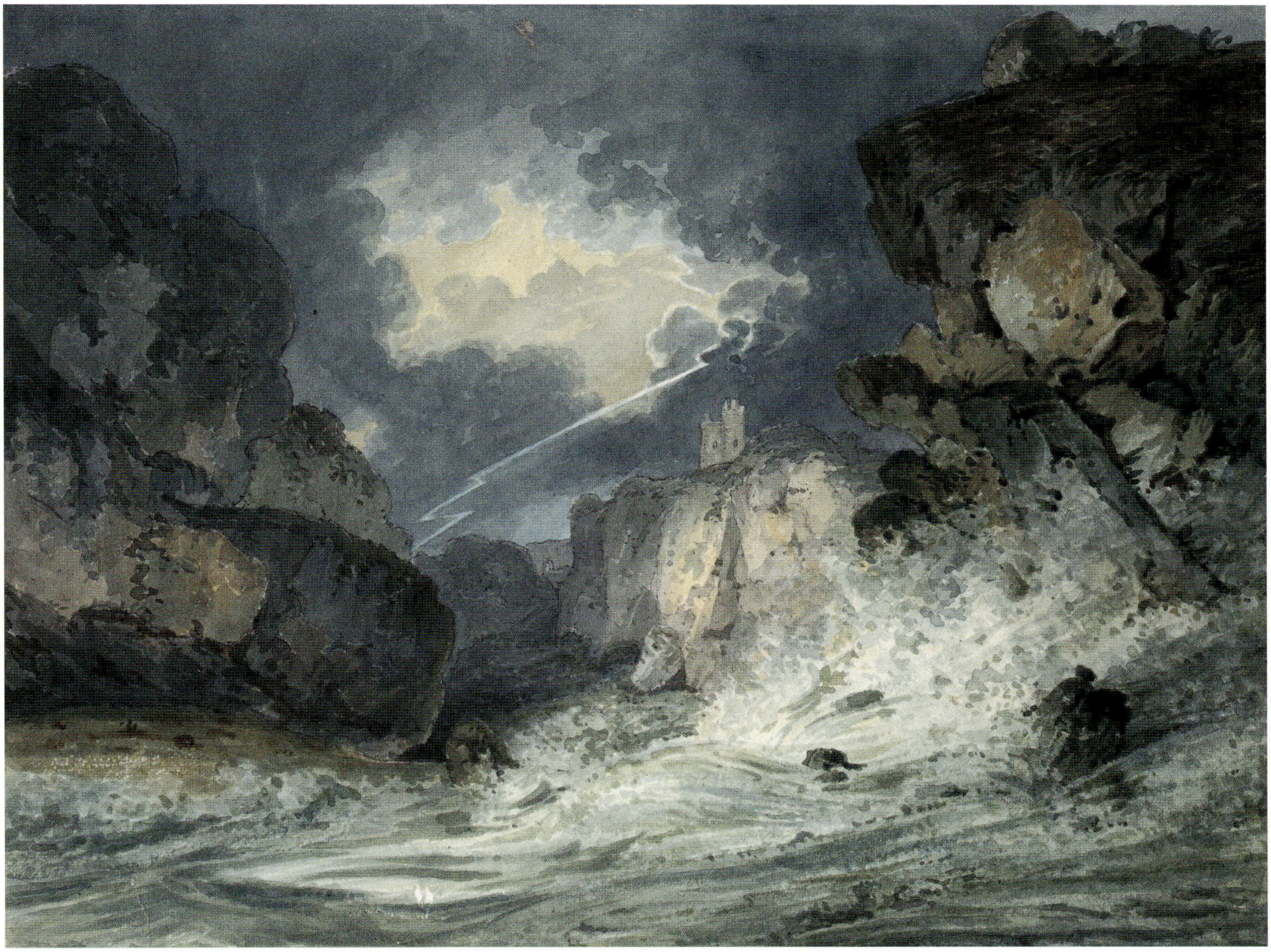

29

THOMAS GIRTIN 1775–1802

The Falls of the Ogwen, North Wales, c. 1799–1800

Watercolour touched with reed pen over indications in graphite on paper
53.6 × 44.5 cm
Signed: *Girtin*
Presented by A. E. Anderson in memory of his brother, Frank Anderson, through The Art Fund, 1931
WA1931.11

LITERATURE: Girtin and Loshak (1954) no. 432ii; Brown (1982) no. 745; Smith (2002), no. 121

After a period of about two years making copies of antiquarian subjects for James Moore, Girtin embarked on his first sketching tour in 1794. His trips to the West Country in 1797 and to Wales in 1798 liberated him from close architectural views, and he began to produce the panoramic landscapes that dominated his final years. They were generally painted on coarse, absorbent, cartridge paper, which allowed him to apply his colours very wet, and encouraged spontaneity and immediacy of effect. He was thus able to combine breadth of handling with great delicacy.

After his death in 1802, Girtin's great friend and rival, J. M. W. Turner, is supposed to have said that 'If Tom Girtin had lived, I should have starved'. The remark is probably apocryphal, but recognises that, at that date, Girtin was much the more advanced artist, and preferred by some patrons. So, Lady Sutherland and Edward Lascelles, heir to the Harewood estate in Yorkshire, were reported by Joseph Farington to have been 'disposed to set up Girtin against Turner who they say effects his purposes by industry – the former more genius – Turner finishes too much'.[1]

Girtin visited Harewood several times between 1796 and 1801, so frequently that it was said that his room was always kept in readiness. Lascelles bought nearly 20 works from Girtin, nearly twice as many as from Turner, and also employed him as a drawing master. Most of his commissions were of Yorkshire subjects, including views of the house and park at Harewood, but Lascelles also owned two large watercolours of Welsh subjects. One, a monumental *View near Beddgelert, North Wales*, was shown at the Royal Academy in 1799, to unanimous praise.[2] It was universally recognised as marking an important step in the development of the Romantic watercolour.

The other Welsh view was *The Falls of the Ogwen, North Wales*. It forms a highly appropriate contrast with the panoramic sweep of its companion, in its upright format and low, relatively close viewpoint. It is among Girtin's most powerful expressions of the sublime; one can almost hear the roar of the falls as they cascade down the steep gully. A pair of diminutive sheep gaze in amazement from a vantage point high above, while on the slope below, their companions are tended by a shepherd. CH

1. Quoted in Hill (1999) pp. 19–20.
2. Girtin and Loshak (1954) no. 266ii; Smith (2002) no. 116.

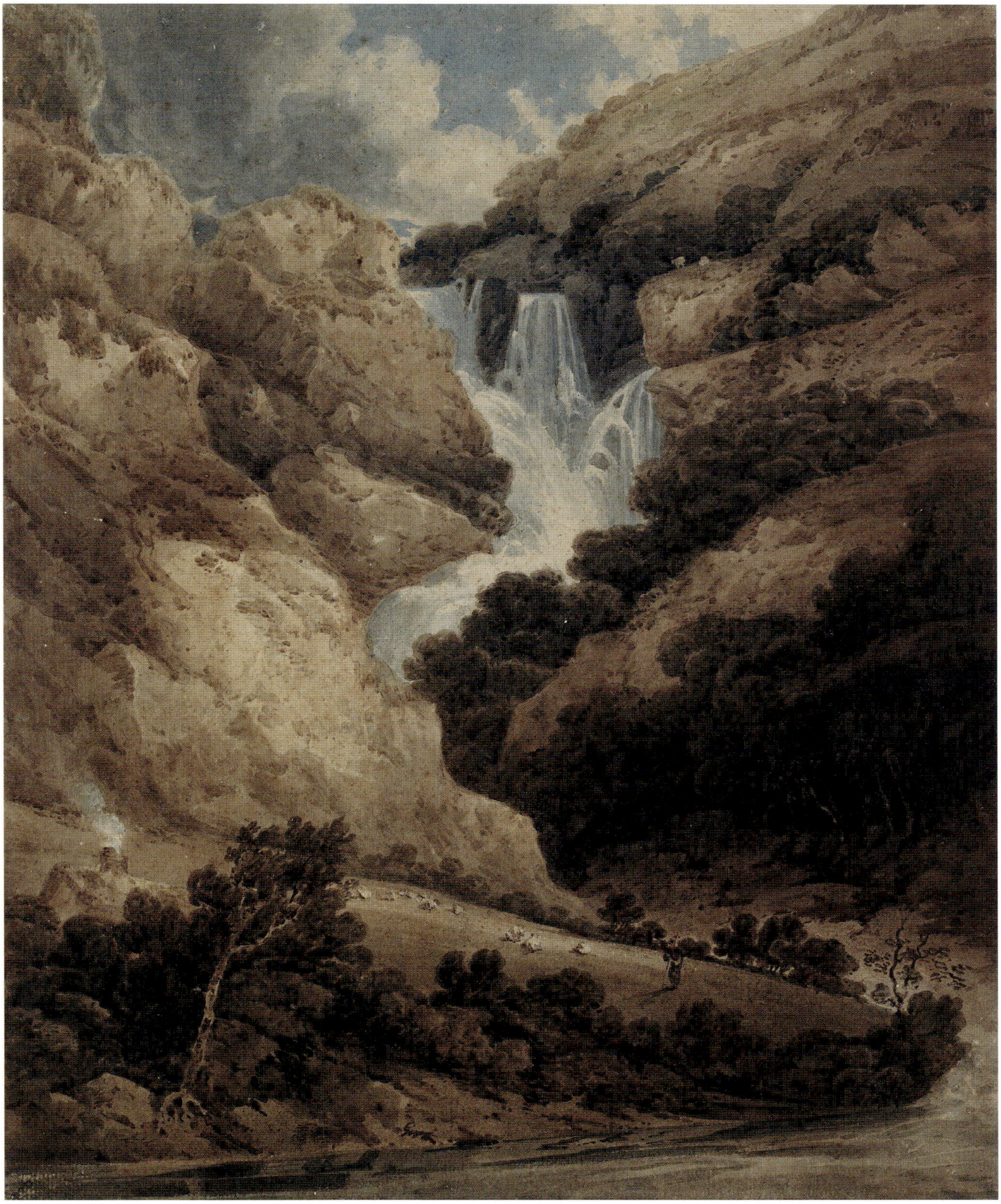

30

EDWARD DAYES 1763–1804

Magdalen College and Bridge, Oxford, from the River, 1794

Watercolour over indications in graphite on paper
30 × 44.6 cm
Signed and dated: *Edwd. Dayes / 1794*
Deposited by the Delegates of the Oxford University Press, 1850
WA1850.46

LITERATURE: Petter (1974) pp. 80–1; Brown (1982) no. 510; Smith (2002) no. 4

The Oxford Almanack has been produced annually since 1674 as the official calendar of the University of Oxford. The earliest examples were grand allegorical engravings on the lines of Continental thesis prints. Later they included views of individual colleges or university buildings with portraits of founders or benefactors, but it was not until the 1760s that they took their most characteristic, and current, form. The Oxford violinist and drawing master John 'Baptist' Malchair (1730–1812) provided two landscapes which were reproduced as the headpieces in 1767 and 1768. Since then the Oxford Almanacks have included a picturesque view at the top of the sheet, and the calendar, with lists of University officials, beneath. Malchair was followed by Edward and Michael 'Angelo' Rooker, who made a long series from 1769 to 1788, and a few by local artists. In 1794–5 Edward Dayes was commissioned to make six views, for which he was paid 40 guineas. Apart from the accounts, there is no evidence as to how the Delegates of the Clarendon (later University) Press chose the artists for the Almanacks.

Although he came to specialise in watercolours of topographical and architectural subjects, Dayes had studied with a portrait painter and at the Royal Academy Schools; he always maintained that landscape painters should have a thorough training in drawing the human figure. By the early 1790s he had established his reputation as a painter of topographical watercolours, and was employed by the antiquary James Moore, to work up his sketches of views in Scotland.

Dayes's watercolours for the Oxford Almanack were all based on pencil sketches made on a visit in July 1794. This view of Magdalen College and Bridge was reproduced as the *Oxford Almanack* for 1797. It shows the banks of the River Cherwell in front of Magdalen Bridge, the most splendid and formal of all the bridges in Oxford, begun as a consequence of the Mileways Act of 1771 but not completed until 1790. Beyond is the distinctive late Gothic form of Magdalen Tower, one of the most famous landmarks in Oxford, and the first notable building for travellers approaching the city from the east. On the horizon are the spire of the University Church of St Mary the Virgin and the dome of the Radcliffe Camera, while an elegant group of cows gives the scene an essentially bucolic quality. In the foreground a man in mortarboard and gown converses with two fishermen who, from their dress, might be wealthy undergraduates, attended by a dog. CH

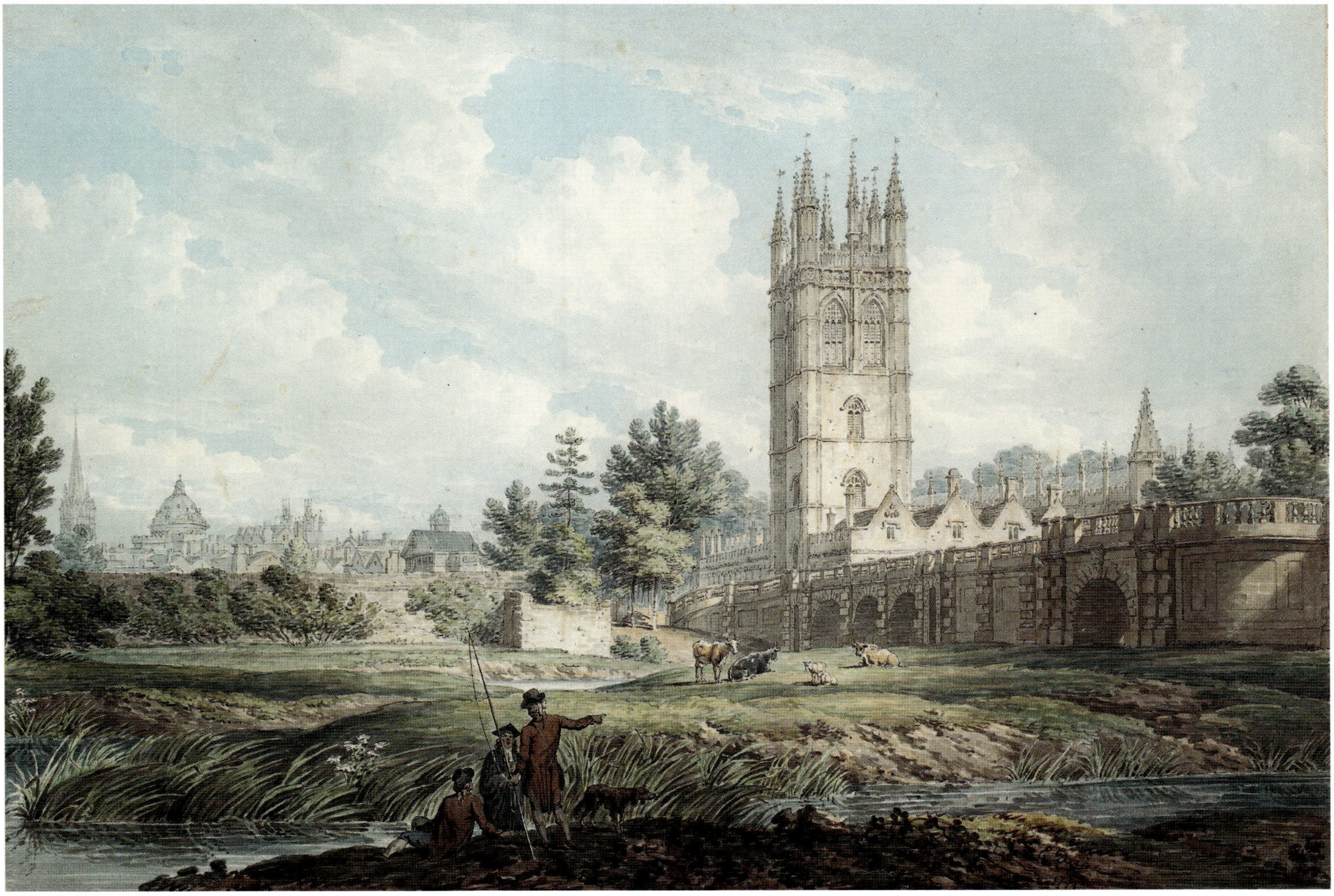

31

EDWARD DAYES 1763–1804

Durham Cathedral seen through an Arch of Ralph Flambard's Bridge, 1797

Watercolour over indications in graphite on paper
10.7 × 16.2 cm
Verso inscribed: *Durham Cathedral seen through an arch of the Old Bridge with the Prebends or New Bridge in the Distance*
Presented in memory of Percy G. F. Allen, Assistant Keeper in the Ashmolean Museum (1914–5), 1916
WA1916.11

LITERATURE: Brown (1982) no. 515

Durham Cathedral and Castle both occupy a dominant position high above a bend in the River Wear. In the seventeenth and eighteenth centuries they were depicted in numerous antiquarian engravings, but it was not until the 1780s that they attracted the attention of artists in search of the Picturesque. Among the first of these was Thomas Hearne (1744–1817), who made lively watercolours of the monuments and bridges of Durham in the 1780s.[1] He was followed by Edward Dayes, whose views influenced those of his pupil, Thomas Girtin, and his rival, J. M. W. Turner. Dayes seems to have visited Durham in the early 1790s, when he made a sketch of the cathedral with the western tower swathed in scaffolding. He later worked this up into a finished watercolour, published in the *Copper Plate Magazine* on 1 February 1796.[2] Girtin made a copy of Dayes's watercolour in 1795, and a sketch of the same view on his own tour to Durham in 1796; the latter formed the basis for two further watercolours by Girtin, one of which is dated 1799.[3] They all show the cathedral and castle looming high over the Prebends' Bridge. Less sublime, but no less conventional, was Turner's watercolour based on sketches from his tour of the north of England in 1797.[4]

For this later watercolour, Dayes adopted a completely original viewpoint: the cathedral is seen through an arch of the Framwellgate Bridge. One of three bridges crossing the Wear, this was originally built by Ranulf Flambard, Bishop of Durham, in 1120, shortly after he had ordered the completion of the cathedral itself. Flambard's bridge was swept away in a flood in 1400, and reconstructed according to the present design under Bishop Langley. Dayes shows the cathedral's western tower still covered in scaffolding, minutely depicted in pencil, while the bridge is painted in much broader, flatter areas of dark watercolour. The sun sets behind, with a lone figure on the bridge itself, while two men in a boat hurry home as a fresh wind whips up the water. The composition is indebted to Canaletto's extraordinary painting of *The City of London seen through an Arch of Westminster Bridge*, a work made popular by Richard Parr's engraving, published in 1747.[5]

As well as the watercolours he commissioned after his own copies, James Moore bought independent watercolours of antiquarian subjects from his artists. He acquired one of Turner's most poetic views of Tintern Abbey, probably after it was shown at the Royal Academy in 1795.[6] Moore also purchased this dreamily evocative view of Durham by Dayes, for which he paid one guinea on 21 February 1798. CH

1. See for example, Brown (1982) no. 836.
2. The watercolour was sold at Christie's 17 November 2005, lot 47.
3. Smith (2002) nos. 52–5.
4. Wilton (1979) no. 249.
5. 1747; collection of the Duke of Northumberland; Beddington (2006) no. 24.
6. Wilton (1979) no. 58.

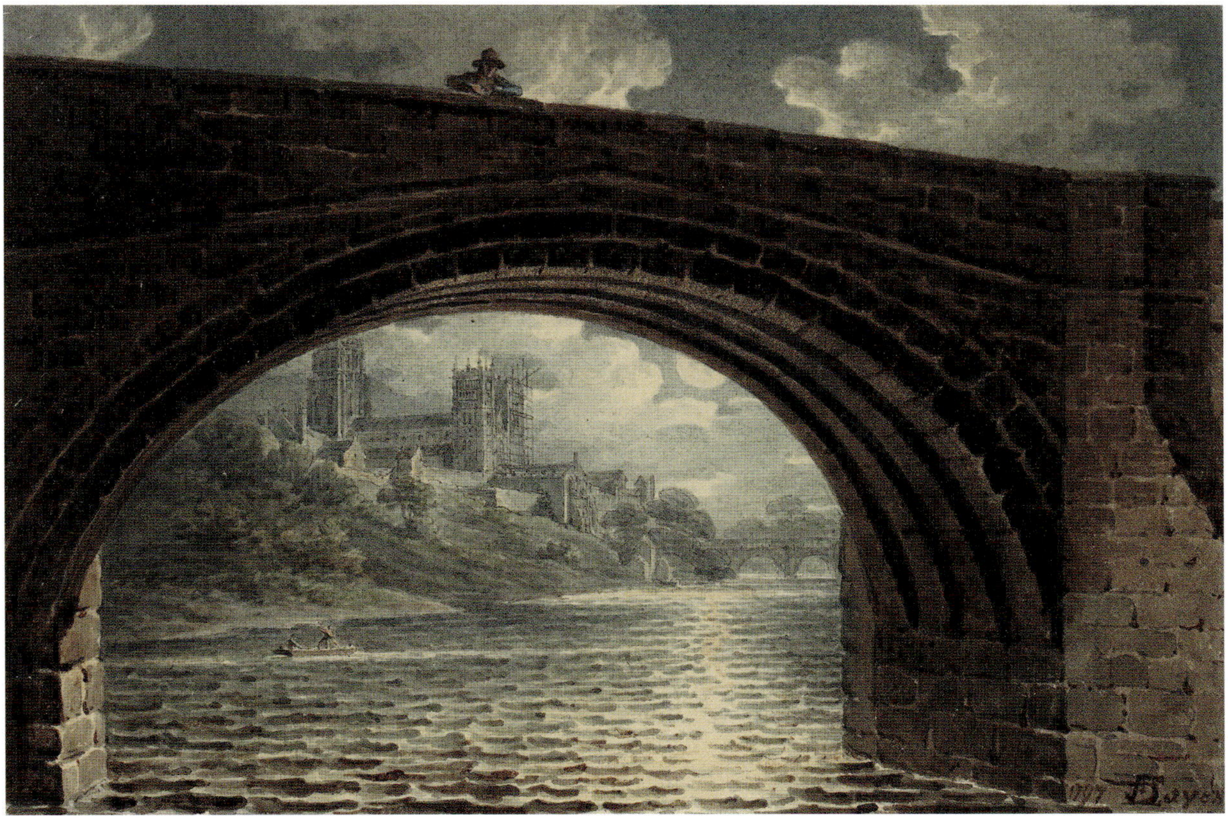

32

JOSEPH MALLORD WILLIAM TURNER 1775–1851

Inside View of the Hall of Christ Church, Oxford, 1803–4

Watercolour over graphite on paper, with some scratching out
32.9 × 44.8 cm
Deposited by the Delegates of the Oxford University Press, 1850
WA1850.55

LITERATURE: Herrmann (1968) no. 7; Petter (1974) pp. 83–4; Wilton (1979) no. 301; Harrison (2000) pp. 69–71

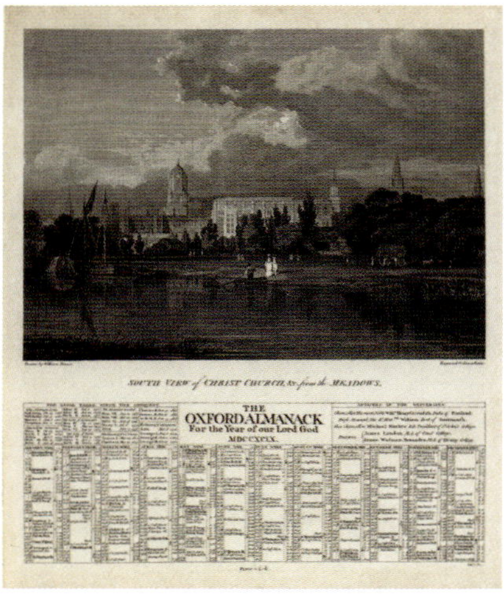

Fig. 33 | James Basire (1730–1802) after J. M. W. Turner (1775–1851), *South View of Christ Church, &c., from the Meadows: Oxford Almanack for 1799*. Engraving. Ashmolean Museum, Oxford, WA.L.55.29

One of Turner's most prestigious early commissions was for a pair of watercolours, to be reproduced as the headpiece for the Oxford Almanack in 1797–8. He was paid 20 guineas for both, the same rate as his friend Edward Dayes, who may have recommended his services to the Delegates of the Press. Turner was, in any case, a familiar figure in Oxford – he had relations at Suningwell, to the south of the city – and may have known at least one of the Delegates personally, Dr Cyril Jackson. He was also an obvious choice as artist, having been trained as an architectural draughtsman with Thomas Malton, who later produced a series of rather dry aquatint views of the colleges. For his first watercolours, and no doubt with an eye to receiving further commissions, Turner produced two contrasting compositions, a distant view of *Christ Church from the Meadows* (fig.33), and a strongly architectural view of the chapel and hall of Oriel College (reproduced in 1799 and 1801 respectively). On the strength of these watercolours, Turner was given a further commission for another watercolour in 1801 and seven more in 1804.

The hall at Christ Church is the most splendid of any Oxford or Cambridge college, and the only part of Wolsey's foundation that still reflects the magnitude of his ambitious building scheme. It was completed shortly before his downfall in 1529, and measures 115 by 40 feet, and 50 feet high. The windows are original, including the bold bay window lighting the high table on its dais. The portraits hanging against the wainscotting show eminent old members of Christ Church surrounding the second founder, Henry VIII; they were at the time considered the most important collection in Oxford. The only surviving study for any of the Almanack drawings is a pencil sketch for this watercolour (Tate), which has indications of perspective together with measurements and colour notes. It also includes details of individual bosses with coats of arms round the walls, shorthand indications of the different styles of picture frames, and the tables laid for dinner. The emphatic scratching out of the picture frames and roof bosses is unusual, and may have been done to assist the engraver. However, the Delegates were not satisfied and in May 1806 they ordered Hugh O'Neill to 'correct' some parts of Turner's watercolour. Nevertheless, the published Almanack for 1807 does correspond in most respects to Turner's original. CH

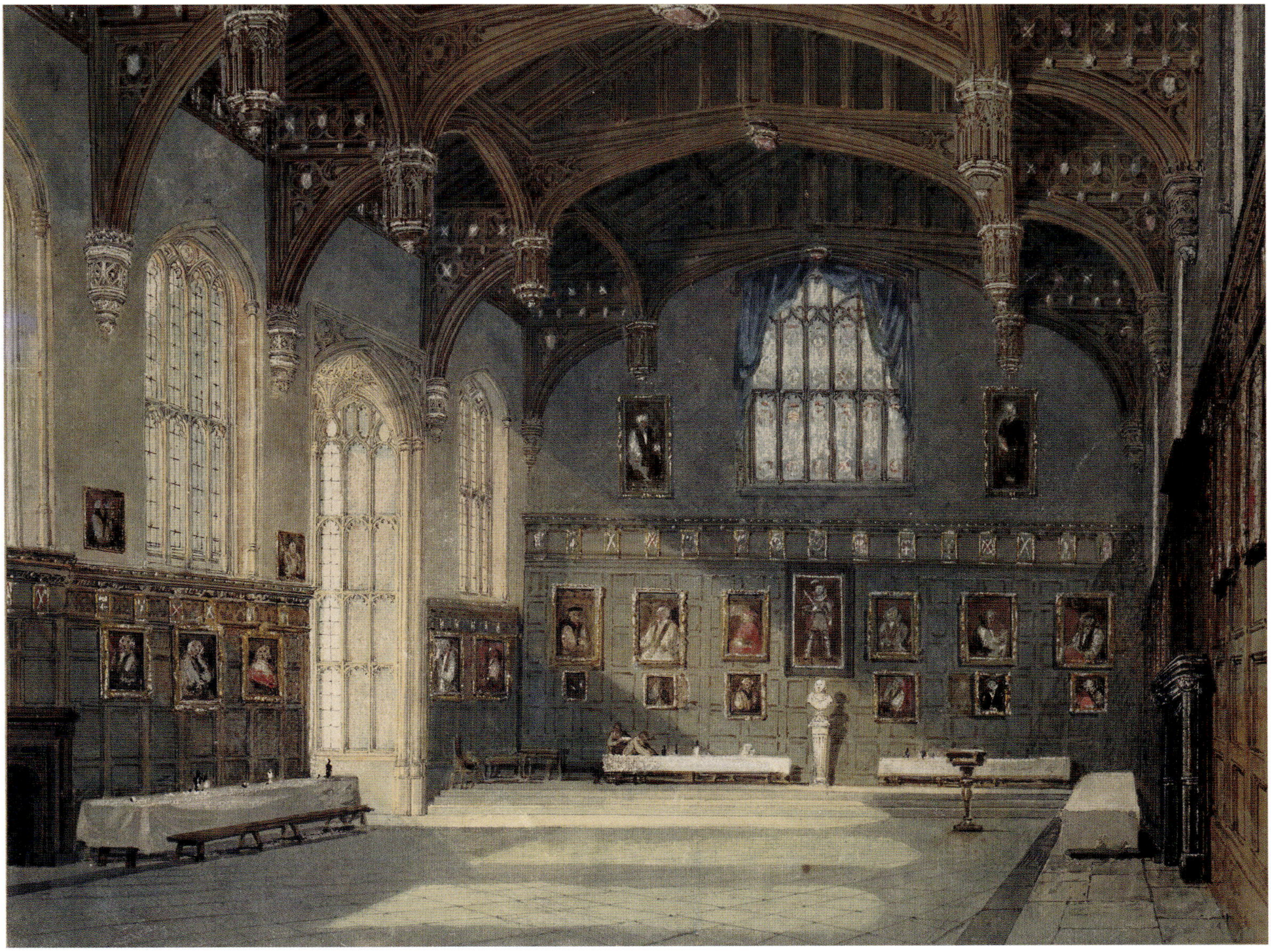

33

JOHN SELL COTMAN 1782–1842

A Ruined House, c. 1807–10

Watercolour over graphite on paper
32.7 × 26.1 cm
Presented by Sir Michael Sadler in memory of Lady Sadler, through The Art Fund, 1931
WA1931.8

LITERATURE: Kitson (1937) p. 112

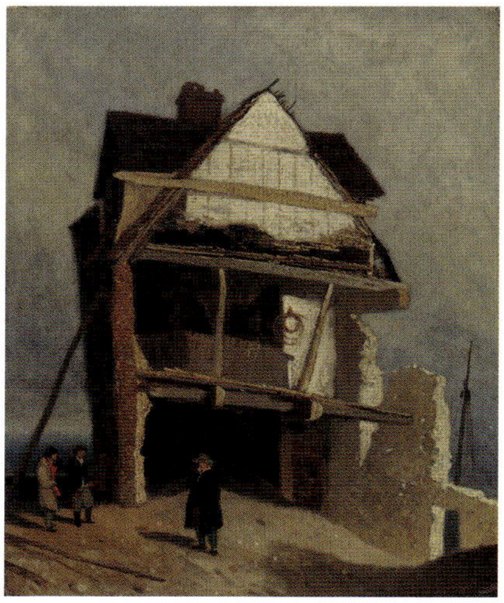

Fig. 34 | John Sell Cotman (1782–1842), *Ruined House, c.* 1807–10. Oil on millboard, mounted on panel. Yale Center for British Art, Paul Mellon Collection, B1975.1.2

The Norwich Society of Artists was founded in 1803, while Cotman was attempting to establish his career in London. Initially employed by the publisher Rudolph Ackermann, Cotman was also involved in both Dr Thomas Monro's Academy and the Sketching Society formed by Girtin. Having successfully exhibited at the Royal Academy, he failed to gain membership of the Society of Painters in Watercolours and returned to his native Norwich in 1806. Persistently ambitious, he quickly secured his place beside John Crome as a leading member of the city's Society of Artists, being elected Vice President in 1810 and as President the following year.

Before he embarked on the series of antiquarian etching projects that dominated his work from 1810 to 1822 Cotman produced a number of oil paintings. This watercolour is a study for a work now in the Yale Center for British Art.[1] Ruins are a recurrent motif in Cotman's work, from dramatic castles and abbeys to modest examples of vernacular architecture. Here, however, the decaying house is treated in restrained terms rather than in a picturesque fashion focusing on elaborate textural *minutiae*. Cotman's evident delight in abstract pattern-making is emphasised by the small graphite plan of the subject in the lower left corner, and enhanced by careful understated details, such as the separate lateral strokes for the exposed bricks echoing the disintegrating roof slats. Delicately handled untinted areas give the impression of brilliant sunshine, off-set by the dense darkness of the building's interior. The close, low viewpoint lends the dilapidated dwelling a bold monumentality, an effect that is slightly reduced in the finished painting.

Cotman's aspirations as an oil painter were largely frustrated by his duties as a drawing master mainly in Norfolk, but from 1834 as a master at King's College, London, where among his pupils was the young Dante Gabriel Rossetti. The full recognition of Cotman's achievement, particularly as a watercolourist, would come only in the twentieth century. He was then lauded by artists such as Paul Nash, Eric Ravilious, and John Piper in their search for a recognisably British tradition that could be reconciled with developments in modern European painting. Cotman was increasingly co-opted to represent this synthesis, with Laurence Binyon even claiming in his survey *English Water-colours* (1933) that 'there was no need to invoke Cézanne, for Cotman was there to show the way'.[2] KW

1. Possibly one of two paintings exhibited with the Norwich Society of Artists in 1809 under the title *An Old House, Norwich*.
2. Binyon (1933) p. 191.

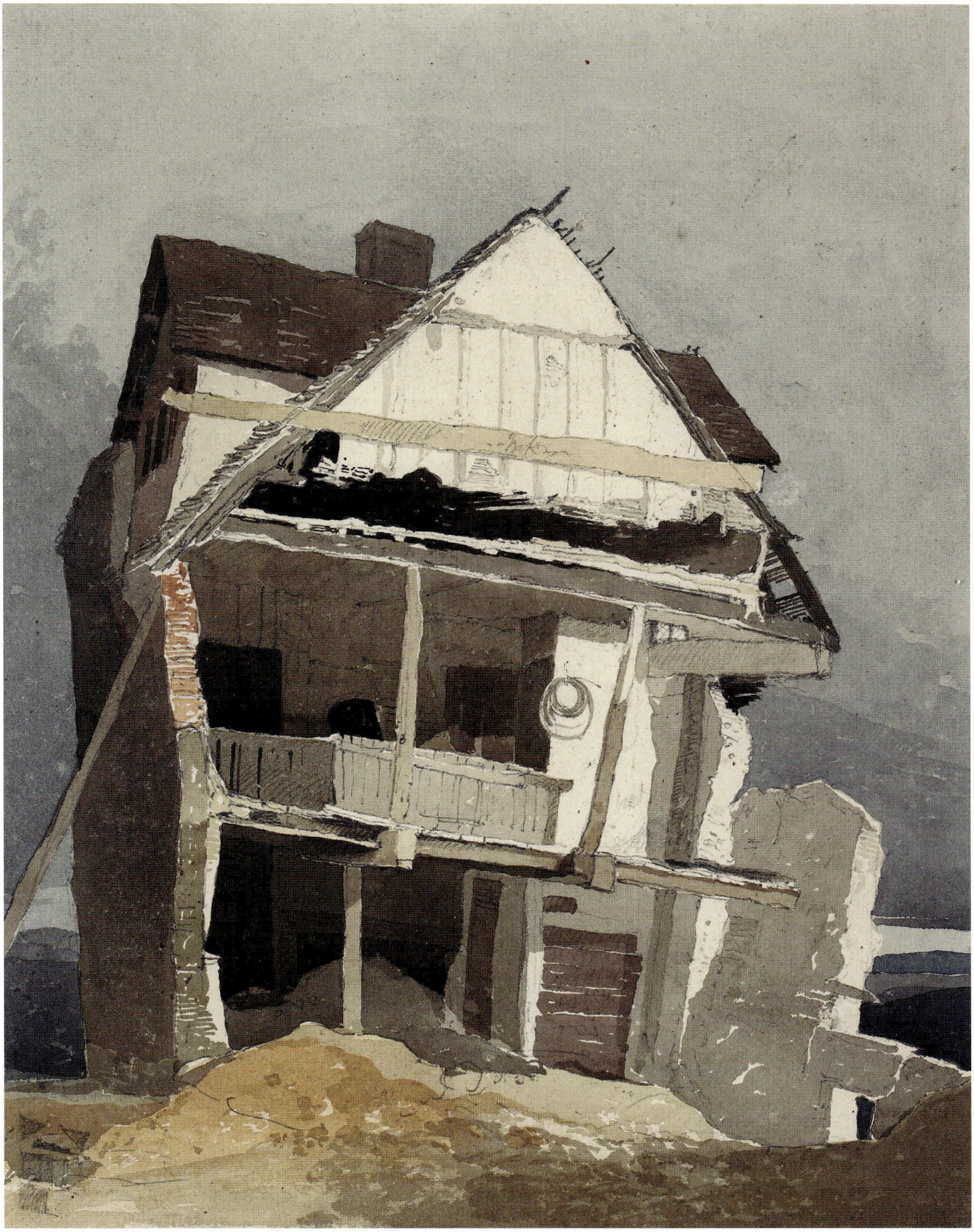

34

JOHN SELL COTMAN 1782–1842

The Tower of West Walton Church, Norfolk, c. 1812

Watercolour over graphite on paper
34.4 × 25 cm
Inscribed: 5
Presented by A. E. Anderson through
The Art Fund, 1923
WA1923.4

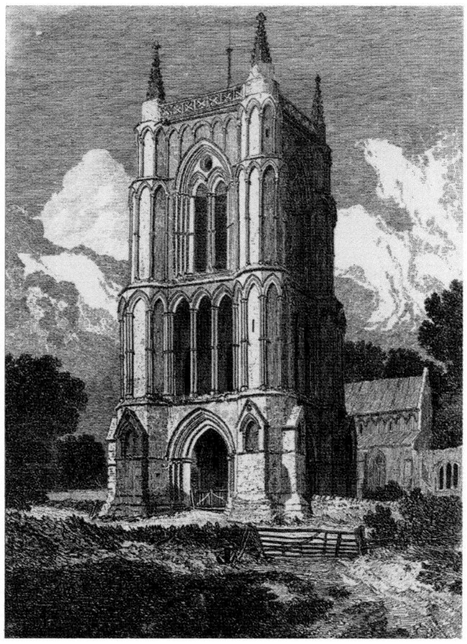

Fig. 35 | John Sell Cotman (1782–1842), *Tower of West Walton Church, Norfolk*, 1814, plate XXXIV from *A Series of Etchings Illustrative of the Architectural Antiquities of Norfolk*, 1818. Etching. Ashmolean Museum, Oxford, WA1932.85

Cotman was still at work on his *Miscellaneous Etchings* (1811), dominated by sites encountered during his travels in Yorkshire between 1803–5, when he wrote to Dawson Turner on 2 February 1811 seeking his advice on his proposed project to etch 'all *Ornamented Antiquities* in Norfolk'.[1] Turner, a noted local banker, botanist, and antiquary, first met Cotman in 1804 and became a committed, if perhaps restrictive, patron. Cotman again sought Turner's advice, regarding the itinerary for his autumn sketching tour of Norfolk, on 25 August, the day after the conclusion of the 1811 Norwich Society of Artists exhibition.

Mid-September found the artist in the north-west of the county. During this time he made studies of West Walton Church, a fine example of Early English Gothic architecture, upon which the present watercolour is based. This served in turn for an etching, originally published in 1814 and later in *A Series of Etchings Illustrative of the Architectural Antiquities of Norfolk* (1818).

An advertisement in the *Norwich Chronicle* signalled Cotman's dual intentions for his forthcoming etchings: 'Although it will be the principal object of the Author to exhibit faithfully the Styles of the various Structures, yet he will not be inattentive to the Selection of the most favourable points of view; being persuaded it will be the wish of his subscribers to see architectural fidelity combined with picturesque effect.'[2] The etching is notably more picturesque in appearance than the watercolour, with the rough grass and tottering gate in the foreground. In fact, some of these details appear in the graphite underdrawing of the watercolour, but are obscured by the deep shadow falling across the base of the tower. Rather than being a topographical observation, this device, favoured by the formidable eighteenth-century draughtsman Giovanni Battista Piranesi, enhances the drama of the composition. Cotman held Piranesi's work in high esteem, and early in 1812 he encouraged Dawson Turner to purchase the Italian's complete etchings, being unable to afford them himself.

After some prevarication, Cotman moved to Yarmouth in April 1812 under Turner's patronage, for £200 per year, succeeding John Crome as the family's drawing master. Turner's own antiquarian interests, including his Grangerisation of an edition of Blomefield's *History of Norfolk* (1805–10), dominated Cotman's work for the next decade – in part accounting for his delay in completing the 60 etchings for *Antiquities of Norfolk*. Despite lacking a chronological scheme or touring narrative the etchings were sufficiently well received to secure Cotman a commission for Longman's *Excursions* as the main contributor of illustrations for the volumes on Norfolk and Suffolk (1818–9). KW

1. Moore (1982) p. 60.
2. *Ibid.*

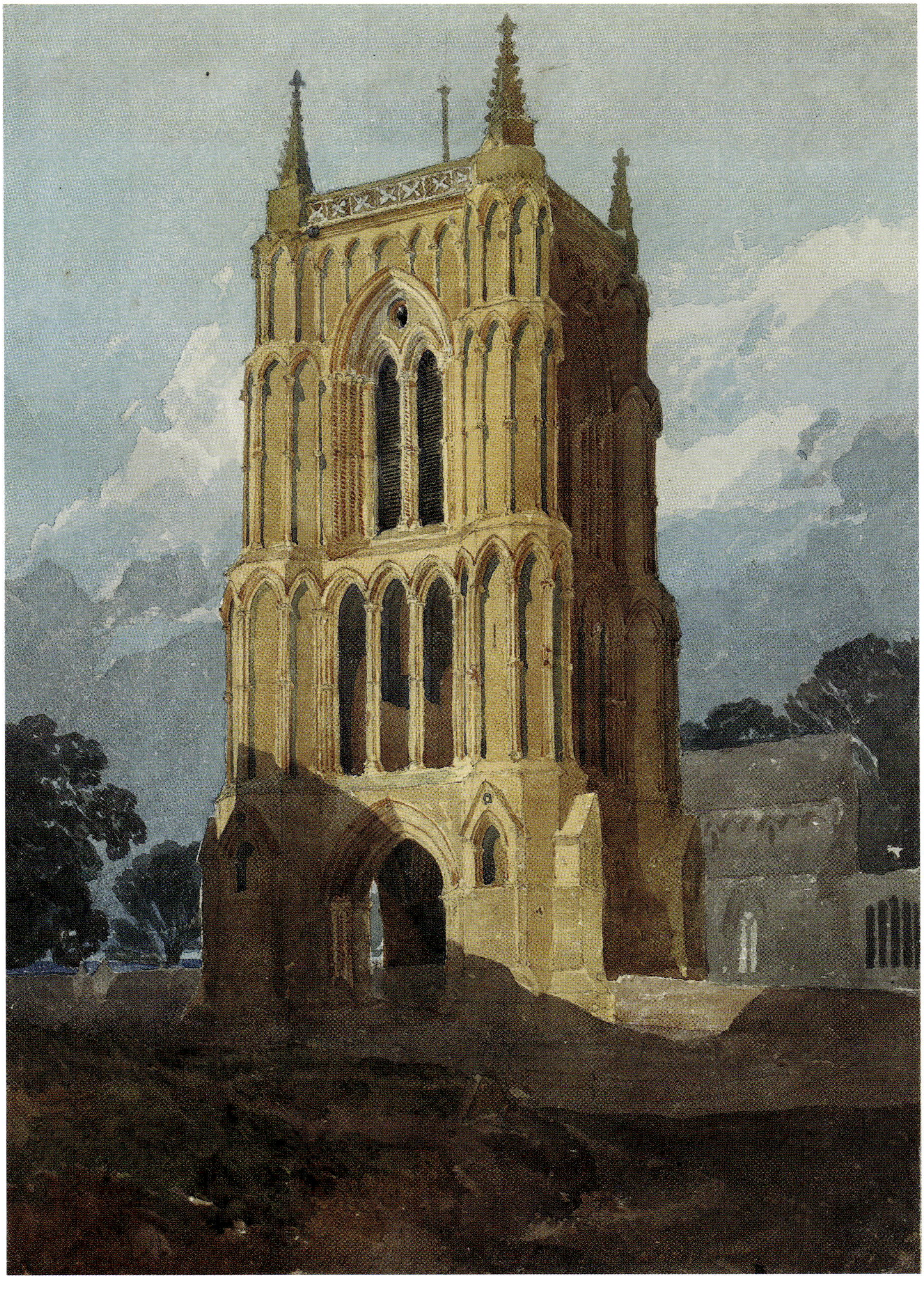

35

DAVID COX 1783–1859

Fishermen on the Thames looking towards Westminster and Lambeth, 1823

Watercolour over graphite on paper
25 × 36.2 cm
Signed and dated: *Cox 1823*
Lent from a private collection
L12224.2

Born in Birmingham, Cox moved to London in 1804 and initially specialised in watercolour, first exhibiting at the Royal Academy in 1805. He quickly became a stalwart of the Society of Painters in Watercolours, which he joined in 1812, having earlier shown at the rival Associated Artists in Watercolours. Between 1813 and 1819 he published a series of drawing manuals which enjoyed great success among amateurs and aspiring professionals, the most notable being his *Treatise on Landscape Painting and Effect in Water Colours* (1813–4). Like many of his contemporaries Cox made several tours of Wales, providing illustrations to Thomas Roscoe's *Wanderings and Excursions in North Wales* (1836) and the companion volume on *South Wales* (1837); and of the Midlands, the Lake District, the north of England, and the Low Countries (1826) and France (1829, 1832). As his style developed, he accepted the challenge of oil painting in the late 1830s.

Although Cox lived in Hereford from 1814 until 1827, teaching privately and at the local grammar school, he remained closely in touch with the Watercolour Society in London. This charming view is an outstandingly fresh example of the kind of work he exhibited in the 1820s. He had shown views of the Thames at his earliest exhibitions with the Associated Artists, but they later became something of a speciality, and he produced a particular concentration in 1823 and 1824. This watercolour may be the *Fishing Boat on the Thames* exhibited in 1823. In part, these must have been painted in the hope of sales. Since the Middle Ages the Thames has been associated with English national pride, and after the victory of Waterloo collectors were eager to reaffirm the significance of this symbol. More importantly, however, the low horizon and wide panorama perfectly suited Cox's talent. Here, two colourfully dressed men sit in a boat, one rowing and the other looking after a fishing net. On the horizon can be seen the massive form of Westminster Abbey and the arches of the old bridge, while the ghost-like dome of St Paul's Cathedral looms in the far distance. There is a great deal of activity on the banks, a reminder of the river's economic as well as symbolic importance. CH

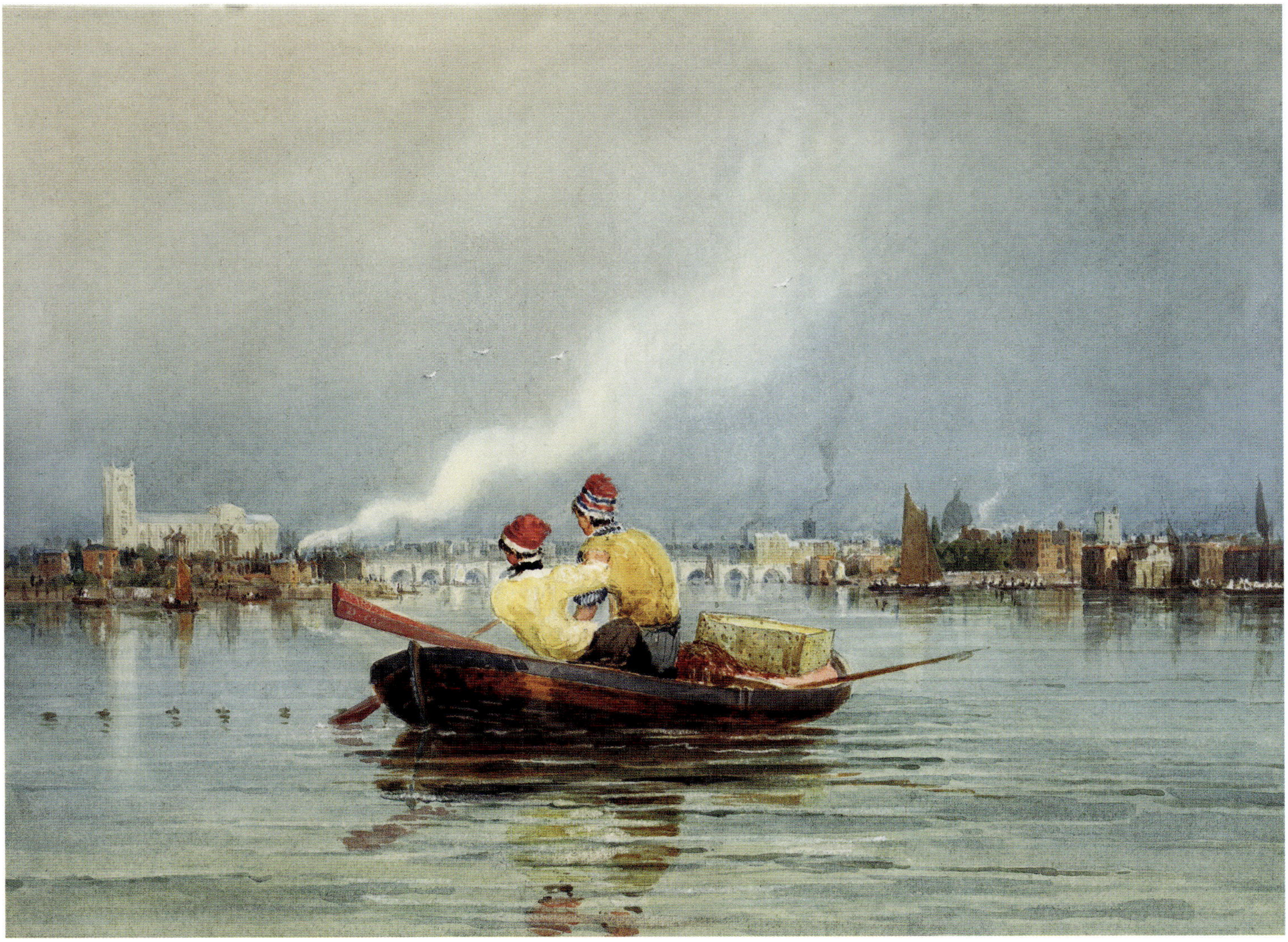

36

SAMUEL PROUT 1783–1852
A View in Strasbourg, 1822

Watercolour and pen and ink on paper
62.1 × 47.7 cm
Inscribed: *HANDLUNG / VON / S. PROUT / Commerce de Jean Dichl / no. 65*
Presented by William Vautier Paterson, through The Art Fund, 1943
WA1943.4.26

LITERATURE: Wilton and Lyles (1993) no. 233

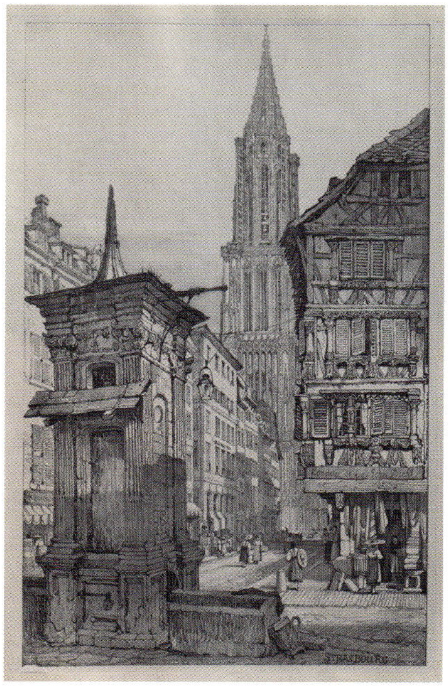

Fig. 36 | Samuel Prout (1783–1852), *The Rue Mercière and west front of Strasbourg Cathedral*, published in *Facsimiles of Sketches made in Flanders and Germany*, 1833. Lithograph on Chine collé. Ashmolean Museum, Oxford, WA.RS.ED.059

Despite persistent ill health, Prout pursued a successful career as a draughtsman and watercolourist. The author of several manuals on drawing and an influential teacher, he counted members of the aristocracy, the artist J. D. Harding and John Ruskin among his pupils, with the latter becoming his most committed advocate. Prout was a contributor to numerous publications of picturesque scenery, as well as a pioneering exponent of lithography.

Appointed as Painter in Ordinary in Water-Colours to Queen Victoria in 1837, Prout's reputation rested on his work of the 1820s. During this decade he made several trips to the Continent, which provided him with novel motifs in astute competition with the picturesque views of the British Isles that by this date had become somewhat hackneyed. 'We had begun to tire,' William Henry Pyne remarked 'of the endless repetitions of Tintern Abbey from within, and Tintern Abbey from without, and the same by moonlight, and twilight, and every other light in which taste and talent could compose variations to the worn-out theme.'[1]

Prout first visited Strasbourg from 12 to 19 September 1821 as part of an extensive trip down the Rhine. His itinerary, recorded in his surviving *Goldsmith's Almanack*, shows that Strasbourg, along with Cologne, was the only city in which he remained for more than two days. This view shows the Rue Mercière looking towards the west front of Strasbourg Cathedral. The composition allows the cathedral to appear gracefully in the background while affording Prout the opportunity to delineate abundant local detail in the foreground, worked up in characteristic broken lines with a reed pen and brown ink. Shadows placed across the buildings create a receding rhythm of light and dark, culminating in the ethereal grey tones of the magnificent north tower. Ruskin's admiration for Prout was based in part upon his accurate record of dilapidated structures that would subsequently be destroyed, such as the water fountain in the foreground. Here, however, the artist ignores the distinctive pink hue of the Vosges sandstone with which the cathedral was renovated following a devastating fire in 1176.

Exhibited at the Old Water-Colour Society in 1822, along with three other views of Strasbourg, this watercolour probably fetched 35 guineas, the highest price for a work by Prout recorded on that occasion. It did not feature in his *Illustrations of the Rhine* (1824), but, slightly adapted, served as the basis of a lithograph for *Facsimiles of Sketches made in Flanders and Germany*, published by the artist in 1833. It was the purchase of this volume by Ruskin's father that inspired the first of his family's Continental tours. KW

1. *Somerset House Gazette*, quoted in Lockett (1985) p. 65.

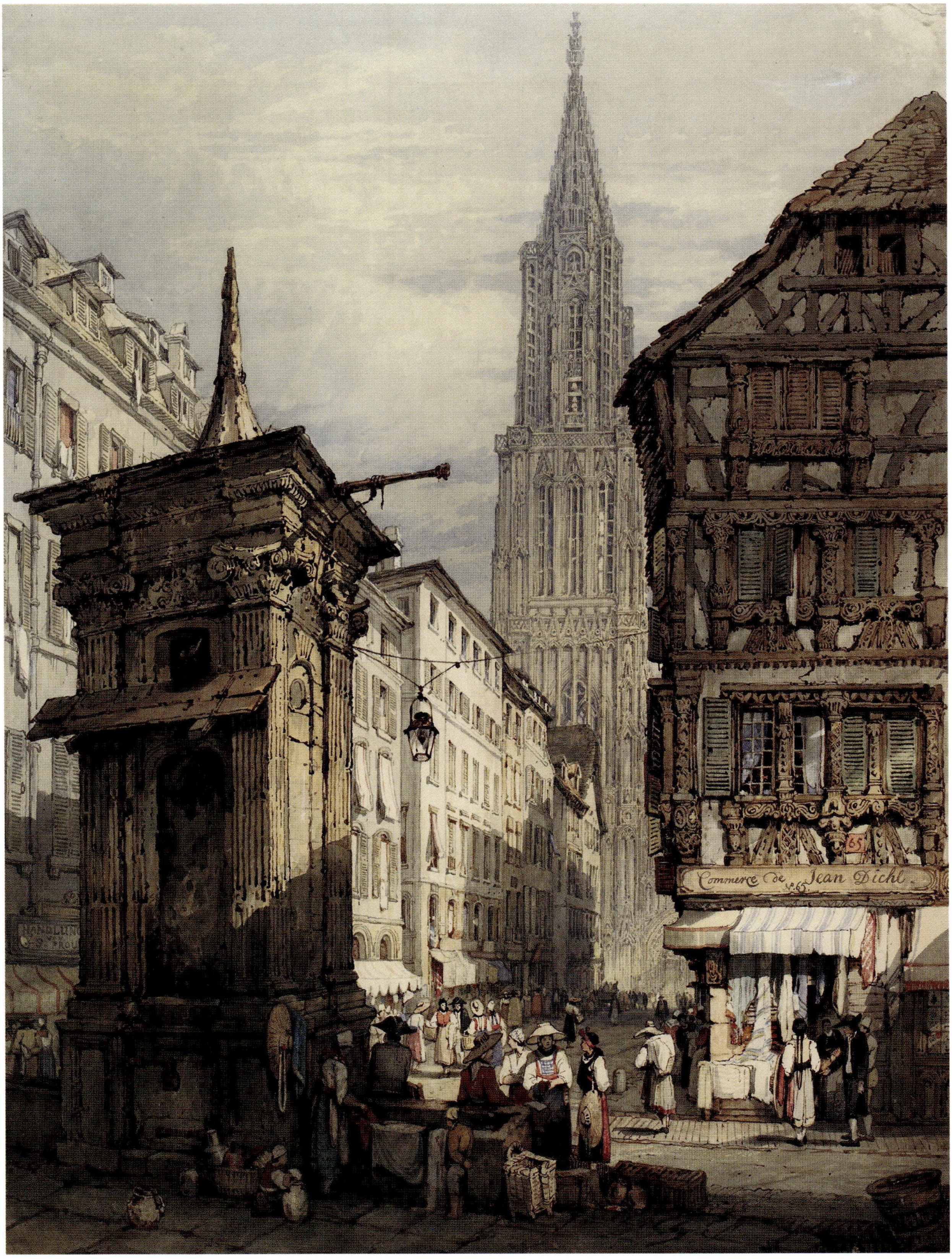
65
Commerce de Jean Dichl
N.65.

37

GEORGE CHINNERY 1774–1852

Ruins in Bengal, 1820–5

Pen and grey ink and watercolour and bodycolour over graphite, on off-white wove paper, on buff-coloured inlay with red framing line
15.2 × 19.9 cm
Signed and dated on the *verso*: *Geo Chinnery. F. / Macao China 1826.*
Presented by Professor Luke Herrmann from the collection of Sir Bruce Ingram, through The Art Fund, 2002
WA2002.21

A colourful character, known as a great raconteur and as 'one of the ugliest men in existence', Chinnery trained at the Royal Academy Schools in the early 1790s. He won success as a painter in Ireland from 1796, before following his brother John, an employee of the East India Company, to Madras in 1802. Chinnery moved on to Calcutta in 1812, where he established himself as a portrait painter, though he preferred landscape 'a thousand times better'.[1]

Despite the inscription on the *verso* locating the scene to Macau, this watercolour must have been painted in Bengal. It is related to a number of Bengali scenes in which the fallen dome of a Muslim mausoleum lies amid crumbling stonework, sometimes accompanied by figures bathing on the banks of a river.[2] Chinnery left for China in July 1825, in an attempt to escape substantial debts in Calcutta.

Rather than depicting a spectacular view of foreign scenery, the scene is one of restful contemplation. Towards the left, however, a sharp dash of bright red catches the eye, drawing attention to the fallen dome in the shadows. The red indicates a small fire from which smoke rises, drifting across the scene. Chinnery was particularly fond of using blue-grey smoke to lighten the more obscure corners of his compositions, which he preferred to be at least two-thirds in shadow – the 'great Engine of Effect', as he described it.[3] In an album entitled 'Scenery in Bengal 1825', once belonging to Lady Harriet Paget, he inscribed an evening landscape drawing: 'Smoke in air in the dark parts would be beautiful' (fol. 18).[4]

The Paget album includes about 50 sketches mostly dating to 1821, when Chinnery travelled up the Hoogli (Hooghly) river to Serampore to evade his creditors. One drawing depicts a riverside village with ruined tombs (fol. 7, September 1821), while another shows a Muslim mausoleum beside a banyan tree, with a seated figure, goat and cow in the foreground (fol. 5). Chinnery no doubt used such carefully observed sketches as reference material from which to construct his imaginary compositions.

Although exotic in its setting, the watercolour is closely related to the Picturesque tradition that dominated English art when Chinnery first trained in London, notably in the diverse textures of the brick and plaster, the invading vegetation and the rickety palmleaf shelter. The precisely laid wash to the right of the wall, leaving the finest strip of light beneath a cloud, is balanced by a similar strip of light on the fallen stonework bottom left, demonstrating Chinnery's masterful handling of the medium. CP

1. Patrick Conner, 'Chinnery, George (1774–1852)', *Oxford Dictionary of National Biography* online edn. (2007) http://www.oxforddnb.com/view/article/5311, accessed 6 January 2015.
2. See, for example, *Sunset*, Rhode Island School of Design Museum, 73.204.6; and *Bengal Landscape with the Ruins of a Mosque*, Christie's 26 September 2007, lot 415, showing a man in the same white clothes with a blue sash.
3. Quoted in Conner (1993) p. 138.
4. British Library, WD3385.

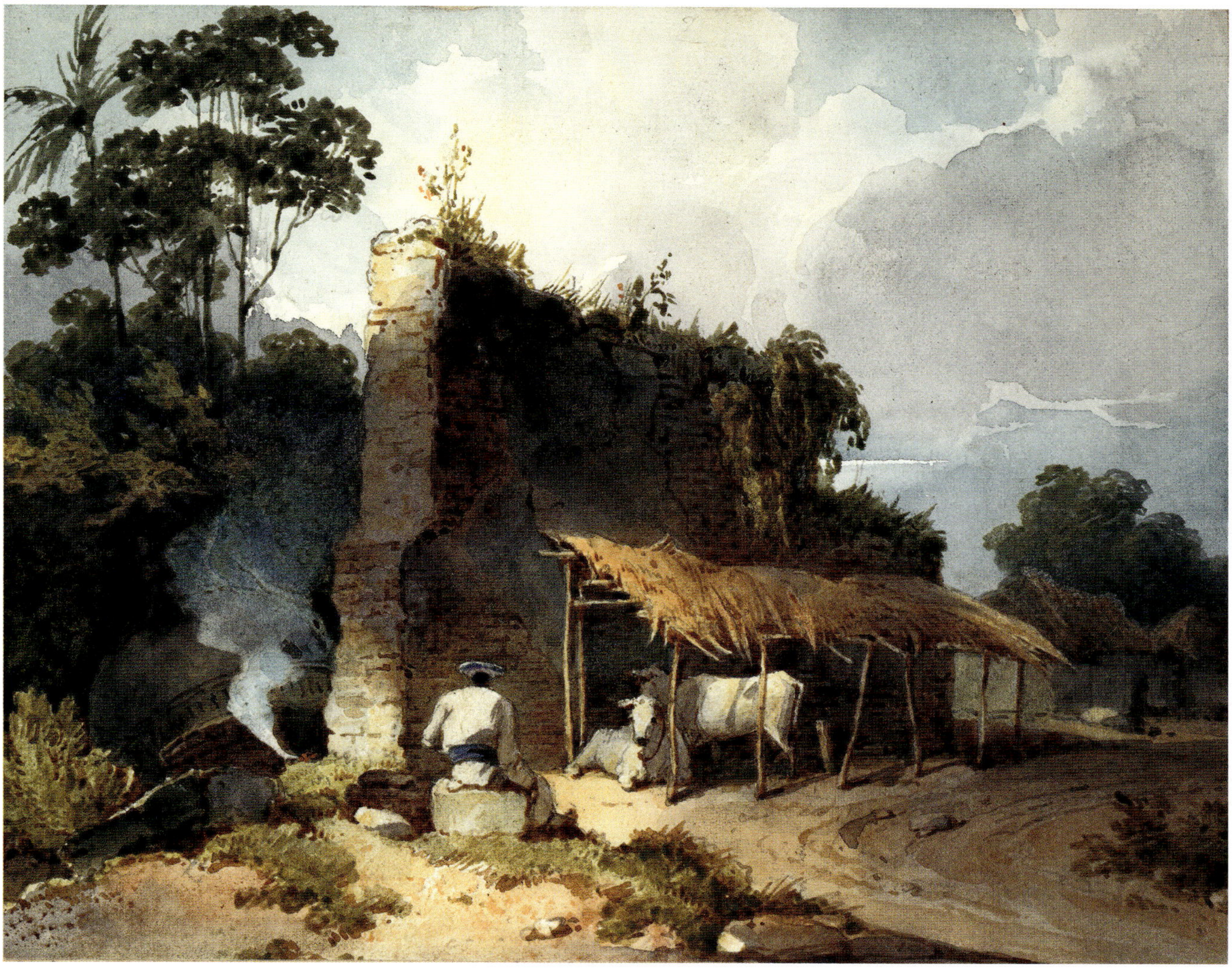

38

DAVID ROBERTS 1796–1864
The Puerta de Alcalá, Madrid, 1832–3

Watercolour over graphite on brown paper
26.9 × 38.8 cm
Inscribed: *Gate of Alcalá. Madrid*
Purchased (Virtue-Tebbs Bequest Fund), 1963
WA1963.89.72

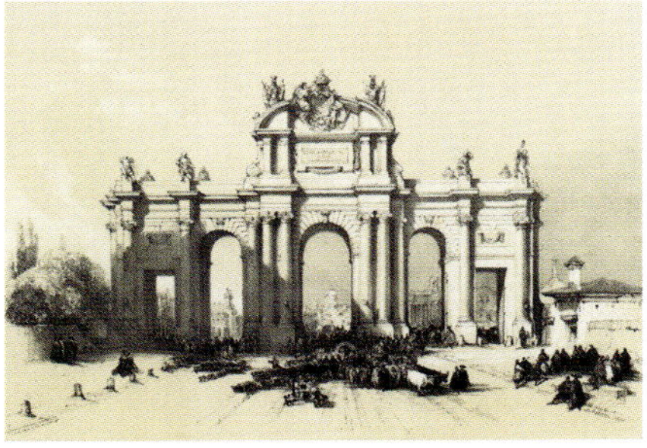

Fig. 37 | David Roberts (1796–1864), *The Puerta de Alcalá, Madrid*, from *Picturesque Sketches in Spain taken during the years 1832 and 1833*, London, 1837. Lithograph © Bodleian Library, University of Oxford.

Balancing precision with facility, this view of the Puerta de Alcalá in Madrid – a monumental gateway designed by the neo-classical architect Francesco Sabatini in 1778 – exemplifies the art of the Scottish watercolourist David Roberts. According to the Redgrave brothers, Roberts was an 'essentially scenic' artist-topographer whose architectural views conveyed 'the splendour and magnificence of his structures, by simplicity … of parts, by breadth of daylight, and by enriching his subjects with groups of accessories'.[1]

Roberts rose from humble beginnings to gain success as a scene-painter – a background evident in the speed of his execution and direct appeal to the eye. The imposing backdrop of the gate resembles a theatre in itself, with the figures spilling out on to the 'stage' to enliven the scene. Roberts has used a ruler in drawing the architecture, but there is extraordinary freedom in his application of paint, which leaves large areas of the paper exposed. Scattered touches of colour draw the eye to key points of focus: two dabs of green are placed either side of the main arch, for example, with another in the cape of a figure directly below the centre. The blue of the sky is picked up in foreground figures to left and right of centre, while red notes link the group on the far right to figures under each curved arch.

This view was published as a lithograph in *Picturesque Sketches in Spain* (1837, plate XVIII). Here the splashes of colour take on the clear forms of travelling farmers with ox-drawn carts, and groups of priests. The gate marked the passage of a *cañada real* (a designated royal route for migrating livestock), so flocks of sheep were regularly driven through the Puerta.

Before Roberts, few artists had travelled to Spain, described by fellow artist David Wilkie as 'the wild unpoached game reserve of Europe'.[2] An advertisement for *Sketches of Spain and Spanish Character* (1833–4) by his friend J. F. Lewis appears in the back of Roberts's volume, indicating one painter who had preceded him. Otherwise it was largely Wilkie who inspired Roberts to set off for Madrid – and perhaps the Murillos and Velázquezs recently acquired by Wallis (see cat. 26).

He arrived in the city in December 1832, braving its piercing winds for three weeks before travelling south to Córdoba. Roberts relished the purity of Madrid's fog-free air, as can be seen from the brilliant clarity of this watercolour. Returning 'laden … like the bees with honey' in the form of a packed portfolio, Roberts transformed his studies into paintings for exhibition and illustrations for the *Landscape Annuals* (1835–8).[3] His *Picturesque Sketches*, which sold 1,200 sets in two months, was frequently reprinted, and brought him considerable recognition, as well as praise from Cotman.[4] CP

1. Redgrave (1947) p. 406.
2. Quoted in Sim (1984) p. 61.
3. Quoted in Sim (1984) p. 70.
4. Guiterman and Llewellyn (1986) p. 65.

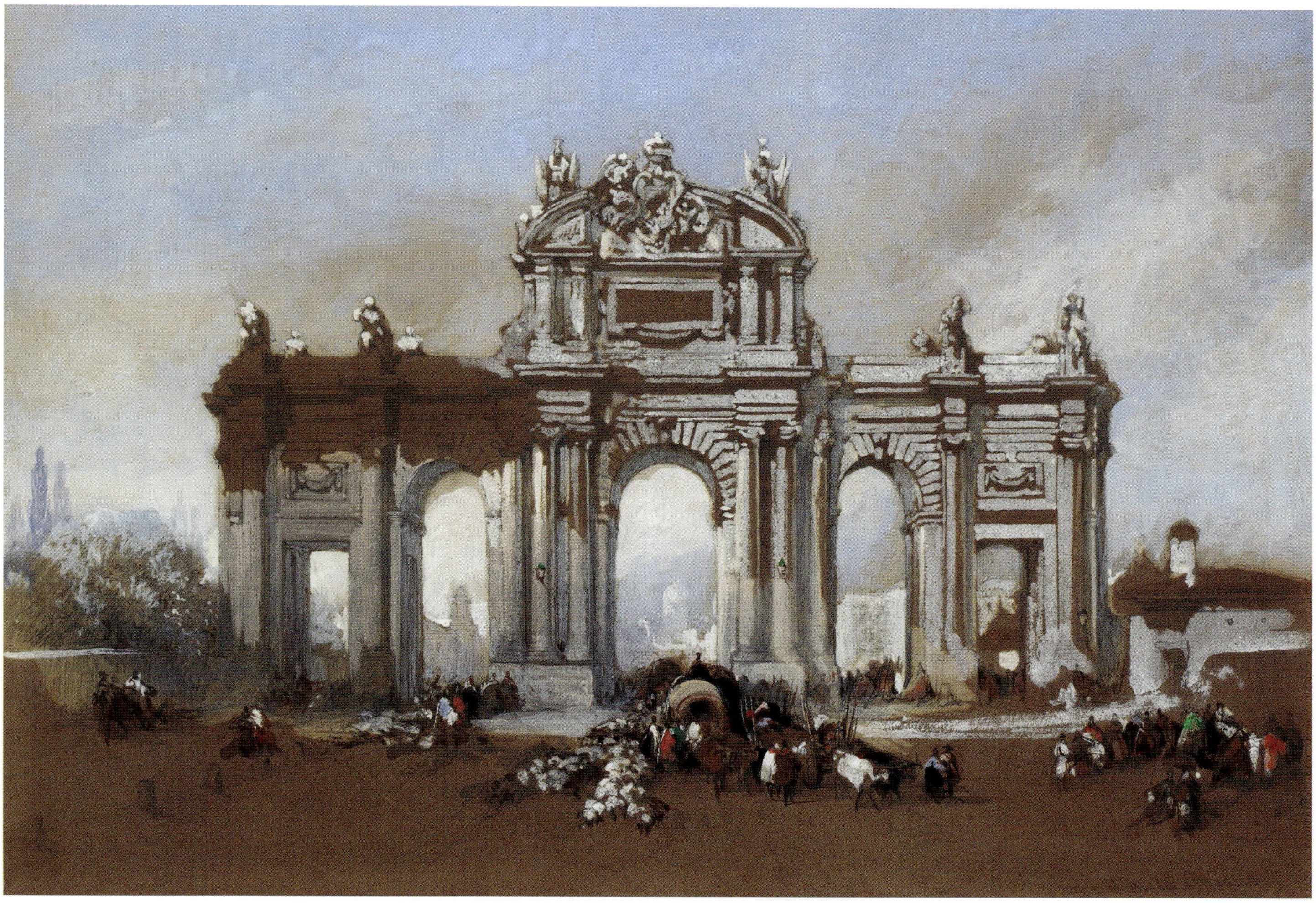

39

JOHN FREDERICK LEWIS 1804–1876

Head of a Girl in a Lace Shawl, 1838

Red and black chalk and Indian ink with watercolour and bodycolour on buff board
37.1 × 26.3 cm
Signed and dated: *J. F. Lewis / 1838*
Presented by Professor Luke Herrmann from the collection of Sir Bruce Ingram, through The Art Fund, 2002
WA2002.24

LITERATURE: Lewis (1978) no. 289

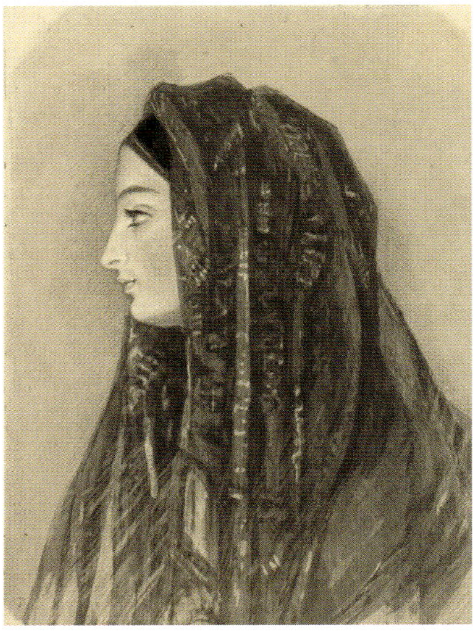

Fig. 38 | Attributed to John Frederick Lewis (1804–1876), *Bust of an Oriental Woman*, c. 1832–56. Mixed media, with etching, engraving, stipple, and drypoint. British Museum, London, 1867,1214.275 © Trustees of the British Museum.

Renowned as one of the foremost Orientalist painters, Lewis began his travels in Spain and Italy before venturing further afield to Egypt in search of more exotic subject matter. Previously exhibited as a *Spanish Girl in a Mantilla*, this exquisite study is more likely, according to Briony Llewellyn, to have been made in Italy, where Lewis is known to have been travelling in 1838. A watercolour in the Ashmolean of a *Girl in Neapolitan Native Dress*, dated 29 August 1838 and inscribed 'Procida', the name of an island off the coast of Naples, would seem to support this theory. It shows a model with a very similar profile and expression, also with her eyes demurely downcast.[1]

Typical of Lewis is the interest shown in the intricate scalloped patterns of the heavy folded lace. It has been suggested that the black veil may represent mourning dress, though such veils were frequently worn as head-coverings in the Catholic churches of both Spain and Italy, symbolising modesty and submission to authority. They are especially characteristic of the Holy Week festivities in Seville. Plate 13 of Lewis's *Sketches of Spain and Spanish Character* (1836) shows a somewhat less modest young girl gazing yearningly upwards, wearing just such a *mantilla* over a traditional hair-comb (*peineta*).[2] As Lewis tended to collect costumes on his travels, it is possible that he provided his model with a Spanish lace shawl he owned, rather than representing an Italian version.[3]

A print in the British Museum now attributed to Lewis also shows a woman in profile wearing a scalloped black lace hair-covering, though she is looking upwards.[4] The fact that the print is in reverse implies that it could have been adapted from the drawing, but the print does not include the model's folded hands, apparently wearing fingerless lace gloves.[5] The drawing is far more sensitively drawn than the print, with delicate touches of red chalk in the hands, nostril and lips, and fine long eyelashes. Although this could be an idealised Mediterranean beauty, created by Lewis for avid readers of the *Annuals*, it certainly has the sense of a carefully observed portrait taken from life.

Reviewing the annual exhibition by the Society of Painters in Watercolours in 1835, Leigh Hunt's *London Journal* remarked 'J. F. Lewis gives us several scenes from Spain in his smart and lively style; but why does he for ever drag in that demure young lady with a black veil over her head?'.[6] Clearly the reviewer's comments did not deter Lewis from repeating this favourite subject. CP

1. WA1942.154
2. British Museum, 1948,0410.131.
3. Selborne (2011) p. 78.
4. British Museum, 1867,1214.275, originally described as F. C. Lewis after J. F. Lewis.
5. See British Museum, 1948,0410.124 for a Spanish woman wearing similar gloves.
6. *London Journal*, 13 May 1835, no. 59, p. 152.

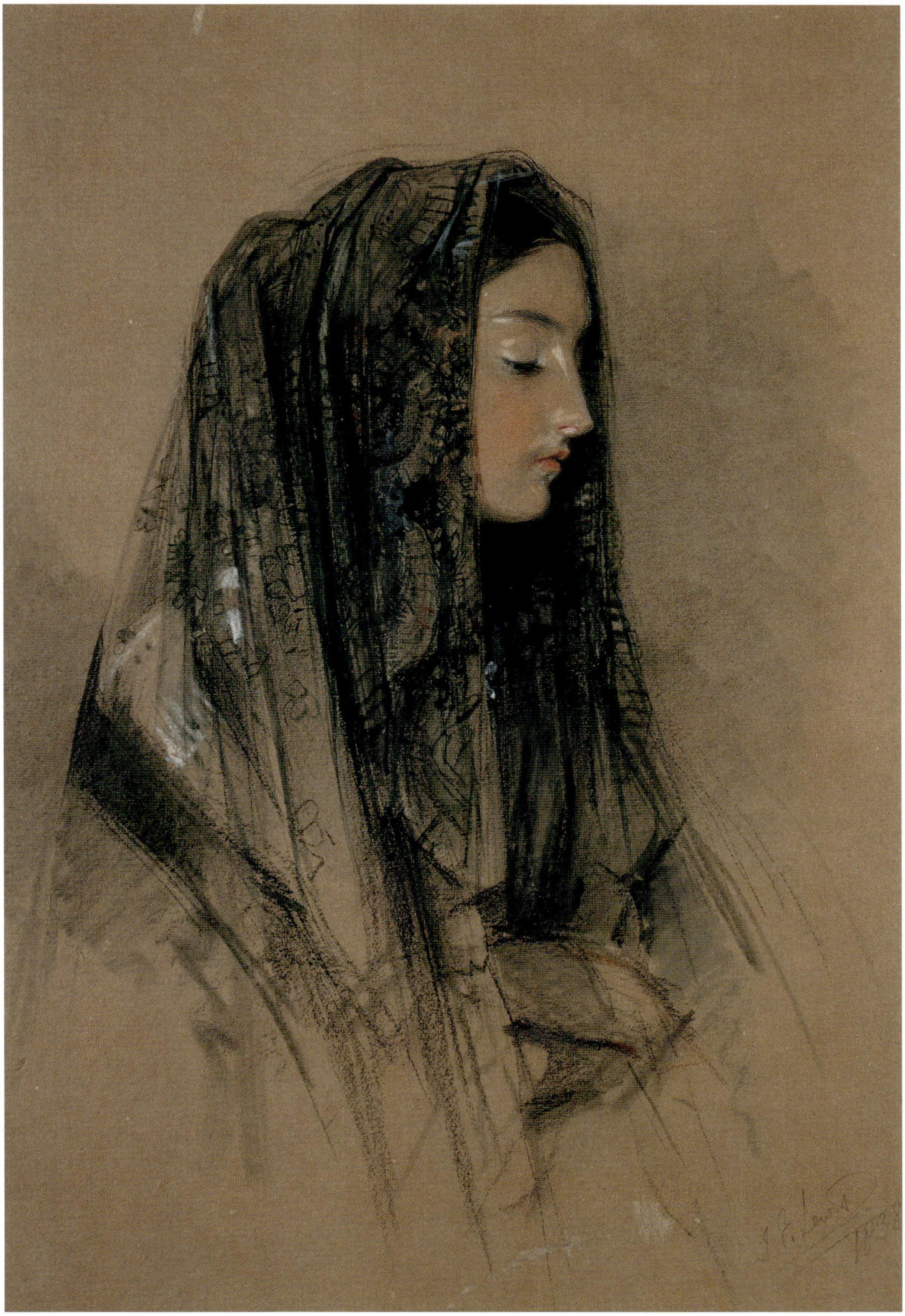

40

GEORGE FREDERIC WATTS 1817–1904
Lady Holland, c. 1843–5

Graphite on off-white paper
20 × 14.5 cm
Purchased (Hope Fund) with the assistance of The Art Fund, 2003
WA2003.196

LITERATURE: Bryant (2004) no. 5

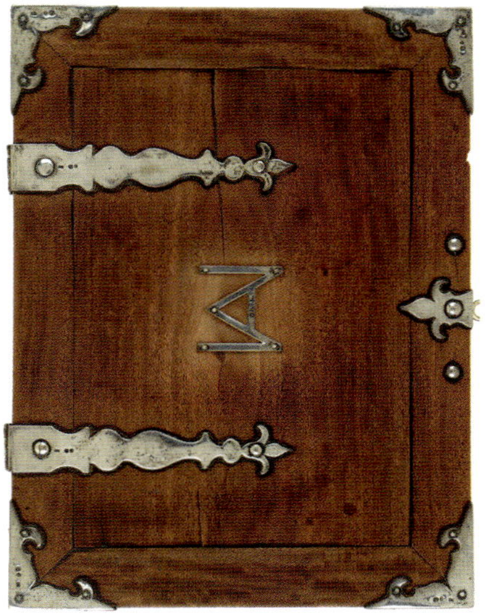

Fig. 39 | Folding frame for *Lady Holland*. Wooden frame and cover with silver mounts and hinges, the lock inscribed *MORDAN & CO. LONDON*; the initials MA in monogram in silver on the front cover hallmarked with the date letter *M* for 1847–8 and the maker's mark *IW*

Lady Mary Augusta (1812–1889) was the daughter of the 8th Earl of Coventry and his wife, Lady Mary Beauclerk, daughter of the 6th Duke of St Albans. She married Henry Fox (1802–1859) in 1833, and accompanied him on diplomatic postings to Vienna and Frankfurt. He served as Minister Plenipotentiary to the Court of the Grand Duke of Tuscany from 1839 to 1846, and succeeded as 4th Lord Holland in 1840. Lady Holland was largely brought up on the Continent and notoriously unconventional; she rode side-saddle, for example, long before it became fashionable. Noted for her tiny stature and small feet, she was described by one contemporary as 'under three feet in height, the very nicest little doll or plaything I ever saw'.[1]

Watts met the Hollands on 3 October 1843, having travelled to Florence to study fresco as one of the winners of a competition to decorate the Houses of Parliament. He soon went to stay with them at the Casa Feroni (now the Palazzo Amerighi) for a few days, and remained for three years. Lord Holland described him as 'full of genius and favourable ambition, without any of the jealous, niggling, detracting vanity of his brother artists'.[2] In addition to formal portraits of Lord and Lady Holland and a number of other notable personages in Florence, both local and visiting, Watts painted several informal portraits of his hostess. For a time, they were clearly very intimate. However, by May 1845 she was worried about propriety, and confessed to her husband that she had 'a strong and determined wish to break the spell, and make him feel that he is ever a welcome guest but not a constant and *necessary* intimate'.[3] Her husband agreed.

During this period of intimacy Watts also made a number of pencil portraits, showing Lady Holland reclining on a day bed or sewing with her feet up. This drawing is the most suggestive of the series; Lady Holland looks out rather coyly, her dress *décolleté* to the point of provocation. It was clearly a very private and cherished portrait, for the sitter exceptionally had it framed in a silver-mounted folding frame on her return to London. The other pencil portraits made at the Casa Feroni, which constitute the only works by an English artist comparable to Ingres's portrait drawings of British Grand Tourists in Rome, were uniformly framed and displayed in an ante-room at the top of the grand staircase at Holland House. Among them are Florentine grandees of the Corsini, Bentivoglio, and Aldobrandini families, the cosmopolitan Lady Dover, as well as Mme de Flahault, Edward Cheney, and the Marquess of Normanby. Unfortunately, most are now in ruinous condition.[4] CH

1. Quoted in Bryant (2004) p. 43.
2. Bryant (2004) p. 40.
3. Quoted in Gaja (1995) p. 20.
4. Private collection; for a list of those executed and those surviving, see Gaja (1995) pp. 116–17.

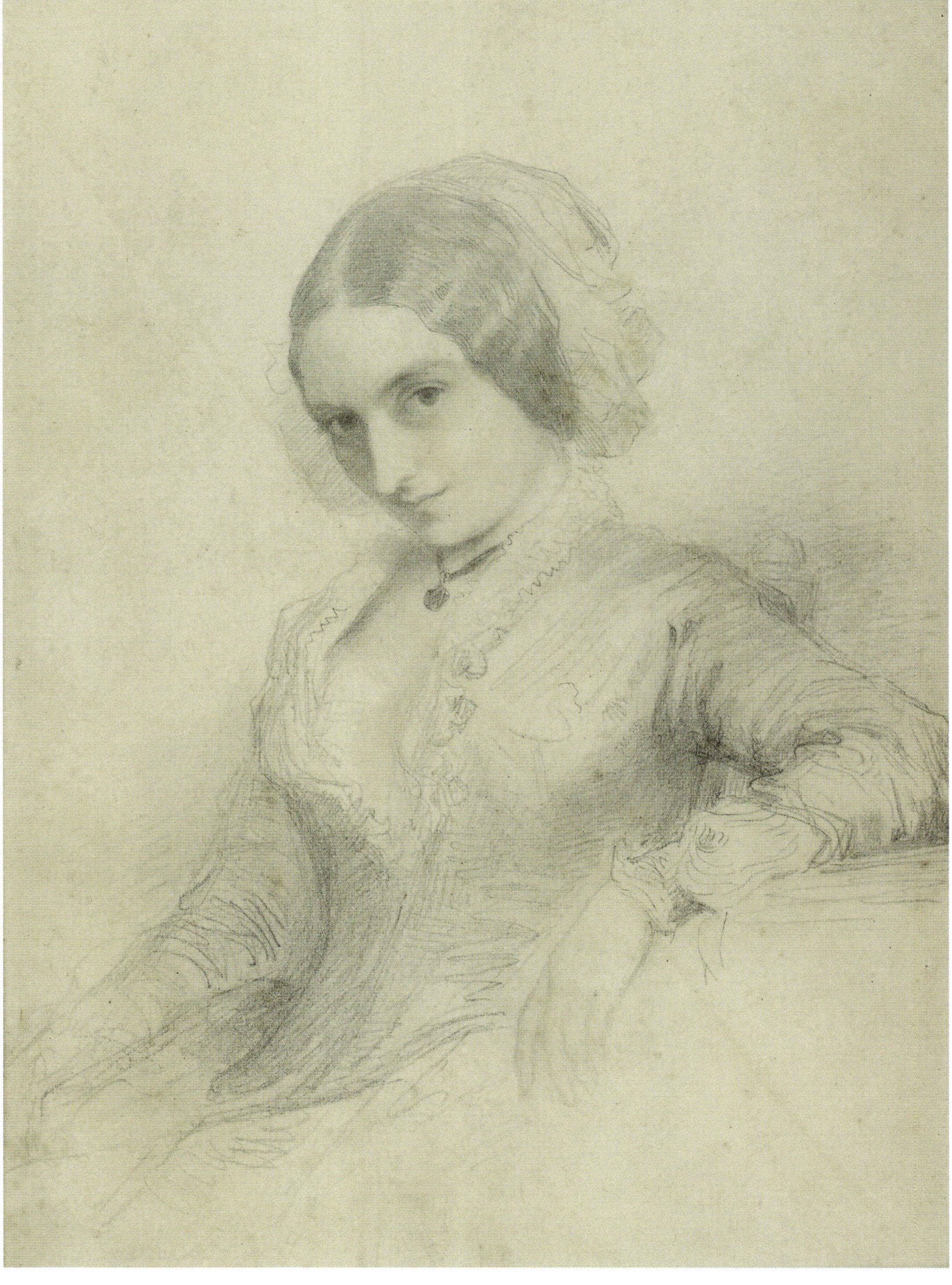

41

SIR DAVID WILKIE 1785–1841

Portrait of Sotiri, Dragoman of Mr Colquhoun, 1840

Watercolour and bodycolour with some oil, over red and black chalk on buff paper
47.5 × 32.7cm
Purchased, 1954
WA1954.53

LITERATURE: Brown (1985) no. 61

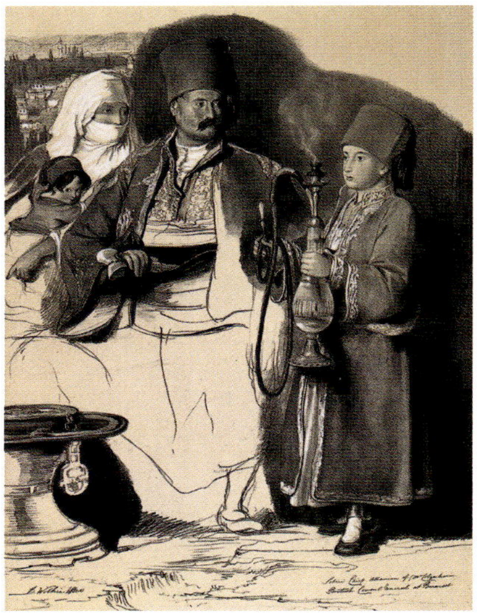

Fig. 40 | Joseph Nash (1808–1878) after David Wilkie (1785–1841), *Portrait of Sotiri, Dragoman of Mr Colquhoun, the British Consul at Bucharest*, from *Wilkie's Sketches in Turkey, Syria and Egypt*, plate 12, 1843. Lithograph. Wellcome Library, London, ICV no. 19680 © Wellcome Library, London

Like Lewis and Roberts, Wilkie was drawn to the Near East in search of unusual subjects to paint – in particular hoping to discover more historically authentic details and scenery for the illustration of biblical narratives, or 'Scripture subjects'. Setting out in August 1840 and travelling via Cologne, Munich and Vienna, he reached Constantinople in October 1840, but was delayed there by the war over Syria between the Turks and Egyptians. The Turks eventually triumphed with British assistance, but Syria remained closed to travellers, and Wilkie reached Jerusalem only in February 1841.

This enforced break gave Wilkie an opportunity to make several portraits while staying in the suburb of Pera (now Beyoğlu). According to Allan Cunningham, he made 53 drawings in Constantinople and six in Pera itself. Here we see Sotiri, an Albanian interpreter and guide in the service of Robert Colquhoun, British Consul-General at Bucharest. The female figure on the left is Wilkie's 'beautiful and accomplished' landlady in the European quarter of Pera, Madame Giuseppina. The young boy on the right is the son of Mustapha, janissary (or bodyguard) of John Cartwright, the Consul-General in Constantinople.[1] Wilkie notes in his journal that he dined with Cartwright on the evening this drawing was begun; Cartwright was frequently hospitable during Wilkie's stay, offering him Christmas dinner and sitting to him on numerous occasions in connection with a drawing for Mr Woodburn.[2] In the background can be seen the suburbs of the city, looking out over the 'Petits Champs des Morts', or Pera cemetery.

While Wilkie takes great painterly delight in improvising straight onto the paper the pure white draperies of Madame Giuseppina, he is clearly intent on recording the exact details of the more exotic accoutrements of the scene – perhaps intended for future compositions in oils: the gold embroidery on the red tunics, the rich blue of the fez tassels, the elaborate hookah pipe, and table in the foreground. Wilkie's studies remained preparatory works only, however, as his return trip ended with his sudden death off Malta. He was buried at sea in June 1841.

This watercolour was lithographed in Joseph Nash's edition of *Wilkie's Sketches in Turkey, Syria and Egypt, 1840 and 1841* (1843). Nash adds further detail to the table, the woman's hand, and to the child on the left, lending it a winsome smirk. In Nash's print the expression of the boy with the hookah becomes resolutely sullen, supporting Cunningham's opinion of the sitters as 'grave and suspicious'. In Wilkie's original, by contrast, they all have more kindly or open expressions.[3] CP

1. *Illustrated London News*, 18 March 1843, supplement, p. 197.
2. Cunningham (1843) III, pp. 330–67.
3. Cunningham (1843) III, p. 341.

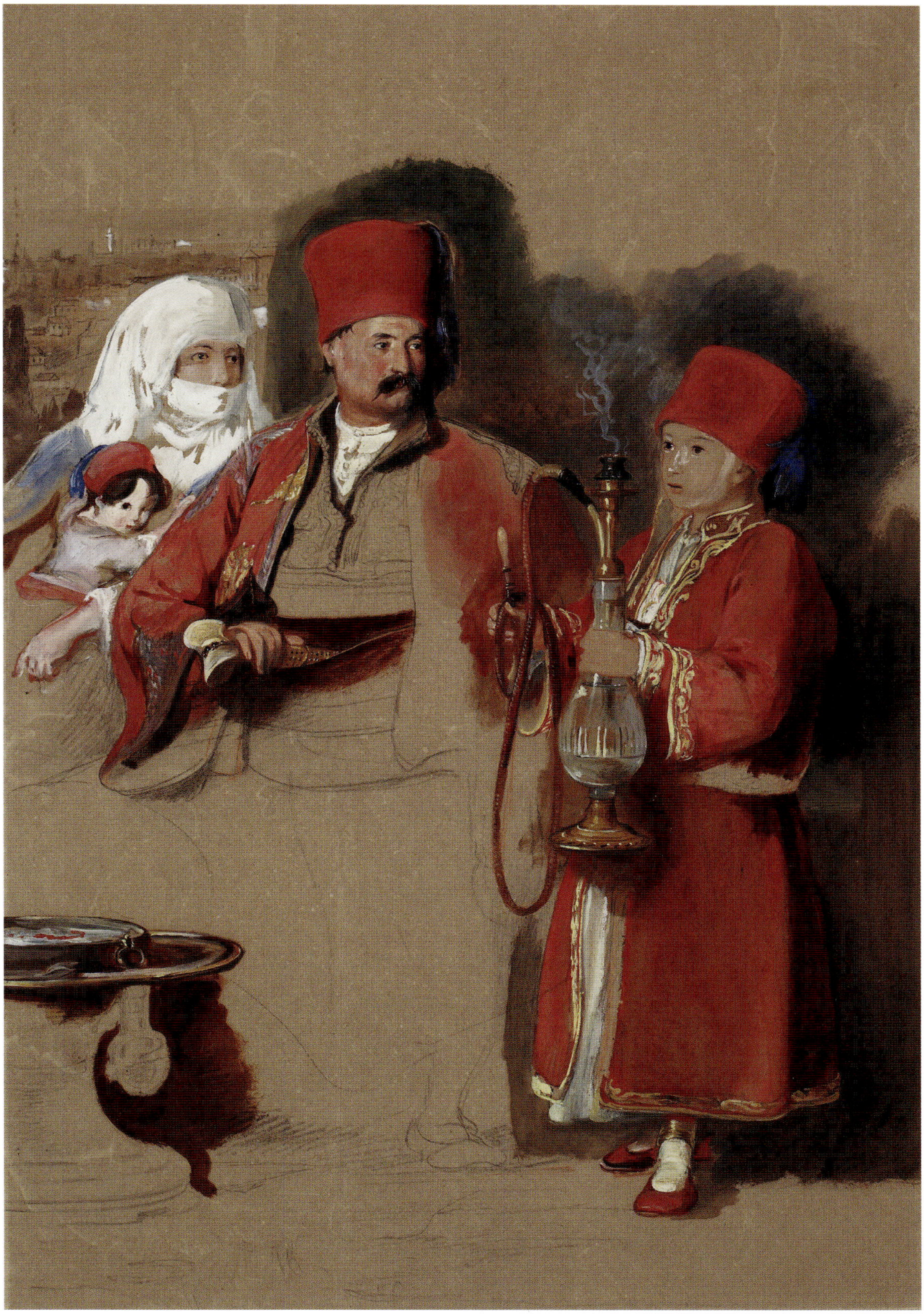

42

EDWARD LEAR 1812–1888

Constantinople from Ayoub, 4 September 1848

Pen and brown ink with watercolour over graphite on wove paper
33.5 × 52.5 cm
Inscribed: *Constantinople from Ayoub. 4 Sept 1848 39 A / many old tombs – turbans fallen off onto ground* and with colour and other notes
Bequeathed by Christopher Gandy, 2009
WA2011.5.17

Having established his reputation as one of the greatest natural history illustrators, Lear decided in 1837 to become a landscape painter, telling his employer John Gould that 'my eyes are so sadly worse, that no bird under an Ostrich shall I soon be able to see to do'.[1] With money from the Stanley and Hornby families, he travelled to Rome for the sake of his health. He remained there until 1848, making drawings for sale, and undertaking sketching expeditions in the Abruzzi and southern Calabria. He published two illustrated travel books, *Views in Rome and its Environs* (1841) and *Illustrated Excursions in Italy* (1846). He then intended to make a tour of the eastern Mediterranean to gather material which would provide the basis for oils and watercolours made in the studio. It was on the journey out to Greece that Lear began his characteristic working practice for topographical drawings, making pencil sketches during the day and inking them out in the evening, or at some later date. He also meticulously inscribed each drawing with the date, time, a running number for the particular tour, colour, and other notes.

Lear visited Constantinople at the invitation of Lady Canning, wife of the British ambassador. He arrived on 1 August, but fell ill, and spent a month convalescing at the ambassador's summer residence. He eventually moved into the Hôtel d'Angleterre in Pera on 1 September, and began an intensive exploration of the surroundings. On 4 September he explored the Muslim cemetery. It had been the burial place of Mohammed's lieutenant, Ayoub (Turkish Eyüp), who was killed in the siege of Constantinople in AD 670. By the nineteenth century it had become a vast area of tombs, and a popular place for walks and picnics. Lear wrote to his sister that 'the view of the whole city and Golden Horn from the cemetery above Ayoub's burial place amazes and delights me. The effect of the whole panorama as the sun sets is like a glorious vision'.[2] Lear made three very similar sketches, numbered 39A, 39B, and 40.[3] They are among his grandest and most complex topographical views, and served as the basis for finished watercolours, one made in 1856, while the central section of this drawing was the subject of an oil painting made for Aubrey de Vere Beauclerk.[4] CH

1. Quoted in Noakes (1985) p. 93.
2. Noakes (1968) pp. 68–71.
3. The former in the Houghton Library at Harvard; the latter sold, Christie's, 12 December 2007, lot 51.
4. Sold Sotheby's, 30 June 2005, lot 296; the latter repr. Hyman (1988) p. 15.

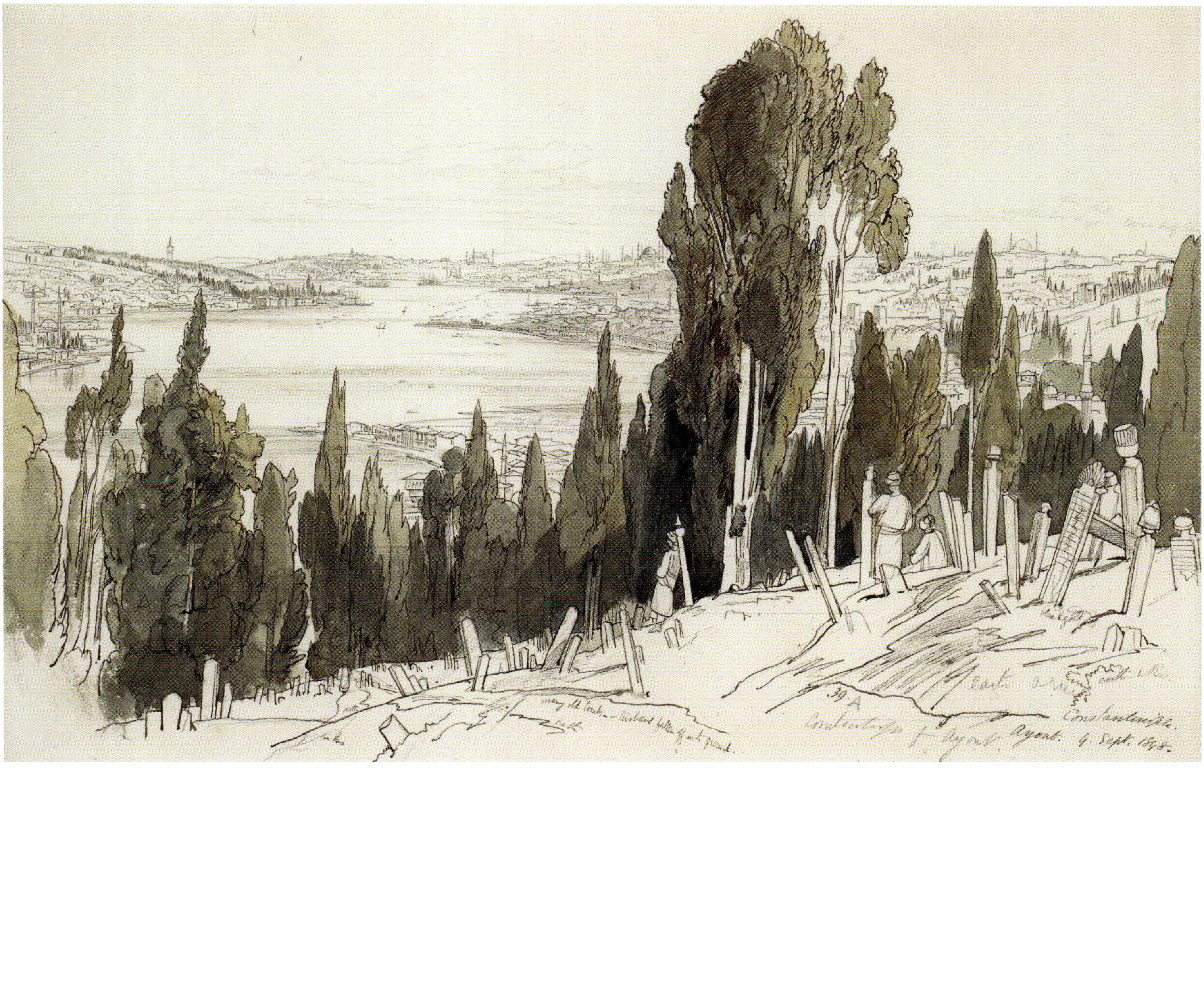

39. A
Constantinople.
Ayoub. 9. Sept. 1848.

43

JOHN FREDERICK LEWIS 1804–1876

Arabs with Camels by a Tomb in the Desert, 1858

Watercolour and bodycolour with black ink over graphite on paper
47.5 × 33.5 cm
Signed: *J.F.L. 1858*
Bequeathed by C. D. E. Fortnum, 1899
WA1899.CDEF.P19

Lewis arrived in Cairo in 1841 and remained there for ten years. He produced a large number of drawings of local scenes, including several studies of camels with their Bedouin drivers in the Sinai desert. Having begun his career as an animal painter, Lewis made careful observations of these strangely aloof creatures, which he later incorporated into some of his most famous works – including the *Frank Encampment* so praised by Ruskin (see fig. 15). According to Thackeray, whose account of visiting the artist in Cairo was published in 1846, Lewis's 'great pleasure of pleasures' was life in the desert with no crowds to jostle him.[1] His desert scenes were well received, encouraging him to produce several variations on this theme.

Lewis appears to have taken the foreground figure and camel of this study from a composition entitled *Halt in the Desert*, exhibited at the Society of Painters in Watercolours in 1854 (no. 248; now private collection). A review of this work praised the 'microscopic textures ... of the coats and trappings of the animals' as 'marvellous in execution'. The writer pointed to the way in which the 'minute pebbles which are strewn at the feet of the camels' relieve the eye as it gazes across the 'unbroken, arid plain' under a glaring sun.[2]

Ruskin encouraged viewers to examine the eyes of Lewis's camels with a magnifying glass to appreciate the depth of painting in them. Certainly enlargement of the foreground of this work reveals an extraordinary attention to detail.[3] The texture of the surface is dazzling in its almost abstract use of colour. A light cream is scumbled on with a broad dry brush, allowing the brown paper to show through, and splashes of pure blue, red, yellow, and white have also been added, probably using smaller sable brushes. The sky, by contrast, is barely modulated; a single shade of blue is used throughout to convey the intensity of the desert light.

Touches of black seem to have been inked in with a fine pen, especially in the tassels, the distant camels, and around the eye of the camel in the foreground. Parallel strokes of cream applied to the robe and to the legs of the camel link the two visually, and the picture plane as a whole is unified with accents of pure red; these draw the eye from the turban to the elaborate woven trappings, and to the robe and blankets of the distant group. As the Redgrave brothers put it, through his 'exquisite dexterity of handling' Lewis is able to combine 'the utmost finish without oppressing you with any sense of the labour of execution'.[4] CP

1. Selborne (2011) p. 78.
2. *Art Journal* (1854) p. 174.
3. *Academy Notes* (1856) in Ruskin (1903–12) XIV, p. 74.
4. Redgrave (1947) p. 412.

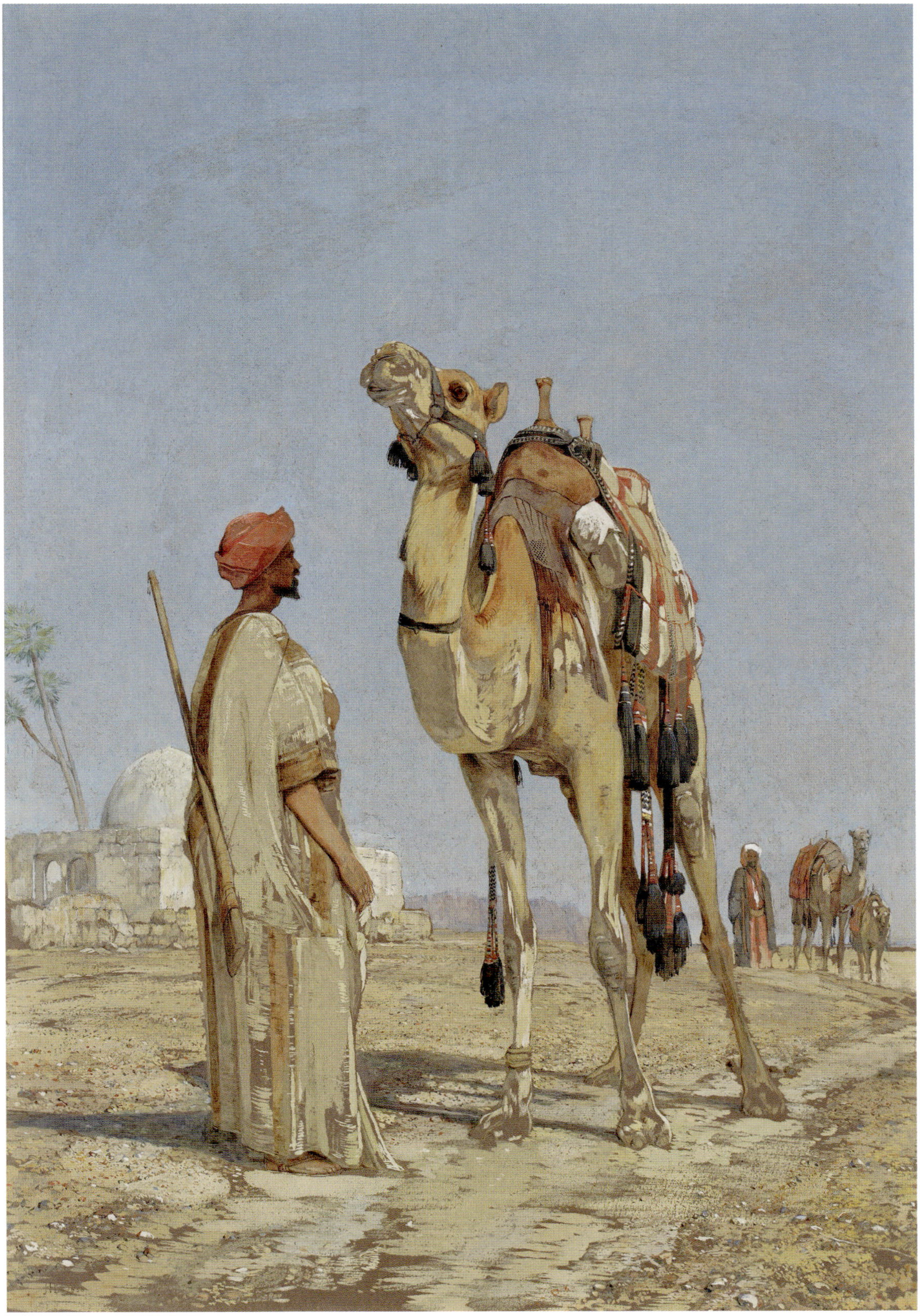

44

JOSEPH MALLORD WILLIAM TURNER 1775–1851

Walton Bridge, c. 1825–8

Watercolour and bodycolour and scratching out on paper
28.9 × 45.7 cm
Lent from a private collection, 2010
LI1160.1

LITERATURE: Wilton (1979) no. 824; Shanes (1979) no. 36

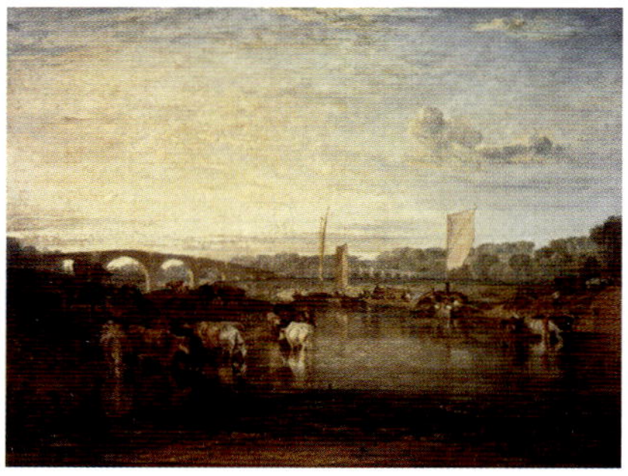

Fig. 41 | J. M. W. Turner (1775–1851), *Walton Bridges*, 1806–7. Oil on canvas. The Loyd Collection, on loan to the Ashmolean Museum, Oxford, LI197.3

In 1824 the London publisher Charles Heath commissioned from Turner a series of watercolours which would be published as engravings and eventually collected as *Picturesque Views in England and Wales*. The venture was fraught with difficulty, not only because of Turner's notorious demands over the quality of the engravers and his habit of retaining the best proofs for himself, but also due to prosaic financial difficulties with the publishers. Heath initially envisaged 120 watercolours, but Turner completed only about 100, of which 96 were engraved before the project was abandoned in 1838. Turner was paid £30 for each watercolour, the engravers £100 for each plate. The watercolours were based on sketches often made many years earlier, and the subjects chosen to tell a visual history of England and Wales in the late 1820s and early 1830s, a period of great social, political, agricultural, and industrial change. In June 1829 Heath exhibited 35 watercolours from the series at the Egyptian Hall, Piccadilly. Among them was *Walton Bridge*.

The bridge over the Thames at Walton had been a favourite subject for artists ever since Canaletto had painted the old wooden structure in 1754. This was replaced by an elegant and graceful stone bridge, which was opened in 1788 and survived until 1859. Turner had first sketched it in 1805, and painted two magisterial views exhibited separately in Turner's Gallery in 1806 and 1807. One shows the view looking downstream, bought by Sir John Leicester; the other, looking in the opposite direction, was bought by the Earl of Essex.[1] They show Turner at his most poetic and idyllic, the Arcadian landscape in England bathed in Claudean light.

In his watercolour for *England and Wales*, Turner chose the view looking upstream, the first arch of the bridge seemingly echoed by the second in the distance. Under a vivid and windswept sky of intense purple clouds, life on the river continues. On the far bank, a team of horses strain, while numerous figures are at work and play in a barge and other boats. In the foreground a young man stands in the river fishing; to his right a huge flock of sheep is driven to drink by their shepherd. Farther upstream, a woman carries a heavy load on her shoulders. No longer does Walton Bridge seem to be transplanted from Italy; it is a point of reference for one of the most evocative of all the views of England in this series, in a perfect state of preservation. CH

1. Fig. 39; Wilton (1979) no. P60; and National Gallery of Victoria, Melbourne; Wilton (1979) no. P63.

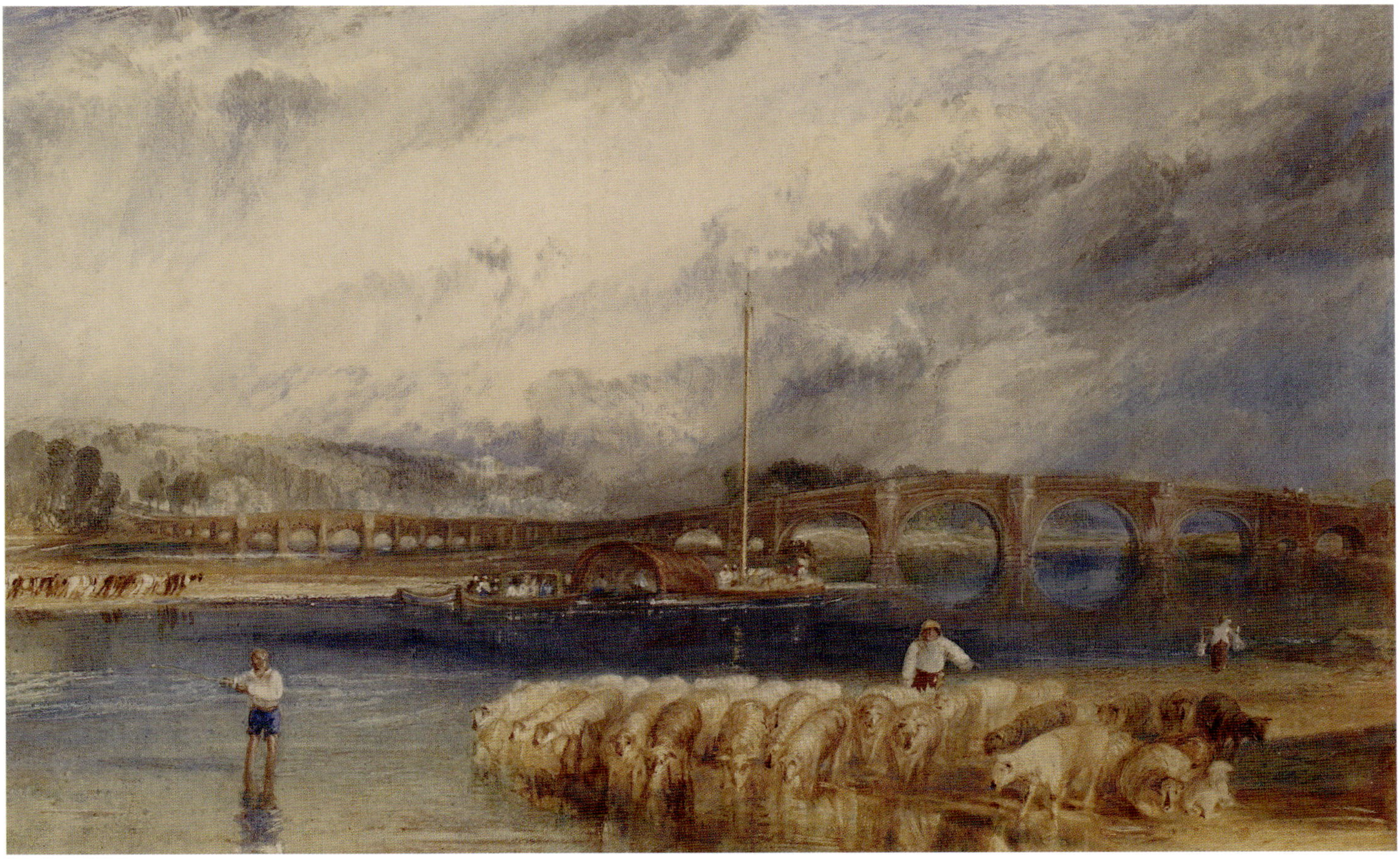

45

JOSEPH MALLORD WILLIAM TURNER 1775–1851

Christ Church College, Oxford, 1832–3

Watercolour and bodycolour over graphite with scratching out, on paper
29.5 × 41.7 cm
Purchased (B. D. H. Miller Bequest Fund) with the assistance of The Art Fund (including a contribution from the Wolfson Foundation), the MGC/V&A Purchase Grant Fund, and donations in memory of Evelyn Joll, 2002
WA2002.28

LITERATURE: Shanes (1979) no. 62; Wilton (1979) no. 853; Harrison (2000) pp. 86–91

When he came to consider suitable subjects of Oxford for his *Picturesque Views in England and Wales*, Turner revisited the city, probably in September–October 1830, as part of the tour of the Midlands recorded in his 'Kenilworth' sketchbook. He made sketches of the High Street and Magdalen Bridge, as well as a new view of Christ Church from St Aldates. Unlike Turner's watercolours of this college in the 1790s, which generally incorporate the distinctive shape of Tom Tower into picturesque compositions of trees and meadows, cottages or gardens, this rather formal view shows the college from the road to the south-west.

The finished watercolour is full of excitement and incident. The afternoon sunshine bathes the great front range of Christ Church in a golden light, while a pair of dons walk resolutely past a table loaded with prizes, their minds on more elevated matters. The serenity of the east side of St Aldate's contrasts strongly with the activity in the middle of the road and, especially, with the demolition taking place opposite. This provides a highly topical reference, which Turner would have observed on his sketching tour. Since the passing of the Mileways Act in 1771, it had been thought desirable to widen St Aldate's and provide a more imposing entrance to Pembroke College. This could only be achieved by demolishing Cardinal Wolsey's almshouses, part of the original foundation of Christ Church. Eventually, in 1829, the two colleges agreed to proceed. Turner shows the demolition in full swing, with men up ladders or manoeuvring huge blocks of stone, and a great mess of rubble. In the middle of the road, men struggle with a waggon, while in front of them, a group of carefree boys fly kites. On the right, Turner has introduced a note of humour, as two dogs sniff each other suspiciously. The watercolour was one of nearly 80 for *England and Wales* exhibited by Moon, Boys and Graves in 1833, and the engraving was published in the following year.

A few years later, Turner considered including a second view of Oxford in the series, and made fresh studies of the High Street and other subjects in his 'Oxford' sketchbook. This resulted in the finished watercolour *Merton College*, which could almost be described as a pendant to *Christ Church College*, though it was never engraved.[1] CH

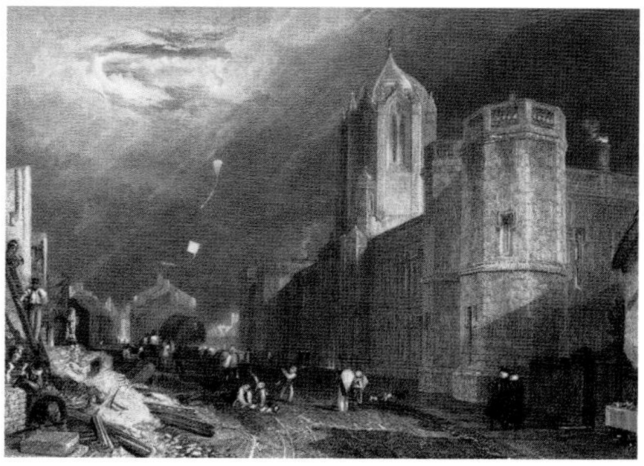

Fig. 42 | James Redaway (1797–1858) after J. M .W. Turner (1775–1851), *Christ Church College, Oxford*, 1834. Engraving. Ashmolean Museum, Oxford, WA2002.29

1. Shanes (1979) no. 87; Wilton (1979) no. 887.

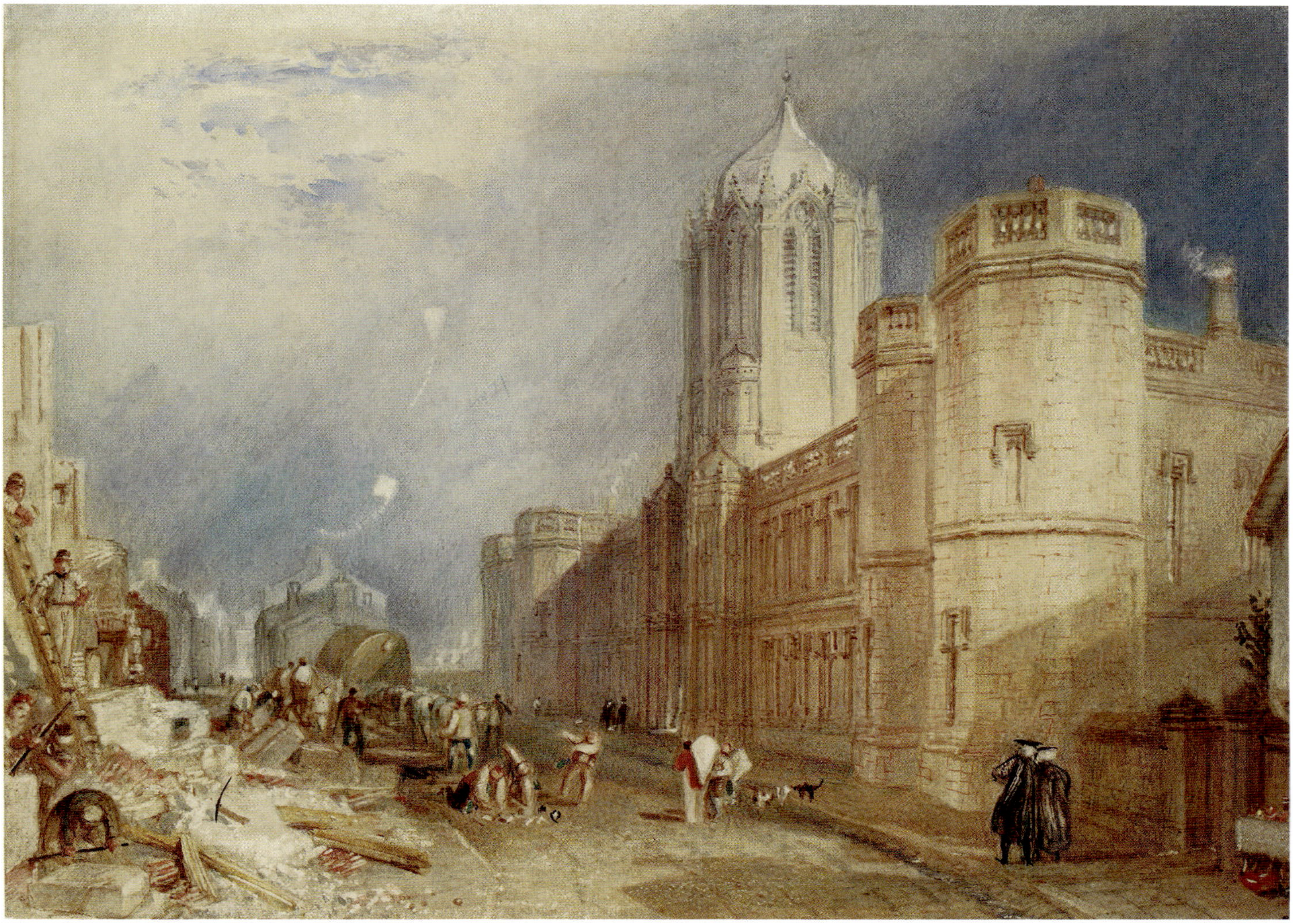

46

JOSEPH MALLORD WILLIAM TURNER 1775–1851

Blois, c. 1826–30

Watercolour with bodycolour and pen and brown and black ink on blue paper
13.5 × 18.3 cm
Presented by John Ruskin, 1861
WA1861.32

LITERATURE: Herrmann (1968) no. 42; Wilton (1979) no. 933; Warrell (1997) pp. 133–9, 229

At the end of his long tour of north-west France in 1826, Turner travelled up the Loire. He spent about a fortnight on the journey from Nantes to Orleans in early October, sketching as he went. In addition to the usual sketchbooks, he took for the first time a number of sheets of blue paper made at the De Montalt mill near Bath. Each sheet could be folded in 16 and provided a mid-tone for Turner's compositions in both pencil and watercolour; they were thus ideal for the purpose. The tour was rather hurried, so Turner concentrated on the main riverside towns, and did not venture far from the river itself.

As he approached Blois from the west, Turner would have been reminded of a similar view he had copied over 30 years earlier.[1] Since there are no surviving sketches for the present watercolour of *Blois*, it is generally assumed to have been begun on the spot. The disposition of the town on the hilly riverbanks meant that, in order to depict the principal buildings distinct from each other, it was necessary to take quite a distant view, which in reality resulted in the details becoming unclear. As Warrell has noted, it is a measure of Turner's mastery that he has managed to combine detail with accurate topography in such a small composition. The view is dominated by the early eighteenth-century bridge constructed to the design of the architect Jacques Gabriel (1666–1742), with the obelisk on the east (upstream) side. Turner shows only 9 of the 11 arches of the bridge, and adjusts it to be seen frontally, rather than to the side, which would have been more accurate. On the far right is the church of St Saturnin, and on the left the white facade of the famous Château. Below this, moving right, are the spire and towers of the abbey church of St Laumer, the cathedral, and the bishop's palace, also designed by Gabriel.

Like others from the journey, including views of the bridge and château at Blois, this watercolour was worked up in London to be engraved. Twenty-one plates were published by Charles Heath as *Turner's Annual Tour, 1833*. The collection was received in January 1833 as 'the most extraordinary collection of landscapes ever published in a body'.[2] Most of the published watercolours were acquired by John Ruskin, who gave them to his old University in 1861. In a long letter to his friend Sir Henry Acland, of March 1861, he said that Blois was one of two drawings which 'are full of repentirs and are entirely bad'. However, in his Slade lectures for 1871, Ruskin acknowledged that the Loire drawings were chiefly notable for 'their infallible decision' and 'their extreme modesty in colour'.[3] They are among the most miraculous of Turner's works, detailed, atmospheric, suggestive, and tiny. CH

1. Repr. Warrell (1997) p. 15.
2. Warrell (1997) p. 17.
3. Herrmann (1968) p. 29.

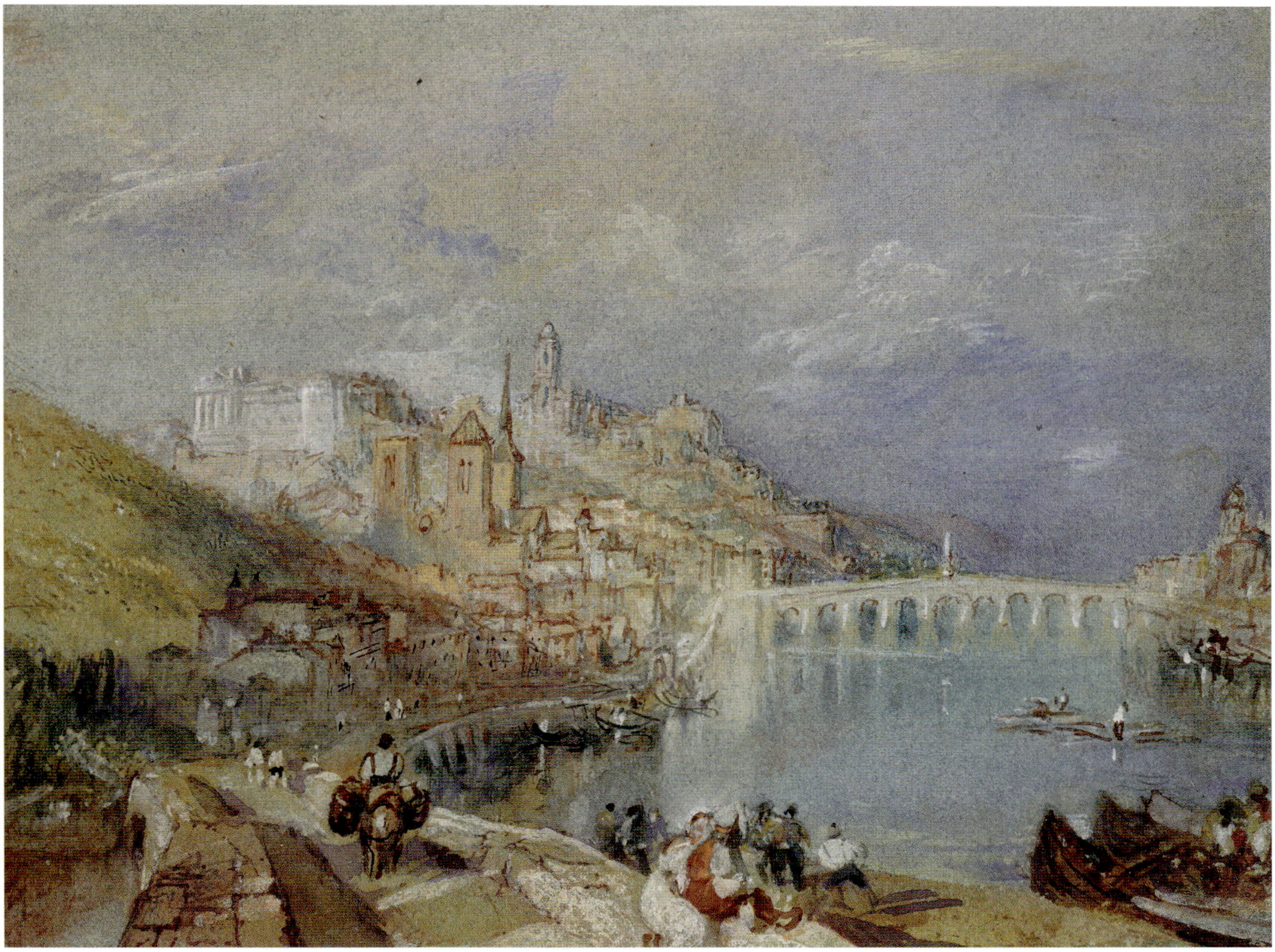

47

PETER DE WINT 1784–1849

View of Iffley from the River, 1840–1

Watercolour with scratching out on paper
33.2 × 52.5 cm
Deposited by the Delegates of the Oxford University Press, 1850
WA1850.89

LITERATURE: Petter (1974) p. 93; Smith (1982) p. 184; Lord (2007) no. 60

For Ruskin and many of his contemporaries, the art of Peter de Wint was quintessentially English. He

despises all rules of composition, hates Old Masters and humbug – synonymous terms with him – never was abroad in his life, never sketches anything but pig-styes and haystacks, and is a thorough-going John Bull of an artist in all respects. But, to make amends for all this, he is a most ardent lover of truth, hardly ever paints except from nature, attends constantly and effectually to colour and tone, and produces sketches of … miraculous truth of atmosphere, colour and light'.[1]

Like his near-contemporary David Cox, De Wint was a long-standing and prolific member of the Society of Painters in Watercolours, exhibiting almost annually from 1814 until his death. He became well known for his riverside landscapes and harvesting scenes, though his range was much wider, taking in picturesque views in Wales and the Lake District, as well as architectural subjects and ruins. He was also a prolific illustrator of topographical books, including W. B. Cooke's *Thames Scenery* (1814–29) and George Cooke's *Views in London and its Vicinity* (1834).

It was no doubt through such work that De Wint came to the notice of the Delegates of the Clarendon Press in Oxford. After the difficulties over the later watercolours by J. M. W. Turner for the Oxford Almanack (cat. 32), they had been rather unadventurous in their choice of artists. Most commissions had been given to modest watercolour painters, including Henry O'Neill, Charles Wild, and Frederick Mackenzie. Perhaps as a result of representations from the engravers, they also seem to have preferred small drawings in monochrome washes roughly the size of the prospective engraving, rather than full watercolours.

In January 1834 the Delegates paid De Wint £83 5s. 0d. for an unspecified number of watercolours. Six of his small monochromes were reproduced in the Almanack between 1833 and 1855, featuring views of Oxford from the surrounding hills, or prominent landmarks and bridges over the Thames. In addition, two large watercolours were engraved. It has been reasonably suggested that these resulted from a separate, unrecorded commission, this *View of Iffley from the River* for the Oxford Almanack of 1841, and a *View of Oxford from the West*, published in 1852. Here, the village of Iffley, about a mile downstream from Oxford, is seen on a windy day, nestling among trees and dominated by the tower of its Romanesque church. A horse tows a barge along the river, accompanied by two men and a dog. The watercolour is notable for the emphatic scratching out to highlight the effect of the wind as it blows across the landscape. CH

1. Quoted by Jim Cheshire in Lord (2007) p. 60.

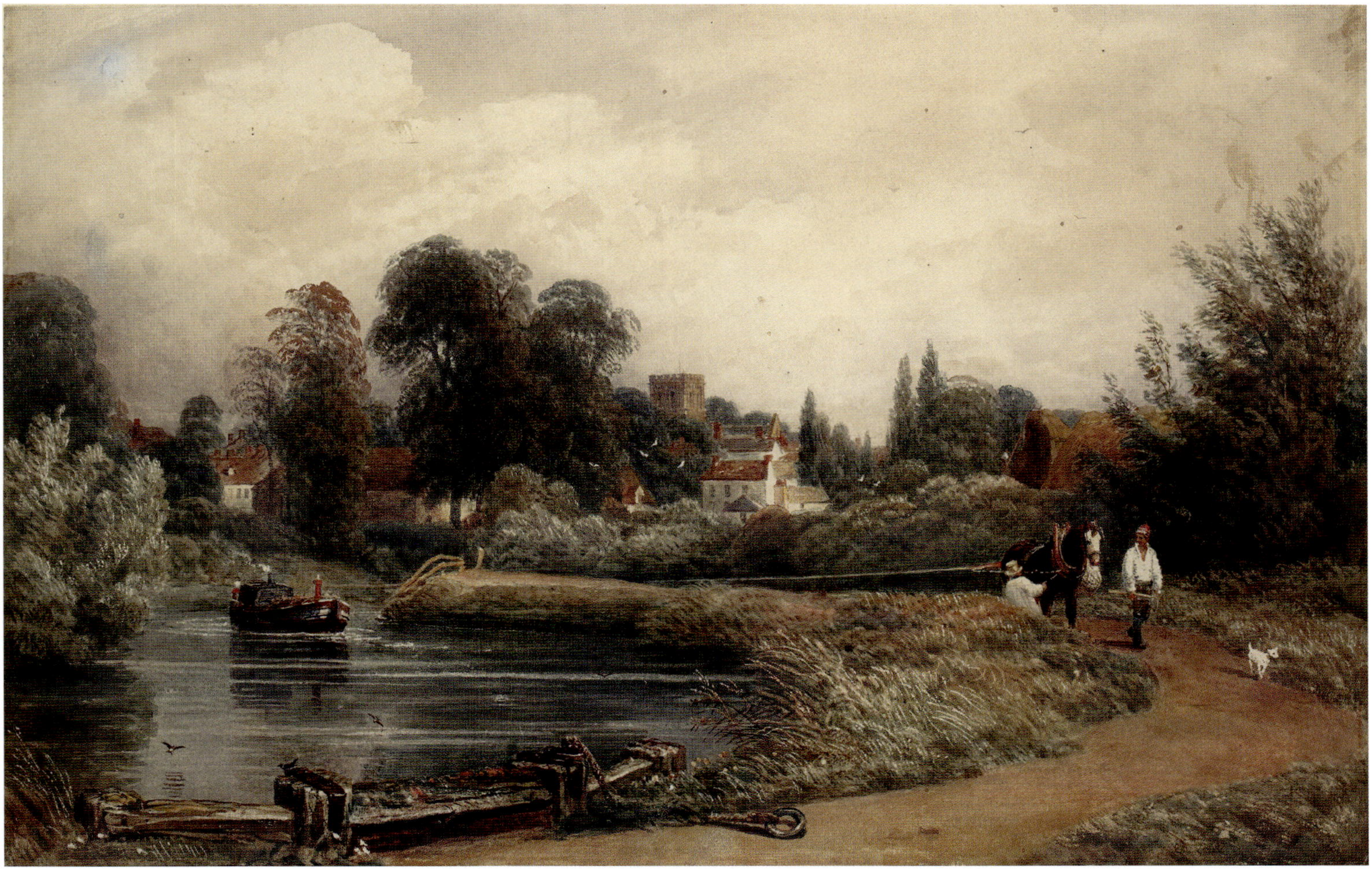

48

WILLIAM TURNER OF OXFORD 1789–1862

Stonehenge: Stormy Day, 1846

Watercolour over graphite on paper
45.7 × 67.8 cm
Inscribed *verso*: *No. 5 / Stonehenge - Stormy day / W. Turner / 16. St John's Street./ Oxford*
Purchased, 1961
WA1961.39

LITERATURE: Wilcox and Titterington (1984) no. 69

Since the Middle Ages, the monument of Stonehenge on Salisbury Plain has attracted the interest of antiquaries and artists, many of whom have speculated over its origins and function.[1] From Thomas Girtin in the early 1790s onwards, Stonehenge became associated with the highly Romantic motif of the thunderstorm, a symbol of prehistory almost as old as the Earth. Among Girtin's most notable successors was J. M. W. Turner, who, in a watercolour for his *Picturesque Views in England and Wales*, portrayed the stones at the heart of a cataclysm, with a shepherd and much of his flock struck down by lightning, and his sheepdog howling dejectedly.[2] A few years later, in 1836, John Constable sent a large watercolour of Stonehenge to the Royal Academy, explaining in the catalogue that 'the mysterious monument of Stonehenge ... carries you back beyond all historical record into the obscurity of a totally unknown period'. In a note to a plate in his earlier *English Landscape Scenery*, Constable had gone so far as to claim that 'no kind of effect could be introduced too striking or too impressive to portrait it; and among the various appearances of the elements, we naturally look to the grander phenomena of nature as according best with the character of such a scene'.

William Turner of Oxford exhibited a number of distant views of Stonehenge in the late 1830s, but it was generally agreed that a much closer treatment was more effective. Indeed, as early as 1798, William Gilpin, in his *Observations on the Western Parts of England*, noted that

Stonehenge, at a distance, appeared only as a diminutive object. Standing on so vast an area as Salisbury Plain, it was lost in the immensity around it. As we approached, it gained more respect ... but when we arrived on the spot, it appeared astonishing beyond conception ... it is not the elegance of the work, but the grandeur of the idea that strikes us.

This large watercolour, exhibited at the Society of Painters in Watercolours in 1846, is one of Turner's most magisterial. After his tour of Scotland in 1838, he had mastered not only the picturesque pastoral landscape around Oxford, but also the sublime scenery beloved by his namesake. Indeed, it is clear that his watercolour of Stonehenge pays homage to that of J. M. W. Turner, and politely suggests that a less extreme composition might be equally imposing. The flock of sheep, the shepherd, and his dog are integral components of the landscape. So are the sea birds circling above, picked out against the lowering sky, with a shower of rain approaching from the right, and a clearing in the clouds directly above the monument. CH

1. See Pitts (2007)
2. Private collection; Wilton (1979) no. 811.

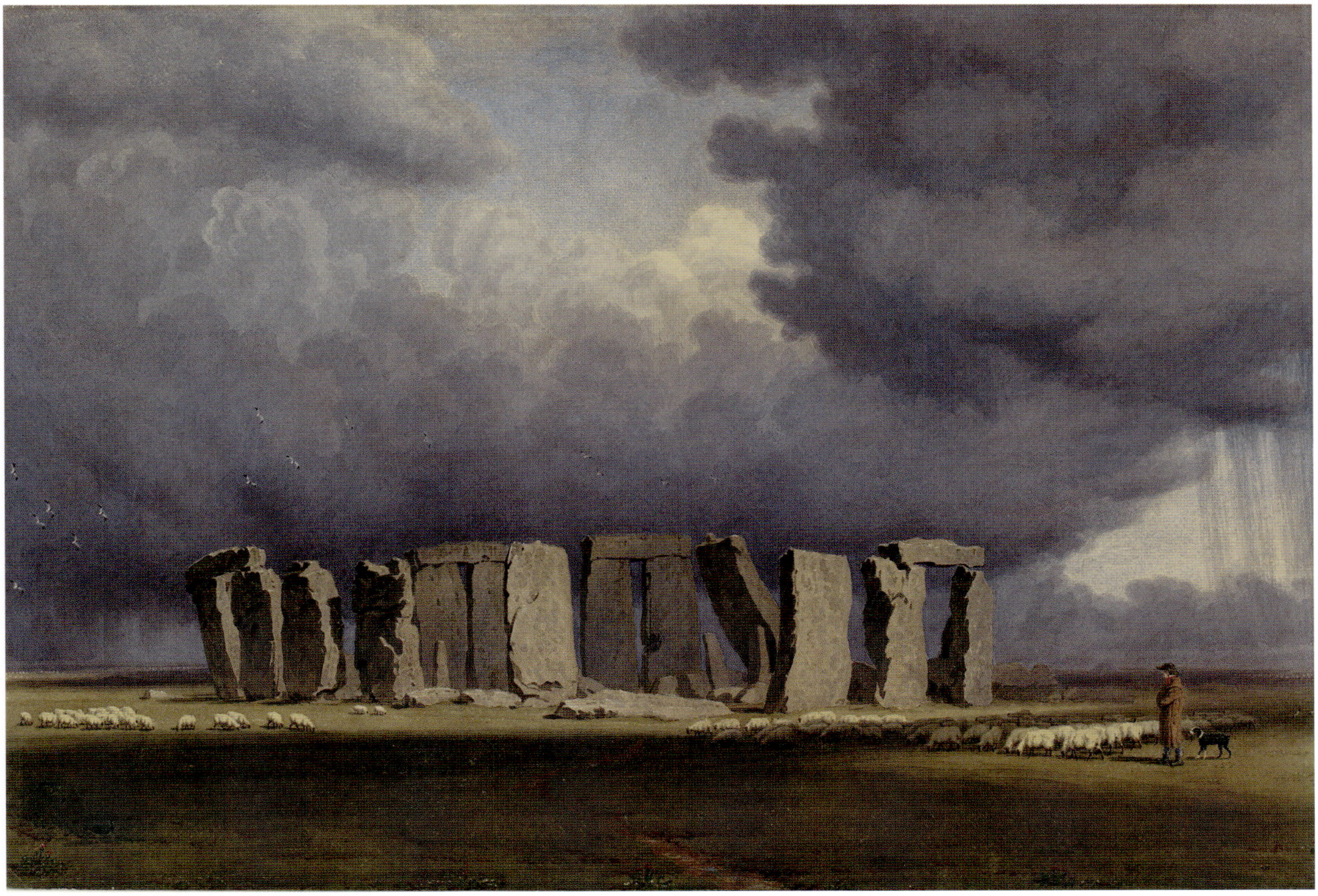

49

WILLIAM TURNER OF OXFORD 1789–1862

Waterlilies in the Cherwell, 1850s

Watercolour and bodycolour on paper
38 × 58.4 cm
Bequeathed by Miss Annie Symonds, 1938
WA1938.34

Ruskin apostrophised William Turner of Oxford as 'this patient and unassuming master'.[1] Born near Burford, he was brought up by an uncle who purchased the Manor House and parish of Shipton-on-Cherwell in 1804. Turner studied in London with John Varley between 1804 and 1807, joined the Society of Painters in Watercolours in 1808, and settled in Oxford in about 1810–11. Thereafter he lived modestly, became a popular drawing master, and exhibited in London every year. Apart from views of Oxford and the surrounding countryside and villages, Turner's range extended to the mountainous regions of the British Isles. His tour of Scotland in 1838 provided him with subjects for the rest of his life.

Turner's first exhibit at the Society of Painters in Watercolours, in 1808 had been *On the River Charwell* [*sic*], *Oxfordshire* and he was to show several pictures of this title over the course of his career. In 1837 his view of *The River Cherwell, near Woodstock, Oxfordshire* was appended with the line, 'Know that the lilies have spread their bells … ' from Felicia Hemans's 'Water-Lilies: A Fairy Song'. This sentimental lyric exhorts elves to use the water lilies as boats, making music as they sail, but being careful of the midday heat, since 'the life of the lily may not be long'.

It would seem that Turner enjoyed the association of water lilies both with the supernatural and with intimations of mortality, for he appended various lines from Mrs Hemans's poem to later versions of this subject exhibited in 1846 (bought by the Duke of Sutherland) and in 1849 (given to the Society of Painters in Watercolours after Turner's death).[2] In 1851 he produced yet another version, the title supplemented with the line, *'Conscious of the earliest beam' Mrs C Smith*. Charlotte Smith's poem 'The Horologe of the Fields' extols the beauties of nature and the natural manner of telling the time, not with an expensive clock, but by looking at flowers such as the *Nymphaea* or water lily. Turner exhibited a final version of the subject in 1854.

The present example probably dates from the 1850s. It shares with other late versions a close examination of water lilies in the calm waters of the Cherwell, shaded from the heat of the sun by the arching boughs of willow overhead. The work's high colouring, and attentive, almost obsessive, observation of nature, including a moorhen and a kingfisher, give it an almost hallucinatory quality, appropriate to the texts that Turner associated with the subject. CH

1. Quoted in Herrmann (1966) p. 246.
2. Wilcox and Titterington (1984) no. 75.

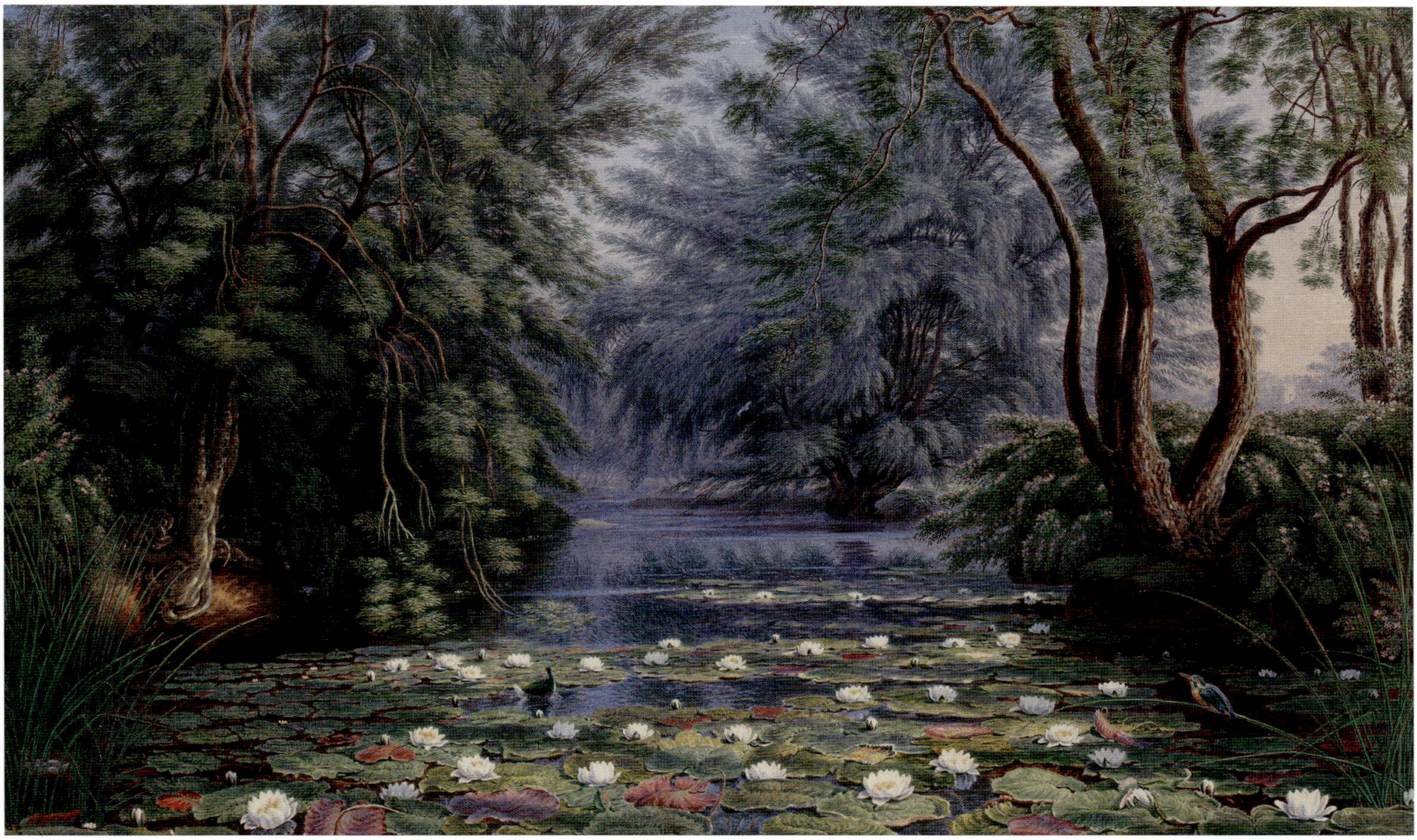

50

DAVID COX 1783–1859

Rhyl Sands, c. 1854–5

Charcoal and watercolour on rough paper
26.7 × 36.9 cm
Lent from a private collection
L12224.3

Cox first painted panoramic beach scenes in France in the early 1830s, perhaps inspired by J. M. W. Turner's *Calais Sands, Low Water, Poissards Collecting Bait*, shown at the Royal Academy in 1830 (now in the National Gallery), which in turn was a homage to the Anglo-French artist Richard Parkes Bonington (1801–1828). As Cox's son noted, such compositions 'attracted him from the opportunity of displaying space over sands with bright figures'.[1] Soon afterwards, in July 1834, Cox visited Morecambe Bay; the sight of travellers crossing Lancaster and Ulverston Sands at low tide provided material for numerous watercolours and oils, characterised by low horizons and vast skies in different weather.

During his annual summer sketching tour in 1842, Cox once again explored North Wales. He already knew the area well, having, among other projects, provided illustrations to Thomas Roscoe's *Wanderings and Excursions in North Wales* (1835). On this occasion he spent a day or two making studies of Rhyl Sands, which provided the basis for one of his exhibits at the Society of Painters in Watercolours in the following year. More important, however, were his two visits to Rhyl in 1850 and, especially, in 1854.

Cox had suffered a stroke in 1853, and was ostensibly on holiday with his son in August 1854. He went armed with some sheets of what he called 'Scotch' paper, which he used to produce some of his most informal and luminous sketches. He had discovered this paper, which Peter Bower has established was made as wrapping paper at Langley Mill, County Durham, in 1836, and was so taken with it that he bought a whole ream, which cost £11 and weighed 280 pounds.[2]

This watercolour is one of a group of sketches made on the spot in August 1854. The horizon is higher than in other representations of Rhyl Sands, dividing the composition exactly in half. On the right are very brief indications of holidaymakers and bathing machines in front of the boarding houses that lined the seafront. Otherwise, in a few apparently haphazard strokes of charcoal, and thinly applied watercolour in blue-grey and pinkish-brown, the artist has successfully evoked a windy day on a timeless anonymous coast. Such a sketch was made for its own sake, and not for sale. It is tempting to view these late works as precursors of Boudin and the Impressionists, but they are more appropriately considered as the personal meditations of an elderly artist in ill-health. CH

1. Quoted in Wilcox (2008) p. 179.
2. Bower in Wilcox (2008) p. 101.

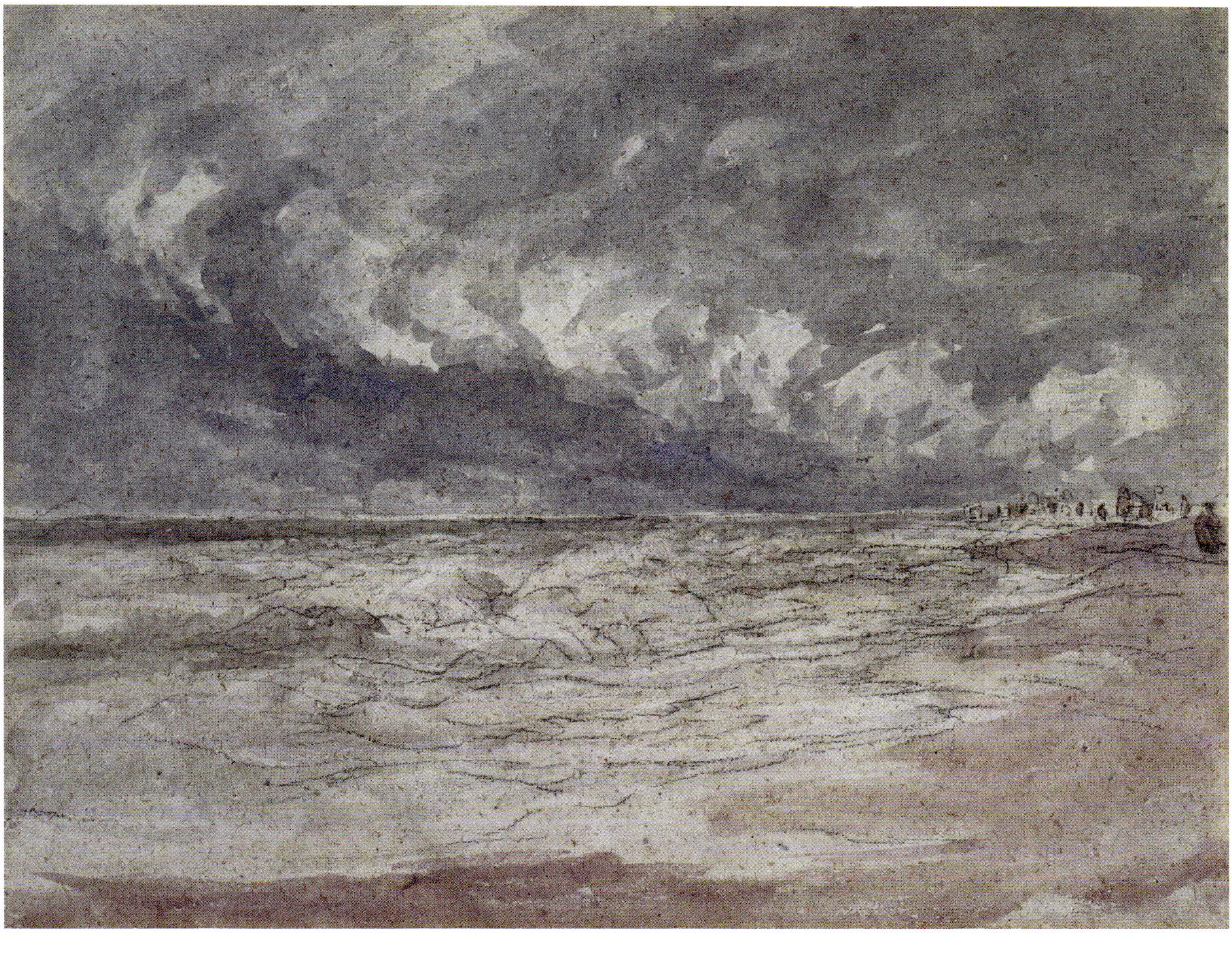

51

SAMUEL PALMER 1805–1881

Tintagel Castle: Approaching Rain, 1848–9

Watercolour and bodycolour, mixed in parts with gum arabic, over indications in graphite and black chalk on paper
30 × 44.4 cm
Presented by Percy Moore Turner, 1942
WA1942.27

LITERATURE: Brown (1983) no. 31; Lister (1988) no. 453; Vaughan, Barker, Harrison (2005) no. 122

Following his return from an extended honeymoon and study trip in Italy in 1839, Palmer found it difficult to reconcile the intense light and infinite distances of the Italian countryside with the familiar landscapes of England and Wales. For a few years he continued to send oil paintings to the Royal Academy and the British Institution, but it became clear that watercolour now suited him better. Following his election in 1843 as an Associate of the Society of Painters in Watercolours, Palmer regularly sent the maximum eight works to their annual exhibition. His main income at this period was derived from teaching.

Palmer had first visited the West Country in 1834, when he made sketches in North Devon which provided him with the basis for a number of oil paintings.[1] In the summer of 1848 he made a further tour of Devonshire and Dorset which extended to Cornwall. He wrote to his old friend and fellow artist, Edward Calvert (1799–1883) that

The north Cornish coast is very wild, but the country above treeless and desolate. There is one most curious place on the peaks of two cliffs, which are gradually tumbling by huge fragments into the sea, viz. Tintagel Castle, the birth-place and palace of King Arthur. It was a mouldered ruin in the days of Henry the Eighth. Some turreted fragments remain which are very quaint and strange.[2]

Unusually, Palmer made a large sketch of the scene in chalk and watercolour (now in the British Museum). The ruins sit on top of a massive rock formation, facing a second outcrop, the chasm between cluttered with boulders. Under the castle is a deep cavern.

This study formed the basis for the finished watercolour, shown at the Society of Painters in Watercolours in 1849. The viewpoint has shifted slightly to the right and further back, so that the castle is now almost in the centre of the composition, with a waggon bearing a huge anchor travelling along a road on the right. In the foreground, gulls fly disconsolately above the mast and wreckage of a sailing vessel, while goats forage for vegetation up a path on the left. An approaching rainstorm adds drama to the lighting. This has justifiably been described as one of the greatest of Palmer's watercolours. Its highly wrought technique of stippling evokes the complete assimilation of the ruins with the geological formation of the rocky promontory. CH

1. Notably *Scene from Lee, North Devon* (Fitzwilliam Museum); Lister (1988) no. 219; Vaughan, Barker, Harrison (2005) no. 97.
2. Quoted in Vaughan, Barker, Harrison (2005) p. 201.

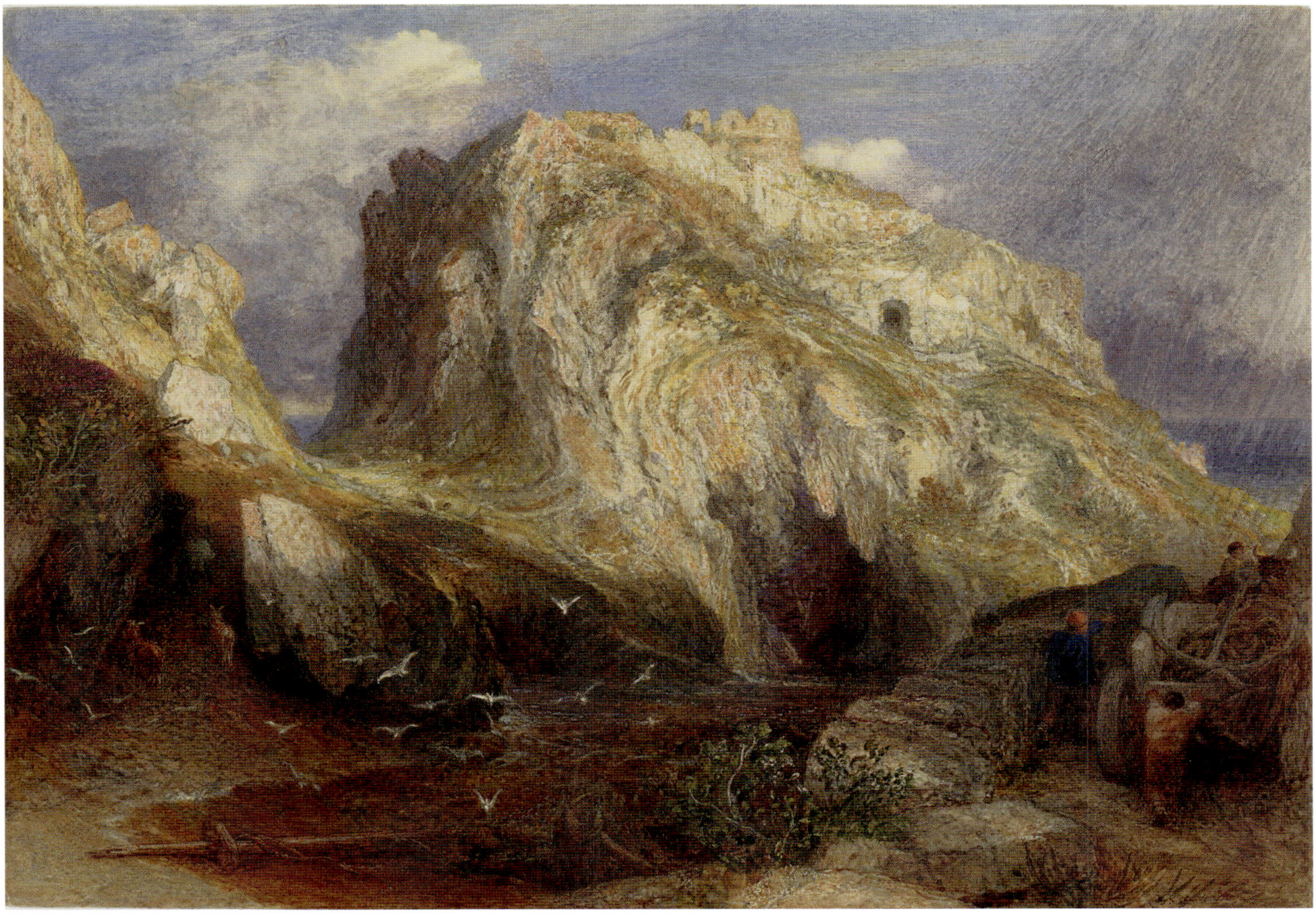

52

SAMUEL PALMER 1805–1881

The Prospect, 1864–81

Watercolour and bodycolour with gum arabic, on London board
50.8 × 70.5 cm
Signed: *Samuel Palmer*
Purchased with the assistance of The Art Fund (including a contribution from the Wolfson Foundation), the National Heritage Memorial Fund, the MLA/V&A Purchase Grant Fund, the Headley Trust, the Friends of the Ashmolean, and numerous private donations, 2005
WA2005.165

LITERATURE: Lister (1988) no. M12; Vaughan, Barker, Harrison (2005) no. 146

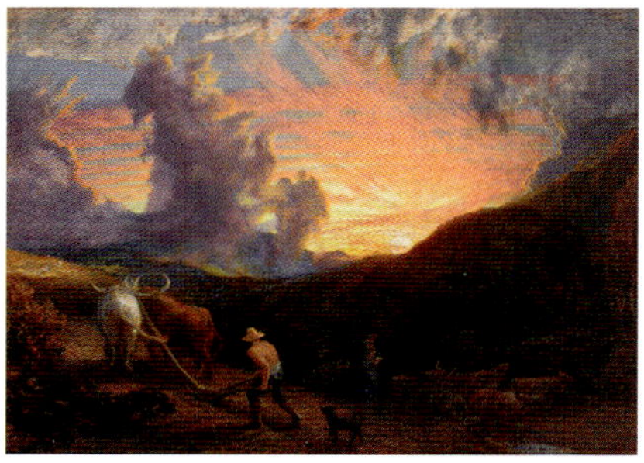

Fig. 43 | Samuel Palmer (1805–1881), *The Eastern Gate*, exhibited 1881. Watercolour and bodycolour on London board. Private Collection

When she died in 1837, Palmer's beloved nurse left him her copy of Tonson's edition of Milton, which he cherished all his life. He was brought up on Milton, and had a particular admiration for the 'minor poems', 'L'Allegro' and 'Il Penseroso', which he could recite by heart. In 1863 the solicitor and collector Leonard Rowe Valpy invited Palmer to paint something that appealed to his 'inner sympathies', and he responded that he had long considered making a series of illustrations to 'L'Allegro' and 'Il Penseroso'.[1] Initially, there were to be four contrasting pairs, divided equally between the two poems; but Palmer eventually produced three illustrations to 'L'Allegro' and five to 'Il Penseroso'. The project preoccupied the artist for the last 18 years of his life. Each watercolour was exhibited at the Society of Painters in Watercolours, three in 1868, one each in 1870 and 1877, two in 1881, and the last, *The Bellman*, which he considered unfinished, posthumously in 1882.[2]

The Prospect was the last watercolour to be completed: Palmer was still working on it a few months before his death in May 1881. It illustrates lines from 'Il Penseroso': 'Straight mine eye hath caught new pleasures / Whilst the landscape round it measures ... ' In an undated letter to Valpy, Palmer expresses the difficulty in capturing the scene: 'The other day I think the true "vision" came of "The Prospect". It is a curious subject, for there seems no medium between a mappy Buckinghamshire treatment and a genial poetic swoon.'[3] By February 1881 he was able to report to Valpy that 'I *have* worked upon, and I think, finished the part I was most anxious about, namely, the little town by the blue river. So I hope all is safe, and, if so, it will be a wonder, for never man ran riot with a hobby as I have done here. I always, from a child, expected to see a great deal when I was taken to see a "prospect"'.[4] The view is over an imaginary bay reminiscent of the Bay of Baiae which Palmer had drawn in 1838, the sun shining brilliantly on an Italianate hill town on the left. In the shadow of the foreground, a traveller points out the prospect to his two female companions. Behind them, in the valley, a hamlet very like Shoreham nestles among the trees.

The Milton watercolours were painted on thick London board, best suited to take Palmer's accumulated layers of pigment. They form a splendid culmination to his life. When *The Prospect* and *The Eastern Gate* (fig. 43) were exhibited in 1881, the critic and former member of the Pre-Raphaelite Brotherhood, F. G. Stephens, rightly called them 'epoch-making'.[5] CH

1. Vaughan, Barker, Harrison (2005) p. 227.
2. Lister (1988) nos. M10, M12, M14, M16, M20, M22, M25, M27.
3. Quoted in Vaughan, Barker, Harrison (2005) p. 227.
4. *Ibid.*
5. *Ibid.*

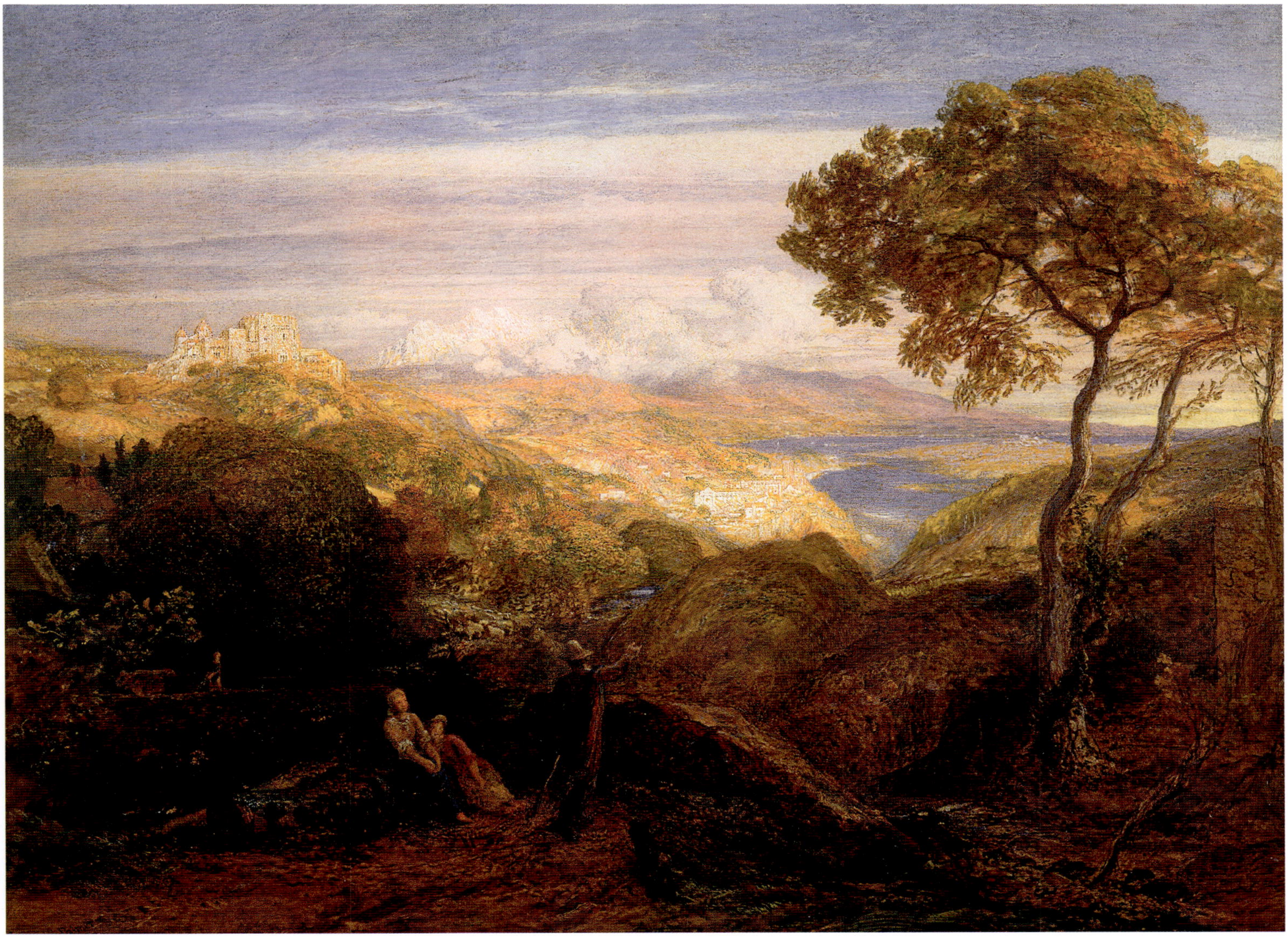

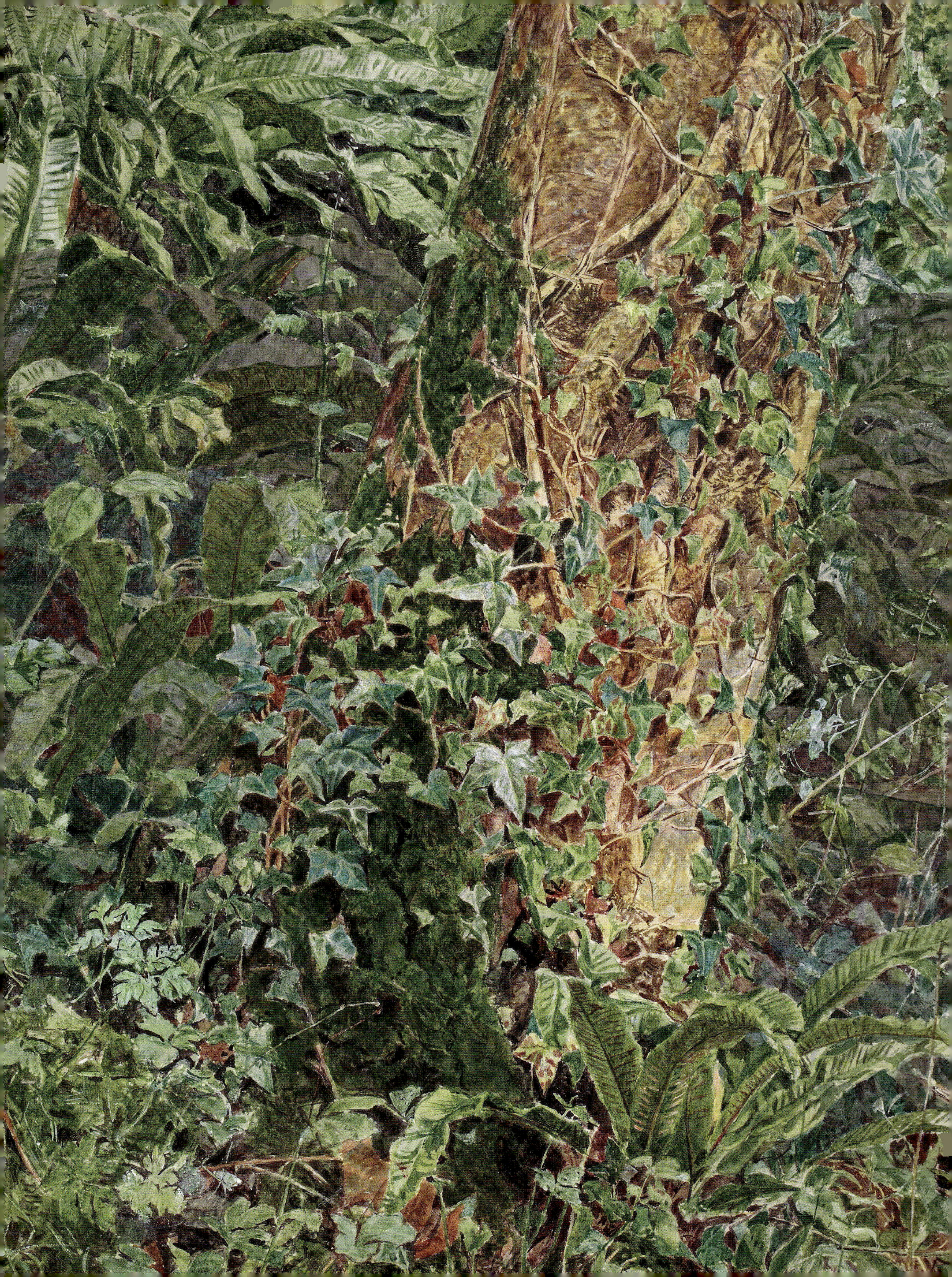

Ruskin & the Pre-Raphaelites

Observation & Imagination

Detail from Albert Moore,
Study of an Ash Trunk (cat. 59)

53

JOHN RUSKIN 1819–1900

Morning in Spring, with North-east Wind, at Vevey, May–June 1849, or 1 May 1869

Watercolour and bodycolour over graphite on pale grey wove paper
17.7 × 26.4 cm
Presented by John Ruskin to the Ruskin Drawing School, 1875
WA.RS.ED.298.b

Ruskin frequently visited Switzerland, at first with his parents and later independently. He was inspired by the example of J. M. W. Turner, several of whose Swiss watercolours he owned; but his purpose was very different. His father's birthday gift in 1834 of a copy of Horace de Saussure's *Voyages dans les Alpes* (1779–96) taught him the scientific importance of mountains and their formation. The lessons in geology provided by this and other books always informed Ruskin's own drawings, and were to play a major role in his discussion of landscape painting in *Modern Painters*. Like Saussure, he had a particular affection for Mont Blanc and the mountains around Chamonix, and made some of his most elaborate drawings of the glaciers and peaks in the vicinity.

Elsewhere in Switzerland, he painted a number of watercolours of panoramic views across the lakes. These are often difficult to date accurately, because after about 1845 Ruskin used a number of different styles for his drawings, depending on their subject and function. Consequently, there is no consensus on the dating of this atmospheric view of Lake Geneva. It may have been produced in May or early June 1849, when Ruskin stayed at Vevey as part of a tour of Switzerland; this resulted in a remarkable group of watercolours of alpine scenery inspired by Turner. On the other hand, when Ruskin gave *Morning in Spring* to his Drawing School he placed it in the same frame as a view of *Afternoon in Spring, with South Wind, at Neuchâtel* (fig. 44). The latter is generally dated to 1866, but may have been made on 30 April 1869, the day before Ruskin was in Vevey. Whereas the Neuchâtel watercolour is one of the most vividly coloured of all Ruskin's works, the wind-flecked water of the lake an intense emerald green, this view towards the north-east across the rippling waters of Lake Geneva is much more subtle, with a greatly restricted palette. The buildings of the town of Vevey are silhouetted against the Molard and the Dent de Lys beyond, the early morning sky is streaked with bright white clouds, and a cushion of mist lies above the shore. Ruskin placed these watercolours in the section 'Rocks, Waters, Clouds' in his Educational Series. CH

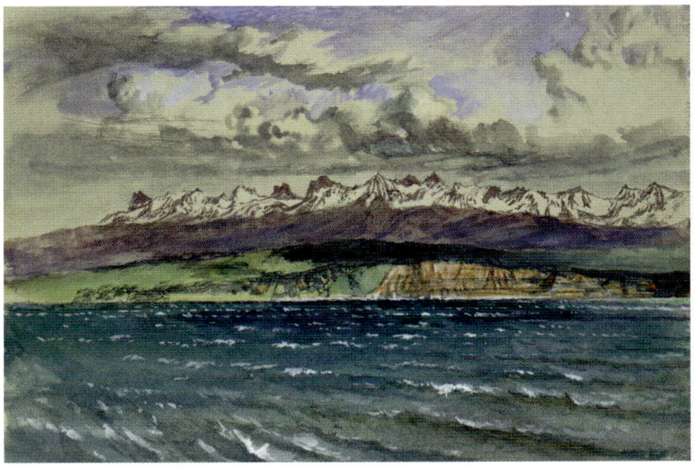

Fig. 44 | John Ruskin (1819–1900), *Afternoon in Spring, with South Wind, at Neuchâtel*, 30 April 1869. Watercolour and bodycolour over graphite on pale grey wove paper. Ashmolean Museum, Oxford, WA.RS.ED.298.a

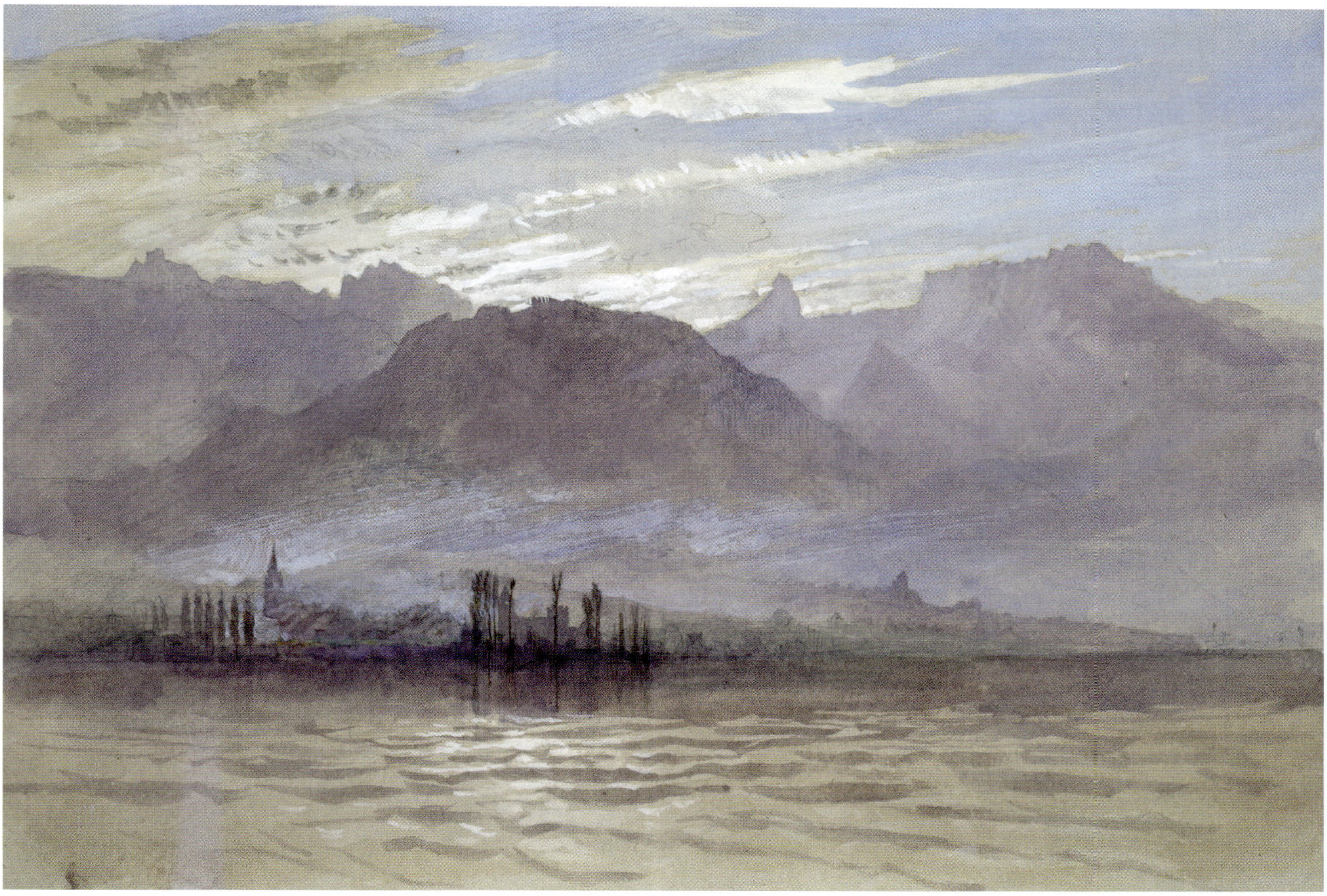

54

JOSEPH MALLORD WILLIAM TURNER 1775–1851

Venice: The Riva degli Schiavoni, 1840

Brush and pen and ink, with watercolour on paper
21.7 × 31.8 cm
Presented by John Ruskin, 1861
WA1861.10

LITERATURE: Herrmann (1968) no. 58; Wilton (1979) no. 1364; Warrell (2003) no. 108

From his earliest days Turner was an inveterate sketcher, filling books of various sizes with studies in pencil, watercolour, and occasionally pen and ink. Over 300 survive, mostly in the Turner Bequest in the Tate. Some were broken up by the artist, and a few dismembered after his death. He had a phenomenal memory, and the sketches served to remind him of the precise disposition of buildings and other features of the landscape, more than any effects of atmosphere or weather. They were generally bound in hard covers, though from the late 1820s onwards Turner also used books with more flexible covers which he could roll up and put in his pocket. These 'roll' sketchbooks, as they are known, were especially useful for sketching in watercolour.

Turner first visited Venice in 1819, spending a few days there on his extensive tour of Italy, which concentrated on Rome. He returned in 1833, making intensive sketches in the so-called 'Venice' sketchbook, and a number of watercolours, especially of night scenes and dark interiors. His third visit to Venice, from 20 August to 3 September 1840, resulted in his most ethereal watercolour studies of the city, originally contained in two roll sketchbooks, which Ian Warrell has identified as the 'Grand Canal and Giudecca' sketchbook (Tate) and the 'Storm' sketchbook. The latter was broken up shortly before or after Turner's death, and the individual sheets dispersed through the artist's dealer, Thomas Griffith. It consisted of nearly 20 watercolours, many of squally atmospheric effects. John Ruskin bought six; he gave three to his old University in 1861 and the others to Cambridge. Apart from the delight in Venice and its unique light, these watercolours were probably made as patterns to show possible patrons for future commissions, either of oil paintings or of watercolours. However, there are no finished watercolour views of Venice at this late period, although Turner continued to exhibit oils of Venetian subjects until 1846.

This view of the Riva degli Schiavoni shows the area between St Mark's Square and the church of the Pietà, the marble facade only partly constructed. Behind rises the ghostly campanile and domed church of S. Zaccaria. Most of Turner's attention is focused on the buildings at the water's edge and the shipping in front of them. The sailing boats, canoes, and gondolas are depicted in an extraordinarily free network of fine lines, made with the pen rather than the brush. The shimmering reflections in the calm waters of the Bacino and the hazy atmosphere give this scene an air of unreality characteristic of Turner's Venice. CH

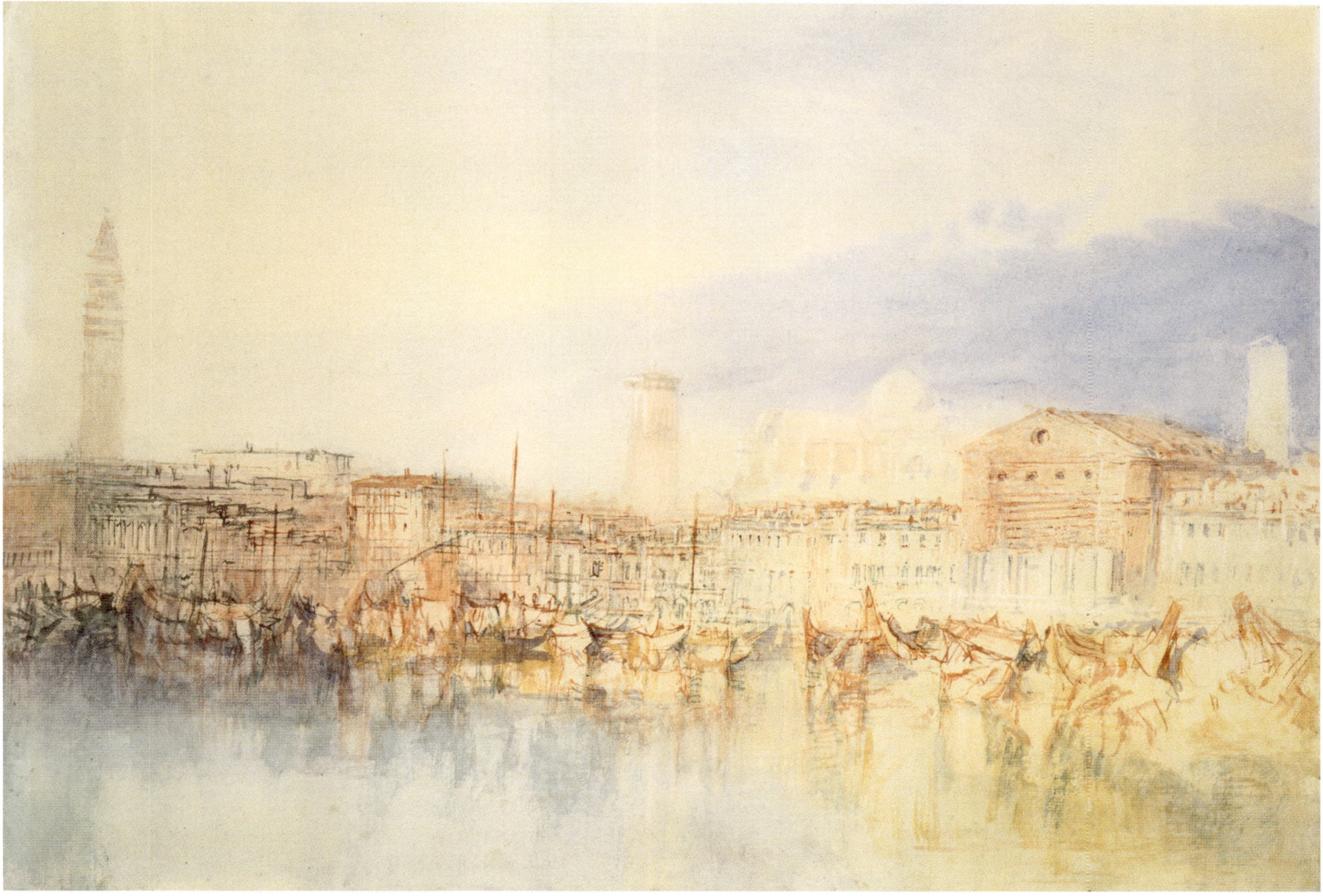

55

JOHN RUSKIN 1819–1900
The Exterior of the Ducal Palace, Venice, 1852

Watercolour over graphite on off-white paper, some lines ruled, and with some scratching out
36.2 × 50.2 cm
Inscribed: *intervals of pillars on top of balustrade* and with numbers and measurements
Presented by John Ruskin to the Ruskin Drawing School, 1875
WA.RS.REF.067

LITERATURE: Ruskin (1903–12) XXI, p. 31

Ruskin first visited Venice as a tourist with his parents in 1835. However, it was not until he was allowed to travel there alone, in 1845, that he began the careful study of the city which resulted in several of his most influential books. The immediate stimulus was the profound changes that were taking place in the city, such as the construction of a railway bridge across the lagoon, which destroyed the romantic approach by gondola. Above all, Ruskin was appalled by the wholesale 'restoration' of buildings such as St Mark's Cathedral and the palaces on the Grand Canal, the facades of which were being removed and replaced. He also detested other general 'improvements', for example the installation of gas lamps 'of the last Birmingham fashion' along the canals.[1] Returning in the following year, he observed that 'The rate at which Venice is going is about that of a lump of sugar in hot tea'.[2] It was only in the winters of 1849–50 and 1851–2 that Ruskin was able systematically to record the buildings of Venice, intending to incorporate his observations into a general history of Venetian architecture and its relationship with the society that had produced it. The publication of *The Stones of Venice* in 1851–3 was to prove a landmark in the preservation of Venice, and the chapter on 'The Nature of the Gothic' inspired William Morris to champion the hand-crafted over the industrial.

The Doge's palace occupied a prominent position in Ruskin's thesis; he considered it 'a mode of perfection'.[3] This drawing, made from a boat, shows the right-hand half of the facade towards the sea, together with the Ponte della Paglia and part of the Bridge of Sighs, as well as the prison beyond. Ruskin has concentrated on particular architectural details, and the rest of the drawing is rapidly sketched in broad wash. Although it was intended principally as a record, a group of gondolas enlivens the scene.

Ruskin was proud of the accuracy of this drawing, noting that it was 'sketched … by measurement, with extreme care; and showing the sharp window traceries, which are rarely seen in photographs'.[4] Indeed, he claimed that 'No one had ever drawn the traceries of the Ducal Palace till I did it myself. Canaletti, in his way, is just as false as Prout; Turner no better. Not one of them painted anything but their general impressions; and not a soul in England knew that there was a system in Venetian architecture at all, until I made the measured (to half and quarter inches) elevation of it.'[5] CH

1. Quoted in Hewison (2000) p. 20.
2. Quoted in Hewison (2000) p. 25.
3. Ruskin (1903–12) VIII, p. 111.
4. Ruskin (1903–12) XIX, p. 456.
5. Ruskin (1903–12) XIV, p. 424.

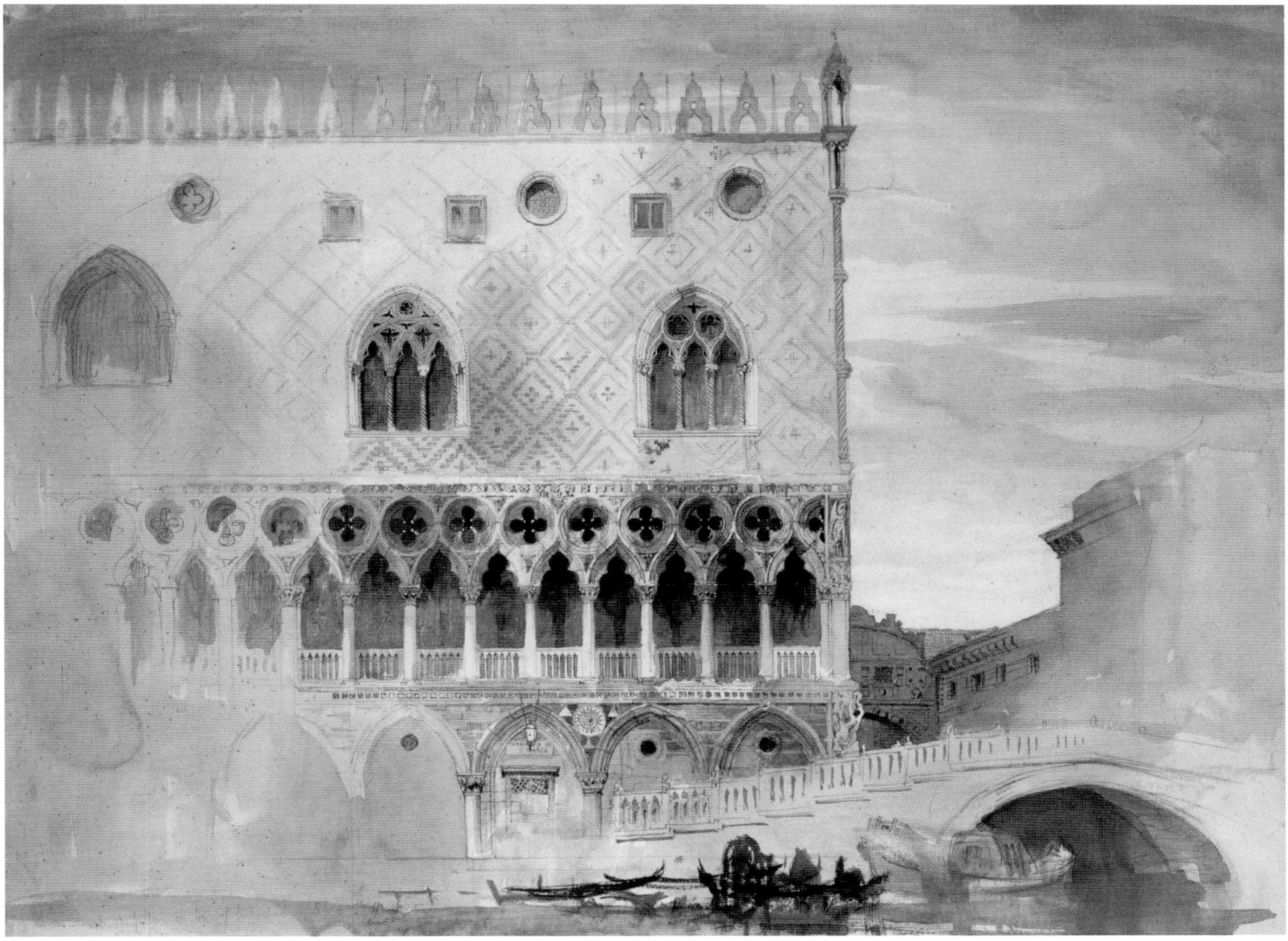

56

JOSEPH MALLORD WILLIAM TURNER 1775–1851
Sketch of Mackerel, c. 1835–40

Watercolour over graphite on Whatman Turkey Mill paper dated 1818
22.4 × 28.7 cm
Presented by John Ruskin to the Ruskin Drawing School, 1875
WA.RS.ED.182

LITERATURE: Herrmann (1968) no. 80; Wilton (1979) no. 1399

It was at Farnley Hall in Yorkshire, the seat of his close friend Walter Fawkes (1769–1825), that Turner was able to indulge most consistently his love of fishing and shooting. On his visits between 1808 and 1825 he also made numerous watercolour landscapes and, especially after 1815, still lifes for his patron. Fawkes assembled a fine library, in which natural history occupied a prominent part. In addition to acquiring the standard texts, he compiled an *Ornithological Collection* based on Thomas Bewick's *History of British Birds*. This included 20 watercolours by Turner, who also painted a number of other studies of birds at Farnley, among them a *Sketch of a Pheasant* later owned by John Ruskin.[1]

For the last 18 years of his life, Turner lived with Sophia Booth (1798–1875). She was recently widowed when they met in 1833 at Margate, where she kept a lodging house facing the harbour. While staying with her, he made a number of studies of mackerel. One of these is inscribed by Mrs Booth, 'sketched from Fish brought in for dinner at Margate of which Fish Mr Turner partook of for his dinner'.[2] The watercolours of mackerel have one, two, and three fish respectively; a fourth shows a single mackerel and some prawns, while another depicts rather less appetising species, again with prawns.[3] In this *Sketch of Mackerel* the three fish are consummately captured in brief but suggestive brushstrokes, their colours bright, their scales opalescent.

Ruskin greatly admired this study, inviting Frederic Leighton in June 1863 to visit him in Denmark Hill 'if it be but to look at some dashes in sepia by Reynolds [*sic.* Romney, cat. 12], and a couple of mackerel by Turner'. Later, he wrote of the whole group that 'These sketches ... are all executed with a view mainly to colour, and, in colour, to its ultimate refinements, as in the grey down of the birds and the subdued iridescences of the fish. There is no execution in watercolour comparable to them for combined rapidity, delicacy, and precision – the artists of the world may be challenged to approach them'.[4] CH

1. Now in the Ashmolean, WA.RS.ED.183; Herrmann (1968) no. 78; Wilton (1979) no. 634; Lyles (1988) no. 38.
2. Wilton (1979) no. 1401.
3. Herrmann (1968) no. 81; Wilton (1979) no. 1043. The other studies of mackerel are Wilton (1979) nos. 1400–1402.
4. Quoted in Herrmann (1968) pp. 97–8.

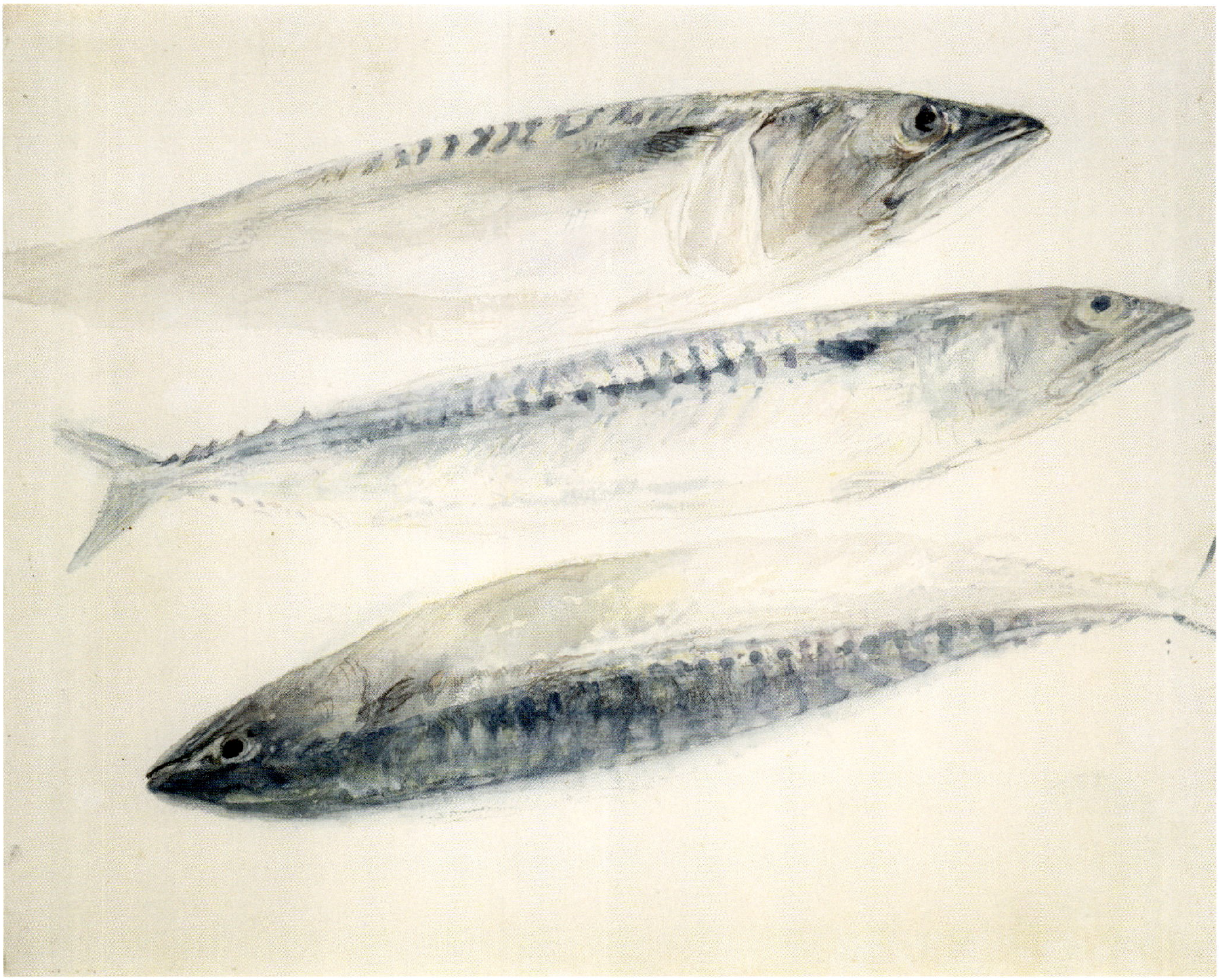

57

WILLIAM HENRY HUNT 1790–1864

Peach and Grapes, c. 1850

Watercolour and bodycolour over graphite on paper
12.4 × 17.5 cm
Signed: *W HUNT*
Presented by John Ruskin to the Ruskin Drawing School, 1875
WA.RS.ED.213

LITERATURE: Witt (1982) no. 689

A tradesman's son, Hunt was trained by John Varley and at Dr Monro's Academy alongside Turner and Linnell. 'Bird's Nest' Hunt, as he came to be called, may appear limited in his subject matter to modern viewers, but his range is in fact far wider than the still-lifes for which he is best known. In his earlier career he worked on landscapes, genre scenes and even scene-painting. The Ashmolean's large drawing of the *Portico of St-Martin-in-the-Fields* (1822) demonstrates that he was equally skilled in tackling large-scale architectural subjects.[1]

The illusionistic technique of this exquisitely detailed watercolour would have been frowned on by eighteenth-century viewers for its excessive 'minuteness'. However, Ruskin saw Hunt's work as exemplifying the sincere observation of nature that he was trying to inculcate in his students, and this work formed part of the Educational Series at his Drawing School in Oxford, demonstrating imitative colour. Ruskin asserted that the peach and grapes are 'not to teach you anything you didn't know about those familiar fruits'; they seek rather 'to show what is meant by Painting, as distinguished from daubing ... from chromo-tinting, from tray-varnishing, ... from the sort of things that people in general do when you put a brush into their hands'.[2] A very similar work is seen hanging in Ruskin's bedroom at Brantwood, indicating just how highly he valued Hunt's work.[3] He particularly admired his keen eye for truth, though the compositions were in fact artfully contrived, arranged on a table-top so that Hunt could observe the mossy 'bank' at eye-level.

The late works are primarily concerned with balancing complementary colours. Hunt even entitled one of his still-lifes *The Contrast: Red and Green Apples*, complaining in a letter to John Linnell in 1863 that the public still considered his fruit as something to eat rather than as studies in colour.[4] The delicate stippling in this work conveys the soft furry texture of the peach and the purple-grey bloom of the grapes. Under magnification the tiny strokes of colour are revealed to be laid alongside each other as pure tints, allowing the colours to blend in the eye at a distance. Hunt was fascinated by subtle gradations within a single hue, for example floating mottled flecks of blue over a reddish-purple underlayer in the grapes. Reflected blue from the grapes can be found in the yellow peach; rather than being clearly outlined, the fruits melt imperceptibly into coloured shadows.

Hunt's techniques, in particular his glazing with transparent washes over an opaque white underlayer, had a lasting impact on the Pre-Raphaelites. Through Ruskin's *Elements of Drawing* (1857) they also influenced Monet, Seurat and Signac, who were to apply the theory of simultaneous contrasts and optical colour-mixing more systematically in their Divisionist paintings. CP

1. WA1935.161
2. Ruskin (1880) p. 83.
3. Engraving after Arthur Severn, reproduced in Witt (1982) pl. 105.
4. Quoted in Jones (1981) p. 47.

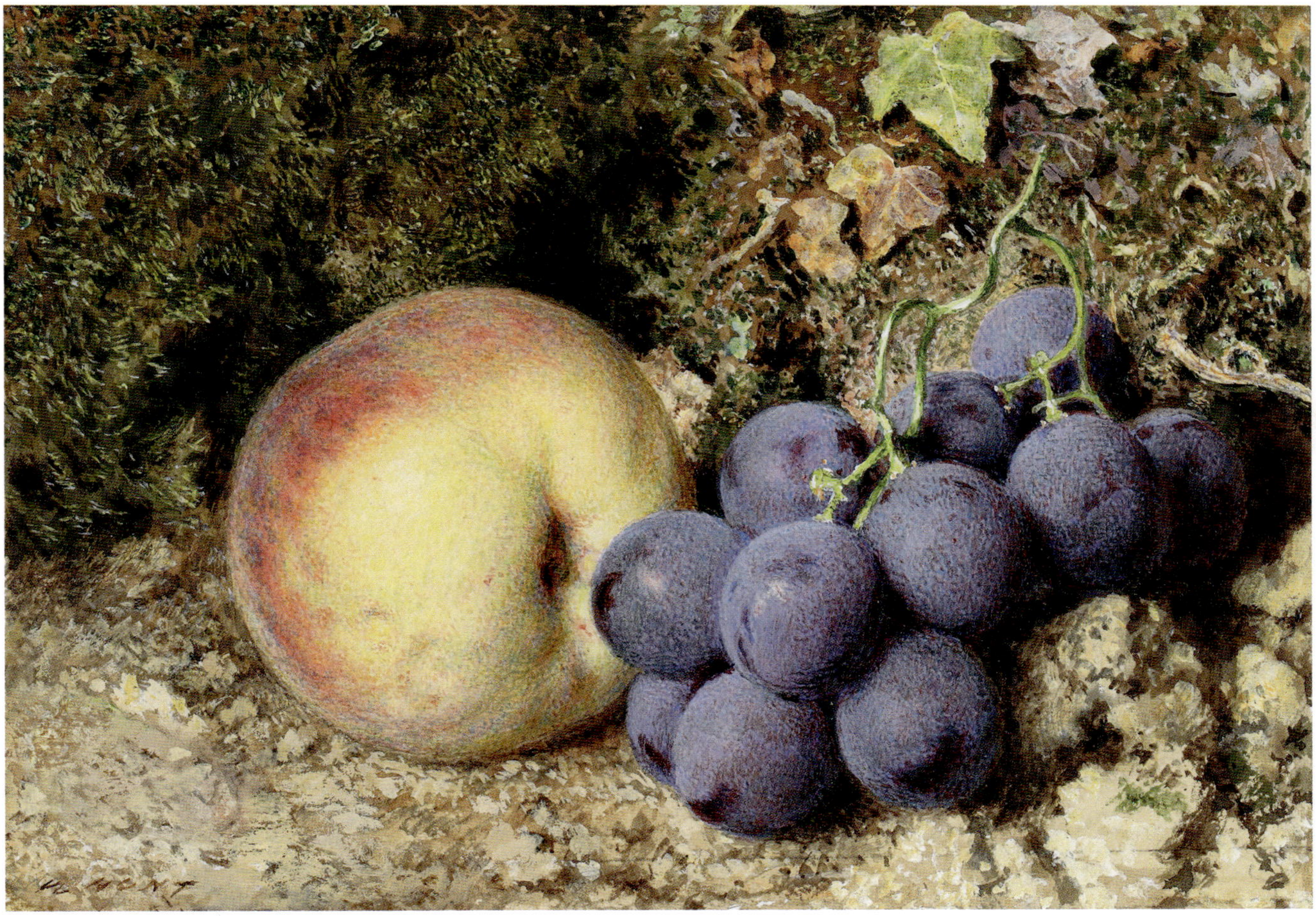

58

JOHN RUSKIN 1819–1900

Enlarged Studies of the Feathers of a Kingfisher's Wing and Head, and a Study of a Group of the Wing Feathers, real Size, July 1871

Watercolour and bodycolour over graphite on paper
37.5 × 25 cm
Presented by John Ruskin to the Ruskin Drawing School, 1875
WA.RS.RUD.204

LITERATURE: Lyles (1988) no. 58

On his visits to Farnley Hall (see cat. 56), Ruskin especially admired Turner's study of a dead kingfisher; on his second visit in 1884, he examined it 'for a long time with a microscope, and he said he could not find words to describe its exquisite beauty'.[1] His own study of a kingfisher is one of his most meticulous and closely observed watercolours, apparently made from a stuffed specimen belonging to his friend, Sir Henry Acland (fig. 45).[2] It was placed in the Rudimentary Series in the Drawing School, together with four other studies of a kingfisher, under the general title 'Exercises in Colour with Shade, on Patterns of Plumage and Scale'. This included two contrasting drawings, a watercolour *Study of a Kingfisher with dominant reference to colour* and a pencil *Study of a Kingfisher with dominant reference to shade*. In addition, there was a *Feather of a Kingfisher's Back, enlarged*, an *Enlarged Drawing of a Kingfisher's Wing*, and this sheet of three different portions of the plumage from the head and wing. All were probably drawn in October 1871. Together they provided the student with a uniquely comprehensive examination of a single specimen, Ruskin's other studies of feathers generally being isolated examples.

Ruskin discussed birds and their plumage in *Love's Meinie* (1881), based on lectures given at Oxford between 1873 and 1881; and *The Laws of Fesole* (1877–8), intended as a sequel to *The Elements of Drawing* (1857). In the latter, he wrote eloquently of the 'elementary organic structure' of a bird, and, in a truly scientific manner, explained the different textures of a bird's plumage, and the nomenclature of the different parts of a feather: 'A feather always consists of the quill and its rays; a ray of the shaft and its barbs. Flexible shafts are filaments; and flexible barbs, cilia'.[3] His watercolours of these individual elements of the kingfisher's feathers are among his most breathtaking in their confidence, delicacy, and microscopic attention to detail. CH

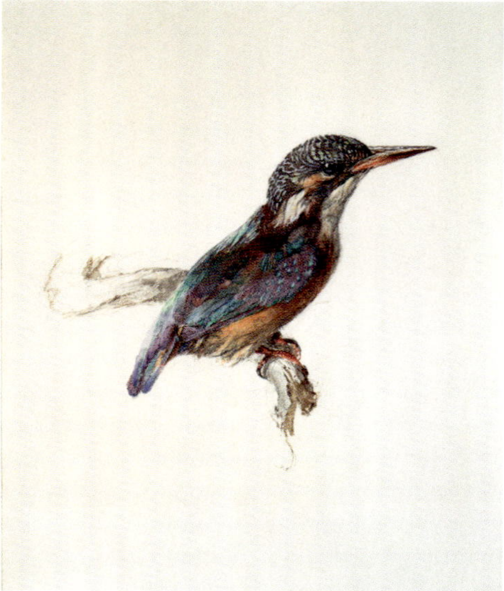

Fig. 45 | John Ruskin (1819–1900), *Study of a Kingfisher, with dominant reference to colour*, 1871. Watercolour and bodycolour over graphite on wove paper. Ashmolean Museum, Oxford, WA.RS.RUD.201

1. Quoted in Lyles (1988) p. 57.
2. This specimen is preserved in the Oxford University Museum of Natural History.
3. Quoted in Lyles (1988) p. 66.

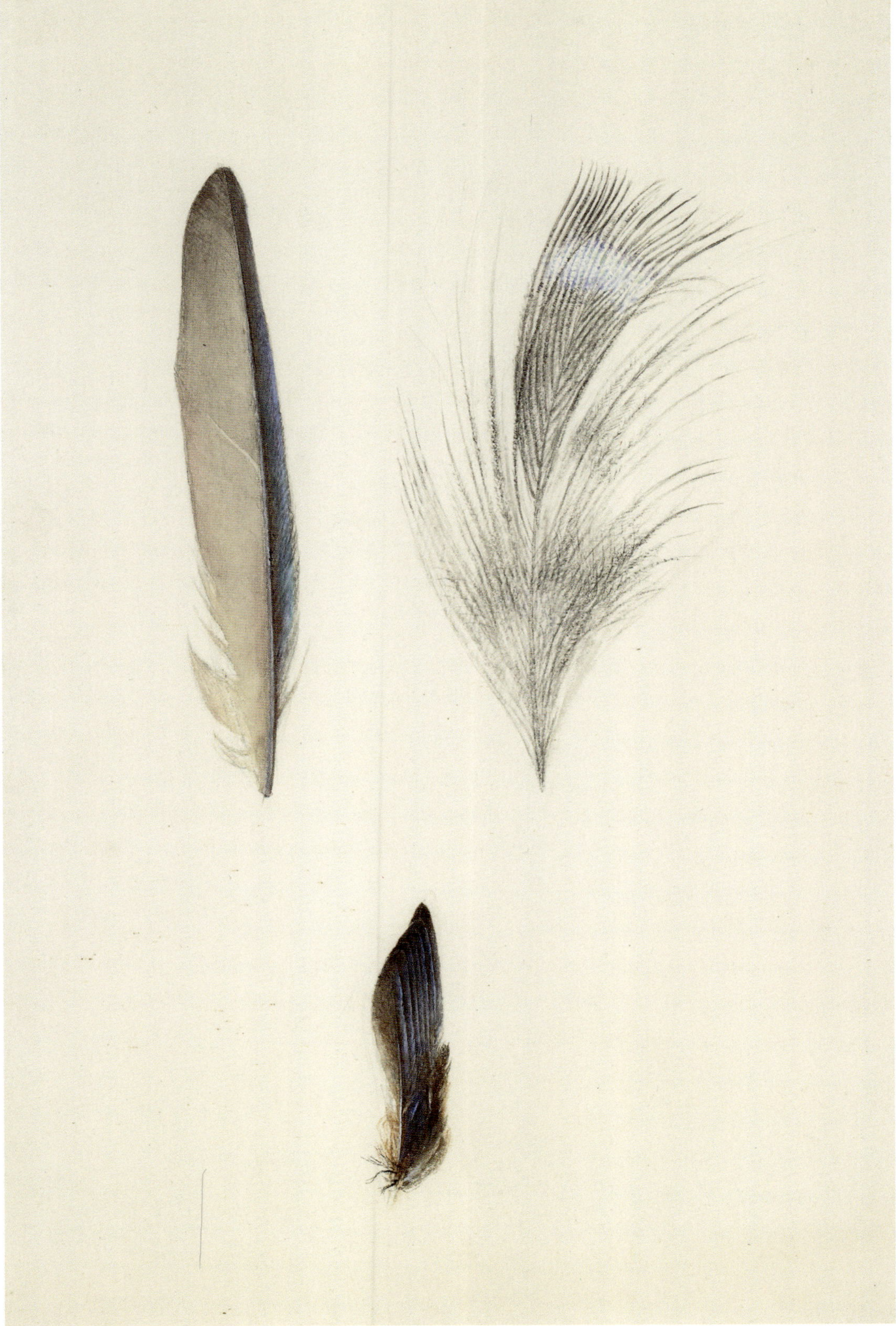

59

ALBERT JOSEPH MOORE 1841–1893
Study of an Ash Trunk, 1857

Watercolour on paper
30.3 × 22.9 cm
Signed in monogram and dated: *AM 1857*
Purchased, 1959
WA1959.59

LITERATURE: Staley and Newall (2004) no. 14

In the first volume of *Modern Painters* (1843), John Ruskin exhorted every painter to 'go to Nature in all singleness of heart, and walk with her laboriously and trustingly, having no other thoughts but how best to penetrate her meaning, and remember her instruction; rejecting nothing, selecting nothing, and scorning nothing; believing all things to be right and good, and rejoicing always in the truth'. For a few years the members of the Pre-Raphaelite Brotherhood, founded in 1848, followed this prescription, painting in a minutely detailed manner in bright colours on a white ground.

The backgrounds to Millais's paintings of *Ophelia* (1851–2) and *John Ruskin* (1853–4) represent the most intently Ruskinian examination of nature by a member of the Brotherhood.[1] It was not until the mid-1850s that landscape artists realised the potential of Ruskin's words. The true pioneer was John William Inchbold (1830–1888), who exhibited *A Study, in March* at the Royal Academy in 1855, and *Mid-Spring* in the following year.[2] Ruskin observed that the latter was 'as close and wonderful a piece of work as there is on the room walls'.[3]

A further impetus to the habits of microscopic examination of nature came in 1857 with the publication of Ruskin's *Elements of Drawing*, in which he specifically advocated that 'In woods, one or two trunks, with the flowery ground below, are at once the richest and easiest kind of study: a not very thick trunk, say nine inches or a foot in diameter, with ivy running up it sparingly, is an easy and always a rewarding subject'.[4]

Among the artists who must have read these lines was Albert Moore. The younger brother of the landscape artist Henry Moore (1831–1896), he entered the Royal Academy Schools in 1858. His first exhibits at the Royal Academy were wholly Ruskinian: two watercolours of dead birds in 1857, followed by this *Study of an Ash Trunk* in 1858. The close focus on a small section of a tree trunk with ivy growing up it, partly covered with moss, the careful delineation of the individual leaves of the ferns, and the general untidiness of the undergrowth all follow Ruskin's recommendation. So too does the limited palette of greens and browns. It was an exercise that Moore never repeated: he later became a distinguished painter of historical subjects, especially featuring classicised females.

1. Tate and Ashmolean Museum respectively; Rosenfeld and Smith (2007) nos. 37–8.
2. Ashmolean Museum and private collection; Newall (1993) pp. 11–13 and no. 6.
3. Quoted in Staley and Newall (2004) no. 12.
4. Quoted in Cruise (2012) p. 86.

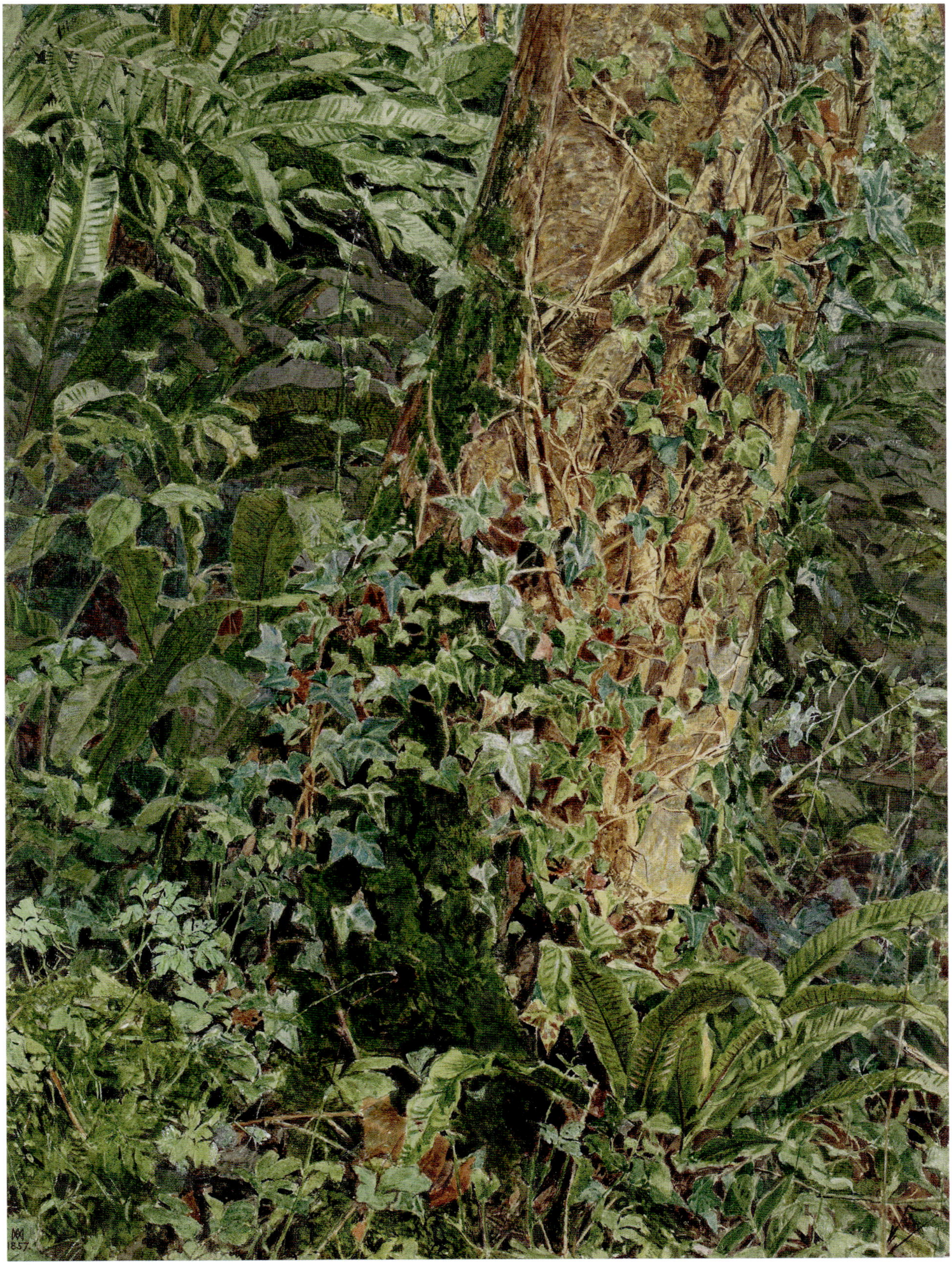
1857

60

ALFRED WILLIAM HUNT 1830–1896

A November Rainbow – Dolwyddelan Valley 11 November 1866, 1 p. m., 11 November 1866

Watercolour on paper
50.3 × 75.5 cm
Purchased with the assistance of The Art Fund, 1922
WA1922.1

LITERATURE: Newall (2004) no. 35

The son of a minor landscape painter from Liverpool, Hunt was admitted as a scholar of Corpus Christi College, Oxford, in 1848. He won the Newdigate Prize for Poetry in 1851 and was elected a Fellow of his College in 1857. Even as an undergraduate he travelled widely, and frequently exhibited landscape paintings. He no doubt read Ruskin's volumes of *Modern Painters*, and will have found the third, 'Of Mountain Beauty' (1856), of particular interest, since it encouraged a close geological examination of the structure of the mountain landscapes that Hunt had already been painting in the Lake District and North Wales. Stimulated by Ruskin, Hunt adopted a style that was at once minutely detailed yet richly atmospheric, whether in panoramic views in Snowdonia, or the patient examination of the bough of a tree or a piece of rock. Ruskin recognised Hunt's prowess, describing a picture shown at the Royal Academy in 1856 as 'the best landscape I have seen in the exhibition for many a day – uniting most subtle finish and watchfulness of Nature, with real and rare power of composition'.[1] He was not always so complimentary, however, calling Hunt's exhibits in 1859 'extremely well meant, but suffering under the same oppression of plethoric labour', while in 1873 he tried to instruct him in capturing form before colour. Nevertheless, Hunt remained closer to Ruskin than any other landscape artist.

A November Rainbow is one of the artist's most celebrated works. It was shown at the Old Water-Colour Society in 1867 with the elaborate title insisting on a precise, momentary effect of weather, emphasised by a subtitle from Book IV of Tennyson's *The Princess: A Medley*: 'A stroke of cruel sunshine on a cliff, when all the glens are drown'd in azure gloom.' Christopher Newall has established that the viewpoint is taken from the hill to the south of the valley of the Lledr, near the hamlet of Bertheos, and about a mile and a quarter to the west of the village of Dolwyddelan. In the middle distance on the right is Dolwyddelan Castle, while in the foreground a cowherd protects himself from the rain with a piece of sacking. As one reviewer noted, the meteorological effect was one favoured by the artist, 'a rainbow among mountains, with his peculiarly hard, dark shadows and pale sunlight'.[2] Technically, this watercolour is one of Hunt's most sophisticated, in composition, and in the variety of effects in the paint, ranging from minute stippling to vigorous scratching out. The result is a work of astonishing breadth and power, far eclipsing a similar composition created by the artist ten years earlier.[3] CH

1. Quoted in Newall (2004) p. 7.
2. Quoted in Newall (2004) p. 120.
3. Stainton (1985) no. 192.

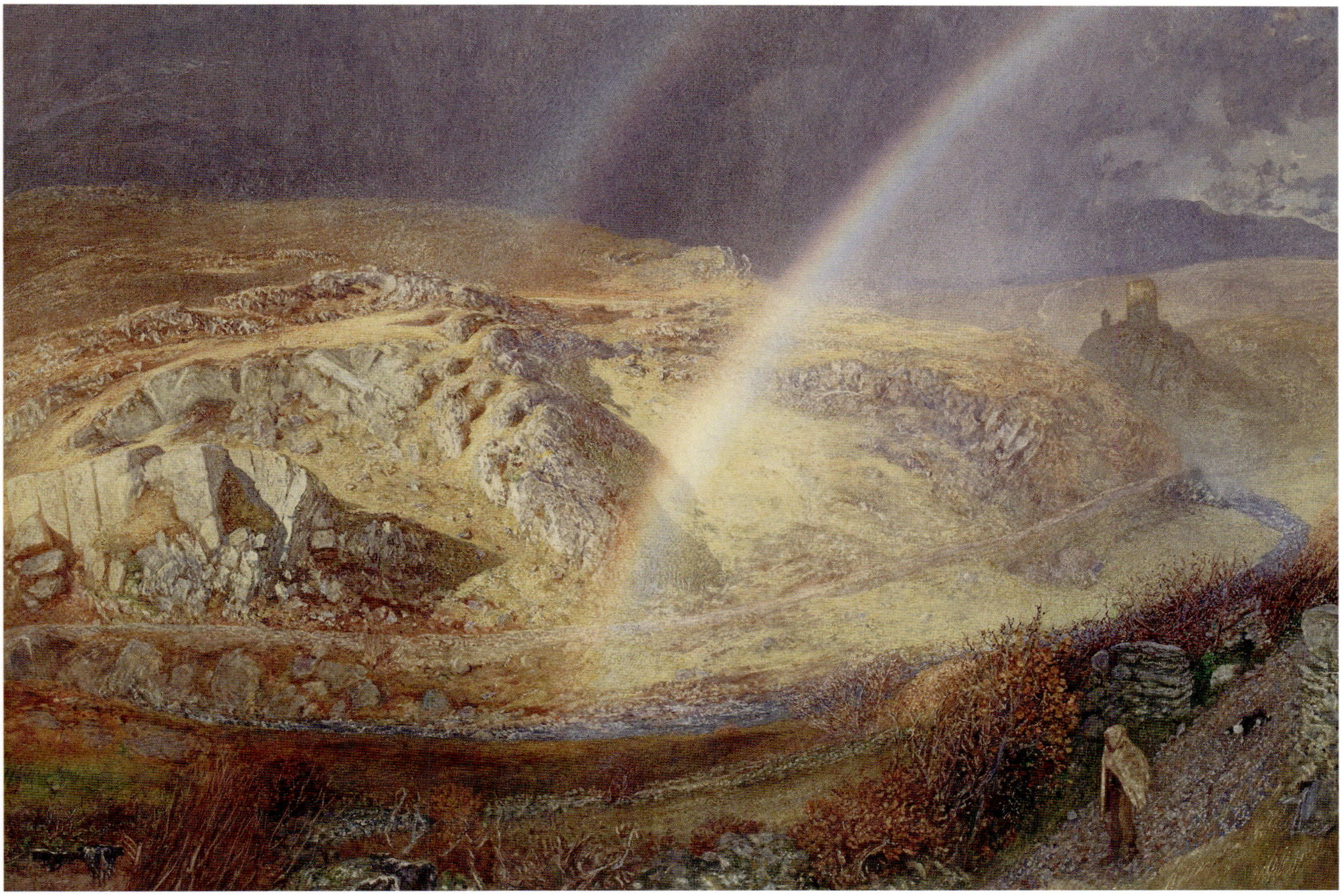

61

WILLIAM HOLMAN HUNT 1827–1910

The Sleeping City: the Cemetery of Pera, Constantinople, 1856–88

Watercolour on paper
50.4 × 35.2 cm
Bequeathed by Mrs Thomas Combe, 1893
WA1894.7

LITERATURE: Bronkhurst (2006) no. D138

Hunt wrote to Mrs Combe on 28 September 1888 that

The drawing was done in January 1856, but it was brought home with the lower part left blank. My dear friend your husband liked it so much that I gave it to him, asking him to keep it until I could complete it. When I was in Florence in 1868 on my way East Mr Combe brought it out for me to take with me, and I have had it ever since, sometimes taking the opportunity of advancing my subject a little, but until this spring I was never able to take it in hand to finish. I promised it for exhibition to the Royal Society of Painters in Water-Colours, but when the time came for delivering it up although I had completed all the facts I had not been able to give the complete general effect, and so after the exhibition this had to be secured by further fastidious study, which was prolonged so far that I feared you would almost lose faith in my energy.

His account vividly demonstrates the difficulties in pursuing the true Pre-Raphaelite principles of painting in minute detail and only in front of the subject. It is not surprising that none of the original Brotherhood continued in this vein much after 1854.

The watercolour was begun at the very end of Hunt's extended excursion to the Holy Land, while he was waiting for a steamer to take him to Malta after spending about a month at Constantinople. The site is one of two cemeteries in Constantinople, either the Petits Champs des Morts in Pera (modern Beyoğlu) or the larger one at Eyüp overlooking the Bosphorus. Unlike Lear (cat. 42), who found such a scene effortlessly picturesque, for Hunt it was intensely poignant, and his watercolour is loaded with symbolism. The doves are symbols of peace, perhaps a reaction to the massacres of the Crimean War, while the cedars represent timelessness, and the crocuses, the rebirth of spring. This watercolour is one of Hunt's most elaborate. Every element is painstakingly studied, from the trunks of the trees to the inscriptions on the tombs and the feathers of the pigeons in the foreground. CH

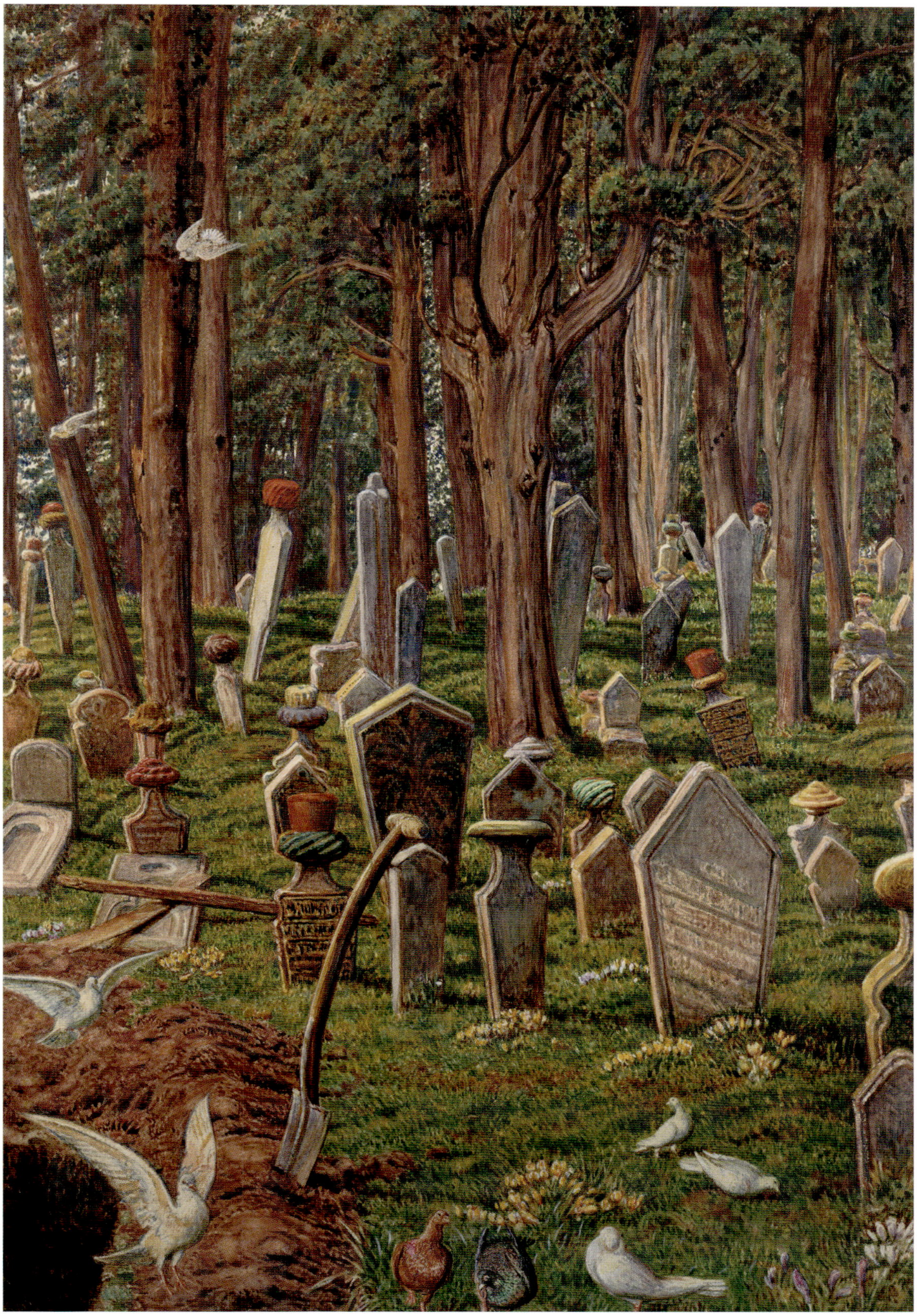

62

DANTE GABRIEL ROSSETTI 1828–1882

Dante drawing an Angel on the Anniversary of Beatrice's Death, 1853

Watercolour and bodycolour on paper
42 × 61 cm
Signed in monogram and dated: *DGR 1853*
Bequeathed by Mrs Thomas Combe, 1893
WA1894.16

LITERATURE: Surtees (1971) no. 58; Treuherz (2003) no. 42; Harrison and Newall (2010) no. 8

Rossetti nurtured a life-long affinity with the work of his namesake, the thirteenth-century Florentine poet Dante Alighieri, whose autobiographical romance, *La Vita Nuova*, he translated during the 1840s. He had produced an earlier pen and ink drawing on the subject of *Dante drawing an angel* (1848–9) as one of 12 episodes with which he planned to illustrate his translation of the poem.[1] So intense was Rossetti's identification with his poetic predecessor that the following year he changed his name from Gabriel Charles Dante Rossetti to the form by which he would henceforth be known.

This watercolour, the largest and most elaborate that Rossetti had produced to date, was commissioned by Francis McCracken, a Belfast cotton-spinner. It took over a year to complete. The absorbed poet-artist was modelled by Rossetti's brother William Michael. Dante's facial features were based on the recently discovered supposed portrait of the poet by Giotto, a copy of which was sent, along with the poet's death mask, to Rossetti's father, Professor of Italian Literature at King's College and a Dante scholar. Realising that he has neglected his visitors, Dante rises with the salutation 'Another was with me'. The highly detailed symbolic setting, absent from *La Vita Nuova*, owes much to paintings by Van Eyck and Hans Memling, which Rossetti and Hunt had admired while in Bruges in 1849; the mirror recalls Van Eyck's *The Arnolfini Marriage*, the first 'Primitive' painting to enter the National Gallery's collection in 1842. Modelled by Elizabeth Siddal (cat. 66), the woman may represent Dante's future wife, Gemma Donati, or the pitying woman who watches him from her window. The conflation of these episodes is consistent with Rossetti's promotion of fidelity of spirit over literalness in translation.

Rossetti painstakingly applied the almost dry pigment, giving a deep saturation of colour quite unlike the effect of traditional watercolour washes, but akin to the appearance of medieval manuscript illumination. The figure of Dante is preoccupied in producing a drawing by the same means as Rossetti, as demonstrated by the flasks of the three primary colours glowing on the windowsill. While bright sunshine illuminates the landscape of Florence beyond, the poet-artist is intent upon depicting Beatrice among the heavenly host – not abiding by the Pre-Raphaelite principle of 'truth to nature', but employing a combination of memory and imagination. The work is a highly personal exploration of artistic vocation, so it is unsurprising that when Burne-Jones saw it in Thomas Combe's collection in 1855 it filled him with particular 'wonder and delight', and was instrumental in his decision to devote himself to art rather than to holy orders.[2] KW

1. Birmingham Museums and Art Gallery; Surtees (1971) no. 42; Treuherz (2003) no. 11.
2. Burne-Jones (1904) I, p. 110.

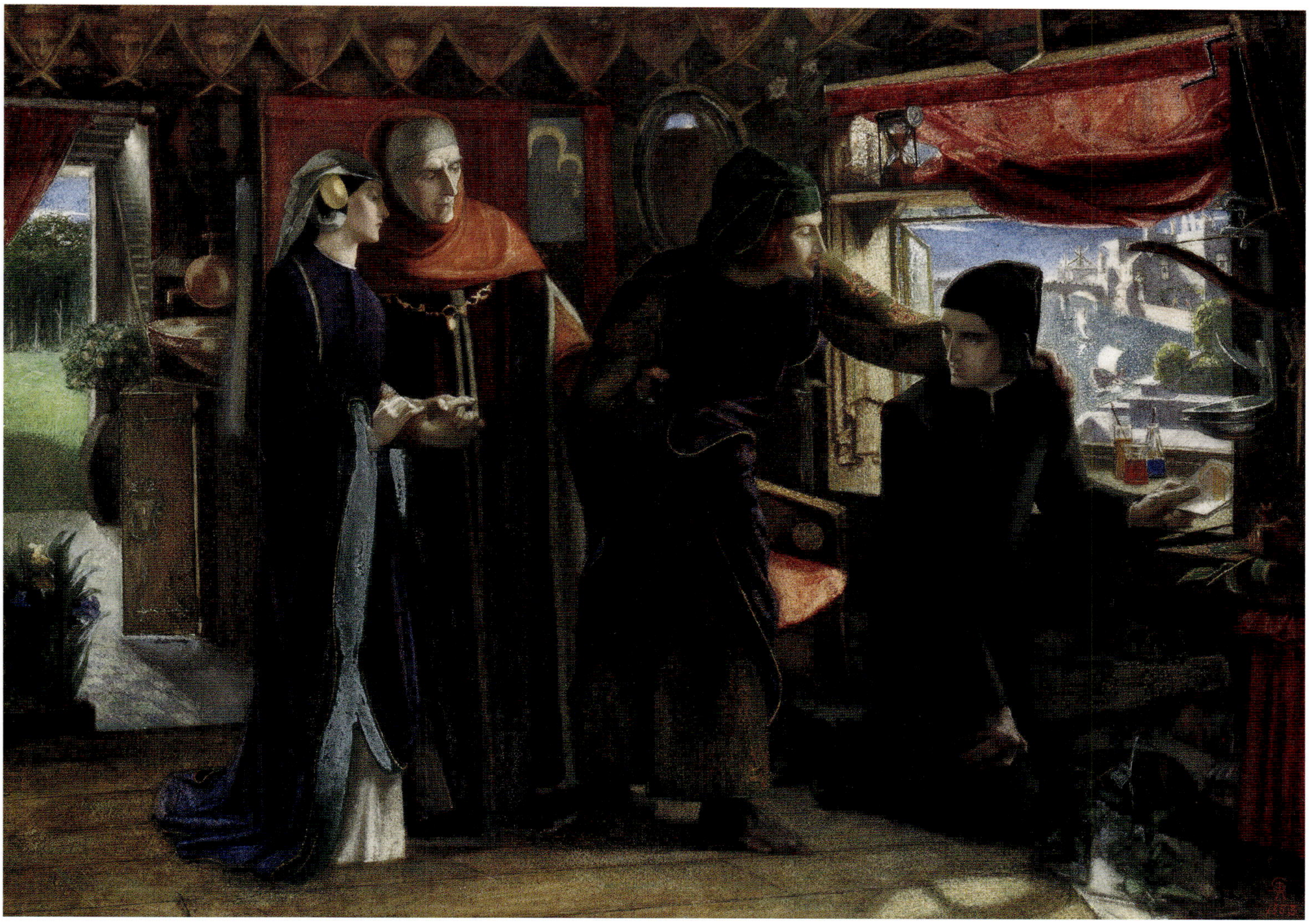

63

SIR JOHN EVERETT MILLAIS 1829–1896

William Holman Hunt, 1854

Black chalk with brown wash on cream paper
22 × 17.5 cm
Signed in monogram and dated: *JEM / 18 × 54*
Bequeathed by Mrs Thomas Combe, 1893
WA1893.8

LITERATURE: Funnell (1999) no. 27; Rosenfeld and Smith (2007) no. 36

In common with other artistic brotherhoods, notably the Nazarenes, the Pre-Raphaelite Brotherhood made portrait drawings of each other on several occasions. For example, Millais drew his friend Charles Allston Collins (1828–1873) while they were both staying with Thomas and Martha Combe in Oxford in the winter of 1850–1; and Collins reciprocated.[1] The Brotherhood lasted less than five years: Rossetti never really fitted in, and the departure of the sculptor Thomas Woolner in 1853 to seek his fortune in the gold fields of Australia broke up the group. On 12 April 1853 the Brothers all made portraits of each other to send to Woolner: Millais drew Stephens and *vice versa*, Hunt drew Millais and D. G. Rossetti, D. G. Rossetti drew Hunt and W. M. Rossetti, and W. M. Rossetti drew the whole group. When Hunt, who had long been hoping to travel to the Holy Land in search of real biblical landscapes and types, eventually announced his departure later the same year, the Combes asked Millais to make a portrait of him. Millais made a drawing of Hunt in December 1853, but wrote to Combe that 'I am so pleased with it, that as I have no other, I must keep it for myself, but will copy it for you and send it in the course of a week or two. Now that Hunt is going I don't know what will become of me'.[2] The portrait made for Combe was, in fact, much more successful. It was drawn from memory on 8 January 1854, and Millais wrote to Combe on 12 January that 'I have made a drawing of Hunt, which I think you will find very like. It is not a copy of the one I have got but another I drew on Sunday evening. I will get it framed for you (as it would rub sent as it is), and forward it as soon as it is out of the framemaker's hands'.

Much more informal than contemporary portrait drawings of, for example, John Ruskin, this work adopts a similar pose, but is less highly wrought. Hunt wears a high collar, long hair parted in the centre and hanging over the ears, with well-developed sideburns and beard, giving him an older appearance than in the portrait Millais kept for himself. The whole work is very rapidly drawn in graphite, brown wash applied only in the hair and on the striped stock, and accents added on top of the wash in the hair. Nonetheless, it is a very vivid portrait of Hunt, the most committed to Pre-Raphaelite ideals of all the Brotherhood. CH

1. Both drawings are now in the Ashmolean, WA1894.57–8.
2. Now in the National Portrait Gallery, NPG 5834.

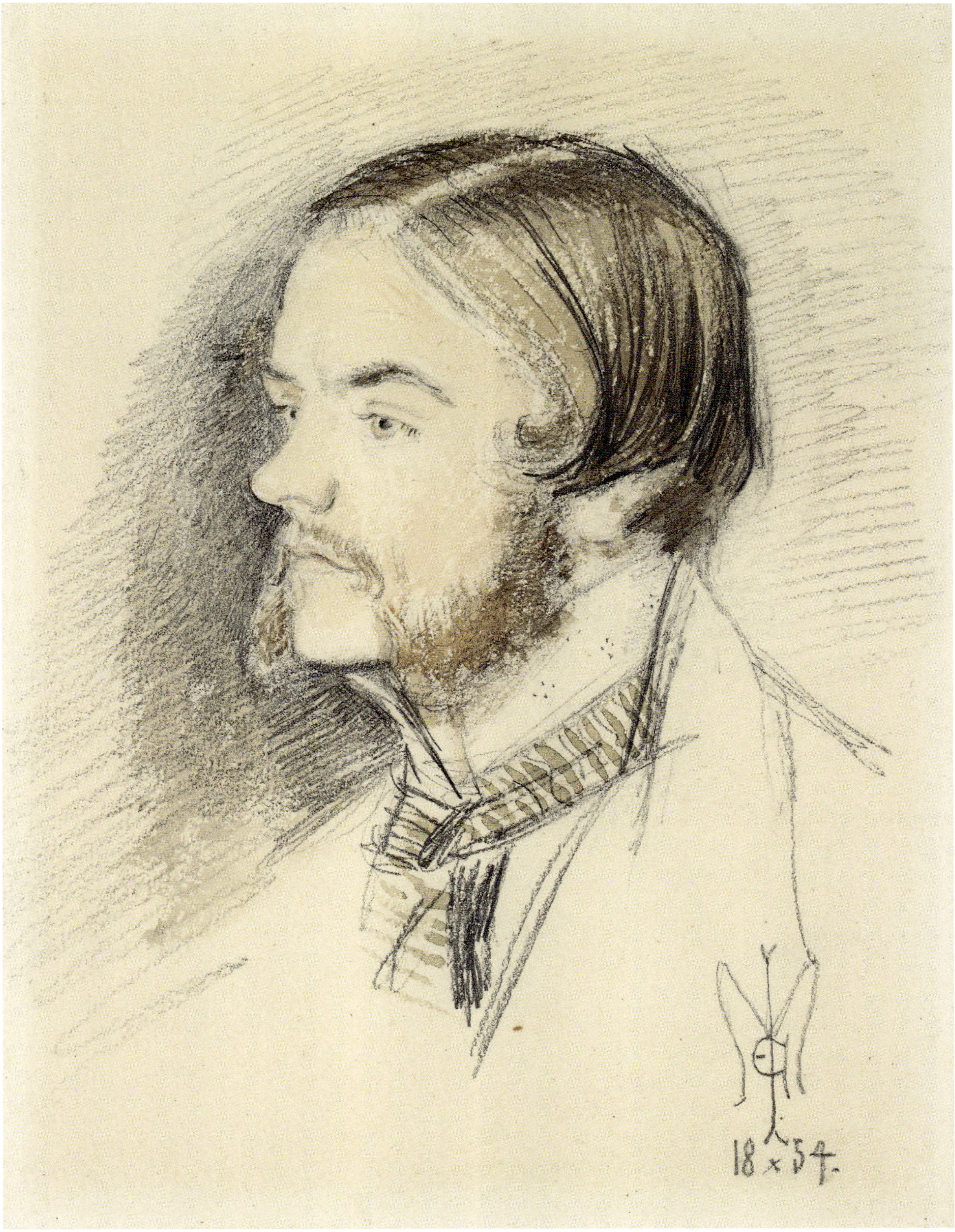
18 x 54.

64

SIR JOHN EVERETT MILLAIS 1829–1896

Five Illustrations for 'The Moxon Tennyson', 1855–7

The Sleeping Palace
Mariana
The Death of the Old Year
St Agnes Eve
The Lord of Burleigh
Pen and ink on paper
8.3 × 9.6 cm, 9.6 × 7.9 cm, 9.7 × 8.4 cm
9.7 × 7.2 cm, and 8.3 × 9.6 cm
Purchased, 1954 and 1958
WA1954.58 and WA1958.53.1–4

LITERATURE: Goldman (2004), no. 5; Rosenfeld and Smith (2007) no. 71

Millais's career as an illustrator was longer and more productive than any of his Pre-Raphaelite contemporaries. Lasting from 1852 until 1883, it resulted in over three hundred illustrations for a wide variety of books and periodicals. Apart from a handful of early etchings, all Millais's drawings were reproduced by other artists, generally as wood engravings, and most often by the firm of Dalziel Brothers.

The Moxon Tennyson was conceived by the publisher Edward Moxon to rival, indeed to eclipse, the success of William Allingham's *The Music Master* (1855), illustrated by Rossetti, Millais, and Arthur Hughes. The new edition of Tennyson's poetry, based on the text published in 1842, was to be heavily illustrated by established artists such as William Mulready, Daniel Maclise, and Thomas Creswick, as well as the more radical members of the Pre-Raphaelite Brotherhood. Holman Hunt later remembered that

> *The greater proportion were in favour of the work done by prominent artists of the old school, and their admirers were scandalised by the incorporation of designs by members of the Pre-Rapahelite Brotherhood; while our fewer appreciators would not buy the book in which the preponderance of work was by artists they did not approve.*[1]

Millais was the first artist to be approached by Moxon, and he discussed the project while visiting Tennyson at Farringford on the Isle of Wight in November 1854. He provided more designs than either Rossetti or Holman Hunt, 18 in total, and they rank with his most accomplished and atmospheric works. These highly finished drawings would have been preceded by rough sketches, and it has even been suggested that they are not working drawings but repetitions of the wood engravings made for sale. They are undoubtedly among the artist's most beguiling creations. On a tiny scale, using the finest of pen nibs, Millais has succeeded in evoking not only the details of architecture and dress, but also the mood of each poem. His long familiarity with the texts gave him an unerring facility in selecting the best lines to illustrate. For *Mariana*, for example, Millais chose the same lines that he had illustrated in one of his first major oils for the Royal Academy in 1851 (now in the Tate): "Then', she said, 'I am very dreary, / He will not come', she said; / She wept, 'I am aweary, aweary, / Oh God, that I were dead!"

When Moxon died in 1858, over three-quarters of the print run of his edition of *Poems by Alfred Tennyson* (1857) remained unsold. After the stock had been bought by Routledge, however, it quickly sold out, and remains one of the greatest of all English illustrated books. CH

1. Quoted in Sanders (2001) p. 78.

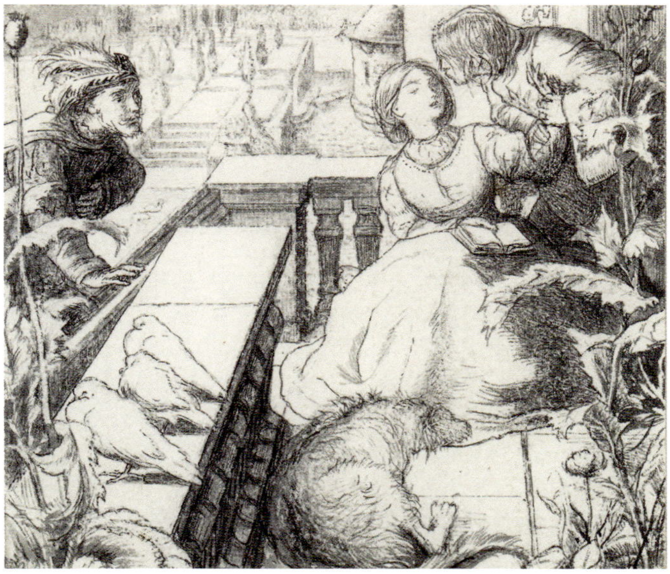

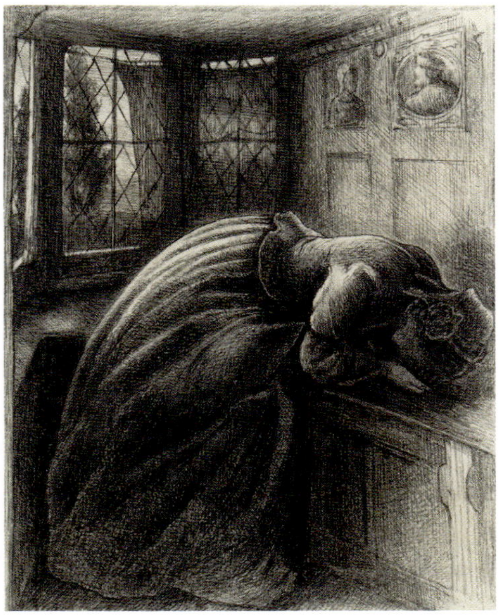

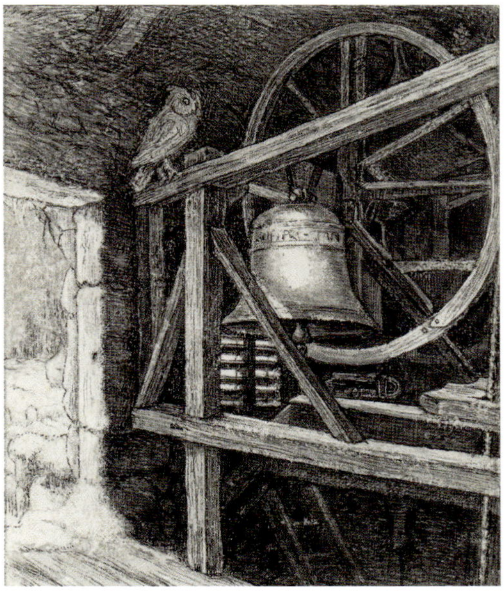

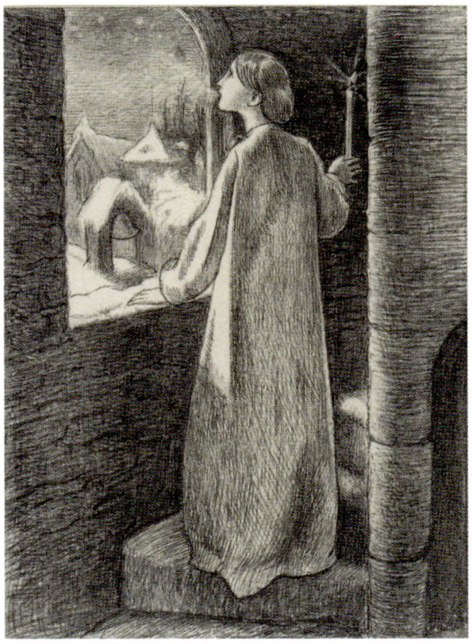

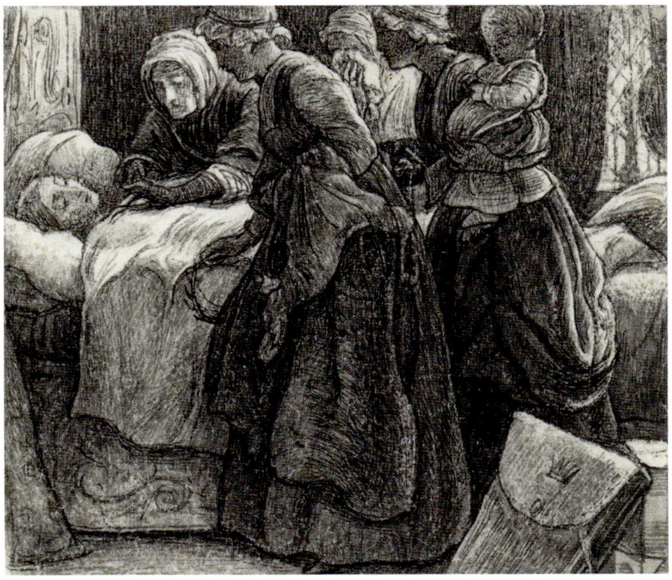

65

WILLIAM HOLMAN HUNT 1827–1910

Thomas Combe, 1860

Red and black chalk on paper
67.6 × 47.9 cm
Signed and dated: *Whh /1860 / Oxford*
Bequeathed by Mrs Thomas Combe, 1893
WA1894.20

LITERATURE: Bronkhurst (2006) no. D197

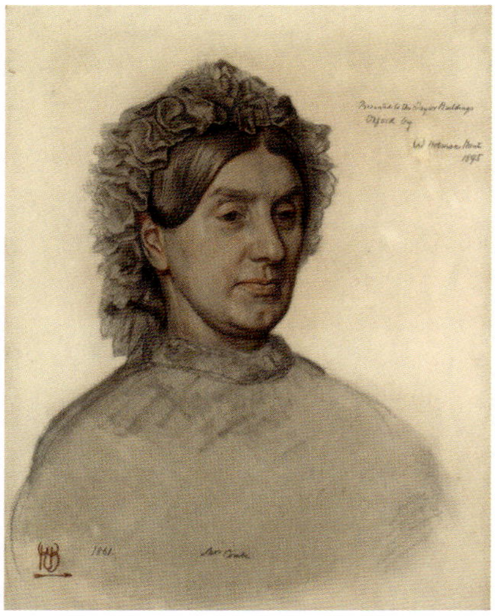

Fig. 46 | William Holman Hunt (1827–1910), *Mrs Thomas Combe*, 1861. Red and black chalk. Ashmolean Museum, Oxford, WA1895.11

Thomas Combe (1796–1872) was the son of a Leicester bookseller. He continued in that profession in London, Oxford, and Leicester before moving permanently to Oxford in 1838 to be superintendent of one division of the University Press, the side devoted to 'learning', i.e. classical texts. He was married to Martha Bennett by John Henry Newman in 1840 and bought his first shares in the 'bible' side of the Press in the following year. By 1851 he was the majority shareholder and relinquished his interest in the 'learning' side. The Combes were deeply committed to the Tractarian, or High Church, movement, and made their first major acquisition as collectors in 1850, when they bought Holman Hunt's *A Converted British Family*. They subsequently acquired the major exhibits by Millais and Charles Allston Collins in 1851, and a Rossetti water-colour in 1855, but later concentrated on their patronage of Hunt. In 1853 the couple bought Holman Hunt's *The Light of the World* (Keble College, Oxford), for 400 guineas (Combe's income at this period was over £4,000 a year). All their major purchases were bequeathed to the University Galleries, Oxford (now the Ashmolean Museum), on the death of Mrs Combe in 1893.

Hunt remained close to the Combes all his life. On a visit to Oxford in 1852, he declared that Combe was 'such a glorious fellow as to be perfectly delightful as a companion although 60 years of age, or nearly … I must say that he comes more nearly up to my conception of a good practical happy Christian than any man ever met by me'.[1] Combe acted as Hunt's banker during his journey to the Near East in 1854–6, and he later made regular visits to the quadrangle of the University Press, spending Christmas 1859 in Oxford, followed by a summer holiday in June 1860, when this portrait was presumably taken. In the following year he made a companion portrait of Mrs Combe, which he presented to the University Galleries after her death (fig. 46).[2]

Hunt had made a number of small chalk or pen and ink portraits in the early 1850s. However, he later adopted a much broader and grander scale in black and coloured chalks, to depict his disciples Edward Lear (1857) and Robert Braithwaite Martineau (1860), his patrons Thomas and Martha Combe (1860–1), his first and second wives (1866, 1881), and his daughter (1891).[3] The portrait of Combe is probably the most successful. Combe had grown a beard in the late 1850s and was frequently termed 'the Patriarch'. Hunt shows him with abundant grey hair, bushy eyebrows and a full white beard, looking in a conspiratorial manner towards the artist or viewer, a man of great character and resolution as well as a close friend.

1. Bronkhurst (2006) I, p. 47.
2. Bronkhurst (2006) no. D214.
3. Bronkhurst (2006) nos. D72, D196, D175, D214, D242, D246, D348, D385.

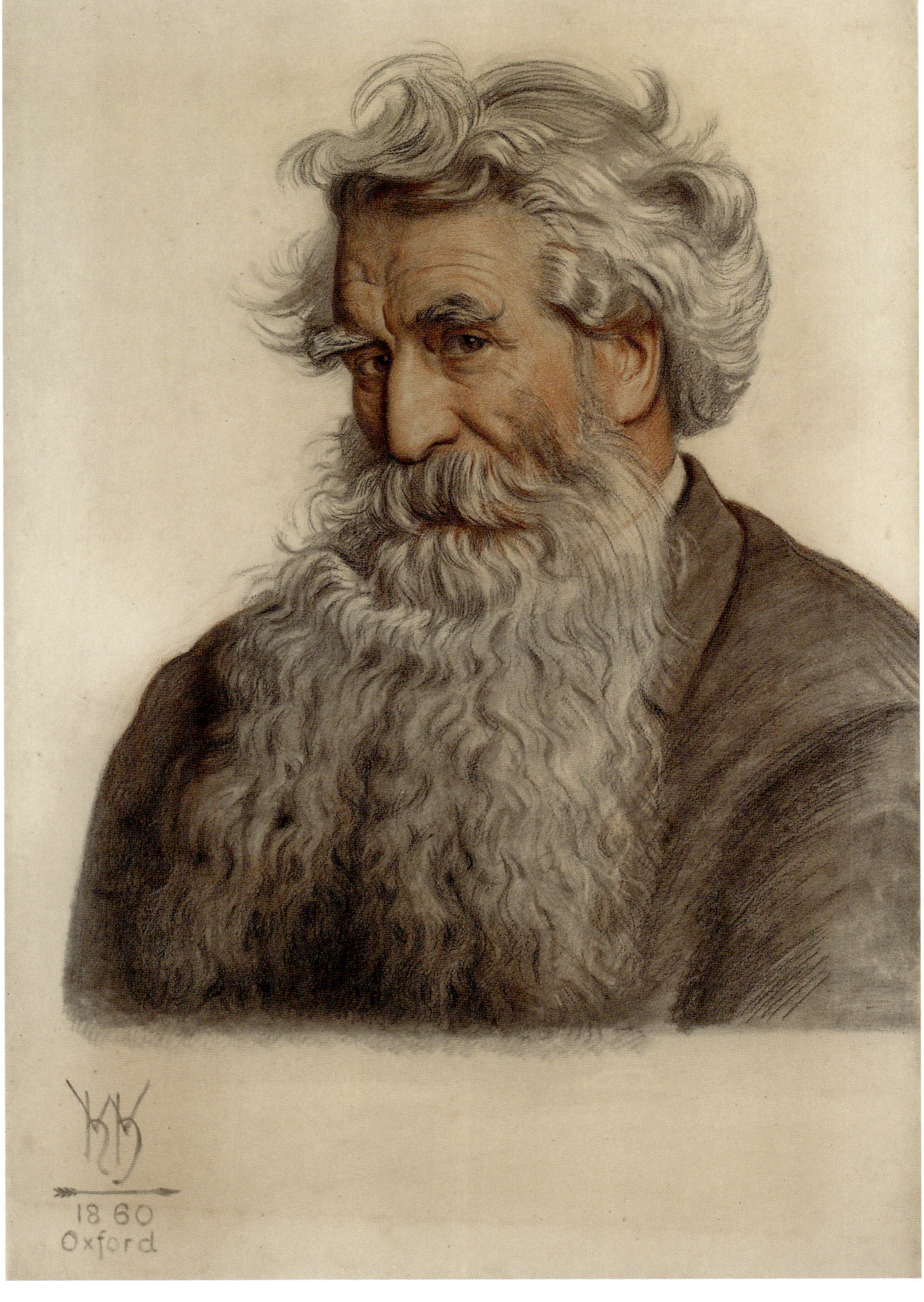
1860
Oxford

66

DANTE GABRIEL ROSSETTI 1828–1882
Elizabeth Siddal, 1855

Pen and brown and black ink on paper, with some scratching out
13 × 11.2 cm
Signed and dated: *DGR / Feb. 6 / 1855*
Bequeathed by Francis Falconer Madan, 1962
WA1962.17.77

LITERATURE: Surtees (1971) no. 472; Surtees (1991) no. 26; Treuherz (2003) no. 28

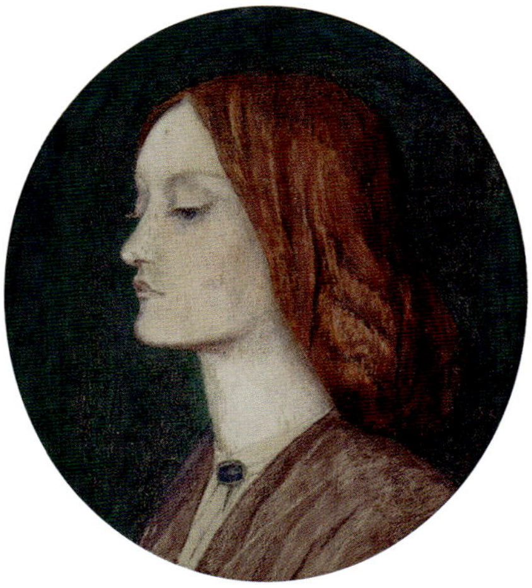

Fig. 47 | Dante Gabriel Rossetti (1828–1882), *Elizabeth Siddal*, 1854. Watercolour on wove paper. Ashmolean Museum, Oxford, WA2011.57

Born on 25 July 1829 in Hatton Garden, Holborn, Elizabeth 'Lizzie' Siddal was the daughter of a Sheffield cutler. She entered the Pre-Raphaelite circle around 1849 or 1850, having been spotted by Walter Deverell working in a milliner's shop near Leicester Square. Rossetti would later remark that having met her he 'felt his destiny was defined'.[1] Siddal initially modelled for a number of Pre-Raphaelite artists, including Holman Hunt and Millais, but from 1852 she sat exclusively to Rossetti, becoming both his muse and pupil, and eventually in 1860 his wife. Siddal suffered protracted periods of ill health and emotional upheaval, partly owing to Rossetti's apparent infidelities. She gave birth to a still-born daughter in 1861 and died from an overdose of laudanum in 1862.

Fifty-eight drawings by Rossetti of Siddal survive, all created in the period 1850–61 (although none from October 1856 to 1860, during which time the couple were partially estranged). In 1854 Ford Madox Brown, Rossetti's former teacher and mentor, recorded after a visit to the artist that Rossetti had a drawer filled with studies of the lovely 'Guggums' (one of several pet names by which Siddal was known) 'each one a fresh charm, each one stamped with immortality', exclaiming 'God knows how many, it is like a monomania with him'.[2] With her queenly physique, dreamy expressive eyes and heavy, copper-red hair, Siddal's appearance became a keynote in the Pre-Raphaelite articulation of female beauty. However, she was not merely an object of desire and reverence but had latent talent as an artist and poet in her own right. In April 1855 John Ruskin bestowed on Siddal an annual sum of £150 in return for all of the work that she produced, and he encouraged her in 1857 to attend art classes in Sheffield. Several of her works were shown in the Pre-Raphaelite exhibition at Russell Place that same year.

Of all Rossetti's drawings of Siddal, this most poignantly captures both the sitter's evasive melancholy and the artist's tender response to her delicate beauty. Unusually she is shown full-face, although with her eyes typically downcast. The gleam of gaslight from the right, achieved by scraping away the inked surface, accentuates the lustre of the sitter's hair and casts half of her expression into shadow, epitomising her reserved and enigmatic character. KW

1. Treuherz (2003) p. 37.
2. Surtees (1991) pp. 101 and 148.

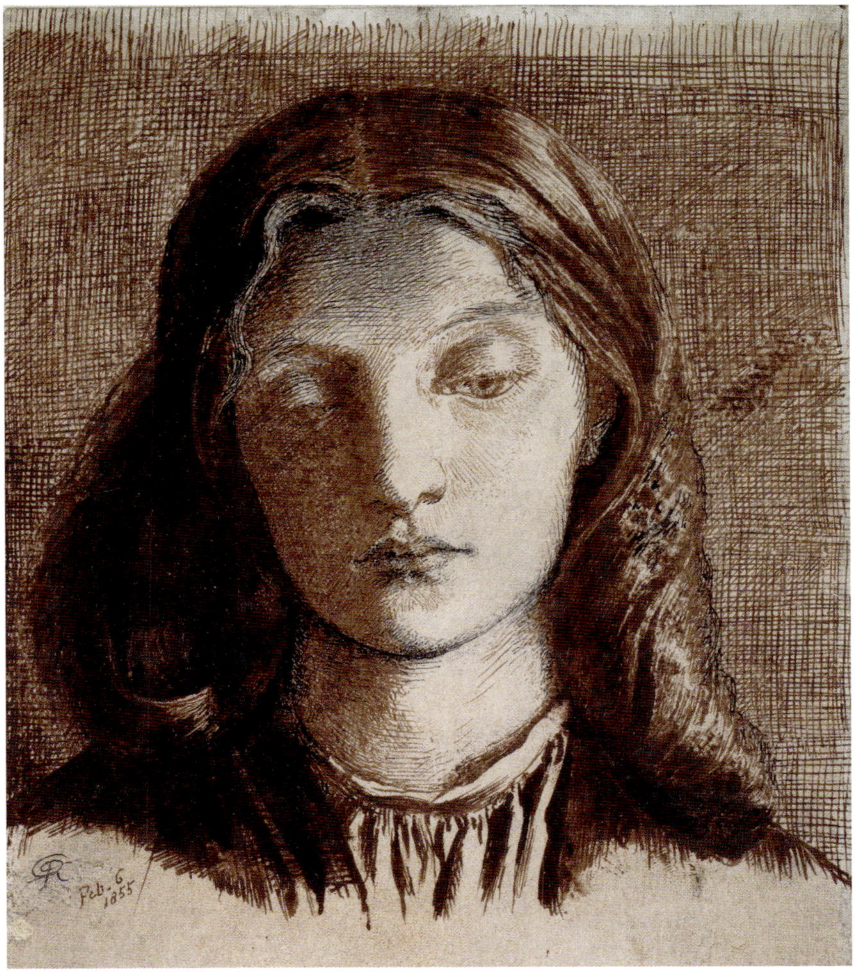
Feb. 6
1855

67

DANTE GABRIEL ROSSETTI 1828–1882

Louisa Ruth Herbert, 1858

Graphite on wove paper
framed as an oval
50.8 × 43 cm (frame)
Inscribed: *Ruth Herbert / 1858 / DGR delt*
Presented by Virginia Surtees, 2014
WA2014.38

LITERATURE: Surtees (1971) no. 325

Miss Herbert made her official debut in London at the Strand Theatre in October 1855. Rossetti discovered her in February 1856 at the Olympic Theatre and captivated by beauty, made a quick sketch, which he annotated 'Stunner No I'.[1] Two years later, he wrote excitedly from his studio at 14 Chatham Place, Blackfriars to William Bell Scott, 'I am in the stunning position this morning of expecting the actual visit, at ½ past 11, of a model whom I have been longing to paint for years – Miss Herbert of the Olympic Theatre – who has the most varied and highest expression I ever saw in a woman's face, besides abundant beauty, golden hair etc. … O my eye she will sit to me for Mary Magdalene in that picture I am beginning. Such luck!'[2]

Known to Rossetti as Ruth Herbert, although formally Mrs Crabbe, the actress embodied a type of female beauty that would dominate Rossetti's work in the 1860s, one quite distinct from that of the imperious but fragile Lizzie Siddal. Her glorious hair, frequently mentioned by contemporary theatrical reviewers, is depicted with alluring softness in Rossetti's portrait. The undulating waves of her coiffure are echoed with great subtlety by the modelling of her throat, the ripples of her simple collar and the sensual curve of her lips. The earrings, ubiquitous in her portraits, are used to great dramatic effect in the gesture of their removal in Rossetti's *Mary Magdalene at the Door of the House of Simon* (completed 1859).[3] The profession of actress was synonymous with that of courtesan in Victorian society, and Miss Herbert's marital status the source of considerable complication, making the casting particularly apt.

Rossetti's fervent and contradictory reverence for her is encapsulated by the inscription he gave to one of his watercolours, 'BEATRICE HELEN GUENEVERE HERBERT'.[4] The quality of Miss Herbert's appearance was such that the artists gathered around the hospitability of Mrs Prinsep, at Little Holland House, would admire her as though she were, in her own later words, 'a holy thing'.[5] Ruskin urged Rossetti to use her for his altarpiece *The Seed of David* at Llandaff Cathedral, although in 1861, her features were supplanted in this painting by those of Jane Morris, whose husband William sat for the figure of David.

In exchange for sittings over the course of about a year, Rossetti made portraits of Miss Herbert, and 17 such works were in her possession at the time of her death. This particular drawing served as an illustration to Georgiana Burne-Jones's biography of her husband, Edward, published in 1904. It was recently given to the Ashmolean by the sitter's great grand-daughter. KW

1. Surtees (1997) p. 22.
2. Surtees (1997) p. 35.
3. Surtees (1997) no. 109.
4. Surtees (1971) no. 335.
5. Marsh (1999) pp. 193–4.

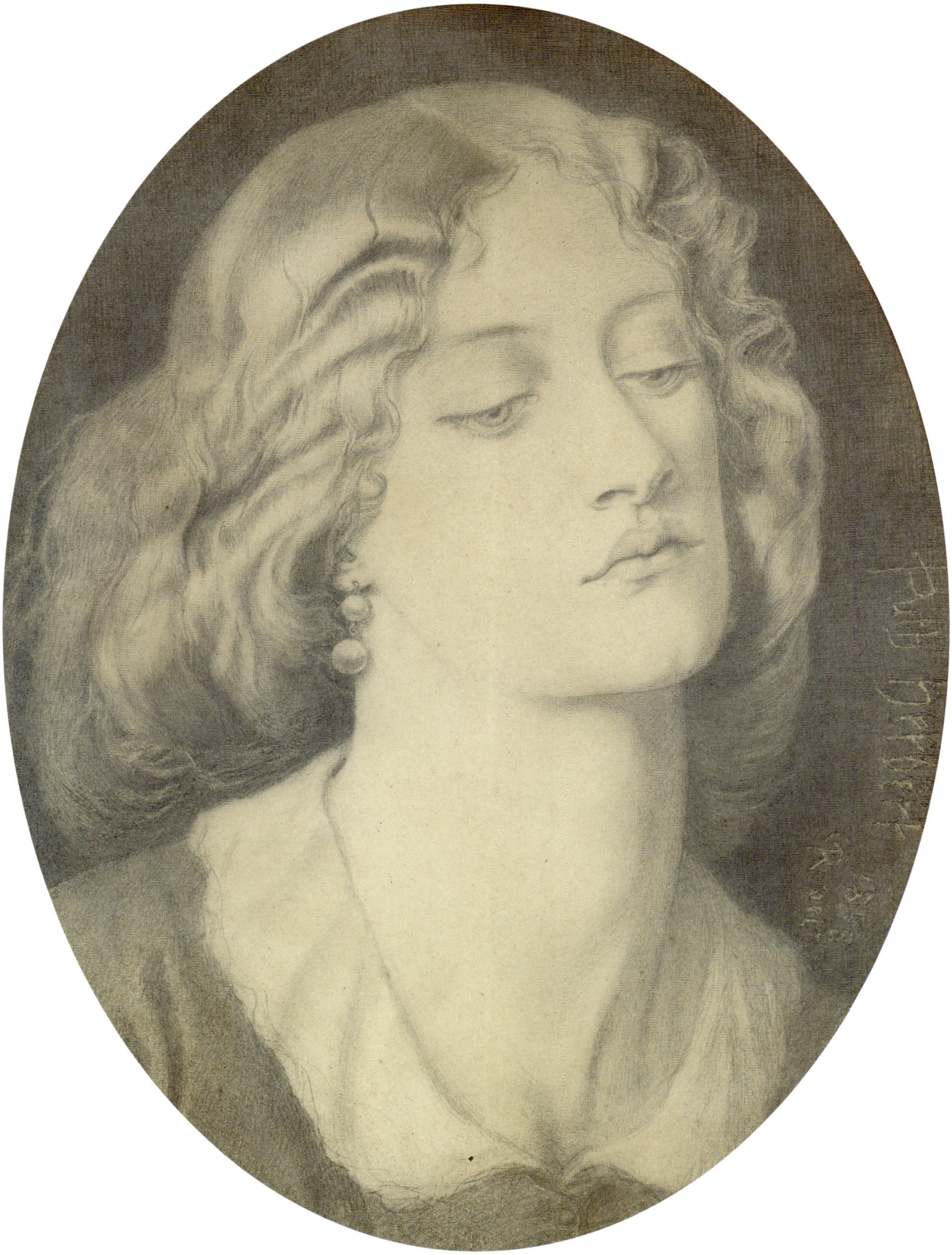
Ruth Herbert

68

DANTE GABRIEL ROSSETTI 1828–1882

Proserpine, 1871

Pastel on two sheets of paper
97 × 46 cm
Signed in monogram and dated: *DGR 1871*
Bequeathed by May Morris, 1939
WA1939.5

LITERATURE: Surtees (1971) no. 233A; Cruise (2012) no. 286

Of all Rossetti's 'stunners', the features of Jane Morris recur in his work with the greatest intensity. Over 25 years the artist would portray her more than 40 times – both as 'herself', in formal and informal portraits, and in the guise of mythical, historical, and literary characters from Dante to classical legend.

Rossetti first met Jane Burden in 1857, while in Oxford working on the sequence of murals for the interior of the new Union Library. She would be cast, with uncanny prescience, in the role of Guinevere, while Burne-Jones modelled Launcelot in Rossetti's *Launcelot at the Chapel of the San Graal*. Jane married William Morris in 1859 but by late 1869 Jane and Rossetti were intimately involved, and her image came to dominate his work. Writing to her in February 1870 he declared, 'No-one seems alive at all to me now, and places that are empty of you are empty of all life'.[1]

Between 1871 and 1877 Rossetti produced at least eight oil paintings of Jane as Proserpine, along with numerous other versions on paper in various media. This work was probably executed during the first idyllic summer that Jane and Rossetti spent together at Kelmscott Manor, near Lechlade in Oxfordshire, while William Morris magnanimously travelled in Iceland. The drawing remained in Jane's possession, and was bequeathed to the Ashmolean by her daughter May in accordance with her mother's wishes.

The subject of Proserpine abducted to the Underworld and trapped there for half of every year has clear resonances with the triangular relationship of Morris, Jane, and Rossetti. Yet the imposing, monumental stature of the brooding figure, together with the sonnets in Italian and in English that Rossetti inscribed on to other versions of the composition, make it clear that *Proserpine* is an exploration of death, hope, and the imagination. While her consumption of the pomegranate partially condemns Proserpine to the Underworld, in Christian symbolism the fruit was an emblem of the Resurrection. The light in the background is thus not only a tantalising glimmer from the (for now) unattainable world above, but a possible suggestion of hope. This tale of opposing halves is replicated in the construction of the drawing from two pieces of paper, chamfered together, as well as the contrasting articulation of surfaces in the work. The figure's flesh is conveyed in rich blended pastel, distinct from the background and folds of her green-blue silk robe, which are swiftly worked in free, individually discernible strokes. The enduring power of the image derives from its ability to encompass both a personal and a primal meaning, encouraging wide-ranging meditation in the viewer. KW

1. Quoted in Spencer-Longhurst (2000) p. 25.

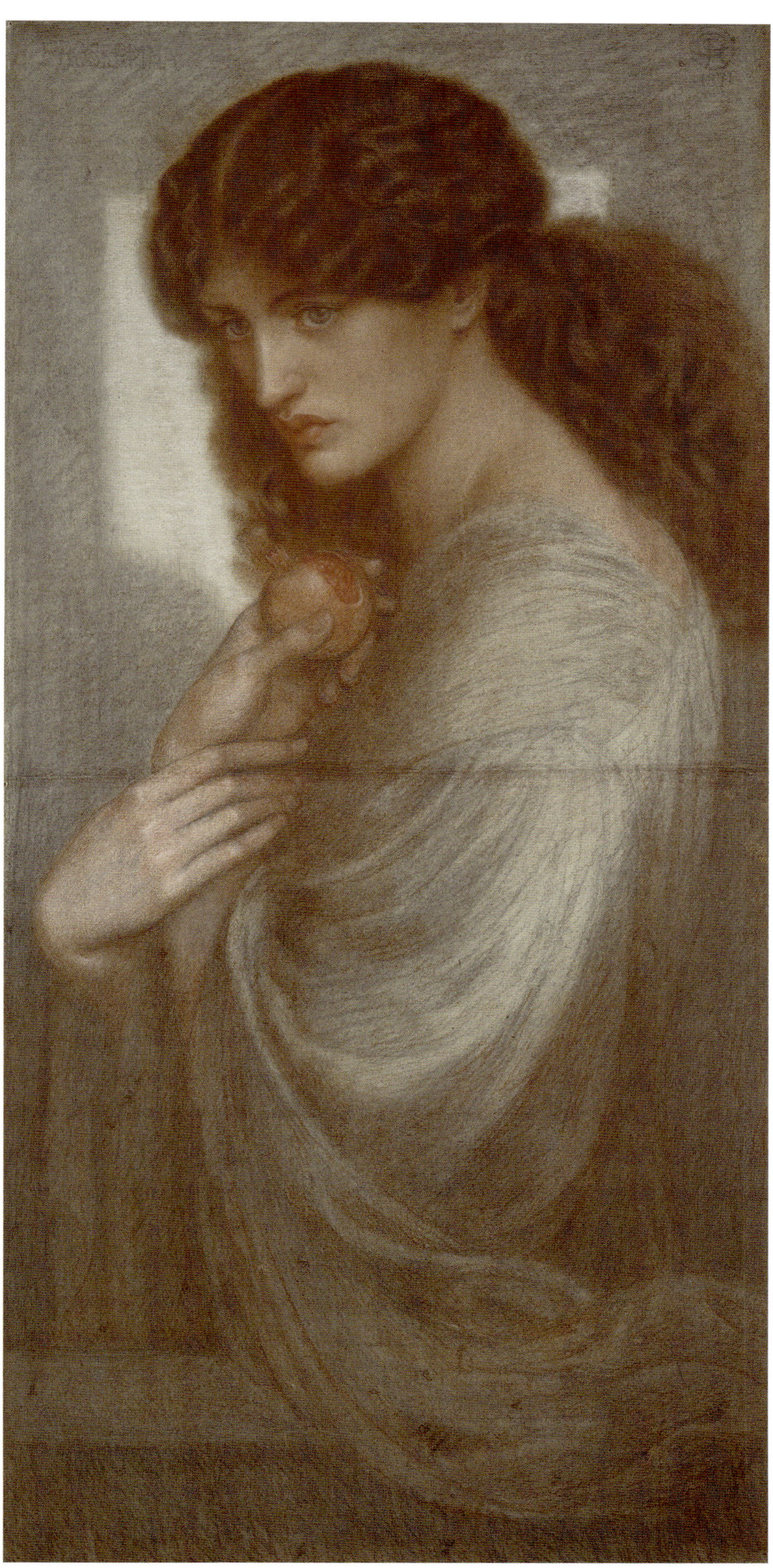

69

EMILY MARY OSBORN 1828–1925

Study for 'Nameless and Friendless', c. 1857

Black and red chalk heightened with white on buff paper
80 × 72 cm
Inscribed: *Millais, 1854*
Purchased, 1965
WA1965.60

LITERATURE: Cherry (1987) pl. 10, pp. 78–81

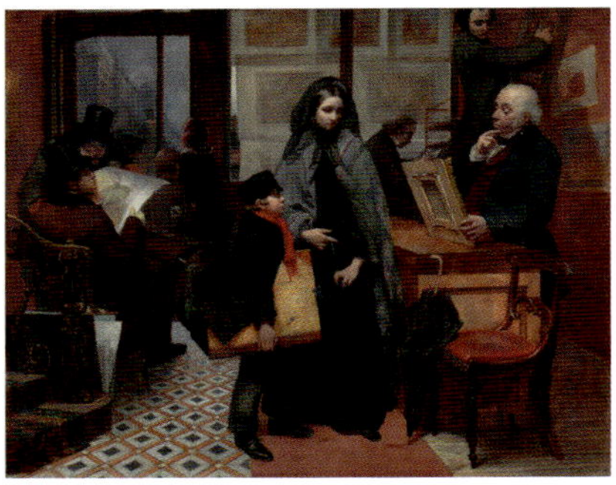

Fig. 48 | Emily Mary Osborn (1834–1925), *Nameless and Friendless*, 1857. Oil on canvas. Tate, London, T12936 © Tate, London 2014

This drawing is a finished study for the painting *Nameless and Friendless*, exhibited at the Royal Academy in 1857 and the International Exhibition in 1862.[1] It incorporates a ruled perspective construction related to the full composition, and scored lines are visible throughout, following the main outlines. This indicates that it was probably traced for transfer using a stylus, so it is likely to have been used as a cartoon for the final painting. The work shows a young woman standing; she nervously winds a length of string around her fingers as a corpulent dealer considers her work. Next to her stands a boy, probably a younger brother for whom she has responsibility, clutching a portfolio of drawings. The young boy, in particular, is beautifully drawn, the delicate red in his ear indicating his exposure to the elements. It has been suggested that the image is based on the novel *Self-Control* by Mary Brunton (1810, reprinted 1855), but the similar incidents described in chapter IX of the book make no mention of this boy.

In the finished painting we see two top-hatted gentlemen, and a well-dressed woman leaving the shop followed by a servant. They clearly illustrate the contrast between wealth and poverty underlined by the lines from Proverbs (10.15), which were attached to the painting in the Royal Academy catalogue: 'The rich man's wealth is his strong city: the destruction of the poor is their poverty.' The painting called attention to the difficulties faced by respectable middle-class women forced to make a living through their art in a society that frowned on their participation in the marketplace. The distressed gentlewoman – struggling to survive as a governess, writer or dressmaker – was a familiar figure in the art and literature of this period, and the 'Woman Question' would continue to be debated for much of the century. The year 1857 also marked the formation of the Society of Female Artists, designed to support such women. Osborn became a member of the Society, and in 1859 signed a petition calling for women to be admitted to the Royal Academy Schools.[2]

Osborn pursued a highly successful career as a genre and landscape painter. The daughter of a clergyman, she trained at James Leigh's drawing school in London and exhibited widely. Two of her paintings were purchased by Queen Victoria, and *Nameless and Friendless* sold for £250. Through such lucrative sales, Osborn financed her own studio. Several of her works demonstrate 'protest in favour of the afflicted and down-trodden classes'.[3] *Half the World Knows not how the Other Half Lives* was awarded a prize at the Crystal Palace exhibition of 1864 as the best figure subject in oil by any British artist. CP

1. An oil sketch for the full composition is in York City Art Gallery (YORAG 1483).
2. Charlotte Yeldham, 'Osborn, Emily Mary (1828–1925)', *Oxford Dictionary of National Biography* (2004), http://www.oxforddnb.com/view/article/48916, accessed 6 January 2015.
3. *The Queen*, 4 December 1880, p. 501.

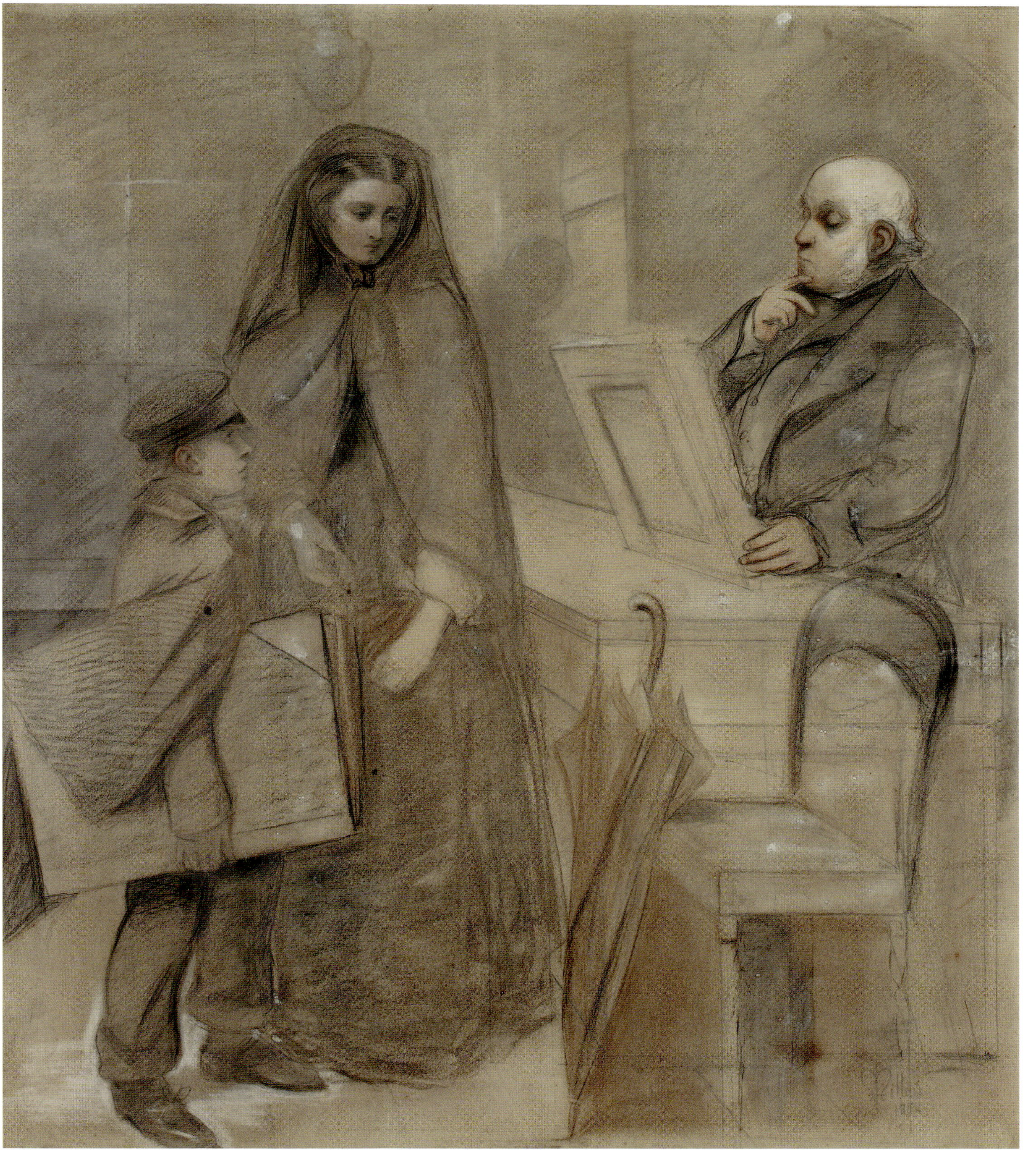

70

FORD MADOX BROWN 1821–1893

The Nosegay, 1865

Watercolour and oil on paper
47.5 × 31.9 cm
Signed in monogram: *FMB*
Presented by Mrs W. F. R. Weldon, 1933
WA1933.5

LITERATURE: Bennett (2010) no. A84; Treuherz (2011) no. 93

Ford Madox Brown was never a member of the Pre-Raphaelite Brotherhood, indeed never suggested as a member, though he was closely associated with them in the 1850s. Unlike his younger friends, he enjoyed a cosmopolitan education, studying at the Academies in Bruges, Ghent, and Antwerp, and then in Rome, where he worked out his first masterpiece, the huge *Geoffrey Chaucer Reading the 'Legend of Custance' to Edward III and his Court* (1847–51).[1] For a brief period in the 1860s he produced a number of Aesthetic subjects, female figures with little narrative content, in emulation of Dante Gabriel Rossetti's *Bocca Bacciata* (1859; Museum of Fine Arts, Boston).

In 1865 Brown held a one-man exhibition at 196 Piccadilly, where he came to the attention of the Manchester collector, Frederick Craven (1818–1895). Through the intermediary of Rossetti, Craven commissioned from Brown a pendant to a watercolour by William Henry Hunt of *A Boy Praying* (now in Manchester City Art Gallery), of 'a golden headed female party'.[2] Brown considered and rejected the possibility of making a watercolour repetition of an earlier subject, and noted that 'the subject of "The Nosegay" on the other hand being not as yet fixed in any way, I could make it accord more perfectly as to size of figure and general proportions with Hunt's design, without thinking of giving up my own feelings or style'.[3]

The model for the figure was Brown's daughter Cathy (born in 1850), and the setting the garden of their home at Grove Terrace, Kentish Town. According to his diary, the artist worked most intensively on the subject in the autumn months of 1865, finishing it on 25 October. A smaller watercolour was completed at much the same time and, though generally described as a sketch, is more probably a repetition.[4] The subject is a comely young woman in white holding a large bouquet of garden flowers, with a cat nuzzling at her legs through her skirt. The high garden wall appears in many early Pre-Raphaelite paintings, and derives from the medieval concept of the *hortus conclusus*.

Craven was initially pleased with *The Nosegay*, finding it a 'very charming work'.[5] In 1868, however, he decided to offer it back to Brown, having persuaded himself that the artist's more high-minded history subjects would suit him better – he later bought versions of Elijah and Cordelia. Nevertheless, Brown managed to sell the work easily to the great Pre-Raphaelite collector, William Graham (cat. 75). CH

1. Art Gallery of New South Wales; Bennett (2010) no. A40.
2. Bennett (2010) I, p. 221.
3. *Ibid.*
4. Lady Lever Art Gallery, Port Sunlight; Bennett (2010) no. A84a.
5. Bennett (2010) I, p. 222.

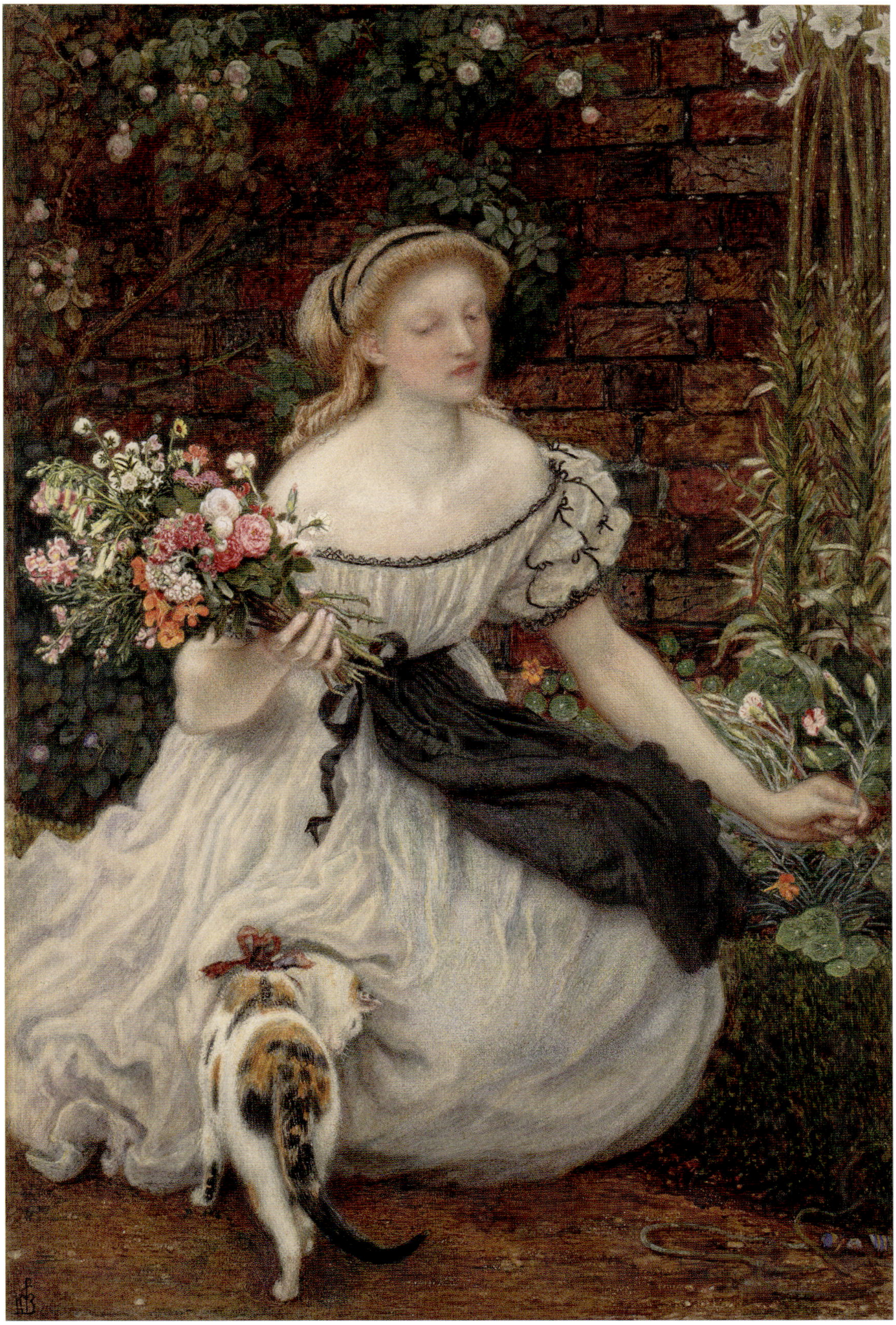

71

SIR EDWARD COLEY BURNE-JONES 1833–1898

The Knight's Farewell, 1858

Pen and black ink over graphite on vellum
17.6 × 24.2 cm
Signed in monogram and dated: *EBJ 1858*
Inscribed: *ROMAN / DU QUESTE / DU / SADGRAIL*
Bequeathed by John Bryson, 1977
WA1977.34

LITERATURE: Arts Council (1975–6) no. 12; Wildman and Christian (1998) no. 5; Prettejohn (2000) p. 103

In 1855 Burne-Jones discovered a copy of Southey's edition (1817) of Sir Thomas Malory's *Le Morte d'Arthur* (1485). He was unable to afford the purchase, however, and his friend and fellow student at Exeter College, Oxford, William Morris, acquired the book. So began Burne-Jones's life-long exploration of Arthurian romance and the *Legend of the San Grael* in particular – an affinity he shared with Morris, who later purchased *The Knight's Farewell*. The following year Burne-Jones met Rossetti and subsequently left Oxford to study under him in London.

Prevented by fragile health in the late 1850s from working in oils, Burne-Jones produced a series of fine, densely worked pen and ink drawings inspired by medieval chivalry; all were on the theme of the departure for battle. Familiar with the medium from his earlier illustrations for Archibald Maclaren's *Fairy Family* (1854–6), he now refined his technique, having encountered Rossetti's drawings. Rossetti in turn described Burne-Jones's drawings to William Bell Scott as 'marvels in finish and imaginative detail, unequalled by anything except perhaps Albert Dürer's work'.[1] Through Rossetti, in 1856 Burne-Jones was introduced to John Ruskin, who in *The Elements of Drawing* (1857) recommended Dürer's engravings as models for pen and ink drawing. In all likelihood Ruskin lent the young Burne-Jones examples of Dürer's prints from his own collection.

Burne-Jones spent the summer of 1858 at Little Holland House, whose grounds his widow, Georgiana, later described as an 'enchanted circle'; and at Summertown near Oxford, where her husband read aloud from Malory in the garden.[2] The composition and stylised figures of *The Knight's Farewell* owe much to Rossetti's 'Froissartian' watercolours. However, the enclosed space in the foreground where an anguished male figure is comforted, as well as the suggestion of violent action confined to a narrow strip above, also resemble Hunt's *A Converted British Family* (1850; Ashmolean Museum), which Burne-Jones had seen when he visited Thomas Combe in 1855 (cat. 65). The inclination of the woman's head recalls Siddal's *Lady Clare* (*c.* 1854–7; private collection).

The vellum support imitates the medieval manuscripts that Burne-Jones and Morris had admired in the Bodleian Library, while the drawing is painstakingly executed with a metal pen, over indications in graphite which glint in the outline of the figures. Elaborate patterns and curious details, such as the shadow of the dove swooping in front of the knight's pennant, crowd the entire surface. The obsessive articulation of textures includes the technique of scratching out to soften some elements, such as the contours of the facial features. The viewer is encouraged to linger intently over the meticulous details yet the narrative remains enigmatic, with the principal figure's face hidden from sight. KW

1. Fredeman (2002) II, p. 171.
2. Burne-Jones (1904) I, pp. 181 and 183.

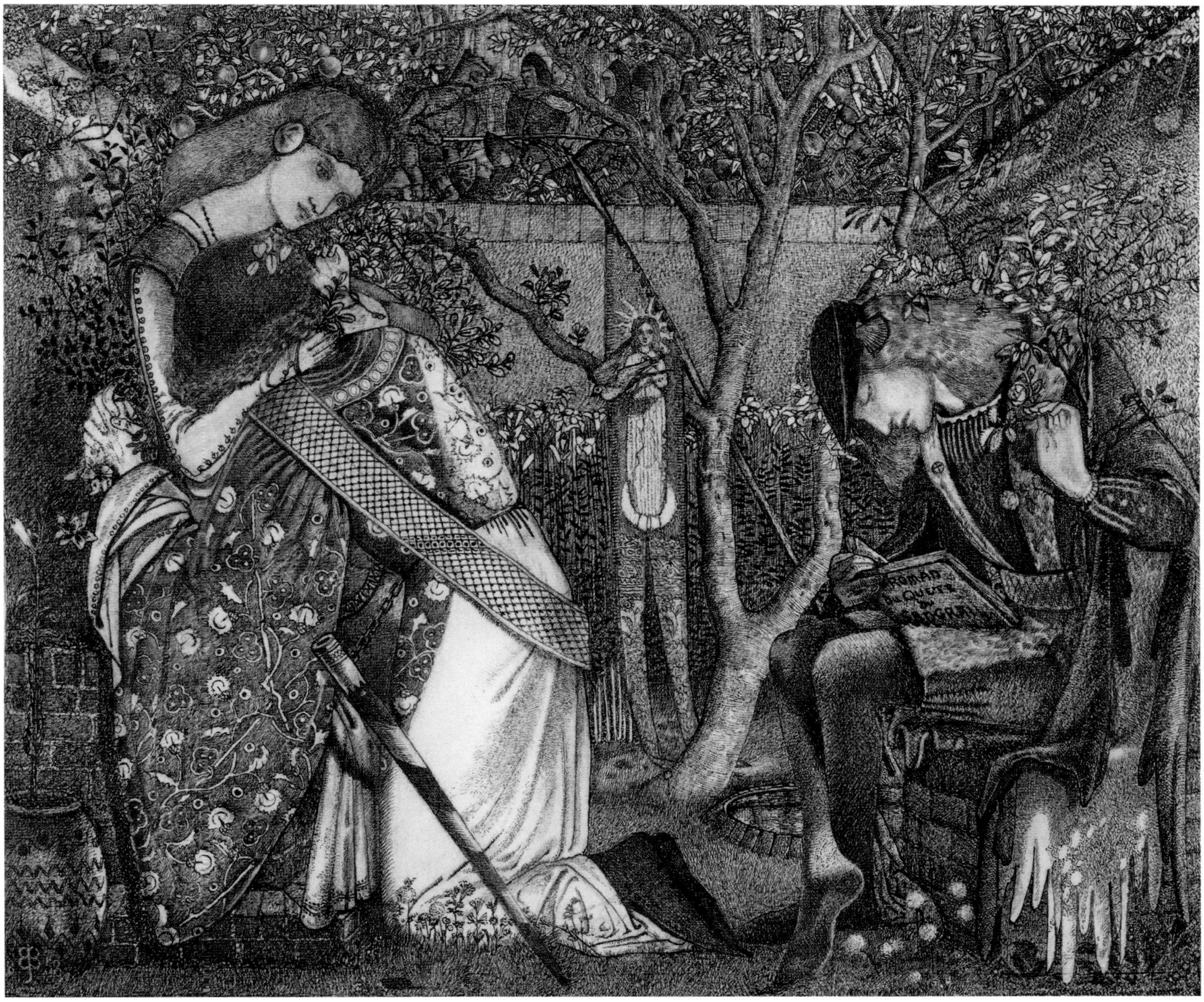
ROMAN

72

ARTHUR HUGHES 1832–1915
The Knight of the Sun, 1860–1

Watercolour and bodycolour on paper
22.3 × 31.6 cm
Signed: *A HUGHES*
Presented by Mrs Reginald Cripps, 1949
WA1949.189

LITERATURE: Brown (1987) no. 32; Roberts and Wildman (1997) no. 43.8

Like the members of the Pre-Raphaelite Brotherhood, Hughes studied at the Royal Academy Schools, but always claimed that his life had been changed by an issue of *The Germ* which included a 'strangely interesting and pathetic etching' by Holman Hunt and a 'quaint but inspiring sonnet' by William Michael Rossetti.[1] He soon became an associate of the Pre-Raphaelites, and participated in the decoration of the Oxford Union in 1857, painting *The Passing of King Arthur*.

The experience encouraged Hughes to explore medieval subjects, and he exhibited *The Knight of the Sun* at the Royal Academy in 1860, where the title was appended in the catalogue with lines from George Macdonald's poem 'Better Things': 'Better a death when work is done / Than earth's most favoured birth'.[2] According to the artist, 'a study of the sky reflecting river seen thro' a wild cherry tree autumn turned … gave me the idea first for the subject'.[3] He later described the scene as 'an aged warrior mortally wounded, being carried by his men-at-arms to the shelter of a religious house'; though F. G. Stephens explained that '*The Knight of the Sun* illustrates a legend, an incident of which declared how an old knight, whose badge was a sun, and who had led a Christian life throughout his career, was borne out of his castle to see, for the last time, the setting of the luminary he loved'.[4]

This watercolour was painted for Benjamin Godfrey Windus, probably soon after the oil was exhibited. The knight in armour is draped in red, and carried by three of his warriors. Behind him a page carries his shield, blazoned with the emblem of the sun, and his horse and two other warriors bring up the rear. The setting sun shines most strongly on the knight's face, and is reflected in the river on the right, a symbol of the passing of life. The landscape is painted with Pre-Raphaelite detail, each leaf of the autumn trees, the fallen twigs and boughs, carefully delineated. The richness of the colouring owes much to Rossetti's watercolours, though the strong but subtle lighting reflects Hughes's technique in oils, with clear outlines and defined masses. CH

1. Quoted in Roberts and Wildman (1997) pp. 12–3.
2. Lord Lloyd-Webber; Roberts and Wildman (1997) no. 43.
3. Quoted in Roberts and Wildman (1997) p. 146.
4. *Ibid.*

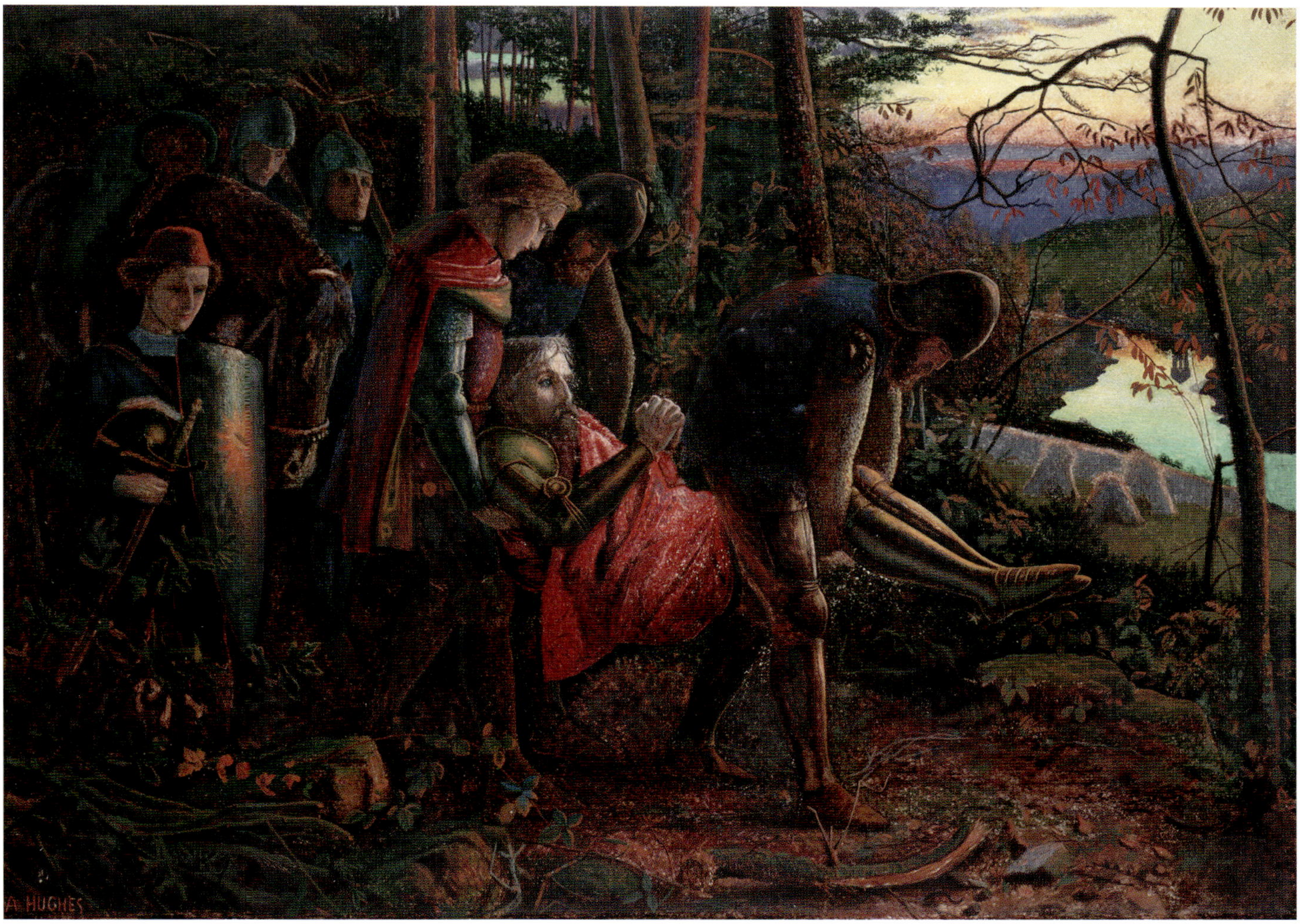
A. HUGHES

73

ARTHUR HUGHES 1832–1915

The Dial, 1870

Pen and Indian ink over graphite on card
23.4 × 17.5 cm
Signed in monogram: *AH*
Presented by Charles Emanuel, 1950
WA1950.178.263

LITERATURE: Roberts and Wildman (1997) no. 23.3

Arthur Hughes occupies a distinguished place within the extraordinary flowering of book illustrators in the 1860s. The historian of the movement, the novelist Forrest Reid (1875–1947), wrote that although he never became a 'first-rate draughtsman ... he had what is rarer than clever draughtsmanship, a spark of genius, and a personal charm so persuasive that it goes far to make up for a somewhat wobbly technique'.[1] His earliest success in this genre came with the illustrations to William Allingham's *The Music Master* in 1854, but it was not until the next decade that he produced his best work. Reid reserved a special admiration for Hughes's illustrations for *Good Words for the Young*, to which he contributed 231 drawings over five years, as well as the cover design for the issue of November 1870. This periodical was founded in 1868 by the evangelical Scottish publisher, Alexander Strahan, offering a junior version of the most popular magazine of the period, *Good Words*. The plates to George MacDonald's 'At the back of the north wind' (1868–70) are generally considered the high point of Hughes's career as an illustrator, although his earlier designs for the same author's 'Dealing with fairies', and in particular Thomas Hughes's *Tom Brown's Schooldays* (1867–8), for which he produced 43 illustrations, are also well known.

Hughes first worked for the parent publication, *Good Words*, in 1864. In 1871 he produced what Reid described as 'four drawings in his best manner'.[2] Three of these were made for an illustrated edition of Tennyson's *Loves of the Wrens* (Sullivan supplying the music), and it was only after the cantankerous poet had discovered that he did not really want illustrations that the pictures were cut down and issued in *Good Words*.[3] Tennyson's 'The Window; or, the Songs of the Wrens' was published in *Good Words* in January–March 1871, but only two of Hughes's designs were used.

This famous drawing was originally intended as an illustration to Tennyson's 'The Window', but was published by Strahan to accompany lines from a poem by F. W. Simmons: 'She pluckt a rose with tender care; Brooding she panted o'er the flower; The sunlight toucht her golden hair, and mark'd the hour.' A pair of lovers, perhaps modelled on William and Jane Morris, are seen dallying over a sundial in a luxuriant country garden in high summer. The motif of the sundial was a favourite with Victorian illustrators, who used it to denote the transitory nature of human existence. The drawing shows nothing of the 'wobbly technique' noted by Reid, but rather demonstrates Hughes's complete mastery of the pen. CH

1. Reid (1928) p. 84.
2. Reid (1928) pp. 86–7.
3. *Ibid.*

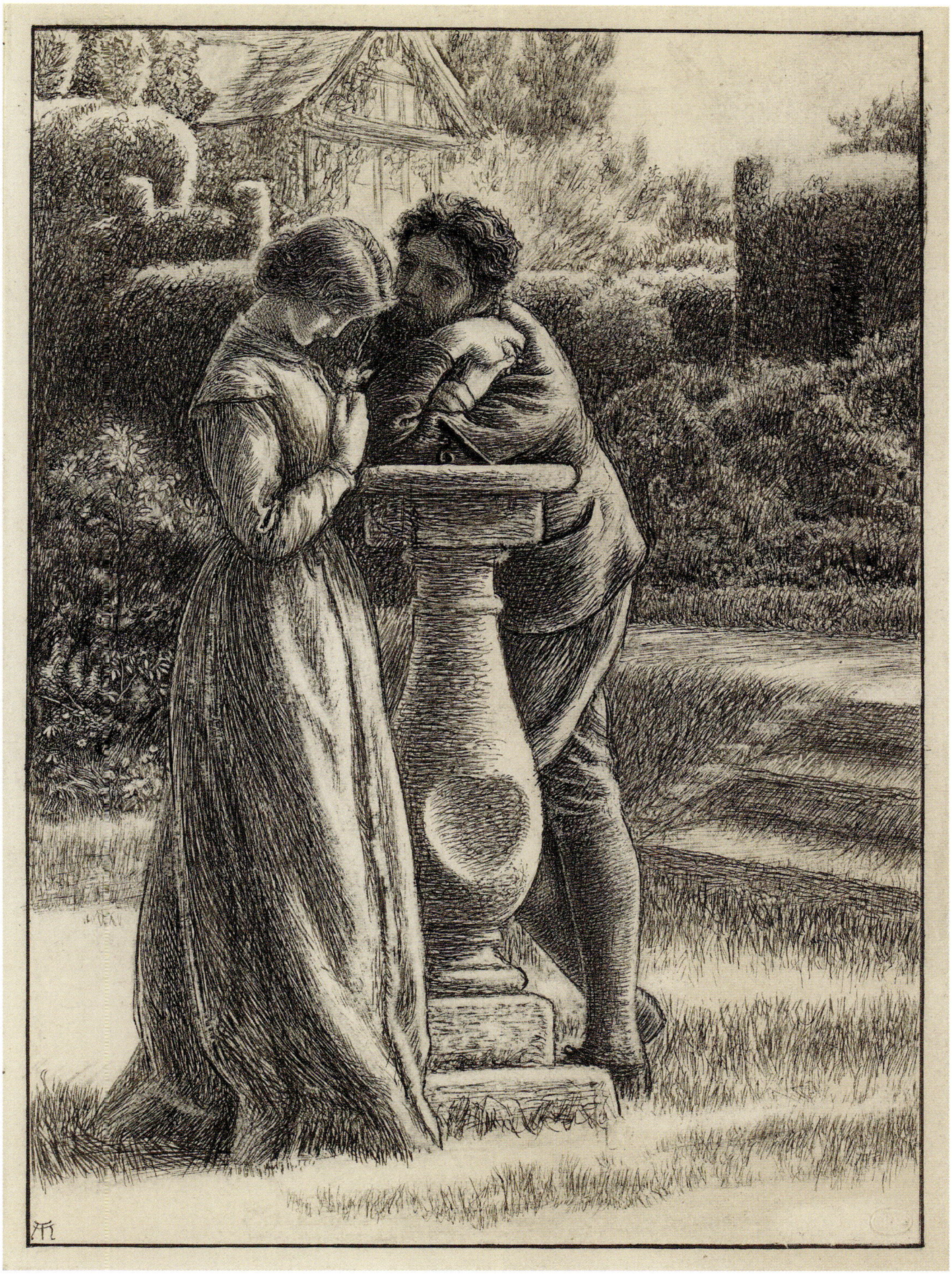

74

SIR EDWARD POYNTER 1836–1919

Study of a Man holding a Spear and a Shield, and a Study of a Leg, ?1869

Brown chalk on green paper
35.4 × 25.2 cm
Stamped in black ink at centre: *EJP*
Dated *1871*. Inscribed: *Study for medal for Ashanti War*
Presented by Miss Clarissa C. Bell, 1971
WA1971.33

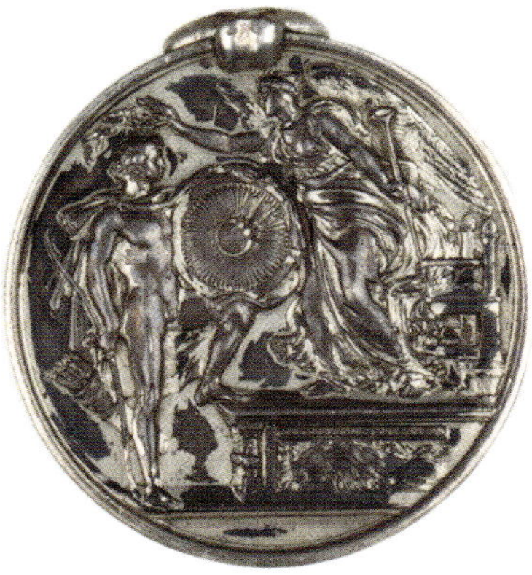

Fig. 49 | Sir Edward John Poynter (1836–1919), *Army Best Shots Medal or Queen's Medal*, 1877. Silver. Fitzwilliam Museum, Cambridge, CM.1150–2009 © Fitzwilliam Museum, Cambridge

Although he established his reputation in 1867 with the huge painting of *Israel in Egypt* (Guildhall Art Gallery), Poynter had even earlier become known as a designer for the decorative arts. He received his first commissions for decorated furniture and stained glass when he was a student in Paris in the late 1850s, and he continued to make designs for stained glass after his return to London in 1860, notably for the firm of James Powell of Whitefriars. He later designed large decorative schemes for the Victoria and Albert Museum, the Royal Albert Hall, and the Palace of Westminster.

This drawing is a study for a medal awarded to the best shot in the British army, instituted in 1869 as the Queen's Medal and awarded annually until it was discontinued in 1883. The reverse shows the portrait of Queen Victoria, while the obverse has a nude archer holding a target shot with three arrows, being crowned with a laurel wreath by the female personification of Victory. Poynter's technique owes much to his training in the studio of Charles Gleyre (1806–1874) in Paris, and from his particular interest in Michelangelo, both as a draughtsman and a sculptor. The traditional medium favoured by the Academy, reddish brown chalk, is applied with great sensitivity, describing the contours and volumes, with white used discreetly for highlights. The separate study of the right leg is reminiscent of drawings by Michelangelo which Poynter might have seen in Oxford or exhibited in London. At this stage, he had apparently envisaged the composition simply including the single figure of the archer, as the subsidiary study of the medal at the top left of the sheet makes clear.

Poynter later designed the medal awarded in the first Ashanti War, a much more compact composition of Roman soldiers attacking tribesmen in the bush of the Ashanti Confederacy, for which several preparatory drawings survive.[1] The inscription on the Ashmolean drawing mistakenly associates it with this project, and the date was probably added much later and may be erroneous. He went on to participate in the revival of the artistic medal which flourished under the immigrant French artist, Alphonse Legros (1837–1911), who made his first design in 1881 and whose influence culminated in the foundation of the Society of Medallists in 1885. CH

1. See Bell (1905) plates IX, XI.

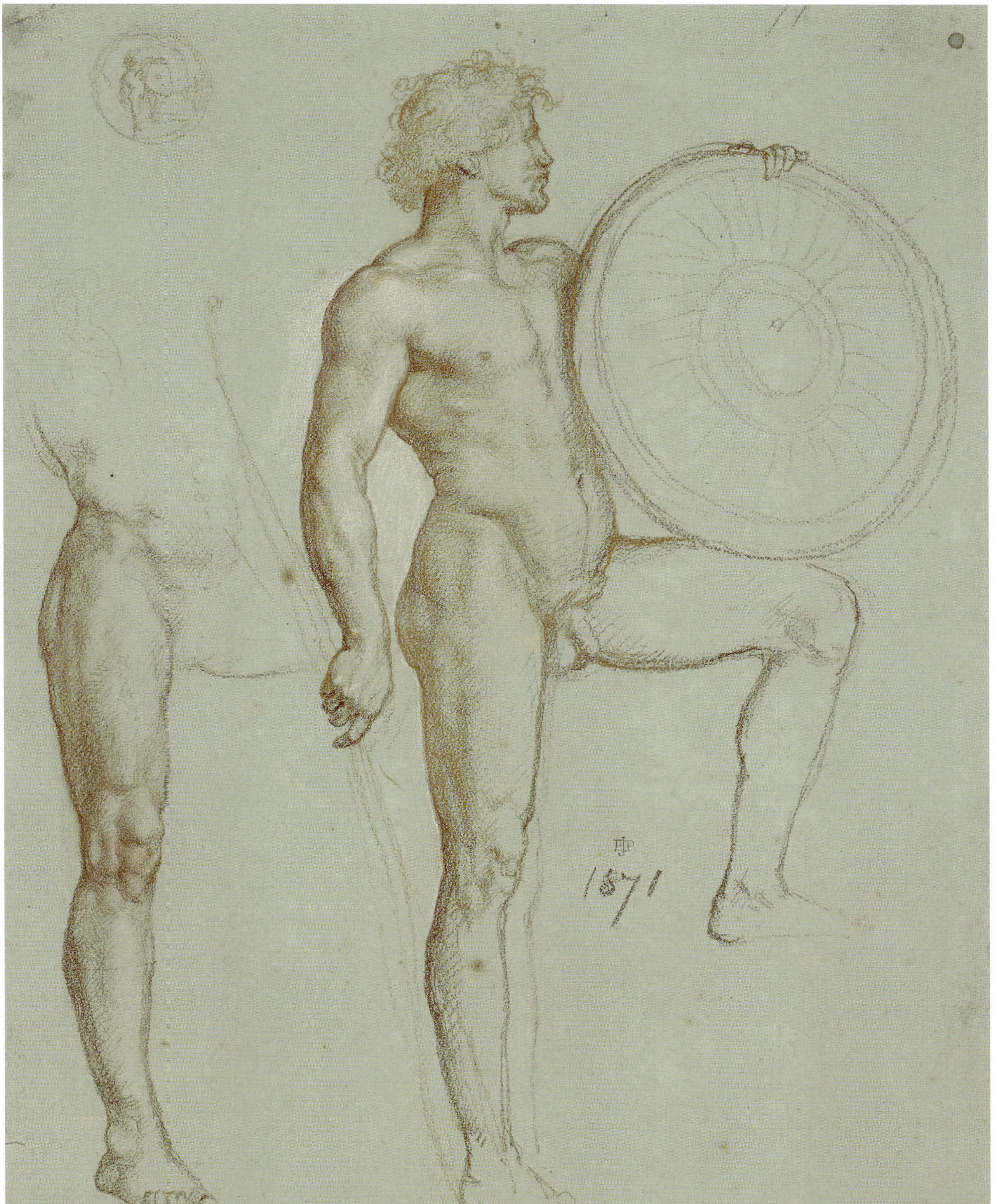
FJP
1871

75

SIR EDWARD COLEY BURNE-JONES 1833–1898

The Garden Poisoned, 1875

Graphite on paper
24.6 × 24.4 cm
Signed and dated: *EBJ 1875*
Bequeathed by Sir Philip Burne-Jones, 1926
WA1926.24

LITERATURE: Wildman and Christian (1998) no. 126

Soon after the inception of Morris Marshall Faulkner and Company in 1861, Burne-Jones, a friend of William Morris's from their undergraduate days at Exeter College, Oxford, became the principal designer. His main role was to provide designs for figure subjects for stained glass and tiles, and later embroideries and tapestries. He also turned his hand to jewellery, costumes and set designs for the theatre, and even a pair of shoes. Yet for much of his life, Burne-Jones yearned for a commission to decorate a grand piano. Indeed, in 1878 he designed a wholly new shape of piano, with straight rather than bulbous lines and plain rather than turned legs. As he wrote to Kate Faulkner, 'I have been wanting for years to reform pianos since they are as it were the very altar of homes, and a second hearth to people'.[1]

In his record of work for 1872, Burne-Jones noted that he had 'designed the story of Orpheus'. This entry is generally associated with the 11 drawings dated 1875 now in the Ashmolean. They illustrate an unpublished poem by William Morris, *The Story of Orpheus and Eurydice*, retelling the Greek myth. In 1879 the designs were painted on to a piano commissioned by Burne-Jones's great Scottish patron, William Graham, for his daughter, Frances. The outside of the lid features the figure of a poet and muse, while the inside has one of the artist's most exuberant designs, *Terra Omnipotens* (Mother Earth) and 21 *putti* clambering on the tendrils of an extravagant vine.

Covering the sides are the roundels telling the story of Orpheus, painted in grisaille. Burne-Jones's episodes are entitled *The Garden*, *The Garden Poisoned*, *The Gates of Hell*, *The Doorkeeper*, *Across the Flames*, *The House of Pluto*, *The Regained Lost* (three designs), and *The Death of Orpheus*. *The Garden Poisoned* shows Eurydice dying in the arms of her husband, having been bitten by a snake, precipitating the tragedy of their eternal separation. The drawings are among Burne-Jones's most exquisite creations, demonstrating his consummate mastery of graphite. Every fold in the diaphanous draperies is rendered with the utmost subtlety, and the compositions fit perfectly into the roundels. CH

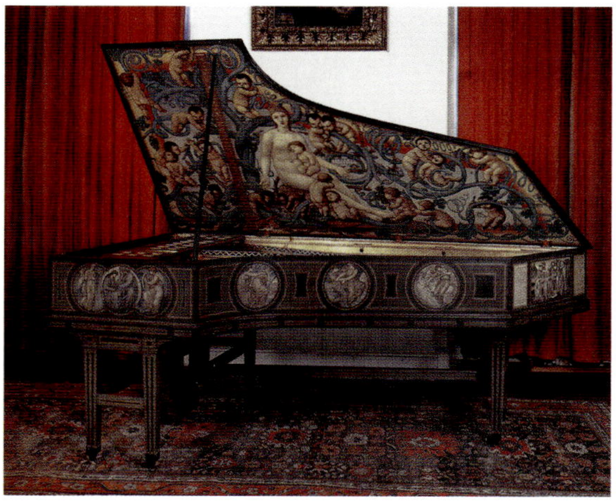

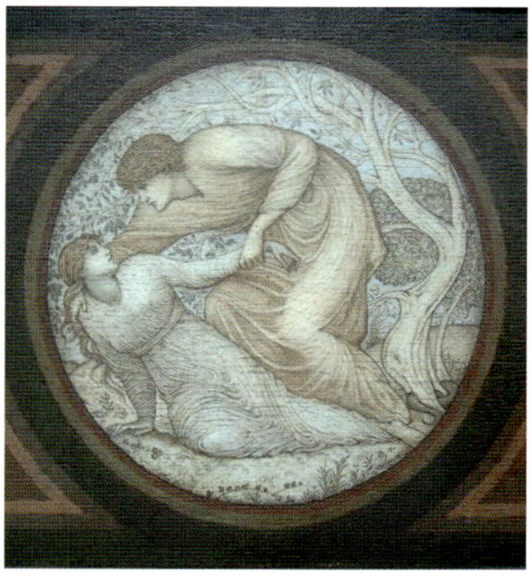

Fig. 50 | Sir Edward Coley Burne-Jones (1833–1898), *'Orpheus' or 'Graham' piano*, 1879–80. Painted wood. Private Collection

Fig. 51 | Detail of *'Orpheus' or 'Graham' piano*, showing *The Garden Poisoned*

1. Quoted in Wildman and Christian (1998) p. 276

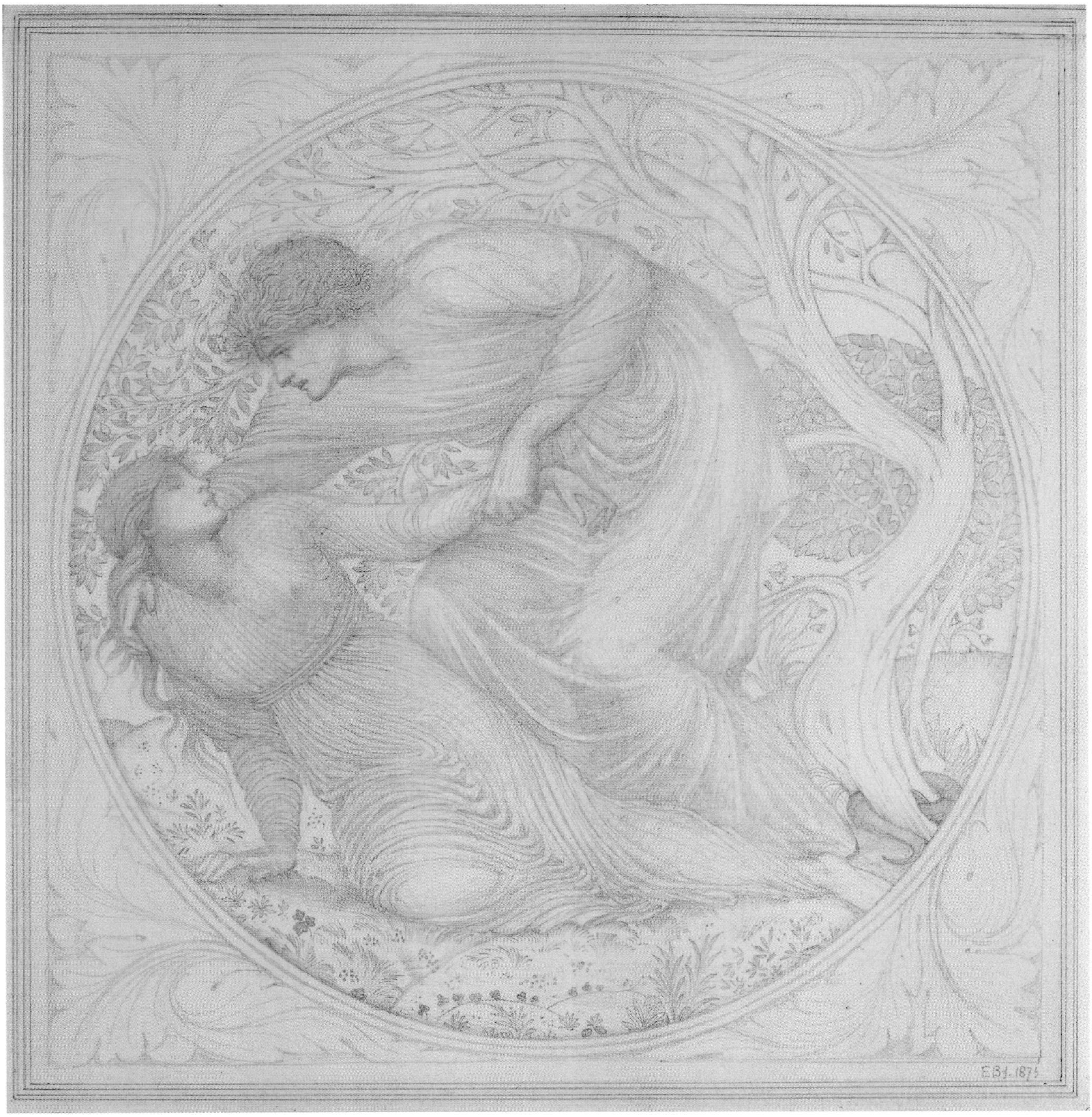
EBJ. 1875

76

SIR EDWARD COLEY BURNE-JONES 1833–1898

Antonia, 1877

Silverpoint, graphite and bodycolour on paper with a grey prepared ground
32 × 15.2 cm
Inscribed: *ANTONIA*. Signed and dated: *EB-J / 1877*. Inscribed: *to HMG*
Presented by Mrs Helen Mary Gaskell, 1939
WA1939.15.2

LITERATURE: Arts Council (1975–6) no. 139; Wildman and Christian (1998) no. 110

Fig. 52 | Sir Edward Coley Burne-Jones (1833–1898), *The Golden Stairs*, 1880. Oil on canvas. Tate, London, N04005 © Tate, London 2014

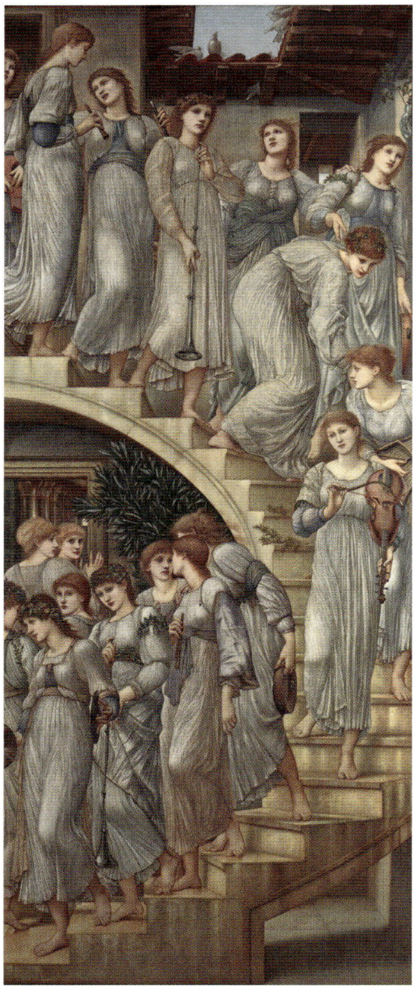

Having returned from his third trip to Italy in 1871, a visit made in the wake of his affair with Maria Zambaco, Burne-Jones conceived an impressive array of designs for paintings. Among them was *The Golden Stairs*, for which this drawing is a study. The painting was finally completed in 1880 under considerable pressure; Burne-Jones's wife Georgiana reported in her diary that: 'The picture is finished, and so is the painter almost. He never was so pushed for time in his life.'[1] The painting was the artist's only submission for exhibition at the Grosvenor Gallery that year, and proved both enduringly popular and immensely influential.

The figure is that of Antonia Caiva, a professional model frequently employed by Burne-Jones. She sat for each of the figures in *The Golden Stairs*, as well as for many other eminent Victorian artists, including Burne-Jones's brother-in-law, Edward Poynter. This particular study is for the girl at the bottom left of the painting who holds the cymbals. Her head was modelled by a young woman for whom Burne-Jones had an intense affection, Frances Graham, daughter of the Glasgow MP William Graham, one of the artist's most significant patrons (cat. 75).

Burne-Jones had received scant formal artistic training. From the mid-1860s, seeking to improve his draughtsmanship, he adopted the academic practice of making nude studies for the figures in his paintings. However, this example is unusual in employing silverpoint, in direct emulation of Quattrocento Florentine drawings, of which Burne-Jones collected photographic reproductions with particular assiduity following his time in Italy. The other surviving studies for *The Golden Stairs*, including those of the hands with cymbals, and the feet of this figure (Fitzwilliam Museum, Cambridge), are executed solely in hard graphite. This imitates the precise quality of silverpoint, but allows for easier erasure.

This work was given by the artist to Helen Mary 'May' Gaskell as a birthday gift. After allowing his intimate friend and confidante to select a drawing from his portfolio, Burne-Jones reportedly remarked at her choice, 'Ah, my dear, you have chosen the finest drawing I have ever done'.[2] Slight alterations are visible in the line of the right shoulder, the bend of the right arm and knee, as well as the placement of the ear. Yet these do nothing to detract from the exquisite *contrapposto* grace of the figure, enlivened by white highlights, which articulate delicate details as well as the play of light over the cool sculptural contours of the body. KW

1. Burne-Jones (1904) I, p. 103.
2. Dimbleby (2004) p. 257.

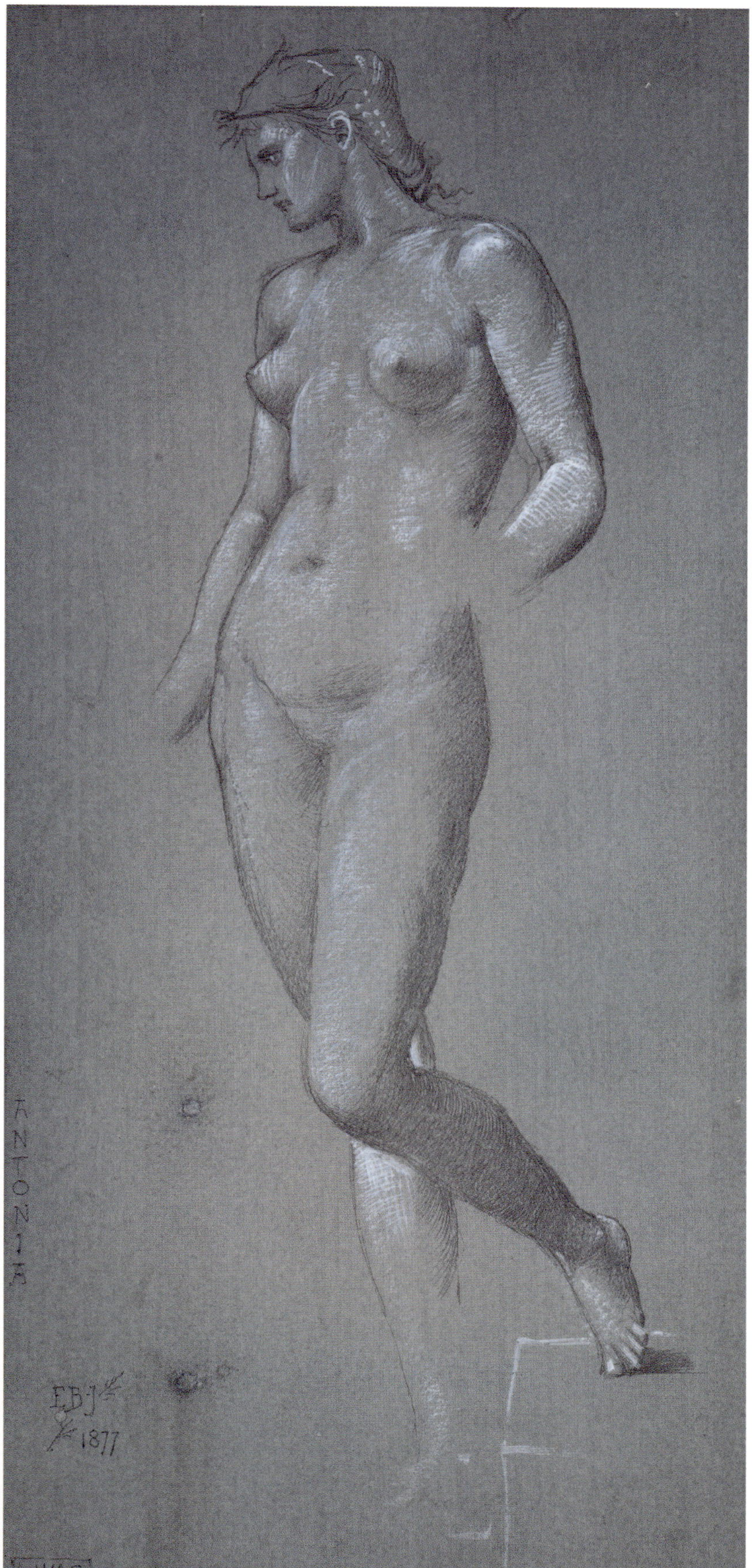
ANTONIA
E.B.J
1877
to HMG

77

SIR EDWARD COLEY BURNE-JONES 1833–1898

Studies for 'The Wheel of Fortune' from a sketchbook of figure and drapery studies, c. 1882–3

Graphite on paper, in a cream clothbound sketchbook of 21 folios
26.7 × 15.3 cm (sheet); 27.6 × 16.2 × 1.7 cm (volume), open at fol. 13
Inscribed by the artist's son: *Study for 'Fortune'* and *for 'Fortune'*. Front cover inscribed by the artist: *XVIII*
Presented by Sir Philip Burne-Jones and Mrs J. W. Mackail, children of the artist, 1920
WA1920.55

LITERATURE: Arts Council (1975) no. 125

Fig. 53 | Sir Edward Coley Burne-Jones (1833–1898), *The Wheel of Fortune*, 1875–83. Oil on canvas. Museé d'Orsay, Paris © Museé d'Orsay, Paris, France / Bridgeman Images

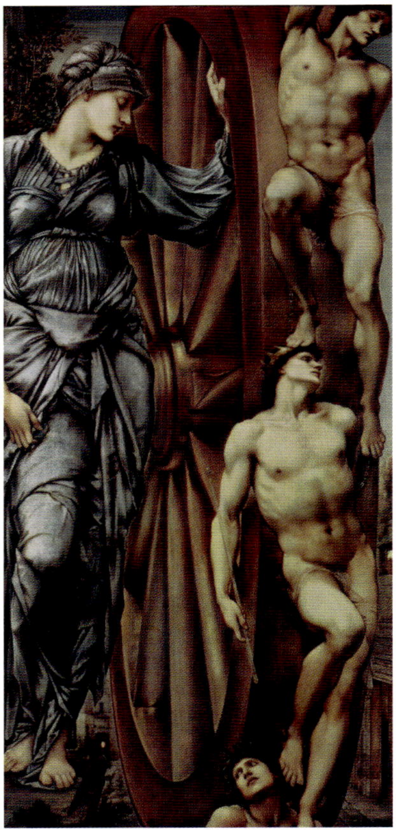

During his third visit to Italy in 1871, Burne-Jones fell comprehensively under the spell of Michelangelo. To study the Sistine Chapel frescoes he 'bought the best opera glasses he could find, folded his railway rug thickly, and lying down on his back, read the ceiling from beginning to end, peering into every corner and revelling in its execution'.[1] Galvanised, once home he began working on a range of new designs including *The Troy Triptych* (1870–98), inspired by the form of Italian Renaissance altarpieces.[2] The *predella* was divided by four figures, *Fortune* appearing at the far left.[3]

According to his son, *Fortune* was the artist's favourite design. He produced at least six painted versions, of which the largest and most compelling is now in the Museé d'Orsay; it was exhibited at the Grosvenor Gallery in 1883 and bought by the future Prime Minister, Arthur Balfour.[4] This sketchbook contains 16 studies for Fortune, exploring different dispositions of drapery; the knot of fabric depicted here is closer to the other versions of the composition than to the canvas of 1883. The cap in that version was designed by Mrs Comyns Carr, wife of one of the directors of the Grosvenor Gallery, who also devised several costumes for the actress Ellen Terry. Here, however, the head-scarf derives from the example of Michelangelo's Sistine Sibyls and the elaborate coiffures of his drawings of *Ideal Heads*. By contrast, the intricate folds of the costume owe much to the work of Botticelli. Burne-Jones consummately articulates not only the exquisitely creased drapery, but the powerful presence of the body beneath.

Burne-Jones's graceful costumes were frequently provided by Aglaia Coronio (neé Ionides), a cousin of Maria Zambaco, the woman with whom he had an intense affair in the late 1860s. They recall the free-flowing dresses favoured by the women of the Pre-Raphaelite circle, in contrast to conventional Victorian fashions. In William Morris's utopian *News from Nowhere* (1890), he approvingly described women 'decently veiled with drapery, ... clothed like women, not upholstered like arm-chairs, as most women of our time are', dressed in something between 'ancient classical costume and the simpler forms of the fourteenth-century garments, though ... not an imitation of either'.[5]

This marriage of the classical and the medieval is similarly evident in the self-conscious presentation in this sketchbook of a series of anatomical drawings in ochre chalk, as well as further studies in graphite for *The Morning of the Resurrection* (1883–6) and *The Sleep of Arthur in Avalon* (1881–8).[6] In March 1893 Burne-Jones described himself as broken on Fortune's wheel, yet together, these three paintings characterise his work as profoundly spiritual rather than simply pessimistic.[7]

1. Burne-Jones (1904) II, p. 26.
2. Unfinished; Birmingham Museums and Art Gallery. Wildman and Christian (1998) no. 50.
3. The remaining three figures were *Fame*, *Love*, and *Oblivion*.
4. Other versions of *The Wheel of Fortune*: Cecil French Bequest, Hammersmith; National Gallery of Victoria, Australia; Tullie House Museum, Carlisle; National Museum of Wales, Cardiff; ex-Watts Gallery, Compton.
5. Morris, ed. Wilmer (1993) p. 53.
6. Tate and Museo del Arte de Ponce, Puerto Rico.
7. Letter to Helen Mary Gaskell, quoted in Wildman and Christian (1998) p. 155.

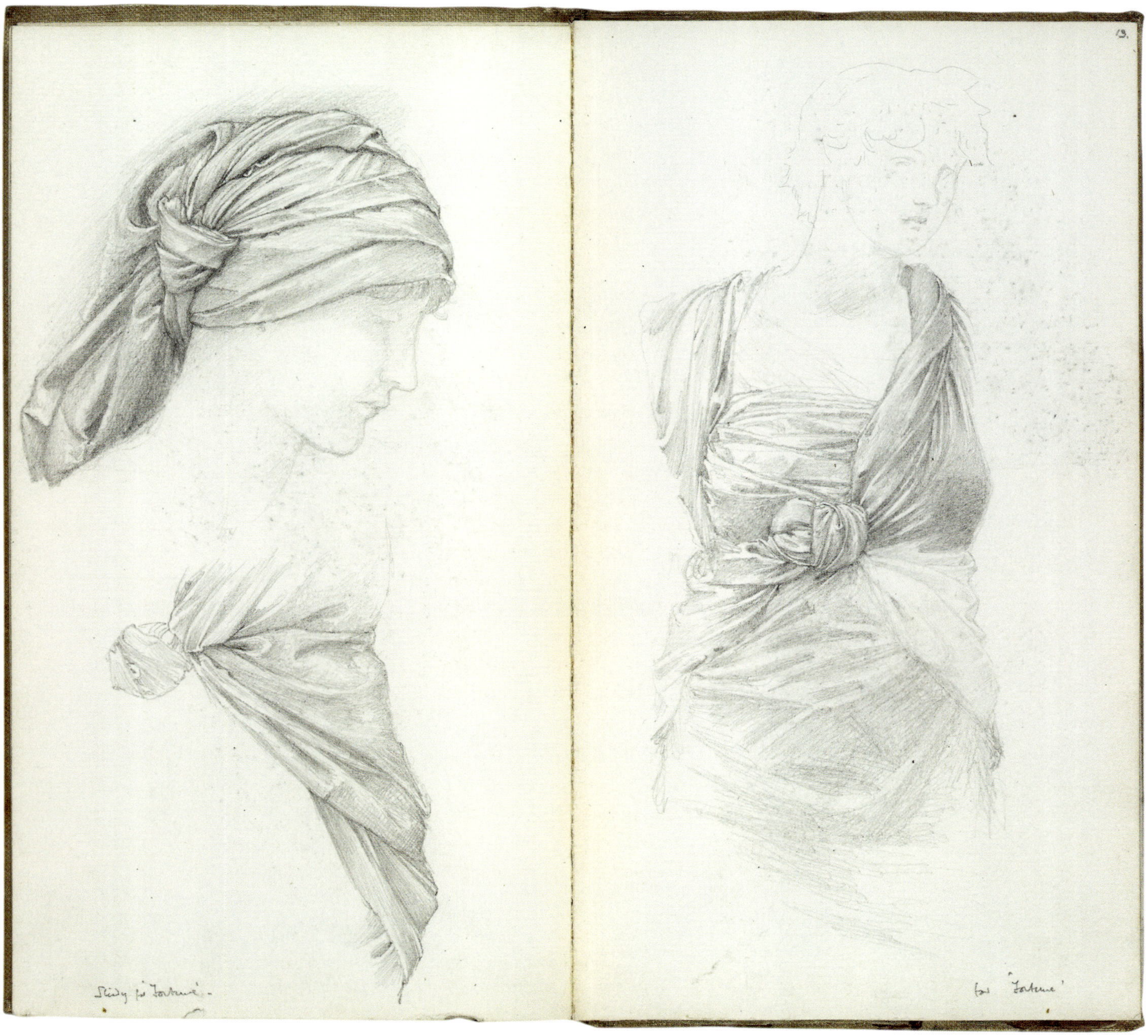
13.
Study for 'Fortune' -
for 'Fortune'

78

SIR EDWARD COLEY BURNE-JONES 1833–1898

Study for 'The Depths of the Sea' from an album of 48 drawings, 1884–8

Watercolour and bodycolour on paper
22.3 × 9.8 cm
Album bound in dark brown leather, tooled and gilded, 37.1 × 27.7 × 4.5 cm, open at fol. 48
Presented by Helen Mary Gaskell, 1939
WA1939.9.48

LITERATURE: Harrison and Waters (1973) pp. 140 and 142

Fig. 54 | Sir Edward Coley Burne-Jones (1833–1898), *The Depths of the Sea*, 1887. Watercolour and bodycolour on wove paper mounted on panel. Fogg Museum, Harvard Art Museums, 1943.462 © President and Fellows of Harvard College

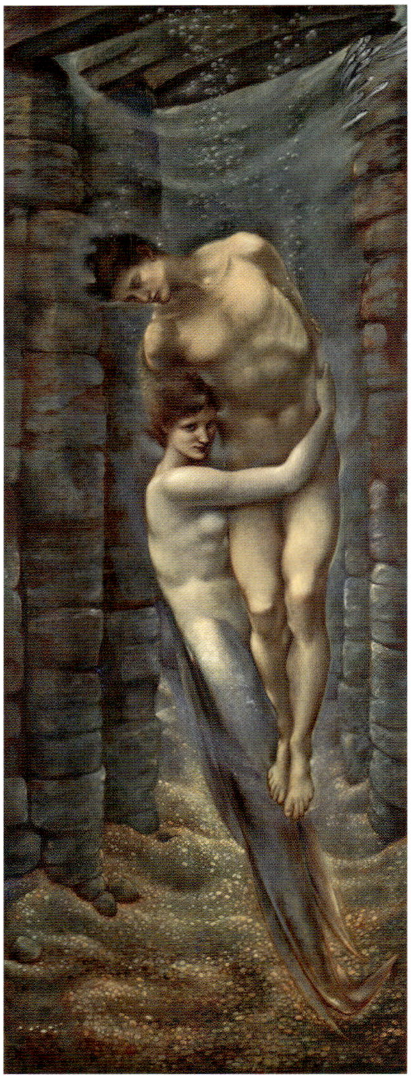

In June 1885 Burne-Jones was unexpectedly elected an Associate of the Royal Academy of Arts, and the following year exhibited his haunting submarine painting, *The Depths of the Sea*.[1] This was the only work that Burne-Jones displayed at the Academy and he resigned in 1893, having repeatedly failed to gain full membership.

The poet, Gerard Manley Hopkins described *The Depths of the Sea* as 'the stroke of true artistic genius'.[2] F. G. Stephens praised its charming colour but criticised the weak anatomy of the male figure, observations that are equally relevant to this vibrant study. In the finished painting Burne-Jones enhanced the plunging motion of the figures, conjoining the pair more tightly, with the mermaid's hair streaming above her head. She looks towards the viewer with a glance as mesmerising as it is mysterious. However, in this drawing her imploring gaze recalls the controversial *Phyllis and Demophoön* (1870), the work that had precipitated Burne-Jones's resignation from the Old Water-Colour Society.[3] Intriguingly, the year in which he exhibited *The Depths of the Sea* also witnessed his re-election to this institution.

Burne-Jones's preoccupation with mermaids is usually dated from his purchase of the property he named North End House, in Rottingdean, near Brighton, in 1880. Indeed, a room in the house was designated 'The Mermaid Inn'. In the early 1880s he produced a number of pictures of merfolk, often with a humorous or maternal aspect, but another study from the Gaskell Album shows a nude male clinging to a cluster of coral, vigorously resisting a mermaid's grasp.[4] In fact the dangerously ambiguous nature of mermaids featured in Maclaren's *Fairy Family* (1857), for which Burne-Jones had provided his earliest commissioned illustrations.

The astonishing versatility of Burne-Jones's draughtsmanship, unceasingly experimenting with a range of media, is encapsulated in the Gaskell Album. Formed with drawings given by the artist to Helen Mary Gaskell (cat. 121), it demonstrates the impressive variety of Burne-Jones's work. The album not only contains studies for paintings such as *The Annunciation*, *King Cophetua and the Beggar Maid* and *The Masque of Cupid*, but also designs for stained glass (*St Luke* and *Sibylla Cimmeria*), as well as illustrations (both used and discarded) for Kelmscott Press publications, including *The Golden Legend*, Morris's *The Well at the World's End*, *The Romance of Sire Degrevant*, *The Romance of Sir Isumbras* and the magisterial *Kelmscott Chaucer*. These are interspersed with delicately rendered female faces, garlands, and anatomical studies that are absolutely characteristic of Burne-Jones's other-worldly artistic language. KW

1. Private collection; Wildman and Christian (1998) no. 119. Burne-Jones made a copy of this painting in 1887, see fig. 54.
2. Quoted in Mancoff (1998) p. 88.
3. Burne-Jones later recast this composition, removing the element of nudity, as *The Tree of Forgiveness* (1882; Lady Lever Art Gallery).
4. WA1939.9.46. A further study in graphite for the mermaid's face was also given to the Ashmolean by Mrs Gaskell, WA1939.13.

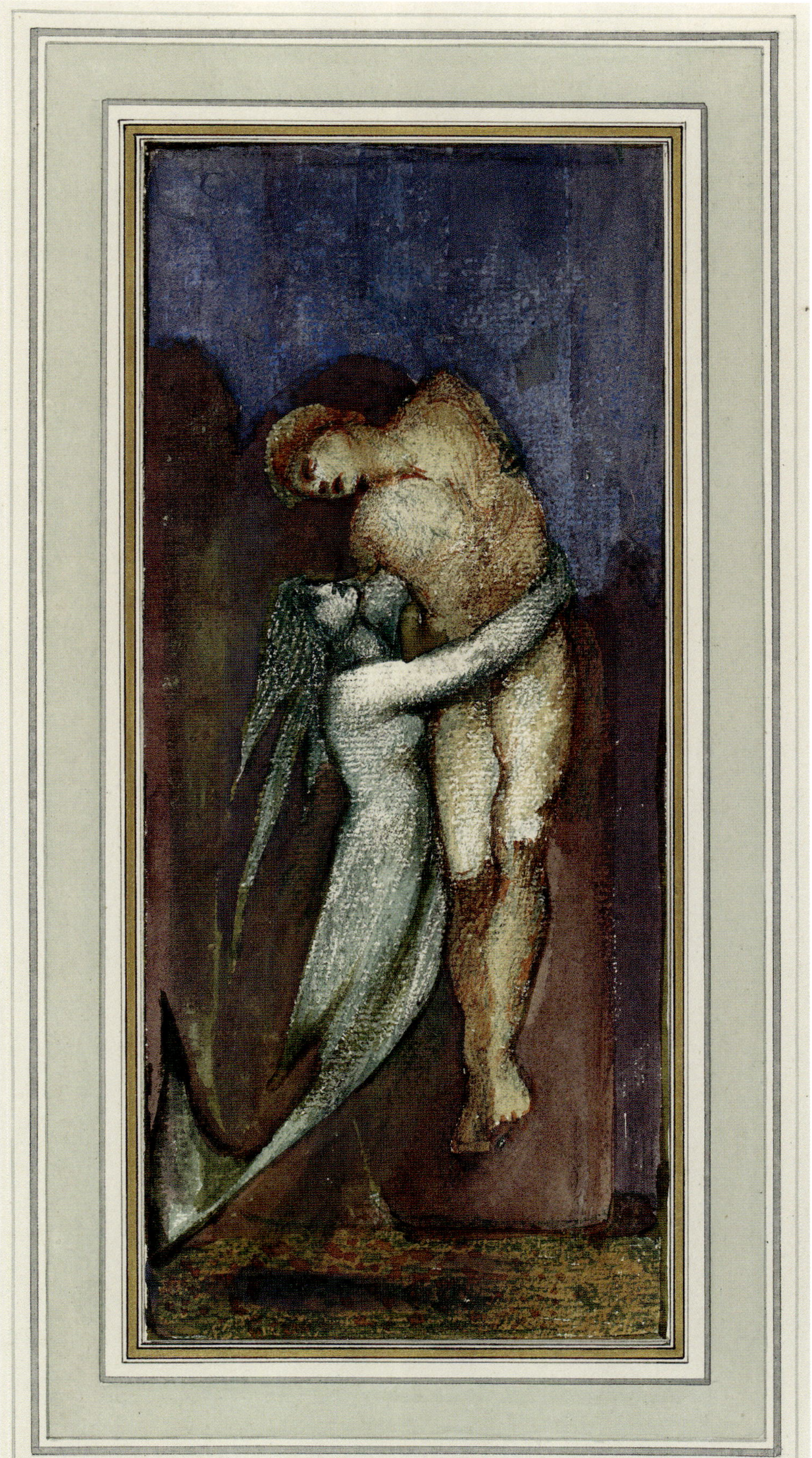

79

FREDERICK SANDYS 1829–1904

Nepenthe, 1892

Black and white chalks on paper
32 × 24.5 cm
Signed and dated: *FF Sandys 1892*
Inscribed: *Nepenthe* (in Greek characters)
Presented by Sir Karl Parker, 1942
WA1942.81

LITERATURE: Elzea (2001) no. 5.5

From an early age Sandys had a reputation as a consummate draughtsman, which he said he owed to the studies of antiquities that he made as a boy in Norfolk for the Revd James Bulwer. His first exhibit at the Royal Academy, in 1851, was a large chalk portrait drawing, a genre in which he later came to specialise. After his meeting with Rossetti in 1857, he painted and drew a succession of half-length or head and shoulders portraits of women. From *Queen Eleanor* in 1858, the oils were executed in true Pre-Raphaelite fashion, with meticulous detail and using bright colours on a white ground.[1] Gradually, the narrative became less important, and the titles largely a pretext for the depiction of a beautiful model, sometimes a *femme fatale*.

In the early 1870s Sandys made a large, full-length drawing of *Lethe*, for which his sister Emma probably posed.[2] She illustrates lines from Dante's *Purgatorio*, Canto 29, in which the poet meets Mathilda singing and gathering flowers beside a brook, intended to evoke the twin rivers of Lethe and Eunoe, Oblivion and Remembrance. Nearly 20 years later Sandys resumed the head of Lethe, creating one of his most beguiling and symbolist images, *Nepenthe* – named after a drug of forgetfulness mentioned in the *Odyssey*, and more recently by Edgar Allan Poe in his celebrated poem, 'The Raven' (1845).

Since Emma Sandys died in 1877, it is perhaps fanciful to associate this drawing of 1892 with her memory. In any case, it is possible that Sandys still had the drawing of Lethe in his studio, so he was able to make an accurate transcription of the head. Behind it are the flowers associated with forgetfulness, in particular the opium poppy. This treatment is reminiscent of Sandys's early masterpiece, *Gentle Spring* (1865), in which the figure of Proserpine returning from the land of the dead is seen against a blossoming garden. An orchard and meadow lie beyond, while prominent opium poppies grow in the foreground.[3] The drawing is made on an appropriately greenish sheet of paper, in black and white chalks applied with extraordinary subtlety. The textures of flesh, fabric, and flowers are perfectly differentiated, while the smoke swirling round her head is almost ethereal. CH

1. National Museum of Wales, Cardiff; Elzea (2001) no. 1.A.159.
2. William Morris Gallery, Walthamstow; Elzea (2001) no. 3.11.
3. Ashmolean Museum, WA1923.2; Elzea (2001) no. 2.A.70.

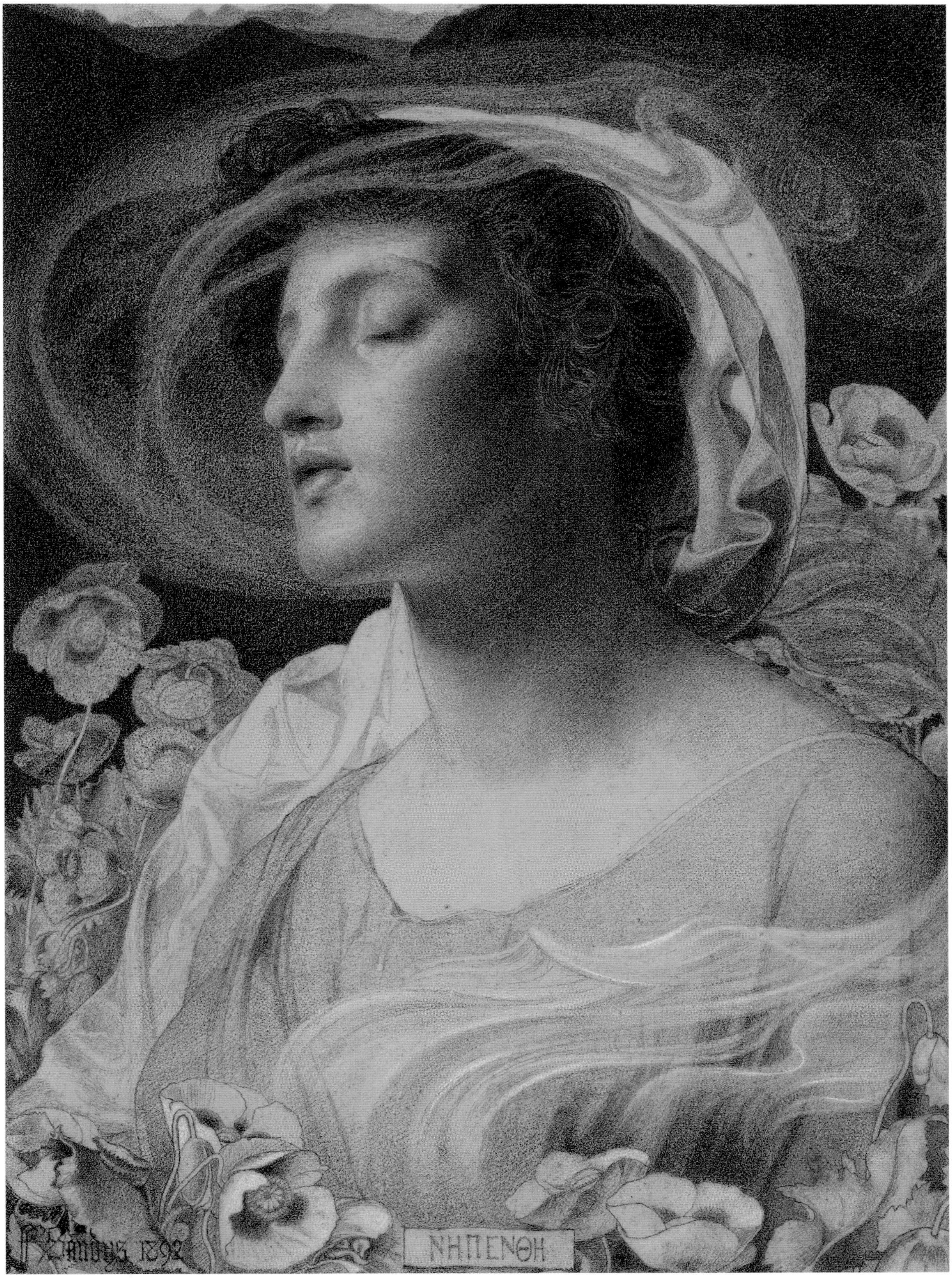
ΝΗΠΕΝΘΗ

80

AUBREY VINCENT BEARDSLEY 1872–1898

Vignettes for 'Le Morte d'Arthur': Female Figure (book 11, chapter 7) and A Faun (book 6, chapter 9), 1893

Pen and black ink on white paper
11.2 × 7.6 cm and 10.6 × 7.7 cm
Purchased, 1941
WA1941.110–11

In 1892 the 20-year-old Beardsley was working in London as a clerk for the Guardian Fire and Life Assurance Company and frequenting Frederick Evans's bookshop in nearby Queen Street, obtaining books in exchange for his drawings. Through Evans, Beardsley was introduced to the publisher John Dent, who was seeking an illustrator for his edition of Malory's *Morte d'Arthur*. Beardsley thus secured the first commission of his artistic career.

Dent promised a fee of £250 for around 400 illustrations 'in the manner of Burne-Jones'.[1] He planned to produce a popular volume rivalling those of Morris's Kelmscott Press, and to employ the cheaper photo-reproductive line-block process rather than printing from hand-carved woodblocks. There can be no doubt that Beardsley initially considered Burne-Jones's work worthy of emulation. He and his sister, Mabel, had first met the elder artist in July 1871 at his studio, where Burne-Jones encouraged Beardsley to attend the Westminster School of Art. He also provided him with a letter of introduction to Puvis de Chavannes, whom Beardsley met in Paris in mid-1892. However, the onerous obligations of the commission weighed heavily on Beardsley and his satirical nature and characteristic love of the grotesque prompted him to parody his previous mentor. Both Morris and Burne-Jones, for whom Malory's *Morte d'Arthur* was tantamount to a sacred text, were subsequently appalled by Dent's edition (1893–4).

Beardsley's genius lay in adapting his draughtsmanship to the limitations of the line-block process and the rigours of punishing deadlines. Influenced by both Japanese woodblock prints and the art of *fin-de-siècle* Paris, Beardsley radically simplified his backgrounds, persuasively playing off expanses of dense black against areas of blank white. His masterly economy of line produced the faintly malevolent expressions of these two figures. Concentrating upon creating compelling designs rather than convincing depictions of space, Beardsley's illustrations abound with unsettling disruptions of expected scale, as here in the relative proportions of the faun and the framing trees. His sheer inventiveness, often unhampered by a need, or desire, to illustrate the text in any traditional sense, nevertheless conveyed the element of the sinister or uncanny undoubtedly present in Malory's narrative, but ignored by previous interpreters. While the lady agitating the incense fumes with a suggestively malicious demeanour may not have been conceived as a particular character, she aptly opens the account of the second enchanted seduction of Launcelot by Elaine, mother of Galahad, assisted by her maid Dame Brisen. The shame of this unintended infidelity when discovered by Guinevere prompts Launcelot to jump out of the chamber window and to run mad in the forest for a spell of two years. KW

1. Quoted in MacCarthy (2011) p. 440.

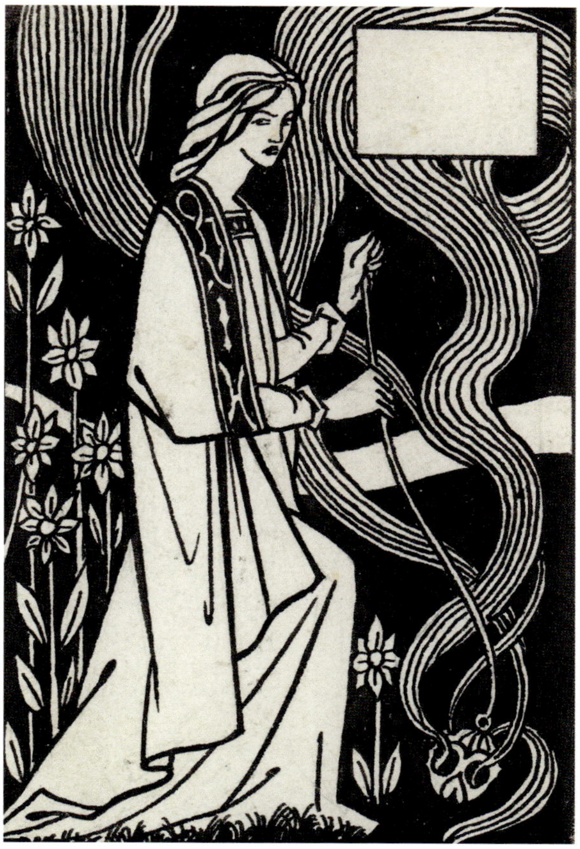

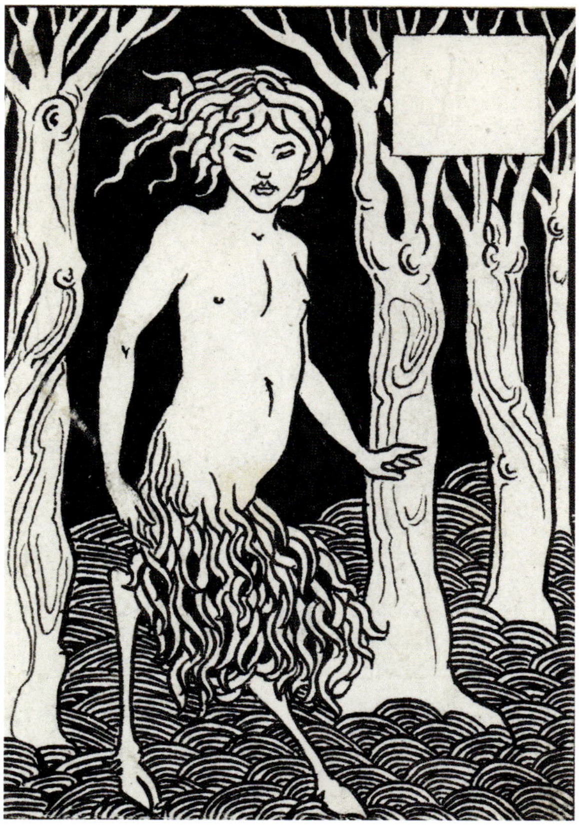

81

ANNA ALMA-TADEMA 1865/7–1943
Girl in a Bonnet with her Head on a Blue Pillow, 1902

Watercolour and bodycolour with some graphite on board
36.6 × 26.5 cm
Signed and dated: *Anna Alma Tadema 1902*
Purchased, 1964
WA1964.81

Anna Alma-Tadema is best known for her highly detailed studies of the ornate and exotically furnished interiors of Townshend House near Regent's Park (1883–5), where her father, the Dutch painter Sir Lawrence Alma-Tadema (1836–1912), made his home.[1] As Anna was only in her late teens when these were produced, she was clearly highly skilled at a young age, conveying the sumptuous details of the mosaics, tiles and textiles using a jewel-like colouring technique similar to the Orientalist interiors of J. F. Lewis. Described by her father's biographer Helen Zimmern as a 'delicate, dainty artist who has inherited so much of her father's power for reproducing detail', Anna was probably encouraged by him, as well as by her step-mother Laura (née Epps, *c.* 1852–1909), herself a painter.[2] Anna exhibited regularly at the Royal Academy and elsewhere, winning a prize at the World's Columbian Exposition in 1893.

The sitter in this striking portrait is unknown. Nonetheless, with her dark eyes and long oval face she bears a striking resemblance to the model gazing out at the viewer from the bottom right of Lawrence Alma-Tadema's *The Roses of Heliogabalus* (1888; private collection).[3] The reclining female, languidly arranged on soft furnishings in a domestic interior, is a familiar theme in this period, but the turning of the woman's face towards us gives the work a very different effect from those in which she is distanced from us, enabling us to view her more voyeuristically. Pressed close up against the picture plane, she engages us as an individual, despite her absent, slightly melancholic gaze.

As in many Aesthetic paintings, the artist delights in evoking a sensuous variety of textures – the gauze cap with its lace edging, the soft velvet of the cloak, the fluffiness of the swan's-feather collar, and the cushion's crisp silk. Like Whistler's *Symphony in White, No. 1* (1861–2), this work plays with subtle shades of white on white, set against the green-white wood panelling behind and white couch beneath. The Japanese-style butterflies on the blue pillow may also be a reference to Whistler. The painting by Lawrence Alma-Tadema of his two young daughters, *This is Our Corner* (1873; Van Gogh Museum, Amsterdam), may indicate that the blue pillow held a particular significance for Anna, as she is seen reclining with her head on a blue pillow in the background. Alternatively, it may simply have been an opportunity to introduce a spectacular colour note into the composition.

Marion Hepworth-Dixon's description of Laura Alma-Tadema's approach to painting also seems apt in relation to Anna's careful and meditative technique: her 'love and reverence of nature seems to make her handle her pigments as a nun might count her rosary'.[4] CP

1. These are in the Royal Academy, London; Nelson-Atkins Museum, Kansas; Cooper Hewitt, Smithsonian Design Museum.
2. Zimmern (1902) p. 8.
3. Becker and Prettejohn (1996) pp. 236–7.
4. *The Studio*, 50 (June 1910), p. 54.

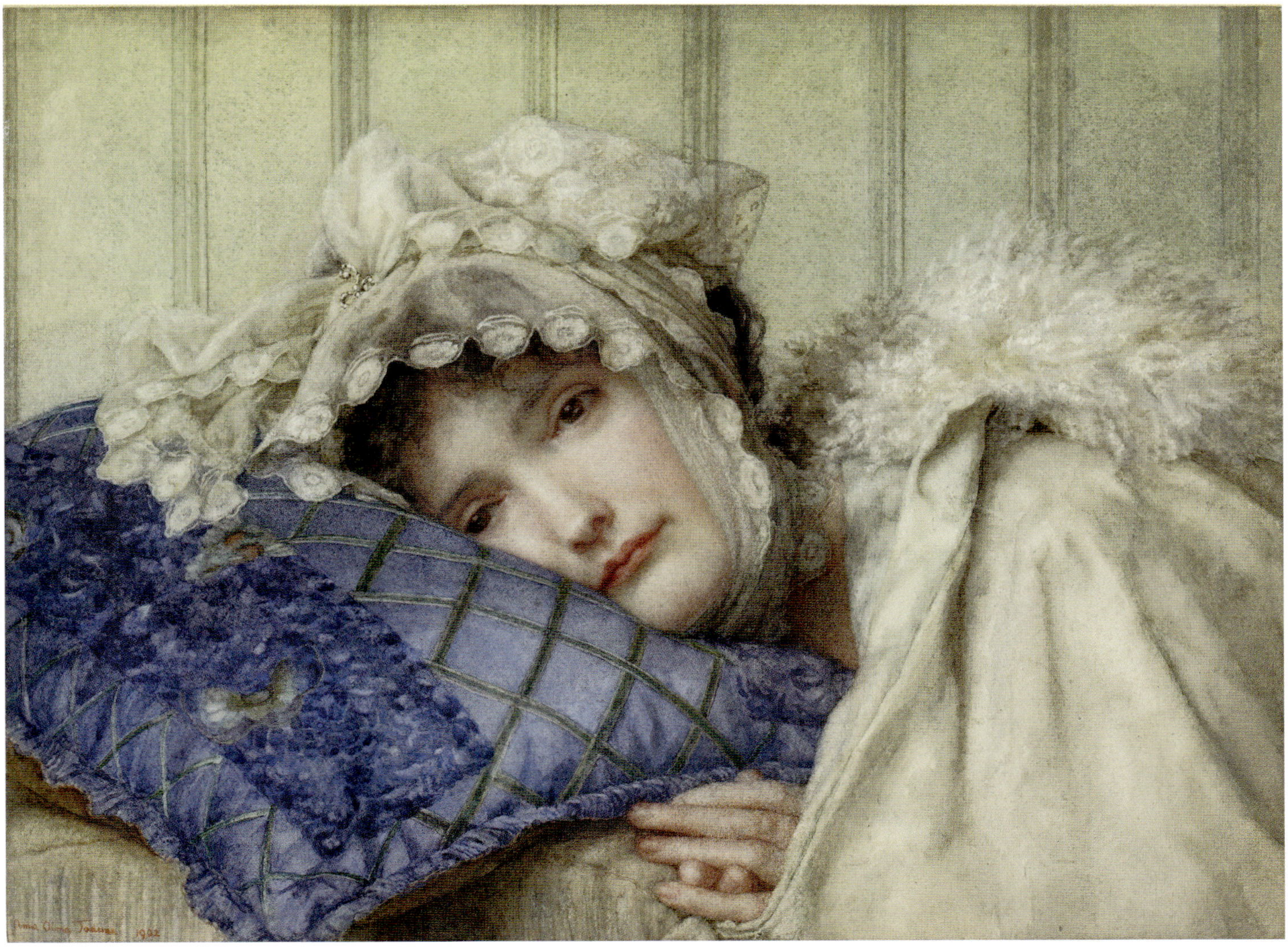

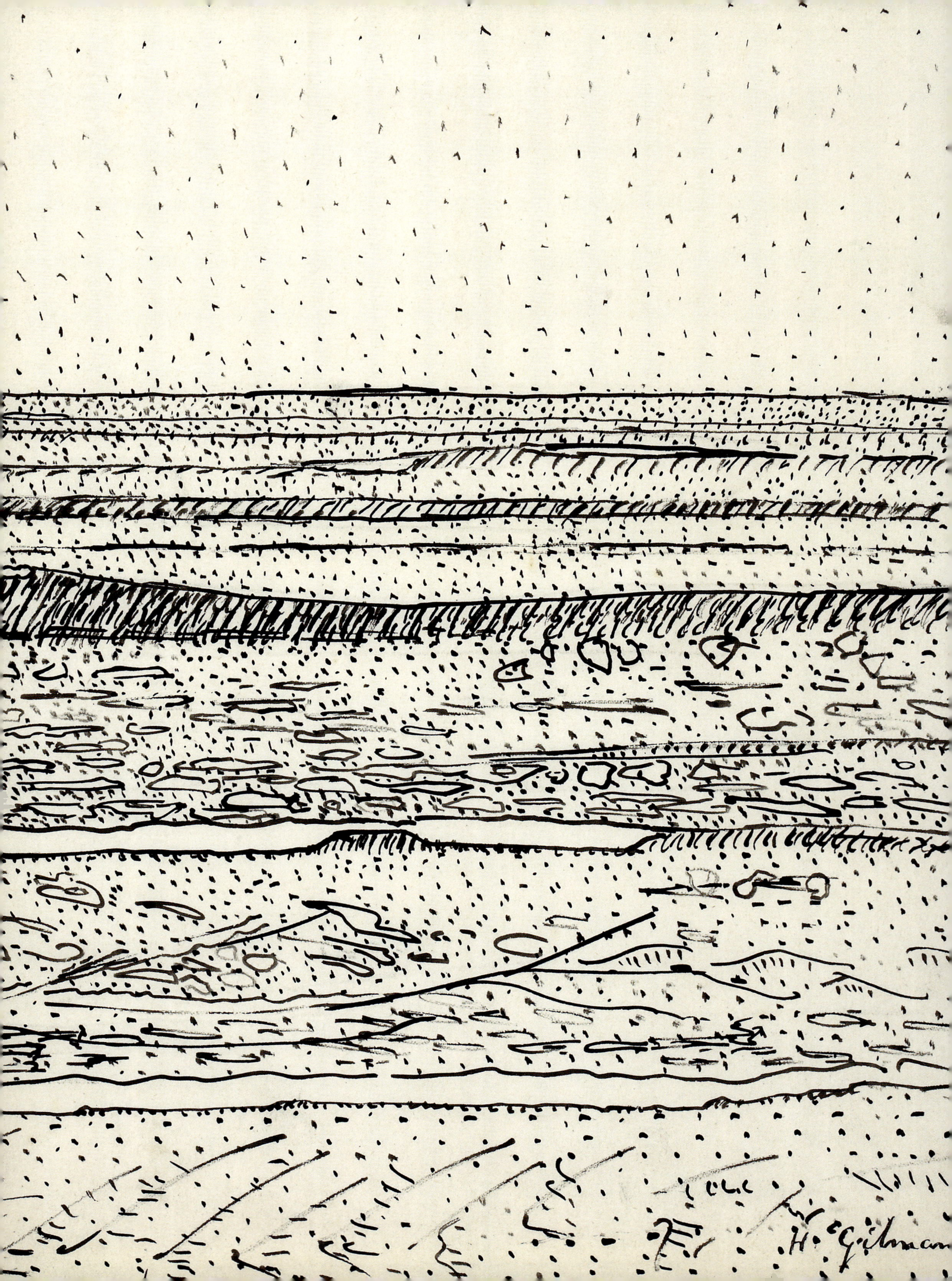
H. Gilman

Diversity & Conflict

The Modernist Century

Detail from Harold Gilman,
Seascape: Breaking Waves (cat. 89)

82

AUGUSTUS EDWIN JOHN 1878–1961

Caspar, 1906

Black chalk on paper
27.3 × 22.2 cm
Signed: *John*
Lent by the Christopher Sands Trust, 2001
LI054.60

LITERATURE: Holroyd, Evans, John (1996) no. 23

In 1906 Augustus John's wife Ida (née Nettleship, 1877–1907) wrote to her friend Margaret Sampson from Paris: 'Caspar has just come up from the studio remarking "he gave me a penny". I suppose he's been sitting ... He is still very fat and solid, and can't run at all quickly.'[1] Caspar (1903–1984) was her second son; he would have been aged about three when this drawing was made. It is ironic that, in a further sketch (private collection) made at about the same time, he is seen wearing a cocked hat given that he entered naval college aged 13 (despite his father's objections). He became a flying officer in the fledgling Fleet Air Arm and eventually Admiral of the Fleet.[2] As First Sea Lord and Chief of Naval Staff (1960–3), Caspar came to embody a level of military discipline that was entirely absent from his early, rather Bohemian upbringing.

Augustus John's portraits of his sons are some of the most sensitive, psychologically astute images of children ever produced. Like his sister Gwen, he seems to have wished to penetrate the mysterious inner world of a child's mind. A number of wonderfully fluent black chalk drawings of John's children, most purchased directly from the artist, are currently on loan to the Ashmolean from the collection of Morton Sands.

In this rapid sketch, taken from life, the soft but elaborate curls of Caspar's long hair are sketched in fluently, while the artist focuses on capturing the unsettling intensity of the child's gaze, with his distinctive almond-shaped eyes. Sharp accents around the eyelids, pupils, and lips give way to loose hatching for the shading on the left side of the face, suggesting the need for a speedy transcription of the impatient toddler's features.

A slightly older and more introspective Caspar can be seen in an oil portrait of *c.* 1909 at the Fitzwilliam Museum, Cambridge.[3] His more serious expression may reflect the fact that his mother Ida had died following the birth of her fifth son, Henry, in 1907. CP

1. Quoted in Holroyd, Evans, John (1996) p. 41.
2. Holroyd, Evans, John (1996) no. 24.
3. PD.23–1976.

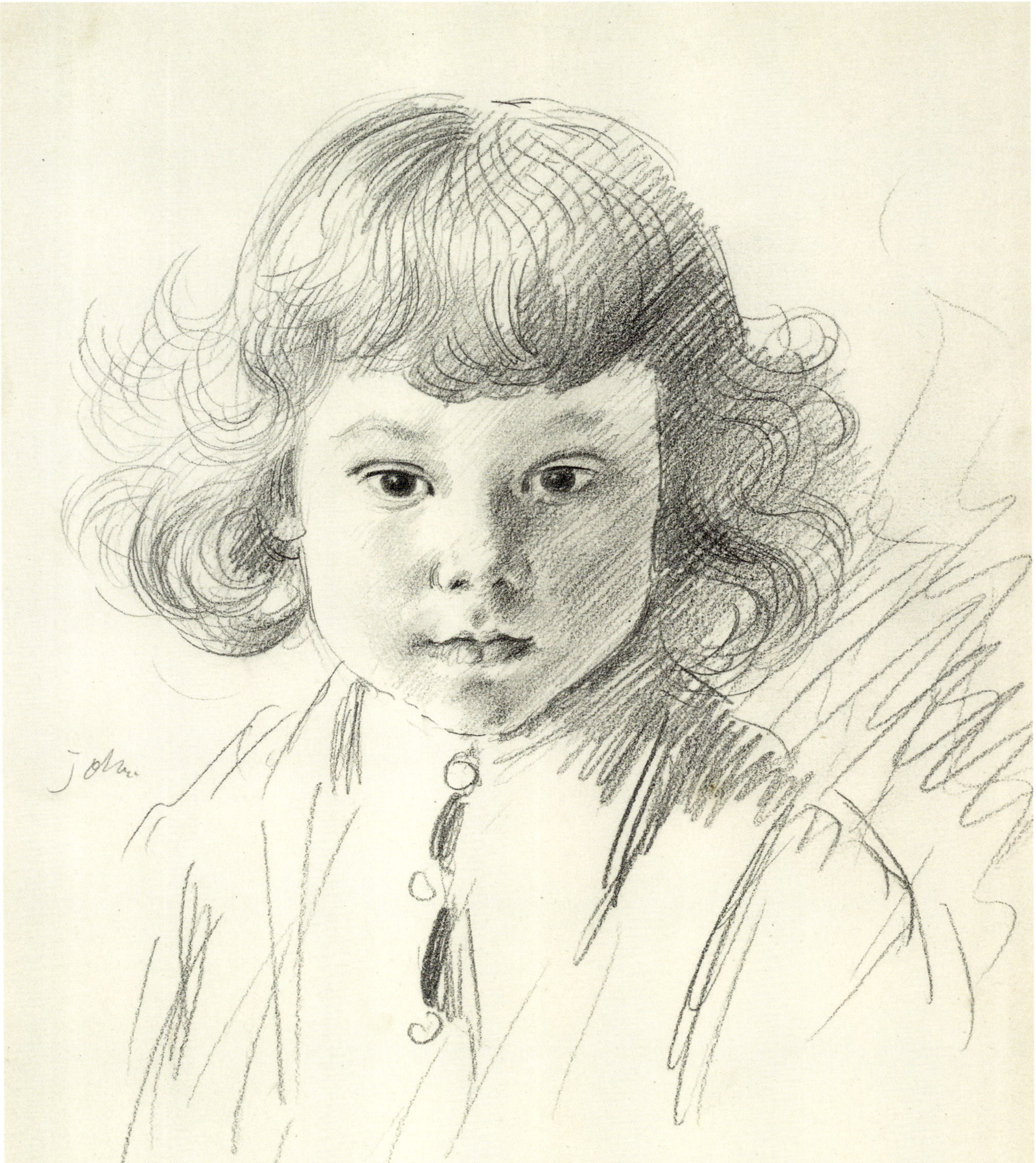
John

83

AUGUSTUS EDWIN JOHN 1878–1961

Standing draped figure, c. 1909

Graphite on paper
54.5 × 35.4 cm
Signed: *John*
Lent by the Christopher Sands Trust, 2001
L1054.101

LITERATURE: Jenkins (1978) pp. 104–11; Jenkins and Stephens (2004) no. 75

The model in this drawing is probably Dorothy McNeill (1881–1969), nicknamed 'Dorelia' by John. A student at the Westminster School of Art, she became a friend of Gwen John and subsequently joined Augustus in a *ménage à trois* with his wife, Ida. The work most closely resembles the large study of a *Standing Woman Draped in a Shawl*, of *c.* 1907–10 (Fitzwilliam Museum, Cambridge).[1] In general the large drawings of Dorelia from this period show her more heavily clothed, in characteristically loose skirts and peasant blouses, but a study for the painting *Forza e Amore* (exhibited 1911; now destroyed) also shows her in a scantily clad state, draped in a more classical garment (*c.* 1909–11; Ashmolean Museum).[2]

Around 1909 Augustus John began making large-scale drawings of standing female figures in connection with a commission from the art dealer Sir Hugh Lane for mural decorations in his new home, part of Lindsey House in Cheyne Walk, Chelsea. Although this drawing is probably associated with these unfinished murals (abandoned after Lane was drowned on board the *Lusitania* in 1915), it cannot be directly related to any existing works. It is most similar to a figure in the same pose, though in reverse, in a compositional drawing of *c.* 1910 at the National Museum of Wales. This features six classically posed and draped female figures on a bank with the sea behind them, and is thought to be a study for *The Lyric Fantasy* (1911–4; Tate).[3] The woman's open left arm is also similar in gesture to the figure of Ida in *The Way Down to the Sea* (exhibited 1909; private collection). Both the classical draperies and expansive gestures of these figures reflect John's interest in the work of the French artist Puvis de Chavannes (1824–1898), which he had encountered in Paris around 1900.

The confidence with which John approaches this complex subject reflects his training under Henry Tonks and Wilson Steer at the Slade School. There, the painter William Rothenstein recalled, 'we did *draw* at a time when everywhere else in England students were rubbing and tickling their paper with stump, chalk, charcoal and india rubber'.[4] There is some smudging of the pencil in the model's left arm and torso, but otherwise John uses sweeping lines and a great economy of touch, for example employing shorthand squiggles for fabric folds on the shoulder. His work reflects the importance he gave to draughtsmanship, quoting Ingres's 'magisterial dictum' in a National Gallery exhibition catalogue of his drawings of 1940: 'Le Dessin, c'est la Probité de l'Art.'[5] CP

1. Jenkins and Stephens (2004) no. 74; see also *Dorelia Wearing a Shawl*, in Hazlitt Holland-Hibbert (2004) p. 30.
2. L1054.93
3. Jenkins (1978) no. 106 (NMW 3976).
4. Rothenstein (1931) I, chapter III.
5. National Gallery (1940) p. 17.

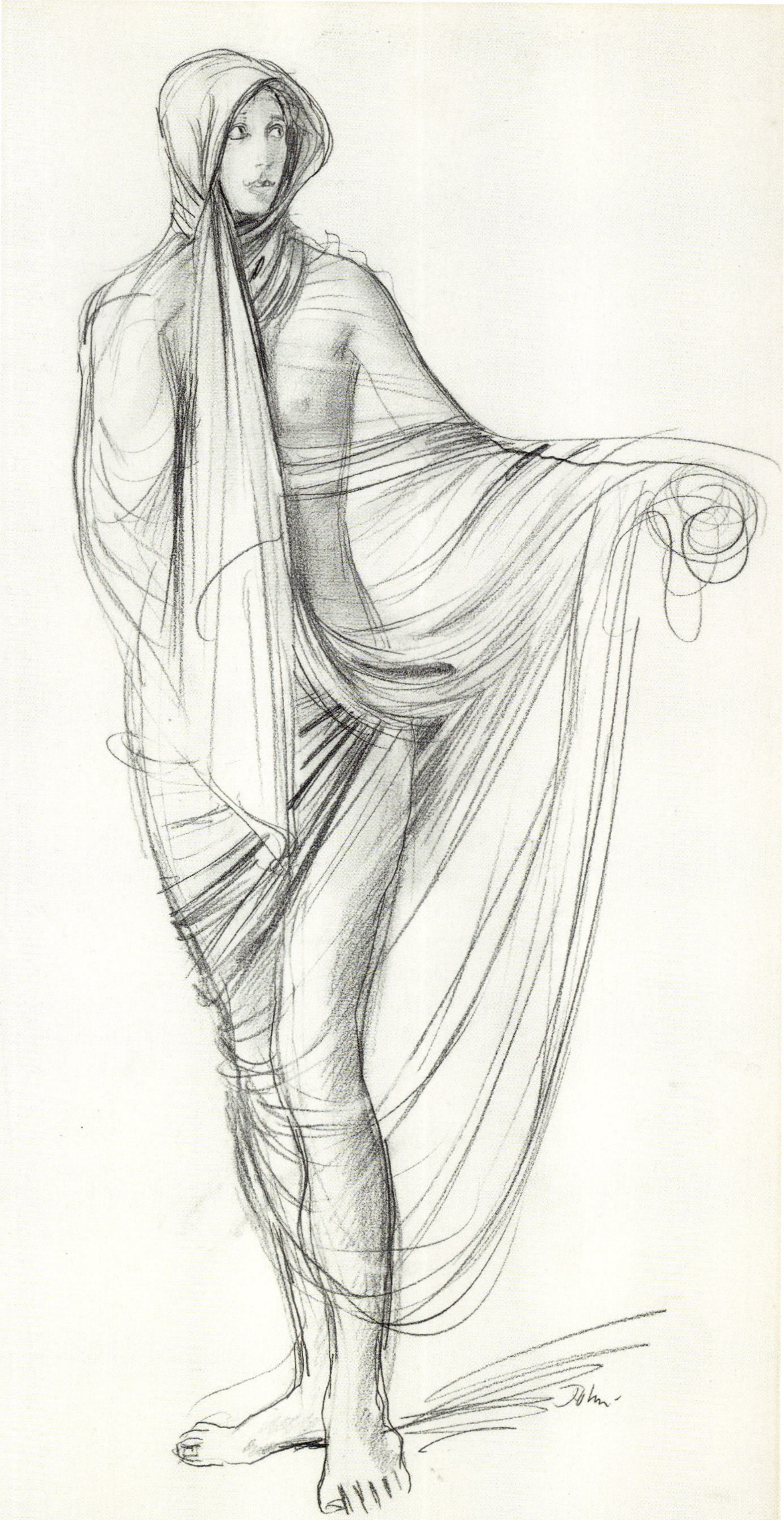
John

84

GWEN JOHN 1876–1939

Boy with a Blank Expression, 1928

Black chalk and bodycolour with some white chalk on paper
20.9 × 16.4 cm
Bequeathed by Miss Anna Hornby, 1996
WA1996.29

LITERATURE: Arts Council (1968) no. 95

Gwen John trained with her brother Augustus at the Slade School 1895–8. She won the figure composition prize in 1898 before going on to study with Whistler in Paris and to work as a model for Rodin. From late December 1926, living in Meudon, she became spiritually very close to her neighbours, the charismatic Catholic theologian Jacques Maritain and his wife Raïssa, to whose younger sister Véra Oumançoff Gwen became obsessively attached. Seeing her as a form of 'spiritual mother', she wrote to Véra virtually every day, expressing the inner struggle between the demands of her religion and her art in a form of private confessional.

Restricted to visiting Véra just once a week, Gwen would give her a regular 'dessin de lundi' (Monday drawing), so that by the time Véra ended the friendship in late 1930 – having found Gwen's intensity too smothering – she owned around a hundred drawings. This study of a young boy appears to have been one such drawing. It is closely related to another version that bears Gwen's studio stamp, *Boy with a Blank Face*.[1] The Ashmolean version was given to Véra on 29 May 1928. The close similarity between the two drawings implies that Gwen could have traced the outlines, using a technique she had learned in Rodin's studio, by holding the work up against a window.[2] This may explain why the fluid contours are so much more assured than the broken lines of the portraits of Breton children that Gwen had sketched in the late 1910s. In the paring down of the form to its bare essentials, the work has something of Rodin's drawings, of Gaudier-Brzeska, and of nineteenth-century Japanese prints. In 1909 Gwen John wrote to Ursula Tyrwhitt of the need to practise 'putting things down with decision', noting that 'I want my drawings ... to be definite and clean like Japanese drawings'.[3]

According to Susan Chitty, Gwen John saw this boy waiting on a station platform on a journey into Paris. A brief sketch on the *verso* of the Ashmolean drawing of a sleeping man in a bowler hat, might also have been drawn on the train. She offered Véra this drawing together with one of a 'Little Girl with a Large Hat and Straw-coloured Hair', inscribing them on the back of the original mounts, 'Little girl in the train (you)' and 'At the station (me)'.[4] Indeed, the boy bears a striking resemblance to a photograph of Gwen as a child, in the angle of the head, the outline of the face, and his hauntingly mournful expression, described by Gwen herself as one of 'stupid fear'.[5] CP

1. Present location unknown; Langdale (1987) no. 309.
2. Lloyd-Morgan (2004) p. 49.
3. Lloyd-Morgan (2004) p. 49.
4. Bristol City Art Gallery, K1829; Langdale (1987) no. 294.
5. Chitty (1981) p. 187; photograph reproduced in Langdale (1987) p. 3.

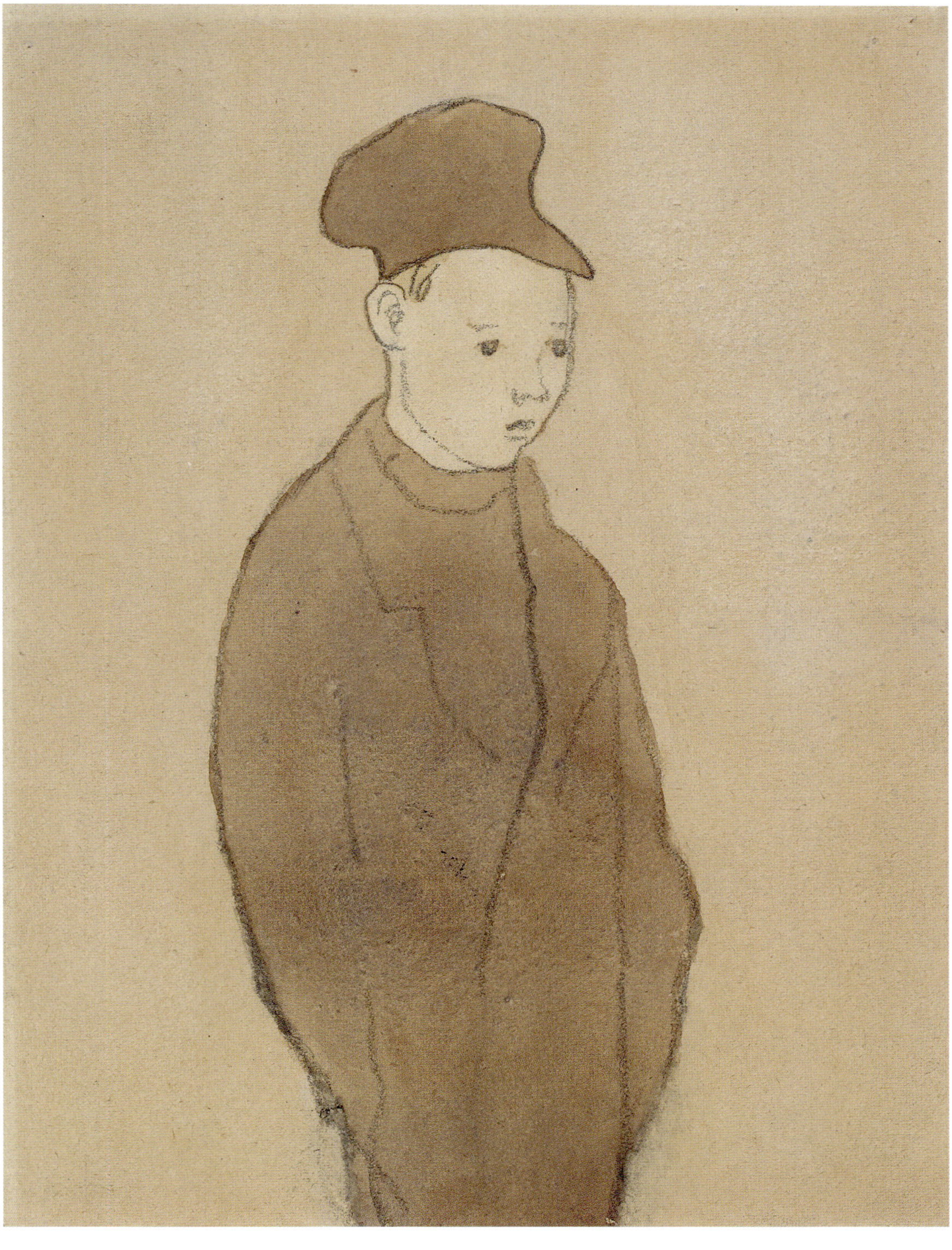

85

PAUL NASH 1889–1946
The Wood on the Hill, 1912

Pen and black ink over graphite with wash on paper
33.9 × 33.3 cm
Signed with monogram: *PN*
Purchased (Christopher Vaughan Bequest Fund), 2001
WA2001.60

LITERATURE: Eates (1948) no. 7; Causey (1980) no. 55; Jenkins (2010) no. 39

The Wittenham Clumps, near his uncle's farm at Sinodun House outside Wallingford, came to fascinate Nash in 1911; he described them as 'the Pyramids of my small world'.[1] They reappeared frequently in his works of the 1930s and 1940s. Although Nash found fame as an official war artist from 1917–8, the domed forms of Round Hill and Castle Hill crowned with beech woods became synonymous with his artistic identity at the outset and conclusion of his career. In 1913 the poster for his joint exhibition with his brother John, at the Dorien Leigh Gallery, included the Wittenham Clumps as a backdrop. John's book jacket for Paul's posthumously published autobiography *Outline* (1948) also featured this distinctive Oxfordshire landscape.[2]

Initially, Nash had been under the sway of the Pre-Raphaelites, primarily that of Dante Gabriel Rossetti. However, having spent four terms at the Slade School from autumn 1910, and on the advice of Sir William Blake Richmond that he 'should go in for nature', Nash began to develop his skills as a landscape artist.[3] He was profoundly engaged by the mystery of the encounter between himself and particular places, which especially in his early work often focused on trees. Writing to his mentor Gordon Bottomley, he explained, 'I have tried ... to paint trees as tho' they were human beings ... because I sincerely love and worship trees and know they *are* people'.[4]

Describing his first conscious experience of the Clumps nearly 30 years later, Nash highlighted his solitariness, having strayed from a shooting party in which he was a beater. The unexpected, vivid revelation of the landscape surprised him. The following day he sought the best position from which to depict the motif, likening his sketch to successfully hunted quarry, allowing him to make his 'living out of the land as much as my ancestors ever had done'.[5] Captured with formal austerity and delicacy of colour, the timeless autumn landscape, in which the stooks of corn recall the imposing group of trees, is so calm as to give the sensation of a place brimming with concealed significance. The path from right to left (reinforced by the placement of Nash's monogram), then ascends the hill, implying a metaphysical journey. Yet the contemplation of this monumental vision is not entirely divorced from the wider landscape, which Nash punctuates at the left with a tiny church spire. KW

1. Nash (1948) p. 122.
2. Rothenstein (1983) p. 20 and Gough (2014) p. 126.
3. Causey (1980) p. 24.
4. Letter *c.* 1 August 1912, Nash and Bottomley (1955) p. 42.
5. Nash (1948) p. 123.

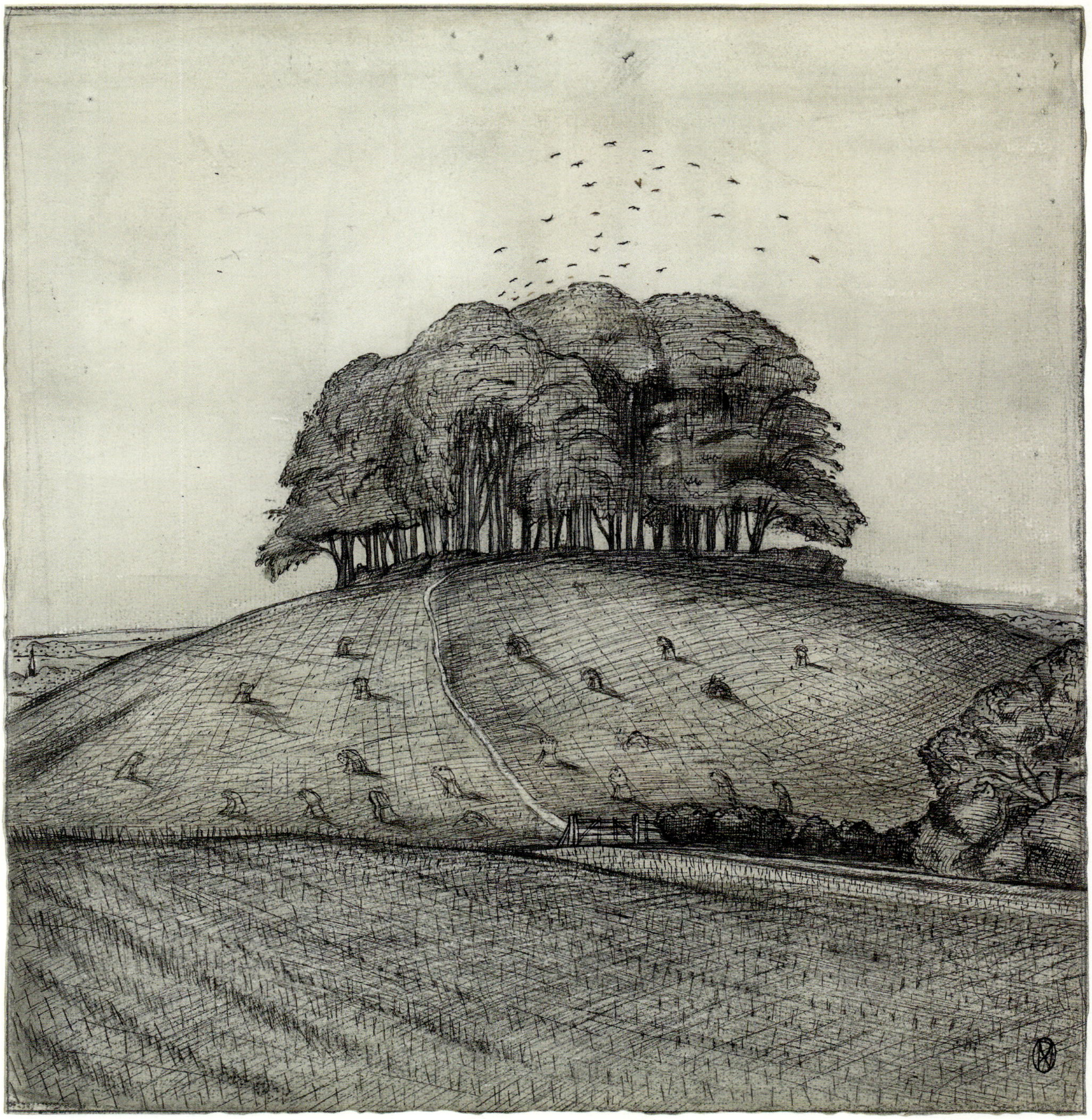

86

WALTER RICHARD SICKERT 1860–1942

Study for 'Ennui': Hubby and Marie, 1913–4

Pen and brown ink over black chalk, with red ink, on pale brown paper
38 × 28 cm
Inscribed: *O I say I wish if I'd never / cared for him, in [...] of this / free from the stars / O I say ...*
Purchased, 1943
WA1943.95

LITERATURE: Manchester (2004) no. 5.06; Baron (2006) no. 418.5

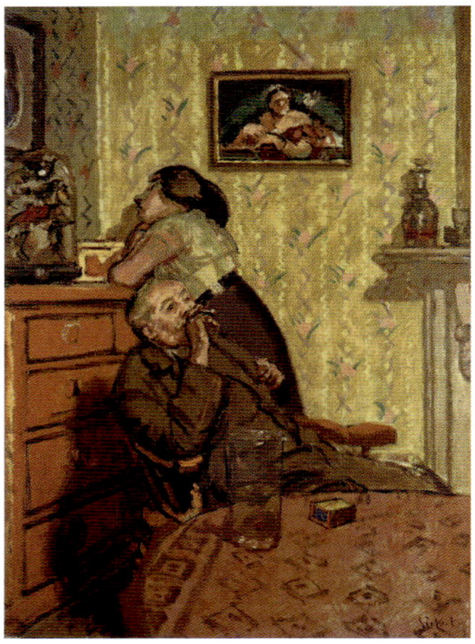

Fig. 55 | Walter Richard Sickert (1860–1942), *Ennui*, 1917–8. Oil on canvas. Ashmolean Museum, Oxford, WA1940.1.92

After his return to London in 1905, Sickert occupied a number of houses and studios in Camden Town, an area of London described by the novelist Ford Madox Ford as a place of 'grimy boxlike houses, yellow gas and perpetual ring of tram-horse hoofs'.[1] Camden Town was never fashionable, and in 1907 it became notorious owing to the murder of the prostitute Emily Dimmock, a crime known as 'the Camden Town Murder'. Sickert used the title for a series of paintings, drawings, and etchings depicting a naked woman and a clothed man. He continued the theme of two figures in an interior in numerous other paintings. *Ennui* marks the climax.

The first, and largest, painting of this title was exhibited at the New English Art Club in 1914, and preceded by an unusually complex preparatory process.[2] The models were Hubby, an old schoolfriend of the artist's and a reformed alcoholic, and Marie Hayes, who may have been Hubby's wife. Both had joined Sickert's household towards the end of 1911. They are seen in Sickert's studio on the corner of Granby Street and the Hampstead Road, which was appropriately down-at-heel, and which he furnished with unfashionable furniture and ornaments, such as the Victorian bell-jar of stuffed birds and the religious painting. In addition to three oil sketches of the figures, Sickert also made a large number of preparatory drawings, both of the whole composition and of individual elements, concentrating on the precise pose of the figures and their relationship, and the elements of still life – decanter, bell-jar, and picture frame. The present drawing is the final compositional study, to which Sickert seems to have returned as he worked out various problems in other paintings and drawings. Marie's back is therefore drawn three times, reflecting its changing position in one of the oil sketches. The drawing is squared up, and Sickert probably used an adjustable grid to transfer the composition to canvas. He reported to Miss Sands that he was pleased by this new method of painting:

I find this painting from drawings works out very well. You work in such properly ordered stages from general to particular statement. It also naturally dictates a somewhat larger scale as drawings can be so delicate and paint is so thick. I expect it is the solution to that puzzle.[3]

The title, *Ennui*, suggests the boredom of married life, in which a wife finds a glass of stuffed birds more interesting than her husband, who has to resort to beer and a cigar for pleasure. In the final, and most satisfactory, painting of the subject, now in the Ashmolean, Sickert intensified the mood by including a jaunty wallpaper, suggested in this drawing by the circular patterns to the right of the figures. CH

1. Quoted by Lynda Nead in Upstone (2008) p. 40.
2. Tate; Baron (2006) no. 418.
3. Baron (2006) p. 93.

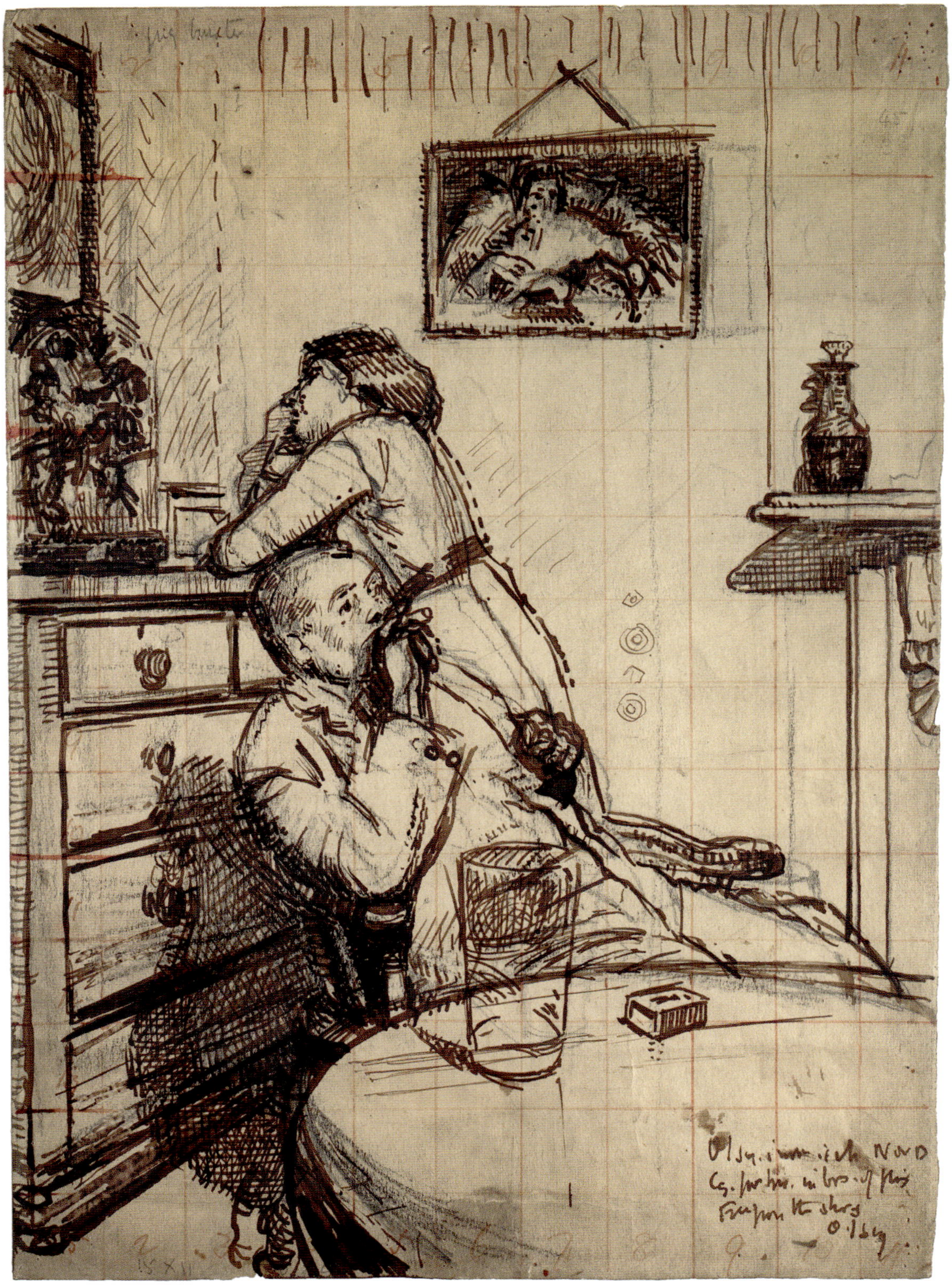

87

WALTER RICHARD SICKERT 1860–1942

Still Life: the Music Room in Morton Sands's House, 91 Cheyne Walk, London, 1913

Pencil, pen and ink and watercolour, on paper, squared for transfer and numbered
29.2 × 26 cm
Accepted by HM Government in lieu of Inheritance Tax and allocated to the Ashmolean Museum, 2011
WA2011.194

LITERATURE: Baron (2006) no. 429

Morton Sands (1884–1959) was the younger brother of Ethel Sands (1873–1962). Their father was a wealthy American drug manufacturer and their mother, Mary Hartpence, a great society beauty. Both parents died young. Morton was brought up by his sister, a painter who was a member of Sickert's Fitzroy Street Group and his close friend and confidant for many years. Ethel undoubtedly influenced her brother's taste, and in about 1911 he began to build up one of the most important collections of works by Sickert formed during the artist's lifetime; most of the paintings and drawings it contained are now in the Ashmolean Museum. Some years after leaving New College, Oxford, Morton moved into a handsome, mid-eighteenth-century house known as Belle Vue Cottage, 91 Cheyne Walk; here he lived until his death. He was musical, and had political aspirations.

This unusual drawing was made in March 1913, at a period when Sickert declared to Miss Sands that 'your technical salvation is my present mission'.[1] She had begun a painting of Morton's sitting room, but found it inexorably turning black. In line with his current practice of making elaborate preparatory drawings for his paintings, Sickert therefore made a study for Ethel to work on. She wrote to her companion, Nan Hudson, on 7 March that 'It's a lovely drawing but you can't imagine how funny it is, for him!'[2] Four days later Sickert squared it up, and added the figures of Ethel and Morton on separate pieces of paper. At the same time he made four 'adorable little sections from his drawing which he wants me to work into, they are much too pretty to touch'.[3]

Neither Miss Sands nor Miss Hudson ever completed the large oil, in spite of Sickert's encouragement, but they were both very fond of the drawing. However, Sickert instructed them to 'keep it as a private drawing and not frame or put it up ... Let us treat it as a compromising letter and not show it either to J.B. Lady O. or anyone'.[4] As a vivid and intensely personal study, described by Sickert as 'the picture of Morton's "objects de luxe and articles de virtue" (As I once saw on a bric-a-brac window)', it is both rare and touching.[5] CH

1. Quoted in Baron (1977) p. 104.
2. *Ibid.*
3. Quoted in Baron (1977) pp. 104–5.
4. Quoted in Baron (1977) p. 105.
5. *Ibid.*

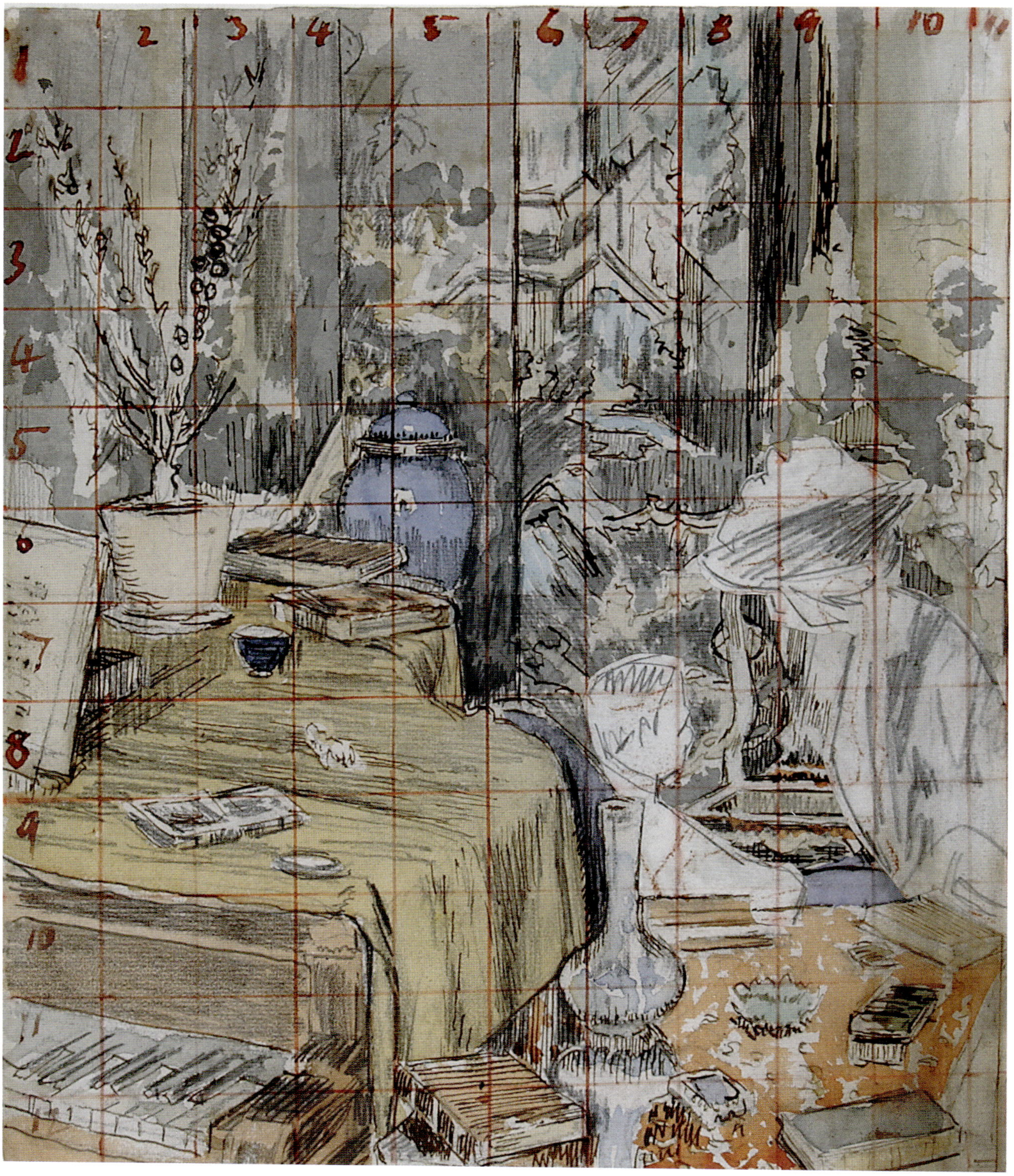

88

HAROLD JOHN WILDE GILMAN 1876–1919

Mrs Mounter at the Breakfast Table, 1916–7

Pen and black ink, partly scratched, squared in red ink, on paper
28.5 × 18.9 cm
Signed: *H Gilman*. Inscribed with numbers for transfer
Presented by R. A. Bevan, 1957
WA1957.28

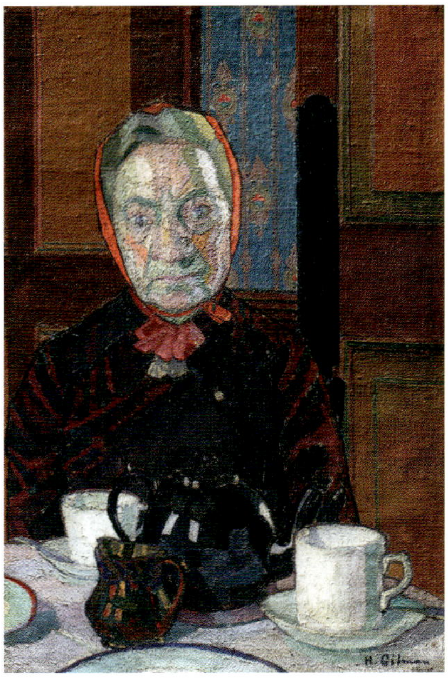

Fig. 56 | Harold Gilman (1876–1919), *Mrs Mounter at the Breakfast Table*, 1916–7. Oil on canvas. Tate, London, N05317 © Tate, London 2014

Gilman was already over 30 when he and his contemporary from the Slade School, Spencer Gore (1878–1914), joined Sickert in the Fitzroy Group, initially called 'Mr Sickert at home', in rented premises at 19 Fitzroy Street. Together, the members of the group developed their individual styles of painting in response to recent developments in France. The exhibition of 'Manet and the Post-Impressionists' in 1910 was decisive for Gilman, who admired Van Gogh above all, but experimented with a variety of styles. He was instrumental in the formation of the Camden Town Group in 1911, and shared his fellow members' love of essentially urban subjects, interiors and townscapes, painted in bright colours.

It was not until 1914 that Gilman moved permanently to London. He lodged at 47 Maple Street, W1, only a few yards from Fitzroy Street, where he painted a number of portraits of Mrs Mounter, until recently assumed to be his landlady, but in fact a fellow lodger. She was Anna Emma Mounter (1850–1932), who lived with her husband, Frederick, in another set of rooms in the same house.[1] Gilman occupied two rooms, probably on the first floor; the larger at the front where he ate and slept, with the smaller at the back serving as his studio.

This drawing, its function indebted to Sickert's similar practice of making elaborately squared-up studies for his oil paintings (cat. 87), was made in preparation for Gilman's portrait of Mrs Mounter. He was to paint two versions of different sizes *c.* 1916–7, the study corresponding more closely to the larger work.[2] Mrs Mounter has joined Gilman in his rooms, and is sitting at the breakfast table, ready to pour tea from the brown Betty for the two of them. In the paintings, the dazzling scarlet of her headscarf and the brilliant turquoise of the wall paper relieve the strict geometry, emphasised in the drawing by the squaring for transfer. The critic Frank Rutter wrote of this composition that it was 'the apotheosis of the charwoman, the transfiguration of homeliness, age, and toil into a spiritual loveliness of colour that time cannot wither'.[3]

1. See Rolfe (2010)
2. Walker Art Gallery, Liverpool; and Tate, London. See http://www.tate.org.uk/art/research-publications/camden-town-group/harold-gilman-mrs-mounter-at-the-breakfast-table-r1156198, accessed on 27 January 2015.
3. Quoted in Upstone (2008) no. 55.

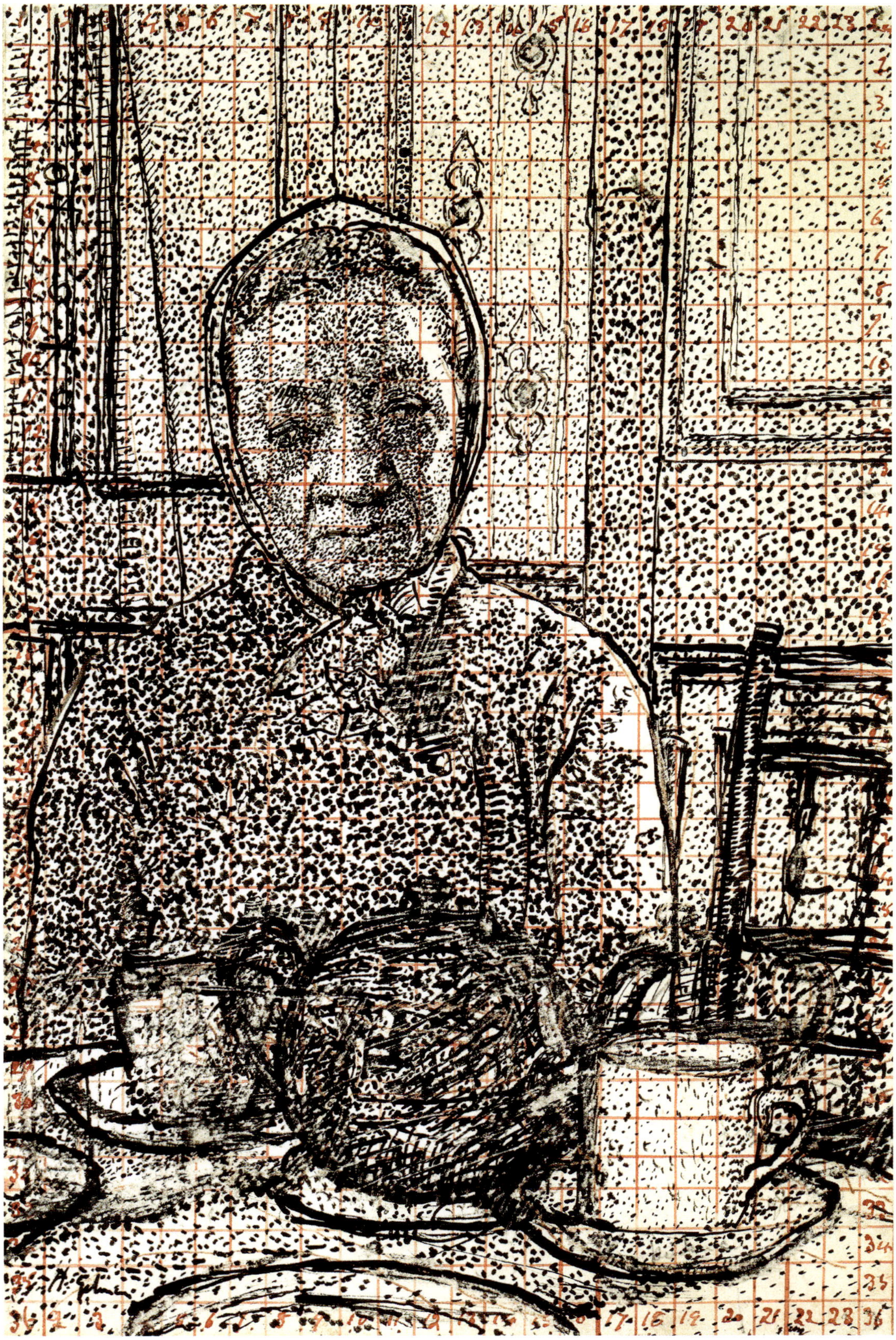

89

HAROLD JOHN WILDE GILMAN 1876–1919

Seascape: Breaking Waves, 1917

Pen and black ink on paper
29.8 × 43 cm
Signed: *H. Gilman*
Purchased (Bevan Fund), 1958
WA1958.32

In their ambition to remain resolutely modern, the members of the Camden Town Group generally eschewed landscapes without identifiably contemporary subjects. The notable exception was Robert Bevan (1865–1925), who painted numerous agricultural landscapes in Devonshire and elsewhere. Ginner, Gilman, and Gore also painted landscapes, but these only serve to emphasise the urban character of their usual subjects.

This seascape is exceptional in Gilman's work, indeed in the whole production of the Camden Town Group. The subject has come to epitomise the Romantic view of man's isolation in the face of the infinity of God's creation, as described by Robert Rosenblum in his seminal text, *Modern Painting and the Northern Romantic Tradition* (1975), based on his Slade lectures at Oxford in 1972. He traced the contemplation of the sea from Caspar David Friedrich's *Monk by the Sea* of 1809 through the aggressively 'realist' *The Artist on the Seashore at Palavas* (1854) by Gustave Courbet, and on to the American painter J. A. McNeill Whistler's *Harmony in Blue and Silver*, subtitled *Courbet at Trouville*, of 1865.[1] The motif of the beach and sea was repeated frequently by Whistler, generally without a figure, as Impressionist studies of ephemeral effects of weather and light and shade. Whistler's seascapes would have been known to Gilman, who visited the great memorial exhibition of his work in 1905 and stayed in Whistler's house at Neuville outside Dieppe in the summer of 1907.

Gilman made a handful of landscapes on Romney Marsh, where his father served as rector of Snave with Snargate from 1890 until his death. The flat expanses of the countryside were therefore familiar to him from his adolescence. This drawing may date from a visit to the area shortly before or after the death of his father in 1917. It is executed with a broad reed pen, a medium frequently used by Van Gogh, whom Gilman particularly admired.[2] In the drawing school that he and Charles Ginner ran in Soho between January 1916 and December 1917, the two reproductions on the walls were of paintings by Van Gogh and Toulouse-Lautrec. This seascape shares with its iconographical precedents an intention to merge the sea and the sky into a whole composed of identifiable elements. Yet its technique transcends the conventional Romanticism of such a subject, creating a pattern of marks which, while evoking a seascape, tend towards the abstraction of nature. CH

1. See Rosenblum (1978) pp. 69–70.
2. Ives (2005) p. 37.

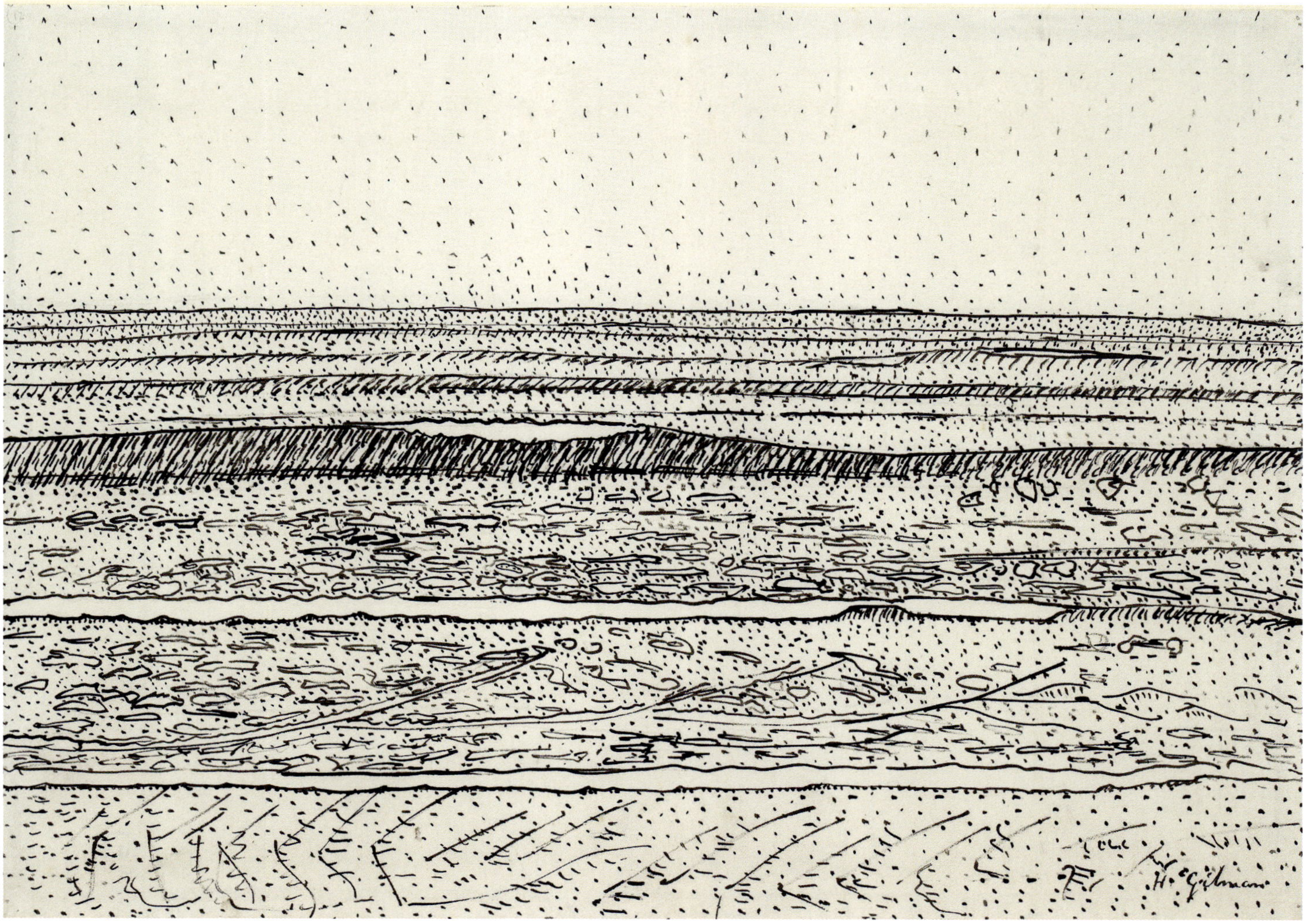
H. Gilman

90

CHARLES GINNER 1878–1952
Flask Walk: Rain, c. 1924

Pen and black ink with watercolour on paper
34.6 × 23.2 cm
Signed: *c. GINNER*
Presented by the Misses Kitson, 1940
WA1940.8.7

In an article entitled 'Neo-Realism' in *New Age*, 1 January 1914, Ginner set out the beliefs of his colleagues in the Camden Town Group that art should concern itself with life 'in all its effects, moods, and developments. Each age has its landscape, its atmosphere, its cities, its people'.[1] Among the themes the Group treated were those specifically favoured by the Impressionists: streetscapes, intimate interiors, and portraits of friends, family, and the working classes.

Ginner had trained as an architect, and he enjoyed painting the complexity of the interlocking and superimposed planes of the industrial or residential townscape. He habitually used a home-made viewfinder, with black cotton to find the exact view. His oil paintings thus have the appearance of complex geometrical puzzles, painted in thick impasto, which give them an air of unreality. In the creation of a new and highly imaginary realism, he may be seen as the precursor of L. S. Lowry (1887–1976).

From 1919 until 1938 Ginner lived at 61 Hampstead High Street, where he occupied the four floors above the shop. The view over the High Street towards Flask Walk frequently provided him with a convenient subject. His sitting room had three windows, so he was able to vary the viewpoint, concentrating on the buildings on the left or the right side of the street. He also painted or drew the scene in different effects of weather, or on special occasions such as Guy Fawkes' Day in 1936 or Coronation Day in 1937.[2]

This highly finished drawing has been dated *c.* 1924. Ginner shows more of the room than usual, and the foreground is occupied by an elaborate still life, including the top of his desk with a ginger jar and other objects, and the windowsill crowded with flowers, scales, and ink bottles. In his oil paintings, Ginner used heavily encrusted, carefully applied pigment with thick black outlines, and his watercolours share these qualities. This splendid example is drawn in his characteristically meticulous technique, the black ink delineating every detail, and the saturated watercolours applied with painstaking deliberation. CH

1. Quoted in Upstone (2008) p. 139.
2. See http://www.tate.org.uk/art/research-publications/camden-town-group/charles-ginner-flask-walk-hampstead-on-coronation-day-r1159221, accessed on 27 January 2015.

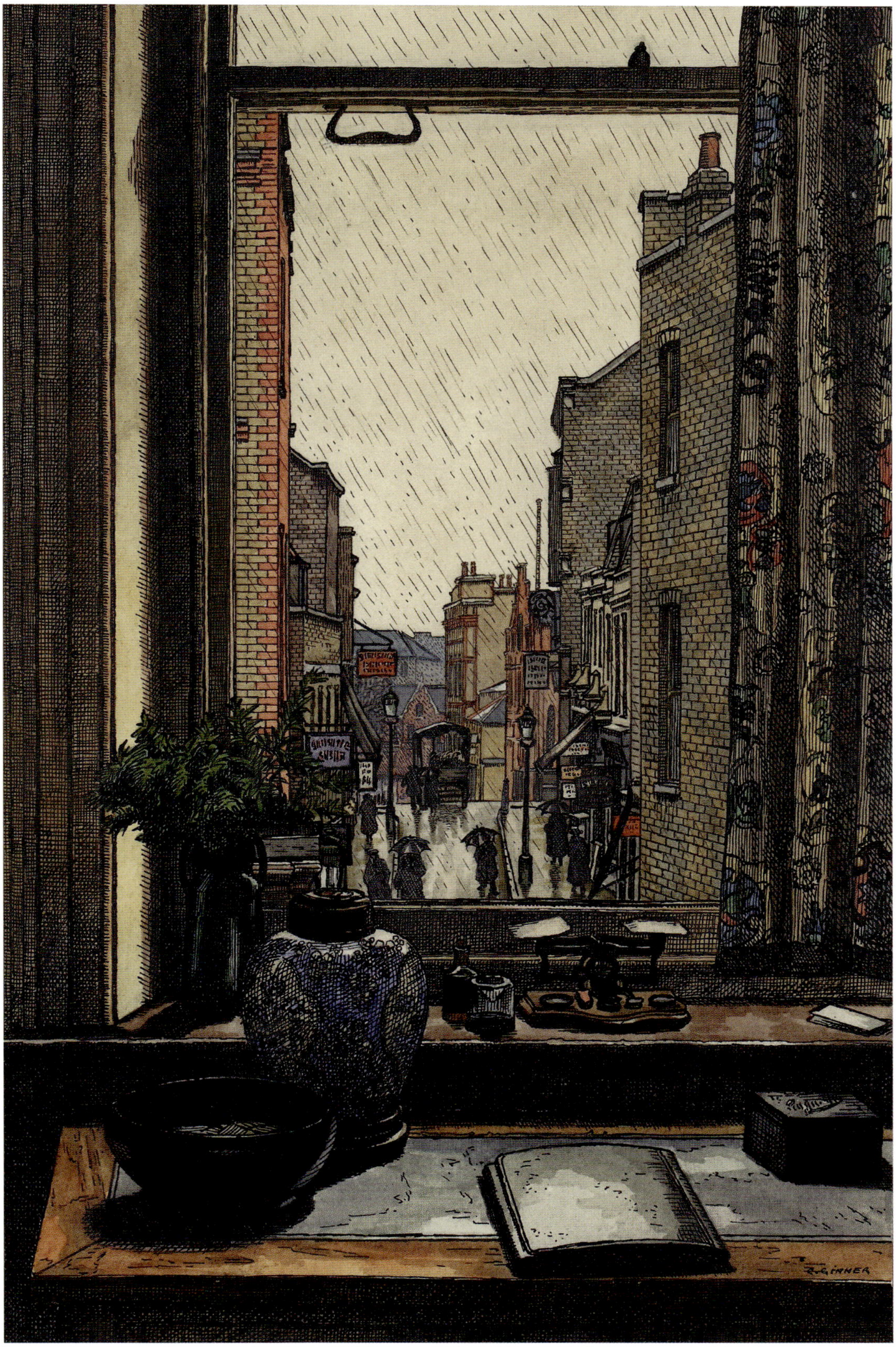
R.GINNER

91

ERIC HENRI KENNINGTON 1888–1960

William Rothenstein, 1917–8

Black chalk touched with red chalk and heightened with white chalk on grey paper
49.5 × 41.5 cm
Accepted by HM Government in lieu of Inheritance Tax on the Estate of Lady (John) Rothenstein and allocated to the Ashmolean Museum, 2005
WA2005.16

On the outbreak of the First World War Kennington volunteered, and went on to serve as a private in the 13th territorial battalion of the London Regiment, known as 'the Kensingtons'. His first war painting, *The Kensingtons at Kaventie: Winter 1914* (1915; IWM), was described by Campbell Dodgson, an influential Keeper in the British Museum, as 'decidedly the finest picture inspired by this war as yet produced by an English artist'.[1] Following an unofficial visit to France in December 1916, Kennington showed a series of portraits of soldiers at the Goupil Gallery, which enjoyed great success. His claims to be appointed an official war artist were promoted by Thomas Derrick, who thought his portraits would be useful propaganda, because 'most people are more interested in soldiers than shell-holes'; and Dodgson, who proclaimed him 'a born painter of the nameless heroes of the rank and file'.[2] After his appointment in August 1917 he travelled out to the Western Front, where he was much in demand: 'a portrait draughtsman is welcomed out here, everybody wanting to be drawn from Generals to Privates and, consequently, I am treated magnificently.'[3] His aim was to 'get as much as possible of the magnificence of the men, all their fine qualities, varied characters and appearances'.[4] For much of the time, he was not at the front line, but, as he wrote to William Rothenstein, 'near enough to get the war and far enough for safety'.[5]

Rothenstein was only appointed an artist to the Ministry of Information on 17 December 1917, after persuading the authorities that his German name and slight German accent should not be perceived as handicaps. He joined Kennington on the Somme at Montigny Farm near Roisel, some 10 miles from Péronne, where British and American troops were quartered, 'a desolate spot, where a few tin huts were grouped together in a flat muddy landscape'.[6] He was surprised to find that Kennington 'seemed content to draw tents and shacks and camp rubbish'.[7] During their few days together Kennington made this very striking portrait of his friend and fellow artist, in the quick, confident strokes of black chalk for which he was renowned. The features of the bald, short-sighted Rothenstein are admirably characterised, rather uncomfortable in his tommy's tin hat, and looking every inch the displaced intellectual or aesthete. CH

1. Black (2001) p. 4
2. Quoted in Black (2001) p. 6; Dodgson and Montague (1918) p. 1.
3. Black (2001) p. 4.
4. Quoted in Black (2001) p. 8.
5. Black (2001) p. 6.
6. Harries (1983) p. 62.
7. Harries (1983) p. 50.

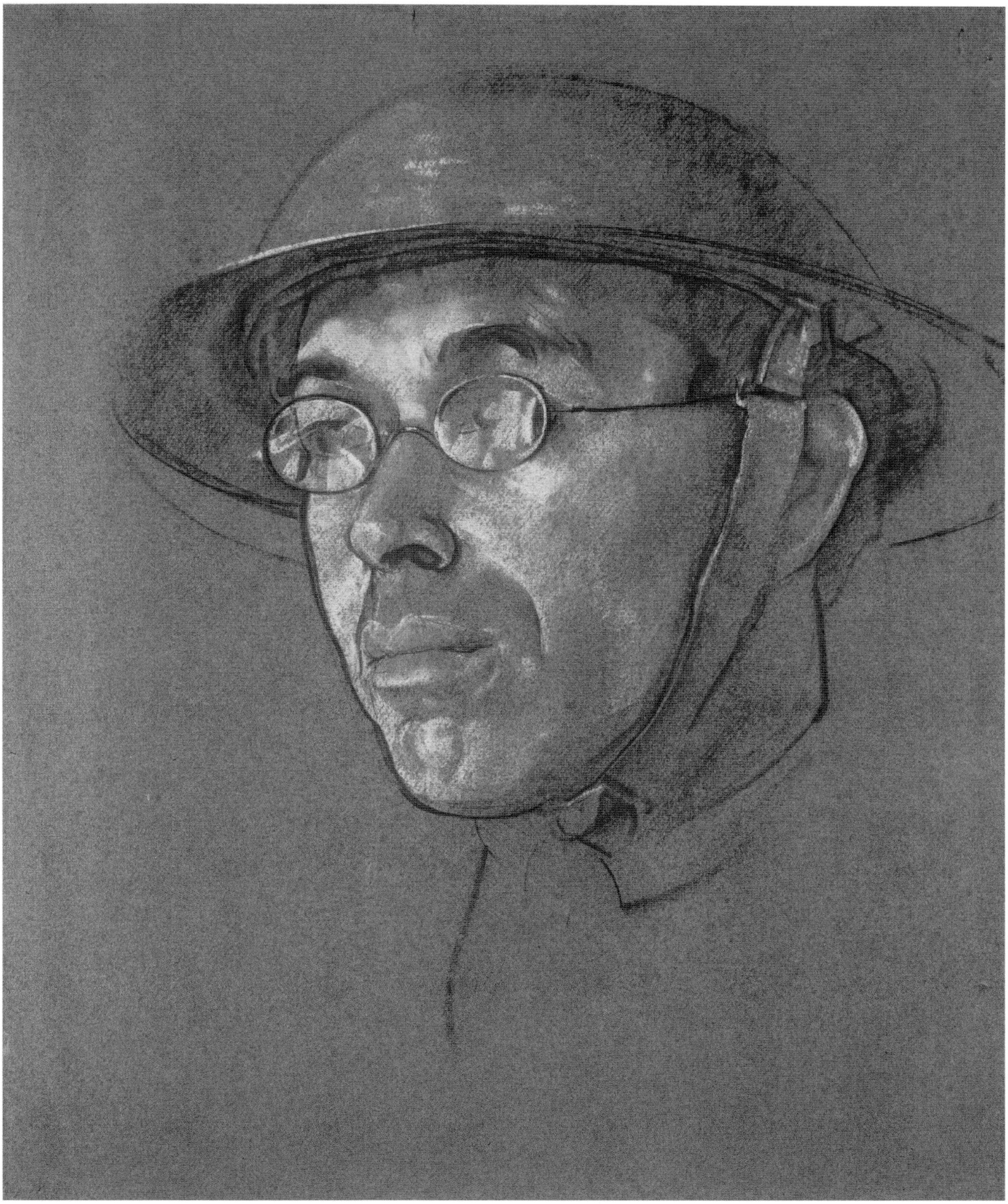

92

AUSTIN OSMAN SPARE 1886–1956

A Dressing Station, 1919

Pastel on Ingres paper
52.1 × 39.5 cm
Presented by Mrs Elizabeth Mitchell, 2004
WA2004.110

When Spare first exhibited at the Royal Academy in 1904, he was hailed as a genius and confessed that his ambition was to be President of that institution.[1] He was already inventing what he called his own 'religion' and in the following year, published his first book, *Earth: Inferno*. Whilst his drawings were frequently compared with those of Aubrey Beardsley and Edmund Sullivan, his style was much more mannered, and his imagery became increasingly weird and sexual. His abstruse mysticism can be seen in the article he published in 1916 on 'Automatic Drawing', in which he argued that, just as the character of handwriting is due to the subconscious, so automatic drawing enables the artist to release 'the fundamental static truths which are repressed by education and customary habit and lie dormant in the mind'.[2]

In spite of this intensely personal imagination, Spare became an effective war artist. He was conscripted as a private in the Royal Army Medical Corps on 16 May 1917, working in a hospital in Blackpool before moving back to London to paint records of events in the First World War that he had never witnessed. Between 13 May and 6 September 1919, he was in France, making drawings of dressing stations and other medical installations. These were no longer considered primarily as material for propaganda, but instead as accurate representations of the reality of the Front. Many were made in coloured chalks, avoiding the need for cumbersome painting equipment whilst at the same time offering the possibility of colouring on the spot rather than later in a studio.

This drawing of a dressing station shows a medical orderly in a long white smock looming out of the darkness of the trench, holding a jar of chloroform. On the right, one invalid props himself up in his bunk, while above him, a second lies awkwardly on his side. Opposite is a soldier whose face is partly in shadow, his appearance gaunt and pallid, as he sits with his legs swinging above the floor, his boots and puttees crumpled. Spare has invested the scene with an extraordinary atmosphere of foreboding, emphasised by the deathly stillness, as all four men stare attentively at the artist.

In later years, Spare was ashamed of his war work, going so far as to say that 'I am hoping all my work is dead and buried as there is nothing worth seeing'.[3] Fortunately, a number of pastels survive, mostly in the Imperial War Museum, providing a distinctive and valuable account of the work of the RAMC. CH

1. *Daily Chronicle*, 3 May 1904.
2. Spare (2007) p. 11.
3. Baker (2012) p. 127.

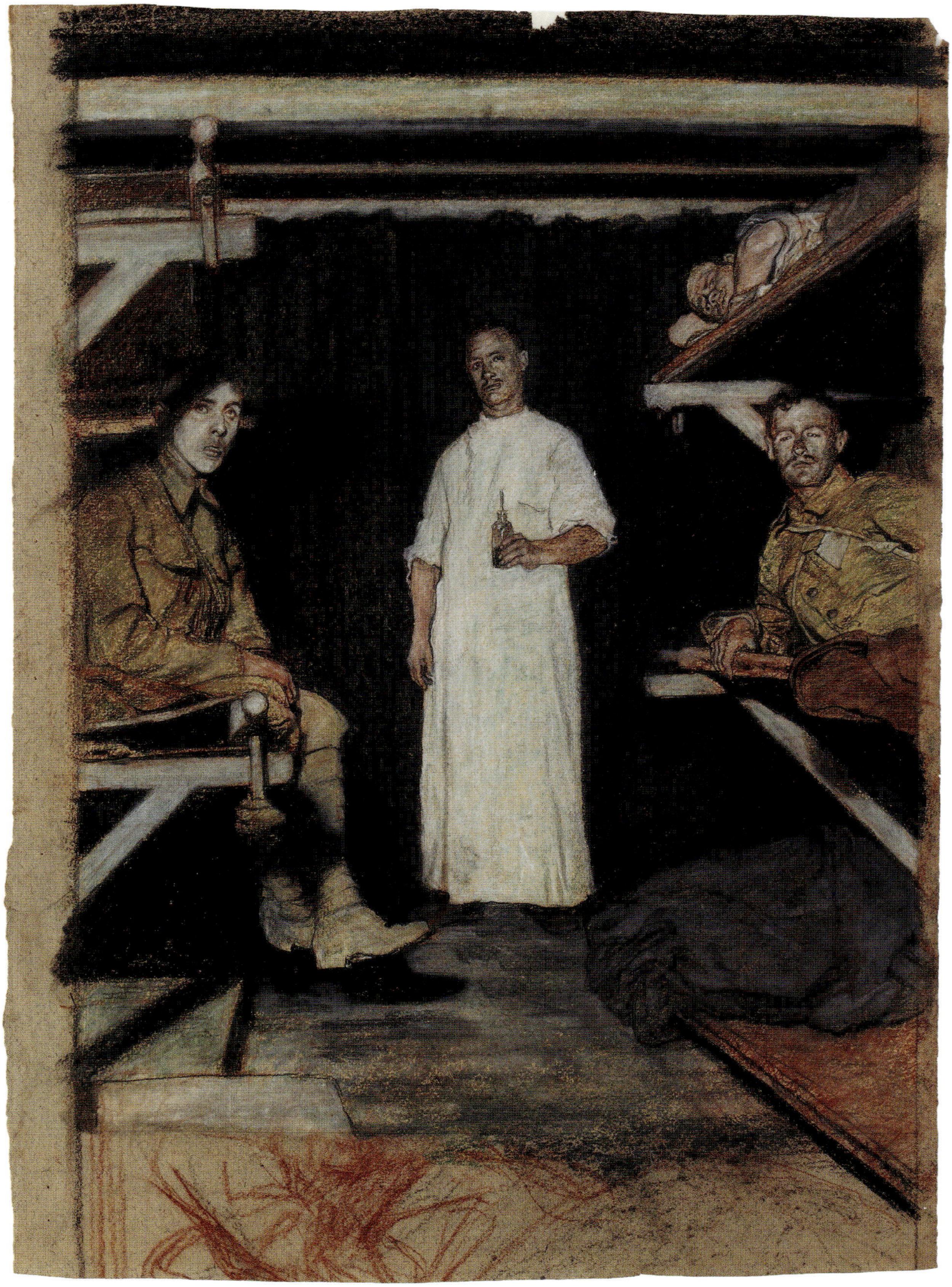

93

BEN NICHOLSON 1894–1982

1929 (view of the harbour at St Ives)

Graphite on paper
33 × 42 cm
Inscribed: *Ben Nicholson / one of the dwgs made on / first visit with Kit Wood to St Ives / + worked on later / One of the first dwgs he drew / St Ives 1929. for / the day / Kit Wood / 198*
Accepted by HM Government in lieu of Inheritance Tax on the Estate of the Artist, and allocated to the Ashmolean, 1986
WA1986.358

The son of one of the most successful artists of his day, Ben Nicholson quickly rejected all that his father represented, and soon after the First World War began a long period of experimentation with various forms of the *avant-garde*. With his new wife, Winifred Roberts (1893–1981), he looked particularly at the work of Cézanne, the Douanier Rousseau, and the Cubists Picasso and Braque in Paris. His own pictures show Nicholson restlessly playing with paint and pencil, often combining the two, in a succession of bold experiments in perspective, seeking to reduce his compositions to an ultimate condition of simplification, and populating his landscapes with deliberately naive figures and animals. He produced his first abstract paintings in 1924, but not until nearly ten years later did he resume these experiments in his abstract sculptural reliefs.

In August 1928 Nicholson visited St Ives with his friend Christopher Wood (1901–1930), who had become a close friend of Winifred's. Together they discovered the art of the self-taught 'primitive' painter Alfred Wallis (1855–1942). Wallis seemed to epitomise the innocence the modernists sought; his paintings were devoid of any accuracy of description, but possessed an innate untutored vitality and expressiveness. As Nicholson later recalled, 'One finds only the influences one is looking for and I was certainly looking for that one'.[1] Stimulated by Wallis's example, his painting gained a new boldness and confidence.

Wallis was much less influential on Nicholson's drawings. They remained consistently spare and linear from his first attempts at St Ives until the early 1950s, when he began to add rudimentary washes. The outline is firm and continuous, with almost no shading, space being suggested simply by interlocking lines. Nicholson found painting landscape difficult because he felt unable to assimilate so many different elements into a single composition; but drawing enabled him to convey the essence of a scene without losing immediacy or vitality. This sheet, taken from a sketchbook made on the artist's first visit to St Ives, shows a view down a passage from Bethesda Place to the harbour. The buildings, the pier and lighthouse, and the distant hills, are all drawn in economical outline, while the boats in the harbour and one of the cats in the foreground are more fully described, deliberately distorting the perspective. Nicholson has paid particular care to the geometric shapes of the steps up to the doors on the left and right, and the Victorian streetlight. The lightly drawn animals on the quayside add a playful note to what is otherwise an austere drawing. CH

1. Quoted in Stephens (2008) p. 25.

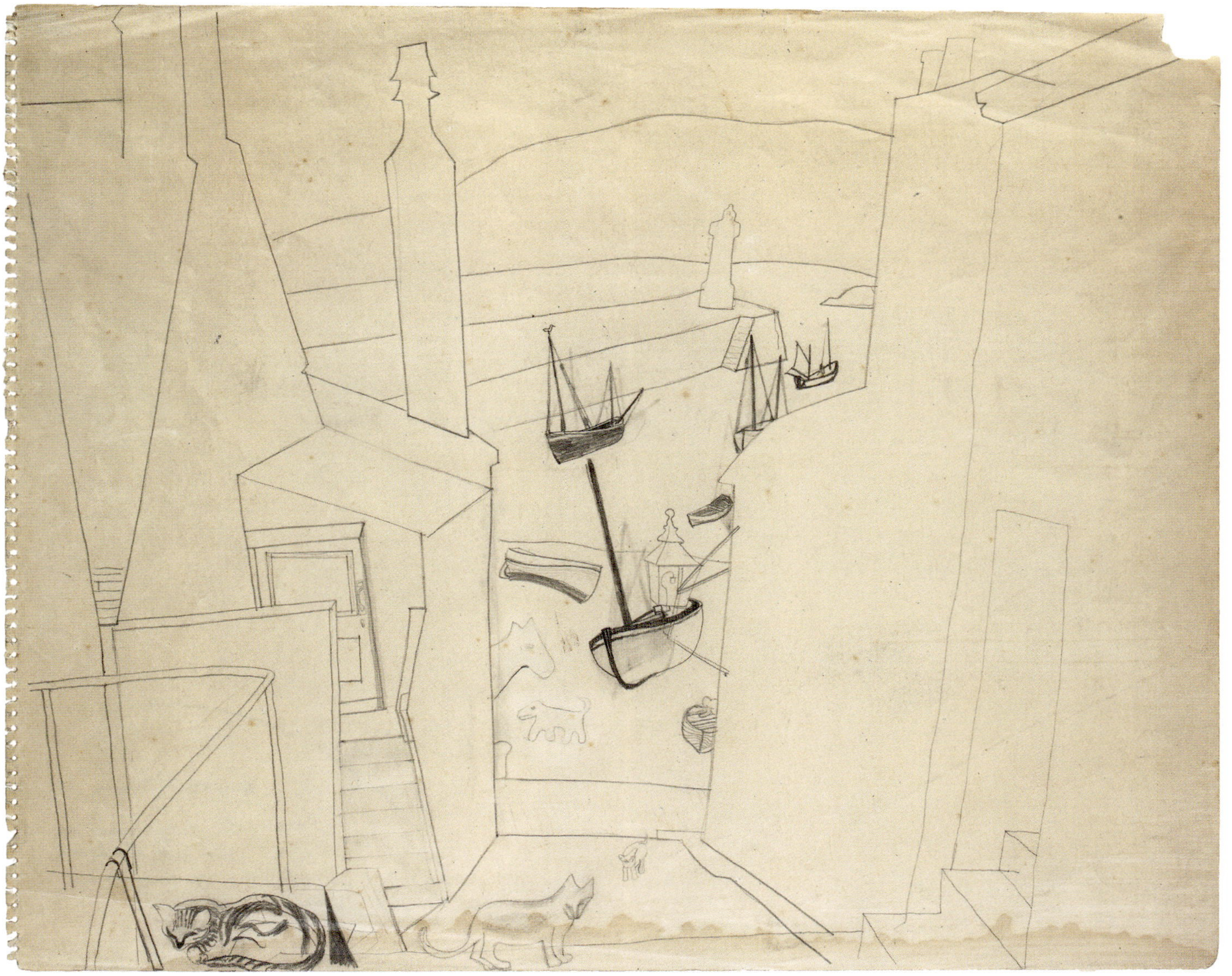

94

ERIC ARTHUR ROWTON GILL 1882–1940

Sketchbook: 'Drawings of B.W. 1928–1930 & S.M.'s hands', 1928–30

Graphite on paper, 53 folios, bound in linen open at fol. 3
28.5 × 22 cm
Purchased (Madan, Blakiston Funds) with the assistance of The Art Fund, the Resource/V&A Purchase Grant Fund, the Friends of the Ashmolean, and Michael Barclay, 2003
WA2003.197

Gill was already in his mid-forties when he enrolled in the life drawing class at the Grande Chaumière in Paris in May 1926. He later argued that an artist should come to drawing from the nude 'rather late in life, when the experience of living has filled the mind'.[1] (These drawings were later published as *First Nudes* in 1954.) Thereafter, he studied the nude assiduously, and what might hitherto have seemed unnecessary for an artist-craftsman with firm Christian beliefs quickly became a dominant feature of his work.

One of his most important models was the American typographer Beatrice Warde (1900–1967), who frequently visited Gill's home at Pigotts in the Chilterns, where he had moved in October 1928. This sketchbook, one of the few by Gill to remain intact, includes drawings of Beatrice Warde and Stanley Morison, together with a few miscellaneous subjects. Gill met Morison, who was the Typographic Adviser to the Monotype Corporation, before the First World War, and it was he who introduced Gill to the redoubtable Mrs Warde. Whereas the relationship between Morison, a strict Catholic, and Mrs Warde, was not physical, Gill was typically less restrained, as his diary makes clear. Exceptionally, on 1 May 1930, he noted, 'To BW in eve – sup with her. SM came later and I drew his hands and drew BW after. Slept with BW and she with me but did *not* commit adultery – we really slept'.[2]

The 49 drawings in this sketchbook are all precisely dated between 21 December 1928 and 1 May 1930. Of these, 38 represent Beatrice Warde in a variety of poses: crouching, leaning, sitting, some provocative, others more demure. There is a particular focus on her breasts, stomach, and buttocks, and her arms and legs are very often truncated. Many sketches show variations on a similar pose. Gill's line is outstandingly confident, and the shading characteristically on the outside of the outline, giving the forms a distinctly sculptural quality. He had first mastered this technique in a sketchbook dated 1927, in which the study on fol. 29 is inscribed 'first drawing in this method'.[3]

Although Gill believed that drawing could be a pleasure and an end in itself, several of these drawings were later reproduced in *Twenty-Five Nudes* (1938). One became *La Belle Sauvage*, the colophon for the publisher Cassell and Company, which occupied premises in an inn of that name. The final drawing in the sketchbook, showing Morison's hand resting on a book, was engraved for the last edition of *The Fleuron* (1930), which contained an essay on Gill's typography by Mrs Warde. CH

1. Gill (1938) unpaginated.
2. Quoted in MacCarthy (1989) p. 235.
3. 39 Life studies, Victoria and Albert Museum, P.D. 24.

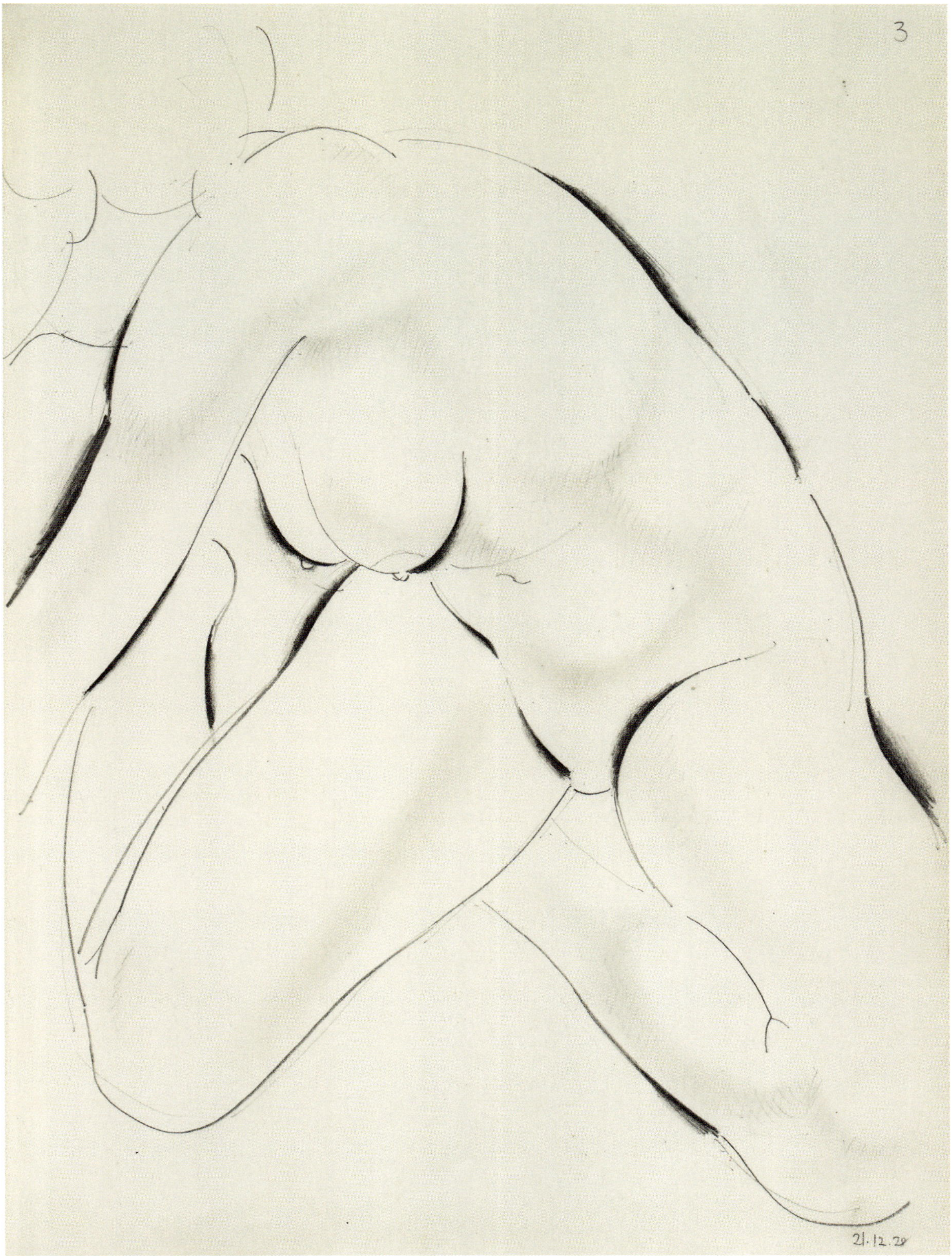
3
21.12.28

95

WILLIAM PATRICK ROBERTS 1895–1980

Study for 'The Park Bench', 1933

Graphite and brown ink on paper
22.4 × 28 cm
Signed: *Roberts*
Presented by Sir Muirhead Bone, Leonard Huskinson, Albert Rutherston, and Professor Randolph Schwabe, 1939
WA1939.113

As one of the signatories to the Vorticist manifesto, 'Vital English Art', in 1914, Roberts was in the forefront of the radical movement, dedicated to reconciling the abstract with the figurative in an innovative manner. His early works were resolutely cubist, not unlike those of his friend, David Bomberg. Later, as an official war artist during the First World War, he developed a more realistic style, the angular forms gradually becoming more rounded and plastic. Among the paintings he showed at his first solo exhibition in 1923 was the celebrated portrait of T. E. Lawrence as *Aircraftman Shaw* (Ashmolean Museum).[1] Apart from portraits, Roberts painted complex compositions of numerous human figures engaged in everyday activities, often in the area near Regent's Park or Camden Town, where he lived.

The Park Bench (fig. 57) marks the culmination of a series of paintings begun in 1921 which depict people enjoying time off work in a park. As usual, Roberts made a detailed preparatory drawing, as well as a coloured sketch, before beginning work on the canvas, although he made very few changes as he proceeded.[2] Crowded into a narrow focus is a group of people sitting on a park bench. Their arrangement is apparently haphazard and they are facing in all directions. Most are in motion; the man on the farthest left smokes a pipe, while his elder daughter stands between his legs and makes her younger brother clap his hands. Their mother is in the middle, playing with another toddler who holds a ball and looks at a black dog, reclining on the right. On the end of the bench, a bearded man holds his pipe away from his mouth, his slipper dangling nonchalantly, while he looks back at the children. A bald man on the other side of the bench watches a woman to his left lifting up another child, and she in turn looks at the woman in the middle. Behind them two men play football, one shooting while the other acts as goalkeeper. The simplified forms and strongly contrasting areas of light and dark are offset by the remarkable vitality of the poses. CH

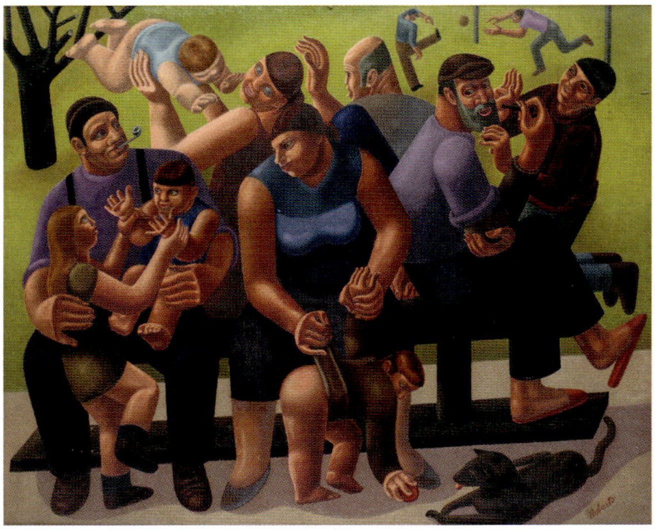

Fig. 57 | William Roberts (1895–1980), *The Park Bench*, 1933. Oil on canvas. Private Collection. Photograph courtesy of Sotheby's Picture Library © Estate of John David Roberts. By permission of the William Roberts Society

1. WA1946.267.
2. The bodycolour sketch is in the British Museum; see http://www.users.waitrose.com/~wrs/catchron.html under 1933. The painting was sold at Sotheby's, 19 November 1988 lot 229.

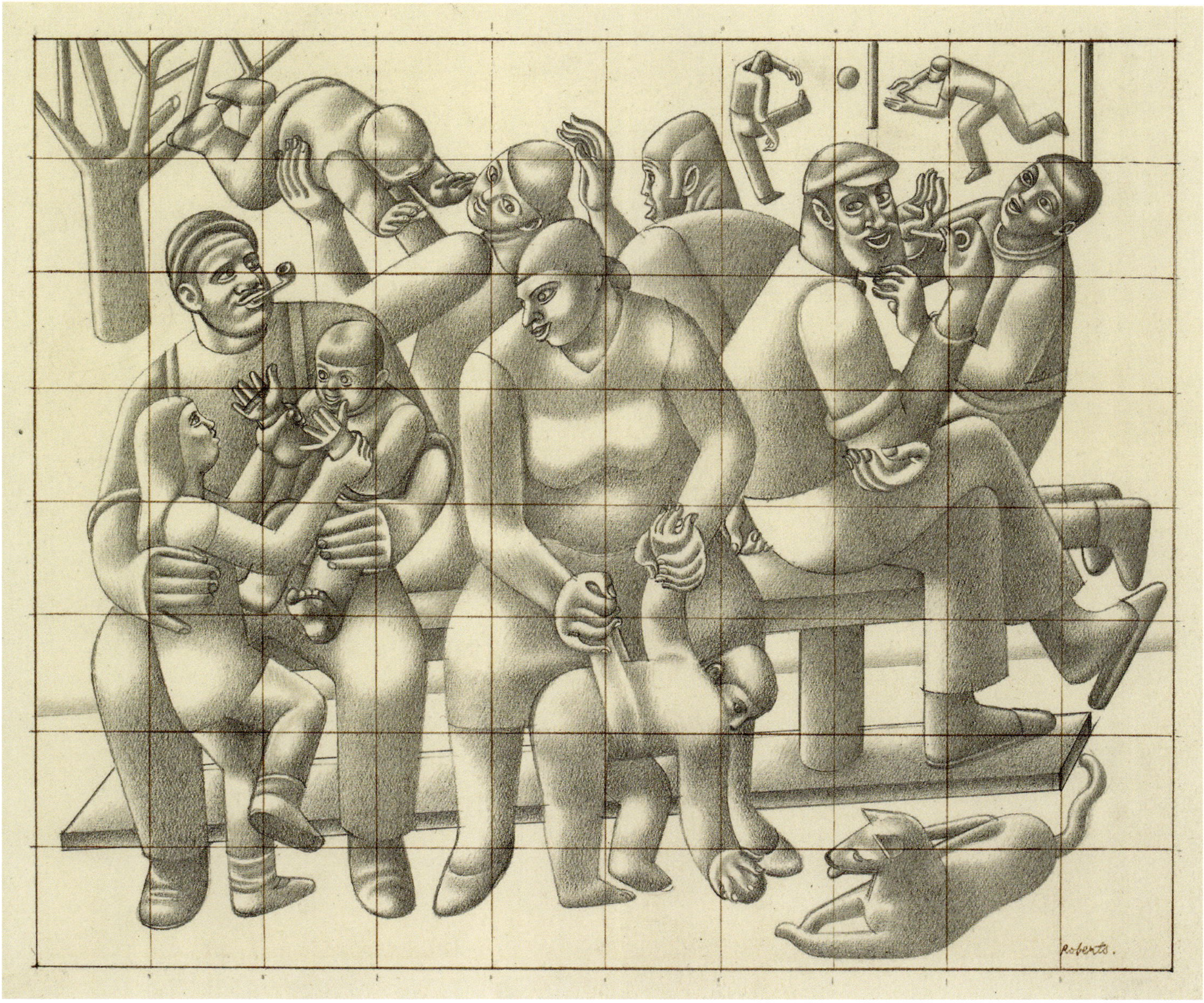
Roberts.

96

ERIC WILLIAM RAVILIOUS 1903–1942

The Brickyard, c. 1935–6

Watercolour over graphite on paper, with a small sheet of added paper
47.8 × 56.6 cm
Signed: *Eric Ravilious*
Bequeathed by Thomas Balston, through The Art Fund, 1968
WA1968.38

LITERATURE: Zwemmer Gallery (1936) no. 23; Graves Art Gallery (1958) no. 55; Russell (2011) p. 24

Trained as a wood engraver and mural painter at the Royal College of Art, where he was taught by Paul Nash, Ravilious worked as a book illustrator and designer but turned increasingly to watercolour during the 1930s. He first explored Essex with Edward Bawden, his friend and fellow student, when they part-rented the handsome Georgian Brick House, in Great Bardfield, in 1931. In 1934 Ravilious and his wife bought Bank House in nearby Castle Hedingham. He discovered the Victorian Tortoise Brickworks outside Sible Hedingham the following year, while preparing works for his second one-man show at the Zwemmer Gallery of Feburary 1936.

Ravilious never felt Bawden's affinity for the Essex landscape, preferring the beguiling beauty of the Sussex Downs, which he had begun to visit early in 1934.[1] His discovery there of Asham Cement Works prompted a series of five watercolours exploring the relationship of industry to the ancient chalk landscape. In *The Brickyard*, the old-fashioned steam engine is the main actor in the apparently abandoned wintry scene. While Ravilious was aware of Surrealism, the objects are a realistic part of the landscape, nonetheless embodying the distillation of heightened experience. The effect is akin to 'the rusty harrow, the plough / Long worn out, and the roller made of stone' described in Edward Thomas's 'Tall Nettles'. Thomas's poetry featured in Ravilious's wide-ranging reading, and both men were intrigued by the silent eloquence of commonplace things.

The numinous atmosphere depends greatly on the sober colour palette – inspired as much by the example of John Sell Cotman and Francis Towne, whose work Ravilious knew from visits to the British Museum and the Victoria and Albert Museum, as by the scene itself. A sophisticated variety of mark-making combined with the luminosity of the paper creates dynamic patterns redolent of Ravilious's wood engravings. Ravilious built up the composition on one sheet without making preparatory studies, destroying around four out of every five works he produced. Here, a final amendment has been made to the foreground, with a patch to obscure a hand-barrow. Carefully attuned to the nuances of the landscape, the regimented row of pollarded willows is contrasted with the free forms of the other untouched trees. The brickworks are not an industrial incursion into a pristine landscape, but an episode in the continuing narrative of man's manipulation of nature. KW

1. Powers (2013) p. 89.

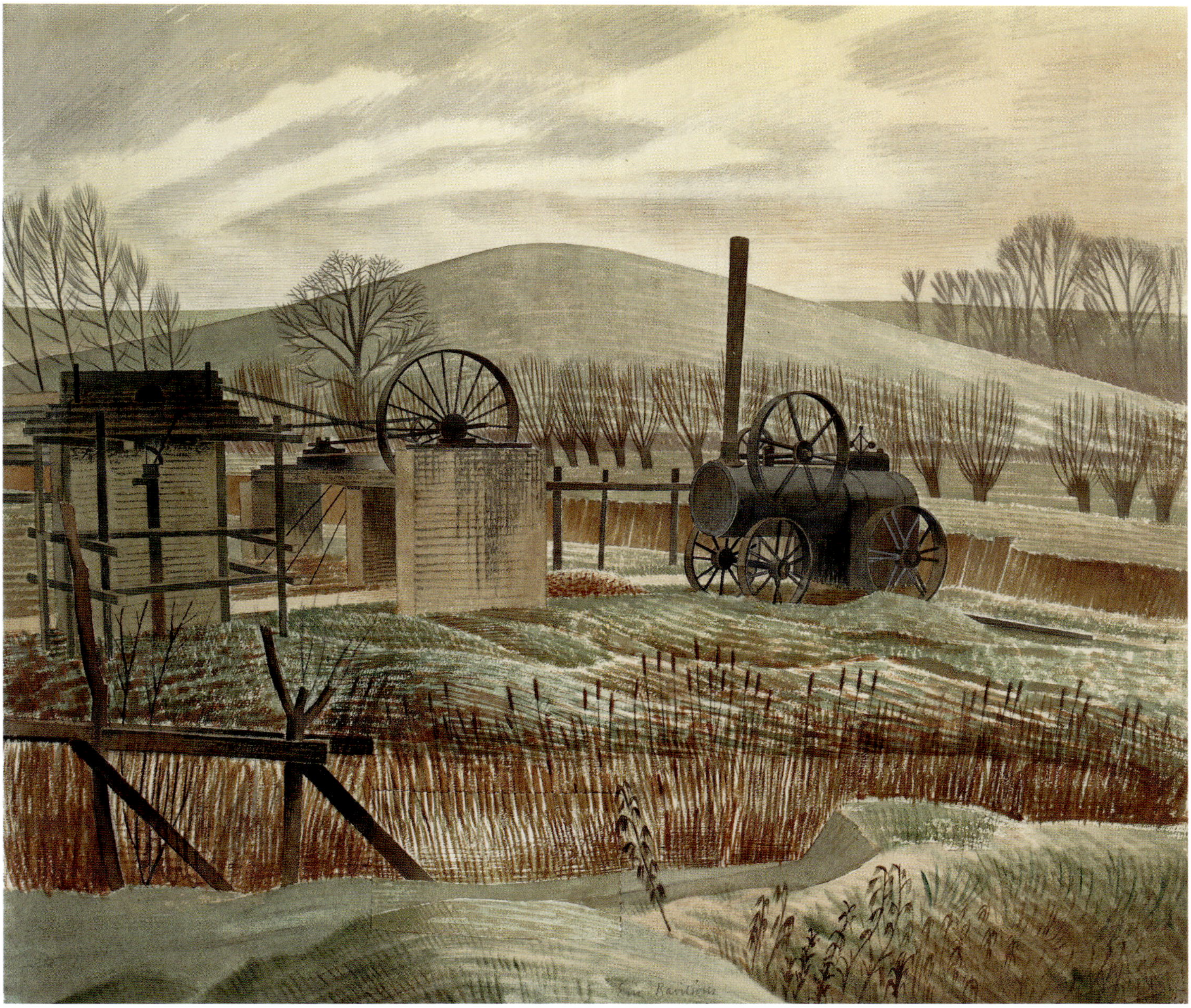

97

CECIL COLLINS 1908–1989

Study for 'The Quest', 1936

Watercolour and bodycolour on paper
32 × 33 cm
Signed and dated: *Cecil Collins 1936*
Promised gift, 2015
L12202.2
© Tate, London 2014

From the early 1930s Cecil and Elisabeth Collins lived in relative seclusion in rural Buckinghamshire, but in late 1936 they moved to Totnes in Devon. Their relocation was prompted in part by Mark Tobey, the American artist who was at that time Director of the Art Studio at Dartington Hall, which Leonard and Dorothy Elmhirst had founded on the estate they purchased in 1925. The couple quickly became involved in the life of Dartington Hall.

From 1934 Dartington became an important base for exiles fleeing Nazi Germany, indeed Hein Heckroth, Tobey's successor as Director, had fled to Britain with his Jewish wife. Heckroth's forced resignation as an enemy alien in 1940 and his subsequent internment in Australia during the war, catapulted Collins, exempt from military service due to longstanding ill health, into the position of Director.

The present work was made in preparation for an oil painting completed in 1938, which Elisabeth Collins bequeathed to the Tate Gallery in 2001. The origins of *The Quest* have been described by William Anderson as specifically arising from Collin's involvement at Dartington:

In one instance, the stimulation at Dartington had an unintended effect. Collins had gone to a lecture with slides on the subject of the Arctic. The lecture was so boring he fell asleep, but there remained with him the images of the ice floes and a deserted land.[1]

A subsequent holiday on the Dartmouth coast in the summer of 1938 reinforced this image: 'the unusual view of the mere, a lake divided from the sea by a long sandbank, brought about a synthesis with the Arctic images, and this prompted him to paint *The Quest* with its Arthurian overtones'.[2]

This enigmatic work has been interpreted in several different ways. Principally, it has been linked with T. S. Eliot's poem *The Waste Land*, with its references to Arthurian legend and the search for the Holy Grail. It also evokes an episode from Dante's *Inferno* in which Dante and Virgil are ferried across the river Acheron to Hell. The rowing boat, rudderless and without visible means of propulsion, is set adrift in a threatening sea, perhaps symbolising Collins's anxiety regarding the increasingly hostile political situation in contemporary Europe. HD

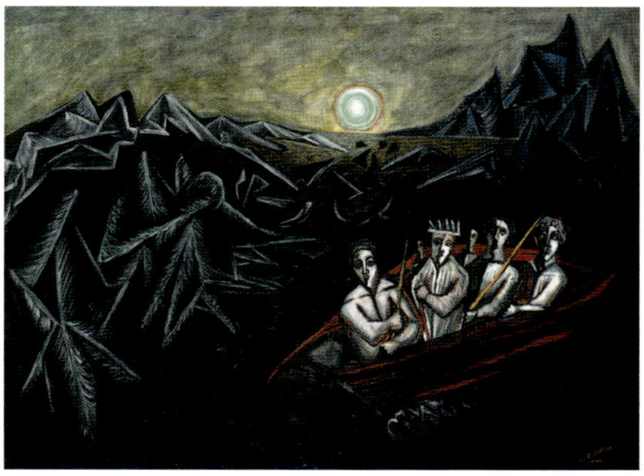

Fig. 58 | Cecil Collins (1908–1989), *The Quest*, 1938. Oil on board. Tate, London, T07732 © Tate, London 2014

1. Anderson (1988) p. 49.
2. *Ibid.*

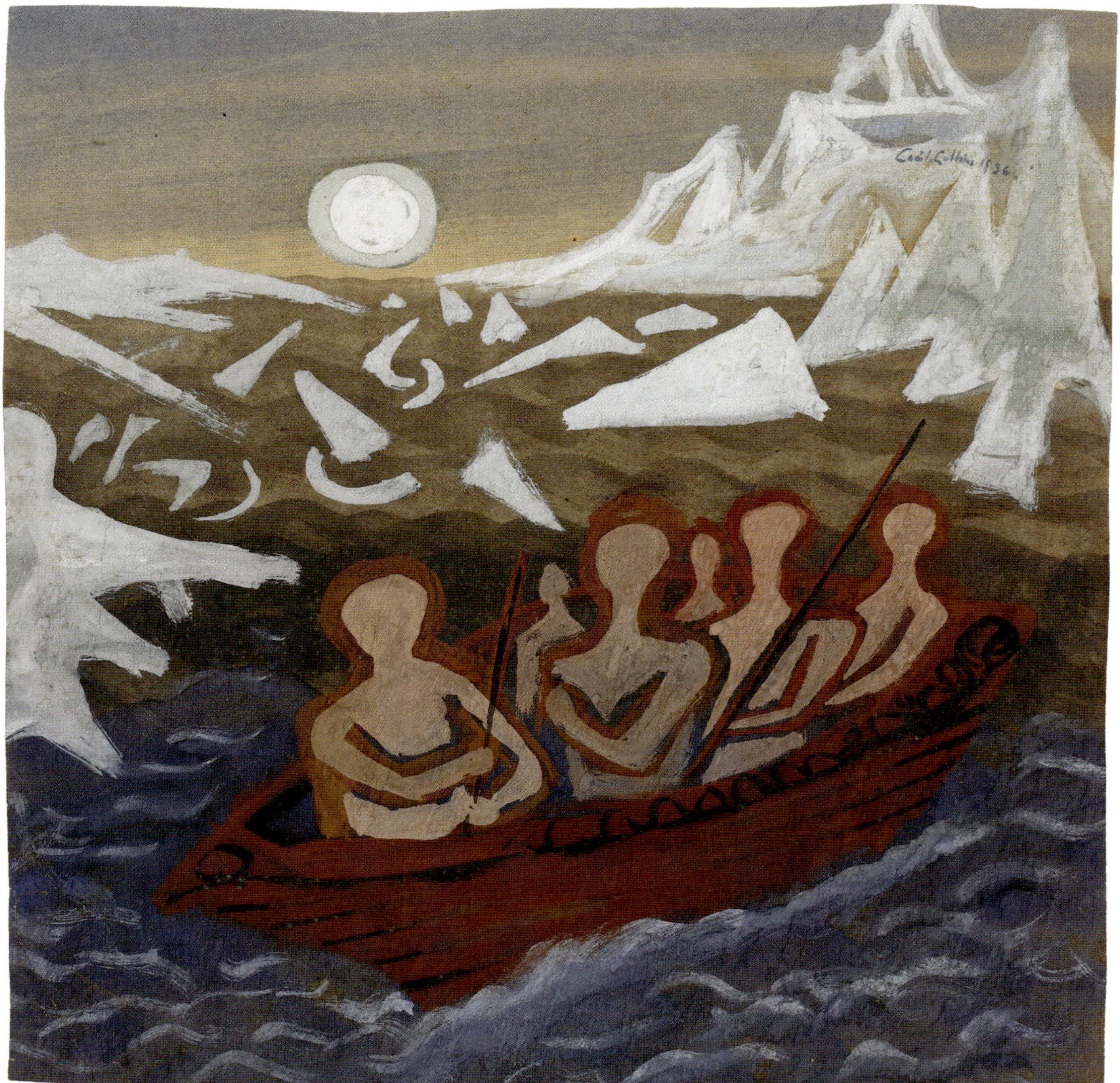

98

SIR MUIRHEAD BONE 1876–1953

Low Tide on the Portsmouth Hard, 1940

Pen and ink and wash over black chalk on paper
39.8 × 59.3 cm
Signed and dated: *Muirhead Bone / 1940*
Presented by HM Government (War Artists' Advisory Committee), 1947
WA1947.392

During the First World War, the British government had employed a number of artists to record scenes in France. In 1939, as the Second World War loomed, Sir Kenneth Clark succeeded in establishing an official War Artists' Advisory Committee. His aims were both 'to keep artists at work on any pretext', and 'to use the work produced as propaganda'.[1] Initially, there were five official war artists: Muirhead Bone, Edward Ardizzone, Barnet Freedman, Reginald Eves, and Edward Bawden. Bone was the oldest, and greatly admired by Clark, who declared that, 'for technical skill Bone must be the only one who can be compared with the great Italians Piranesi and Bibiena'.

Bone was the most prominent and influential of all the war artists, having been the very first appointed in 1916. His training as an architect, and his childhood familiarity with the Clydeside docks, the Gorbals, and other outlying districts, enabled him to capture a scene in rapid sketches, to be worked up later. He was particularly pleased with his 'splendidly generalled armies of dutiful details' of shipyards on the Clyde.[2] On occasion he felt that this gave his drawings a somewhat impersonal character, admitting that, 'I do not like to imagine war scenes and so only drew what I saw, and this only when I had a chance to digest it. This limited me very much and I am afraid resulted in rather prosaic work'.[3] Two hundred of his drawings were published in *The Western Front* (1917), which sold 30,000 copies.

In 1940 Bone was commissioned as a major in the Royal Marines. As he wrote to D. S. MacColl, 'It is a grand chance, seldom given to anybody, to improve on last time'.[4] Once again his subjects were largely ruins, such as the destruction of the docks in London, or the blitzed cityscape around St Paul's Cathedral, or shipping in the Firth of Forth and on the Clyde. This spectacular drawing of one of the most important strategic ports in the English Channel was presumably made some time before the first bombing of Portsmouth, on 11 July 1940. It exemplifies Bone's ability to orchestrate large complex townscapes and industrial sites. Many figures are shown scurrying across the bridge to the installations beyond, skirting a huge deposit of logs, while several destroyers and other vessels manoeuvre in the Channel, under the protective cover of a host of barrage balloons. CH

1. Weaver, O'Neill, Bawden (2008) p. 9.
2. Quoted in Harries (1983) p. 12.
3. Quoted in Bone (2009) p. 100.
4. Quoted in Bone (2009) p. 128.

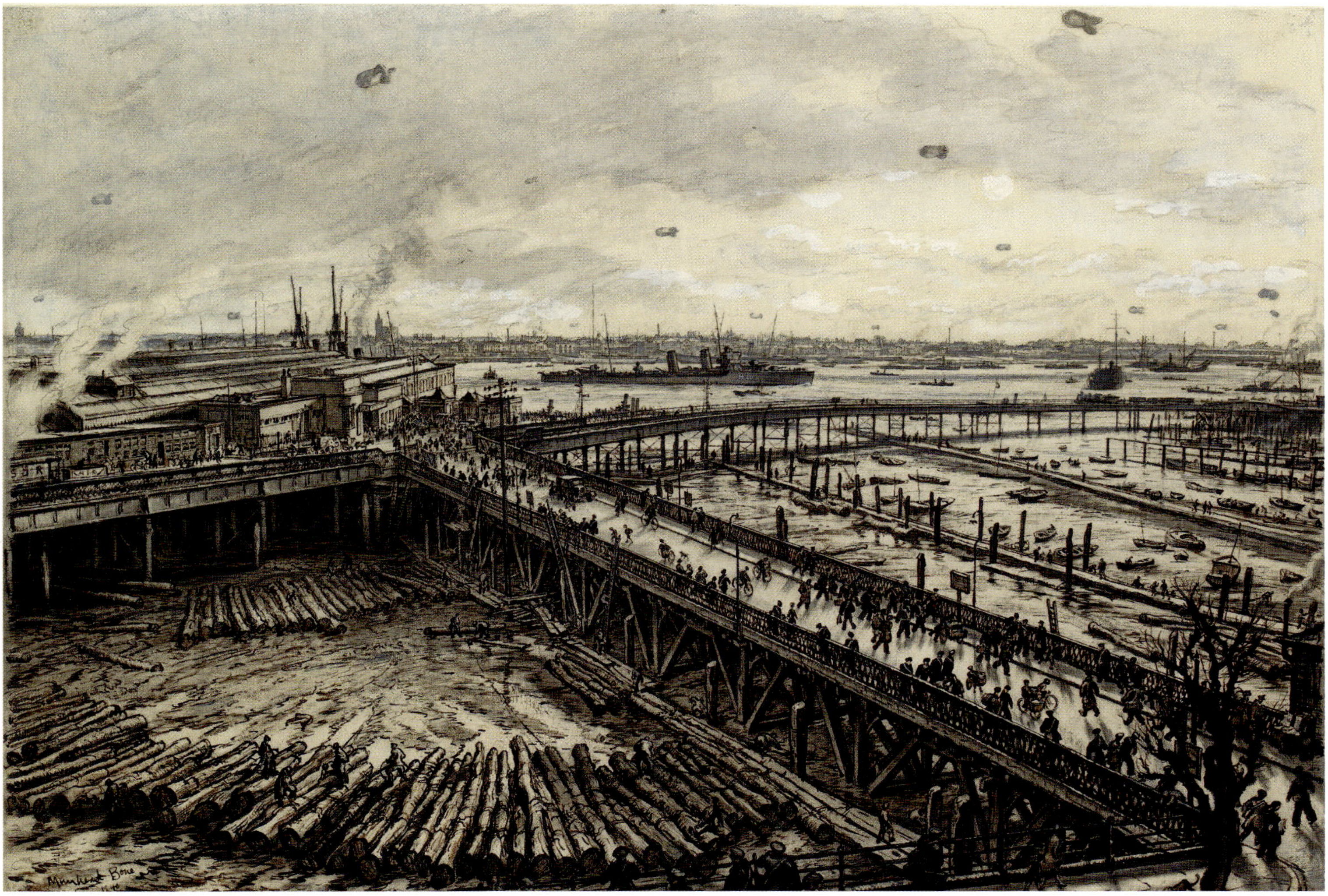

99

PAUL NASH 1889–1946
Under the Cliff, 1940

Watercolour and white bodycolour over black chalk on paper
38.7 × 56.8 cm
Signed: *Paul Nash*
Presented by HM Government (War Artists' Advisory Committee), 1947
WA1947.408

LITERATURE: Causey (1980) no. 1041; Hall (1997) no. 22

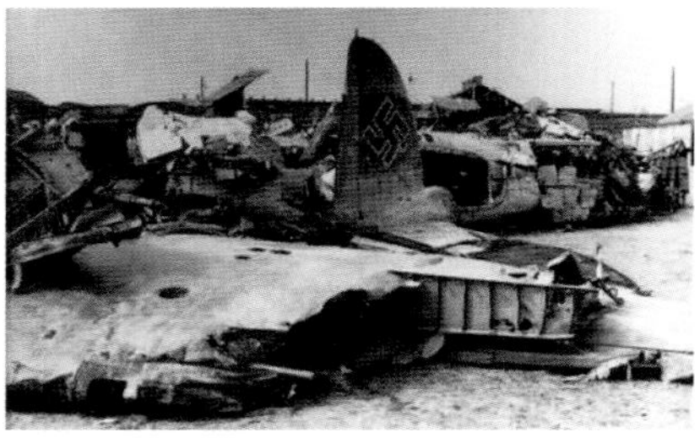

Fig. 59 | Unknown photographer, *Wrecked planes at Cowley Aircraft Dump*, c. 1940. © reserved

While his service as an official war artist from 1917–8 assured Nash's fame and changed the direction of his work, his reappointment during the Second World War found him imaginatively prepared and predisposed to explore his current themes in a new, urgent context. Eric Newton, in *The Sunday Times* in 1939, likened his appointment to 'asking T. S. Eliot to cover a boxing match', but Nash, with his fierce hatred of the Nazis' aesthetic intolerance, was adamant that his images should be used as propaganda.[1] As he insisted to Sir Kenneth Clark, 'I aim at something more than a picture to be exhibited in the National Gallery'.[2]

During the 1930s Nash had used the 'found object' to create a unique synthesis of Continental Surrealism and English Romanticism, exploring the poetic enigma of human interaction with nature. He exhibited at the International Surrealist Exhibition in 1936, and Henri Magritte reportedly regarded him as 'Master of the Object'.[3] In 1938 Nash discovered the site that he named 'Monster Field' on Carswalls Farm, near Newent, Gloucestershire. Here he photographed two large elms, violently felled by lightning, whose forms reminded him of William Blake's *Pity* (*c.* 1795) and Pablo Picasso's *Guernica* (1937). The elms inspired a series of works including *Monster Shore* (Art Gallery of Hamilton, Ontario), which he finished just prior to his appointment on a six-month contract to the Air Ministry in 1940.

Fascinated by how the stricken trees were transformed by their demise, Nash transferred this preoccupation to wrecked or grounded aircraft, conceiving them as objects 'out of their element'.[4] He quickly created a series of watercolours of crashed German bombers, situated within landscapes with which he was intensely familiar. A number of these, like *Under the Cliff*, feature the Jurassic Coast, near Swanage, which had appeared in his earlier works such as *Event on the Downs* (1934). Nash also continued to rely heavily on photographic images, including those of Cowley Aircraft Dump, near Oxford, the city to which he and his wife had moved in 1939. The high horizon of Nash's Cowley photographs is recalled here in the looming cliffs. The landscape appears to have reared up against the invading German aircraft, obliterating all but the tail section, which languishes on the beach, partly submerged in the sand. Nash's 'Albion' has defeated the forces of Fascism. The propagandist message is reinforced by the repetition of the fin shape of the tail in the monumental contours of the cliff face: the sheer, dominating white of the paper triumphant over the dark, battered machinery. KW

1. Quoted in Hall (1997) p. 7.
2. Letter from Paul Nash to Kenneth Clark, 18 March 1940, quoted in Causey (1980) p. 308.
3. Gough (2014) p. 97.
4. 'The Personality of Planes', *Vogue*, March 1942, quoted in Causey (1980) p. 305.

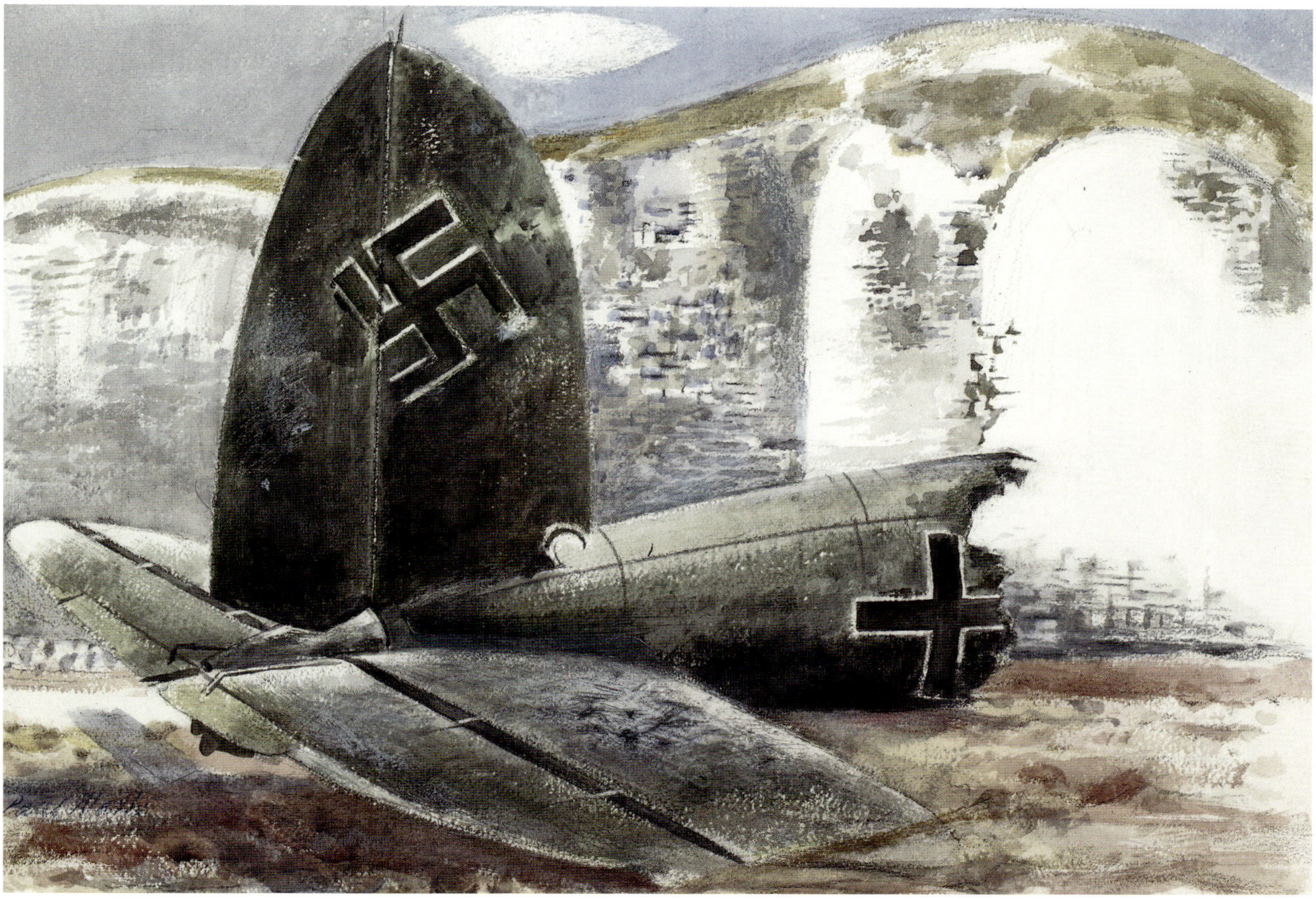

100

GRAHAM VIVIAN SUTHERLAND 1903–1980
The Smelting Works, 'Twin Ladles', 1941

Watercolour, wax crayon and bodycolour over indications in graphite, with varnish, some pen and ink and scratching out, on paper
56.8 × 38.7 cm
Presented by HM Government (War Artists' Advisory Committee), 1947
WA1947.416

LITERATURE: Hammer (2005) no. 57; Gough, Allen, Gosher (2013) p. 62

At the outbreak of the Second World War Sutherland applied to train as a munitions gauge maker. Thanks to his close friend Sir Kenneth Clark, however, he received an invitation to serve as an official war artist in June 1940. Tasked with recording bomb damage sustained in Swansea and London during the Blitz, he created his forcefully expressive 'Devastation' pictures, in which the contorted forms of architectural wreckage potently suggest the destruction of human life.

In September 1940, Sutherland was dispatched to record steel works in Cardiff. This was the first of a series of commissions in which he was asked to portray the industries contributing to Britain's war effort. From 1920–1, prior to attending Goldsmiths Art College, Sutherland had been a Privileged Apprentice at the Midland Railway Works, Derby. On the 80-acre site he had received training in precision drawing, as well as in boiler construction and repair. This fostered a life-long fascination with machinery, and his war work explores the transformation of materials in manufacturing, creating visions of industry as an 'eternal war; a constant conflict between the forces of man and nature'.[1] He later described the process of steel-making as a 'rite … being performed'.[2]

Sutherland was especially drawn to the forms of the slag ladles, used for transporting molten waste from the blast furnaces, but it is the relationship between the figures and the brutal environment of the smelting works that is at the heart of this work. As the dwarfed figures emerge, seemingly struggling, their contorted poses evoke figures from seventeenth-century Old Master paintings such as El Greco's *The Purification of the Temple* (*c.* 1600, National Gallery, London). The vivid egg-yolk yellow, carmine and sooty black recalls the work of William Blake, whom Sutherland had described as the paradigm of the imaginative artist in his *Signature* article of July 1936. In his pre-war Pembrokeshire landscapes Sutherland had employed a similar colour palette, but the layering of different media here evokes the intense heat and acrid atmosphere of the factory – a visceral assault on all the senses. The bold geometry of the design, emphasised by the grid of the ceiling and the parallel rails in the foreground, is countered by the swirl of the raging flames and the murky smoke. The exact articulation of the figures evidently caused Sutherland difficulties, and the drawing is patched here in three places.[3] KW

1. Sutherland to Eric Newton, quoted in Hammer (2005) p. 31.
2. Quoted in Alley (1982) p. 97.
3. A similar sheet, Christie's 15 November 2006, lot no. 196, shows the figures in an earlier, less resolved state.

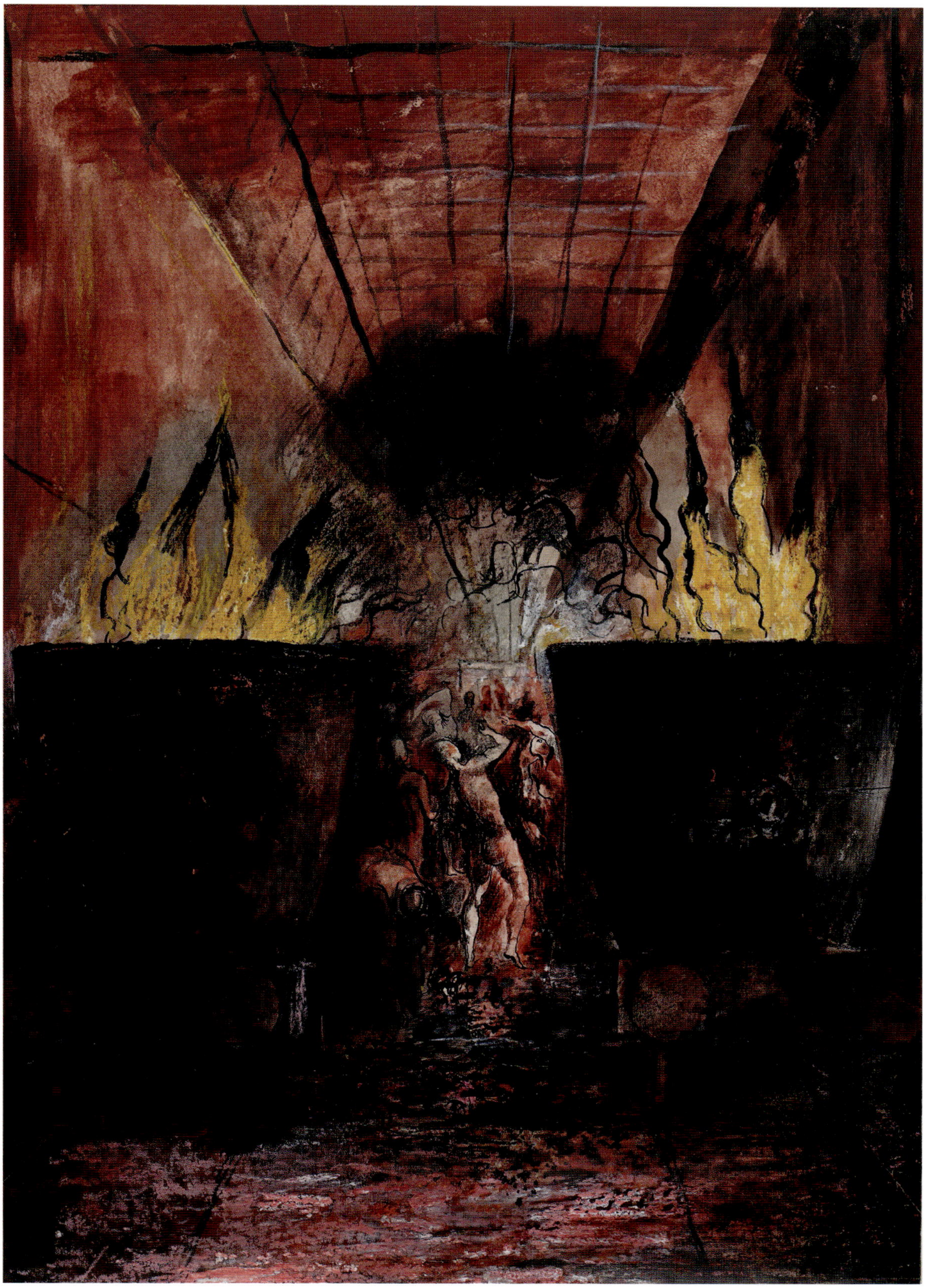

101

EDWARD BAWDEN 1903–1989

Private Kimoi Chemeri, ?1942

Pen and brush in Indian ink, and waxy sepia chalk on paper
35.3 × 25.3 cm
Verso inscribed: *K.A.R. Askanies / Pte.* KIMOI CHEMERI */ orderly / tribe Elgeyo / drawn at Adama.*
Presented by HM Government (War Artists' Advisory Committee), 1947
WA1947.388

Bawden might have seemed a surprising choice to be included among the first five artists appointed under the War Artists' Advisory Scheme, since he was largely known for his commercial work, designing posters and advertising material for London Transport, Shell, and the Westminster Bank. With his friend Eric Ravilious, he also painted murals at Morley Working Men's College in Lambeth (completed in 1930). Bawden, Ravilious and their wives moved into a handsome townhouse at Great Bardfield, Essex, in 1932, and began to paint the countryside in stylised and idiosyncratic watercolours. Although Bawden did not have much relevant experience, his appointment by Sir Kenneth Clark proved to be inspired. J. M. Richards later wrote that his war work 'gave him an entirely new standing among contemporary artists ... he rose powerfully to the translation from rural Essex to the raw strangeness of the Middle East endowing all things with a touch of poetry and peculiarity'.[1]

After witnessing the debacle of Dunkirk in May 1940, Bawden was posted in the rank of Captain to East Africa, where he remained between September 1940 and August 1941. At first he travelled down the Nile to Khartoum and Omdurman, where the extreme heat obliged him to concentrate on making portraits of soldiers and natives. He then joined the campaign to liberate Abyssinia, which had been occupied by the Italians since 1936. Bawden's was the smallest of the three parallel columns advancing on Addis Ababa, consisting only of an English colonel on a white horse, a number of officers and sergeants commanding 80 Abyssinian cadets, and a train of camels. 'There was generally an uproar in which the camels joined, of course. Oh, a most enjoyable experience.'[2]

This drawing was taken at Adama, some 60 miles south-east of Addis Ababa, perhaps shortly before the liberation of the capital on 5 May 1941. It shows Kimoi Chemeri, of the Elgeyo or Keiyo tribe of Kenya, in the uniform of a private in the Kings African Rifles. This regiment, formed by the amalgamation of various others in British East Africa, included a large number of 'askaris', native African soldiers. Such portraits are among Bawden's most successful, though he noted that 'When the model is the colour of a grape it is difficult to disassociate form and colour, more especially in the region of the cheek and cheek bone, a rounded expanse of fat with no geographical features and impossible to map with accuracy'.[3] CH

1. Richards (1946) unpaginated.
2. Harries (1983) p. 224.
3. Harries (1983) p. 226.

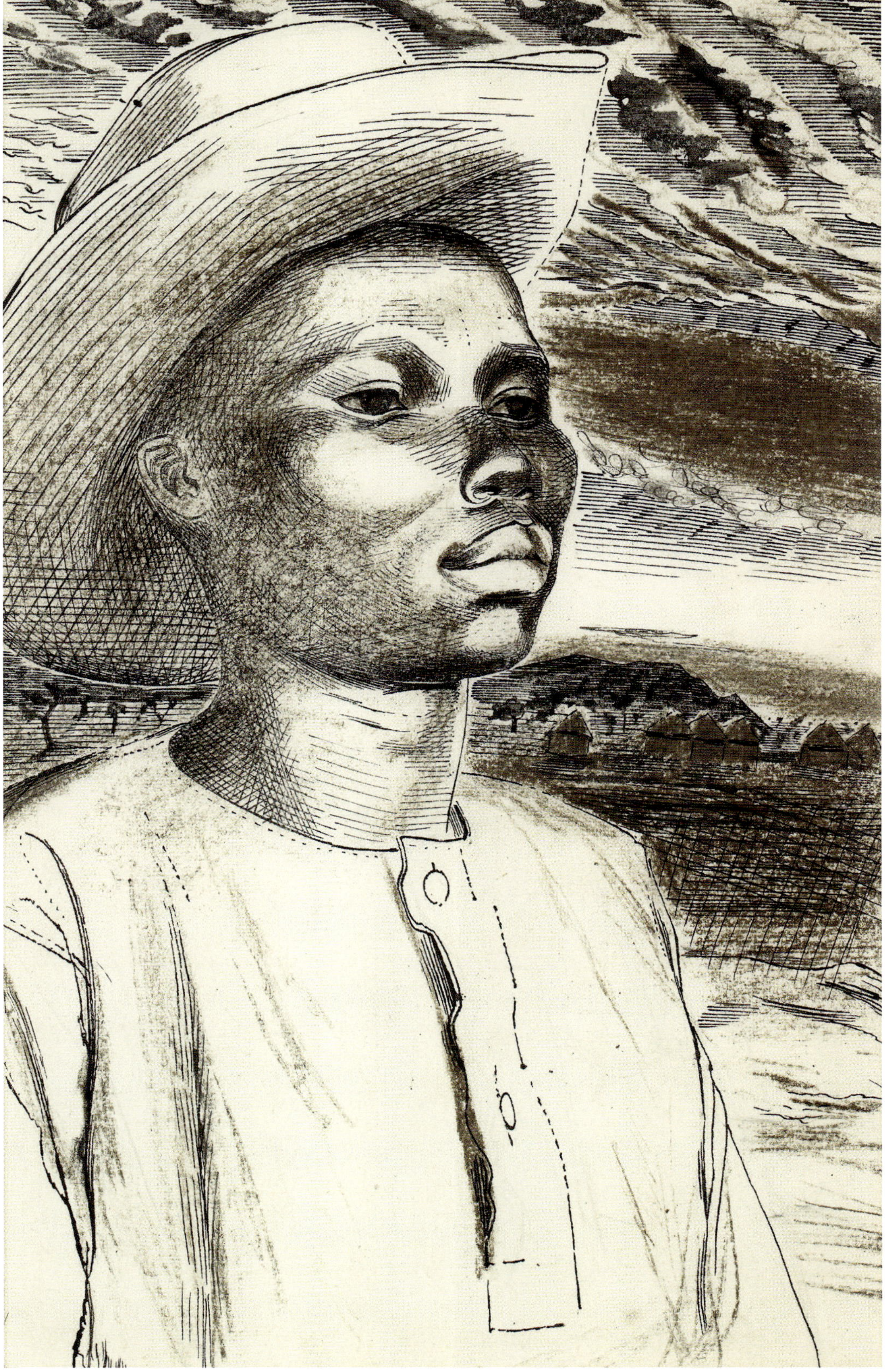

102

WYNDHAM LEWIS 1882–1957

The King Plays, 1942

Black crayon, wax crayon, pen and Indian ink, charcoal, and bodycolour on wove paper
30 × 45.4 cm
Signed and dated: *W. Lewis 1942 / Wyndham Lewis 1942–49*. Inscribed *verso*: *The King Plays*
Presented by Mrs Bronia Steiner, 2011
WA2011.170

LITERATURE: Michel (1971) no. 995

The publication of the first issue of *Blast* magazine in 1914 proposed a new and specifically English *avant-garde*. The intention was to 'blast' British culture out of its complacent mediocrity, and promote Vorticism as the way forward. As the prime instigator, Wyndham Lewis was well placed to further this manifesto. Always an outsider, he was equally influential as a writer and an artist, and fully informed of all the latest developments in Europe as well as England. He had studied at the Slade School and then in several European capitals, and exhibited with the Camden Town Group, but did not fit in. In his search for a modern figurative art, Lewis experimented with French Cubism, Italian Futurism, and German Expressionism, before settling on Vorticism, whose principles he applied to both images and text. In his paintings and drawings, the forms became fragmented and geometric, being theoretically based on the idea of the vortex as the point of maximum energy.

During the 1920s, Lewis began to feel that geometric shapes were 'bleak and empty', and he added portraiture to his repertoire, painting and drawing such figures as Edith Sitwell and James Joyce.[1] His reputation suffered severely when he published an article in praise of Adolf Hitler in 1931, and, although he later repudiated his views, he felt obliged to cross the Atlantic, spending a dreary year in New York before moving to the 'sanctimonious icebox' of Toronto in December 1940.[2]

In spite of loneliness and isolation, Lewis enjoyed a brilliantly creative period over the next two years. His drawings became increasingly personal, and were often on religious themes. This evocation of King David, the most musical of Old Testament monarchs and the author of many of the Psalms, playing the harp to a disparate group of courtiers, reflects Lewis's long interest in the theatre. Indeed, the sloping ground and enclosed space give the impression of a stage set, with the viewer sitting above, an impression emphasised by 'prompter's box' at the front, and the strange figure on the right, whose eyes resemble binoculars.

This drawing belonged to Robert Lewin (1918–2004), one of the most distinguished dealers in *avant-garde* art in London, and founder of the Brook Street Gallery in Mayfair; it was presented to the Ashmolean by his sister-in-law. CH

1. Quoted in Richard Cork, 'Lewis (Percy) Wyndham (1882–1957)', *Oxford Dictionary of National Biography*, online edn. (2010), http://www.oxforddnb.com/view/article/34517?docPos=2, accessed 6 February 2015.
2. Quoted in Edwards (1992) p. 48.

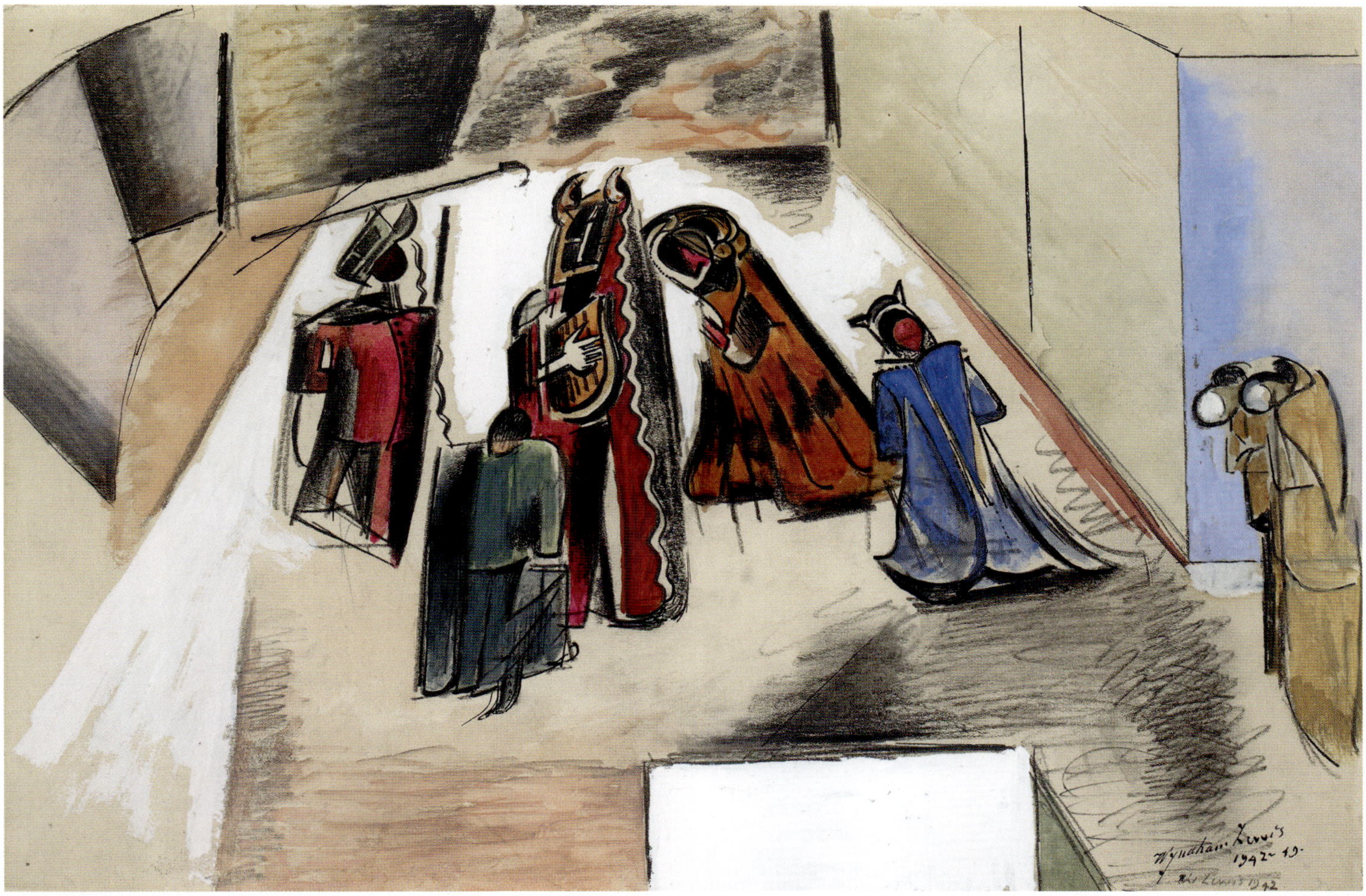
Wyndham Lewis
1942-49.

103

WILLIAM GEAR 1915–1997

Palestine Scrapbook – Costume Notes No.2, July 1943

Pen and ink and watercolour on paper
24.4 × 32.5 × 0.7 cm (volume), open at fol. 3
Inscribed on front cover: *PALESTINE / SCRAP BOOK / July – 1943 / COSTUME NOTES / No 2*. Signed: *WG*. Drawing inscribed: *BAB EL WADI* and with colour and other notes
Lent from a private collection
L12202.6

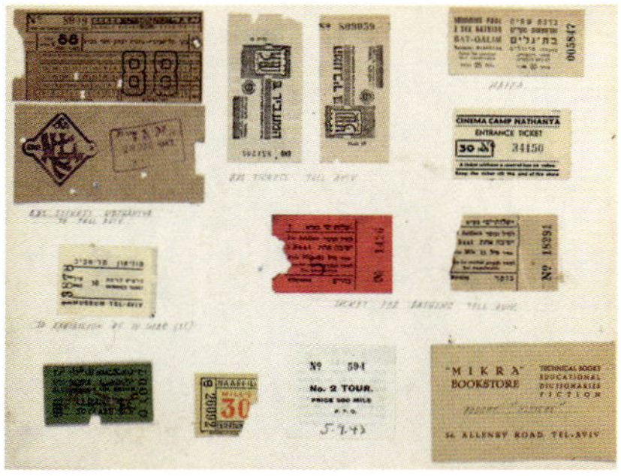

Fig. 60 | William Gear (1915–1997), *Page from 'Palestine Scrapbook' showing tickets, facing 'Bab-El-Wadi'*, July 1943. Private Collection © The William Gear Estate

The son of a coal miner, Bill Gear was born in Methil, Fife, in 1915. By dint of considerable natural talent nurtured by successive teachers, he was able to study at the Edinburgh College of Art, supported by a grant from Fife Education Authority with financial assistance from the Miners' Welfare Fund and the Carnegie Trust. The curriculum was rigidly traditional, with a highly disciplined emphasis on drawing for the first two years and painting only in the third and fourth years. A postgraduate scholarship allowed Gear to continue working independently, as well as to study the history of art at Edinburgh University. During this period he spent a year abroad, in Paris, including three months at Fernand Léger's *académie* in Montparnasse in 1937, as well as spending time in Italy, Greece, and the Balkans. Later that year he graduated with a first class degree, followed by a teacher training course in Edinburgh.

Like many of his generation, Gear's artistic career was interrupted by military service. He was teaching in Dumfriesshire when he received his call-up papers in May 1940. Assigned to the Royal Corps of Signals, he was quickly selected as officer material and, after a spell at the Officers' Training Unit at Aldershot, was despatched to the Middle East, initially to Cairo, and subsequently to Palestine. His biographer, John McEwen, has commented that 'it was darkly ironic that Palestine, that country of ceaseless conflict, enjoyed virtually undisturbed peace' during the war.[1] Gear's duties allowed him ample time for drawing and painting.

This charming scrapbook, a combination of visual diary and assorted memorabilia, including a ticket for Gear's own exhibition at the Museum Tel-Aviv, is carefully annotated and provides a glimpse into the leisure time of a young officer on leave. Most of the drawings date from early July 1943. They include landscapes, as well as street scenes and figure studies in Jerusalem. Although some of Gear's work had a surrealist tone at this period, these drawings have no such quality; they reveal a fluent and grounded drawing style, with an assured sense of colour.

The subject of this drawing, Bab-El-Wadi, 'the Valley Gate', lies on the road from Tel-Aviv to Jerusalem, where there is a narrow defile between a series of ridges. Owing to its strategic location, Bab-El-Wadi was the site of notorious ambushes and clashes, both during the Arab uprising of 1936–9 and the War of Independence in 1948. HD

1. McEwen (2003) p. 19.

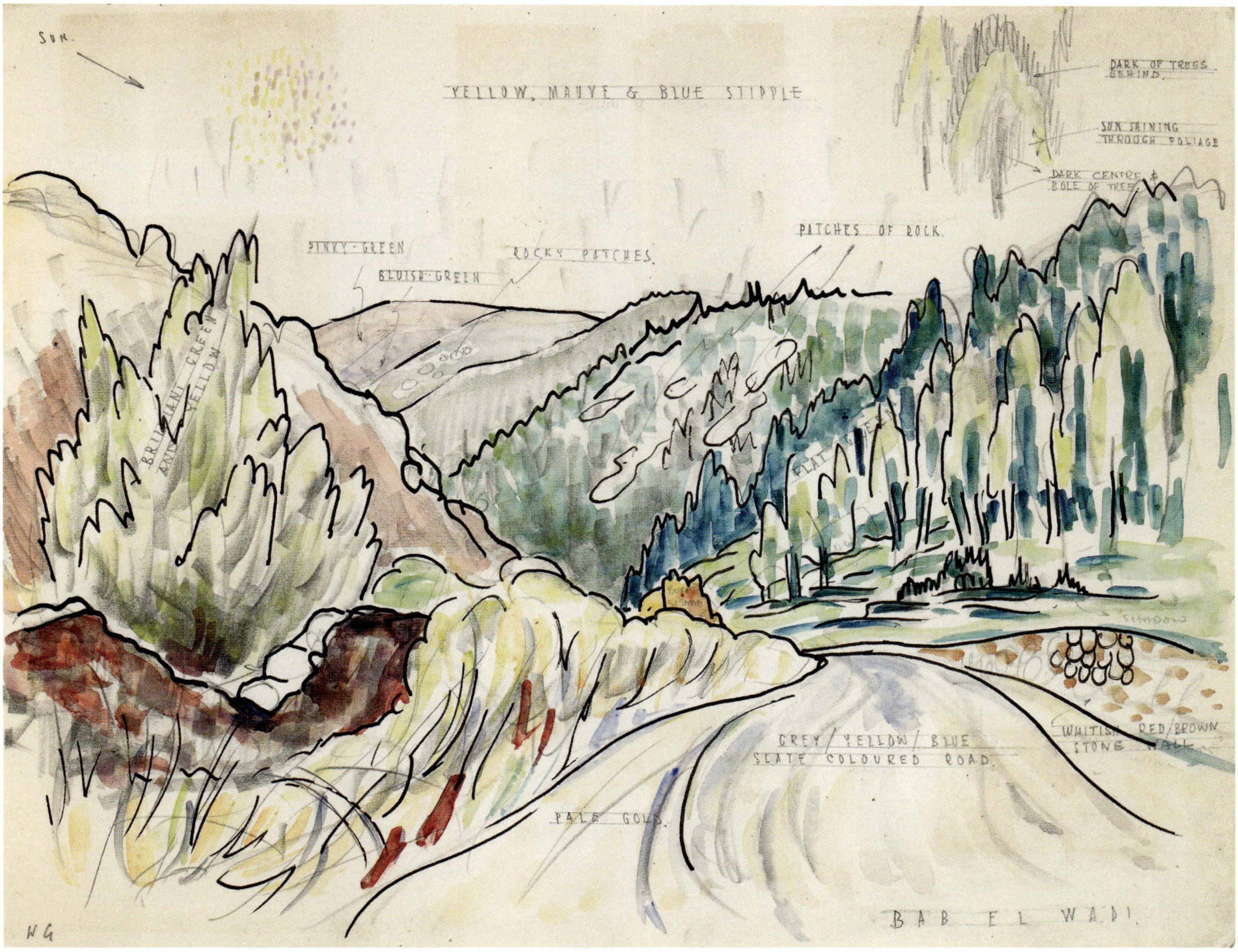
SUN.
YELLOW, MAUVE & BLUE STIPPLE
DARK OF TREES BEHIND.
SUN SHINING THROUGH FOLIAGE
DARK CENTRE & BOLE OF TREE
PATCHES OF ROCK.
PINKY GREEN
BLUISH GREEN
ROCKY PATCHES.
GREY/YELLOW/BLUE SLATE COLOURED ROAD.
PALE GOLD.
BAB EL WADI.
HG

104

DAVID GARSHEN BOMBERG 1890–1957

Evening in the City of London, 1944

Charcoal on paper
46.4 × 59 cm
Signed and dated: *Bomberg 44*
Presented by Mr and Mrs James Newmark in memory of the artist, through the Contemporary Art Society, 1981
WA1981.606

LITERATURE: Cork (1988) no. 158

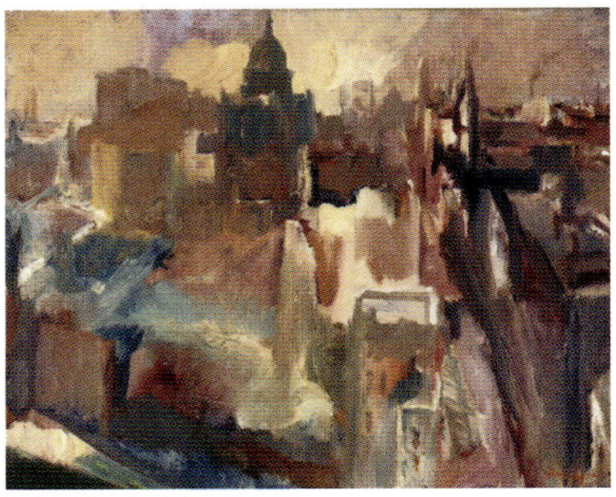

Fig. 61 | David Bomberg (1890–1957), *Evening in the City of London*, 1944. Oil on canvas. Museum of London, 85.219 © Museum of London

The son of Polish Jewish immigrants, Bomberg was one of the most audaciously experimental artists to attend the Slade School prior to 1914. Flirting with Vorticism, he produced works simplifying the human figure in extremely geometric terms within Cubist-inspired splintered perspectives, declaring, 'I want to translate the life of a great city, its motion, its machinery, into an art that shall not be photographic, but expressive'.[1] Despite successive changes of style, a strong formal sense of the cityscape continued to dominate his work in locations as diverse as Jerusalem, Toledo, and Ronda.

Bomberg's active service during the First World War left him profoundly disillusioned with the Machine Age. Despite his urgent desire for work, his services were twice rejected by the War Artists' Advisory Committee before he was awarded a token commission in February 1942 of 35 guineas for a painting of the subterranean bomb store near Burton-on-Trent. Bomberg's painting, dwelling upon the appalling destructiveness inherent in the accumulated weaponry, was rejected by the WAAC, which instead accepted three charcoal drawings.

Such treatment was typical of the dispiriting artistic neglect Bomberg suffered for much of his career. 1944 found him giving drawing instruction to gun crews in Hyde Park and serving as a firewatcher in Kensington, having applied unsuccessfully for over 300 teaching positions during the previous five years. He secured permission to sketch St Paul's from the church of St Mary-le-Bow, at great risk as the timing of air-raids was always unpredictable. The survival of Christopher Wren's cathedral had become a symbol of British defiance in the face of the brutal bombardment of the Blitz. Bomberg handled his favourite drawing medium with vehement urgency; jagged sooty strokes delineating the charred skeleton of the city. To the right stands the tower of St Vedast-alias-Foster, another Wren church, gutted by a devastating raid in December 1940. The curved dome of St Paul's resiliently presides over the otherwise fractured angularity of the scene. The cathedral's prominence might also represent Bomberg himself, but it equally chimes with his insistence that fostering spiritual life could combat an increasingly menacing mechanised culture.[2]

This drawing was one of a series depicting the London Blitz-scape that Bomberg hoped to turn into a book with John Rodker of the Imago Press. Sadly, his drawings were not deemed topographically accurate enough to be of interest to the general public. Nonetheless, this work served as preparation for an oil painting displayed in the London Group exhibition of 1944 and praised by Ivon Hitchens as 'the only painter's painting of bombed London he had seen.'[3] KW

1. *Jewish Chronicle* 8 May 1914, quoted in Cork (1988) p. 17.
2. See Cork (1988) p. 49.
3. David Bomberg to Lilian Bomberg, 13 October 1944. Tate Gallery Archive.

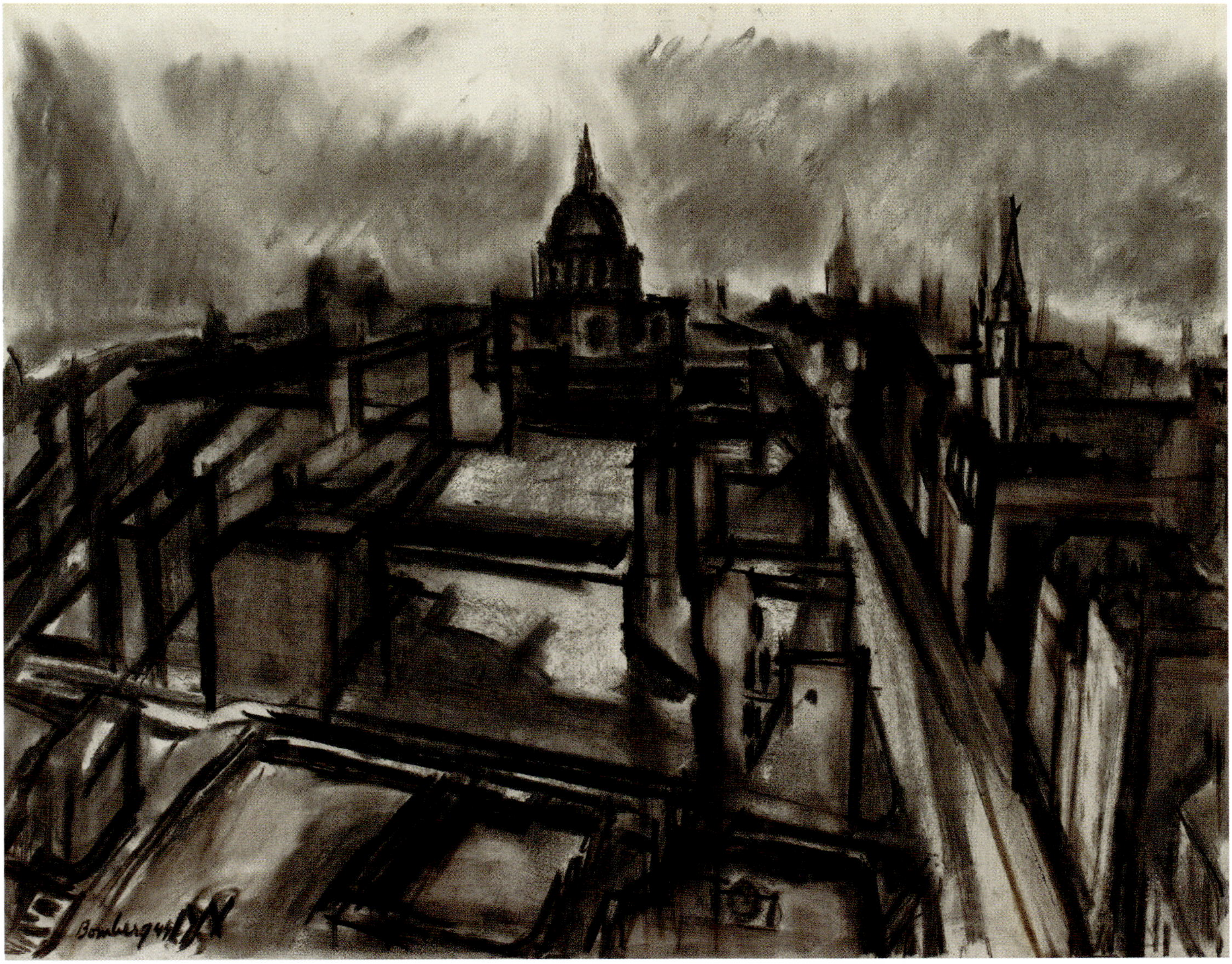
Bomberg 44

105

GRAHAM VIVIAN SUTHERLAND 1903–1980
Thorn Head, 1945

Indian ink, black crayon, grey wash and gum arabic on discoloured laid paper
24.2 × 18.5 cm
Signed and dated: *Sutherland 1945*
Inscribed: *To Curt / January 10th 1945*
Bequeathed by Paul Clark, 2010
WA2010.11

LITERATURE: Shaw (2011) p. 94

Fig. 62 | Graham Sutherland (1903–1980), *The Crucifixion*, 1946. Oil on hardboard. St Matthew's Church, Northampton © Saint Matthew's Church, Northampton, Northamptonshire, UK / Bridgeman Images / The Estate of Graham Sutherland

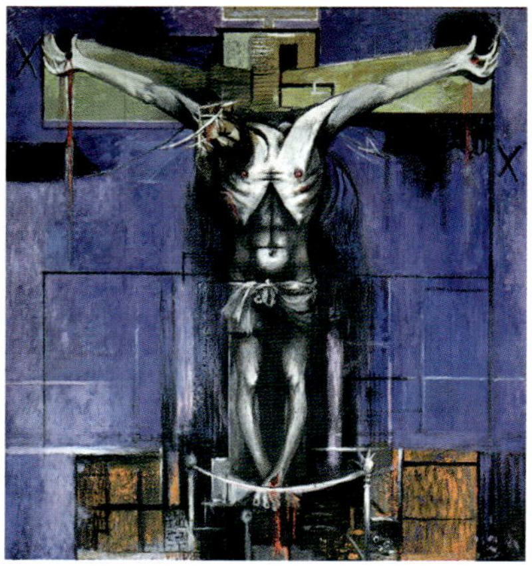

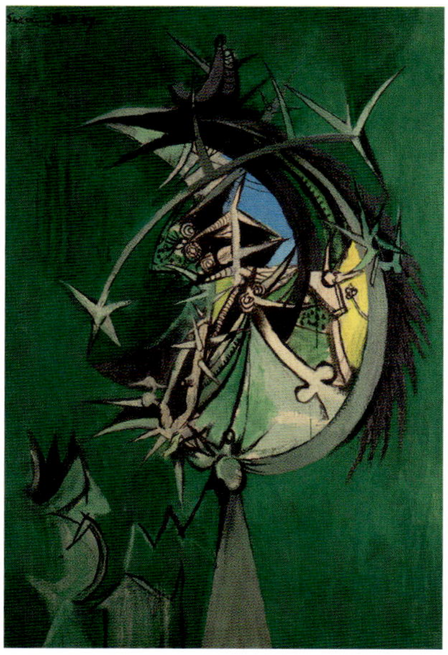

In early 1944 Sutherland attended the unveiling of Henry Moore's sculpture of the Virgin and Child in St Matthew's Church, Northampton. Its commissioner, Revd Walter Hussey, proposed that Sutherland undertake a painting of Christ's Agony in the Garden to be displayed in the opposite transept. Sutherland suggested instead that he tackle the Crucifixion.

Sutherland converted to Roman Catholicism in 1926, shortly before his marriage. He later described how this gave him the 'conception of a system whereby all things created, human and otherwise ... are integrated'.[1] The Crucifixion embodied both agonising tragedy and redemptive salvation. In the wake of the atrocities of the Second World War it became for many artists, including Sutherland's friend Francis Bacon, an expression of horror. Yet Sutherland found the duality of the image compelling. Describing the genesis of his Thorn pictures to Curt Valentin of the Buchholz Gallery, New York (to whom this drawing is dedicated), Sutherland emphasised his preoccupation with the St Matthew's commission and the Crown of Thorns. In spring 1945, revisiting the Pembrokeshire countryside that had been integral to his work since 1934, he noticed thorns 'like dividers pricking out points in space in all directions'.[2] This galvanised his imagination, and he produced a series of thorn trees and heads, according to his customary self-termed 'paraphrasing', or in this case 'pruning', of his natural observations, creating a lasting addition to his pictorial vocabulary.[3]

While *Thorn Head* undoubtedly suggests aggressive cruelty, the form also stems from Sutherland's pre-war paintings, including *Entrance to a Lane* (1939) and his images of roots as meditations on organic growth. Such a synthesis of forms is typical of Sutherland's work, echoed in his orchestration of influences as diverse as Picasso's *Guernica* (1937) and Grünewald's *Isenheim Altarpiece* (*c.* 1515). The application of gum arabic gives the darkest areas a scorched, gleaming appearance reminiscent of the 'gorse burnt and blackened after fire', which delighted Sutherland in the Pembrokeshire landscape.[4] Attempting to follow the progressive construction of the motif, the viewer is immersed in the mysterious, improvisatory vitality of the drawing, in which sickle-shaped elements are juxtaposed with angular spikes. The result is a disquieting exploration of the 'precarious tension of opposites'.[5] KW

Fig. 63 | Graham Sutherland (1903–1980), *Thorn Head*, 1947. Oil on canvas. Private Collection. Photograph courtesy of Sotheby's Picture Library © The Estate of Graham Sutherland

1. Conversation reported by Robert Melville, *World Review*, February 1952, quoted in Hammer (2005) p. 171.
2. Sutherland to Curt Valentin, 24 January 1946, quoted in Hammer (2005) p. 156.
3. The elimination of unnecessary elements to construct his Thorn paintings was described by Sutherland 'almost as if one had taken a pruning knife' in *The Listener* 68, 1962, quoted in Alley (1982) p. 174.
4. Sutherland in *Horizon*, April 1942, quoted in Hammer (2005) p. 70.
5. Sutherland, 'Thoughts on Painting', *The Listener*, 6 September 1951, quoted in Hammer (2005) p. 145.

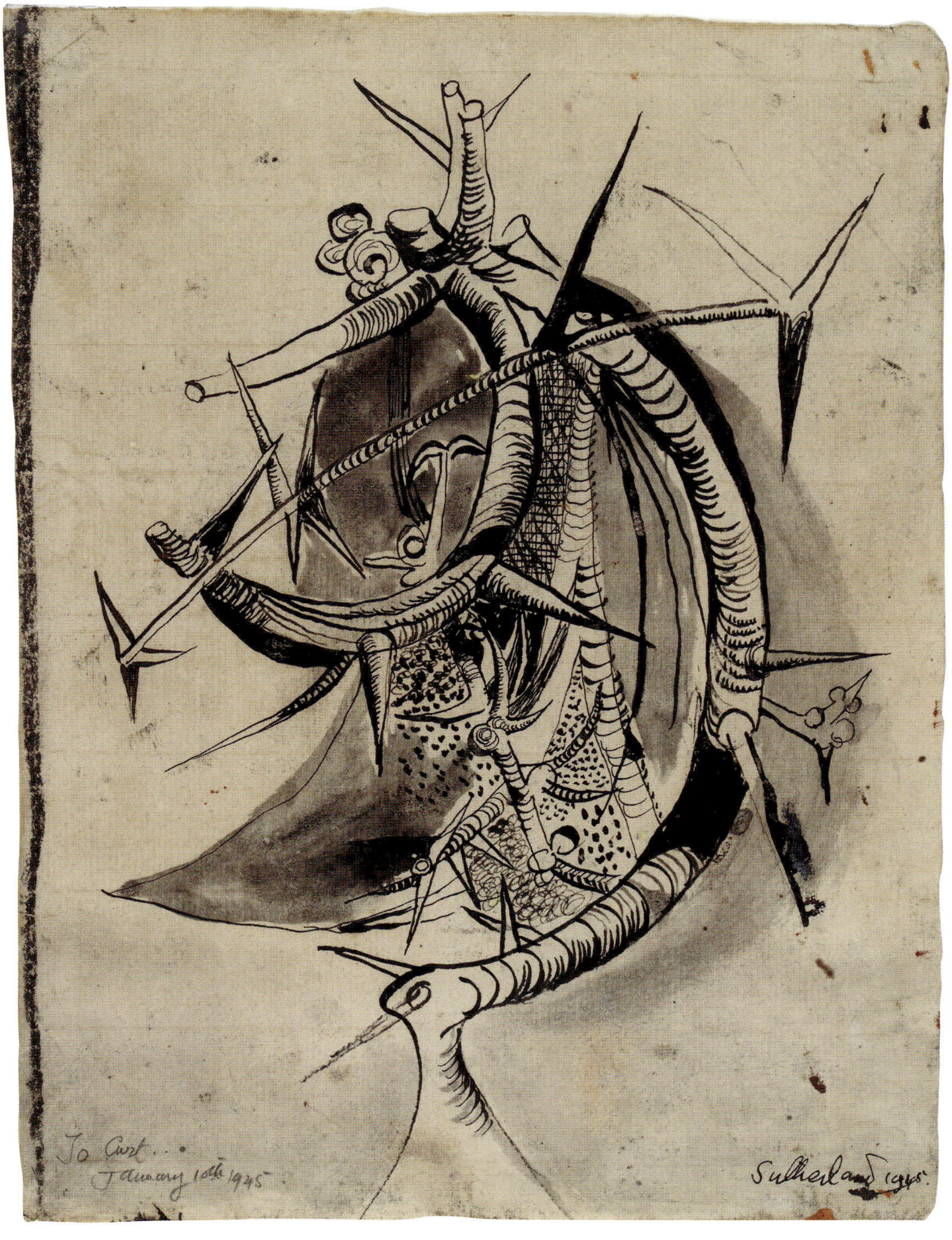
To Curt..
January 10th 1945
Sutherland 1945

106

KEITH VAUGHAN 1912–1977

Two Gardeners, 1946

Bodycolour and Indian ink on paper
26 × 35 cm
Signed and dated: *Keith Vaughan 1946*
Lent from a private collection
LI2202.1

Keith Vaughan had little in the way of formal artistic training, despite showing great promise in his school years. Instead of going to art school, he joined the Art Department of Lintas, the advertising section of Unilever, from which he resigned on the outbreak of war in 1939. He entered the war period in his twenty-seventh year, 'alone, with no very great liking for life, without much ambition for the things most people pursue, but simply a dumb and mule-like persistence in continuing the struggle'.[1]

When his call-up papers arrived, Vaughan registered as a conscientious objector. After his tribunal he was assigned to the Pioneer Corps, initially doing heavy manual work in the countryside. From 1943 he helped to establish a prisoner of war camp for captured German soldiers, where he acted successively as a clerk and an interpreter. These years, among the happiest of his life, brought Vaughan into close contact with working men. As he was later to note, 'I believe a painter has only one basic idea which probably lasts him a life time. Mine is the human figure'.[2] Any landscape setting for the figures, as in *Two Gardeners*, was used as a vehicle for mood and atmosphere. In this he owed much to Graham Sutherland, whom he met during the war and who, apart from Palmer, Blake, and Cézanne, was perhaps the greatest influence on his artistic development until he reached his maturity.

Between 1941 and 1946 Vaughan produced well over 400 works in body-colour. These were all small, intensely worked pieces which relied for their effects on the quick-drying properties of the medium, and the manner in which it can be washed over water-resistant crayon or drawn over in Indian ink when dry. In *Two Gardeners* we see two dimly-lit figures portrayed in an almost monotone colour range; they emerge from an even darker background in which there are hints of a building and a lifeless tree. As a critic of the *New York Times* wrote on reviewing an exhibition in 1948, '[Vaughan's] chief discovery is a particular vision of the human form as a piece of landscape'.[3] HD

1. Vaughan (1966) p. 11.
2. Barber (1954) p. 79.
3. *New York Times*, 15 February 1948.

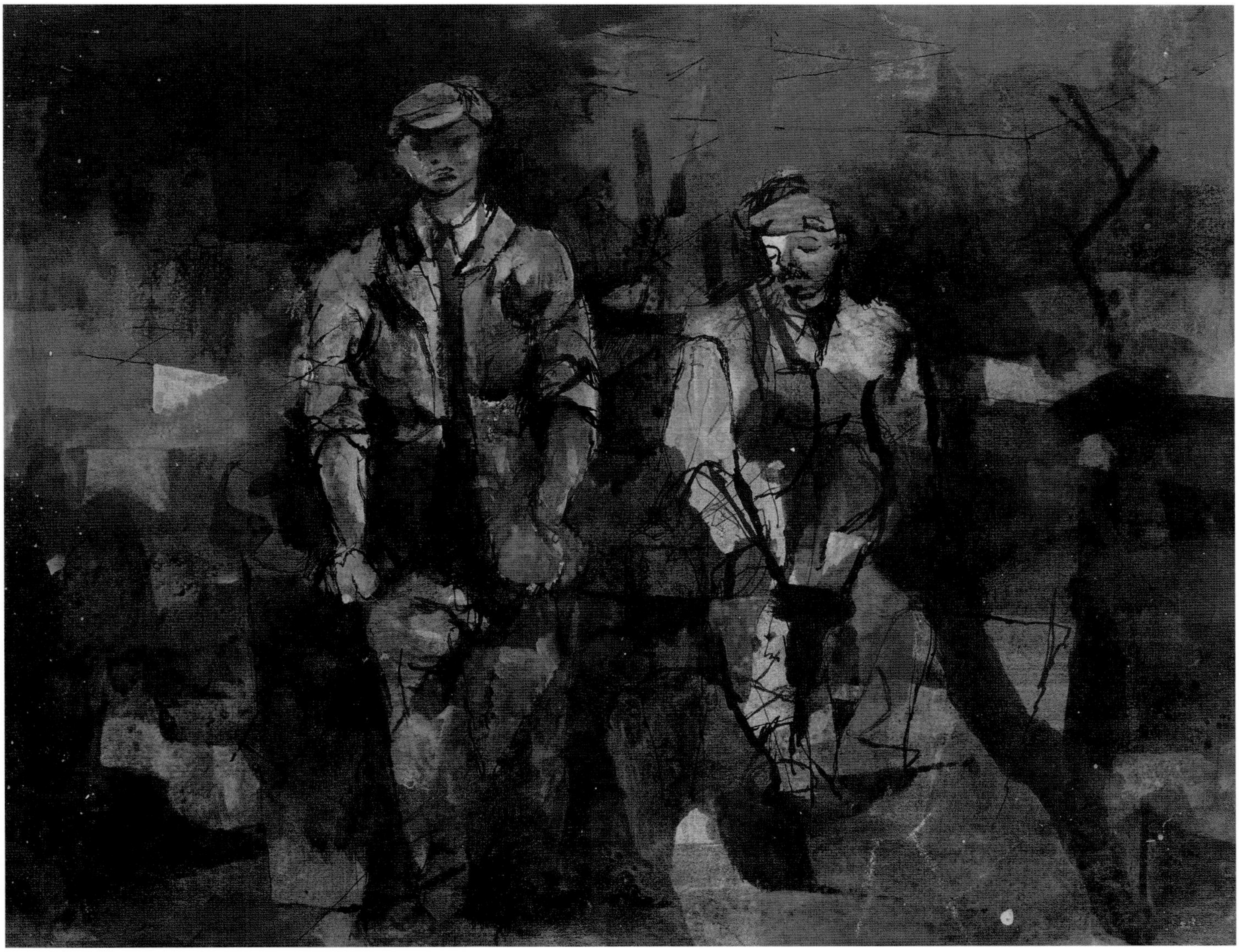

107

JOHN FRANCIS MINTON 1917–1957

Young Fellow Asleep in a Barn, 1946

Pen and ink and wash laid on card
25.1 × 35.6 cm
Signed and dated: *John Minton 1946*
Inscribed: *To Malcolm for Christmas*
Bequeathed by A. L. Rowse, 1998
WA1998.56

While they were students at the St John's Wood School of Art, John Minton and Michael Ayrton (1921–1975) read James Thrall Soby's influential book, *After Picasso* (1935), which showed a route back to progressive figurative painting. They studied and imitated the work of the Paris-based Neo-Romantics, notably Pavel Tchelitchew, and the Surrealists such as Giorgio de Chirico.

With the beginning of the Second World War, Minton declared himself a conscientious objector, but in December 1941, he relented and joined the Pioneer Corps. In early 1943, while he was stationed in North Wales, a friend sent him a copy of *Horizon* magazine with an article by Graham Sutherland on his 'Welsh Sketch Book', which led Minton towards a more recognisably English tradition. Sutherland himself was deeply indebted to Samuel Palmer's works of the Shoreham period, intensely poetic visions of the English countryside executed in a dazzlingly unorthodox technique. On his discharge from the army in June 1943, Minton would no doubt have seen reproductions in an earlier issue of *Horizon* of two of Palmer's sepia drawings of 1825, then newly acquired by the Ashmolean Museum. One of them, *The Valley Thick with Corn*, showing a poet in a landscape, inspired numerous tributes from younger artists. For a brief period, from 1943 to 1946, Minton's work reflected his love of the English countryside and of Palmer's depictions of it. As Ayrton wrote in his seminal account of *British Drawings* (1946), 'Minton is English and Palmer shines through him, but his work is personal none the less'.[1]

While living in London with two fellow artists, Robert Colquhoun and Robert MacBryde, Minton made expeditions to Kent and Cornwall. He produced a series of landscapes inspired by Palmer, highly wrought, idealised, with compressed perspective, and usually incorporating a single male figure. The scenes were often illuminated by moonlight, for, as he joked, 'moons are in! Half-moons are really selling this year!'[2] *Young Fellow Asleep in a Barn* is one of the last of these pastoral idylls, a timeless evocation of rest after labour. Minton adapted the composition of the great barn with double doors beside a twisting road for an illustration to Alain Fournier's *Le Grand Meaulnes*, translated as *The Wanderer* and published by Paul Elek in 1947.[3] CH

1. Quoted by Colin Harrison in Vaughan, Barker, Harrison (2005), p. 59.
2. Quoted in Martin, Butlin, Meyrick (2007), p. 95.
3. Repr. in Spalding (2005) p. 116.

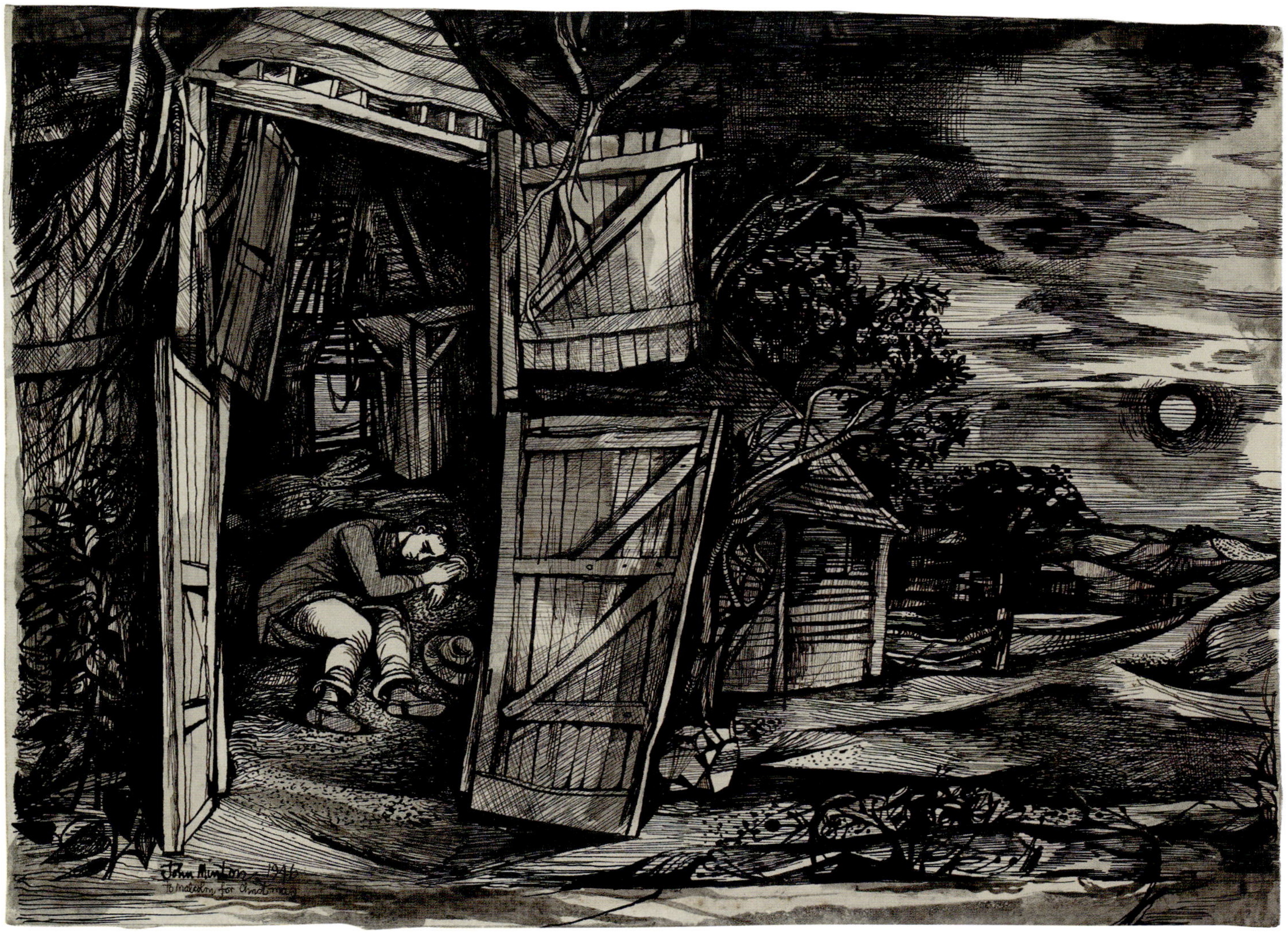
John Minton 1946
To Malcolm, for Christmas

108

BRYAN WYNTER 1915–1975

Tin Mines, 1947

Monotype ground with added bodycolour, stencil and woodcut on paper
22.3 × 28.5 cm
Signed and dated: *Wynter 47*
Lent from a private collection
L12202.3

Having spent five years struggling to conform to his father's wish that he succeed him in the family business, Bryan Wynter was already 23 when he began his studies at the Slade School in 1938. He was still studying there when the School was evacuated to Oxford in 1940. When his call-up papers arrived, he registered as a conscientious objector. Wynter spent a dispiriting war, first engaged in land work and later looking after laboratory animals (especially Rhesus monkeys) housed for vivisection in the Department of Anatomy, Oxford, under Solly (later Lord) Zuckerman. At night he was regularly posted on fire-watching duty in the Ashmolean Museum.

After the end of the war in 1945 Wynter left for St Ives, a place he had known for some years. He quickly found 'The Carn', an isolated granite cottage with no running water or electricity, on the windswept moors above Zennor. It was to be his home until 1960. He became absorbed into the artistic community in St Ives, and was closely associated with artists such as Peter Lanyon, Patrick Heron, Adrian Ryan, and John Wells. He was a founder member of the Crypt Group (1946) and the Penwith Society of Artists (1949).

Wynter was continually making things, and his work displays great evidence of having been crafted and improvised. Indeed, *Tin Mines* raises fundamental questions about the definition of a drawing, so varied are the techniques he used in its creation. From 1946 to 1952 his work was mainly small in scale and mixed in media, often incorporating a monotype as a ground, and frequently using transfer drawing, so that the basic elements of a work could be resolved before printing. Here, Wynter has used a variety of techniques to build up the image. The sea, for example, is monoprinted using a piece of wood with a light wash, so that the grain of the wood shows up as the waves in the harbour. He has also used stencils, most notably to produce the foliage effect at the lower right. This image is an evocation rather than a naturalistic representation, the most striking elements being the chimneys of the tin mines, an immediately recognisable element of the Cornish landscape. Every building is in a state of dereliction, a melancholy addition to the images of ruin that proliferated during and after the Second World War. HD

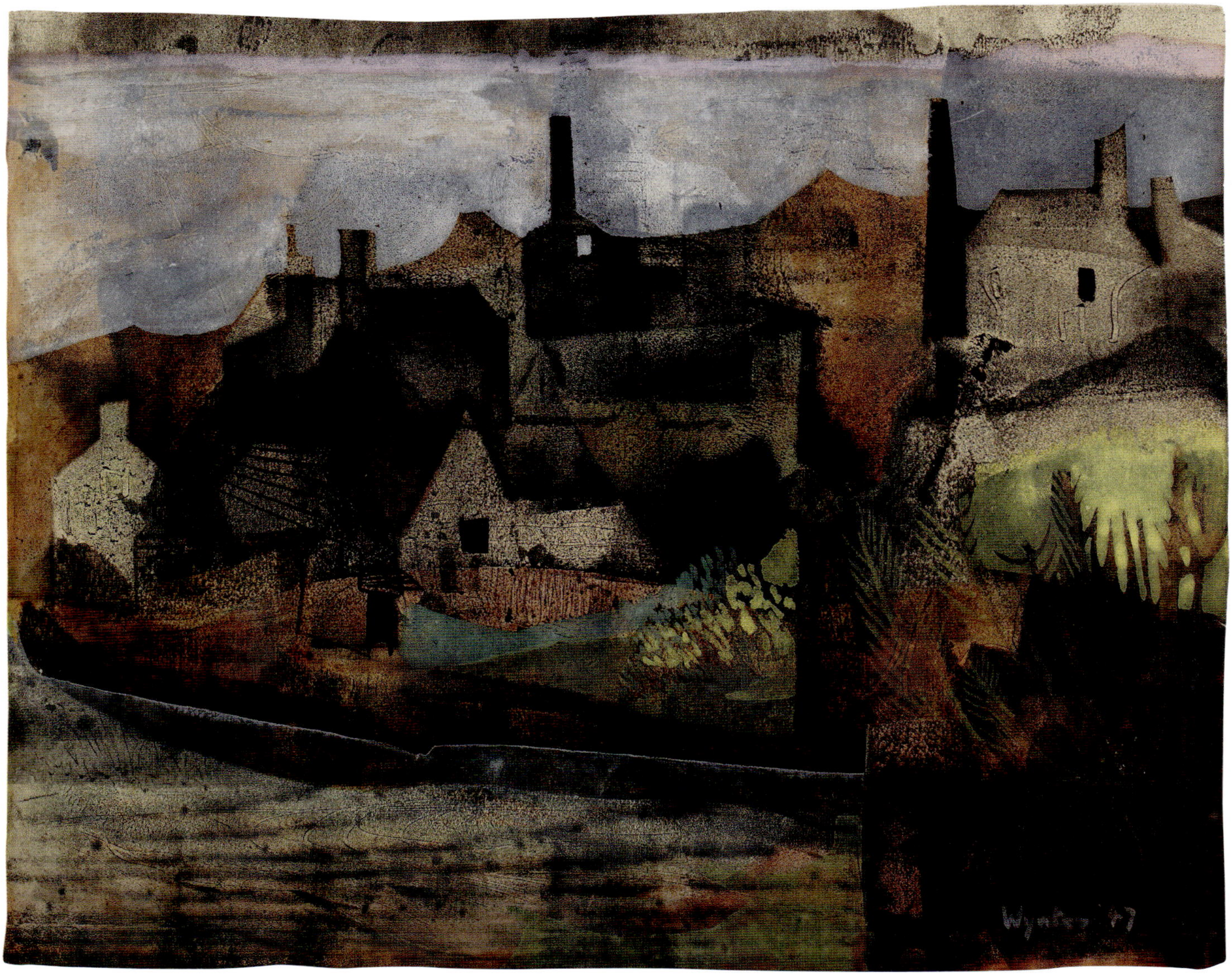

109

WILLIAM GEAR 1915–1997

Paysage, 1947

Mixed media on monotype ground
30 × 49 cm
Signed and dated: *Gear / 47*
Lent from a private collection
L12202.4

Paysage is a transitional drawing. Made in Germany in early 1947, it reveals a dramatic change from the naturalistic style evident in *Palestine Scrapbook, July 1943* (cat. 103). Within another year Gear's work was to become completely abstract, and would remain so for the rest of his life.

Following VE Day on 8 May 1945, Gear was posted at his own request to Germany. He was quickly seconded to the Monuments, Fine Arts and Archives department of Control Commission, with responsibility for safeguarding Germany's cultural heritage. There he was exposed to German Expressionist art and established close links with Karl Otto Götz, a German artist who worked in an Expressionist, Surrealist style. Gear soon began utilising black armatures as a framework, as in *Paysage*. The sources of the armatures was likely to have been 'subconscious memories of the pit-head winding gear; the engineering marvel of the Forth Bridge … and silhouetted trees on that stormy coast [of Fife]'.[1]

It was in 1945, while on leave in London, that he was reintroduced to monotype by Jankel Adler (1895–1949). Adler was a Polish wartime refugee who had himself learned the technique from Paul Klee when the two had adjacent studios in Düsseldorf in the early 1930s. For a time in the late 1940s, Gear used monotype as a ground in mixed media works, often in combination with oil transfer drawing, bodycolour, and pen and ink. He would establish the 'drawing' in monochrome and then rework the image, building up the textures of the monotype with bodycolour. In *Paysage*, the monotype and transfer drawing are clearly visible, providing depth, texture and structure, on to which pen and ink have been added in sweeps of black. Bodycolour has also been applied, in strong, clashing colours. Gear's purpose was to convey mood as well as destruction in this fractured landscape.

Demobbed in 1947, Gear went straight to Paris, becoming one of only two British artists to exhibit with CoBrA between 1947 and 1950. After returning to Britain, he went on to have a distinguished career, both as Curator of the Towner Art Gallery, Eastbourne (1958–64), and Head of the Faculty of Fine Art, Birmingham College of Art (1964–75). HD

1. Tessa Sidey, National Sound Archive, 1995, quoted in McEwen (2003) p. 7.

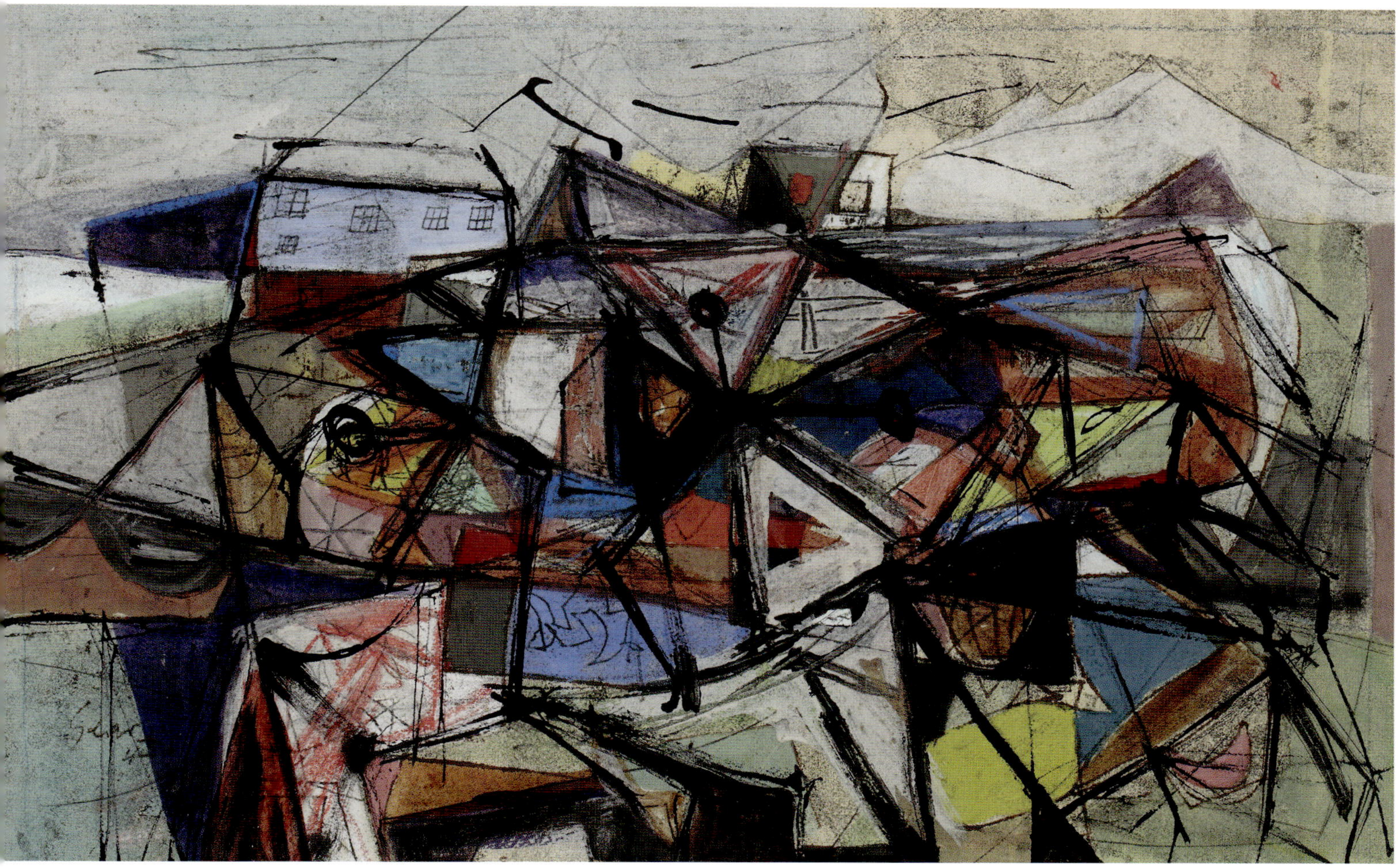

110

JOHN PIPER 1903–1992
The Abbey from the Churchyard, Arbroath, 1982

Brush in Indian ink with watercolour, bodycolour and coloured chalks on paper
57.7 × 67.5 cm
Signed: *John Piper*
Bequeathed by Robert and Rena Lewin, 2004
WA2006.21
© The Piper Estate / DACS 2015

LITERATURE: Jenkins (1992) no. 39

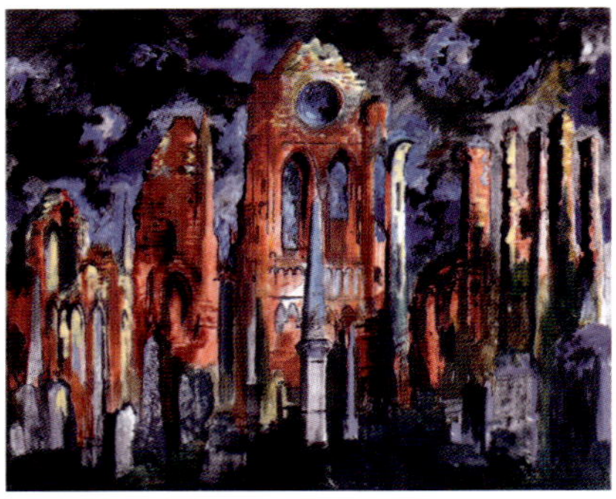

Fig. 64 | John Piper (1903–1992), *Arbroath*, c. 1987. Oil on canvas. Image courtesy of Waddington Custot Gallery © The Piper Estate / DACS 2015

Piper's distinguished career ranged over six decades and proved prodigiously diverse. As an artist he produced paintings, graphic work and collages, as well as designs for the theatre, stained glass, ceramics, and textiles. He was also a writer and editor, and with John Betjeman had a long-standing involvement in the *Shell Guides*. Although Piper embraced a variety of subjects, he was primarily an artist of the *genius loci* and particularly responsive to architecture, claiming in 1962 that his work was based upon 'a feeling for places … just going somewhere, anywhere really, – and trying to see what hasn't been seen before'.[1]

In 1934 Piper was elected to the 7 & 5 Society and at the forefront of the British *avant-garde*. Four years later, however, he pronounced abstraction a 'luxury' that could be ill-afforded in the hostile world of contemporary European politics.[2] His abandonment of pure abstraction was cemented by his appointment as an official war artist; he was assigned to make images of bomb sites, including the shattered remains of Coventry Cathedral in November 1940. Inspired by J. M. W. Turner and John Sell Cotman, Piper attempted in his own idiom what Paul Nash and Eric Ravilious pursued in theirs: the union of British Romanticism with European Modernism.

Scotland was a country little explored by Piper, but during the last decade of his life he created a series of images of Arbroath Abbey, near Dundee, a significant site for Scottish history owing to the Declaration of Arbroath in 1320. This large watercolour served as a study for one of two monumental oil paintings, while a monochrome watercolour of the same view was issued as a screenprint in 1988.[3] The looming ruins of the late-twelfth to early-thirteenth-century abbey appear theatrically lit against a thunderous sky. The attenuated fragments are crowded by obelisks and grave monuments, one of which has been elongated to pierce the iconic round window of the south transept. Truncating the nave and rotating the east end through 90 degrees enabled Piper to include all the abbey church's most distinctive elements; these are concentrated together while the swift brushwork suggests a perilous dissolution of architectural forms. The oil painting retains a striking sense of drama, but softens the urgent anguish of the watercolour with greater topographical clarity in the transept arcading and more solidly rooted structures. The present drawing, a troubled meditation on impending mortality is nonetheless a bravura performance full of the calligraphic verve and the revelling in weathered surfaces that characterises Piper's finest work. KW

1. *The Sunday Times*, quoted in Ingrams and Piper (1983) p. 9.
2. Quoted in Jenkins and Spalding (2003) p. 48.
3. Watercolour, *Ruined Church, Arbroath* (c. 1982), Christie's 17 November 2006, sale 7277, lot 70; screenprint, *Arbroath Abbey*, Levinson (1996) no. 407.

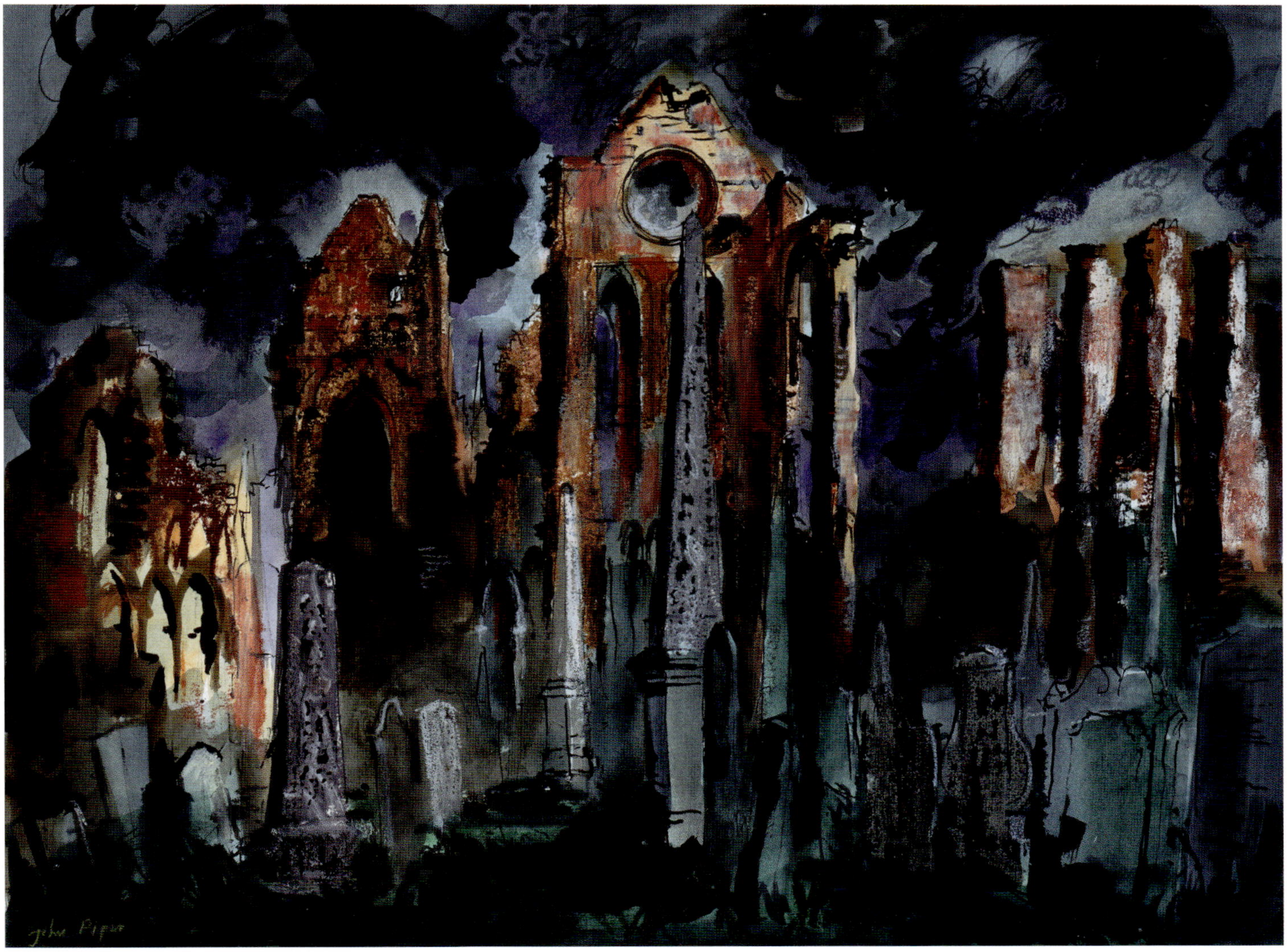
John Piper

III

COLIN SELF B. 1941
Four Studies for 'Victims of Hiroshima', 1966

Pen and ink, wash and charcoal on letter paper with bodycolour and oil paint on paper
29.5 × 25.5 × 3.7 cm and 29.5 × 17 × 3.7 cm
Signed and dated: *Colin Self / 3-4-66 / 16-3-66 / 30-6-66 / 3-6-66*
Lent from a private collection
L12202.5

The art of Colin Self has always been difficult to categorise. Early in his career, he was labelled as a Pop artist, but his path has been so quirky and idiosyncratic, and his work at times so preoccupied with political themes, that he has never properly fitted into Richard Hamilton's famous summary of Pop Art as 'Popular / Expendable / Low Cost / Mass Produced / Young / Witty / Sexy / Gimmicky / Glamorous / Big Business'.

Coming from a large working-class family in Norwich, Self studied at the Norwich School of Art and the Slade School (1961–3). Pop Art represented for him 'both a specifically working-class rebellion against obscurantism' and 'the first movement for goodness knows how long, to accept and reflect the world in which it lives'.[1]

A long visit to the USA in 1965, in particular his reaction to New York, fostered a new nuclear theme in Self's work, notably in his *Fallout Shelter* drawings. However, it was while he was in Santa Monica, California, together with David Hockney, Patrick Prockter, and Norman Stevens, that he conceived the idea of *Beach Girl*, a sculpture of a young woman as a charred corpse, dead on a beach as a result of a nuclear explosion. He worked on this theme in 1966 following his return to Britain, and the principal picture is now in the Imperial War Museum. Self's preoccupation had its roots in his adolescence, as he later explained:

I spent my teenage years … having been psychologically devastated by the preachings of Bertrand Russell and thought Armageddon would have exploded its nuclear end when he predicted. By 1967 or 8. For seven years I worked towards that end, thinking the most civilised thing we could do (with what time was left) would be a 'record' of 'how come' the world ended? [2]

The four studies for *Victims of Hiroshima* were executed at much the same time, and were based on photographs of casualties of the Hiroshima bombing in 1945. Instead of the glamorous female icons so familiar from glossy magazines and typical of Pop Art, Self presents us with images of appallingly mutilated women, the victims of nuclear warfare. HD

1. Letter from Colin Self to Marco Livingstone, 1 December 1987, quoted in Livingstone (1990) p. 162.
2. Letter from Colin Self to Marco Livingstone, 23 September 1987; Livingstone (1990) p. 257.

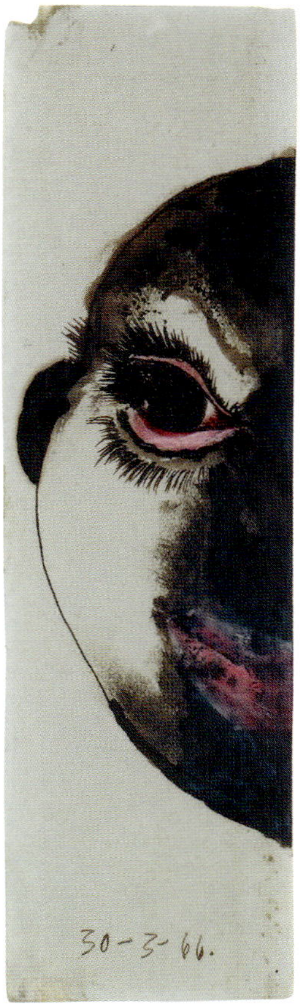
30-3-66.

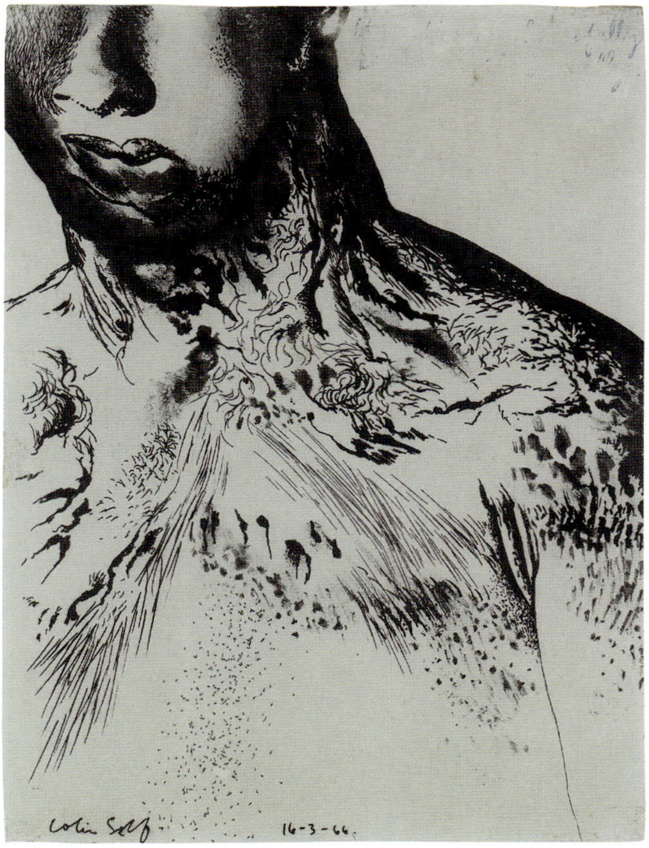
Colin Self
16-3-66.

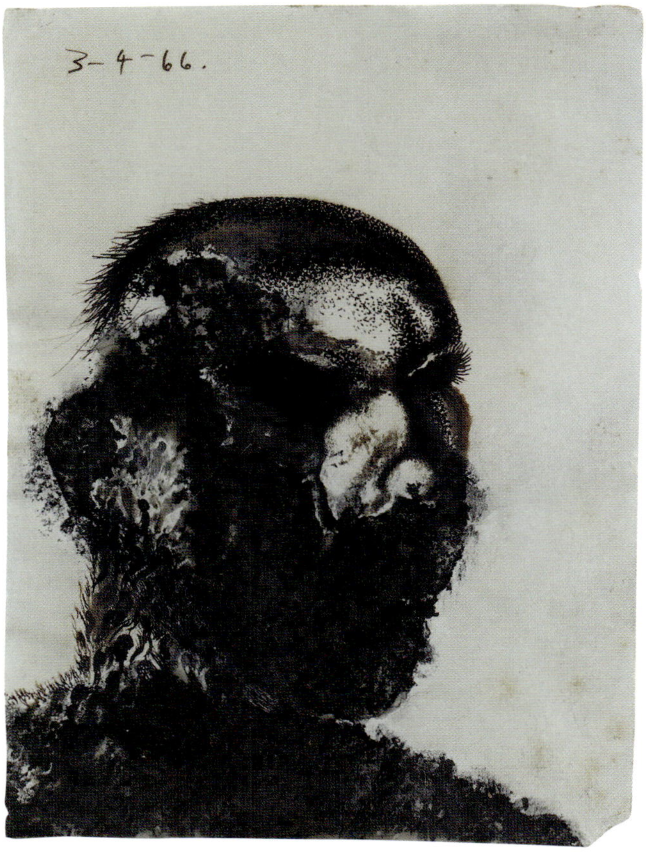
3-4-66.

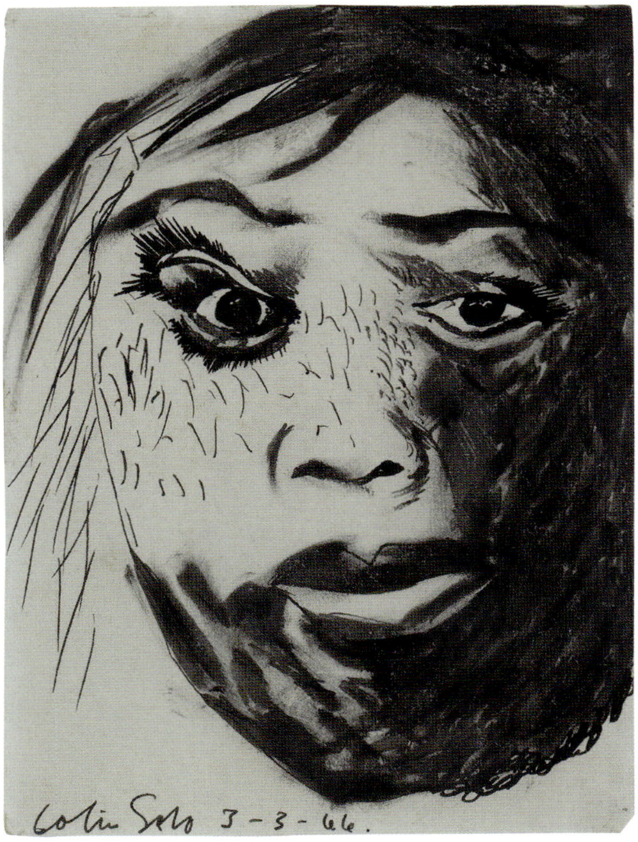
Colin Self 3-3-66.

112

DAVID HOCKNEY B. 1937
Henry writing, Lucca, 1973

Pen and black ink on white paper
43.1 × 35.4 cm
Signed: *D.H.* Inscribed and dated: *Henry writing / Lucca. Aug 73*
Presented by the Friends of the Ashmolean, to commemorate Lord Bullock's Chairmanship of the Friends, 1976–96, 1996
WA1996.28

LITERATURE: Brown (2013) no. 71

Picasso's death in April 1973 may have inspired Hockney to create this wonderfully fluid line drawing a few months later by way of homage, reigniting the admiration he had felt for Picasso's work at the Tate Gallery retrospective exhibition of 1960. An etching of similar date, *Artist and Model* (1973–4), shows a naked Hockney sitting opposite the Spanish master across a table, using spare, clean lines akin to those employed in this portrait of Henry Geldzahler (1935–1994), art critic and curator at the Metropolitan Museum of Art, New York.

Andy Warhol first introduced the young Hockney to Geldzahler in 1963. They became close friends, staying together while on holiday in the summer of 1973 at a villa in Lucca. Hockney produced a number of drawings of Henry in the 1970s, many in pared-down style, showing him in relaxed poses – lounging with his leg over a tubular modern chair, sitting cross-legged on a sofa smoking a cigar, or buried deep in an armchair reading a book. He is most often shown with one leg crossed over the other, as here, in what must have been a characteristic posture.[1]

Flowing over the sheet with apparently effortless control, Hockney's fine pen line is economical and elegant. Longer phrasing lines contrast with short, staccato strokes in the hair and beard, with repeated rhythmical striping in the T-shirt and chair seat. The barest indications suggest a spatial context – a diagonal bottom left and two vertical lines framing Henry's profile – while the curlicue of Henry's bottom lip is wittily repeated in his slightly bulging waistline, as well as in the typewriter and carving of the chair and table leg. Hands raised above the keyboard in a moment of thought or suspended animation, Henry is recorded in the process of creating *Hockney on Hockney*, first published in 1976. His body appears in repose while his mind is clearly in motion.

Although Hockney is famed for experimenting with bold colour, he has always practised draughtsmanship as a disciplined exercise in observing and recording. This may reflect his early training at the Royal College of Art (1959–62). Following a minor stroke, Hockney has recently returned once again to drawing, using charcoal rather than pen and ink as a medium. In an exhibition catalogue of 2014 he emphasises his continuing loyalty to the use of black and white on paper: 'The Chinese say black and white contains colour, and so it can.' Declaring that his stroke has not affected his ability to draw, but has made him concentrate all the more, he writes, 'I'm OK so long as I can draw'.[2] CP

1. Luckhardt and Melia (1995) nos. 87, 97; Livingstone and Heymer (2003) pp. 98–107.
2. Annely Juda (2014) preface.

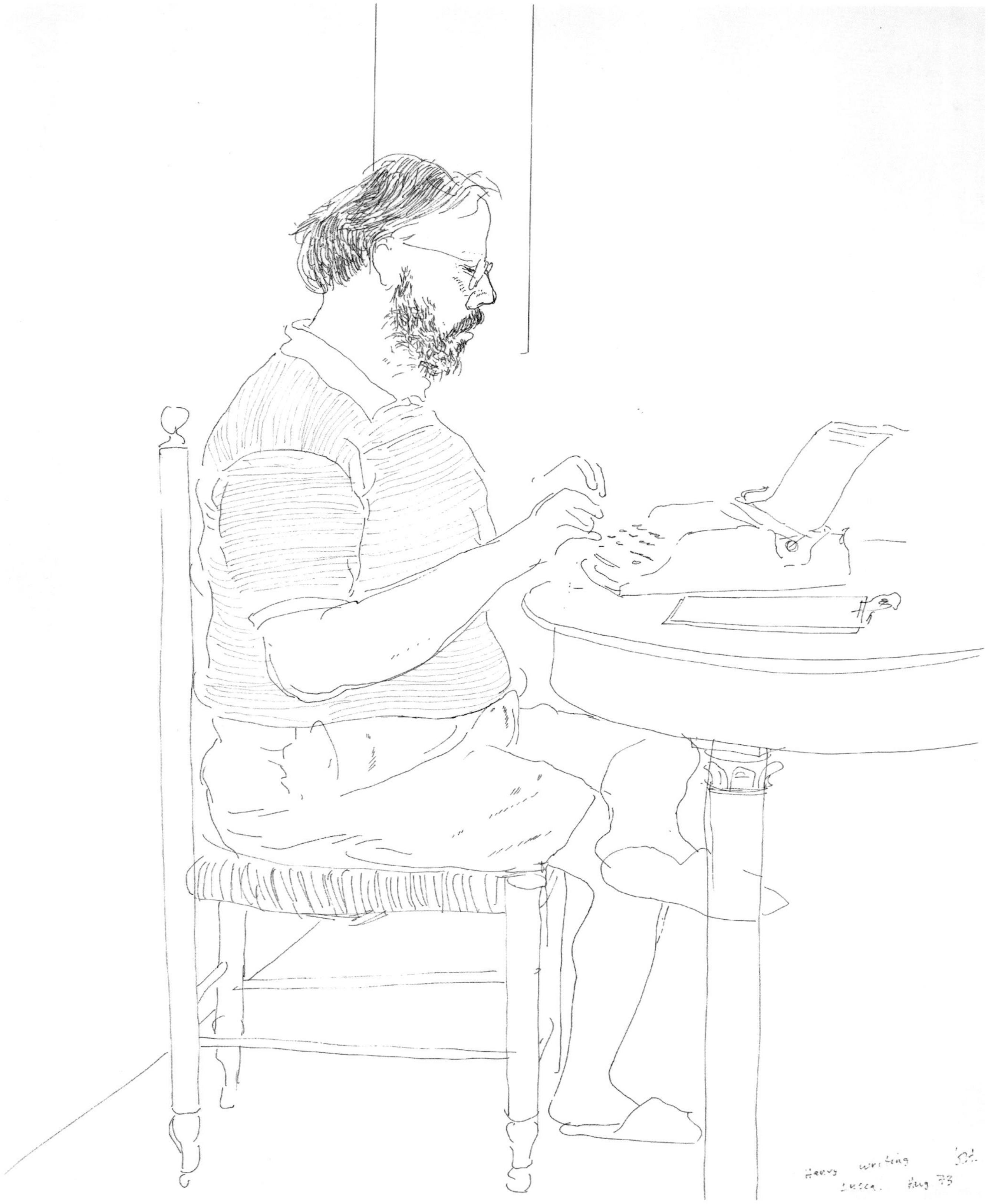
Henry writing
Lucca. Aug 73

113

FRANK AUERBACH B. 1931

Head of Julia, 1985–6

Charcoal and chalk on paper
92.7 × 76.2 cm
Signed and dated: *Auerbach / 85 – 86*
Accepted by HM Government in lieu of Inheritance Tax on the estate of Lucian Freud and allocated to the Ashmolean Museum, 2015
WA2015.6

LITERATURE: Lampert, Rosenthal, Carlisle (2001) no. 108

Although he studied at St Martin's School of Art (1948–52) and then at the Royal College of Art (1952–5), Auerbach learnt most from the weekly life classes held by David Bomberg at the Borough Polytechnic. Like Bomberg himself, Auerbach began to draw in charcoal on large sheets of paper, working quickly because the models did not hold their poses for long periods. Since then, he has worked obsessively, for ten hours a day, every day of the week, his only interruptions being a weekly visit to the National Gallery. His range of subjects is deliberately limited, the majority being portraits of sitters familiar to him, and landscapes near his studio in Camden Town. Auerbach has intently studied a succession of models, the principal being Estella Olive West (EOW) from 1948 to 1973, his cousin, Gerda Boehm, and Julia Yardley Mills. In the late 1970s, he began to use other models, sometimes for only one or two works, often for a long series. One constant presence has been that of Julia Wolstenholme, whom he met when they were studying at the Royal College of Art; they were married in 1958.

Robert Hughes has vividly described Auerbach's working method when drawing a portrait. He habitually uses two sheets of stout paper glued together, pinned to an easel.

As he scribbles and saws at the paper, the sticks of willow charcoal snap; they make cracking sounds like a tooth breaking on a bone. When he scrubs the paper with a rag clouds of black dust fly … The studio is like a colliery; the drawing easel is black and exquisitely glossy from years of carbon dust mixed with hand-grease.

As the portrait develops, sometimes over a period of weeks, 'the creature will mutate, becoming dense and troll-like one day and dissolving in *furioso* passages of hatching the next' but 'in the end, the likeness is retrieved, but as a ghost, the colour of very tarnished silver'.[1]

Auerbach worked on this portrait of Julia over many sittings, adding and subtracting lines in charcoal and chalk not simply to create a likeness of his wife, but to capture her character, and only with the final thick strokes emphatically defining her hair, face, and neck. It was one of the representative collection of 40 works by the artist owned by his friend, the painter Lucian Freud (1922–2011), which has recently been distributed to museums and galleries throughout the United Kingdom.

1. Hughes (1990) p. 15.

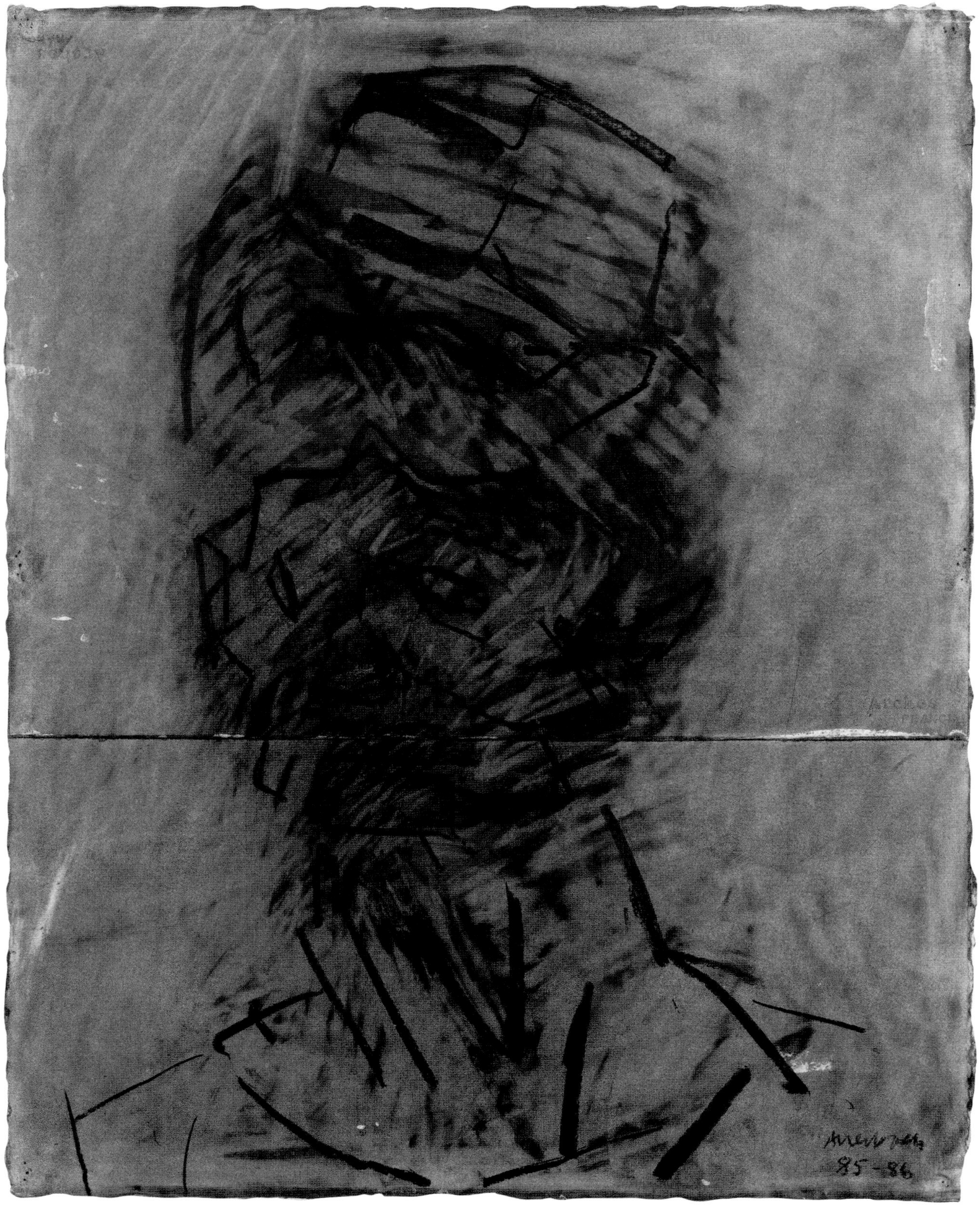

114

TOM PHILLIPS B. 1937

Salman Rushdie, 1993

Charcoal, pastel, black and red bodycolour, brown mud bound in Liquitex Matte medium on white paper
70 × 55.8 cm
Inscribed: *NOT TO SHUT UP / TO SING ON*
Purchased (Vaughan and Blakiston Funds) with the assistance of The Art Fund and the MLA/V&A Purchase Grant Fund, 2009
WA2009.81

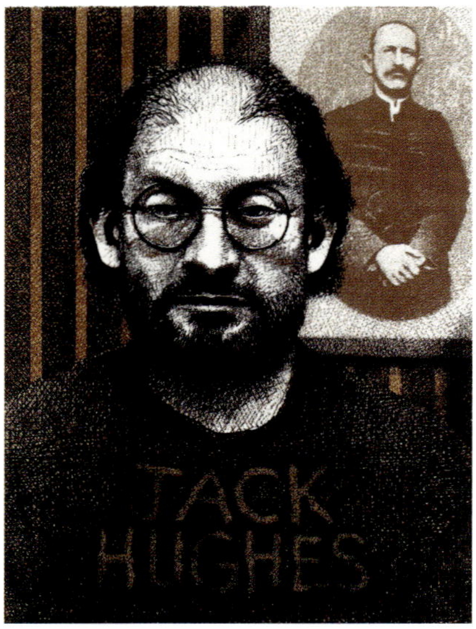

Fig. 65 | Tom Phillips (b. 1937), *Salman Rushdie as DIY Zola*, 1993. Colour lithograph. Ashmolean Museum, Oxford, WA1993.469 © Tom Phillips. All rights reserved, DACS 2015

Tom Phillips first turned to portrait painting in the 1980s, and in 1992–3 created several portraits of the author Sir Salman Rushdie (b. 1947), partly in response to the *fatwa* issued by the Ayatollah Khomeini following publication of his controversial novel, *The Satanic Verses* (1988).[1] A large head-and-shoulders lithograph of Rushdie bears an ancient cuneiform inscription which translates as 'How can we say what blasphemy is; we do not know the thoughts of the Gods'.[2] A further lithograph (fig. 65) shows Rushdie wearing a T-shirt emblazoned 'JACK HUGHES', standing before a portrait of Captain Dreyfus, the falsely imprisoned Jewish army officer famously defended in Emile Zola's letter 'J'accuse' (1898).

In this, the most powerful of the portraits, Rushdie's image is almost obliterated by the scratched lines and savagely overlaid marks of charcoal, pastel and thick black paint. Over the surface is spattered red-brick mud – a novel drawing medium. It is dripped in trails and smeared across the paper in a manner reminiscent of Jackson Pollock. The inscription on the portrait is taken from Rushdie's poem entitled '6 March 1989', the date of the *fatwa*, first published in *Granta* (autumn 1989): 'Still, nameless-and-faceless or not, here's my choice: / not to shut up. To sing on'.

The second verse of the poem describes the imagined violence done to Rushdie's face by his attackers, who have poked out his eyes and knocked out his teeth so he can barely recall how his face used to look. Phillips's drawing expresses the anger of this poem, conveying the damage done to Rushdie's image by his detractors while endorsing his right to speak out against the 'mud-slinging'. Despite the artist's 'attack' on his subject, employing all the media he can throw at him, the face remains recognisably that of Rushdie, stoically enduring the onslaught.

In his description of the sittings for these portraits, however, Phillips appears far from angry. He remembers Rushdie as 'a fearsome table-tennis opponent' rather than as a tortured man of letters, despite his virtual house arrest while confined under police protection.[3] Rushdie and Phillips collaborated on a limited edition artist's book entitled *Merely Connect* (1993), which incorporated some of these wittily defiant political portraits. CP

1. Paschal (1992) pp. 176–7.
2. Ashmolean Museum, WA1993.468.
3. http://www.tomphillips.co.uk/works/portraits/item/5453-salman-rushdie, accessed 9 January 2015; Hurrell (1997) p. 20.

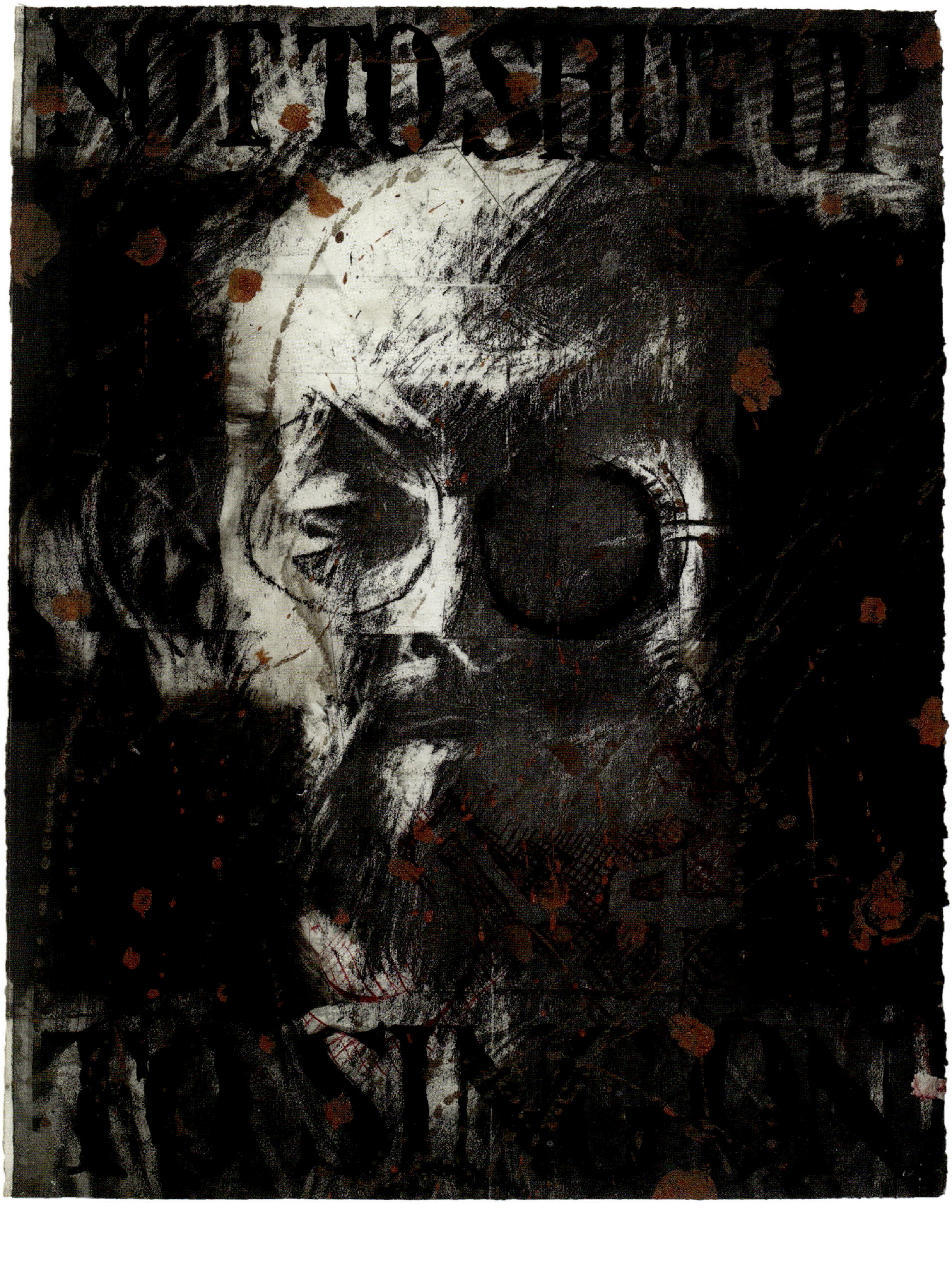
NOT TO SHUT UP

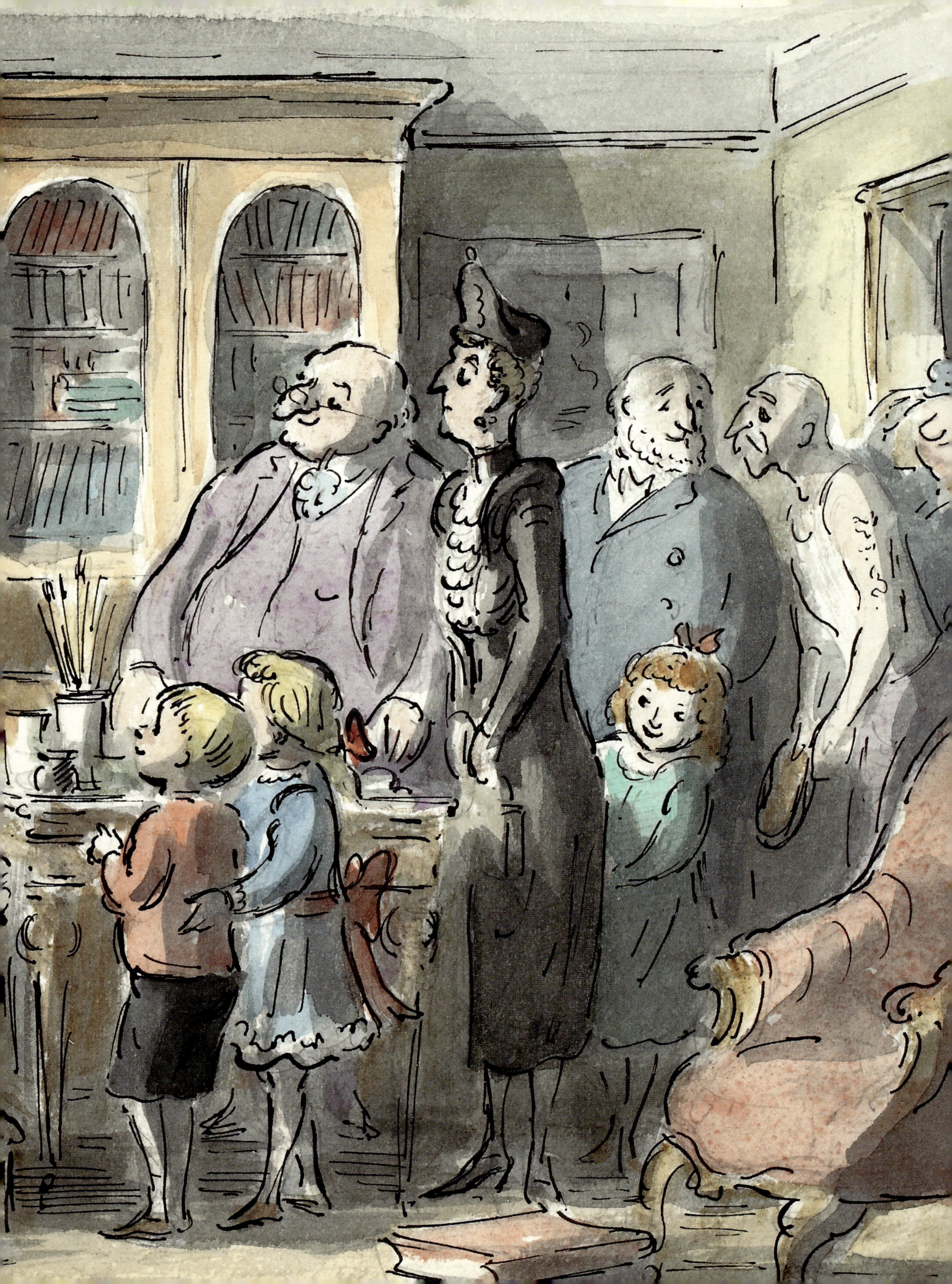

Caricature & Satire

A British Sense of Humour

Detail from Edward Ardizzone,
A Homage to Jock Cumberlege (cat. 129)

115

FRANCIS BARLOW ?1626–1704

The Fox and the Eagle, 1667–8

Pen and black ink with grey wash on paper, many of the outlines incised for transfer
25.4 × 18.4 cm
Bequeathed by Francis Douce, 1834
WA1863.997

LITERATURE: Hodnett (1978) pp. 197, 202; Brown (1982) no. 59

According to George Vertue, Barlow had originally intended to become a portrait painter, but quickly realised that 'his fancy did not lye that way, his Genious leading him wholly to drawing Fowl, Fish, and Beasts'.[1] By 1656 he was described by the diarist John Evelyn as 'the famous Paynter of fowle, Beastes and Birds'.[2] Barlow was the first British-born specialist in this genre, though better known for drawings and prints than for oil paintings. His work was based on a long and scientific study of his animal subjects, and an exceptional familiarity with their behaviour and environment. He was nevertheless aware of his predecessors, and used their prints for more exotic animals, specimens of which were not available in London. Among his series of prints of birds, only one seems to have been engraved by Barlow's own hand, the grandiosely entitled *Multae et diversae avium species multifarijs formis et pernaturalebus figures* (reprinted in 1671). Similar collections of his drawings engraved by other artists circulated widely.

Barlow's most celebrated plates are the illustrations to the perennially popular *Aesop's Fables*, which he published in his own edition of 1666. In contrast to earlier artists such as Francis Cleyn (*c.* 1582–1658), Barlow shows an extraordinary naturalism in his approach; his animals dominate the composition rather than being incidental, while the backgrounds are integral and convincing. The plates were so successful that when he came to publish a third, expanded edition of his *Aesop Paraphras'd* (1651, 1665), John Ogilby enlisted Barlow's help.

This drawing of *The Fox and the Eagle* was one of several that Barlow provided for the *Aesopics* of 1668. It takes up his composition from the edition of 1666, but in an upright rather than a horizontal format. An eagle has carried off a fox cub to feed to her chicks, while the vixen, carrying a lighted brand, stands on a high branch of a tree, preparing to set fire to the nest. In the background, the episode is echoed several times with variations: another eagle attacks a fox's lair, a second fox carries an eagle in its teeth, and a third howls at an eagle perched out of reach. Like most of Barlow's drawings for illustrations, it is drawn with a quill pen in brown ink over graphite underdrawing, with diluted grey ink added to convey light and shade. The heavy and rather hard outlines were intended to facilitate the task of the engraver, in this case Richard Gaywood. CH

1. Quoted in Hodnett (1978) p. 13.
2. Quoted in Hodnett (1978) p. 12.

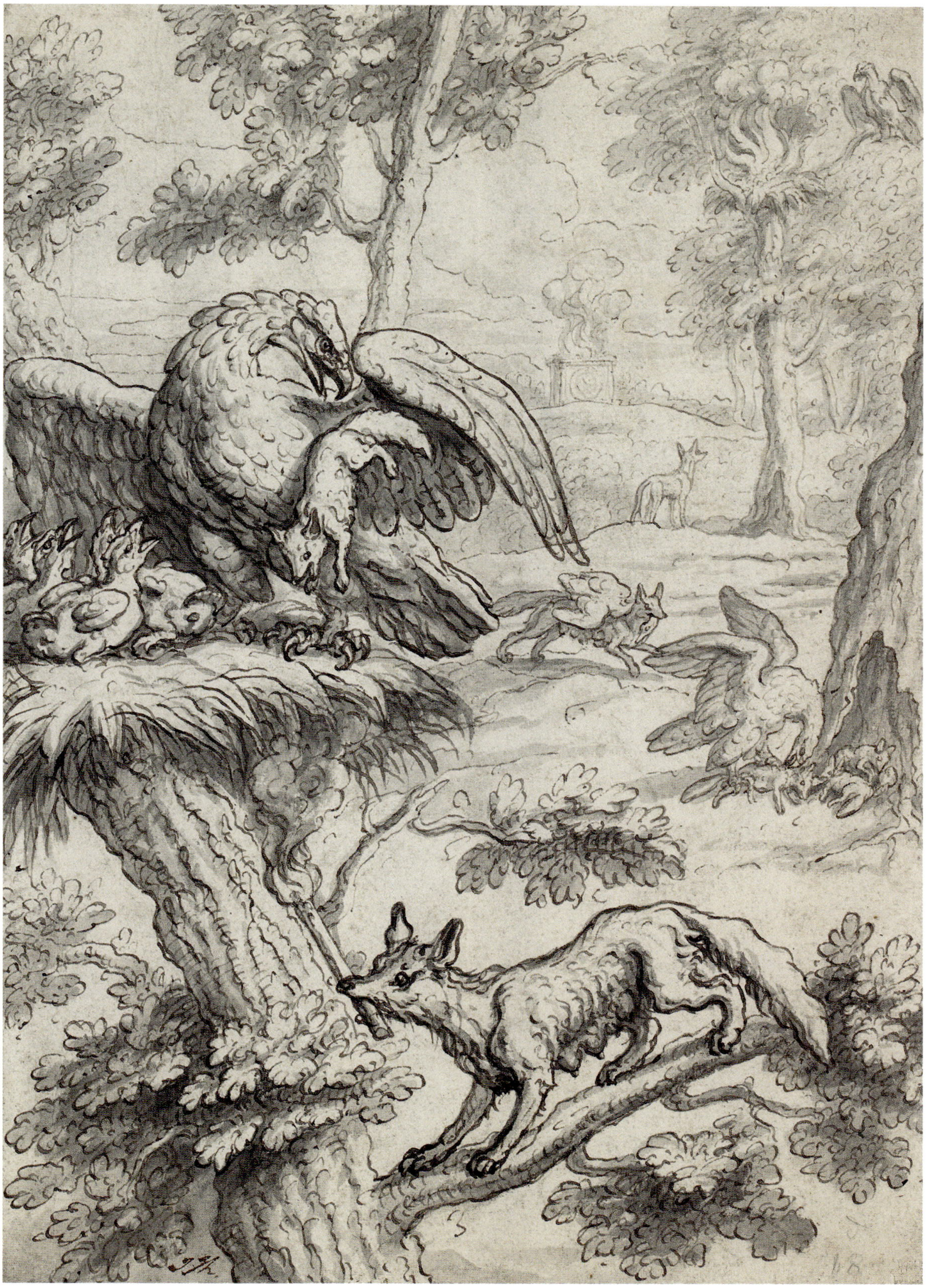

116

FRANCIS BARLOW ?1626–1704

A Political Satire, 1679

Pen and brown ink with grey wash on paper
21.2 × 31.4 cm
Signed and dated: *F. Barlow 1679*
Inscribed: *we walk but slow but Aps face we be shure / And these Afronts no longer shall indure; Come Mounsure [crossed out and altered in a different hand to] good sa hust I shall so pault your Brayne / Ile make you spue my aple up agayne / your Shabrone rout shall soene my Cuntrey fly / Lyke Shitlecoke Ile make them mount the sky; Began [crossed out and altered in a different hand to] Gadone you are soone of an Hure and know / Ile have your countrey where de Aple grow / no matter where the warre be false or right / Tis for my Glory that I now doe fight; Sa sah along ten towsand pug me slay / then turn my arse and bravely run away*
The pages inscribed *magiour / Liktren / cher and Captayne Suckplume.*
Bequeathed by Francis Douce, 1834
WA1863.999

LITERATURE: Hodnett (1978) pp. 26–30; Brown (1982) no. 63; Stainton and White (1987) no. 110

Political cartoons were published regularly in England in the seventeenth century, but were usually made by untrained artists with no great technical skill. Barlow was the first major artist to turn his hand to the genre, but only three of his designs survive, of which this is the most elaborate. The drawing is prepared for engraving as a large broadside, but seems never to have been published.

The subject has been convincingly interpreted by Hodnett. It refers to the extensive territorial conflicts which were resolved by the Treaty of Nijmegen in 1679. On the left is an ape intended for the Holy Roman Emperor, Leopold I, riding a bear. He is accompanied by his monkey attendant, 'major Likterncher', representing Charles V, Duke of Lorraine. Opposing him in this mock joust is the French king, Louis XIV. He is personified as an ape riding a boar, with the *fleur de lys* on his shield and the Gallic cock on the boar's armour. The king is attended by 'Captayne Suckplume', probably Charles II of Great Britain and an ally of the French. Above the Emperor is an owl blowing a horn, to which is attached a banner bearing a pair of crossed artichokes. Above Louis XIV is a snipe with a different horn, and a banner emblazoned with three mushrooms. The birds represent the Papacy (with reference to the crossed keys of St Peter) and Charles XI of Sweden (the three crowns being an emblem of Sweden and referring to the united kingdoms of Norway, Sweden, and Denmark). In 1678–9, at the conclusion of a series of wars, Louis XIV formally ceded Lorraine, symbolised by the apple that is the object of this joust, to the Holy Roman Empire. In other contemporary treaties France gained possession of the Franche Comté and Artois from Spain, and ceded Maastricht to the Dutch Republic. Iconographically, Barlow's cartoon is indebted to Aesop's fable of the kite, the frog, and the mouse.

The circumstances of the commission of this drawing are not known. However, Barlow's patron, William Cavendish, later 1st Duke of Devonshire, had succeeded in 1677 in persuading Charles II to withdraw British troops from supporting the French, and the cartoon may have been made at his behest. CH

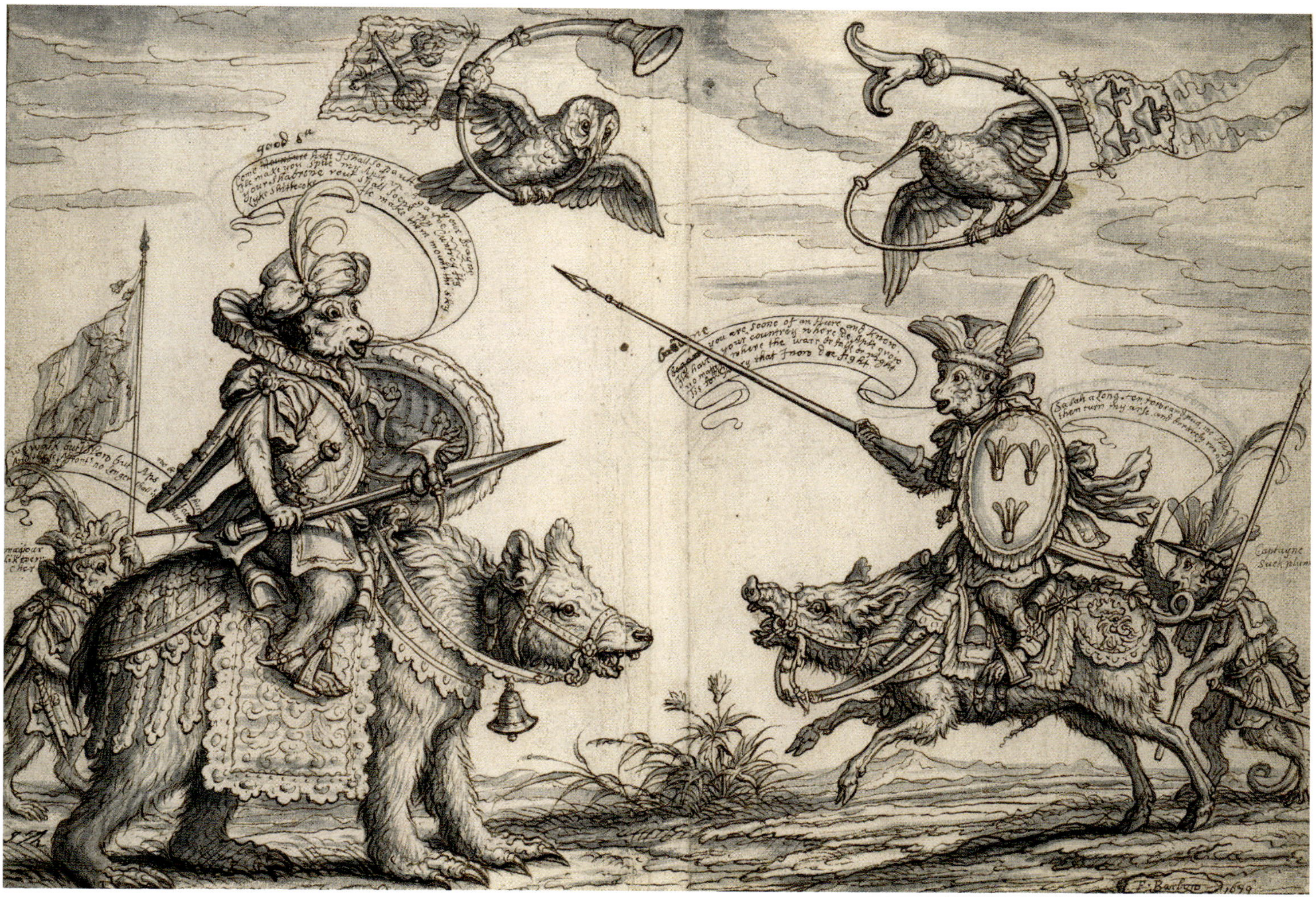
Captayne

117

JAMES GILLRAY 1756–1815

Consequences of a successful French Invasion, No. VI Plate 1st: We fly on the Wings of the Wind to save the Irish Catholics from Persecution, 1798

Pen and brown ink and watercolour on paper
31 × 40 cm
Lent from the Jeffrey Archer Political Cartoon Collection
LI2225.1

LITERATURE: George VII no. 9183; Beetles (2013) pp. 32–3

Gillray was the first political caricaturist in Britain. The son of a member of the Moravian Brethren, who believed in the essential depravity of existence, he maintained a misanthropic attitude to life, and a keen interest in politics. As a draughtsman, he was so precocious that he was already able to support himself by selling caricatures while studying at the Royal Academy Schools.

Like many in Britain, Gillray initially welcomed the outbreak of the French Revolution and the downfall of Louis XVI in 1789, producing a print entitled *France Freedom, Britain Slavery*. As atrocity succeeded atrocity, however, his attitude changed completely, and from 1791 the French became the targets for some of his most ferocious caricatures. Following the execution of Louis XVI in 1793, Gillray reserved his greatest animosity for the *sans-culottes* and their supporters, among whom he counted Charles James Fox. Even before France declared war on Britain in February 1793, Gillray attacked Fox as a regicide and traitor. The fall of Fox gave way in Gillray's repertoire to the rise of Napoleon. *Little Boney* was to become one of his greatest creations: small, haggard, manic, and almost insane.

In 1798 Sir John Dalrymple of Cousland (1726–1810), an enthusiastic but rather ineffectual Scottish writer, published a prospectus advertising a series of caricatures illustrating *The Consequences of the French Invasion*, in the hope of attracting funding from the government. His intention was to 'rouse all the People to an active Union against that Invasion; at a time when about five Millions of Cultures, with Beaks and Claws, hover over them; and when the Indolence and Divisions of the people themselves are more alarming than all foreign Enemies'. Two years earlier, Gillray's companion, Mrs Humphrey, had already published his print of *Promis'd Horrors of the French Invasion, or, Forcible Reasons for negotiating a Regicide Peace*, against the proposed peace treaty with the revolutionary government. Now he provided plates showing the French instructing the House of Lords, the House of Commons, and the peasantry in their iniquitous ways.[1] The present drawing, in Gillray's most vigorous style, depicts two bloodthirsty French soldiers ejecting a priest from his church; a third stamping on a pile of crucifixes and mitres, while a judge looks on with approval. Dalrymple admired Gillray's drawing, telling him that 'The Irish Roman Catholic one is excellently executed & will do Good in Ireland in opening the eyes of these poor people'.[2] Unfortunately, the British government did not agree, and the series was discontinued with only four plates completed. CH

1. George VII nos. 9180–2.
2. Quoted in George VII, p. 430.

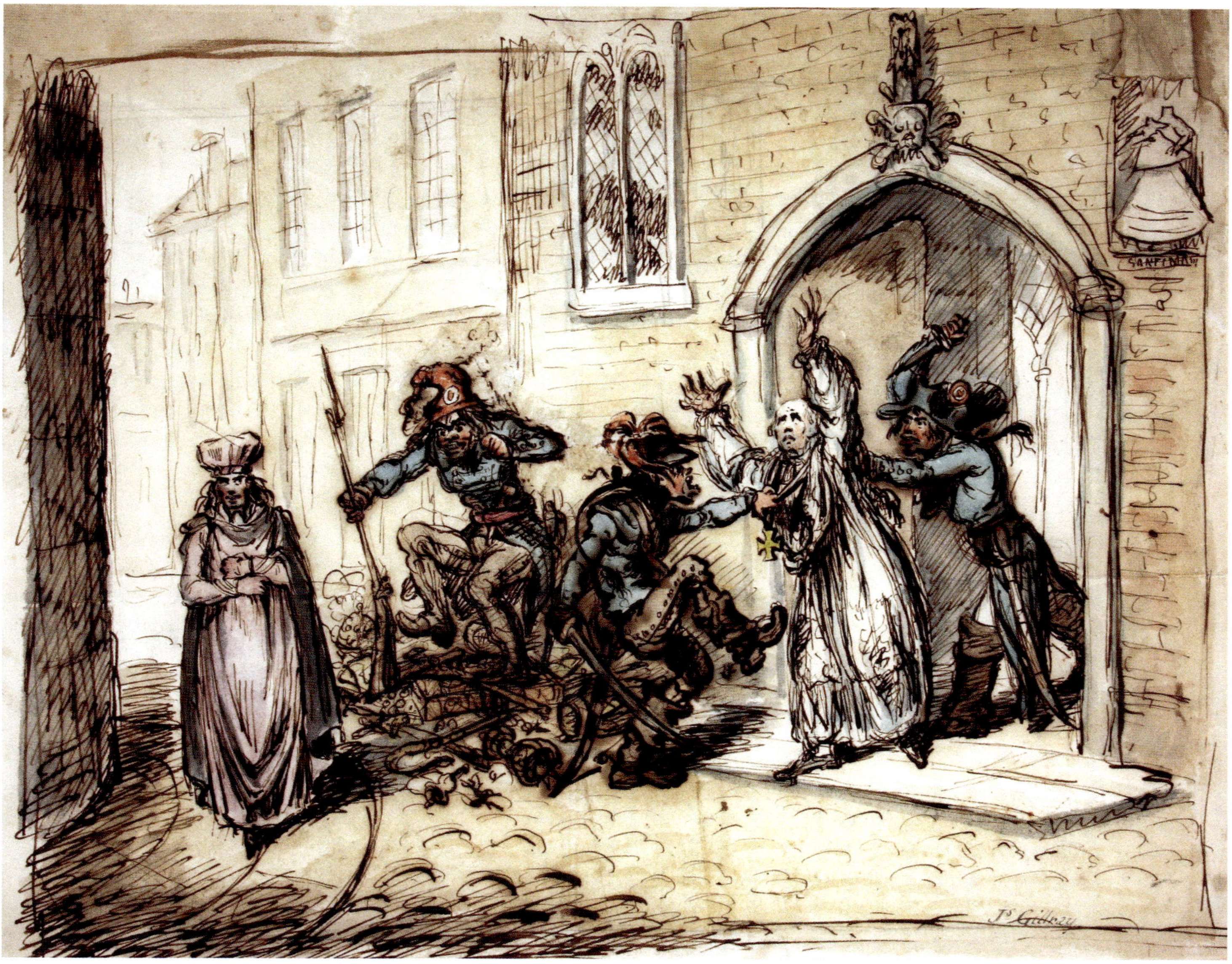
Js Gillray

118

THOMAS ROWLANDSON 1756/7–1827

The Corsican, his Two Friends and his Bloodhounds at the Window of the Tuileries looking over Paris, 1815

Pen and brown ink and watercolour over graphite on paper
23.5 × 35.8 cm
Inscribed: *The Corsican, his two friends, and his Blood Hounds / at the window of the Thuilleries Looking over Pari*, and: *MORE HORRERS DEATH HELL AND / DESTRUCTION*
Presented by Gerald Reitlinger, 1972
WA1978.47

LITERATURE: Grego (1880) II pp. 292–3; Brown (1982) no. 1620

For most of his professional life, Rowlandson loved ridiculing the French. He first visited France in 1774, while still a student at the Royal Academy Schools, and returned several times in the 1780s. His caricatures mocked all aspects of French life, from royalty to beggars, with favourite targets being the military and the clergy, as well as the eating habits of all classes.

Napoleon was an obvious target for an English caricaturist, but Rowlandson did not begin drawing him in earnest until he had himself crowned as Emperor of France in 1804. Thereafter, Napoleon's tribulations and foibles became frequent subjects. In one of Rowlandson's most memorable works, published in 1808, Napoleon is portrayed as the 'Corsican spider', sitting in the middle of his web waiting for all the countries of Europe to become ensnared. Elsewhere, he appears as the Corsican bloodhound, the Corsican toad, or the Corsican Munchausen. Increasingly, he was accompanied by a skeleton personifying Death; the two appear to great effect in *Nap and his Friends in their Glory*, with Joseph Bonaparte and the Devil drinking a toast of 'success to plunder and massacre'. Five years later Napoleon and Death appeared sitting disconsolately on the battlefield under the title *The Two Kings of Terror*.[1] With great relish, Rowlandson drew caricatures of each episode of Napoleon's discomfiture.

Following a succession of defeats by the Allied Coalition, Napoleon was deposed by the French Senate. Eventually accepting the inevitable, he was obliged to abdicate in April 1814. Under the terms of the Treaty of Fontainebleau, he was exiled to the island of Elba, but escaped on 26 February 1815. After landing in France, he rallied the army against King Louis XVIII, but after 100 days, on 18 June 1815 his forces were defeated by the allied armies under the Duke of Wellington at Waterloo.

This caricature is one of several by Rowlandson that closely follows the events after Napoleon's escape from Elba. It portrays him in Paris, on the balcony of the royal palace of the Tuileries, wearing his uniform but no orders. Standing beside him is his henchman, Marshal Ney, who had risen from lowly origins in Napoleon's army, turned against him in 1814, and recently re-joined his forces. Both men are embraced by the Devil. Death is perched on the balustrade, holding a dart dripping with blood, and looking into Napoleon's eyes, tempting him to perpetrate more horror, death, and destruction. However, the sand runs quickly through the hourglass of Time. Below, the crowds hold aloft pikes and bayonets, some skewering human heads. The drawing was published with modifications by Rudolph Ackermann on 16 April 1815. CH

1. Grego (1880) II pp. 100–1, 255–7.

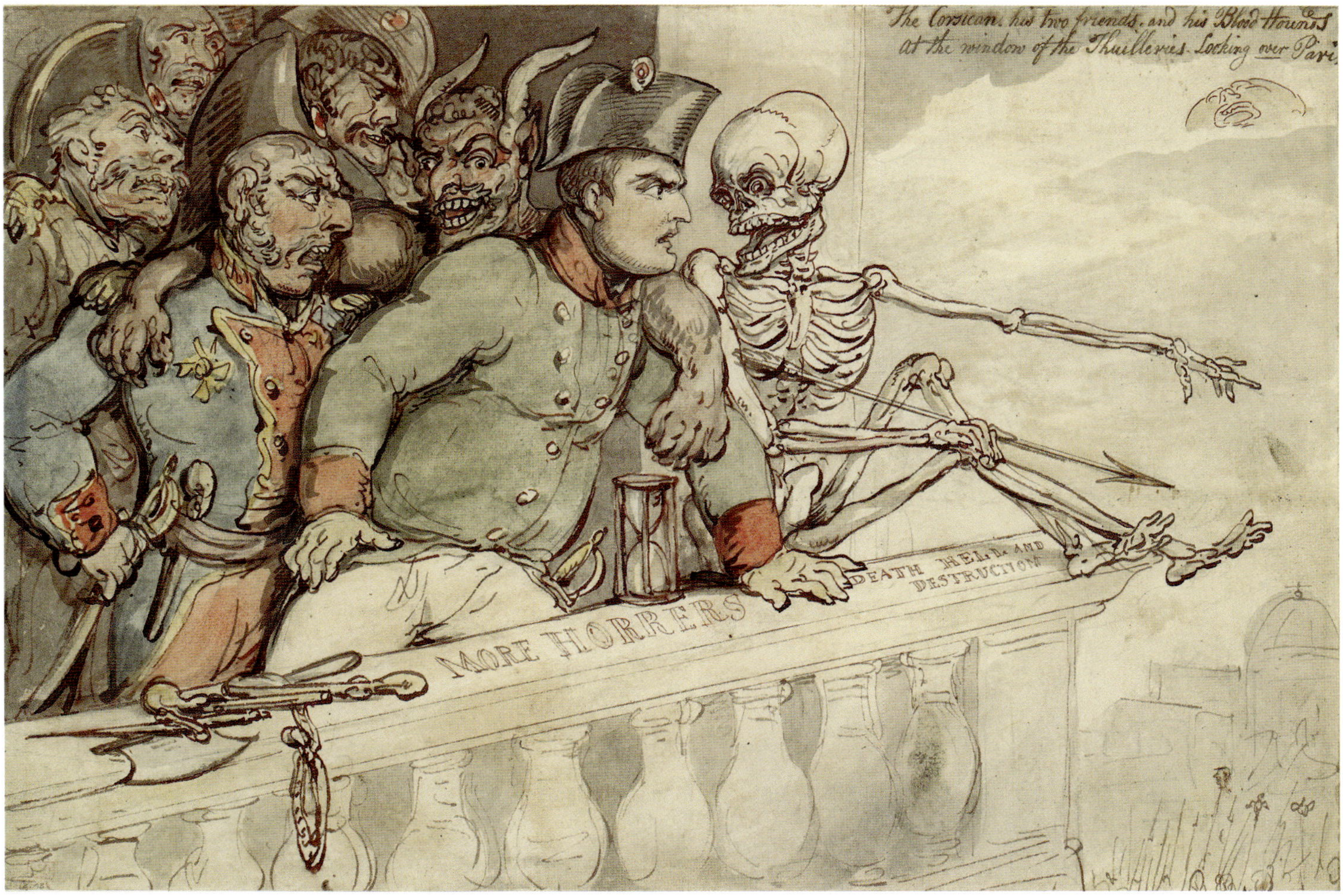
The Corsican. his two friends. and his Blood Hounds
at the window of the Thuilleries. Looking over Paris
MORE HORRERS
DEATH HELL AND DESTRUCTION

119

THOMAS ROWLANDSON 1756/7–1827

Off Spithead, or 'Cattle not Insurable', c. 1809

Pen and grey and brown inks and watercolour over indications in graphite on paper
23.7 × 34.6 cm
Purchased (Virtue-Tebbs Bequest Fund), 1963
WA1963.89.78

LITERATURE: Paulson (1972) no. 31; Brown (1982) 1603

Rowlandson produced many lively images of soldiers and sailors during the period of Napoleonic conflict. Although he was a close friend of the caricaturist James Gillray, his satire generally focused on wry social observation rather than ascerbic political comment.

Spithead is a sheltered body of water at the mouth of the Solent, between Portsmouth and the Isle of Wight, in which the Royal Navy Fleet would anchor. Here two ships await the arrival of rowing boats laden with carousing, buxom women, apparently eager to entertain the crews on board. Sailors were not permitted to go ashore when they returned to port, but 'wives' were allowed to visit them, and as the sailors received their pay when the ship docked, prostitutes needed little encouragement. When the *Royal George* foundered off Spithead in 1782, over 400 prostitutes were found below decks. In 1784 Rowlandson made a brief visit to the Isle of Wight with his friend, the painter Henry Wigstead (1760–1800), possibly to see the wreck of this ship. A less finished version of this drawing is in the Huntington Library, together with nearly 70 watercolours resulting from the trip. They may have been intended for publication with texts by Wigstead, as in the case of Rowlandson's tours to Brighton (1789) and Wales (1797).[2]

Never afraid to tackle scenes of rollicking sexuality, Rowlandson produced many semi-pornographic images. However, this scene is in a lighter vein: the woman at the centre of the boat, waving her hat and handkerchief to a man leaning out of a porthole, may well be a genuine spouse, reunited with her husband. Her handkerchief mirrors the billowing skirts of the woman scrambling up the ship's ladder, while the vast anchor above echoes the curve of her behind. There is a joyful, optimistic quality to the scene, despite the dark context of war and prostitution. The ship's figurehead is a British lion bearing the cross of St George, to which the woman on the far left appears to raise her glass in a patriotic salute.

Rowlandson's designs were widely reproduced as prints during his lifetime; within the mount of this drawing is a copy of the hand-coloured etching and aquatint published by Rudolph Ackermann in 1809 as 'Cattle not Insurable'.[3] In 1813 a cruder version was produced by William Elmes, in which barrels of 'Smugled Coniac Brandy' and 'Hollands Gin' are roped to the stern of the boat.[4] Such prints perhaps contributed to the decline in Rowlandson's reputation, proving too ribald for Victorian tastes. His work went rapidly out of fashion, and did not re-emerge as worthy of serious consideration until after the First World War. CP

1. Blake and Lawrence (2005) p. 120.
2. Wark (1975) no. 137.
3. Ashmolean Museum, WA.OA1964.
4. British Museum, 1872,1012.5035; George (1949), IX, BM Satires 12158.

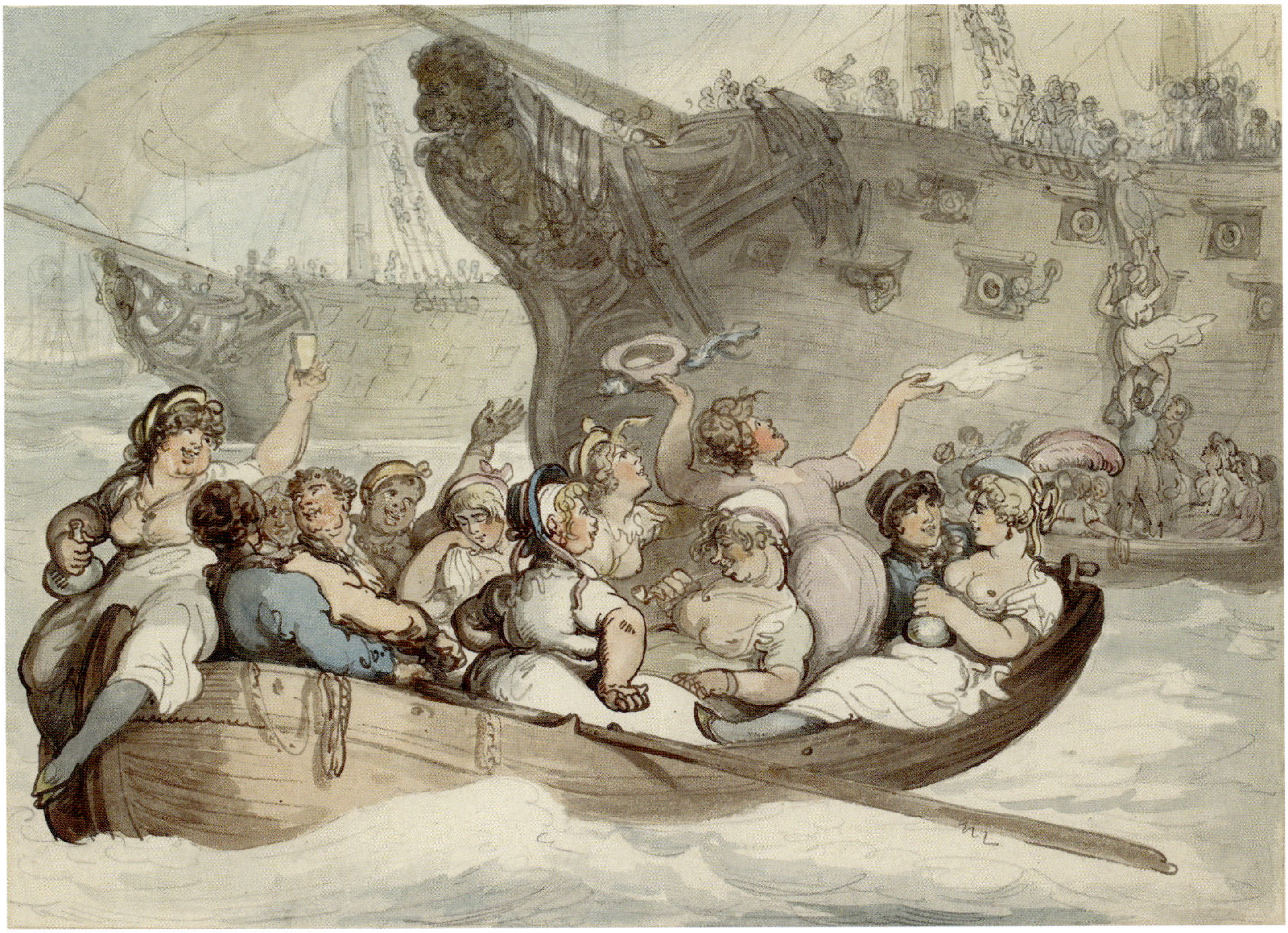

120

EDWARD LEAR 1812–1888
Nonsense Alphabet, 1862

26 sheets, pen and ink on blue paper backed with linen
31.7 × 20.5 cm (volume)
31.1 × 19.6 cm (sheet)
Open at the letter R: *R was a Rabbit / Who had a bad habit / Of eating flowers, / In gardens and bowers. / r! / Naughty fat rabbit!*
Bequeathed by James Farquharson, 2011
WA2013.24

LITERATURE: Noakes (1985) no. 81b; Hyman (1988); Harrison (2012)

It was in the 1830s, while he was staying with his great patron the 13th Earl of Derby at Knowsley Hall, that Lear began to amuse himself and the children of the household by writing nonsense verses illustrated with his own drawings (he never called them limericks). Although most of the nonsense was originally composed for specific children on specific occasions, some of the best were published as *A Book of Nonsense* in 1846, under the pseudonym Derry Down Derry, taken from a character in the medieval mummers' plays. Lear finally acknowledged his authorship publicly in the third, much expanded, edition of 1861. This was also the first to enjoy wide currency, the plates being printed from woodblocks rather than lithographic stones. He later published nonsense in other genres, notably *Nonsense Songs, Botany and Alphabets* (1871), which included for the first time 'The Owl and the Pussy Cat'.

Several of Lear's nonsense alphabets survive; six were published in the posthumous edition of *Nonsense Botany and Nonsense Alphabets* (1889). The present alphabet was made for the infant Ruth Decie. Her parents, Captain Richard Decie and his wife Bella, were stationed in the British garrison on Corfu in the winter of 1861–2, when Lear met them. He already knew Mrs Decie's parents, William and Arabella Prescott, who lived at Clarence House, Roehampton, christened 'Hospitality Hall' by Lear. William Prescott was a partner in the private bank of Prescott, Grote, Cave, and Co., and 'a hearty, gentlemanly man', the head of a 'merry & pleasant family'.[1]

Lear spent Saturday to Monday, 21 to 23 June 1862 with the Prescotts at Clarence House. He recorded in his diary for Sunday 22 that he 'rose at 6:30 & made an alphabet for the Decie baby till 9', and completed it after lunch. The first draught (now in the Houghton Library, Harvard) shows that he must have made the verses for each letter, then copied them out with rough drawings, and finally made the fair copy on blue, linen-backed writing paper after lunch. The subjects, a mixture of animals and domestic articles, would have been familiar to any child. The rabbit is particularly appealing, as he glances sidelong while naughtily munching the flowers. This alphabet, together with illustrated letters, a suite of four 'Eggstracts from the Roehampton Chronicle' and other items, became treasured family heirlooms. They passed from the Decies to James Farquharson, who in turn bequeathed them to the Ashmolean.

1. Lear, *Diary*, 22 June 1862.

R

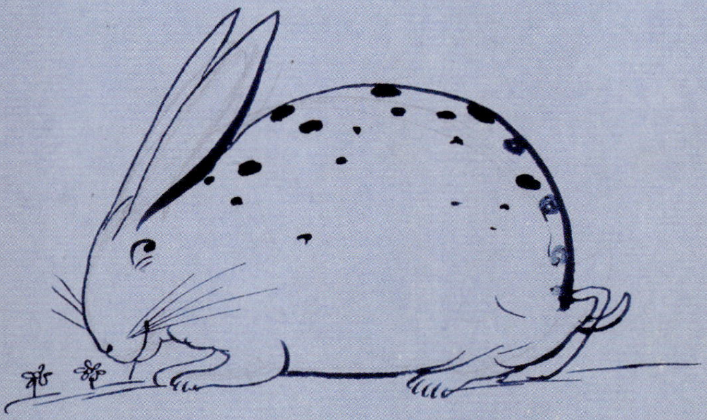

R. was a Rabbit
Who had a bad habit
Of eating the flowers,
In gardens and bowers.
r!
Naughty fat rabbit!

121

SIR EDWARD COLEY BURNE-JONES 1833–1898

Album of Illustrated Letters from Burne-Jones to Mrs Gaskell, 1893–8

Pen and ink on writing paper, mounted on to an album page
40.5 × 28 cm (page)
41 × 30.5 × 3.5 cm (album), open at fol. 3
Lent from a private collection, 2009
L11075.4

Throughout his married life, Burne-Jones maintained intense friendships with a succession of women. The last was Helen Mary Gaskell (1853–1940), known as May, whom he met in 1892. She was the wife of a cavalry officer of considerable wealth but little culture, and Burne-Jones soon became dependent on her, declaring that she had 'reached the well of loneliness that is in me'. He sent her intimate and revealing letters several times a day, and, shortly before his death, recalled 'six years of the most beautiful friendship that ever there was'. In spite of Burne-Jones's instructions to burn all their correspondence, Mrs Gaskell carefully preserved their letters. She bequeathed most of them to her surviving daughter, Daphne, because 'you who knew him will understand that they are so precious and tender and wise and witty, but not for the eye of the scoffer, or for the eye of the casual reader'.

In addition to these private and often deeply emotional letters, Burne-Jones also sent more light-hearted, illustrated letters, which Mrs Gaskell had mounted into two matching albums; a third album, containing only six letters, was given to Lord Balniel (later 28th Earl of Crawford) in 1936.[1] Their cast of characters is to some extent familiar from humorous letters written to other correspondents, notably Katie Lewis.[2] It includes the artist himself, in a series of cartoon-like tales of mishap and misadventure. Beneath the surface lies the black humour endemic to Burne-Jones's frequent moods of depression and insecurity; there is, for example, a superb sequence of caricatures of the artist suffering from flu.

One special character who appears frequently in Mrs Gaskell's letters is a fat lady with 'abominable' dress sense, whom Burne-Jones christened Julia Parkington. In this sequence, she is seen making a deep curtsey – 'as for our deportment in the presence of Royalty, I'll just trouble you to look'; remarking on a picture, her fan dangerously close to the canvas – 'we can point out the beauties of pictures with the best of them'; sleeping on a day bed, the drawing so saturated in ink that the artist wondered 'whether she will dry in time for the afternoon post'; and sleeping in a hammock. Elsewhere, she is captured walking on the cliffs at Rottingdean, near the artist's country residence, North End House, on a windy day; deliberating over propriety in the bathroom; and sitting in a very tight-fitting bath. The last is annotated by Burne-Jones, 'I like this best'. CH

1. Sold at Sotheby's, 28 November 2002, lot 27, and now in the collection of Lord Lloyd-Webber.
2. Now in the British Museum; see Christian (1988) and Christian (2011).

Ah! what have we here – this is indeed a surprise.

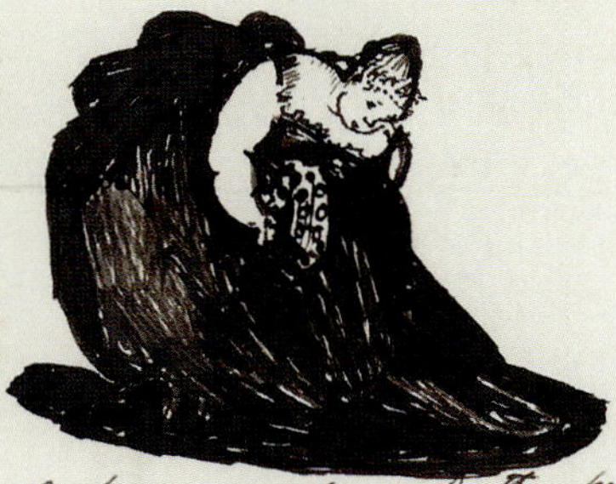

As for our deportment in the presence of Royalty I'll just trouble you to look — but I have blotted her bouquet nearly out.
Is the village of Kiddington pretty? is it of grey stone & grey stone roofing everywhere – is it a lovely village?

Tuesday 2

To-day isn't nice at all – & tomorrow will not be nice either – & I am dull – it is all so different to yesterday & I am quite spoilt – quite.

THE GRANGE.
49, NORTH END ROAD.
WEST KENSINGTON, W.

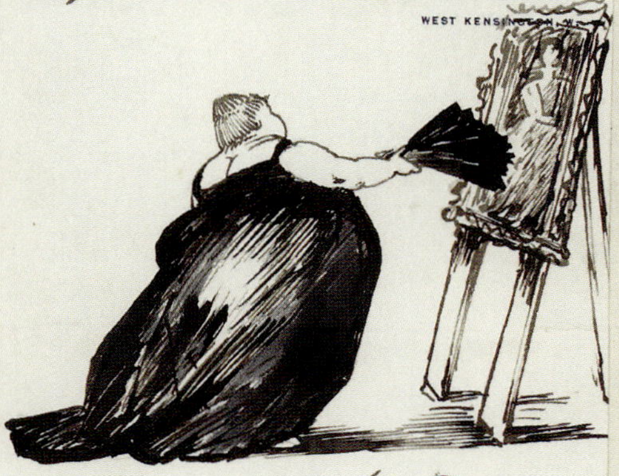

but can point out the beauties of pictures with the best of them –

Evening
I am dictating letters to Miss Anderson and while she folds up letters & seals them I can send a little word to you. She has just come from Brantwood & tells me all about my blessed Ruskin – & on the whole I am glad I didn't go away from you

Tuesday. 1

I wonder whether she will dry in time for the afternoon post – and after all the people came while I was out, & my telegram missed them – I could easily have gone to Oxford with you

THE GRANGE.
49, NORTH END ROAD.
WEST KENSINGTON, W.

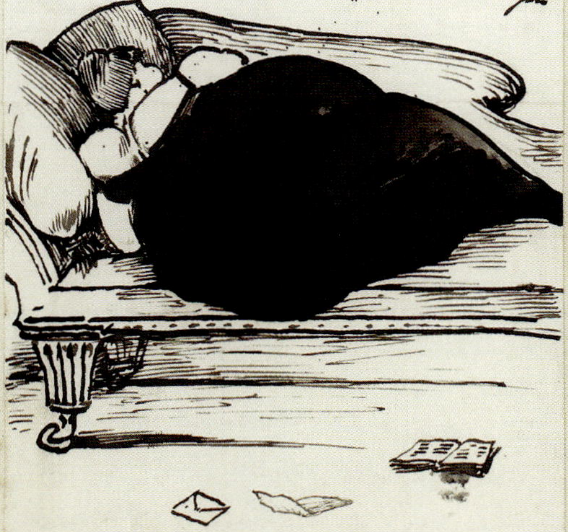

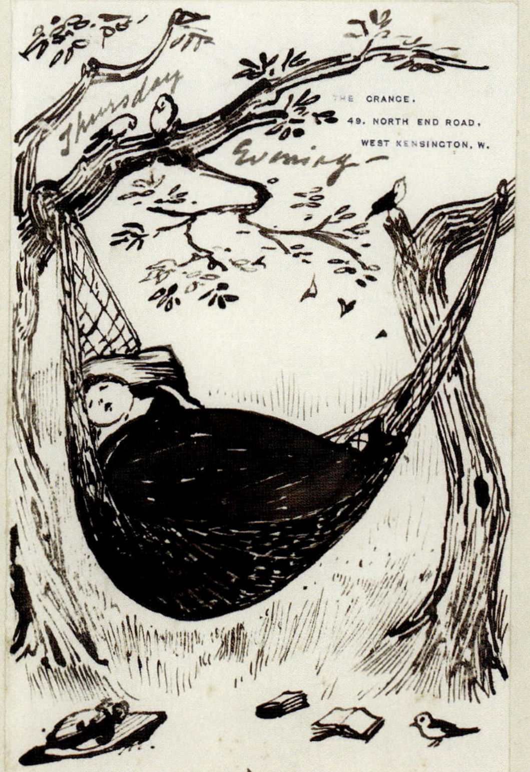

122

SIR EDWARD COLEY BURNE-JONES 1833–1898

Daphne's Album, open at a letter including a self-portrait of Burne-Jones with a cat, 1893–8

Pen and blue ink on writing paper
17.7 × 22.5 cm (letter)
27.5 × 37.5 × 4 cm (volume)
Lent from a private collection, 2009
L11075.5

Daphne Gaskell (1887–1964) was the younger daughter of May Gaskell (see cat. 121). Her elder sister, Amy (1874–1910) was a haunting beauty whose portrait Burne-Jones painted in 1893–4.[1] Daphne was only six when she met the artist, and he took an affectionate and fatherly interest in her, sending numerous letters written in phonetic spelling, and illustrated with whimsical birds and animals, including such fantastic inventions as the 'phlumbudge', the 'paddiflab', the 'flapdabble' and the 'grabblethwacker'. Burne-Jones greatly disliked dogs, and in one rather gruesome letter he complains of being kept awake by a dog barking, so that he was obliged to get dressed and take a 'choper' to it. The question he asked Daphne was, inevitably, what should he do with the pieces – 'I think of sending to have them made up for sossidges for some horsepittle'.

On the other hand, Burne-Jones was very fond of cats. The text of this letter refers to the Gaskell family cat, Thomas.

Darlink dafny

i foregot to say i do want a cat but I think i want a fat hevy tabby chap like Tommus, how is Tommus by the by? and i think persian pusseys are delikit and i want a heavy fellow with a face like a poik py and waying many pounds with being tite and fat so that when it sits on my lapp it will feel hevy and rest me because it is a nice felink to be sat upon and I should like to rest in a armchar like this and have a hevy cat crecher sitting all up me and perring. Now i must conclewd dear and i send you my love.

Your efxiontate B. J.

In later life, Daphne Gaskell married Frank Rose (1874–1914). He was the son of Sir Charles Rose of Hardwick House, Oxfordshire (1874–1913), a politician and keen motorist, who was one of the models for Mr Toad in Kenneth Grahame's *The Wind in the Willows* (1908). Shortly after succeeding as second baronet, Daphne's husband was killed in action at Ypres. CH

1. Now in the collection of Lord Lloyd-Webber; London (2003) no. 50.

i want a heavy felow
with a face like
a poik pig - and
waying many pounds
with being tite and
fat so that when
it sits on my lapp
it will feel hevy
and rest me becausa
it is a nice felink
to be sat upon

I should like to
rest in a arm chair
like this

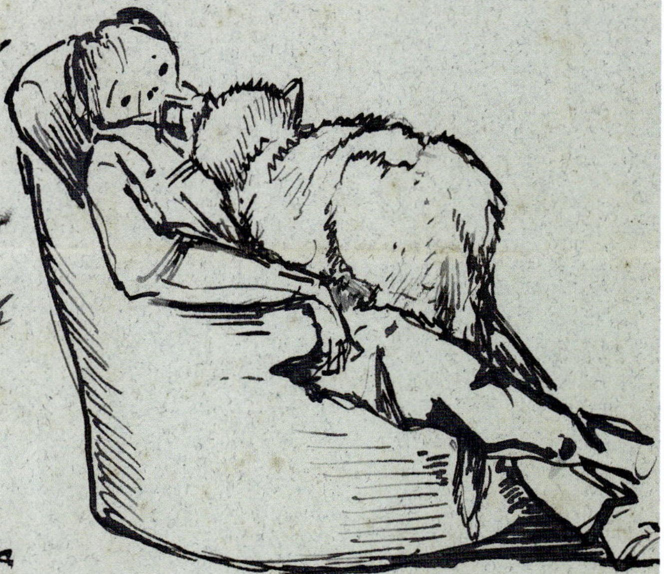

and have a hevy
cat crecher sitting

123

SIR MAX BEERBOHM 1872–1956

Oscar Wilde, 1894

Pen and black ink on off-white paper
30.9 × 19.1 cm
Signed: *Max*. Inscribed: *Oscar Wilde*
Presented by Mrs Philip Guedalla, 1945
WA1945.1

LITERATURE: Hart-Davis (1972) no. 1779; Hall (1997) pp. 18–9

Beerbohm was an undergraduate at Merton College, Oxford, when he first met Oscar Wilde (1854–1900) in 1890. Their relationship blossomed through a circle of mutual friends, among them Robert Ross and Reginald Turner. The Irish writer was rising to the height of his fame as the author of short stories and criticism. A succession of plays, culminating in *The Importance of Being Earnest*, which opened on 14 February 1895, consolidated his reputation as the wittiest man in London. Beerbohm's first publication was an article on 'Oscar Wilde by an American' in 1893; it elicited flattering comments from the subject, who called him, 'incomparably brilliant ... he knew no other undergraduate who could have written it'.[1] At the same time Beerbohm was publishing his first caricatures, and he contributed both essays and caricatures to such periodicals as *The Yellow Book* and *Sketch*. The appearance in 1896 of collections of essays as *The Works of Max Beerbohm* and of drawings as *Caricatures of Twenty-Five Gentlemen* confirmed his accomplishments in both areas.

This caricature of Wilde was published in *Pick-me-Up* magazine on 22 September 1894. Drawn in the thin, nervous, swirling line of Beerbohm's earliest drawings, it portrays Wilde in a bejewelled shirt front and ring and with an extravagant buttonhole; his features puffy and his hair unfashionably long. In private, Beerbohm was not uncritical of his friend; he wrote to Turner in April 1893 that, 'I am sorry to say that Oscar drinks far more than he ought ... he has deteriorated very much in appearance: his cheeks being quite a dark purple and fat to a fault'.[2] Although he always maintained, somewhat disingenuously, that 'caricature implies no moral judgement on the subject ... it eschews any kind of symbolism, tells no story, deals with no matter but the personal appearance of its subject', Beerbohm came to regret his first and most famous portrayal of Wilde.[3] Many years later, he wrote that it 'showed only the worst side of his nature ... I hardly realised what a cruel thing it was: I only realised that after Oscar's tragedy and downfall'.[4] CH

1. Quoted in Hall (1997) p. 17.
2. *Ibid.*
3. Hall (1997) pp. 15–16.
4. Hall (1997) p. 19.

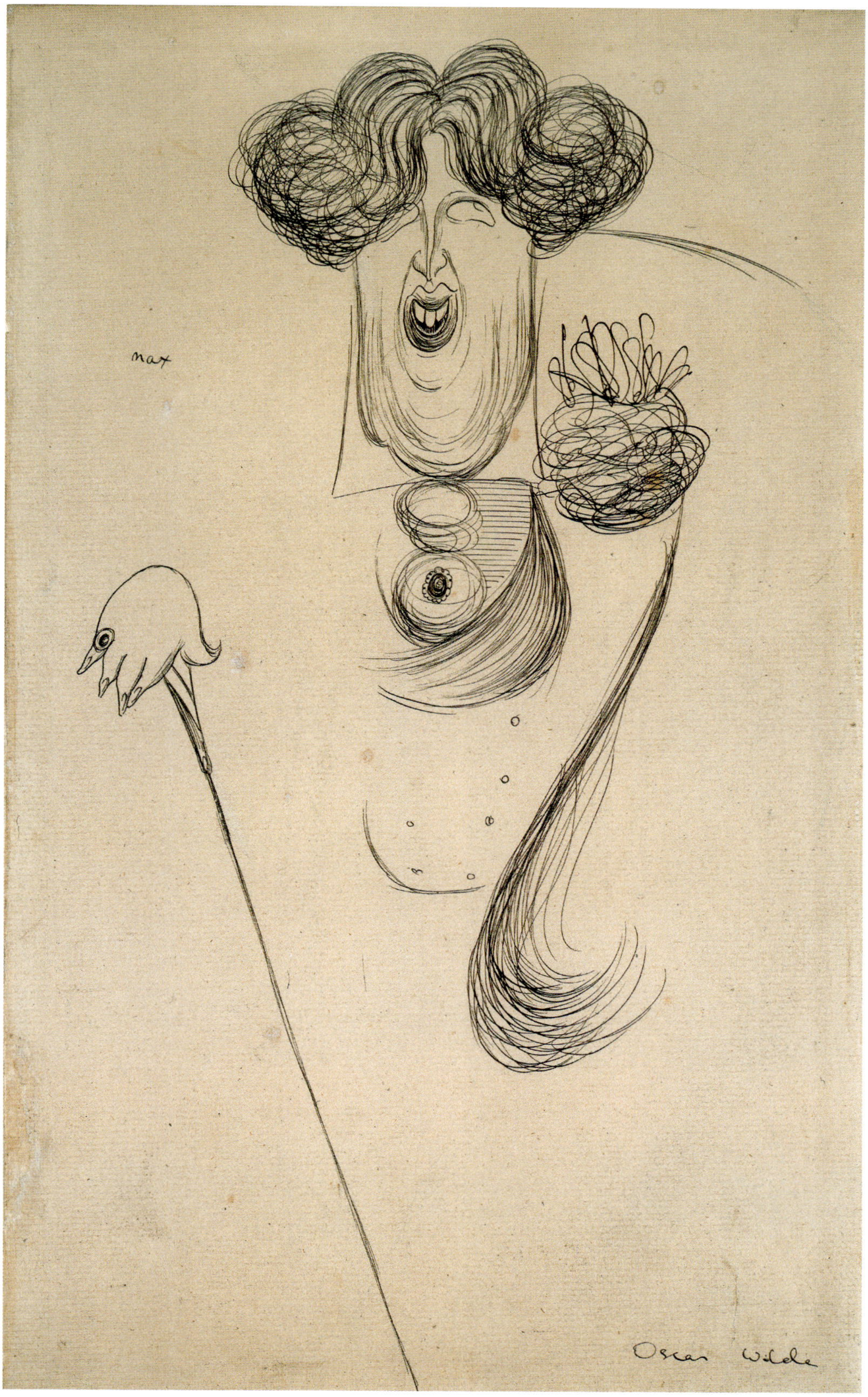
max
Oscar Wilde

124

SIR MAX BEERBOHM 1872–1956

Mr G. K. Chesterton, 1912

Watercolour, black chalk and graphite on off-white paper
32.5 × 21.4 cm
Presented by Mrs Philip Guedalla, 1945
WA1945.47

LITERATURE: Hart-Davis (1972) no. 312; Hall (1997) pp. 55–6

By 1912, when this caricature was drawn, Gilbert Keith Chesterton (1874–1936) had become one of the most recognisable writers in England. The author of apparently innumerable essays, he had also published several novels, ranging from *The Napoleon of Notting Hill* (1904) and *The Man who was Thursday* (1908) to *The Innocence of Father Brown* (1911), the first collection of stories featuring the Roman Catholic priest whose insignificant appearance belies extraordinary powers of observation and deduction. Having been slim in his youth, Chesterton had become notoriously obese. Encouraged by his wife, he adopted extravagant dress, habitually wearing a huge cloak and wide-brimmed hat. He frequented the taverns of Fleet Street with his pockets stuffed full of books and papers, somewhat in the guise of a latter-day Dr Johnson.

Even before Chesterton had become famous, Beerbohm went out of his way to meet him. He wrote in 1902 of an

Enormous apparition. Head big for body – way of sinking head on chest. Like a mountain and a volcanic one – constant streams of talk flowing down, paradoxes flung up in the air – very magnificent.[1]

This caricature exemplifies his view that

The perfect caricature (be it of a handsome man or a hideous or an insipid) must be the exaggeration of the whole creature, from top to toe. Whatsoever is salient must be magnified, whatsoever is subordinate must be proportionately diminished. The whole man must be melted down, as in a crucible, and then, as from the solution, be fashioned anew. He must emerge with not one particle of himself lost, yet with not a particle of himself as it was before. And he will stand there wholly transformed, the joy of his creator, the joy of those who are privy to the art of caricature. … The perfect caricature is not a mere snapshot, it is the epitome of its subject's surface, the presentment (once and for all) of his most characteristic pose, gesture, expression.[2]

Chesterton is seen in all his magnificent corpulence at the dinner table, smoking a cigar but apparently before the food and wine have been served. Great folds of flesh are scarcely contained by his suit, while his waistcoat is far from meeting the top of his trousers, revealing his straining braces. In keeping with the subject, the style of the drawing is smooth and round, with wash carefully applied only to the figure. This caricature was published in the *Bystander* for 24 July 1912. CH

1. Quoted in Hall (1997) p. 55.
2. Quoted in Hall (1997) p. 15.

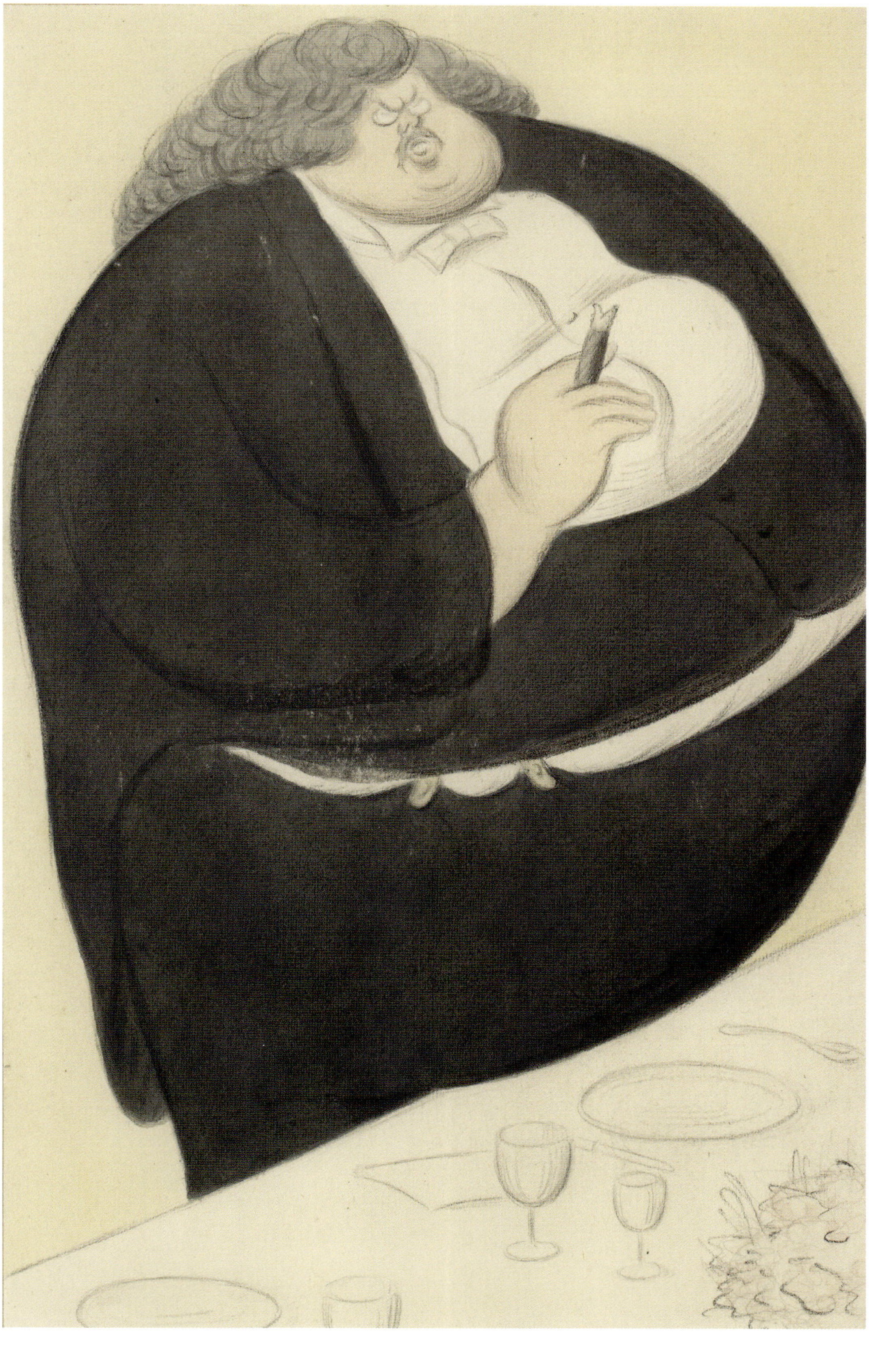

125

SIR WILLIAM NEWENHAM MONTAGUE ORPEN 1878–1931

Seeing Himself as Others See Him: A Caricature of Kaiser Wilhelm II, 1919

Pen and brush and black ink with wash, over graphite indications on paper
30 × 20 cm
Inscribed: *Seeing himself as others see him / 28.6.19*
Purchased, 1964
WA1964.54.2

LITERATURE: Konody and Dark (1932) pl. XII, p. 58; Upstone (2005) p. 39

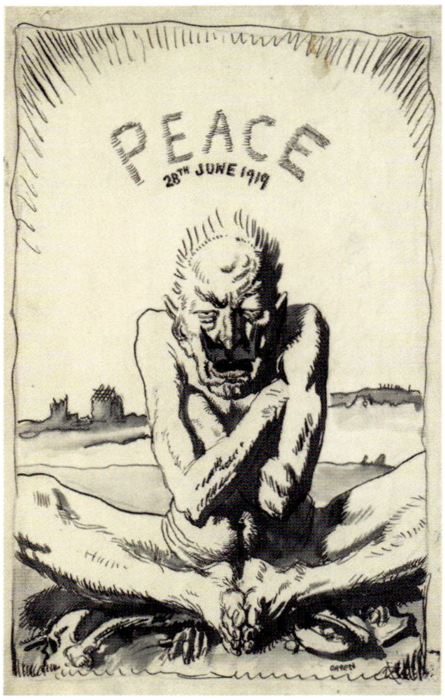

Fig. 66 | Sir William Newenham Montague Orpen (1878–1931), *Peace, 28th June 1919: Caricature of Kaiser Wilhelm II*, 1919. Pen and brush and blue ink on paper. Ashmolean Museum, WA1964.54.1

A product of the Slade School, where he was a close contemporary of Augustus and Gwen John, the Irish painter William Orpen was appointed an official war artist in 1916 and visited the Western Front in April 1917. His early idealism turned to disillusionment as a result of his bitter wartime experiences on the Somme, and the powerful paintings he produced – devastated battlefield landscapes, portraits of fighting men, and haunting victims of shell-shock – convey his horror. An exhibition of his work for the Ministry of Information was held at Agnew's in spring 1918, simply entitled 'War'.

Orpen created a number of caricatures of Kaiser Wilhelm, including one of him as the Devil stalking abroad (1914; private collection). Here he uses the Kaiser's nakedness to emphasise his vulnerability, though the crouching figure, like some grotesquely aged and moustachioed foetus, has a threatening coiled strangeness to it – reminiscent of Japanese Netsuke carvings or the nightmarish figures of Hieronymus Bosch. Orpen felt enormous empathy for those damaged by the war, and his anger is reflected in the savagery of this image. Yet his prints and drawings of German prisoners of war (many in the Imperial War Museum) acknowledge their humanity and show great sympathy for their plight.

A second caricature drawing in the Ashmolean collection, inscribed *PEACE / 28th June 1919*, was used as a poster for the *News of the World* (fig. 66). This shows an emaciated, shivering Kaiser sitting cross-legged in the manner of an Indian *sadhu*, or holy man, on a pile of bones; it may be that the prickly bed of graveyard crosses in the present drawing was also intended to evoke an Indian mystic's bed of nails. The drawings employ the same paper, medium and style of border, so were undoubtedly produced for the same commission, marking the signing of the Treaty of Versailles.

Propaganda was a vital part of the war effort, and many talented artists contributed. The liberal politician Charles Masterman (1873–1927), in charge of the War Propaganda Bureau from August 1914, declared 'It is absurdly difficult to explain ... why any particular piece of propaganda is desirable ... Every little piece of it easily looks ridiculous; it is only by the concentrated effect of all that the result we desire is obtained.'[1] Far from appearing ridiculous, this drawing still carries a powerful emotive charge that transcends its original political context. CP

1. Quoted in Harries (1983) p. 77.

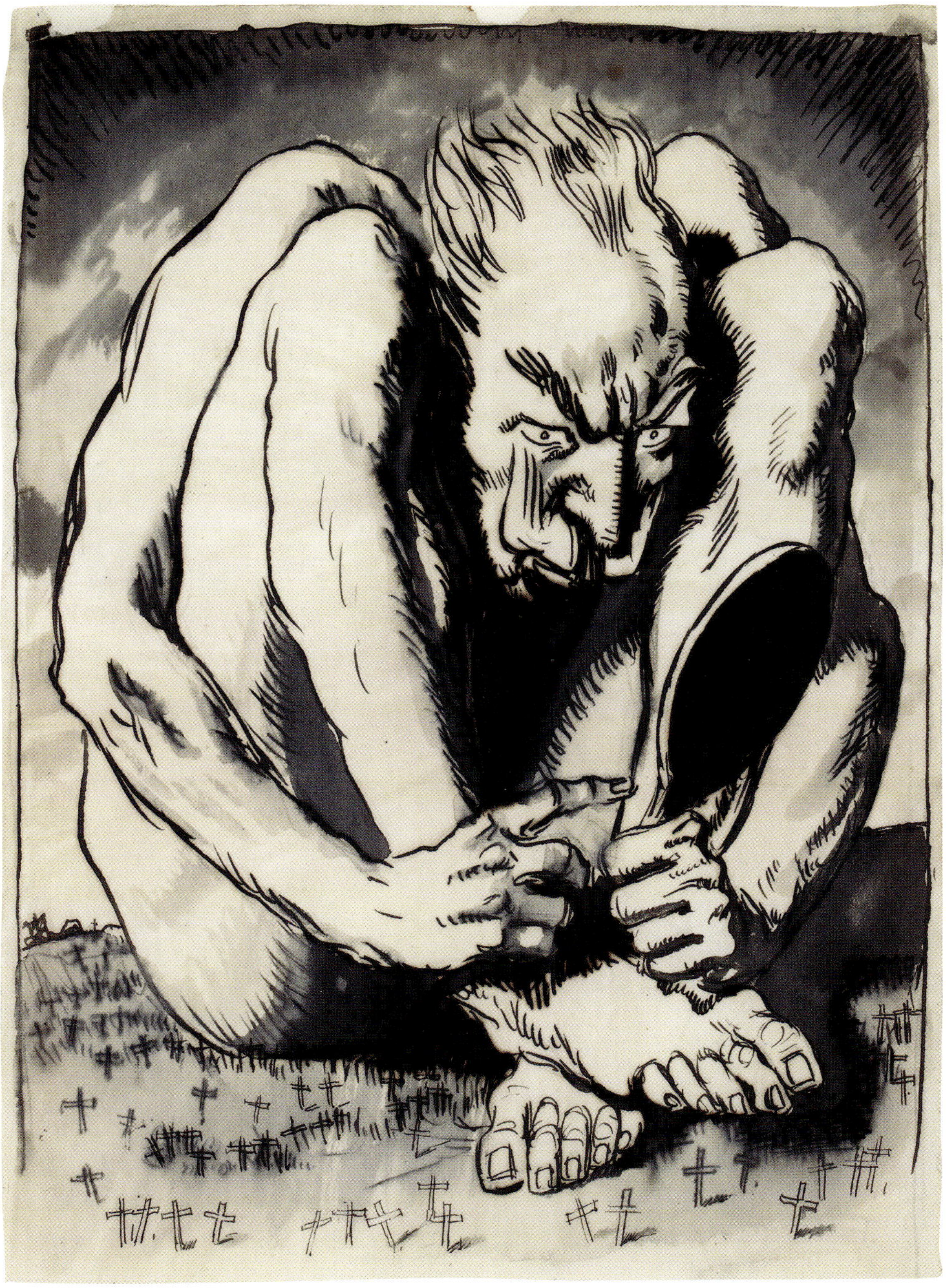

126

SIR DAVID ALEXANDER CECIL LOW 1891–1963

Max, Lord Beaverbrook, 1926

Black crayon and white bodycolour over graphite on paper
43.1 × 31.2 cm
Signed: *Low*. Inscribed: *Max, Lord Beaverbrook*.
Purchased (Dr John Fuggles Bequest Fund), 2003
WA2003.130

LITERATURE: National Portrait Gallery (1985–86) no. 74; Mumford (2002) no. 88

Born in New Zealand, Low moved to London in 1919 and joined the *Star* as a political cartoonist. In October 1927 the Canadian-born Lord Beaverbrook, proprietor of the *Evening Standard*, persuaded Low to join his staff, and Low was to work for him until 1950, despite his cartoons often opposing the Conservative policies that Beaverbrook espoused. Winston Churchill described Low as a 'green-eyed ... Antipodean radical, a master of black and white; he is the Charlie Chaplin of caricature'.[1] Although chiefly remembered for his character 'Colonel Blimp', Low's proudest achievement was probably his anti-Appeasement and anti-Nazi cartoons of the 1930s.

This caricature of William Maxwell 'Max' Aitken, first Lord Beaverbrook (1879–1964), was published in a supplement to the *New Statesman* on 27 March 1926. It also appeared as the frontispiece to A. J. P. Taylor's biography of Beaverbrook (1972), as according to Taylor it was the best likeness of all his portraits. Beaverbrook was a business tycoon, Conservative MP (1910–7) and peer. Appointed Minister of Information in the last months of the First World War, he was responsible for Allied propaganda together with Charles Masterman, and created the British War Memorials Committee. In 1940 Winston Churchill brought him into the War Cabinet, where he held a number of important posts before being appointed Lord Privy Seal (1943–5).

Low produced two series of caricatures of politicians for the *New Statesman* in 1926 and 1933, of which Lord Beaverbrook considered those of Lloyd George as a 'lovable cherubic little chap' to be some of the best.[2] Low emphasised the salient points of each subject's character; in his image of Beaverbrook he reveals his impish propensity to stir up trouble, a hint of malicious puckishness in his over-wide grin and elfin pointed shoes. The dynamic Beaverbrook had a reputation as an unscrupulous master of intrigue, and A. J. P. Taylor described him as 'a clever restless little boy always up to mischief'.[3]

Some of Low's most characteristic work is in ink applied with a brush. Here, however, he demonstrates equal facility in his use of black crayon, although his caricatures are always underpinned by careful drawing in graphite beneath. White bodycolour, or possibly process white, is applied to highlight the telephone mouthpiece, all-important to the newspaper proprietor for barking orders through to his editors and journalists. His fellow cartoonist Ronald Searle has expressed admiration for Low's sureness of touch, but Ralph Steadman considered him to lack the viciousness of a Gillray. For Steadman, Low was always 'the insider playing the maverick, hand-in-glove with Lord Beaverbrook'.[4] CP

1. Mumford (2002) p. 11.
2. Ashmolean Museum; WA2008.34–8.
3. Reynolds (2014) pp. 168–9.
4. Mumford (2002) pp. 16–7.

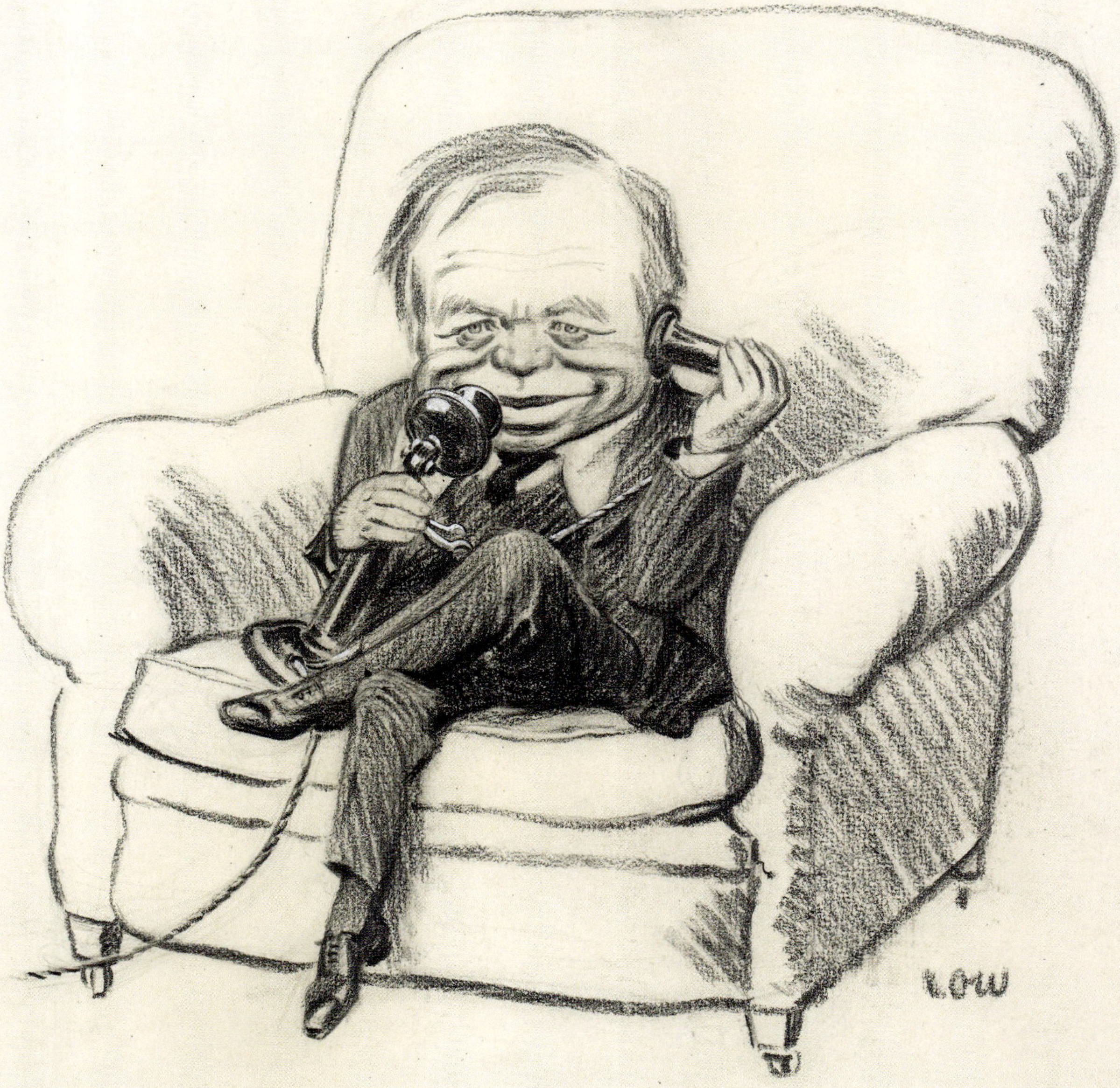

Max, Lord Beaverbrook.

127

ERNEST HOWARD SHEPARD 1879–1976

The Pre-Raphaelite Cocktail Party, 1934

Pen and Indian ink and white bodycolour over pencil with scratching out on board
26.9 × 37.9 cm
Signed: *Ernest H. Shepard*
Inscribed: '*The Pre-Raphaelite Cocktail Party*' (*a thought that came to our artist after visiting the William Morris centenary exhibition*)
Purchased with funds bequeathed by Miss Elizabeth Woods, 2003
WA2003.328

Shepard was conventionally educated at the Royal Academy Schools, but always hoped to work for the satirical magazine *Punch*. His first drawing was accepted in 1906, but it was not until 1914 that he became a regular contributor. In 1921 he was finally appointed as a member of staff. This position required him to produce at least one humorous drawing for each weekly issue, and assured him of a regular income. It was through his contributions to *Punch* that he came to the attention of the author A. A. Milne (1882–1956). They collaborated on a volume of children's verses, published in 1925 as *When we were Very Young*. This was quickly followed by the first of the immortal volumes featuring a stuffed bear of very little brain, his young owner Christopher Robin, and a group of finely characterised animal friends. *Winnie the Pooh* appeared in 1926 and was an instant success, with Shepard's illustrations perfectly complementing Milne's whimsical stories. As early as 1927 Milne could write that 'Anybody who has heard of me has certainly heard of Shepard. Indeed our names have been associated on so many title pages that I am beginning to wonder which of us is which'.[1]

In spite of this fame, Shepard continued to work for *Punch*, and was promoted second cartoonist in 1935. His subjects were very familiar to the artist and his middle-class readers, and dealt with the domestic difficulties of children, servants, and the rapid changes in society after the First World War. A number of the cartoons portray historical subjects, though Shepard exploited this vein most intensively in the volumes he illustrated for George Bell, *Everybody's Pepys* (1926), *Everybody's Boswell* (1930), and *Everybody's Lamb* (1933). Occasionally, his work was inspired by a current exhibition, for example the cartoon published in *Punch* on 9 February 1927. Entitled 'Maniers en Moden: The Effect of the Exhibition of Flemish Pictures', it illustrated the Royal Academy's 'Exhibition of Belgian and Flemish Art 1300–1900'.

The Pre-Raphaelite Cocktail Party was reproduced in *Punch* on 28 February 1934. As the inscription makes clear, it was prompted by a visit to the exhibition celebrating the centenary of the birth of William Morris at the Victoria and Albert Museum, an event opened by the former Prime Minister, Stanley Baldwin, on 9 February 1934. The idea may owe something to Beerbohm's cartoons of *Rossetti and his Circle* (1922). Among the figures incongruously participating in this thoroughly modern form of entertainment are Morris and his wife, Jane Burden, and Dante Gabriel Rossetti and his wife, Elizabeth Siddal. As Shepard wrote on a preparatory study for this drawing, 'I am now come to the conclusion perhaps as well that cocktail parties were not the thing in artistic circles 40 years ago'.[2] CH

1. Shepard (1927) 'Introduction'.
2. Private collection; with the Maas Gallery, 2012.

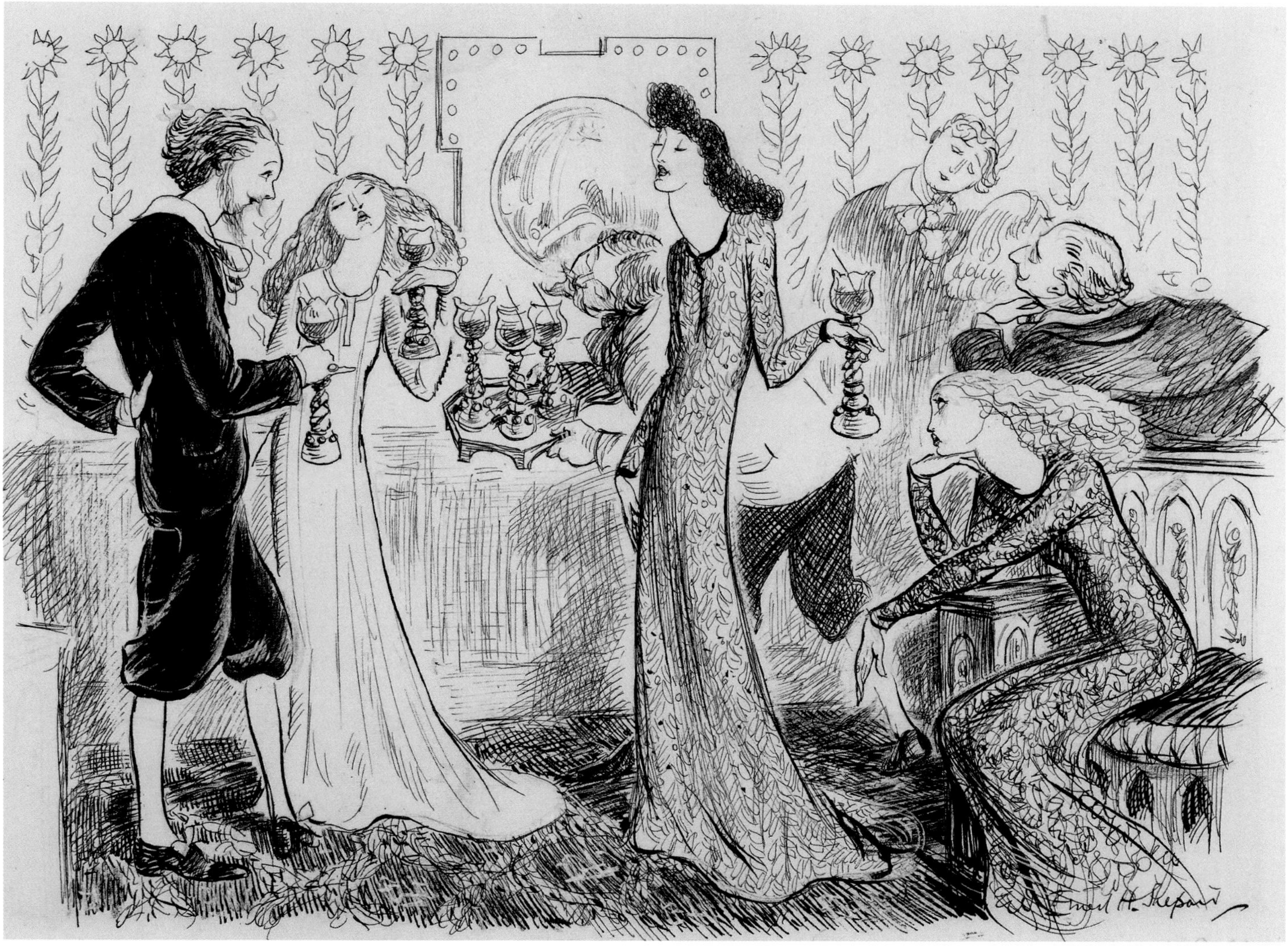
Ernest H. Shepard

128

EDWARD JEFFREY IRVING ARDIZZONE 1900–1979

Diary of a Visit to Dieppe: Sketchbook 12, 1950

Pen and ink and wash on paper
25.7 × 19.6 × 1.6 cm (volume), open at fol. 29
Inscribed: *Dieppe with / David & Barnett Freedman*
Accepted by HM Government in lieu of Inheritance Tax and allocated to the Ashmolean Museum, 1994
WA1994.87

LITERATURE: Clemence and Ardizzone (2000) no. 46

In 1994 the Ashmolean Museum received 64 sketchbooks by Ardizzone, an extraordinary wealth of material by this gifted draughtsman. These date from 1940 to 1979 and contain thousands of lively sketches in graphite, pen and ink, and watercolour depicting beach scenes, public house and law court interiors, together with figure studies and portraits. They also include preparatory ideas for some of Ardizzone's book illustrations. The good humour of his work and the ease of his penmanship are both reminiscent of Rowlandson.

Occasionally, Ardizzone kept a form of visual diary, as during his wartime stay in Southsea or his visit to the west of Ireland in 1958.[1] This sketchbook of 1950 is an especially whimsical record of a short trip to Dieppe with his brother David and the artist Barnett Freedman, a teacher at the Royal College of Art and Ruskin School in Oxford. The visit seems to have entailed much bibulous over-indulgence; even before the trio leave the cross-Channel ferry they 'Drink much whisky in the bar so arrive rather elated' (fol. 25). There follows a detailed list of gastronomic delights, such as a 'mountain' of mussels, lobster mayonnaise, duck terrine *trufflé*, and roast pigeon with garlic toast – in addition to the landlady's fine kidneys (*rognons*). Here we see folios 28 *verso* and 29, towards the end of their stay. The diary closes with all three walking by the sea under the cliffs of Dieppe, silhouetted against a spectacular sunset.

The contrast with Ardizzone's earlier visit to the Normandy coastline could not be more telling. Appointed an official war artist in February 1940, he worked with the British Expeditionary Force, travelling through North Africa, Sicily, and Italy. Joining the Allied forces on 12 June 1944, he landed at Sword Beach near Caen, to the west of Dieppe. Ardizzone spent his first night lying 'cold as the grave' in a collapsing foxhole under bombardment, before hitch-hiking inland as far as Bayeux and back.[2] As a fellow war artist, Freedman had also been in northern France just after D-Day (6 June 1944) to record scenes around the landing beaches and at the invasion headquarters. Just six years later they are watching fireworks rather than shells exploding on the French coast, and being warned of the grave dangers to health of taking snuff. CP

1. Ashmolean Museum; no. 46, WA1994.118 and no. 26, WA1994.100.
2. Ardizzone (1974) pp. 125–30, especially p. 126.

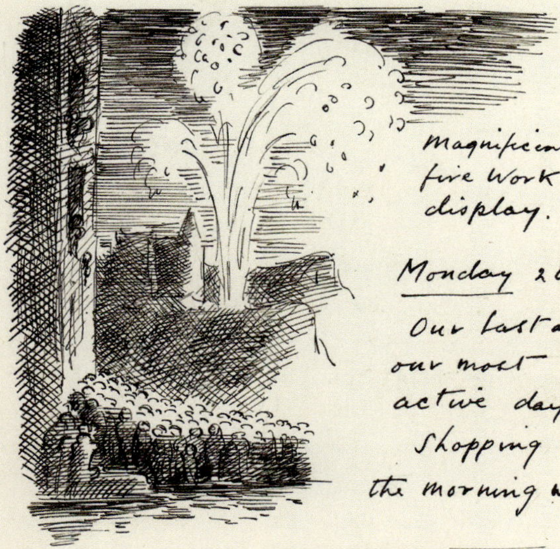

Magnificent
fire Work
display.

Monday 28st

Our last and
our most
active day.
Shopping in
the morning with
an amusing interlude
in an antique shop.
David + Barnett
buy various
objects and we
are treated to
Old Calvados by
the proprietor +
his Wife.

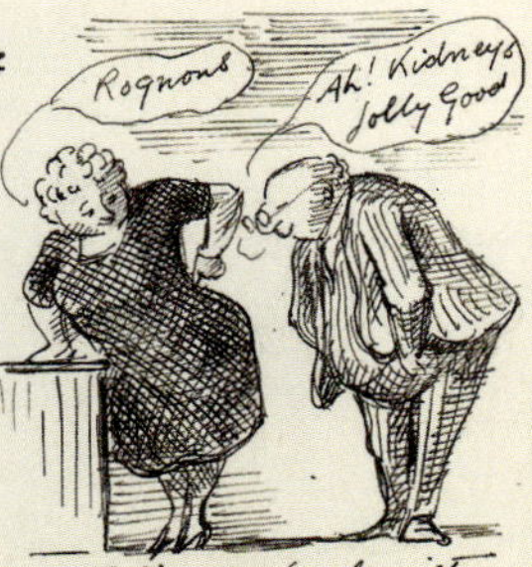

Barnett discusses lunch with
Mademoiselle Elaine

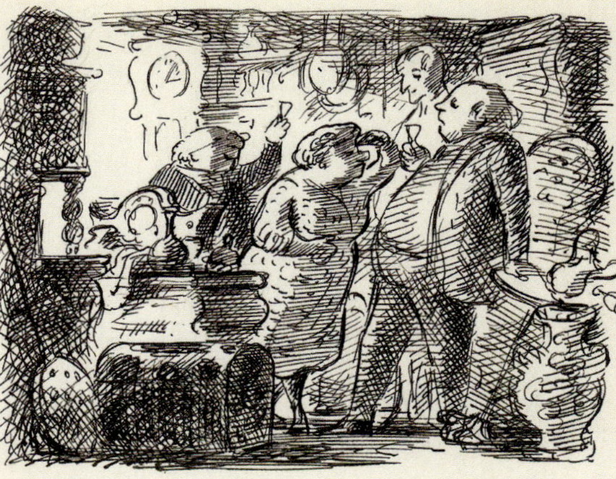

The Wife told me with such
assurance that my snuff would
collect in a ball behind my forehead
and destroy my wits, that I felt
quite alarmed.

The Rognons for
lunch were
delicious

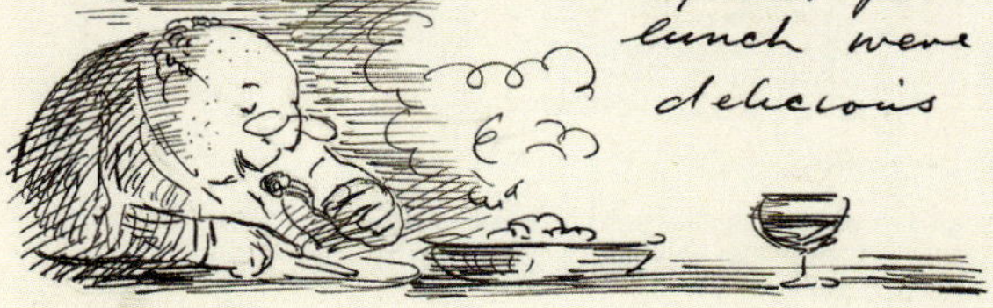

129

EDWARD JEFFREY IRVING ARDIZZONE 1900–1979

A Homage to Jock Cumberlege, c. 1955

Pen and ink and watercolour over graphite on paper
21.8 × 29.5 cm
Signed: *E. Ardizzone.* Inscribed: *To Jock Cumberlege in gratitude for his courage & perspicacity in being Tim's first publisher / Alas I can't get all my characters in, but I hope you will recognise those that are there – Ted. / 5555*
Presented by Geoffrey Cumberlege, 2000
WA2000.126
© The Estate of Edward Ardizzone

LITERATURE: Clemence and Ardizzone (2000) no. 17; Taylor (2000) pp. 81–92

Best known for illustrating books for children, Edward Ardizzone is in fact far broader in the range of his draughtsmanship. The Ashmolean collection has, for instance, three war-related watercolours and a series of pen and ink studies for the Gospels.[1] Ardizzone's formal training – consisting of evening classes at Westminster School of Art under Bernard Meninsky (1891–1950) – was minimal, and the distinctive personal style he evolved through constant repetition and practice altered little through his lifetime. As his daughter Christianna describes, Ardizzone was a compulsive doodler and sketcher, though he preferred (like Cruikshank and Daumier) to create his illustrations not from life, but from his head, storing up a visual dictionary of pictorial ideas and 'symbols for forms'.[2]

This drawing was created as a gift for Ardizzone's American publisher Geoffrey 'Jock' Cumberlege, to whom he owed publication of his first 'Little Tim' story by Oxford University Press in 1936. It shows the prolific illustrator welcoming some of his best-known characters into his first-floor studio at 130 Elgin Avenue, much to the alarm of his cat. Peering over the edge of the drawing board in typically cheeky fashion is Tim's friend Ginger. Tim and Lucy take centre stage, with Lucy's kindly guardian Mr Grimes, his housekeeper Mrs Smawley, and Charlotte to their right. Captain McFee, Joey Adze, the ship's carpenter, and the second mate are entering far right. The gaze exchanged between Tim and 'Uncle Ted' is one of great affection.

Ardizzone sits on a raised dais normally used for posing an artist's model, in front of his tilted drawing board – just as in a profile self-portrait that immediately follows the 'Visit to Dieppe' in Sketchbook 12 (cat. 128).[3] Demonstrating Ardizzone's typical technique, the flowing calligraphic lines in black ink are confidently improvised with a nibbed pen over loosely applied, soft watercolour washes, covering a faint tonal underdrawing in hard graphite. This drawing balances line and colour in a way that Ardizzone complained was difficult to achieve in reproduction, as colour printing techniques entailed creating a separate black line drawing on a transparent overlay. He emphasised the value of original works that united the two elements, permitting a last-minute accenting and balancing of the composition, or 'working over', which added depth to the image. Only this, he felt, was a proper record of the illustrator's skill.[4] CP

1. WA1947.385–7 and WA1991.13–9.
2. Clemence and Ardizzone (2000) pp. 3–6; Alderson (2003) pp. 259–63.
3. See also Clemence and Ardizzone (2000) no. 44 (from Sketchbook 65, fol. 25).
4. Alderson (2003) pp. 264–7.

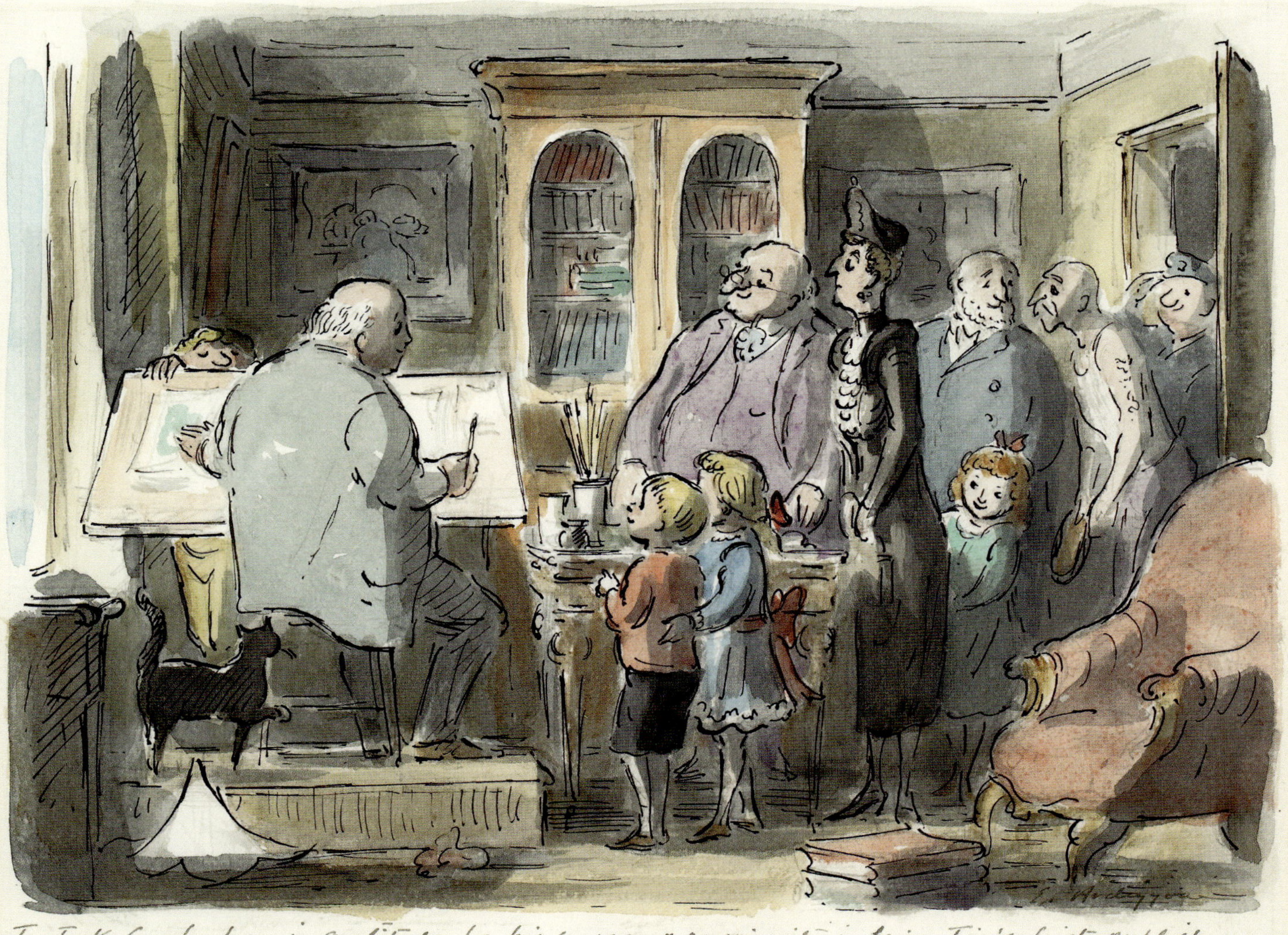

To Jock Cumberlege in gratitude for his courage + perspicacity in being Tim's first publisher —

130

RONALD WILLIAM FORDHAM SEARLE 1920–2011

Design for the Cover of 'How to be Topp', 1991

Pen and ink and bodycolour
and crayon on paper
41.9 × 29.2 cm
Inscribed: *MOLESWORTH / How to be Topp / GEOFFREY WILLANS & / RONALD SEARLE*
Lent from the Jeffrey Archer Cartoon Collection
L12225.3

Ronald Searle illustrated two of the most endearingly awful fictional schools in history, St Trinian's (for girls) and St Custard's (for boys). The former began life while the artist was imprisoned in the notorious Changi jail, where he drew the first cartoons of the series which were published monthly from November 1945 in the periodical *Lilliput*. He eventually tired of the schoolgirls' anarchic activities, and killed them off in his book, *Souls in Torment* (1952). However, by then others had assumed responsibility for their future, and the girls' fame spread much wider with the first of the films by Frank Launder and Sidney Gilliatt, *The Belles of St Trinian's*, released in 1954.

St Custard's, on the other hand, was created by the author Geoffrey Willans (1911–1958), based on his own experiences as a schoolboy and schoolmaster before the Second World War. Searle made his first illustrations to Willans's stories in the magazine *The Young Elizabethan*, and the two collaborated closely on four books: *Down with Skool!*, published in 1953, followed by *How to be Topp* (1954), *Whizz for Attoms* (1956), and *Back in the Jug Agane* (1959). All four books relate the tribulations of 'nigel molesworth the curse of st custard's', a senior boy at a preparatory school, whose spelling is phonetic and erratic, whose cynicism is unbounded, and who maintains that

the only good things about skool are the BOYS wizz who are noble brave fearless etc. although you hav various swots, cissies, milksops, greedy guts and oils with whom I am forced to migle hem-hem.

How to be Topp is subtitled 'a guide to Sukcess for tiny pupils, including all there is to kno about space', and explains how to succeed in most aspects of school life – academic, sporting, and social. The final chapters give advice on 'how to cope with grown ups', especially at Christmas. The dust jacket of the first edition shows Molesworth looking extremely self-satisfied and wearing a mortar board. For the reissue published by Pavilion Books in 1992, Searle adapted an earlier cover used by Puffin Books. 'Sir Molesworth' is now shown triumphing over the dragon of his enemies, shield and sword aloft in an unmistakably balletic pose which might have been censured by his younger self in the 1950s. CH

MOLESWORTH

How to be Topp

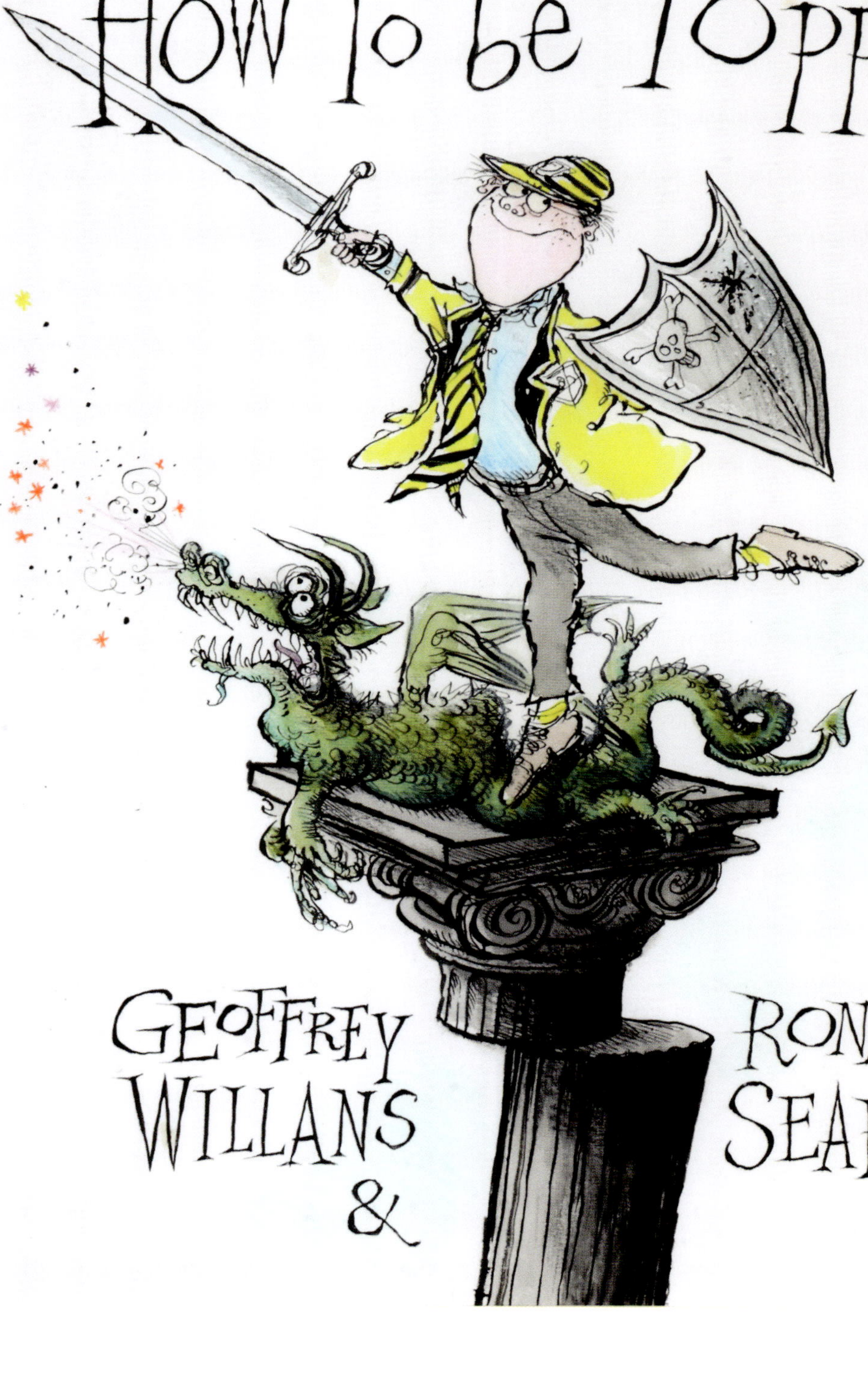

GEOFFREY WILLANS & RONALD SEARLE

HOW TO BE TOPP Willans & Searle

131

GERALD ANTHONY SCARFE B. 1936

Victory Celebrations, 1975

Pen and ink on paper
75.6 × 54.6 cm
Inscribed: *VICTORY CELEBRATIONS*
Lent from the Jeffrey Archer Political Cartoon Collection
L12225.2

Scarfe has worked for *Punch* and *Private Eye*, but is best known as the political cartoonist for *The Sunday Times*, with which he has been associated since 1967. This drawing was reproduced on 29 June 1975, and refers to the Conservative Party's victory in the by-election in Woolwich West. Following the death of the sitting Labour Member of Parliament, the Conservative candidate was again Peter Bottomley (b. 1944). He had been beaten in the general election in the previous year. He succeeded in overturning the Labour majority of 3,541, winning by 2,382 votes. This represented a considerable swing away from the beleaguered government of Harold Wilson, though it was not for another four years that the Labour-Liberal alliance was ousted at the general election on 3 May 1979.

The two figures congratulating each other are Edward Heath (1916–2005) and Margaret Thatcher (1925–2013). Heath had served as Prime Minister from June 1970 until the Conservative Party was narrowly beaten by Labour in the general election of March 1974. He remained as leader of the party until he was succeeded by Mrs Thatcher on 11 February 1975. The Woolwich West by-election thus represented her first significant success as party leader. In emulation of Sir Winston Churchill's frequent signal of 'v' for victory during the Second World War, Heath and Mrs Thatcher are seen making 'v' signs to each other, not palm outwards, as Churchill had done, but palm inwards, in an insulting gesture more typically associated with juvenile rudeness. Scarfe's caricatures are freely and confidently drawn, with very regular hatching to define forms and volume.

Mrs Thatcher went on to become the longest-serving British Prime Minister of the twentieth century (1979–90), while Heath became Father of the House of Commons in 1992, retiring from politics in 2001, and remaining bitter about his rival's success all his life. The two were frequent subjects for Scarfe, who chronicled Mrs Thatcher's rise from Education Secretary in 1971, when she was responsible for withdrawing the daily allowance of free milk for schoolchildren and became known as the 'Milk Snatcher', to her defeat as leader of the Conservative Party in 1990. CH

VICTORY CELEBRATIONS.

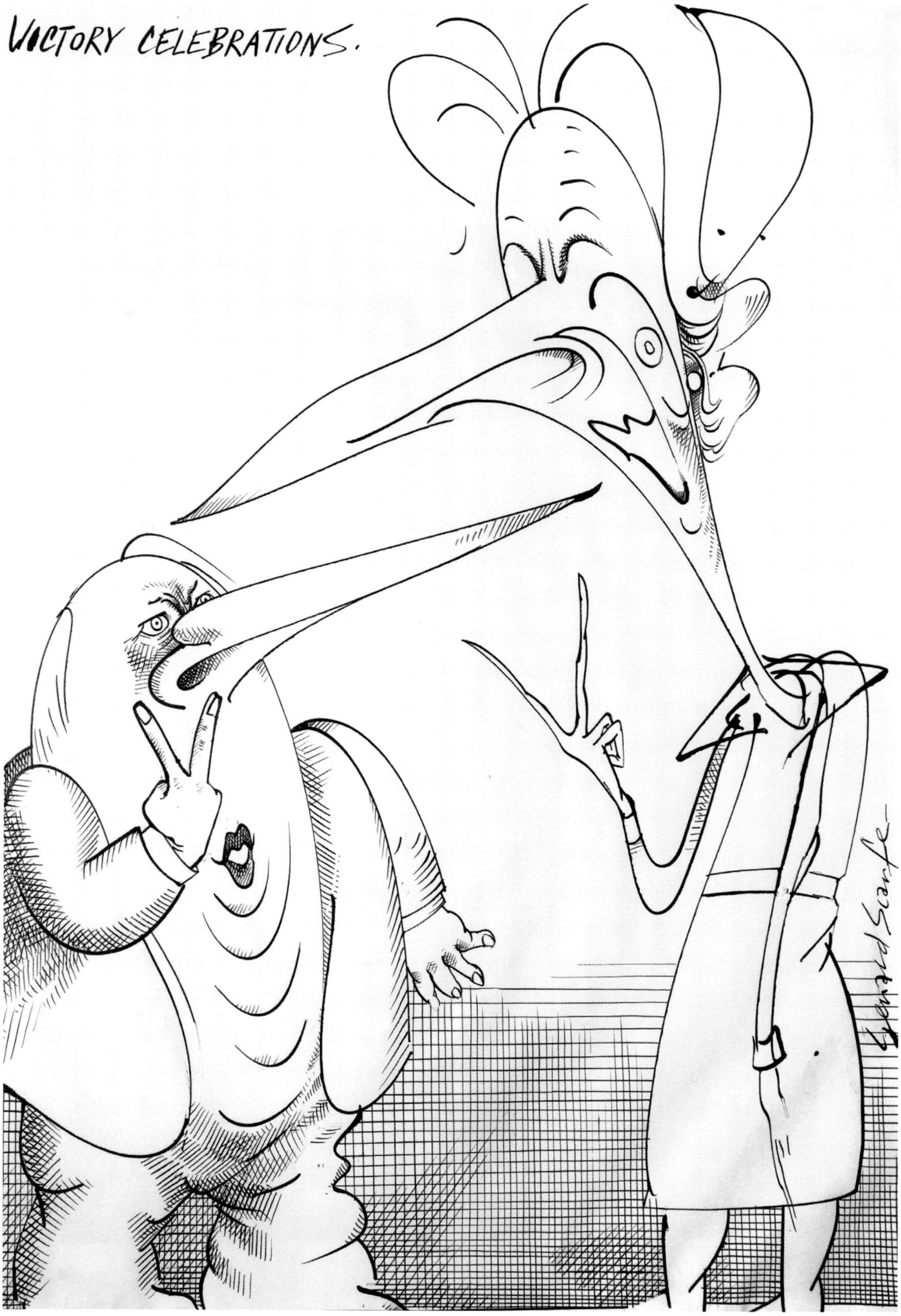

132

TOM PHILLIPS B. 1937

Studies for 'Merry Meetings', 2002–5

Pen and red, green, blue, brown, and black inks on paper
29.7 × 21 cm (each sheet)
Purchased (Vaughan and Blakiston Funds) with the assistance of The Art Fund and the MLA/V&A Purchase Grant Fund, 2009
WA2009.107.51, 91, 93 and 101

LITERATURE: Phillips (2005) nos. 51, 85, 87 and 96

In his essay 'Pleasures of Boredom: Four Centuries of Doodles', the art historian E. H. Gombrich traced the practice of doodling as far back as the Middle Ages. He argued that not only did contemporary art influence the style of the doodles, but also that, in the case of a true artist, the doodles themselves, to some extent unconscious, affected more deliberate acts of creativity.[1] In general, doodles are based either on images, or on words, and often a combination of the two. This explains their appeal to Tom Phillips – an artist who has always combined text and images in imaginative new ways (cat. 114).

Most artists have a compulsive need to set pen or pencil to paper as a means of exploring the subconscious or experimenting stylistically, but when does a doodle become 'art'? Going one step further than Paul Klee's famous notion of 'taking a line for a walk', Phillips turns actual doodling into an art form in his *Merry Meetings*, published in 2005. (The ironic title is taken from the opening lines of Shakespeare's *Richard III*: 'Now are our brows bound with victorious wreaths, ... / Our stern alarums changed to merry meetings.') A total of 107 images sketched at board meetings of the British Museum, Royal Academy, National Portrait Gallery and elsewhere, the doodles playfully undermine the stuffy formalities of these august institutions, represented by their printed agendas and business plans.

Shown here are just four sheets that demonstrate the variety of Phillips's doodling techniques, ranging from simple patterning, mazes and amorphous shapes to portraits of fellow board members. These were not originally intended for display, though the use of colour seems to imply – far more than would a simple black penline – a conscious aestheticising intrusion into the process. The imaginative incorporation of one image into another and the use of line are strongly reminiscent of Picasso's drawing technique, as recorded in 1956 by Henri-Georges Clouzot in his film, *Le Mystère Picasso*.

These works represent a subversive exploration of the gap between boredom and concentration, questioning what is allowable in such official contexts. Phillips insists that, far from distracting him, his drawing acts as an aid to concentration; it occupies the visual part of his brain while freeing his mind to focus on what is being said. 'The inner narcolept,' as he puts it, 'can be triumphed over by any of the techniques of shading, especially the rhythmic bliss of cross-hatching.'[2] CP

1. Gombrich (1999) pp. 212–25.
2. Phillips (2005) introduction, p. 9, unpaginated.

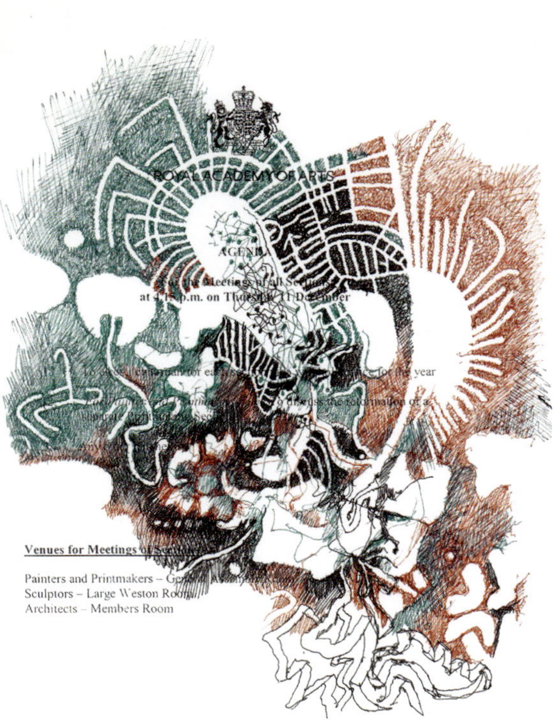
ROYAL ACADEMY OF ARTS
Venues for Meetings of Sections
Painters and Printmakers –
Sculptors – Large Weston Room
Architects – Members Room

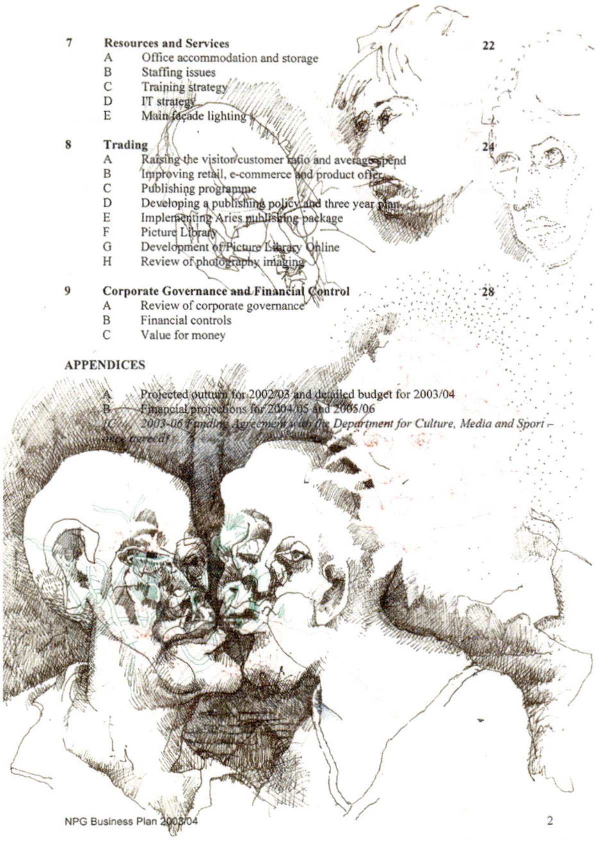
7 Resources and Services 22
A Office accommodation and storage
B Staffing issues
C Training strategy
D IT strategy
E Main façade lighting
8 Trading 24
A Raising the visitor/customer ratio and average spend
B Improving retail, e-commerce and product offer
C Publishing programme
D Developing a publishing policy and three year plan
E Implementing Aries publishing package
F Picture Library
G Development of Picture Library Online
H Review of photography imaging
9 Corporate Governance and Financial Control 28
A Review of corporate governance
B Financial controls
C Value for money
APPENDICES
A Projected outturn for 2002/03 and detailed budget for 2003/04
B Financial projections for 2004/05 and 2005/06
NPG Business Plan 2003/04
2

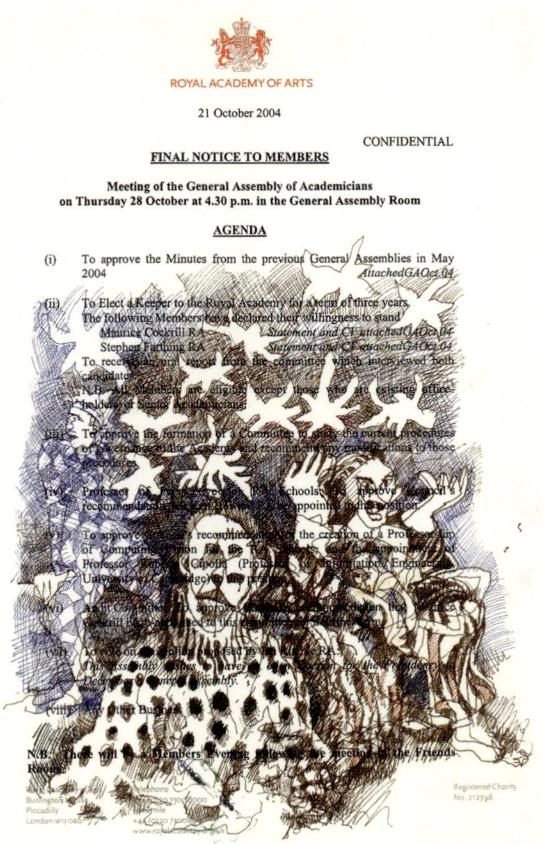
ROYAL ACADEMY OF ARTS
21 October 2004
CONFIDENTIAL
FINAL NOTICE TO MEMBERS
Meeting of the General Assembly of Academicians
on Thursday 28 October at 4.30 p.m. in the General Assembly Room
AGENDA
(i) To approve the Minutes from the previous General Assemblies in May 2004
AttachedGAOct.04
(ii) To Elect a Keeper to the Royal Academy for a term of three years.
The following Members have declared their willingness to stand
Maurice Cockrill RA
Stephen Farthing RA
Registered Charity
No. 212798

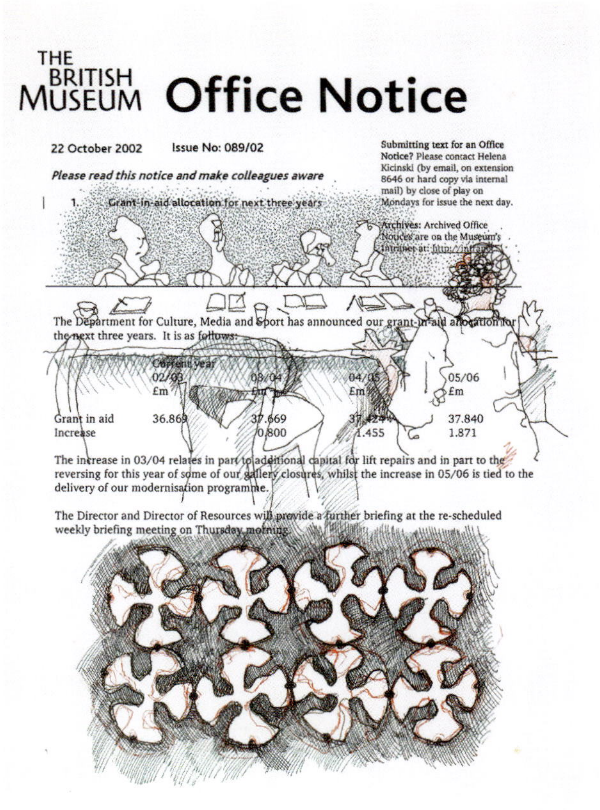
THE BRITISH MUSEUM Office Notice
22 October 2002
Issue No: 089/02
Please read this notice and make colleagues aware
Submitting text for an Office Notice? Please contact Helena Kicinski (by email, on extension 8646 or hard copy via internal mail) by close of play on Mondays for issue the next day.
1. Grant-in-aid allocation for next three years
The Department for Culture, Media and Sport has announced our grant-in-aid allocation for the next three years. It is as follows:
Grant in aid 36.869 37.669 37.840
Increase 0.800 1.455 1.871
The increase in 03/04 relates in part to additional capital for lift repairs and in part to the reversing for this year of some of our gallery closures, whilst the increase in 05/06 is tied to the delivery of our modernisation programme.
The Director and Director of Resources will provide a further briefing at the re-scheduled weekly briefing meeting on Thursday morning.

Bibliography

ALDERSON, Brian, *Edward Ardizzone: A Bibliographic Commentary* (Pinner, Middlesex, 2003)

ALLEY, Ronald, *Graham Sutherland* (exh. cat., Tate, London, 1982)

ANDERSON, William, *Cecil Collins: The Quest for the Great Happiness* (London, 1988)

ANNELY JUDA FINE ART, *David Hockney: The Arrival of Spring* (exh. cat., London, 2014)

ARDIZZONE, Edward, *Diary of a War Artist* (London, 1974)

ARTS COUNCIL OF GREAT BRITAIN, *Gwen John: A Retrospective Exhibition* (exh. cat., London, 1968)

ARTS COUNCIL OF GREAT BRITAIN, *Burne-Jones: The Paintings, Graphic and Decoration Work of Sir Edward Burne-Jones 1833–1898* (exh. cat., London, 1975)

BAILEY, Colin, 'The English Poussin – an Introduction to the Life and Work of George Augustus Wallis', *Annual Report and Bulletin*, Walker Art Gallery, Liverpool, 7 (1975–6), pp. 34–57

BAKER, Phil, *Austin Osman Spare: The Life and Legend of London's Lost Artist* (Devizes, 2012)

BARBER, Noël, *Conversations with Painters* (London, 1954)

BARON, Wendy, *Miss Ethel Sands and Her Circle* (London, 1977)

BARON, Wendy, *Sickert: Paintings and Drawings* (London and New Haven, 2006)

BECKER, Edwin, Elizabeth Prettejohn, Edward Morris, Julian Treuherz *et al.*, *Sir Lawrence Alma-Tadema* (exh. cat., Van Gogh Museum, Amsterdam, and Walker Art Gallery, Liverpool, 1996)

BEDDINGTON, Charles, *Canaletto in England: A Venetian Artist Abroad, 1746–1755* (exh. cat., Dulwich Picture Gallery, London, 2006)

BEETLES, Alexander, 'James Gillray' in *The Long Nineteenth Century: Treasures and Pleasures I From the French Revolution* (exh. cat., Chris Beetles Gallery, London, 2013)

BELL, Charles Francis, and Reginald Lane Poole, *English 17th-century Portrait Drawings in Oxford Collections*, *Walpole Society*, 14 (London, 1926)

BELL, Charles Francis, and Thomas Girtin, *The Drawings and Sketches of John Robert Cozens: a catalogue with an historical introduction* (Oxford, 1934–5)

BELSEY, Hugh, *Thomas Gainsborough: A Country Life* (London, 2002)

BELL, Malcolm, *Drawings of Sir E. J. Poynter* (London, 1905)

BENNETT, Mary, *Ford Madox Brown: A Catalogue Raisonné*, 2 vols (New Haven and London, 2010)

BINYON, Laurence, *English Water-colours* (London, 1933)

BLACK, Jonathan, *The Graphic Art of Eric Kennington* (London, 2001)

BLAKE, Nicholas, and Richard Lawrence, *The Illustrated Companion to Nelson's Navy* (first publ. London, 1999; Mechanicsburg, PA, 2005)

BONE, Sylvester, *Sir Muirhead Bone: Artist and Patron* (London, 2009)

BRONKHURST, Judith, *William Holman Hunt: A Catalogue Raisonné*, 2 vols (New Haven and London, 2006)

BROWN, Christopher, ed., *Master Drawings* (exh. cat., Ashmolean Museum, Oxford, 2013)

BROWN, David Blayney, *Catalogue of the Collection of Drawings at the Ashmolean Museum, Oxford, IV: Early English Drawings* (Oxford, 1982)

BROWN, David Blayney, *Samuel Palmer 1805–1881: A Catalogue Raisonné of the Paintings and Drawings, and a Selection of the Prints in the Ashmolean Museum* (Oxford, 1983)

BROWN, David Blayney, 'A Chinaman found in Western Art', *The Ashmolean*, 6 (Oxford, 1984–5), p. 10

BROWN, David Blayney, *Sir David Wilkie: Drawings and Sketches in the Ashmolean Museum* (Oxford, 1985)

BROWN, David Blayney, *The Pre-Raphaelites in Oxford* (exh. cat., Tokyo, Shiga and Osaka, 1987)

BRYANT, Barbara, *G. F. Watts Portraits: Fame and Beauty in Victorian Society* (exh. cat., National Portrait Gallery, London, 2004)

BUCKERIDGE, Bainbrigg, 'An Essay towards an English School of Painters', in Roger de Piles, *The Art of Painting, and the Lives of the Painters*, transl. John Savage (first publ. London, 1706; 3rd edn., 1754)

BURNE-JONES, Georgiana, *Memorials of Edward Burne-Jones*, 2 vols (London, 1904)

BUTLIN, Martin, *The Paintings and Drawings of William Blake*, 2 vols (New Haven, 1981)

CAMPBELL, Mungo, *Allan Ramsay: Portraits of the Enlightenment* (exh. cat., Hunterian Museum, Glasgow, 2013)

CAUSEY, Andrew, *Paul Nash* (Oxford, 1980)

CHERRY, Deborah, *Painting Women: Victorian Women Artists* (London, 1987)

CHITTY, Susan, *Gwen John 1876–1939* (London, 1981)

CHRISTIAN, John, *Letters to Katie from Edward Burne-Jones* (London, 1988)

CHRISTIAN, John, *Edward Burne-Jones: The Hidden Humorist* (London, 2011)

CLEMENCE, Christianna, and Nicholas Ardizzone, *Edward Ardizzone RA, 1900–1979, Ashmolean Museum, Oxford: A Centenary Celebration* (exh. cat., Ashmolean Museum, Oxford, 2000)

CONNER, Patrick, *George Chinnery 1774–1852: Artist of India and the China Coast* (Suffolk, 1993)

CORK, Richard, *David Bomberg* (exh. cat., Tate, London, 1988)

CRUISE, Colin, *Pre-Raphaelite Drawing* (exh. cat., Birmingham Museums and Art Gallery, Birmingham, 2012)

CUNNINGHAM, Allan, *The Life of Sir David Wilkie: his Journals, Tours and Critical Remarks on Works of Art; and a Selection of his Correspondence*, 3 vols (London, 1843)

DIMBLEBY, Josceline, *A Profound Secret: May Gaskell, her daughter Amy and Edward Burne-Jones* (London, 2004)

DODGSON, Campbell, and C.E. Montague, *British Artists at the Front*, IV, *Eric Kennington* (London, 1918)

EATES, Margot, *et al.*, *Paul Nash: Paintings, Drawings and Illustrations* (London, 1948)

EDWARDS, Paul, *Wyndham Lewis: Art and War* (London, 1992)

ELZEA, Betty, *Frederick Sandys, 1829–1904: A Catalogue Raisonné* (Woodbridge, 2001)

FAGAN, Louis, *A Descriptive Catalogue of the Engraved Works of William Faithorne* (London, 1888)

FOSKETT, Daphne, *Samuel Cooper and his Contemporaries* (London, 1974)

FREDEMAN, William E., ed., *The Correspondence of Dante Gabriel Rossetti: the Formative Years 1835–1862*, 2 vols (Cambridge, 2002)

FUNNELL, Peter, *Millais: Portraits* (exh. cat., National Portrait Gallery, London, 1999)

GAJA, Katerine, *G. F. Watts in Italy: A Portrait of the Artist as a Young Man* (Florence, 1995)

GEORGE, Mary Dorothy, *Catalogue of Political and Personal Satires preserved in the Department of Prints and Drawings in the British Museum*, 11 vols (London, 1870–1954)

GIBSON-WOOD, Carol, 'Jonathan Richardson as a Draftsman', *Master Drawings* 32, 3 (autumn 1994) pp. 203–29

GILL, Eric, *Twenty-Five Nudes* (London, 1938)

GILL, Eric, *Autobiography* (London, 1992)

GIRTIN, Thomas, and David Loshak, *The Art of Thomas Girtin* (London, 1954)

GOLDMAN, Paul, *John Everett Millais, Illustrator and Narrator* (exh. cat., Birmingham Museums and Art Gallery, Birmingham, 2004)

GOMBRICH, Ernst H., *The Uses of Images: Studies in the Social Function of Art and Visual Communication* (London, 1999)

GOUGH, Paul, Sally Allen, and Tehmina Goshar, *Graham Sutherland: From Darkness to Light – Mining, Metal and Machines*, (exh. cat., Penlee House Museum, Penzance, and National Waterfront Museum, Swansea, 2013)

GOUGH, Paul, *Brothers in Arms: John and Paul Nash and the Aftermath of the Great War* (Bristol, 2014)

GRAVES ART GALLERY, *Eric Ravilious 1903–42: A Memorial Exhibition of Watercolours, Wood Engravings, Designs* (Sheffield, 1958)

GREGO, Joseph, *Rowlandson the Caricaturist: A Selection from his Works, with Anecdotal Descriptions of his Famous Caricatures and a Sketch of his Life, Times, and Contemporaries*, 2 vols (London, 1880)

GUITERMAN, Helen, and Briony Llewellyn, *David Roberts* (Oxford, 1986)

HALL, Charles, *Paul Nash: Aerial Creatures*, (exh. cat., Imperial War Museum, London, 1997)

HALL, John N., *Max Beerbohm Caricatures* (New Haven and London, 1997)

HAMLYN, Robin, Michael Phillips, Peter Ackroyd, and Marilyn Butler, *William Blake* (exh. cat., Tate, London, 2000)

HAMMER, Martin, *Graham Sutherland: Landscapes, War Scenes, Portraits 1924–1950* (exh. cat., Dulwich Picture Gallery, London, 2005)

HARRIES, Meirion and Susan, *The War Artists: British Official War Art of the Twentieth Century* (London, 1983)

HARRISON, Colin, *Turner's Oxford* (exh. cat., Ashmolean Museum, Oxford, 2000)

HARRISON, Colin, and Christopher Newall, *et. al.*, *The Pre-Raphaelites and Italy* (exh. cat., Ashmolean Museum, Oxford, and Museo d'Arte della Città di Ravenna, 2010)

HARRISON, Colin, *Edward Lear's Alphabet of Nonsense* (Oxford, 2012)

HARRISON, Martin and Bill Waters, *Burne-Jones* (London, 1973)

HART-DAVIES, Rupert, *A Catalogue of the Caricatures of Max Beerbohm* (London, 1972)

HAWCROFT, Francis, *Watercolours by John Robert Cozens* (exh. cat., Whitworth Art Gallery, Manchester, 1971)

HAWCROFT, Francis, *Travels in Italy 1776–1873: based on the Memoirs of Thomas Jones* (Manchester, 1988)

HAYES, John T., *The Drawings of Thomas Gainsborough*, 2 vols (London, 1970)

HAYES, John T., *The Art of Thomas Rowlandson* (exh. cat., Frick Collection, New York, and Baltimore Museum of Art, Baltimore, 1990)

HAZLITT HOLLAND-HIBBERT, *Augustus John: Masterworks from Private Collections 1900–20* (exh. cat., Hazlitt's, London and New York, 2004)

HERRMANN, Luke, '"This patient and unassuming master": William Turner of Oxford', *Connoisseur* CLXII (1966) pp. 242–7

HERRMANN, Luke, *Ruskin and Turner: A Study of Ruskin as a Collector of Turner, based on his gifts to the University of Oxford; incorporating a Catalogue Raisonné of the Turner Drawings in the Ashmolean Museum* (London, 1968)

HEWISON, Robert, *Ruskin's Venice* (Yelvertoft Manor, Northamptonshire, 2000)

HILL, David, *Thomas Girtin: Genius in the North* (exh. cat., Harewood House, Yorkshire, 1999)

HODNETT, Edward, *Francis Barlow: First Master of English Book Illustration* (London, 1978)

HOLROYD, Michael, Mark L. Evans, and Rebecca John, *Themes and Variations: The Drawings of Augustus John 1901–31* (exh. cat., National Museum and Gallery, Cardiff, and Spink & Son Ltd., London, 1996)

HUGHES, Robert, *Frank Auerbach* (London, 1990)

HURRELL, Bill, *Sacred and Profane: Drawing to a Conclusion* (London, 1997)

HYMAN, Susan, *Edward Lear in the Levant: Travels in Albania, Greece and Turkey in Europe 1848–1849* (London, 1988)

HYMAN, Susan, *Edward Lear: A New Nonsense Alphabet* (London, 1988)

INGAMELLS, John, and Brinsley Ford, *A Dictionary of British and Irish Travellers in Italy, 1701–1800* (New Haven and London, 1997)

INGRAMS, Richard, and John Piper, *Piper's Places: John Piper in England & Wales* (London, 1983)

IVES, Colta, *et al.*, *Vincent Van Gogh: The Drawings* (exh. cat., Metropolitan Museum of Art, New York, 2005)

JEFFARES, Neil, *Dictionary of Pastellists before 1800* (London, 2006)

JENKINS, David Fraser, *Augustus John: Studies for Compositions, Centenary Exhibition* (ex. cat., National Museum of Wales, Cardiff, 1978)

JENKINS, David Fraser, *John Piper: The Robert and Rena Lewin Gift to the Ashmolean Museum*, (exh. cat., Ashmolean Museum, Oxford, 1992)

JENKINS, David Fraser, and Frances Spalding, *John Piper in the 1930s: Abstraction on the Beach* (exh. cat., Dulwich Picture Gallery, London, 2003)

JENKINS, David Fraser, and Chris Stephens, eds., *Gwen John and Augustus John* (exh. cat., Tate, London, 2004)

JENKINS, David Fraser, and David Boyd Haycock, *Paul Nash: The Elements* (exh. cat., Dulwich Picture Gallery, London, 2010)

JONES, Tom, *William Henry Hunt 1790–1864* (exh. cat., Wolverhampton Art Gallery, Wolverhampton, 1981)

KITSON, Sydney D., *The Life of John Sell Cotman* (London, 1937)

KLONSKY, Milton, *Blake's Dante: The Complete Illustations to the Divine Comedy* (London, 1980)

KONODY, Paul G., and Sidney Dark, *Sir William Orpen: Artist and Man* (London, 1932)

LAMPERT, Catherine, Norman Rosenthal, and Isabel Carlisle, *Frank Auerbach: Paintings and Drawings 1954–2001* (exh. cat., Royal Academy of Arts, London, 2001)

LANGDALE, Cecily, and David Fraser Jenkins, *Gwen John: An Interior Life* (London, 1985)

LANGDALE, Cecily, *Gwen John: Catalogue Raisonné* (London and New Haven, 1987)

LEVINSON, Orde, *Quality and Experiment: The Prints of John Piper: A Catalogue Raisonné* (London, 1996)

LEWIS, Major-General Michael, *John Frederick Lewis, RA* (Leigh-on-Sea, 1978)

LISTER, Raymond, *Catalogue Raisonné of the Works of Samuel Palmer* (Cambridge, 1988)

LIVINGSTONE, Marco, *Pop Art: A Continuing History* (London, 1990)

LIVINGSTONE, Marco, and Kay Heymer, *Hockney's Portraits and People* (London and New York, 2003)

LLOYD-MORGAN, Ceridwen, *Gwen John: Letters and Notebooks* (London, 2004)

LOCKETT, Richard, *Samuel Prout 1783–1852* (exh. cat., Victoria and Albert Museum, London, 1985)

LONDON, *Pre-Raphaelite and other Masters: The Andrew Lloyd Webber Collection* (exh. cat., Royal Academy of Arts, London, 2003)

LORD, John, ed., *Peter de Wint 1784–1849: 'For the Common Observer of Life and Nature'* (exh. cat., Lincoln, 2007)

LUCKHARDT, Ulrich, and Paul Melia, *David Hockney: a Drawing Retrospective* (London and New York, 1995)

LYLES, Anne, *Turner and Natural History: The Farnley Project* (exh. cat., Tate, London, 1988)

LYLES, Anne and Robin Hamlyn, *British Watercolours from the Oppé Collection; with a selection of drawings and oil sketches* (exh. cat., Tate, London, 1997)

MACCARTHY, Fiona, *Eric Gill* (London, 1989)

MACCARTHY, Fiona, *The Last Pre-Raphaelite: Burne-Jones and the Victorian Imagination* (London, 2011)

MANCHESTER, Whitworth Art Gallery, *Walter Sickert: 'Drawing is the Thing'* (exh.cat., 2004)

MANCOFF, Debra N., *Burne-Jones* (San Francisco, 1998)

MANNINGS, David, and Martin Postle, *Sir Joshua Reynolds: A Complete Catalogue of his Paintings*, 2 vols (New Haven, 2000)

MARSH, Jan, *Dante Gabriel Rossetti: Painter and Poet* (London, 1999)

MARTIN, Simon, Martin Butlin, and Robert Meyrick, *Poets in the Landscape: The Romantic Spirit in British Art* (exh. cat., Pallant House, Chichester, 2007)

MCEVANSONEYA, Philip, '"A thing to be seen": Creating the Crampton Collection of English Watercolours in the 1850s', *Journal of the History of Collections*, 21:1 (Oxford, 2009) pp. 95–110

MCEWEN, John, *William Gear* (Aldershot and Burlington, 2003)

MICHEL, Walter, *Wyndham Lewis: Paintings and Drawings* (London, 1971)

MILLAR, Oliver, *Sir Peter Lely* (London, 1978)

MOORE, Andrew W., *John Sell Cotman 1782–1842* (exh. cat., Norwich Castle Museum, Norwich, 1982)

MORRIS, William, *News from Nowhere and Other Writings*, ed., Clive Wilmer (Harmondsworth, 1993)

MUMFORD, Alan, *Low: The Twentieth Century's Greatest Cartoonist, 40 years of British history through the cartoons of Sir David Low* (London, 2002)

NEWALL, Christopher, *John William Inchbold: Pre-Raphaelite Landscape Artist* (exh. cat., Leeds City Art Gallery, Leeds, 1993)

NEWALL, Christopher, Scott Wilcox, and Colin Harrison, *The Poetry of Truth: Alfred William Hunt and the Art of Landscape* (exh. cat., Ashmolean Museum, Oxford, 2004)

NOAKES, Vivien, *Edward Lear: The Life of a Wanderer* (London, 1968)

NOAKES, Vivien, *Edward Lear, 1812–1888* (exh. cat., Royal Academy of Arts, London, 1985)

NOAKES, Vivien, ed., *Edward Lear: Selected Letters* (Oxford, 1988)

NOAKES, Vivien, *Edward Lear 1812–1888* (exh. cat. Royal Academy of Arts, London, 1988)

NASH, Paul, *Outline: An Autobiography and Other Writings* (London, 1948)

NASH, Paul, and Gordon Bottomley, *Poet and Painter: Letters between Paul Nash and Gordon Bottomley, 1910–1946* (London, 1955)

NATIONAL GALLERY, *The Drawings of Augustus John, RA* (exh. cat., London, 1940)

NATIONAL PORTRAIT GALLERY, *Colonel Blimp and Friends: the Cartoons of Sir David Low (1891–1963)* (exh. cat., London, 1985–6)

PALEY, Morton D., *Samuel Taylor Coleridge and the Fine Arts* (Oxford, 2008)

PALMER, A. H., *The Life and Letters of Samuel Palmer, Painter and Etcher* (London, 1892)

PASCHAL, Huston, *Tom Phillips: Works and Texts* (London and New York, 1992)

PAULSON, Ronald, *Rowlandson*: A New Interpretation (New York and Oxford, 1972)

PETTER, Helen Mary, *The Oxford Almanacks* (Oxford, 1974)

PHILLIPS, Michael, *William Blake: Apprentice and Master* (exh. cat., Ashmolean Museum, Oxford, 2014)

PHILLIPS, Tom, and Salman Rushdie, *Merely Connect: A Questschrift for Salman Rushdie* (London, 1993)

PHILLIPS, Tom, *Merry Meetings* (Nottingham, 2005)

PIPER, David, 'A Chinese Artist in England', *Country Life* (18 July 1952) pp. 198–9

PITTS, Mike, 'Stonehenge', in *Making History: Antiquaries in Britain, 1707–2007* (exh. cat., Royal Academy of Arts, London, 2007) pp. 225–53

POSTLE, Martin, *Sir Joshua Reynolds: The Subject Pictures* (Cambridge, 1995)

POWERS, Alan, *Eric Ravilious: Artist and Designer* (Farnham, 2013)

PRESSLY, William L., *The Life and Art of James Barry* (New Haven and London, 1981)

PRESSLY, William L., *James Barry: The Artist as Hero* (exh. cat., Tate, London, 1983)

PRETTEJOHN, Elizabeth, *The Art of the Pre-Raphaelites* (London, 2000)

REDGRAVE, Richard and Samuel, *A Century of British Artists* (first publ. 1866; London, 1947)

REID, Forrest, *Illustrators of the Eighteen Sixties: An Illustrated Survey of the Work of 58 British Artists* (London, 1928)

REYNOLDS, David, *The Long Shadow: The Legacies of the Great War in the Twentieth Century* (New York, 2014)

REYNOLDS, Sir Joshua, *Discourses on Art*, ed., Robert R. Wark (New Haven and London, 1975)

RICHARDS, J. M., *Edward Bawden: Penguin Modern Painters* (London, 1946)

ROBERTS, Leonard, and Stephen Wildman, *Arthur Hughes: His Life and Works* (Woodbridge, 1997)

ROLFE, John, 'The Identification of the Sitter in Harold Gilman's Portraits of Mrs Mounter', *Burlington Magazine*, 152 (2010) pp. 236–8

ROSENBLUM, Robert, *Modern Painting and the Northern Romantic Tradition: Friedrich to Rothko* (London, 1978)

ROSENFELD, Jason, and Alison Smith, *Millais* (exh. cat., Tate, London, 2007)

ROSENTHAL, Michael, *The Art of Thomas Gainsborough: 'A Little Business for the Eye'* (New Haven and London, 1999)

ROSENTHAL, Michael, and Martin Myrone, *Gainsborough* (exh. cat., Tate, London, 2002)

ROTHENSTEIN, John, *John Nash* (London, 1983)

ROTHENSTEIN, William, *Men and Memories* (London, 1931)

ROWLAND, Christopher, *Blake and the Bible* (New Haven and London, 2010)

RUNCIMAN, Steven, *Watercolours by Edward Lear from the Collection of the Hon. Sir Steven Runciman CH* (exh. cat. National Galleries of Scotland, Edinburgh, 1991)

RUSKIN, John, *Notes by Mr. Ruskin on Samuel Prout and William Hunt* (London, 1880)

RUSKIN, John, *The Complete Works of John Ruskin*, ed., E. T. Cook and Alexander Wedderburn, 39 vols (London, 1903–12)

RUSSELL, James, *Ravilious in Pictures: A Country Life* (Sparham, Norwich, 2011)

RUTHERFORD, Emma, Bendor Grosvenor, *et al.*, *Warts and All: The Portrait Miniatures of Samuel Cooper, 1607/8–72* (exh. cat., Philip Mould & Co., London, 2013)

SANDERS, Andrew, 'Millais and Literature', in *John Everett Millais: Beyond the Pre-Raphaelite Brotherhood*, ed., Debra N. Mancoff (New Haven & London, 2001) pp. 69–93

SCHIFF, Gert, *Johann Heinrich Füssli, 1741–1825* (Zurich and Munich, 1973)

SELBORNE, Joanna, ed., *Life, Legend, Landscape: Victorian Drawings and Watercolours* (ex. cat., Courtauld Gallery, London, 2011)

SHANES, Eric, *Turner's Picturesque Views in England and Wales 1825–1838* (London, 1979)

SHAW, George, *Graham Sutherland: An Unfinished World* (exh. cat., Museum of Modern Art, Oxford, 2011)

SHEPARD, E. H., *Fun and Fantasy: A Book of Drawings by Ernest H. Shepard* (London, 1927)

SIM, Katharine, *David Roberts RA, 1796–1864: A Biography* (London, 1984)

SLOMAN, Susan, *Missing Pages: George Richmond R.A. 1809–1896; Drawings, Watercolours, Letters, Journals, and Notebooks* (exh. cat., Agnew's, London, 2001)

SLOMAN, Susan, *Gainsborough's Landscapes: Themes and Variations* (exh. cat., Holburne Museum, Bath, 2011)

SMART, Alastair, *Allan Ramsay: Painter, Essayist, and Man of the Enlightenment* (New Haven and London, 1992)

SMITH, Greg *Thomas Girtin: The Art of Watercolour* (exh. cat., Tate, London, 2002)

SMITH, Hammond, *Peter de Wint* (London, 1982)

SOTHEBY'S, *Edward Lear: An Exhibition of works by Edward Lear from the Dayton International Collection, assembled by John Dayton* (exh. cat. Sotheby's, 2004)

SPALDING, Frances, *John Minton: 'Dance till the Stars Come Down'*, (revised edn., London, 2005)

SPARE, Austin Osman, *The Writing of Austin Osman Spare* (Sioux Falls, SD, 2007)

SPENCER-LONGHURST, Paul, *The Blue Bower: Rossetti in the 1860s* (exh. cat., Barber Institute of Fine Arts, Birmingham, 2000)

STAINTON, Lindsay, *British Landscape Watercolours, 1600–1800* (exh. cat., British Museum, London, 1985)

STAINTON, Lindsay, and Christopher White, *Drawing in England from Hilliard to Hogarth* (exh. cat., British Museum, London, 1987)

STALEY, Allen, *The Pre-Raphaelite Landscape* (rev. edn., New Haven and London, 2001)

STALEY, Allen and Christopher Newall, *Pre-Raphaelite Vision: Truth to Nature* (exh. cat., Tate, London, 2004–5)

STEPHENS, Chris, ed., *A Continuous Line: Ben Nicholson in England* (exh. cat., Tate, London, 2008)

STEWART, John Douglas, *Sir Godfrey Kneller* (exh. cat., National Portrait Gallery, London, 1971)

STEWART, John Douglas, *Sir Godfrey Kneller and the English Baroque Portrait* (Oxford, 1983)

SUNDERLAND, John, 'John Hamilton Mortimer: His Life and Works', *Walpole Society*, 52 (1986)

SURTEES, Virginia, *The Paintings and Drawings of Dante Gabriel Rossetti 1828–1882: A Catalogue Raisonné*, 2 vols (Oxford, 1971)

SURTEES, Virginia, *Rossetti's Portraits of Elizabeth Siddal: A Catalogue of the Drawings and Watercolours* (Oxford, 1991)

SURTEES, Virginia, *The Actress and the Brewer's Wife: Two Victorian Vignettes* (Norwich, 1997)

SUTTLE, E. F. A., 'Henry Aldrich, Dean of Christ Church', *Oxoniensia* 5 (1940)

TAYLOR, Judy, *Edward Ardizzone: Sketches for Friends* (London, 2000)

TREUHERZ, Julian, Elizabeth Prettejohn, and Edwin Becker, *Dante Gabriel Rossetti* (exh. cat., Walker Art Gallery, Liverpool, and Van Gogh Museum, Amsterdam, 2003)

TREUHERZ, Julian, *Ford Madox Brown: Pre-Raphaelite Pioneer* (exh. cat., Manchester City Art Gallery, 2011)

UPSTONE, Robert, ed., *William Orpen: Politics, Sex and Death* (London, 2005)

UPSTONE, Robert, ed., *Modern Painters: The Camden Town Group* (exh. cat., Tate, London, 2008)

VAUGHAN, Keith, *Journal & Drawings* (London, 1966)

VAUGHAN, William, Elizabeth E. Barker, and Colin Harrison, *Samuel Palmer 1805–1881: Vision and Landscape* (exh. cat., British Museum, London, and Metropolitan Museum of Art, New York, 2005–6)

WARK, Robert R., *Drawings by Thomas Rowlandson in the Huntington Collection* (San Marino, California, 1975)

WARRELL, Ian, *Turner on the Loire* (exh. cat., Tate, London, 1997)

WARRELL, Ian, *Turner and Venice* (exh. cat., Tate, London, 2003)

WEAVER, Nigel, Robin O'Neill, and Edward Bawden, *Edward Bawden in the Middle East* (Woodbridge, 2008)

WHITE, Christopher, Catherine Whistler, and Colin Harrison, *Old Master Drawings from the Ashmolean Museum* (Oxford, 1992)

WILCOX, Scott, *Sun, Wind, and Rain: The Art of David Cox* (exh. cat., Birmingham Museums and Art Gallery, Birmingham, 2008)

WILCOX, Timothy, and Christopher Titterington, *William Turner of Oxford (1789–1862)* (exh. cat., Woodstock, 1984)

WILCOX, Timothy, *Francis Towne* (exh. cat., Tate, London, 1997)

WILD, Monika von, *George Augustus Wallis (1761–1847): Englischer Landschaftsmaler – Monographie und Oeuvrekatalog* (Frankfurt, 1996)

WILDMAN, Stephen, and John Christian, *Edward Burne-Jones: Victorian Artist-Dreamer* (exh. cat., Metropolitan Museum of Art, New York, and Birmingham Museums and Art Gallery, Birmingham, 1998)

WILTON, Andrew, *The Life and Work of J. M. W. Turner* (London, 1979)

WILTON, Andrew, and Anne Lyles, *The Great Age of British Watercolours, 1750–1880* (exh. cat., Royal Academy of Art, London, and National Gallery of Art, Washington DC, 1993)

WITT, John, *William Henry Hunt 1790–1864* (London, 1982)

ZIMMERN, Helen, *Sir Lawrence Alma-Tadema RA* (London, 1902)

ZWEMMER GALLERY, *Eric Ravilious: Catalogue of an Exhibition of Water-Colour Drawings* (London, 1936)

Index

References to catalogue entry numbers are given in **bold**